Thar's Joy in Braveland!
The 1957 Milwaukee Braves

Edited by Gregory H. Wolf
Associate Editors: Russ Lake, Len Levin, and Bill Nowlin

Society for American Baseball Research, Inc.
Phoenix, AZ

Thar's Joy in Braveland!: The 1957 Milwaukee Braves
Edited by Gregory H. Wolf
Associate Editors: Russ Lake, Len Levin, and Bill Nowlin
Copyright © 2014 Society for American Baseball Research, Inc.

All rights reserved. Reproduction in whole or in part without permission is prohibited.

ISBN 978-1-933599-71-7
(Ebook ISBN 978-1-933599-72-4)
Design and Production: Gilly Rosenthol, Rosenthol Design

Cover photograph: Hank Aaron, Eddie Mathews, and Joe Adcock (National Baseball Hall of Fame Library, Cooperstown, N.Y.)
The Society for American Baseball Research, Inc.
4455 E. Camelback Road, Ste. D-140
Phoenix, AZ 85018
Phone: (800) 969-7227 or (612) 343-6455

Web: www.sabr.org
Facebook: Society for American Baseball Research
Twitter: @SABR

Table of Contents

Introduction: The Milwaukee Braves Make History by Gregory H. Wolf 1
Acknowledgements 4

THE OWNER
From Yawkey to Milwaukee: Lou Perini Makes his Move by Saul Wisnia 5

THE BRAVES
Henry "Hank" Aaron by William Johnson 13
Joe Adcock by Gregory H. Wolf 20
Bill Bruton by John Harry Stahl 27
Bob Buhl by Gregory H. Wolf 33
Lew Burdette by Alex Kupfer 39
Dick Cole by Doug Engleman 45
Gene Conley by John R. Husman 49
Wes Covington by Andy Sturgill 54
Del Crandall by Gregory H. Wolf 59
Ray Crone by Gregory H. Wolf 67
John DeMerit by Steven Schmitt 73
Harry Hanebrink by Andy Sturgill 78
Bob Hazle by Nancy Snell Griffith 81
Joey Jay by Joe Wancho 85
Ernie Johnson by Dana Sprague 92
Dave Jolly by Chip Greene 97
Nippy Jones by Dan Fields 102
Johnny Logan by Bob Buege 107
Bobby Malkmus by Gregory H. Wolf 114
Felix Mantilla by Rick Schabowski 119
Eddie Mathews by David Fleitz 124
Don McMahon by John Vorperian 130
Red Murff by Michael J. Bielawa 135
Danny O'Connell by Mel Marmer 139
Andy Pafko by Dale Voiss 144
Phil Paine by Chip Greene 148

Taylor Phillips by Rick Schabowski 153
Juan Pizarro by Rory Costello 158
Del Rice by Norm King 165
Mel Roach by David Fleitz 170
Carl Sawatski by Gregory H. Wolf 174
Red Schoendienst by Kristen Lokemoen 180
Ray Shearer by William Johnson 186
Warren Spahn by Jim Kaplan 189
Chuck Tanner by Dan Fields 199
Hawk Taylor by Steven Schmitt 204
Bobby Thomson by Jeff Findley 208
Frank Torre by Norm King 214
Bob Trowbridge by Nancy Snell Griffith 218

THE MANAGER
Fred Haney by Jim Gordon 222

THE COACHES
Bob Keely by Gregory H. Wolf 227
Johnny Riddle by Nancy Snell Griffith 232
Charlie Root by Gregory H. Wolf 236
Connie Ryan by John McMurray 243

GENERAL MANAGER
John Quinn by Rory Costello 248

County Stadium by Gregg Hoffmann 255
Jane Jarvis by Rory Costello 259

THE SPORTSWRITERS
Headlines and Deadlines: Wordsmiths of the Braves by Bob Buege 266
Lou Chapman by Bob Buege 267
Red Thisted by Bob Buege 271
Bob Wolf by Bob Buege 275

RADIO ANNOUNCERS
Voices of the Braves: Blaine Walsh and Earl Gillespie by Bob Buege............................... 279

REGULAR SEASON SUMMARY
The 1957 Milwaukee Braves Season Timeline and Summary by Gregory H. Wolf 288

WORLD SERIES SUMMARY
1957 World Series Summary by Norm King.... 307

By the Numbers: Milwaukee Braves in 1957 by Dan Fields... 311
Thirteen Years of Magic by Bob Buege 317

Contributors 322

Introduction:
The Milwaukee Braves Make History

By Gregory H. Wolf

FEW TEAMS IN baseball history have captured the hearts of their fans like the Milwaukee Braves of the 1950s. Aaron and Mathews, Spahn and Burdette—those players need no introduction. During the Braves' 13-year tenure in Milwaukee (1953-1965), they had a winning record every season, won two consecutive NL pennants in 1957-58, lost two more in the final week of the season (1956 and 1959), and set big-league attendance records along the way. This book celebrates the Milwaukee Braves' historic 1957 World Series championship, its players, manager and coaches, front office, and others involved with the team.

The National League owners' 8-0 vote on March 18, 1953, to allow the Boston Braves to relocate to Milwaukee signaled a dramatic shift in the demographic alignment of baseball and marked the first franchise move since the Baltimore Orioles moved to New York and became the Highlanders in 1903. In the great westward migration, other teams followed: the St. Louis Browns to Baltimore in 1954, the Philadelphia Athletics to Kansas City in 1955, the Brooklyn Dodgers to Los Angeles and New York Giants to San Francisco in 1958. The owners of those teams saw the Braves' success in Milwaukee, and baseball was never the same.

Critics derided Milwaukee, then as today baseball's smallest market, as "bush" and argued that a city better known for beer and bowling could never support a major-league team. Fans and players were quick to shed their reputation as a minor-league town whose Brewers attracted just over 195,000 spectators to old Borchert Field in 1952. In their inaugural season in the not-yet-completed County Stadium in 1953, the Braves set a new NL attendance record with 1,826,397 and finished in second place. The seventh-place finish and the paltry attendance figure (281,278) of the previous season in Boston seemed like a distant memory.

The nucleus of the 1957 championship team was already with the team in its first year in Milwaukee. Twenty-three-year-old catcher Del Crandall had returned after a two-year stint in the military; hulking first baseman Joe Adcock had just been acquired from the Cincinnati Reds; fiery 21-year-old third sacker Eddie Mathews was in his second season; 27-year-old fleet-footed center fielder Billy Bruton was a rookie; and another 27-year-old, shortstop Johnny Logan, was a three-year veteran. On the mound, lefty Warren Spahn was "just" 32, Bob Buhl a rookie, and Lew Burdette still primarily a reliever and spot starter. In 1954 the last piece of the puzzle arrived: Henry Aaron, a 19-year-old second baseman for the Class A Jacksonville Braves in 1953. Over the course of the decade, this core of players established the Braves as one of the model teams in baseball. Like the Dodgers and Giants, the Braves embraced integration early, and their success on the field and at the gate can be attributed in no small part to the aggressive signing of African-American and

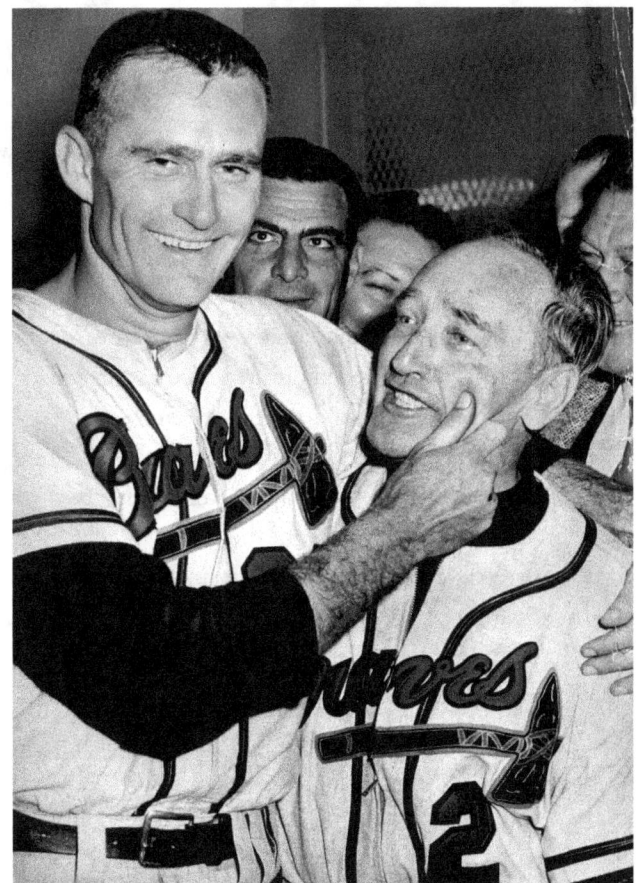

Lew Burdette and Fred Haney Celebrate (National Baseball Hall of Fame Library, Cooperstown, N.Y.)

1957 World Champion Milwaukee Braves
First Row (left to right): Bob Hazle, Phil Paine, Charlie Blossfield (bat boy), Paul Wick (bat boy), John DeMerit, Taylor Phillips
Second Row: Donald Davidson (traveling secretary), Duffy Lewis (traveling secretary), Johnny Logan, Bob Keely, Charlie Root, John Riddle, Fred Haney, Connie Ryan, Andy Pafko, Felix Mantilla, Joe Taylor (trainer)
Third Row: Robert Feron (trainer), Bob Buhl, Don McMahon, Bill Bruton, Bob Trowbridge, Lew Burdette, Frank Torre, Eddie Mathews, Carl Sawatski, Juan Pizarro, Joe Adcock, John Lang (batting practice pitcher)
Fourth Row: Mel Roach, Red Schoendienst, Warren Spahn, Nippy Jones, Hawk Taylor, Del Rice, Wes Covington, Del Crandall, Hank Aaron, Harry Hanebrink, Ernie Johnson, Dave Jolly, Gene Conley
(National Baseball Hall of Fame Library, Cooperstown, N.Y.)

Latino players. Success breeds excitement and the Braves led the NL in attendance every year from 1953 to 1958, setting a major-league attendance record of 2,215,404 in the 1957 championship season.

The 1957 Braves squad was a hard-nosed, take-no-prisoners, ready-to-fight group. After losing two of their final three games and the pennant in 1956, the Braves were determined and battle-tested, yet many prognosticators pegged them for third or even fourth place in 1957. The team was remarkably resilient in the face of adversity. They lost Billy Bruton to a season-ending injury in mid-July, slugger Joe Adcock for 2 1/2 months, and ex-paratrooper Bob Buhl for three tense weeks beginning in mid-August. Teammates stepped up to fill the void, among them hard-hitting outfielder Wes Covington and sure-handed first sacker Frank Torre. And the hitting exploits of a late-season call-up,

outfielder Bob "Hurricane" Hazle, are still stuff of legend. General manager John Quinn was willing to take chances, too. The Braves acquired second baseman Red Schoendienst at the trading deadline to fill the team's one glaring weakness. Warren Spahn, 36 years old but seemingly ageless, kept ticking, led the league in wins, and won his first and only Cy Young Award. But "Hammerin' Hank" Aaron was the key. In his fourth season, he laid claim to the label of Best Player in Baseball by leading the league in home runs and runs batted in (despite batting in the two-hole for almost a third of the season), and won (as unbelievable as it sounds) his only Most Valuable Player Award.

Milwaukee's victory over the New York Yankees in the 1957 World Series may have been considered an upset by some, but not by the Braves and their fans. Lew Burdette's third consecutive complete-game victory, a 5-0 masterpiece on the hallowed grounds of Yankee Stadium in Game Seven, ignited pandemonium in Milwaukee, indeed all over Wisconsin.

The title of this book, *Thar's Joy in Braveland!*, comes from the exuberant headline of the October 7 edition of the *Milwaukee Sentinel* following Eddie Mathews's dramatic, game-winning walk-off home run in the tenth inning in Game Four. Those four words still capture almost 60 years later the excitement, thrill, and sheer enthusiasm of the Braves and their fans upon winning the World Series.

If you are lucky enough to remember the Milwaukee Braves' glorious championship season, recall stories from your family and friends about the time when "David defeated Goliath," or wish to discover the team for the first time, allow the stories and biographies of this book to transport you back to that magical era.

Gregory H. Wolf
Arlington Heights, Illinois
April 15, 2014

Acknowledgements

A labor of love, this book is the result of tireless work of many members of the Society for American Baseball Research (SABR). I express my gratitude to Mark Armour, chairman of SABR's BioProject, and Bill Nowlin, in charge of team projects, for their encouragement and support when I initially suggested a book about the 1957 Milwaukee Braves.

I am indebted to the associate editors and extend to them my sincerest appreciation. Bill Nowlin, the eagle-eyed second reader, fact-checker Russ Lake, and copy editor Len Levin read every word of the text and made numerous corrections to both language and statistics. Their attention to detail has been invaluable.

I thank all of the authors for their contributions, meticulous research, cooperation through the revising and editing process, and finally their patience. It was a long and sometimes frustrating journey from concept to publication. Bob Buege, whose encyclopedic knowledge of the Milwaukee Braves was a precious resource, deserves a special note of gratitude. Thanks also to the Milwaukee Braves Historical Association.

This book would not have been possible without the generous support of the staff and Board of Directors of SABR, SABR Publications Director Cecilia Tan, and designer Gilly Rosenthol (Rosenthol Design). Special thanks to Patricia Kelly of the National Baseball Hall of Fame for supplying the overwhelming majority of photos.

From Yawkey to Milwaukee:
Lou Perini Makes his Move

By Saul Wisnia

He neither slugged like Aaron nor pitched like Spahn, but Lou Perini made his own indelible mark on baseball history. In fact, one can argue that few men ever made a greater impact on the game without playing professionally than the construction giant who moved the Braves from Boston to Milwaukee.

For a half-century from 1903 through 1952, the major leagues consisted of the same 16 teams playing in the same 11 cities. There was no franchise west of St. Louis until Perini gambled that Wisconsinites who enthusiastically supported minor-league clubs would do the same for a major-league outfit. The end result was greater than anybody could have imagined, as the Braves shattered attendance records in their new home and won the 1957 World Series less than five years after relocating.

The move of the Braves was so successful, in fact, that it paved the way for numerous other franchise shifts in the years to come—including the dramatic defection of the New York Giants and Brooklyn Dodgers to the greener pastures of California after the 1957 season. This in turn led to coast-to-coast jet travel and the formation of numerous expansion clubs. By 1969, less than 20 years after Perini's leap of faith, there were 24 major-league teams, including five in California and one in Canada. Lou started it all.

When Perini first became involved with his hometown team, however, moving was the furthest thing from his mind. His large family, and his family business, were firmly entrenched in the Boston area. Perini's father, Bonfiglio ("good son" in Italian) Perini, was a stonemason in Gottolengo, Italy, who immigrated to New York in 1885 and then moved to Massachusetts two years later. He was soon working as a contractor for small dams and roadways throughout and beyond New England, and developed a reputation for taking on jobs—like a 20-mile-long bluestone wall in New York's Catskills—that other men considered too risky or difficult.

Shrewd investments in enterprises like the burgeoning motion-picture industry helped the elder Perini's business grow and withstand equipment shortages during World War I. He and his wife, Clementina, had 13 children, nine of whom survived infancy, and Bonfiglio had sons hauling water around construction sites by age 6. B. Perini and Sons, Inc. incorporated at war's end, in 1918, and as the car became king in the years that followed, the firm took on many large road and highway jobs. Louis Perini recalled for a Boston newspaper how much his father was liked and expressed his admiration for his dad's accomplishments in his adopted homeland.

Work was hard but the family was happy and comfortable. Then, in 1924, came tragedy: Bonfiglio died after a long illness. While they mourned, the children soldiered on with the company—Joseph Perini now

Lou Perini (National Baseball Hall of Fame Library, Cooperstown, N.Y.)

serving as treasurer, daughter Ida as secretary, and 22-year-old Louis (or Lou) as president. The new head man proved quite adept at his job, and nobody was more dedicated; Possessing just an eighth-grade education, Lou took night classes to better understand the business world. Perini and Sons signed its first million-dollar contract around 1930 to build a stretch of the Boston-Worcester Turnpike, and utilized a state-of-the-art high-speed spreader to set new paving records on the job.

By the time the United States entered World War II in 1941, Perini and Sons had developed a great reputation and substantial wealth. A huge wartime defense contract to widen the Cape Cod Canal kept things humming, and a new type of venture also caught the eye of Lou and his familial colleagues—which now included youngest brother Charlie. The Boston Braves baseball club was floundering with a losing record and a tired ballpark, handicapped by a struggling ownership group that could not afford to improve either. Lou Perini, whose own experience with the national pastime had peaked as a teenage catcher for the Ashland Dreadnaughts, saw in the situation a new landscape to conquer.

Perini approached Joe Maney and Guido Rugo, who like him headed local contracting businesses started by their fathers. He encouraged them to join in the venture, and in 1943 this trio picked up majority ownership of the Braves. They also acquired a catchy nickname from sportswriters that perfectly suited their background and take-charge approach: The Three Little Steam Shovels.

"We had been successful as businessmen," recounted Perini, who assumed the role of president (Maney was treasurer). "We knew little about baseball, but we figured that by using sound business methods, we could succeed in baseball as we had succeeded in building bridges, roads, and ammunition dumps."[1] Perini cited their lack of baseball knowledge as an advantage, and said that as contractors they were good planners who could meet any challenge.

A big test was before them. The once-proud Braves franchise, which had played in the first game in National League history, in 1876, and won eight league championships before the turn of the century, was entrenched in a 29-year pennant drought (that would eventually reach 34 years) since their "Miracle" 1914 world championship and had finished no higher than fourth place in 25 years. The team was so bad on the field and at the gate that cash-strapped club executives even ran a contest in local newspapers encouraging fans to come up with a new team nickname that would hopefully change its luck. Boston Bees won out, but the Bees fared no better in the standings from the 1936 through the 1941 seasons. When the Three Little Steam Shovels took control, they were the Braves once more.

A big problem facing the team no matter its name was its crosstown American League rivals, the Boston Red Sox. Once as downtrodden as their neighbors, the Red Sox had risen in the late 1930s and early '40s after being purchased by ore and mining tycoon Tom Yawkey. One of the country's richest men, Yawkey bought the Red Sox shortly after his 30th birthday in 1933 and immediately began spending unheard-of sums to trade for star players like Jimmie Foxx and Lefty Grove. More cash was sent to California in exchange for minor-league standouts Ted Williams, Bobby Doerr, and Dom DiMaggio. Johnny Pesky was snatched up from Oregon.

Yawkey also rebuilt his new team's home of Fenway Park, which always felt cozy and inviting to fans in comparison to cavernous Braves Field. Fenway was right around the corner from bustling Kenmore Square and its numerous hotels, restaurants, and colleges, making it a popular destination point. Braves Field, in contrast, was situated a mile up the road amid nondescript apartment buildings and automobile dealers. It was also hard beside the Charles River and a working railyard, so when the east wind blew cold air in from the river, it mixed with smoke from passing trains and often left fans at Braves Field in a chilly, dusty haze.

There wasn't much the Steam Shovels could do to change their club's hazy fortunes during World War II, but after the war ended in 1945 they went to work in earnest. Not possessing the vast wealth of Yawkey, and with a wife and seven children to support, Lou Perini knew he had to spend money to compete. Starting at the top, he lured former St. Louis Cardinals manager Billy Southworth—a future Hall of Famer then revered as baseball's best skipper—with a record $35,000 annual salary for three years plus bonuses of up to $20,000 for finishing third, second, or first. More cash and savvy trades brought in stars like outfielder Jeff Heath, third baseman Bob Elliot, and college shortstop Alvin Dark, who blended with holdovers including fan favorite and hard-hitting outfielder Tommy Holmes and 20-game-winners Johnny Sain and Warren Spahn to form a contending team.

This group jelled under Southworth to win the 1948 National League pennant, and set a franchise attendance record of 1,455,439 in the process that for once nearly matched what the Red Sox were drawing down the street with a great club of their own. AL champs two years before, the Red Sox in 1948 tied for first with the Cleveland Indians before losing in a one-game playoff at Fenway—an outcome that denied the Braves a chance to beat out their crosstown rivals in an all-Boston World Series. Southworth's troops might still have claimed their spot as top dogs in town with a Series triumph, but Cleveland prevailed in six games.

Hopes for extended success by the Braves were short-lived. Injuries and dissension wracked the 1949 team, which finished in fourth as attendance dropped nearly 35 percent. The Red Sox had another near-miss season, battling with the New York Yankees to the wire before losing the pennant on the season's final day. The gap between Boston's two teams was widening once more.

Perini did everything he could to stop the tide. He fixed up Braves Field with fir trees, fried clams and televisions at the concession stands, neon foul poles, and a $75,000 electronic scoreboard. He poured money into player development, and promoted the team's great young talent with the Rookie Rocket—an airplane that flew sportswriters around nationwide to observe high-school and college players signing Braves contracts. Perhaps most importantly, Lou integrated his team nearly a decade before the Red Sox, acquiring speedy outfielder Sam Jethroe in a deal with the Brooklyn Dodgers before the 1950 season in a move that may have actually done more harm than good for attendance in the then racially divided city.

Nothing Perini tried won back the crowds. The Braves finished fourth in 1950 and 1951, and in the latter year drew fewer than a half-million fans while operating at a $380,000 loss. This was merely a prelude to an even more dismal 1952, when the club fell to seventh with a 64-89 record and was the lowest-drawing team in baseball. Just 281,278 saw games at Braves Field that year, an average of 3,653 a contest in a 40,000-seat ballpark. Attendance topped 10,000 just twice all season, and financial losses for Perini, Rugo, and Maney were listed at $580,000 for the year (and rumored to be closer to $1 million). A glance at the numbers, and it was clearer than ever that Boston was a Red Sox town; despite a lackluster sixth-place club, and Ted Williams's departure for the Marines after April, the Red Sox still drew a respectable 1,115,750 to Fenway Park that summer.

One possible solution for this disparity was never tried. According to his longtime assistant Chuck Patterson, Perini approached Red Sox owner Yawkey in the early '50s and asked about the possibility of the two teams sharing Fenway Park; since they played in different leagues, the Braves and Red Sox could switch off using the ballpark and taking road trips. "Lou tried to sell Mr. Yawkey the same story he tried to tell the press; that it would be good for both ballclubs, that there should be a baseball game in Boston every day, and that he might not be able to stay in town otherwise," said Patterson. "That [last thing] is probably just what Tom Yawkey wanted to hear."[2]

In one area Perini and Yawkey did see eye-to-eye, however: the Jimmy Fund. In 1948, aided by Braves public relations director Billy Sullivan—future founder and owner of the NFL's Boston/New England Patriots—and a giving organization of theater owners known as the Variety Club of New England, Perini helped launch this charitable arm of the Children's Cancer Research Foundation, later known as Dana-Farber Cancer Institute. The Jimmy Fund supports cancer treatment for patients of all ages at Dana-Farber, along with research into possible cures. It was officially unveiled to the public when the starting lineup of the 1948 Braves visited the hospital bedside of a 12-year-old cancer patient—called Jimmy to protect his identity—while a nationwide radio audience listened. "My father died of cancer; so did two of my uncles," Lou Perini explained of his involvement. "I watched my father drop from a robust 260 pounds to about 100 within six months. I made up my mind then that if there was anything I could ever do to help raise cancer research money, I'd do it."[3]

The Jimmy Fund was often trumpeted in its early years by Braves players at cookouts, clinics, and other events, and as of 2013 the Perini family had maintained its commitment to the cause for 65 years. Yawkey pledged when the Braves departed for Milwaukee to continue the Jimmy Fund connection, and it became an official Red Sox charity. For a number of years after the franchise moved to Milwaukee the Braves returned to play the Red Sox in Jimmy Fund Games at Fenway, with all proceeds dedicated to research and patient care at Dana-Farber.

Whether battling cancer or the St. Louis Cardinals, Lou Perini never retreated from the limelight. He was a fan-first owner who drove in with his big brood of kids from their suburban Wellesley home for Sunday doubleheaders, and while at the ballpark he was always accessible to the crowd.

"The owner's box was just to the left of the Braves dugout, which was on the third-base side," recalled Lou's son David Perini, who was a teenager during these years and later succeeded his father as president of the family business. "He would tell us all to spread out so the stands looked fuller, and we could hear the hecklers getting on Dad. It was really difficult for me as a kid to take. But Dad's whole thing was, 'Always stand proud.' After games he would talk and debate with fans while we walked back to the car."[4]

By this point sports columnists were also turning against the Braves, and David Perini recalled that he and his siblings wanted to write a letter to the editor in response to one particularly harsh story. "Our father said, 'I don't think that's the best way to handle it.' His philosophy was it was always better to let sleeping dogs lie. 'If you, as Perini kids, write a letter,' he said, 'the columnist will play that up and blow it all out of proportion.' We never did do it, but it really hurt."

What David and his siblings didn't know then was that their father was considering a decision that would have huge ramifications for the family, Boston, and all of baseball. When the elder Perini bought out partners Maney and Rugo in November 1952, some in the press speculated that Lou was bailing out his buddies while others thought it might be the prelude to a sale or even a move by the Braves. Perini, after all, also owned the team's top minor-league club, in Milwaukee, where fans packed home games and longed for a major-league team. Perini promised he would help them get one, and work had begun on a 36,000-seat city-funded stadium to help sweeten the pot. There was no guarantee there would ever be an MLB club to play there, but that's how hungry Milwaukee's civic leaders were to go big league.

Initially, David Perini attested, his father wanted to give Boston fans at least one more year to show their support for the Braves. Promising young position players like third baseman Eddie Mathews, shortstop Johnny Logan, and catcher Del Crandall boded well for the future, and that summer the club had signed up a young Negro Leaguer named Henry Aaron who also looked solid. Spahn still anchored the pitching staff, and newcomers to the rotation including Chet Nichols and Lew Burdette seemed poised to join him as big winners. "As long as I own the Braves," Lou Perini once said, "they will belong to Boston."[5]

Then circumstances forced his hand. Bill Veeck, the sharp-tongued, iconoclastic owner of the American League's St. Louis Browns, faced a problem similar to Perini's in that his woeful club was having a hard time competing at the gate with its intercity rival, the St. Louis Cardinals of the National League. Veeck wanted to move his club, and saw Milwaukee as an excellent option. He planned to seek permission from his fellow American League owners that winter for a transfer, and even though he was not well-loved among his peers, Veeck was a strong self-promoter who had proved he could pack ballparks.

Since Perini owned the territorial rights to Milwaukee in Organized Baseball, Veeck could not move the Browns there without Lou's permission. The cat-and-mouse game between the two owners played out in the press, and Wisconsin fans and politicians began pressuring Perini to let Veeck have Milwaukee or move there himself. In addition to excitement about the prospects of having a major-league club, these folks knew such a shift would be a huge boon for local and statewide businesses.

Perini realized he might never have a better opportunity to revive his franchise. Boston fans were not responding to his moves to improve the lineup and Braves Field, and less than 500 season tickets had been sold for the coming 1953 season. Milwaukee was a growing city with a strong factory-based economy boosted by World War II contracts and several prosperous breweries, and eventually Lou decided to take the plunge. He called his baseball staff to his Framingham, Massachusetts, construction offices, and, according to Patterson, his assistant, said, "I'm going to tell you fellows something, and I don't even want you to tell your wives. We're going to have to move the team to Milwaukee."

The men, including Perini, kept their word. David Perini said that even his own mother didn't know his dad had made up his mind, and when the Braves headed for spring training in Florida the next February they did so with "B's" on their caps. Then, on Friday the 13th of March, 1953, a reporter from the *Milwaukee Sentinel*, acting on a tip, asked Perini if he was about to go through with shifting his club. "I can't say yes and I can't say no," the owner replied, and that was good enough for headlines like "BRAVES QUIT HUB" to begin appearing in the *Boston Globe*.

Five days later, with a big assist from league president Warren Giles, Perini got the required unanimous vote from his seven fellow NL owners — unlike Bill Veeck, Lou Perini was very well-liked within this fraternity — and the transfer was official. "WE'RE THE HOME OF THE BRAVES!" read the front-page headline of the *Milwaukee Sentinel*, and the Braves' schedule was quickly switched with that of the Pittsburgh Pirates to resolve conflicts with East Coast starting times and night games. The 1953 All-Star Game, ironically scheduled to be played at Braves Field for the first time since 1936, was switched to Cincinnati.

"It basically came down to this — the last thing my father wanted to do was move the team from Boston, but it was an absolute economic necessity to do so," David Perini recalled 40 years later. "The Braves were losing a tremendous amount of money, and I think he felt he needed to go to a territory where there wasn't already a major-league team and the Braves would be accepted and draw well. I think he saw the Braves as sort of a sleeping giant in a way with tremendous potential that wasn't being realized."

As was often the case in matters of business, Lou Perini was correct. The Braves were welcomed to their new home like conquering heroes, greeted by a crowd of 10,000 at the train station and feted by 60,000 in a parade before they even played an inning at brand-new County Stadium — the first major-league ballpark financed entirely by public funds. Lou's daughter Mary, then in college, remembered "being treated like Madonna" by a fan base that saw even the owner's children as celebrities.

Mary's dad hoped his club could draw one million fans that first year in Milwaukee, and it did — in just over half a season. Players like Mathews, Logan, Crandall, and Burdette matured into stars seemingly overnight, making the Braves an instant contender that nearly reversed its record of the previous summer with a 92-62, second-place finish. The final County Stadium tally of 1,826,397 fans set a new National League attendance mark, and the Braves enjoyed a profit of nearly $1.5 million. City officials estimated that the team's arrival generated nearly $5 million in new business for Milwaukee, a city of just 725,000 residents.

Lou's gamble had paid off, and the good times continued for nearly a decade. Aaron came up in 1954, and he, Mathews, and the ageless Spahn formed the nucleus of a team that contended annually and nearly won four straight pennants from 1956-1959. Part of the club's drawing appeal early on stemmed from a decision by Perini not to allow for the televising of any Braves games — home or away — into the homes of Milwaukee residents. If you wanted to see his great club perform, you had to come to the ballpark. And fans kept coming, 2,131,388 strong in 1954 for another record.

The rest of baseball took notice; buoyed by the success of the Braves, American League owners allowed the Browns to move to Baltimore in 1954 (where they became the Orioles) and the struggling Philadelphia

Athletics to shift to Kansas City a year later. Like the Braves, both the Browns and the A's had grown tired of being the second most popular club in two-team towns. In both cases there were brand-new or remodeled ballparks waiting for them in their new homes. Perini, ever the great construction man, had started a new building trend without lifting any of his own shovels.

When the Braves hosted the 1955 All-Star Game, it was like a coming-out party for Perini to show the sporting world what he had accomplished. Among those attending were Brooklyn Dodgers owner Walter O'Malley and New York Giants owner Horace Stoneham, whose legendary franchises had begun struggling at the gate because of aging stadiums in changing urban neighborhoods. "Certainly O'Malley and Stoneham were awakened by the opportunities that lay ahead because of the experience that the Braves had under Perini," said Andrew Zimbalist, the author of several acclaimed books on the business of baseball. "The sleeping sport had a dousing of cold water thrown on its head and any owner with an IQ over 80 noticed and said, 'Wow, here are some opportunities.'"[6]

By 1956 the Braves were poised to come out on top not only at the gate—where they drew 2 million yet again—but also on the field. They wound up just short, finishing a single game behind the defending champion Dodgers, but in 1957 the Braves overcame first Brooklyn and St. Louis for the pennant and then the heavily-favored New York Yankees in a seven-game World Series thriller. Milwaukee repeated as pennant winner in 1958, losing a rematch to the Yankees in another seven-game Series, and then lost a best-of-three playoff in two games to the Los Angeles Dodgers in 1959 after the two clubs tied at the end of the regular season.

O'Malley and Stoneham had by then followed the trend set by Perini, and road games against the Dodgers and Giants now necessitated chartered airline flights to California. As in Milwaukee, the eventual new ballparks in Los Angeles and San Francisco were surrounded by huge parking lots, emblematic of the changing American landscape that Perini had foreseen. "Clearly just as the country was changing to suburbanization, auto mobilization of the late 1940s and early 1950s and the introduction of television on a mass basis throughout the society ... was a westward movement at a very rapid growth indigenously of the population of California," said Zimbalist.[7]

Like the Braves, the Dodgers set a team attendance record of 1,845,556 during their first season (1958) after moving, but in their case they did it with a seventh-place team and in a home venue (Los Angeles Memorial Coliseum) not appropriate for professional baseball. In Los Angeles the good times have never really stopped rolling; thanks to beautiful weather and a majestic ballpark, Dodger Stadium, which opened in 1962, annual crowd numbers have dipped below 2 million just five times in more than half a century (and never since 1972). Through winning seasons and nonwinning seasons, the crowds have kept coming.

In Milwaukee, however, the tremendous surge of the early years began to wane when the Braves' string of championship-caliber seasons ended. During 1960, when the club finished seven games behind the Pittsburgh Pirates and was never closer than five games from the top after early August, average attendance at County Stadium dipped below 20,000 (and season attendance under 1.5 million) for the first time. In addition to not having an exciting pennant race to watch down the stretch, fans were miffed at a decision by the Milwaukee County Board to prohibit them from carrying six-packs of beer into the ballpark. This was, after all, Brew City.

The board lifted the ban in 1961, but the bad taste left in fans' mouths remained. Many who had stopped coming the year before stayed away, and it didn't help that the Braves dropped to fourth place. Even though Aaron, Mathews, Spahn, and other lesser luminaries were still on the roster, crowd numbers fell dramatically again to less than 15,000 per game. For the first time in Milwaukee, the Braves attendance was below the league average.

Perini was not about to go through another free-fall like the one he had in Boston. He began televising Braves games heavily in the early '60s, realizing that TV had become popular and lucrative enough that he could make back hundreds of thousands of dollars in sponsorship and advertising fees to lessen the economic blow of declining crowds. Still, with attendance dipping to just 766,921 in 1962 (eighth in the ten-team National League), Perini lost money for the first time in Milwaukee after making $7.5 million in profits from 1953-1961.

Perini's construction company, now known as the Perini Corporation, had continued to grow. The firm went public in 1961, and the new shareholders were unhappy with declining numbers in the baseball sector. Sharing their concern, Lou Perini sold the Milwaukee Braves to the Chicago-based Lasalle Corporation, led by 34-year-old insurance broker William Bartholomay, on November 16, 1962. The purchase price was $6.2 million.

It was the perfect time for Perini to get out. The love affair between the Braves and Milwaukee was coming to an end, and the new owners made clear their intent to move the team if a suitable suitor city stepped forward. Atlanta showed interest, and Bartholomay began negotiating with Georgia officials to make the change a reality. Milwaukee County officials fought to keep the team in town, but it was too little too late. The move to Atlanta was announced in November 1964, with the team to relocate in 1966 after a final lame-duck season in Wisconsin.

Lou Perini, meanwhile, was back to concentrating full-time about what he knew best, construction. Now nearing a half-century as head of his business, he presided over a firm in the 1960s that built some of the largest dams, tunnels, marine installations, and buildings around the world. "Dad ate and slept the construction business," said son David Perini. "We discussed it at dinner and toured job sites on Sundays after church. It was a constant in our life."[8]

So, for 20 years, had been the Braves. It was tough to get the team out of his blood, so even after he sold it, Lou Perini maintained a 10 percent interest in the franchise and sat on its board of directors. The major-league landscape continued shifting and expanding, to the point where today there are 30 teams playing in six divisions. Many owe their existence to the forward thinking of Lou Perini.

When he died of cancer on April 16, 1972, at Good Samaritan Hospital in West Palm Beach, Florida, at the age of 68, Perini was mourned as a great family man and a giant in the fields of both baseball and building. His acts of charity, including his integral part in the founding of the Jimmy Fund and Dana-Farber Cancer Institute, were duly noted. And while he may never join Aaron, Mathews, and Spahn in the Baseball Hall of Fame, Lou Perini is still making an impact—each time a major-league game is played in California or a cancer patient receives support from the David B. Perini, Jr. Quality of Life Clinic at Dana-Farber, named in memory of his grandson.

"Of all the things we ever did with the Braves in Boston," Lou Perini once said, "the Jimmy Fund gave me the most personal satisfaction."[9] Along with baseball's modern geographical makeup, it remains his legacy.

Sources

Interviews

Author interviews with Louis Perini, Jr., Mary Perini, and Chuck Patterson, 1990s.

Author interviews with David Perini, 1992-2010.

Newspapers

Boston Globe, 1943-1963.

Boston Herald, 1943-1963.

Other printed materials

Herring, Ben, *Constructor* (company newsletter covering construction industry), December 1990.

Hirshberg, Al, "The Man Who Made Milwaukee Happy," *Saga* magazine, July 1954.

"History" section of Perini Building Company website, tutorperini.com.

Kaese, Harold. *The Boston Braves* (New York: G. P. Putnam's Sons, 1954).

Kaese, Harold. "They're Digging a Pennant in Boston," *Saturday Evening Post*, June 28, 1947.

Povletich, William, *Milwaukee Braves, Heroes and Heartache* (Madison, Wisconsin: Wisconsin Historical Society Press, 2009).

Film

Povletich, William. *A Braves New World* (documentary film), Wisconsin Public Television, 2009.

Notes

1   Harold Kaese, "They're Digging a Pennant in Boston," Saturday Evening Post, June 28, 1947.

2   All quotations from Chuck Patterson are from the author's interviews unless otherwise noted.

3   Al Hirshberg, "The Man Who Made Milwaukee Happy," Saga, magazine, July 1954.

4   All quotations from David Perini are from the author's interviews unless otherwise noted.

5   Harold Kaese, "They're Digging a Pennant in Boston," Saturday Evening Post, June 28, 1947.

6   William Povletich, A Braves New World (documentary film), Wisconsin Public Television, 2009.

7   Ibid.

8   Ben Herring, *Constructor*, newsletter covering construction industry, December 1990.

9   Al Hirshberg, "The Man Who Made Milwaukee Happy," Saga magazine, July 1954.

Henry "Hank" Aaron

By William Johnson

"Henry Aaron in the second inning walked and scored. He's sittin' on 714. Here's the pitch by Downing. Swinging. There's a drive into left-center field! That ball is gonna be … outta here! It's gone! It's 715! There's a new home run champion of all time, and it's Henry Aaron!"

— Atlanta Braves announcer
Milo Hamilton, April 8, 1974

WITH THAT SWING of the bat, along with the 714 that preceded it, Hank Aaron not only passed Babe Ruth as the major leagues' career home-run leader, but he also made a giant leap in the integration of the game and the nation. Aaron, an African-American, had broken a record set by the immortal Ruth, and not just any record, but the career home-run record, and in doing so moved the game and the nation forward on the journey started by Jackie Robinson in 1947. By 1974 Aaron's baseball career was within three years of sunset, but the road he'd traveled to arrive at that spring evening in Atlanta had hardened and tempered him, perhaps irrevocably, in ways that only suffering can produce. Aaron finally shrugged off the twin burdens of expectation and fear that evening, and few ever stood taller.

Henry Louis Aaron was born on February 5, 1934, in Mobile Alabama, to Herbert and Estella (Pritchett) Aaron. Among his seven siblings was a brother, Tommie, who later played in parts of seven seasons in the major leagues. For whatever such records are worth, the brothers still hold the record for most career home runs by a pair of siblings, 768, with the elder Henry contributing 755 to Tommie's 13. They were also the first siblings to appear in a League Championship Series as teammates.

The Aarons lived in a poorer neighborhood of Mobile called Down the Bay, but he spent most of his formative years in the nearby district of Toulminville. The family lived on the edge of poverty, in part due to the Great Depression, so every member of the family worked to contribute. Young Henry picked cotton, among other odd jobs, and while his parents could not afford proper baseball equipment for recreation, Henry was able to practice in endless sandlot games and by hitting bottle caps with broom handles and sticks. One of the consequences of this self-coaching was that he developed a cross-handed batting style, a habit he kept until his early days in the professional ranks. Aaron was a gifted athlete and starred in football and baseball at Central High School for two years. On the diamond he played shortstop, third base, and some outfield on a team that won the Mobile Negro High School Championship during his freshman and sophomore years.

In 1949 the 15-year-old Aaron — inspired by the exploits of Jackie Robinson, whom he'd seen on several exhibition passes through Alabama — was allowed to try out with the Brooklyn Dodgers, but did not earn a contract offer, likely due to his unorthodox batting grip. Now a high-school junior, however, he transferred to the private Josephine Allen Institute for his final two

Henry Aaron (National Baseball Hall of Fame Library, Cooperstown, N.Y.)

years of education. He had been playing for the semipro Pritchett Athletics since he was 14, and during those games, and in some of his softball contests, he drew the attention of Ed Scott. The scout convinced Henry and his mother that it would be a good move to sign with the Mobile Black Bears, a semipro team, for $3 a game. Estella granted the boy permission to play, but only on the condition that the he did not travel, thus limiting him to local games.

On November 20, 1951, despite his mother's concerns about his not continuing on to college, Henry signed for $200 a month with the Negro American League champion Indianapolis Clowns. Scout Bunny Downs had seen Aaron playing with the Black Bears, and once with Indianapolis Aaron flourished, helping guide the team to the 1952 Negro League World Series crown. In 26 games that year he posted a .366 batting average, hit five home runs, and stole nine bases. The series, and the season, allowed Aaron to showcase his range of skills not just for regional scouts, but for several major-league organizations as well.

After the championship series, two telegrams reached Henry — one with an offer from the New York Giants, the other with an offer from the Boston Braves. Aaron chose the latter, evidently because of a $50-a-month difference in salary, and Boston immediately purchased his contract from Indianapolis. On June 14, 1952, Aaron signed with Braves scout Dewey Griggs, and reported to the Class C Eau Claire (Wisconsin) Bears. There the coaches helped him eliminate his cross-handed batting grip, and the results were staggering. In 87 games Aaron batted .336 with 9 homers, 19 doubles, and 61 RBIs, earned a spot on the league's All-Star squad, and was selected the Northern League's Rookie of the Year. As impressive as his on-field performance was, though, it may have even been exceeded by his calm mien both on and off the diamond. The teenager's demeanor seemed impenetrable to the occasional bigots in the stands, and the clear absence of racial incidents that season proved his maturity in a way that could not be measured by simple interviews. Aaron not only showed the Braves that he was a wonderful prospect on the field, but also that he could handle the inevitable racism with detachment.

The next season, 1953, found the Braves playing in Milwaukee and Aaron and black teammates Horace Garner and Felix Mantilla on the Jacksonville Braves. Along with two other players from the Savannah Indians, Fleming "Buddy" Reedy and Al Israel, the quintet broke the color line in the South Atlantic (Sally) League, playing in the heart of old Dixie without the top cover of a sympathetic national press. Aaron, playing second base, almost singlehandedly forced the Jacksonville fans to accept him, regardless of race, by leading the league with a batting average of .362 as well as runs (115), hits (208), doubles (36), total bases (338), and runs batted in (115). To cap the first desegregated season in Sally League history Aaron led Jacksonville to the title and was named the league's Most Valuable Player. Because many parts of the South were still governed by Jim Crow laws, circumstances that forced the black players to live in separate accommodations and dining on the road, one pundit wrote, "Henry Aaron led the league in everything except hotel accommodations."[1]

That year Henry also met a young woman named Barbara Lewis. On a lark, she attended a Jacksonville game one night early in the season and watched Aaron single, double, and homer. On October 6, 1953, Aaron, not yet 20, and Lewis were married and within a year welcomed their first child, a daughter they named Gaile.

Aaron spent part of the offseason playing winter ball in Puerto Rico, learning to play the outfield and working with coach Mickey Owen on his batting stance. On March 11, 1954, in spring training, Henry was penciled into the Braves' starting lineup as leadoff hitter and right fielder. He homered and singled. Two days later Milwaukee's left fielder, Bobby Thomson, severely fractured his right ankle. The ensuing lineup shuffle gave Aaron his chance, an opportunity to play as a regular outfielder. The young slugger made the most of his chance.

The Braves purchased Aaron's minor-league contract when spring training ended. On Tuesday afternoon, April 13, 1954, Aaron made his major-league debut in the season opener at Cincinnati, playing left field and batting fifth. Two days later, in Milwaukee, he doubled in the first inning off St. Louis Cardinals pitcher Vic

Raschi for his first major-league hit, and on the 23rd in St. Louis he victimized Raschi again, this time for his first home run. Aaron fractured his left ankle sliding into third base on September 5, ending his season, but in his first 122 big-league games he batted .280, homered 13 times, and finished fourth in the voting for Rookie of the Year. In 1955 Aaron was moved to right field, and there his league-leading 37 doubles, .314 batting average, and .540 slugging percentage helped him earn the first of 21 consecutive All-Star team slots and a ninth-place finish in the National League MVP balloting.

During the early days of Aaron's career, Milwaukee public relations director Don Davidson began referring to him as Hank, not Henry as he was known by those close to him, in an effort to make the quiet player appear a bit more accessible.

In 1956 Aaron hit .328 to win the first of his two batting titles, led the league in doubles (34) and hits (200), and was named *The Sporting News* NL Player of the Year. Aaron would lead the league four times in doubles and twice in hits. It proved to be mere foreshadowing for the following year.

Hank's 1957 baseball season began under less than ideal circumstances when he missed his train in Mobile and reported a day late to spring training in Bradenton, Florida. Since he had signed a new contract during the offseason, one that raised his salary to $22,500, Aaron's tardiness drew the attention of national papers like *The Sporting News*, as well as the Milwaukee press. Another potential omen came with the distribution of his Topps baseball card. It was printed as a photographic reverse, with Hank appearing to bat left-handed. On closer inspection, his uniform number "44" was reversed and clearly underscored the mistake, but the Topps corporate leadership chose not to correct the error and reprint the card.

Regardless of what the baseball card showed, Aaron was not affected on the field. That March in Florida he batted .390 with 11 home runs, despite missing seven games with a sprained ankle. Manager Fred Haney, in the March 27 edition of *The Sporting News*, was quoted as saying: "He hasn't reached his potential yet. I expect him to do better this year. That's how we've got to improve to win the flag." Hank tinkered with his approach in the batter's box, switching from a 36-ounce bat to a 34-ounce model, and he opened the 1957 season by batting safely and scoring in the Braves' first seven games.

The public praise rolled in during those early weeks. In *The Sporting News* on April 24, Dick Young wrote that Dodgers coach Billy Herman "rates Hank Aaron over Willie Mays as a hitter—and over everyone in the NL for my money." The following week, in the same newspaper, Bob Wolf wrote: "Whether or not he wins the Triple Crown, or even two-thirds of it, Aaron certainly must be considered the favorite in the batting derby … and while Aaron isn't high on his chances of leading the league in homers or runs batted in, he agrees that he should repeat as batting king." After 25 games Hank was hitting at a .369 clip and had committed no errors in the field.

Stan Musial, however, was not as impressed as the reporters who followed the team. In a June 26 *Sporting News* article by Cleon Walfoort, Musial left no room for doubt, stating, "[Aaron] thinks there's nothing he can't hit. He'll have to learn there are some pitches no hitter can afford to go for. He still has something to learn about the strike zone." His reference to Aaron as an "arrogant hitter" drew a response, cited in the same article, from Pittsburgh manager Bobby Bragan. "Sure, Aaron's a bad-ball hitter and he always will be, but it would be a bad mistake to try to change him."

Given the late arrival to spring training, Musial's comments, along with a general undertone in the wider reporting on Aaron and what was occasionally dismissed as a lack of effort, Haney again came to his slugger's defense. "That loping gait of Hank Aaron's is deceptive. You'd almost get the impression he wasn't hustling at times, but he'd be about the last player you could accuse that of. He just runs as fast as he has to, and you'll notice he always seems to get to a fly ball or a base in time when there's any chance of making it."

Normally such an offensive outburst would result in a nearly automatic selection to the All-Star team, but ballot stuffing" by Cincinnati fans elected Reds to eight National League starting positions. (The only non-Red was Stan Musial.) Commissioner Ford Frick partly overruled the results and put Aaron and Willie Mays on the starting team.

The All-Star Game was little more than a brief respite in Aaron's terrific season. On July 5 he surpassed his 1956 season home-run total when he hit number 27 off the Cubs' Don Elston. By midmonth Bob Wolf, writing in *The Sporting News,* began touting the hitter's chances for the Triple Crown. Despite Aaron's preseason protestation that he did not see himself as a power hitter, after 77 games he was on pace to tie Babe Ruth's single-season home run record of 60, and on August 15 he smacked career homer number 100. A week later he drove in his 100th run of the season. All the numbers, though, paled in comparison to a single swing of the bat the following month.

On September 23, in the bottom of the 11th inning facing St Louis, Aaron stroked a breaking ball over the fence at County Stadium. The two-run shot was the only homer Cardinals pitcher Billy Muffett surrendered all year, but the walk-off win clinched the pennant for the Braves. Hank was carried off the field that night by his jubilant teammates, and he always remembered that hit, that game, and that night as one of the greatest moments of his career.

A *Milwaukee Journal Sentinel* retrospective on February 26, 2012, quoted Commissioner Bud Selig as saying, "Henry Aaron in '57 was, well, he was a player for the ages. I have never seen a hitter like him. Forget our relationship. I'm telling you, in the '50s, when you watched Hank Aaron, you knew you were watching something really special." That year Aaron led the NL with 44 home runs, 132 runs batted in, 369 total bases, and 118 runs scored, but failed to meet his batting goal of .350. Instead he finished a "mere" fourth in the league race with a .322 average. It was enough to earn him the only Most Valuable Player trophy of his career.

Hank followed that with 11 hits, including three homers, in 28 at-bats in the World Series as the Braves defeated the New York Yankees iu seven games. His .393 average was a fitting conclusion to a remarkable season. Both the man and his team walked off the field after the final out that October as, unquestionably, the best in baseball.

The year 1957 was also special for the Aarons for other reasons. In March Barbara had delivered their first son, Hank Jr., and in December twins Lary and Gary arrived. Gary died in the hospital, but the family carried on. It grew once more, in 1962, with the birth of Dorinda.

In 1958, due in large part to Aaron's 30 home runs, the Braves returned to the World Series, but lost to the Yankees in seven games. Henry finished third in the MVP voting but did win his first Gold Glove award. The following year Aaron appeared on the television show *Home Run Derby* and won six consecutive matches—along with $13,000—before falling to the Phillies' Wally Post. Afterward Aaron noted that he changed his swing to help him hit more home runs because "[T]hey never had a show called *Singles Derby.*"

Aaron's 1959 season was arguably the best of his extraordinary career. Not only did he lead both major leagues in hits (223), batting average (.355), slugging (.636), and total bases (400), he committed only five errors all season while winning his second (of three) Gold Glove awards. The fielding mark is even more impressive in that although he played 144 games as right fielder, he also played 13 in center and even five full games at third base.

Aaron hit his 200th career home run on July 3, 1960, off Cardinals pitcher Ron Kline, and on June 8, 1961, he joined Eddie Mathews, Joe Adcock, and Frank Thomas as the first quartet to hit consecutive homers in a game, a 10-8 loss to the Cincinnati Reds. In 1963 he led the NL in home runs and RBIs, and also became the third member of the majors' 30/30 club, stealing 31 bases and socking 44 homers. That year Aaron barely missed winning the Triple Crown, losing the batting title to Tommy Davis by a scant .007 points, finishing fourth with a .319 batting average.

Aaron continued to excel throughout the decade. In 1966, the first season for the Braves in Atlanta, he hit his 400th home run, off Bo Belinsky in Philadelphia, and in 1968 he crested the 500 plateau, against Mike McCormick of the San Francisco Giants. He moved into third place on the career home-run list on July 30, 1969, when he passed Mickey Mantle with number 537. Despite Aaron's personal successes (a third-place finish in the MVP voting), the Braves were swept in three games by the improbable New York Mets in the new League Championship Series. In that series Aaron batted .357 with three home runs.

The 1960s marked the peak of Aaron's career. From 1960 to 1971, he averaged 152 games per season. In an "average" season, Aaron batted .308, scored 107 runs, amassed 331 total bases, hit 38 homers, and drove in 112 runs. This was all the more remarkable in that the time frame is widely remembered as the "decade of the pitcher," yet Aaron gave no quarter when batting against some of the best pitchers in the game. Don Drysdale was his most frequent home-run victim, yielding 17, but the slugger also punished luminaries like Sandy Koufax and Juan Marichal, along with a wide array of less gifted hurlers.

Aaron's gift in the batter's box flowed through his hands and wrists. In the 1990 book *Men at Work: The Craft of Baseball*, author George Will summarized Hank's approach: "Henry Aaron once said, 'I never worried about the fastball. They couldn't throw it past me. None of them.' That was true, but that was Aaron, he of the phenomenally quick wrists and whippy, thin-handled bat." Despite standing 6 feet tall, Aaron weighed a mere 180 pounds, almost scrawny in comparison to later sluggers, but his unique physical talent allowed him to wait on the pitcher for a split-second longer than most other hitters, to seemingly pluck the ball from the catcher's glove with his bat, and made him one of the most feared sluggers in the league.

With his 3,000th career hit, a single against the Cincinnati Reds on May 17, 1970, Aaron became the first player ever to reach the dual milestones of 3,000 hits and 500 home runs. That year, with his 38 homers, he established a National League record for the most seasons by a player with 30 or more home runs. The following year, on April 28, 1971, Aaron hit homer number 600 off future Hall of Famer Gaylord Perry, joining Ruth and Mays in a most exclusive power-hitting fraternity. With his career-high 47 home runs that year, he also set a league record for most seasons with 40 or more homers, and set an unofficial mark for "close-but-no-cigar" when he finished third in MVP balloting for a sixth time.

On the personal front, things between Henry and Barbara came to a head. The couple had been having marital difficulties since 1966, and had drifted apart. In February 1971 they formalized the separation with a legal divorce. Two years later, in 1973, Aaron married Billye Williams, a former Atlanta television journalist, in Jamaica.

Despite the major leagues' first labor-related work stoppage in 1972, Aaron passed Mays on the home run list when he hammered number 661 off Reds pitcher Don Gullett on August 6. The impact of the strike wouldn't really show until the following season. The two weeks that were lost to pension-benefit negotiations represented eight lost opportunities for Aaron to continue his chase of Ruth's home-run record, and by the end of 1973, with the national media working itself into a lather over Aaron's pursuit of the iconic total, he ended the season with 713, one shy of tying the Bambino.

The stresses on the player, the team, opposing pitchers, and the sport that were spawned—or perhaps revealed—by Aaron's 1973 season have been chronicled in a variety of sources. Henry retained an essential quiet dignity with the media. He never allowed the moment to cause him to break in public, although a lesser man certainly might have cracked. Aaron received, literally, thousands of letters every week, the torment was prolonged over the winter of 1973-74. In 1973 the nation was a scant decade past the passage of the contentious Civil Rights Act, and it was less than a generation since Rosa Parks had refused to move to the back of her bus, so overt bigotry was not nearly as foreign as it might be now. Some of the letters Aaron opened, however, are almost unbelievable for any era.

Some of the notable ones from the collection at the National Baseball Hall of Fame in Cooperstown (spelling and punctuation are verbatim):

"Hi, Hank,
I sees you hit 711 homers. When I goes to sleep every night I pray as follows:
1—That you'se stop hitting these cheap homers
2—That the pitchers stop lobbing in the ball for you to hit.
3—That youse have a good accident when youse hit 713 and never been able to play another game.

4 — That youse get good and sick.

5 — That Babe Ruth is the best homer hitter & 714 is always the record.

6 — That youse get mugged by one of our brothers of the Black Panther Party."

Another one, from mid-1973, read:

"Dear Hank Aaron,

Why are they making such a big fuss about your hitting 701 home runs.? [sic]

Please remember, you have been at bat over 2700 more times than Babe Ruth. If Babe Ruth was at bat 2700 more times he would have hit 814 home runs.

So, Hank what are you bragging about. Lets have the truth. You mentioned if you were white they would give you more credit. That's ignorance. Stupid.

Hank, there are three things you can't give a Nigger. A black eye, a puffed lip or a job.

The Cubs stink, the Cubs stink, Hinky Dinky, Stinky Parlevous. The Cubs are through, the Cubs are through, Hinky Pinky Parlevous."

These are just a tiny sample of the venom and rage directed at Aaron throughout the later stages of his quest. In a third letter, a self-described "50 year old White Woman from Massachusetts" wrote, "*To Hank Aaron: A Rotten Nigger … .you must have made every intelligent white man hate you and your opinions even more…*" Describing those letters as mere irrational raving is reasonable nearly 40 years after the chase, but at the time, with a black player pursuing the record of a white one, the threats seemed very real.

On the positive side, once the nation became aware of the bigotry, public support for Aaron poured in. But Aaron, perhaps channeling his inner Jackie Robinson, took the field without apparent regard for the attention surrounding his play. Atlanta opened the 1974 season in Cincinnati, and although the Braves management wanted Hank to break Ruth's record in Atlanta, Commissioner Bowie Kuhn decreed that Aaron had to play at least two games of the road series.

Henry sat on his 713 total for one at-bat, hitting number 714 on April 4 off Cincinnati's Jack Billingham. On April 8, in front of 53,775 fans in Atlanta, he finally broke the record with a fourth-inning shot off the Dodgers' Al Downing. Dodgers radio announcer Vin Scully captured the moment: "What a marvelous moment for baseball; what a marvelous moment for Atlanta and the state of Georgia; what a marvelous moment for the country and the world. A black man is getting a standing ovation in the Deep South for breaking a record of an all-time baseball idol. And it is a great moment for all of us, and particularly for Henry Aaron. … And for the first time in a long time, that poker face in Aaron shows the tremendous strain and relief of what it must have been like to live with for the past several months."

The euphoria lasted all season, until October 2, when Aaron hammered his 733rd and final homer in Atlanta for the Braves. One month later, on November 2, Atlanta traded the all-time home-run king to the Milwaukee Brewers (of the American League) for minor-league pitcher Roger Alexander and outfielder Dave May. Hank Aaron became a "designated hitter." The next season, on May 1, 1975, he became the all-time RBI leader, and on July 20, 1976, he hit the 755th and final home run of his career, in Milwaukee's County Stadium. He appeared in his final major-league game on October 3, calling it a career after 3,298 games.

In that career, Aaron scored 2,174 runs, and through the 2012 season was the leader in RBIs, with 2,297, total bases, with 6,856, and extra-base hits, with 1,477. His 12,364 at-bats were the second highest total ever, and he was on many "top ten" lists, including doubles, plate appearances, and hits (3,771). All the more remarkable was that he remained on these lists more than 35 years after he last took the field.

After retiring Aaron returned to Atlanta as vice president of player development for the Braves, and on August 1, 1982, he was inducted into the Baseball Hall of Fame. (2.2 percent of the ballots did not contain his name.) He also worked for a time for Turner Broadcasting, and opened Hank Aaron BMW in Atlanta. His auto empire eventually grew to multiple dealerships in Georgia, although he sold all but one in 2007, and he expanded his business venture to include a number of smaller restaurants as well. The 755 Restaurant Corporation grew to 18 fast-food outlets in the Southeast, including several Church's Fried Chicken outlets.

In 1990 Aaron's autobiography, *I Had a Hammer*, was published, and in April 1997 the Mobile Bay Bears of the Southern League christened Hank Aaron Stadium in Mobile. In 1999 Major League Baseball created the Hank Aaron Award for the best offensive performers in each league each season. In 2000 Aaron was named to MLB's All-Century Team. In 2001 he was awarded the Presidential Citizen's Medal by Bill Clinton, and in 2002 was given the Presidential Medal of Freedom by George W. Bush.

That slew of awards underscores Aaron's fame and his relevance not only to baseball's past, but also to America's history. He was a black man who successfully challenged the record of a white player whose legacy borders on mythical, and he did so with a poise so unshakable that it remains a study in professionalism. Naturally taciturn in public, Aaron was only rarely able to convey his inner feelings with words, but he reserved one of his finest moments for the end of another controversy-laden home run chase, by Barry Bonds in 2007. When Bonds hit his 756th homer, Aaron's face appeared on the JumboTron scoreboard in San Francisco, and he offered his congratulations to his replacement:

"I would like to offer my congratulations to Barry Bonds on becoming baseball's career home- run leader. It is a great accomplishment which required skill, longevity, and determination. Throughout the past century, the home run has held a special place in baseball and I have been privileged to hold this record for 33 of those years. I move over now and offer my best wishes to Barry and his family on this historical achievement. My hope today, as it was on that April evening in 1974, is that the achievement of this record will inspire others to chase their own dreams."

Dignity. Pride. Courage. Those are words often reserved for describing heroes. They also describe Henry Aaron.

Sources

Aaron, Henry, and Lonnie Wheeler, *I Had a Hammer: The Hank Aaron Story* (New York: Harper, 1991).

Archives, National Baseball Hall of Fame, Cooperstown, New York (visited: 2011).

Atlanta Journal/Atlanta Journal-Constitution: various issues 1954-1975.

Bryant, Howard, *The Last Hero: A Life of Henry Aaron* (New York: Random House, 2010).

D'Amato, Gary, "Seasons of Greatness: No. 2 Hank Aaron 1957," *Milwaukee Journal Sentinel*, February 26, 2012. Online: http://m.jsonline.com/more/sports/brewers/140517023.htm

espn.com

Furlong, William Barry, "The Panther at the Plate," *New York Times Magazine,* September 21, 1958.

www.biography.com/articles/Hank-Aaron-9173497?part=0

baseball-reference.com

Johnson, Lloyd, and Miles Wolff, eds., *Encyclopedia of Minor League Baseball*, 3rd ed (Durham, North Carolina: Baseball America, 2007).

All Star Results (MLB.com): mlb.mlb.com/mlb/history/mlb_asgrecaps_story_headline.jsp?story_page=recap_1957

Sports Illustrated, various issues 1954-1997.

Stanton, Tom, *Hank Aaron and the Home Run That Changed America* (New York: Harper Collins, 2004).

The Sporting News, various issues.

Will, George, *Men at Work: The Craft of Baseball* (New York: Macmillan, 1990).

Notes

1 http://espn.go.com/sportscentury/features/00006764.html.

Joe Adcock

By Gregory H. Wolf

Joe Adcock smashed some of the longest home runs ever witnessed. Although measuring the distance home runs traveled has historically been an imprecise science, driven by myth and legend, Adcock belongs to a select few sluggers, among them Mickey Mantle, Frank Howard, and Willie Stargell, whose feats still inspire awe. As a vocal leader of the Braves during their halcyon days in Milwaukee, Adcock hit the first ball into the revamped center-field bleachers at the Polo Grounds and the first shot over the 83-foot-high grandstand onto the upper-deck roof in left-center field in Ebbets Field, and was the first right-hander to smash one over the 64-foot-high scoreboard in right-center field at Connie Mack Stadium. One of the most feared sluggers of the 1950s and early 1960s, Adcock became just the 23rd batter to slug 300 home runs and finished with 336 round-trippers in his injury-plagued career that was marred by years of platooning.

Joseph Wilbur Adcock was born on October 30, 1927, in Coushatta, Louisiana, located about 45 miles south of Shreveport on the east bank of the Red River. His father was Ray Adcock, a businessman, farmer, and longtime sheriff of Red River County; his mother, Helen (Lyles) Adcock, was a teacher. Joe and his younger sister, Mary Ann, grew up on the family farm, where they were expected to help out with the chores by the time they were 7 years old.

Joe was always big for his age and gradually drifted toward basketball; baseball, on the other hand, seemed as uncommon as heavy snow in Northwestern Louisiana. "There was no town team, no school team, not even a diamond," said Adcock years later as a big leaguer. "The closest I came was a bit of one old cat as a kid with perhaps five kids playing at a time. I'd hit a rock with a stick out by the roadside down home and I'd knocked corncobs up on the barn roof with a broomstick. But as far as playing baseball, that was just something I heard my dad talk about."[1]

Adcock was a standout basketball player at Coushatta High, leading the school to the state Class B finals as a senior in 1944. Basketball coach Jesse Fatheree at Louisiana State University offered the 6-foot-4, 210-pound Adcock and two of his teammates scholarships to play on the hardwood for the Tigers. Like many colleges (and professional baseball) teams at the time, rosters were depleted because of World War II. Baseball coach A.L. "Red" Swanson took over the team when Fatheree was drafted into the service. "One time in the spring of my freshman year, I was watching the varsity baseball team practice," Adcock recalled of his introduction to baseball.[2] In desperate need of players, Swanson invited Adcock try out for the team. Adcock stumbled learning to throw and catch fly balls, but proved to be a good hitter with an eagle eye. "I was all hit and no field," he recalled. "I'd never worn spikes. I'd never had a uniform. I never played a game with nine men on a side."[3] Adcock's first love remained basketball; he led the Southeastern Conference in scoring (18.6 points per game) in the 1945-1946 season and had offers to

Joe Adcock (National Baseball Hall of Fame Library, Cooperstown, N.Y.)

play professionally.⁴ On the diamond he established his reputation as a right-handed slugger and capable first baseman. Adcock attracted scouts during his junior year when he helped lead the Tigers to the Southeastern Conference championship. Cincinnati Reds scout Paul Florence signed him to a contract in 1947.

Adcock began his professional baseball career as a 19-year-old in Columbia, South Carolina, playing for the Reds' affiliate in the Class A South Atlantic (Sally) League. The second youngest player on the team, Adcock batted .264 with a .414 slugging percentage and earned an invitation to the Reds' spring training in 1948. Among the first cut from camp, Adcock returned to Columbia, where he improved his average to .279 (though his slugging dropped about 30 points), and was named to the Sally League's midsummer all-star team. He also suffered a knee injury, the first of many injuries that plagued him throughout his career.

After another look-see at Reds spring training in 1950, Adcock was assigned to the Tulsa Oilers in the Double-A Texas League. Still a raw fielder, Adcock worked closely with manager Al Vincent to develop his technique. "He changed my whole style," said Adcock of Vincent. "I started from scratch with him and he taught me everything."⁵ Playing with a knee brace, Adcock emerged as one of most promising young sluggers in the league, belting 41 doubles and 19 home runs to go along with a sturdy .298 average for the league champions.

Adcock secured a Reds roster spot in 1950 but encountered a serious problem. An emerging star, big Ted Kluszewski, seemed to be the club's first sacker of the future, leaving Adcock without a natural position. Adcock's three seasons with the Reds were subsequently filled with frustration, missed opportunities, and injuries.

Adcock's impressive debut as a 22-year-old first baseman against the Pittsburgh Pirates on April 23 (2-for-4 with a double) was followed by an embarrassing outing early in the game the next evening. "I'm sitting on the bench … before the game," he recalled, "and [manager] Luke Sewell throws me a glove and says, 'You're playing left field.' It was the first time in my life that I ever had a fielder's glove. The first groundball hit to me should have been held to a single, but I had to chase it all the way to the wall."⁶ Struggling at the plate through June in limited duty, Adcock showed that he could hit big-league pitching in a six-game stretch (10-for-24) in early July, then replaced the weak-hitting Peanuts Lowrey in left field after the All-Star Game. From July 5 through the end of the season Adcock hit a team-high .315 (102-for-324) and earned a berth on *The Sporting News* Rookie All-Star team.

Firmly ensconced as the Reds' left fielder in his sophomore season, "Billy Joe" (a nickname he earned from Dodgers announcer Vin Scully) gradually replaced Kluszewski as the cleanup hitter. Batting a respectable .281 and slugging a team-best .489 during the first seven weeks of the 1951 season, Adcock injured his right knee and ankle while sliding into second base against the Boston Braves on June 3, foreshadowing a much more serious incident six years later. After missing more than three weeks of action, Adcock slumped in his return (he batted just .212 after the injury) and fielded tentatively.

By his third season, Adcock was vocal in his opposition to playing left field because of his home park's distinctive embankment, which bothered his knees. "Every player who came into Crosley Field," said the New York Giants Bobby Thomson, "paid attention to … the unique outfield terrace that ran in front of the left and center field walls."⁷ Increasingly moody, Adcock got off to a hot start (batting .333 and slugging .667) when he aggravated his knee injury on May 22 in Brooklyn, missing three weeks. Hobbled in his return, his average steadily declined to .278 by season's end with little power. He clashed with Rogers Hornsby (the club's third manager during the season), who desired a more athletic and speedy left fielder.⁸ Adcock wanted to play first base, but with just 31 home runs in his first three seasons, he failed to show the consistent power to dislodge Kluszewski, a consistent .300 hitter who had hit 54 home runs during the same period. On February 16 Adcock was traded to the Braves, at the time officially located in Boston, in a complicated four-team, five-player plus cash deal.

Adcock arrived at an exciting yet unsure time in Braves history. After months of speculation, team owner Lou Perini announced on March 13 the club's move to

Milwaukee, bringing baseball to the upper Midwest. "[Adcock] gives us a balanced team," said general manager John Quinn, noting that the Louisiana slugger and another offseason acquisition—outfielder Andy Pafko—would take pressure off left-handed slugger Eddie Mathews.[9]

Adcock's aggressive style of play appealed to manager Charlie Grimm. "Adcock is my kind of player—a holler guy," said Jolly Cholly.[10] Adcock's first home run for the Braves was a prodigious 475-foot blast against the New York Giants at the Polo Grounds on April 29.[11] He launched a pitch from Jim Hearn that landed ten rows up on the left side of the center-field bleachers; he was the first player to do so since the ballpark was renovated in 1923. Another titanic shot, against the Pittsburgh Pirates on July 18, rocketed almost as far, clearing the 457-foot sign in cavernous Forbes Field just to the left of straightaway center. Just as important as Adcock's 18 home runs and 80 runs batted in for the season were his durability (he played in all of the team's 157 games) and his fielding. "He has a good pair of hands and shifts well," said Grimm, a former first baseman with the Cubs.[12] The surprising Milwaukee Braves finished in second place and led the National League in attendance.

A classic pull hitter, Adcock crowded the plate with a locked-in stance and took a big step into the ball, which left him vulnerable to getting hit with inside pitches. Sportswriter Red Smith wrote, "National League strategy insists that he can't pull the ball if it's close to his wrists,"[13] but Adcock continued to make headlines with his slugging in 1954. The power-hitting Braves challenged the supremacy of the Brooklyn Dodgers and their ensuing rivalry throughout the decade proved to be one of baseball's fiercest. On July 31 Adcock became just the seventh big leaguer to belt four home runs in one game when he victimized four Dodgers pitchers at Ebbets Field. "I hit a fastball for the first homer, a slider for the second, a curve for the third, and a fastball for the fourth," he told *The Sporting News*.[14] He also hit a double to set a then major-league record for 18 total bases in one game. In the following game Brooklyn reliever Clem Labine beaned Adcock on the left side of the head. The "distinct thud" heard throughout Ebbets Field came from Adcock's batting helmet, still a relative novelty at the time, but which sportswriters quickly noted may have saved his life.[15] "When they throw at me high and tight," said Adcock, "I can duck, but when they throw behind your head, they mean business."[16] The Braves' next series in Brooklyn proved to be even more dangerous for Adcock. On September 10 the big right-hander walloped his ninth home run of the season in Ebbets Field to set a new record for visiting players. In the first inning of the next game, Don Newcombe plunked the slugger, breaking his right thumb and ending his season during the Braves' stretch drive. Adcock finished with 23 home runs, 87 RBIs, and a career-best .308 batting average.

In 1955 Adcock's season came to a premature end for the second consecutive year. On the anniversary of his four-home-run game against the Dodgers, Adcock's right hand (near his wrist) was broken by an inside pitch from the Giants' Jim Hearn. "That's how I earn my living. Hitting, I mean," Adcock told sportswriter Red Smith. "You've got to make up your mind—do you run away from pitches or stay in there and hit? There are a dozen different stances but I've got to use the one that's natural for me and stay in there."[17]

Given 3-1 odds against winning the World Series in 1956, the Braves got off to a slow start, leading to Grimm's replacement by Fred Haney after 46 games. In his first game as manager, Haney scrapped Grimm's plan of platooning the slumping Adcock at first base with Frank Torre. Adcock responded by belting two home runs in the first game of a doubleheader on June 17 in Brooklyn. His second blast, one of his record 13 against the Dodgers and the game-winner in the ninth inning off Ed Roebuck, was the first ball ever to soar over the 365-foot mark in left-center field, clear a height of 83 feet, and land on the double-deck roof of Ebbets Field before rolling off into a parking lot on Montgomery Street.

A notoriously streaky hitter, Adcock assaulted pitchers for an NL-record 15 home runs and 36 runs batted in during the month of July which included "one of baseball's wildest scenes" in memory.[18] Adcock, increasingly angered by what he perceived as "head-hunting," charged the mound on July 17 at County Stadium after New York Giants pitcher Ruben Gomez hit him on the wrist. In the ensuing melee, Gomez threw another ball at Adcock, striking him in the leg. Adcock then chased Gomez into the Giants' dugout, where by some accounts Gomez found an ice pick but was wrestled to the ground by teammates before he could return to confront Adcock. Two days later Adcock took revenge by clouting two home runs, including one of his ten career grand slams, and driving in a career-high eight runs in a 13-3 Braves victory. The Braves seemed to be headed for their first pennant in Milwaukee, but struggled down the stretch (14-13 in September) and lost the pennant on the final weekend of the season. Adcock enjoyed arguably his best season, ranking second in the NL in home runs (38), RBIs (103), and slugging percentage (.597).

The Braves rewarded Adcock's success with a rare two-year contract worth a reported $25,000 annually.[19] But the big slugger was injury-plagued during the ensuing three years and ultimately forced into an unwanted and frustrating platoon role with Frank Torre. The initial injury occurred 33 games into the 1957 season when Adcock (batting .306 and slugging .562) tore ligaments in his right knee against the Chicago Cubs on May 26. He returned to the starting lineup on June 5 and played through the pain but was platooned thereafter. Adcock's season came crashing down in a game against the Philadelphia Phillies on June 23 when he fractured his right fibula and tore ligaments in his right ankle sliding into second base in an awkward manner trying to protect his already-injured knee.[20] Adcock returned to the Braves roster in September, but was noticeably hampered in the field as the Braves cruised to their first pennant in Milwaukee.

In the World Series against the New York Yankees, Fred Haney followed script by platooning Adcock against left-handers and Torre against right-handers with the exception of Game Three. Adcock started Games One, Two, Three, and Five, but was replaced in the late innings in each game by Torre. Just 3-for-15 in the series, Adcock did line an opposite-field single to right off Whitey Ford to drive in Eddie Mathews in the sixth inning for the only run in the Braves' 1-0 victory in Game Five. Adcock was forced into the uncomfortable role of fan in the final two exciting games as the Braves captured their first and only championship in Milwaukee.

Adcock was confident that the Braves would capture another pennant in 1958. "We could run away with this thing like the Dodgers did in 1955," he told Lou Chapman of the *Milwaukee Sentinel*. "There isn't a ballclub that can touch us outside of Los Angeles."[21] In Haney's platoon system, Adcock played first base primarily against left-handers and started just 71 times; however, when left fielder Wes Covington went down with an injury in June, the big Louisianan took over his spot. "That's a lot of pasture out there," said Adcock in his folksy Southern accent. "You could run several head of cattle out there in all that territory. But we're hurting and I'm going to try to do my best. Let's face it, though, I'm not happy about it."[22] Seeing his first action in the outfield since 1952, Adcock started 24 times despite a painful right knee, which had not fully recovered from the injury the previous year and required surgery following the season. "I couldn't swing a bat right [in 1958]," said Adcock. "Whenever I put pressure on my back leg, out would go the knee. I didn't play a game when my leg didn't lock up on me six to eight times."[23] A team-first player, Adcock complained neither about his role on the team nor his pain. In just 320 at-bats, he belted 19 home runs and slugged .506 to help the Braves secure their second consecutive pennant.

In a rematch of the previous World Series, the Braves and Yankees squared off again in 1958. Adcock started Games One, Four, and Six against Whitey Ford, while Torre started the other contests. In Game One Adcock went 2-for-5 and scored the winning run on Bill Bruton's single in the bottom of the tenth inning to give the Braves an exciting 4-3 victory. With a three-games-to-one lead, the Braves were on the verge of another championship, but lost three consecutive games during which they struck out 25 times and scored just five runs. In the Series, Adcock went 4-for-13 with no runs batted in; Torre had three hits in 17 at-bats with one RBI.

"I don't like playing one day and sitting on the bench the next," said Adcock during a 1959 spring training marred by a holdout and trade rumors. "I can't do either myself or the team justice."[24] Adcock's relationship with

Haney became increasingly acrimonious. He once again split his time at first base and left field. In one of baseball's most memorable games, Harvey Haddix of the Pittsburgh Pirates had a perfect game through 12 innings at County Stadium on May 26. In the 13th inning, with Felix Mantilla on second base courtesy of an error and Hank Aaron on first via an intentional walk, Adcock uncorked the first Milwaukee hit of the game, a towering home run to right-center field. Mantilla scored the winning run; however, in the ensuing melee, Aaron scampered to the dugout after rounding second base while Adcock circled the bases. Adcock was later ruled out for passing Aaron and his home run was scored a double. Three days later Adcock supplied another walk-off game-winner under bizarre circumstances when, as Gene Conley of the Philadelphia Phillies attempted to walk him intentionally, he "reached out over the plate a plucked a dribbler" to drive in Aaron on a fielder's choice.[25] Enjoying his best health in three years, Adcock put together a career-best 20-game hitting streak en route to 25 home runs while playing in just 115 games. In the team's two straight losses in a best-of-three playoff against the Los Angeles Dodgers to determine the pennant winner, Adcock's big bat was silent with no hits and two strikeouts in four at-bats.

Adcock returned to first base in 1960 under new manager Chuck Dressen, and never played in the outfield again in his career. On April 14 he blasted a titanic shot off Curt Simmons that soared over the 390-foot mark in right-center field in Connie Mack Stadium in Philadelphia, becoming the first right-hander (and just the third player) to clear the 64-foot-high scoreboard. Asked about his estimated 500-foot home run, Adcock responded, "I hit one off Seth Morehead [on September 3, 1958] that went over the roof in left center. That's even higher than the scoreboard and just as far."[26] "Billy Joe" never lacked confidence. For the first and only time in his career, Adcock was named to the All-Star team; he started both games of the midsummer classic and rapped three hits in five at-bats. (From 1959 to 1962 two All-Star Games were played each season.) Consistent all season, Adcock led the team with a .298 batting average accompanied by 25 round-trippers while the Braves finished in second place for the fourth time in eight seasons.

Adcock was an accomplished and underrated first baseman whose long arms helped him dig out errant throws. He led first basemen in fielding percentage four times, including three consecutive seasons (1960-1962), and retired with the third-highest fielding percentage (.994) at first base in major-league history.

The Braves were in transition in 1961, though it might not have been apparent at the time. The oldest team in the National League, they got off to poor start, sported a losing record at the All-Star break for the first time since their move to Milwaukee, and needed a surge in August to finish in fourth place at 83-71. More disconcerting to owner Lou Perini was the rapidly declining attendance, which reached its nadir the following two seasons at just over 9,400 per game after leading the NL in attendance for six consecutive seasons (1953-1958). Like his team, Adcock struggled, too, before his bat awoke in the second half of the season (21-for-62, .330) to finish with a team-high 35 home runs and career-best 108 RBIs. On June 8 against the Cincinnati Reds, Mathews, Aaron, Adcock, and Frank Thomas belted a record four consecutive home runs in the eighth inning (since accomplished twice in the American League). Aaron (34), Mathews (32), and Adcock became the first Braves trio to each blast 30 home runs in the same season.

At the age of 34, Adcock showed signs of slowing down in 1962. His precarious right knee limited him to just 112 starts at first base, and he completed just 45 of them. He had difficulty running, but still possessed his awe-inspiring power. On July 21 in Philadelphia, he smashed two home runs, the second of which, reported the *Milwaukee Journal*, soared "over the roof atop the double-decked stands in left center" at Connie Mack Stadium.[27] With rumors of his impending trade widely circulating by season's end, Adcock concluded his final season in Milwaukee with 29 home runs and slugged over .500 for the seventh consecutive season. In their nine years together, Adcock (221), Aaron (298), and Mathews (327) belted 846 home runs, just nine fewer than the Dodgers trio of Duke Snider, Gil Hodges, and Roy Campanella had in ten years.

The offseason signaled an end of an era for Adcock and the Braves in Milwaukee. Owner Lou Perini finalized his sale of the club to the Chicago-based LaSalle Corporation on November 16. Less than two weeks later Adcock was sent to the Cleveland Indians as part of a multi-player trade. "This is just the start [of trading]," said new Braves manager Bobby Bragan, who had succeeded Birdie Tebbetts.[28] Adcock was not surprised by the trade and departed with a lasting shot to the Braves management. "The front office took things for granted too much with guys who won the pennant. They figured they'd keep going. Maybe they sat too long, but then they moved too fast, panicky."[29]

No longer an everyday player, Adcock spent one injury-plagued season with Cleveland platooning at first base with Fred Whitfield. "[Adcock] never once quit on me in Milwaukee," said Tebbetts, now managing Cleveland. "I admire Adcock because he's one of the few players I have ever seen who never has taken a short step … I have never seen him dog it even once."[30]

In a trade widely criticized by sportswriters and fans, the Los Angeles Angels completed a trade of popular outfielder Leon Wagner for Adcock and pitcher Barry Latman on December 6, 1963. Reunited with Haney, then GM of the Angels, Adcock played his final three seasons in Southern California. Still a valuable home-run threat, he platooned at first base and pinch-hit. *The Sporting News* wrote that Adcock retained his boyhood enthusiasm for the game, ran out every grounder despite his aching knees, and was an unselfish player who tutored young hitters.[31] On August 27 he reached a milestone when he launched a pitch from Diego Segui of the Kansas City Athletics for a home run at Municipal Stadium, becoming at the time just the 23rd major leaguer to belt 300 home runs. Playing home games in cavernous Chavez Ravine (Dodger Stadium), Adcock led the Angels in round-trippers in 1964 with 21 in just 366 at-bats. He concluded his playing career in 1966, the Angels' inaugural season in the more batter-friendly Anaheim Stadium. He paced the team with 18 four-baggers (in just 231 at-bats) and launched two of longest home runs in his career. On July 4 he blasted a pitch from Mickey Lolich of the Detroit Tigers into the upper deck just under the left-field roof at Tiger Stadium; and on September 2 he walloped a pitch from Washington Senators reliever Bob Humphreys off a light tower in deep left field at Anaheim Stadium.

Adcock retired as a player after the 1966 season to become manager of the Indians. "The boys can expect me to be strict and I'll stress fundamentals," he said. "I think there are a lot of mental errors made that shouldn't be."[32] He lasted only one season (an eighth-place finish), and was replaced by Alvin Dark. Adcock piloted the Triple-A Seattle Angels in the Pacific Coast League in 1968 before walking away from the game he loved. In his 17-year big-league career, Billy Joe hit 336 home runs, knocked in 1,122 runs, and batted .277.

Adcock retired to his hometown of Coushatta, where he had purchased Red River Farms as a player and spent most of his offseasons. He bred thoroughbred racing horses and was involved in farming. Adcock lived with his wife, the former Joan James, whom he met after his hand and wrist injury in 1955 when she worked as a nurse for the Braves team physician, Dr. Bruce Bower. They married in November 1956 and raised four children.[33] Adcock gradually drifted away from baseball, though he periodically appeared at events commemorating the Milwaukee Braves. In 1975 he was inducted into the Louisiana Sports Hall of Fame.

Suffering from the effects of Alzheimer's disease, Joe Adcock died on May 3, 1999, in Coushatta. He was 71 years old. He was buried in Holly Springs Cemetery in Marin, Louisiana.

Sources

Newspapers

Milwaukee Journal.

Milwaukee Sentinel.

The Sporting News.

Websites

Ancestry.com

BaseballLibrary.com

Baseball-Reference.com

Retrosheet.org

SABR.org

Notes

1. *The Sporting News*, March 11, 1953, 7.
2. Ibid.
3. *The Sporting News*, March 11, 1953, 8.
4. Louisiana Sports Hall of Fame. lasportshall.com/inductees/baseball/joe-adcock/?back=inductee.
5. Walter John, "Joe Adcock, Ex-Columbia Red, May Stick With Cincinnati," *News and Courier* (Columbia, South Carolina), April 14, 1950, 9.
6. *The Sporting News*, March 11, 1953, 8.
7. William A. Cook, *Big Klu. The Baseball Life of Ted Kluszewski* (Jefferson, North Carolina: McFarland, 2012), 43.
8. Ibid.
9. *The Sporting News*, February 25, 1953, 15.
10. *The Sporting News*, April 8, 1953, 14.
11. *The Sporting News*, May 6, 1953, 11.
12. *The Sporting News*, May 13, 1953, 3.
13. Red Smith, "Joe Adcock Philosophical About Injury Jinx," *Milwaukee Journal*, August 4, 1955, 19.
14. *The Sporting News*, August 11, 1954, 13.
15. Bob Wolf, "Adcock is Beaned; Burdette Robinson Feud Flares Again," *Milwaukee Journal*, August 2, 1954, 15.
16. *The Sporting News*, August 11, 1954, 19.
17. Red Smith, "Joe Adcock Philosophical About Injury Jinx," *Milwaukee Journal*, August 4, 1955, 19.
18. "Joe Adcock Hit-Run Victim of Fast Moving Gomez," (Associated Press) *Miami News*, July 18, 1956, 11.
19. *The Sporting News*, January 23, 1957, 24.
20. Bob Wolf, "Braves Beat Phillies Twice. Adcock Breaks Bone in Leg," *Milwaukee Journal*, June 24, 1957, 15.
21. Lou Chapman, " 'We Could Run Away With Flag, Maybe by 12'—Adcock," *Milwaukee Sentinel*, April 14, 1958, 7.
22. Lou Chapman, "Braves Ask OK to Place Buhl on Disabled List," *Milwaukee Sentinel*, June 22, 1958, 28.
23. "Unhappy Adcock Asks Duty Every Day for Champs Braves," (Associated Press) *Reading* (Pennsylvania) *Eagle*, March 28, 1959, 7.
24. Ibid.
25. Cleon Walfoort, "Braves Parlay Careless Conley, Alert Adcock for Winning Run," *Milwaukee Journal*, May 30, 1959, 7.
26. "Big Joe and Booming Bat Make History With Homer," *Milwaukee Journal*, April 15, 1960, 16. The first two batters to clear the scoreboard were Wes Covington and Carl Sawatski.
27. "Adcock's Two Home Runs Help Spahn Beat Phillies," *Milwaukee Journal*, July 22, 192, 23.
28. Joe Reichler, "Joe Adcock Gone, Burdette is Next," (Associated Press) *Ocala* (Florida) *Star Banner*, November 28, 1962, 10.
29. Milton Gross, "Joe Adcock Can't Figure Braves," *Miami News*, March 16, 1963, 22.
30. "Joe Adcock Key Figure in Five-Man Deal with Indians," (United Press International) *Washington* (Pennsylvania) *Reporter*, November 28, 1962, 19.
31. *The Sporting News*, June 27, 1964, 19.
32. "Joe Adcock Chosen As Cleveland Manager," (Associated Press) *Palm Beach Post*, October 4, 1966, 18.
33. "Joe Adcock, Joan James Are Wed Two Days Early," *Milwaukee Journal*, November 16, 1956, 1.

Bill Bruton

By John Harry Stahl

BLESSED WITH SPEED and quickness, Bill Bruton was arguably the fastest man in professional baseball in the 1950s. While prowling center field, he could race back for well-hit long balls and charge in to scoop up potential Texas Leaguers. When batting, he used his speed to intimidate opponents into making throwing and fielding mistakes. He added the important element of speed to the powerful Milwaukee Braves teams of the 1950s.[1]

In addition to his speed, Bruton's development as a player benefited directly from the professional baseball help and advice he received from his father-in-law, Hall of Famer William Julius "Judy" Johnson. Johnson spent 18 years in the Negro Leagues playing third base primarily with the Hilldale Club of Philadelphia and the Pittsburgh Crawfords.[2]

Quiet, thoughtful, and articulate, Bruton also played an important role in sustaining baseball's initial racial integration progress. Anchored by his religious beliefs, he understood that by becoming a successful professional baseball player he could serve as an important role model for youth as well as grow the popularity of professional baseball. Teammate Hank Aaron once characterized Bruton as "like a father to everyone. (He) really saw what needed to be done. … Just keep playing baseball and the system would change."[3]

Bruton played for 12 years (1953-1964) in the major leagues for the Milwaukee Braves (eight seasons) and the Detroit Tigers (four seasons). With the Braves he played on two National League champions and in one World Series. After baseball, he went on to a successful 23-year career as an executive with the Chrysler Corporation.

Born on November 9, 1925, in Panola, Alabama, William Haron Bruton grew up in a world of segregated baseball. As a youngster, he had access only to neighborhood sandlot baseball; his schools had no teams. However, he did have the opportunity to watch Birmingham Black Barons games, at which he saw many early black baseball stars including Satchel Paige and Josh Gibson.[4]

After high school Bruton went into the Army and spent six months in the Far East. Upon his return, he went to live with relatives in Wilmington, Delaware. There, he began playing softball on several community teams. He played catcher and batted from both sides of the plate. He found that when he batted right-handed he tended to hit pop flies. When he batted left-handed, he hit more line drives, so he chose to become a strictly left-handed hitter. He also caught the eye of the young daughter of Judy Johnson. With her encouragement, the elder Johnson went to watch Bruton play, and was impressed.

Bruton became equally taken with Johnson. Judy knew many former Negro Leaguers and they would congregate around his kitchen table and tell baseball stories for hours. Bruton took it all in. He loved talking baseball with Judy.

With Johnson's help, Bruton got a tryout with the Philadelphia Stars, a Negro Leagues team. The Stars

Bill Bruton (National Baseball Hall of Fame Library, Cooperstown, N.Y.)

released Bruton at the end of spring training, and he began playing semipro baseball and barnstorming.

In 1950 Johnson again talked up Bruton to his friend Bill Yancey, who had played with Johnson in the Negro Leagues. Yancey in turn recommended Bruton to Boston Braves scout Jack Ogden. The Braves invited Bruton to their minor-league spring-training camp. He impressed the Braves enough to be offered a professional contract, and signed immediately.[5]

Bruton was 23 years old when he signed his contract. The veteran Yancey knew his age, but fearing that he might be viewed as too old by the Braves, reported it as 21. According to Yancey, the Braves later changed Bruton's reported age to 19. His true age was not publicly disclosed until the day he retired from baseball.[6]

In 1950 the Boston Braves sent Bruton to Eau Claire in the Class C Northern League. Utilizing his tremendous speed, Bruton led the league in stolen bases (66), scored 126 runs, and hit .288. He was chosen the league's Rookie of the Year.

In 1951 Boston moved Bruton up to Denver in the Western League (Class B). This time he hit .303, scored 104 runs, and led the league with 27 triples. His performance caught the eye of Braves general manager John Quinn. On a Western trip, Quinn saw Bruton play and pronounced that he would someday be Boston's center fielder.[7]

How quickly should Bruton, a player with obvious talent and enormous potential, move up toward the major leagues? Many in the Braves organization felt he could neither hit in the high minors nor use his speed effectively in the field. He remained vulnerable to pitcher pickoff moves and did not know how to effectively bunt.[8]

However, Charlie Grimm, manager of the Braves' Triple-A team, the Milwaukee Brewers, saw a potential big leaguer. At the beginning of 1952, the Boston organization decided to let Bruton try to jump from Class B to Triple-A in one season. It would be a make-or-break situation for him.[9]

During 1952 spring training in Florida, *The Sporting News* reported an incident that showed the continued importance Bruton attached to his religion. Bruton and his teammates ate dinner together at their boarding house. Bruton requested that they say grace before each meal. Thereafter, pre-meal grace became an everyday practice.[10]

Grimm let Bruton start the season as the center fielder and leadoff hitter. Bruton quickly found that what he had done in Class B would not work in Triple-A. By midseason, it looked as if Grimm had made a big mistake. Nevertheless, Grimm continued to play Billy.

Bruton later acknowledged that Grimm's patience was critical to his development. "I doubt if I'd even stayed up in Triple-A ball last year if someone besides Charlie was managing Milwaukee (Brewers). I was no help at all to the club. I didn't hit at all, the first two and a half to three months. But Charlie kept me in the lineup. He stuck with me."[11]

On May 31 the Braves fired manager Tommy Holmes and hired Grimm. He quickly made several roster moves, including optioning outfielder Jim "Buster" Clarkson to the Brewers. Bruton became friends with Clarkson, a veteran Braves minor-league player who had also played in the Negro Leagues. A college graduate in physical education, Clarkson began schooling Bruton on how to improve his game.

Bruton quickly turned his disastrous season around. He ended up playing in all 154 games and hit .325 for the season. His 211 hits led the American Association. In the last six weeks of the season, he stole 20 bases.

Bruton gave all the credit to Clarkson. "All I know about baseball, I owe to Bus Clarkson," he said. "He taught me a lot." After the season, Clarkson invited Bruton to play winter ball for a team he managed in the Puerto Rico League. Again, Clarkson provided Bruton with more baseball insight. This time they focused on his bunting.[12]

Based on his minor-league experience with Bruton and Billy's good spring training in 1953, Grimm made him the Milwaukee Braves' leadoff hitter and center fielder. The Braves, who had moved to Milwaukee in the offseason, started the 1953 season with one game in Cincinnati, played in front of an overflow crowd of 30,103. Bruton's major-league debut was described as "sensational." Three times he reached into the overflow crowd and caught certain extra-base hits. The Braves won, 2-0. Leading off, Bruton went 2-for-4 with a single and a double. He stole a base. After the game, winning Braves pitcher Max Surkont raved about Bruton, claiming he had been the primary difference between victory and defeat.[13]

The Braves' next game, in Milwaukee against the Cardinals, marked the return of major-league baseball to Milwaukee after 51 years, and Bruton again provided key plays to help the Braves win. When the Cardinals threatened in the eighth inning, Bruton made a great catch of a Stan Musial blast for the third out. After the Cardinals tied the game in the ninth inning, Bruton hit a walk-off home run. He went 3-for-5. His home run was his only one in 1953.)[14]

Bruton continued to play a great center field. On May 16 the Chicago Cubs' Hank Sauer, batting with a runner on second base, hit a short pop fly to center field. Bruton raced in and caught the ball at his shoe tops, then flipped it to second base to easily double up the runner. The sensational play prompted comparisons to the fielding of Tris Speaker, who also played a shallow center field.[15]

Described his fielding philosophy, Bruton said he played a shallow center field but had "no problems" going back to catch long flies. If somebody "hit a line drive to the center-field fence, he deserved a base hit," Bruton said. If it wasn't a line drive, "I knew I was going to catch it."[16]

In 1953 Bruton played in 151 games and batted leadoff in all but three. He finished with a .250 batting average and stole a league-leading 26 bases. He had 14 triples. From center field he started five double plays, by catching the ball and picking off an advancing runner before he got back to his base. After the season the Milwaukee Chapter of the Baseball Writers' Association of America named Bruton the Braves top rookie of 1953. Bruton was also chosen the year's outstanding athlete from Delaware.[17]

In early 1954 Bruton suffered a string of minor injuries during spring training and in the first week of the season. A foot injury, an ankle injury, a pulled groin muscle, and a virus infection all happened between March 7 and April 18.[18] Still, Bruton starred in the Milwaukee home opener against the St. Louis Cardinals, scoring the winning run from first base on a single and an error. He continued displaying his spectacular, crowd-pleasing speed. In Pittsburgh Hank Aaron hit a fly to deep center field and Bruton scored from second base standing up. During the season, he had a 17-game hitting streak and a 26-game on-base streak.[19] He raised his batting average from .250 to .284. Bruton's 34 stolen bases led the National League, but he was caught stealing a league-leading 13 times.

In his first two seasons, Bruton's contribution to the potent Milwaukee offense was clear. The Braves stole 100 bases in 1953 and 1954. Bruton stole 60 of them, and in 1954 set a major-league record by getting 64.8 percent of his team's stolen bases.[20]

During the offseason, Miller Brewing Company hired Bruton to make speaking appearances. During a trip to Wausau, Wisconsin, Bruton roomed with Bob Allen, the Braves' media-relations director. At bedtime Billy began praying. When Allen asked him why, Bruton told him that as a kid he dreamed of playing in the major leagues but "knew" it could never happen. Now he was paid to play with Hank Aaron and Warren Spahn. So he thanked God every day for watching over him and his family.[21]

Bruton began 1955 focused on lowering his strikeouts and increasing his walks. He had fanned 178 times and walked 84 times in 1953 and 1954. Bruton slightly widened his batting stance and crouched at the plate to get a better view of the pitch and create a smaller strike zone.[22] He still struck out 72 times and got only 43 walks that season.

The Braves started their 1955 season at home against the Cincinnati Reds. With the game tied at 2-2, Bruton singled and scored the winning run on a triple by Hank Aaron. It was the third year in a row that he had scored the winning run in the Braves' home opener.[23] For the season he hit .275, led the league with 636 at-bats and scored 106 runs. He recorded personal bests in home runs (9), doubles (30), and RBIs (47).

Bruton continued to try to use his speed to disrupt opposing teams, leading the National League for the third consecutive year with 25 stolen bases. He set a Braves record by hitting into only two double plays during the season.

Bruton started the 1956 season slowly. The Braves dropped him to seventh in the batting order, and he hit .459 in his first 11 games of the season.[24]

On June 16 manager Charlie Grimm resigned and was replaced by Coach Fred Haney. The change directly affected Bruton. As a player Haney was also a good base stealer. However, he strongly believed things had changed from when he played. With bigger rosters and more power hitters, he believed, base stealing should be more selective.[25]

He decreed that no player could try to steal without his approval. Bruton had only eight stolen bases for the season. Meanwhile Haney highly valued the sacrifice bunt, and Bruton ended with a career-high 18 sacrifices. He finished the season with a .272 batting average for the season. His 15 triples led the NL. On September 23 he hit the first grand slam of his career.

On July 11, 1957, Bruton, going for a Texas leaguer in left-center field, collided with Braves shortstop Felix Mantilla and tore a ligament in his right knee.[26] Bruton knew knee surgery would put him out for the year. Many thought he would never play again. He elected to wait and see if rest and other treatment would help.[27] Upset about his future, the intensely religious Bruton began serving as a radio disc jockey for a Sunday-morning hour program of religious music.[28] The Braves won the pennant. As they played the first game of the World Series against the New York Yankees, Dr. Don H. O'Donoghue was operating on Bruton's knee in Oklahoma City. After the surgery, O'Donoghue predicted that Bruton would be ready for 1958 spring training. Billy was ecstatic.[29] In late January O'Donoghue and the Braves' team doctor agreed that Bruton's knee was healing as expected and he was cleared to report to spring training.[30] But Bruton didn't get into a game until May 25 in Milwaukee. As he approached the plate for the first time, he received a thunderous ovation from the 40,963 in attendance, and then hit the first pitch into right field for a single. Bruton later made a circus catch in center field.[31] For the season he played in 100 games and hit .280.

The Braves again won the pennant, giving Bruton the opportunity to play in his first World Series. In the first game, in Milwaukee, he hit a two-out single in the tenth inning to drive in the winning run against the Yankees. In Game Two Bruton hit a home run to lead off the game in another Braves victory. The Braves lost the Series in seven games, but Bruton hit .412. He later characterized playing in the 1958 World Series as the biggest thrill of his career.[32]

In 1959 Bruton appeared in 133 games primarily as the leadoff hitter (83 games) and hit a career-high .289. On August 2 he became the fourth major leaguer to hit two bases-loaded triples in a game. His hits came against Cardinals left-handers Vinegar Bend Mizell and Dean Stone.[33]

Tied during the regular season, the Los Angeles Dodgers and the Braves had a best-of-three playoff for the pennant. The Dodgers swept, and limited Bruton to one hit in ten at-bats.

In November the Braves fired Haney and hired Chuck Dressen as the manager for 1960. The 34-year-old Bruton remained the leadoff man and center fielder, and had one of his best seasons. He hit .280 and led the National League in runs scored (112) and triples (13). He hit a career high 12 home run, had a 27-game on-base streak and a 15-game hitting streak.

Despite Bruton's 1960 heroics, the Braves dealt him to the Detroit Tigers in a five-player trade. Bruton had spent eight years in Milwaukee and batted .276. For three consecutive seasons (1953-1955), he led the NL in stolen bases. He led the league in triples twice.

Bruton played four years with Detroit before retiring, as a regular the first three years and as a reserve in his final year. He hit .257 in 1961 with a career-high 17 home runs. In 1962 he hit .278 with 16 home runs and a career-high 74 RBIs. He also hit his second grand slam. He posted a .256 average in 1962 and finished with a .277 mark in 1964. In 12 years as a major leaguer Bruton finished with a .273 batting average.

Bruton's retirement came about after the Chrysler Corporation offered him a job paying $15,000 a year. Although he was making $28,000 as a player, Bruton knew he was close to the end of his playing career. He announced his retirement on September 27 before the final home game of the season. In making the move, he said his priority was his wife and four children. "A chance like this doesn't come too often," he said.[34] In his final game in Detroit, before a small crowd, Bruton blasted a home run into the upper deck in right field at Tiger Stadium. Later Bruton's wife confessed, "That had me scared.... I was afraid that Billy might change his mind."[35]

On November 21, at a reception in his honor, Chrysler formally announced his hiring for the automaker's merchandising staff. Tigers vice president Rick Ferrell said, "Bruton is the best player I've ever seen retire. Usually, you have to cut the uniform off a guy to make him quit. Billy can still run and throw and hit the ball."[36]

Bruton spent the next 23 years as an executive with Chrysler, working primarily in the company's Detroit headquarters. He worked in sales, customer service, promotion, and financing. He later owned a Chrysler dealership. He finished his career as a special assistant to Chrysler president Lee Iacocca. He retired in 1988.

In 1989 Billy returned to Delaware with his wife to live in his father-in-law Judy Johnson's old residence in Marshalltown. He continued his work with several churches and charitable organizations, particularly the Big Brothers-Big Sisters of Delaware.

With a history of heart problems, Bruton died of an apparent heart attack on December 5, 1995, while driving near his home. He was 70 years old. The State Police said they found him slumped over the wheel of his car, which had hit a pole. He was buried with an American flag draped over his coffin as an acknowledgement of his military service.[37]

Notes

1. Bill James, *The Bill James Historical Baseball Abstract* (New York: The Free Press, 2001), 768.
2. Tom Tomashek, "Bruton Lauded as quiet force," *The News Journal*, Wilmington, Delaware, December 9, 1998, A16; Jeff Williams, "Judy Johnson home named historic site," *The News Journal*, November 5, 1995.
3. Paula Parrish, "Ballplayer Bill Bruton Dead at 69," *The News Journal*, Wilmington, Delaware, December 6, 1995, A-4.
4. Rich Westcott, *Splendor on the Diamond* (Gainesville: University Press of Florida, 2000), 257.
5. Sam Levy, "Bruton's a Big Man in Milwaukee," *Baseball Digest*, July 1953, 60.
6. Watson Spoelstra, "Luncheon Gives Bruton a Fast Sendoff on Career at Chrysler," *The Sporting News*, November 21, 1964, 9.
7. HOF Bill Bruton Player Clippings File as of September 14, 2012, unidentified author, "Bruton's Triples in '51 Sold Quinn," *The Sporting News*, December 30, 1953, 3.
8. Sam Levy, "Bruton Helps to Banish Cholly's Outfield Worries on the Braves," *The Sporting News*, April 15, 1953, 17.
9. Roger Birtwell, "Braves Bill Bruton for Picket Post," *The Sporting News*, December 24, 1952.
10. Oscar Ruhl, "Ruhl Book," *The Sporting News*, April 2, 1952, 14.
11. Sam Levy, "Bruton's Big Man in Milwaukee, *Baseball Digest*, July 1953, 13, 14.
12. Ibid, 59.
13. Ibid, 60.
14. Sam Levy, "Milwaukeeans Lift Merry Mugs to Braves," *The Sporting News*, April 22, 1953, 13.
15. Ed Prell, "Milwaukee Backing Its Battling Braves in Big League Style," *The Sporting News*, May 20, 1953, 6.
16. Norman Macht, "Billy Bruton Recalls How the Game Was Played in the 1950s," *Baseball Digest*, August 1990, 44-48.
17. "Milwaukee Writers Name Mathews Braves' Top Star," *The Sporting News*, December 9, 1953, 24.
18. "Injury List Already Higher Than in Entire '53 Season," *The Sporting News*, February 28, 1954, 15.
19. "Bruton Still a Card Jinx", *The Sporting News*, April 28, 1954, 21, Red Thisted, "Banjo Cholly Can't Keep His Hurlers and Hitters in Harmony," *The Sporting News*, June 30, 1954, 9 Baseball-Reference.com: Bill Bruton 1954 Gamelogs, Longest Hitting Streak, Longest On Base Streak; Bill Bruton Statistics and History, 1954.
20. "Bruton, Champ Base Thief, Bags His First Steal of Year," *The Sporting News*, May 11, 1955, 19.
21. Tom Tomashek, "Bruton lauded as quiet force," *The News Journal*, Wilmington Delaware, December 9, 1998, A16.
22. "Bruton Credits Speedy Start to Wider Stance and Crouch," *The Sporting News*, May 4, 1955.
23. "Bruton 'Mr. Win' of Braves," *The Sporting News*, April 20, 1955, 24.
24. "Bruton Likes Seventh Spot; Hits .459 in First 11 Games," *The Sporting News*, May 16, 1956, 10.
25. Bob Wolf, "Base Stealing a 'Lost Art,' Moans Ex-Speedster Haney," *The Sporting News*, March 28, 1956, 23.
26. Bob Wolf, "Braves Beaming Despite Rash of Aches' n' Breaks," *The Sporting News*, July 31, 1957, 11.
27. Bob Wolf, "Bruton's Return to Duty Ties Up Hazel Tepee Tale," *The Sporting News*, June 4, 1958, 9.
28. "Tuning In," *The Sporting News*, August 21, 1957, 30.

29 Curt Mosher, "Bruton Undergoes Surgery on Knee, Expected to Be Ready Next Spring," *The Sporting News,* October 23, 1957, 14.

30 "Bruton to Report on Time: Knee Healing Satisfactorily," *The Sporting News,* January 29, 1958, 13.

31 Bob Wolf, "Bruton's Return to Duty Ties Up Hazle Tepee Tale," *The Sporting News,* June 4, 1958, 9

32 Westcott, *Splendor on the Diamond, 262.*

33 "Bruton 4th Major Leaguer to Rap 2 Three-Run Triples," *The Sporting News,* August 12, 1959, 23.

34 Watson Spoelstra, "Bruton Waves Bye: Bengals Eye Farms For Flyhawk Talent," *The Sporting News,* October 10, 1964.

35 Watson Spoelstra, "Luncheon Gives Bruton a Fast Sendoff on Career at Chrysler," *The Sporting News,* November 21, 1964, 9.

36 Ibid.

37 Ibid.

Bob Buhl

By Gregory H. Wolf

"I WAS MEAN on the mound," said Bob Buhl, a tough competitor for the Milwaukee Braves during their heyday in the 1950s.[1] Forming part of the Big Three with Warren Spahn and Lew Burdette, Buhl notched 109 of his 166 career wins for the Braves. Self-confident, brash, and sometimes wild on the mound, Buhl was known for his penchant to challenge and brush back hitters.

The only child of Raymond and Irene Buhl, Robert Ray Buhl was born on August 12, 1928, in the east-central Michigan city of Saginaw. Raised in a hard-working family of modest means during the Depression and war years, Bob was an athletic youngster and started playing sandlot baseball in junior high school. A three-sport star (baseball, basketball, and football) at Saginaw High School, he pitched, but doubted that a scout ever attended any of his games. "My father died when I was a senior in high school," Buhl said of an event that had far-reaching consequences for his baseball career. "I had to get a job from 2:30 to 10:00 each day. I had to drop part of my schoolwork and go back the following semester [in the fall of 1946]."[2] In the summer of 1946 he participated in a Chicago White Sox tryout camp in Saginaw and pitched just one inning. Impressed, the team decided to sign him, but according to major-league rules at the time, they had to wait until he graduated from high school. After completing his classes in the fall, Buhl excitedly signed a minor-league contract with the White Sox in early 1947.

Assigned to the Madisonville (Kentucky) Miners in the Class D Kentucky-Illinois-Tennessee (Kitty) League for the 1947 season, the 18-year-old Buhl set the league on fire, finishing second in wins (19) and earned-run average (3.00), while tossing 216 innings in 40 games. "I was cocky," said Buhl, who walked 126 batters. "I wasn't being groomed for the majors."[3] Despite the paltry $100-a-month salary, Buhl was happy to play baseball; however, at the end of the season, he became upset and insulted when the White Sox offered him a contract paying $200 a month and a promotion to Class C. Having learned about players being declared free agents because they signed contracts while still in high school, he wrote Commissioner Happy Chandler and requested him to investigate, noting that he did not officially graduate until June 1947, well after he signed a contract with Chicago. Chandler declared Buhl a free agent, which permitted Buhl to sign with any team other than the White Sox.

Scouts from 14 teams (all but the Dodgers and White Sox) flocked to Saginaw to try to sign the hard-throwing right-hander. With scout Earle Halstead, Buhl signed an $800-a-month Triple-A contract with the Milwaukee Brewers, a Boston Braves Triple-A affiliate, and received a new car as a bonus. He was assigned to the independent Saginaw Bears in the inaugural season of the Class A Central League. At first he was excited about pitching in his hometown, but later said, "Pitching in my hometown turned about to be a big mistake on my part. Fans expected too much."[4] Struggling most of the season (an 11-12 record was accompanied by a 5.22 ERA and 145 bases on balls), Buhl said years later, "I used to strike out as many as I

Bob Buhl (National Baseball Hall of Fame Library, Cooperstown, N.Y.)

walked. I just threw fastballs and tried to throw a curve."[5] He was assigned to the Hartford Chiefs in the Class A Eastern League in 1949, and his approach to baseball began to change: "Hartford was like a baseball school and I started to learn about fundamentals."[6]

After an 8-8 season in Hartford, Buhl went to spring training with the Brewers in Austin, Texas, in 1950 and made the team. "When the season started," he recalled, "I wasn't used. I got disgusted and told the manager, Bob Coleman, to send me someplace where I'd pitch."[7] He was sent conditionally to the Dallas Eagles, an unaffiliated team in the Double-A Texas League managed by former Chicago Cubs skipper Charlie Grimm. Though just 8-14 for the season and discouraged that he was no longer officially with the Braves, Buhl was relieved when they purchased his contract after of the season.

Buhl's professional baseball career was interrupted for two years while he served as an Army paratrooper stationed in Fort Campbell, Kentucky, in 1951 and 1952. While in the service he married Joyce Miles of Saginaw in October 1951. To keep in shape, he pitched for his base team and for local semipro teams under the alias "Lieutenant Brown" and claimed that he earned more money playing weekend baseball than he did in the Army.

Highly touted by manager Grimm, who took over the helm of the Boston Braves in mid-1952, Buhl arrived at the Braves' spring training in 1953 fully expecting to make the team. "The guy had everything but control," said Grimm. "He throws as hard as any pitcher I ever saw."[8] Landing a spot on the team, which announced its relocation to Milwaukee in March, Buhl followed an inauspicious major-league debut on April 17 (a loss to Cincinnati in 2 1/3 innings of relief) with a two-hitter against the New York Giants in his next appearance. But he also exhibited the wildness that marked most of his career with the Braves by walking six and hitting a batter.

Appearing in 30 games, Buhl was much more effective in his 18 starts than he was as a reliever (a 2.78 ERA as a starter, 3.98 out of the bullpen). In addition to three shutouts, including a two-hitter against the Pirates, Buhl hurled a career-best 14-inning victory over the Cubs on August 22, winning 2-1 and facing 53 batters. As the Braves' 92-62 record and second-place finish did, the 24-year-old rookie surprised fans and sportswriters with an unexpected 13-8 and the third best ERA in the National League, 2.97.

Along with future Braves teammates Hank Aaron, Felix Mantilla, and Ray Crone, Buhl played winter baseball in Puerto Rico after the season and won 12 games while helping lead Caguas to the league title. He was described as a "cinch" to earn a spot as a starter in 1954, but struggled all season, losing his first seven decisions and his spot in the rotation.[9] "Sometimes I was so tired," Buhl said, "that I didn't feel like going to the park. My fastball didn't move."[10]

Following his 2-7 record and 4.00 ERA in 1954, Buhl's future as a major-league starter was in question when he began the 1955 season by losing three of his first four decisions and being taken out of the rotation in May. Given another start against Brooklyn on June 2, Buhl took the loss, but his nine strikeouts and five-hit, three-run ball over seven innings were good enough to earn him the right for another crack in the rotation. Buhl responded by pitching four complete-game victories in five outings. After two losses (one as a reliever) in early July, he reeled off eight wins in his next nine decisions, including a five-hit victory over the Phillies in which he struck out a career-high 12 batters on July 14. His 13-11 finish with an ERA of 3.21, third best in the NL, were a welcome relief to the Braves.

Buhl established his reputation as an intimidating, hard-nosed, no-nonsense pitcher who was not afraid to pitch inside or knock down opponents who crowded the plate. With his bushy black eyebrows and crewcut, he stared down batters, daring them to get a hit. With his control problems, batters were wary of him. "I had a herky-jerky motion," said Buhl, who liked to work quickly on the mound. "I was a short-armed pitcher and instead of moving way back and way forward, I'd let loose tighter to my body."[11] Always blessed with a strong fastball, which *The Sporting News* called the best on the Braves, Buhl attributed his success to pitching coach Bucky Walters, who helped him develop a slider.[12] "It looked like a fastball," Buhl said, "but would break real quick down and away from a right-handed hitter."[13]

After two second-place and one third-place finish in their first three years in Milwaukee, 1956 foreshadowed the future for the Braves as they almost won the pennant and the Big Three of Spahn, Burdette, and Buhl began their five-year run as one of the best starting trios in the majors, if not the best. The Braves' 5 1/2-game league lead on July 26 was fueled by the pitching of Buhl, who had beaten the Brooklyn Dodgers in five consecutive starts and earned the moniker Dodger Killer. "I showed them I was the boss," he said of his contests with the Dodgers. "They knew I'd brush them back. I'd pitch Hodges wide and throw him a lot of curves. I'd throw Campanella nothing but inside fastballs. I'd pitch Duke Snider high and tight."[14]

After his sixth straight victory over the Dodgers on July 30, to raise his record to 14-4, Buhl was the hottest pitcher in the league. In his next start, on August 4 he broke the tip of the index finger on his pitching hand when the Pirates' Lee Walls smashed a line drive back to the mound. Buhl pitched through the pain and beat the Dodgers again on August 26 in the midst of a stretch of three straight complete games, giving the Braves a three-game lead over Brooklyn.

Like the Braves, Buhl had his worst month in September, going just 2-3 and with a 6.39 ERA. The Braves were worn down, especially the Big Three, who pitched 15 of the team's last 17 games and all of the last ten. Despite their swoon, the team entered the final series of the season with a shot at the pennant, but lost two of three to St. Louis while the Dodgers swept Pittsburgh. Buhl finished with a career-high 18 wins and 8 losses and a 3.32 ERA.

"We were better than the Dodgers in 1956," Buhl said, "but we didn't win the pennant."[15] That changed in 1957, when the Braves won their only championship in Milwaukee. When Buhl defeated the Dodgers for a team-leading 14th win on August 4, the Braves were a game behind the Cardinals in a three-team pennant race. The Braves caught fire, going 34-17 the rest of the season, and ran away with the pennant. Leading the National League with 16 wins on August 14, Buhl was sidelined with shoulder problems and missed three weeks. Returning in September, he had his best season in the majors with 18 wins, led the league in winning percentage (.720), ranked fourth in ERA (2.74) and completed a career-high 14 of 31 starts.

With star players Aaron, Mathews, and Spahn having exceptional years, the Braves were also resilient and overcame center fielder Bill Bruton's season-ending knee injury in June and the broken leg that limited slugging first baseman Joe Adock's to 65 games. Manager Fred Haney relied on his pitching, especially his starters, and was known for juggling the rotation to secure the best matchup for his team. The staff posted a 3.47 ERA, second only to the Dodgers, tossed a league-high 60 complete games, and the Big Three won 56 games.

Competitive with one another on and off the field during their nine years together (1953-1961), Spahn, Burdette, and Buhl were close teammates, enjoyed a few beers together, and played practical jokes on each other and teammates, but were also consummate professionals. "We'd talk about hitters," Buhl recalled. "Once you've seen the hitter, you have a pretty good idea how to get them out."[16]

Behind clutch hitting and pitching, the underdog Braves beat the New York Yankees in seven games in the 1957 World Series. With the Series tied, Buhl started Game Three, but was rattled after surrendering a home run to Tony Kubek, the second batter of the game, and didn't make it through the first inning, giving up three runs (two earned), and was the losing pitcher. With a chance to win the deciding game, Buhl started Game Six in New York but was plagued by wildness, walking four, throwing a wild pitch, and giving up a two-run homer to Yogi Berra before being lifted in the third inning to set the stage for a climactic Game Seven. Spahn was due to start but got sick, and manager Haney elected to start Burdette on two days' rest. Buhl and Burdette were roomies for the Series. The night before the game, Buhl said, "We didn't talk about the upcoming game. We just watched television and had room service. Lou could make coffee nervous. ... Lou was invincible. That's why we won the World Series."[17] (Burdette shut out the Yankees, 5-0.)

Buhl began the 1958 season by winning four of his first five starts prompting new pitching coach Whit Wyatt, to comment, "I never noticed how well [Buhl] spotted his pitches. He hits the outside corner like he owns it."[18] However, Buhl's shoulder had been bothering him since the previous year and the pain began to worsen. "It wasn't fun throwing the ball," he said. "I couldn't even lift my arm to put on a jacket."[19] On May 13, after several poor outings, manager Haney shut him down and he was sent to the Mayo Clinic in Minnesota for treatment, but to no avail. By sheer luck, his neighbor, a dentist, suggested that he stop by his office and discovered serious nerve problems in two teeth and removed them. "Two weeks later," Buhl said, "I was pitching with no pain. I was very fortunate. A dentist saved my career."[20]

Tensions arose when Buhl insisted he was ready to resume pitching in mid-August, but Haney refused to clear a roster spot, citing the excellent pitching from the Braves' "Kiddie Korps" of Joey Jay, Juan Pizzaro, and Carl Willey. Added to the roster on September 1, Buhl pitched a complete-game victory over the Cubs and revealed a new delivery to Del Rice, who served as his personal catcher in the mid- to late 1950s. "He throws more overhanded now," Rice said. "His curve is a lot sharper. His delivery is smoother, too."[21] The new delivery put less strain on Buhl's arm and shoulder und undoubtedly helped prolong his career.

Despite Buhl's promising return from arm miseries, he struggled in September and lost his spot in the rotation during the Braves' dominant drive to their second consecutive pennant in 1958, prompting Dick Young in *The Sporting News* to suggest that Buhl would be traded in the offseason.[22] When 32-year-old Bob Rush (winner of 10 games in 1958) started Game Three of the World Series against the Yankees with the Braves up two games to none, Buhl was livid. Spahn pitched his second straight complete game to win Game Four, putting the Braves in command, three games to one, but Haney's decision to pitch Burdette and Spahn on short rest in the final three games backfired. The Braves lost all three and the World Series. Reports of an acrimonious relationship between Haney and Buhl immediately surfaced, and rumors of Buhl's imminent trade persisted throughout the offseason.

The Braves were favored to win their third consecutive pennant when they opened spring training in 1959. Arriving in camp pain-free, Buhl announced that he had worked on his delivery in the offseason, saying, "I used to be straight up and deliver the ball with a snap. Now I bend over more and get my body as well as my arm into the pitch. It gives me more on my breaking stuff."[23] However, when he failed to make it out of the second inning of his first start of the new campaign, he found himself the "forgotten man" in the Braves' bullpen and was dogged by trade rumors.[24]

Given a start on May 11, his first in more than three weeks, Buhl responded by pitching seven innings of five-hit ball to beat the Cubs, and won his way back into the rotation. With the Braves tied with the Dodgers entering the last day of the season, Buhl pitched seven innings of one-run ball to beat the Phillies in one of the most important games of his career. "Other than my first win in the majors," said Buhl, whose victory set up a best-of-three playoff with their archnemesis Dodgers, in their second year in Los Angeles, "that was the most exciting moment of my career."[25]

The Braves lost the playoff series with two straight defeats. The 1959 season proved to be the last year that the Milwaukee Braves competed for the pennant and concluded a four-year run during which they lost two pennants in the last series of the year and won two in convincing fashion. "We figured we'd come back and win [in 1959]," said Buhl years later. "But we didn't. That was a disappointing defeat, but we should have won the pennant prior to a playoff because we had a better team." With 21 wins apiece for Spahn and Burdette and 15 for Buhl, the Big Three won 57 games in '59. The 30-year-old Buhl led the team with a 2.86 ERA (fourth in the league) and led the NL with four shutouts while completing 12 of his 25 starts.

Feisty on and off the field, Buhl and Eddie Mathews, his roommate for almost a decade, enjoyed imbibing with Spahn and Burdette (who were also roommates). "We didn't make a big deal of going out and drinking so much that we wouldn't know what was going on," Buhl recollected. He and Mathews didn't take kindly to hecklers and loudmouths in local taverns either. "Eddie was a tough guy," he said, and the two got into some confrontations. "We weren't looking for trouble and fought only if someone harassed us," Buhl said.[26]

A subtle shift for the Braves in 1960 became more pronounced in subsequent years. Average attendance dropped to less than 20,000 per game for the first time and never reached that height again. Replacing Haney as manager, Charlie Dressen led the aging Braves, with the oldest team and pitching staff in the National League, to another (and last) second-place finish in 1960; but the team never mounted a serious challenge to the Pirates for the pennant. Earning his only All-Star berth (he went 1 1/3 innings and gave up a two-run home run to Al Kaline in the eighth inning of the first of two All-Star games in 1960) and finishing with a 16-9 record and a career-high 238 2/3 innings pitched, Buhl concluded the season with exactly 100 major-league wins.

In 1961 the Braves struggled to stay above .500 for the first 100 games, but were just 6 1/2 games out of first place at the end of August. Birdie Tebbetts replaced Dressen as manager for the last 25 games and vowed to make wholesale changes. He buried the inconsistent and slumping Buhl (9-10 with an ERA over 4.00 at the time) deep in the bullpen, where he saw action in only three games the rest of the season.

Insulted by Tebbetts's treatment and perceived lack of respect and by general manager John McHale's proposed pay cut, Buhl knew his days in Milwaukee were numbered. Actively shopped in the offseason, he surprisingly began the 1962 season on the Braves roster. Starting the third game of the season and seeing action for the last time as a Brave, Buhl was pummeled for five runs in two innings during a loss to the Giants. Two weeks later, on April 30, he was traded unceremoniously to the Cubs for 24-year-old pitcher Jack Curtis.

"I had stopped having fun," Buhl said of his last few months with Milwaukee. "Birdie told me I'd be a spot starter and would work in the bullpen. I didn't want that."[27] In Chicago Buhl was reunited with Charlie Grimm, vice president of the club. "[Buhl] has a pitching style suited to Wrigley Field." Grimm said. "Bob is a low-ball pitcher who makes you hit it in the dirt."[28]

Buhl arrived on a youthful Cubs team coming off a 90-loss season in 1961 and in the middle of a bizarre two-year experiment with a revolving set of head coaches instead of a manager. In 1962 the Cubs lost 103 games, their worst season ever (and still the worst as of the 2012 season). "Everyone was unhappy," Buhl said about the losing and the coaching carousel, "but no one complained." In his Cubs debut on May 2 he pitched two-hit ball over six innings to beat the Dodgers 3-1. At 33 Buhl was the oldest starter on the staff by seven years and noted, "There wasn't nearly as much drinking on this club as there had been in Milwaukee." The staff ace, Buhl finished with a team-high 12 wins (and 13 losses) in 212 innings.

Never known for his hitting, attested by his .089 career batting average in 857 at-bats (without a home run), Buhl set a record for batting futility in 1962 when he went 0-for-70 during the season as part of a hard-to-fathom 0-for-87 streak over the course of three seasons. "When I was going through my hitless streak," he said, "I didn't feel any pressure. Everybody knew I couldn't hit. The infielder was backing up, caught his spikes and fell down and the ball fell. They called time to give me the damn ball. I was embarrassed."[29] Throughout his career Buhl tried everything to improve his hitting, from taking extra batting practice to attempting to bat left-handed. "I don't remember any big hits," he said. "The ones I had were accidental."[30]

From 1963 through 1965 Buhl was a steady pitcher for the Cubs winning 11, 15, and 13 games, but he was no longer the ace of the team with the emergence Dick Ellsworth and the acquisition of workhorse Larry Jackson from the Cardinals after the 1962 season. With a career-high 4.39 ERA and averaging just six innings per start in 1965, the 36-year-old was showing signs of age. Clashing with manager Lou Klein that season, Buhl started just twice after August 27 and was knocked out early in each game.

One week into the 1966 season, Buhl was sent along with his road roommate Larry Jackson to the Philadelphia Phillies in exchange for pitcher Fergie Jenkins, utilityman John Herrnstein, and center fielder Adolfo Phillips. He was reunited with former Braves general manager John Quinn, who had guided the Phillies to four consecutive winning seasons for the first time since 1898-1901. Used as a spot starter and reliever behind Jim Bunning, Chris Short, and Jackson, Buhl lost four of his first five decisions before beating the Braves, then in their first season in Atlanta, on June 13. An aged Eddie Mathews and Hank Aaron were the only players still on the team from its glory days in the 1950s.

Coming off a 6-8 season in 1966, the 38-year-old Buhl appeared in three games before being released on May 16, 1967, as Philadelphia trimmed its roster to the 25-man limit. With no clubs showing interest in acquiring him, he retired with a 166-132 record and a 3.55 ERA in 2,587 innings. He won 46 games in the minor leagues. He saved his best for the Dodgers (30 wins with a 3.00 ERA) and was especially tough on Roy Campanella (.156 batting average in 64 at-bats, Willie Davis (.162 in 74 AB), and Duke Snider (.238 in 130 AB).

Settling in the northern Michigan community of Mio with his wife, Joyce, and their four children after his playing days, Buhl was involved in youth baseball and also coached the baseball team at Hillman High School in the 1970s. Throughout his retirement he participated in Milwaukee Braves reunions and special events, including the emotional closing of Milwaukee's County Stadium on September 28, 2000. Suffering from emphysema, Buhl died on February 16, 2001, in Titusville, Florida, to which he had retired, and his body was cremated. Two days later his longtime roommate Eddie Mathews passed away.

Sources

Newspapers

Chicago Tribune.

Milwaukee Journal.

Milwaukee Sentinel.

The Sporting News.

Websites

Ancestry.com

BaseballLibrary.com

Baseball-Reference.com

Retrosheet.org

SABR.org

Notes

1. Danny Peary, ed. *We Played the Game.* (New York: Black Dog and Leventhal, 1994), 214.
2. Ibid.
3. Peary, 48-49.
4. *The Sporting News*, April 11, 1956, 5.
5. Peary, 112.
6. Ibid.
7. Ibid.
8. *The Sporting News*, April 11, 1956, 5.
9. *The Sporting News*, March 10, 1954, 8.
10. *The Sporting News*, April 11, 1956, 5.
11. Peary, 214.
12. *The Sporting News*, March 6, 1957, 2.
13. Ibid.
14. *New York Times*, February 22, 2001, 23.
15. Peary, 353.
16. Peary, 354.
17. Peary 383.
18. *The Sporting News*, May 7, 1958, 21.
19. Peary, 385.
20. Ibid.
21. *The Sporting News*, September 10, 1958, 20.
22. *The Sporting News*, October 1, 1958, 12.
23. *The Sporting News*, March 18, 1959, 17.
24. *The Sporting News*, May 27, 1959, 13.
25. Peary, 423.
26. Peary, 461.
27. *The Sporting News*, May 9, 1962, 16.
28. *The Sporting News*, May 9, 1962, 23.
29. Peary, 568-69.
30. Gene Fraley, "Buhl Meets Rose Going the Other Way," *Chicago Tribune*, July 30, 1978, 131.

Lew Burdette

By Alex Kupfer

Throughout his 18-year major-league career, Lew Burdette was known for his antics as much as for his success on the mound. One of the best control pitchers of the 1950s, the right-hander paired with his roommate and best friend Warren Spahn to form one of the greatest and most durable pitching combinations in baseball history.

Typically in collaboration with Spahn, Burdette was a notorious prankster who did everything from slipping snakes into umpires' pockets to intentionally posing as a lefty for his 1959 Topps baseball card. On the mound his nervous mannerisms such as fixing his jersey and hat, wiping his forehead, touching his lips, and talking to himself could, in the words of one of his managers, Fred Haney, "make coffee nervous."[1] Burdette's behavior undoubtedly helped to distract batters, but it also led to frequent accusations that he threw a spitball. While the pitcher, supported by his teammates and umpires, always denied that he threw the spitter, he saw the benefit of cultivating the reputation that he did, as he famously stated, "My best pitch is one I do not throw." He relied on a sinking fastball, slider, and changeup to reach the 200-win mark on the way to helping to lead his team to two World Series appearances. Above all, though, Burdette is best remembered for turning in one of the most dominant performances in postseason history when his three complete-game victories over the New York Yankees helped lead the Milwaukee Braves to the 1957 World Series title.

Selva Lewis Burdette, Jr. was born on November 22, 1926, in Nitro, West Virginia, to Agnes Burnett and Selva Lewis Burdette, Sr., a plant foreman at an American Viscose Rayon plant in Nitro. Generally known by his middle name, throughout his life he spelled it "Lou." While he played a lot of sandlot baseball as a child, his first athletic success came with the Nitro High School football team, because the school didn't have a baseball team. He failed to make the local American Legion team, but after graduating from high school in 1944 he used his father's connections to get a job at the Viscose plant (his sister and younger brother also worked there) as a message boy on the condition that he pitch for the company's baseball team. At 17 years old, playing in the Industrial League of the Viscose Athletic Association, Burdette went 12-2 against teams from companies including DuPont, Monsanto, and Carbide.

Burdette's fledgling baseball career was put on hold when he entered the Air Corps Reserve in April 1945. Because the ranks were full, he was never given the opportunity to fly and instead was placed with a welding outfit. Released from active duty after six months, he enrolled at the University of Richmond and joined the baseball team. Burdette quickly drew the attention of scouts from a number of major-league teams, including one from the Boston Braves who told him, "I don't like the way you pitch. You may as well forget about baseball."[2] Signed by the Yankees in 1947 for $200 a month, Burdette was assigned to Norfolk, Virginia, in the Class B Piedmont League to begin his professional career.

Lew Burdette (National Baseball Hall of Fame Library, Cooperstown, N.Y.)

Burdette pitched in only six games in Norfolk, then was sent to Amsterdam, New York, of the Class C Canadian-American League. In 150 innings he showed a great deal of promise, posting nine wins against ten losses and a stellar 2.82 earned-run average. He continued to improve the following season with Quincy, Illinois, in the Class B Three-I League, finishing the season at 16-11, with an ERA of 2.02 and a league-record 187 strikeouts. He moved up the organizational ladder once again, spending 1948 and 1949 with the Yankees' Triple-A affiliate in Kansas City, where he roomed with Whitey Ford. Facing tougher competition, for the first time, Burdette struggled, and was relegated to the bullpen.

During his time in the Yankees system, Burdette occasionally worked with roving pitching coach Burleigh Grimes. Though known as one of the great spitball pitchers, Grimes refused to teach Burdette how to throw the spitter out of a concern that if caught Burdette would be banned from professional baseball. However, Grimes suggested that because of his behavior on the mound and the movement on his breaking pitches, particularly his sinking slider, Burdette could use the spitball as a psychological weapon, so that even though he didn't throw it, batters would convince themselves that he was and come to the plate looking for it.

While with Kansas City, Lew married his fiancée, Mary Ann Shelton. They had met in a bowling alley in Charleston, West Virginia, in October 1948, and decided to get engaged as Lew was leaving for spring training the following March. Upon hearing that the wedding was scheduled for the fall of 1949, the Kansas City front office, wanted to stage the wedding at home plate. Mary nixed the idea and the couple married quietly in Charleston in June 1949. Their first son, Lewis Kent, was born in July 1951.

Despite his pitching struggles in Triple-A, Burdette was called up to the Yankees when the rosters expanded in September 1950. He made his major-league debut for the defending World Series champions on September 26 against the Washington Senators, getting Gil Coan to ground out to end the fifth inning. The next spring he was invited to spring training, then was optioned to San Francisco in the Pacific Coast League. Playing for manager Lefty O'Doul, Burdette started 26 games and did his best to show that he belonged back in the majors, striking out 118 while walking 78 in 210 innings. And although his record stood at 14-12, half of the losses were by one run. Then, on August 29, 1951, Burdette's career radically changed when he was traded to the Boston Braves as a throw-in when the Yankees sent $50,000 for pitcher Johnny Sain to help them with their push for the postseason.

Burdette spent the final month of the season with the Braves, making three short relief appearances. In 1952 he worked mostly out of the bullpen and demonstrated that he could ably shoulder a heavy workload, leading the team with 45 appearances, foreshadowing the durability that highlighted his career. (During his career Burdette was consistently among the league leaders in innings pitched, games started, and complete games.)

Before the 1953 season, frustrated by his team's second-tier status in Boston, owner Lou Perini moved the club to Milwaukee. The Braves were immediately embraced by the fans as the players were showered with everything from cars to free dry cleaning. While the Braves had drawn only 281,278 fans in their final year in Boston, they surpassed the mark after only 13 home games in Milwaukee. That first year, they set a National League attendance record, as 1,826,397 saw the Braves play at the new County Stadium.

The Braves' popularity coincided with their emergence as one of the dominant teams in the National League. Adding Hank Aaron and a number of other key players to the roster, the Braves became perennial pennant contenders, finishing no lower than third in the standings from 1953 to 1960. Beginning the 1953 season in the bullpen, Burdette moved into the starting rotation when Johnny Antonelli and Vern Bickford were injured. Despite making only 13 starts, Burdette finished the season with six complete games, a record of 15-5 and a 3.24 ERA; he was clearly ready to move into the team's rotation as soon as a spot opened up.

The Brooklyn Dodgers became the Braves' biggest rivals during this period, finishing one spot ahead of the Braves in the final standings in each of the Braves' first four years in Milwaukee in races that often went down to the final week. Twice Burdette found himself at the center of run-ins with one of the Dodgers' African-American stars, and was accused of being racially prejudiced—charges that he and his teammates vehemently denied. In August 1953, the Dodgers' Roy Campanella charged Burdette on the mound with his bat in hand after he struck out and the two men exchanged angry words. Both benches emptied, but no punches were thrown and play quickly resumed. After the game Jackie Robinson told the press that Campanella only charged the mound after Burdette had addressed him with a racial slur. A similar incident occurred three years later when during pregame warm-ups Jackie Robinson threw a baseball at Burdette's head (he missed) in response to being called a "watermelon." Burdette emphatically denied that his comment was racially motivated, claiming that he was joking about Robinson's "spare tire, not his race." The two spoke after the game, and Robinson was placated by Burdette's apology and explanation, and put the matter behind him.

Based on Burdette's stellar 1953 season as both a starter and reliever, expectations were high for Burdette and the team coming into 1954. Burdette moved into the starting rotation when Antonelli and Bickford were traded. Throughout the season the Braves were plagued by injuries to position players and inconsistent pitching—at the All-Star break, the Braves' trio of Spahn, Burdette, and Bob Buhl were a combined 15-26 and the Braves sat 15 games out of first place. Burdette had a strong second half, however, going 8-5 to end with a 15-14 record, with an impressive 2.76 ERA, second best in the National League. Despite Burdette's performance, the Braves were never able to seriously contend for the pennant. In 1955 Burdette finished with a 13-8 record and a 4.03 ERA. But once again, the team was never in contention as the Dodgers simply ran away from the rest of the National League en route to their first World Series title.

During his time in the minor leagues and his first few years in the majors, Burdette returned to Nitro each offseason. Lew and Mary's second child, Madge Rhea, was born on Christmas Day, 1954. Her birth was particularly newsworthy because Lew helped deliver the baby in a police ambulance on the way to the hospital. Then the growing Burdette family began to split their time between Milwaukee and Sarasota, Florida, where Lew spent his offseasons as a vice president in a local real-estate firm. The couple's third child, Mary Lou, was born only days before Burdette's masterful performance in the 1957 World Series. A third daughter, Elaina, was born in May 1960.

As his career was taking off, accusations that Burdette threw a spitball became increasingly common from opposing managers and players. Cincinnati manager Birdie Tebbetts (who became Burdette's manager on the Braves in 1961 and 1962) and National League President Warren Giles even went as far as separately commissioning motion pictures of Burdette pitching—though the films never showed that he was using the illegal pitch. Braves manager Fred Haney countered that his pitcher was not doing anything wrong, saying, "He's just a fidgety guy on the mound." Every time the charges arose, Burdette, along with his teammates and even the umpires, would deny them and emphasize the psychological advantage his nervous actions on the mound provided.

Burdette started on Opening Day in 1956 and cruised to a 6-0 win over the Chicago Cubs, allowing only five hits and one walk. The Braves battled Brooklyn and Cincinnati for the pennant until the final game of the season. With the Braves one game behind the Dodgers on the last day, Haney started Burdette against the St. Louis Cardinals needing a win plus a Pittsburgh win over Brooklyn to take the pennant. While Burdette led his team to a 4-2 victory, the Dodgers also won, and the Braves finished one game back. Although the season ended disappointingly, it was another successful season for Burdette. He led the league in ERA at 2.70 (Spahn finished second at 2.78 and in shutouts with 6. His 19 wins, against 10 losses, were the fourth highest in the league, and he received a handful of votes for the Most Valuable Player award.

Expectations were extremely high for the Braves going into the 1957 season. Burdette performed to his now-usual standards, and was named to his first All-Star team. The Braves finally won the pennant, in large part by relying on their top three starters; Spahn, Burdette, and Buhl combined to finish with a record of 56-27. Burdette was 17-9 with a 3.72 ERA.

Spahn lost the World Series opener at Yankee Stadium to Whitey Ford, then Burdette pitched a complete game to defeat Bobby Shantz, 4-2. Taking the mound four days later with the Series knotted at two games apiece, Burdette shut out the powerful Yankees to lead the Braves to a 1-0 victory over his former Kansas City roommate Whitey Ford. When the Yankees won Game Six, it was assumed that Spahn would take the hill for the Braves in the finale. However, with Spahn unable to recover from a bout of Asian flu, Burdette, with only two days of rest, started against Don Larsen. Burdette pitched another complete-game shutout, holding the Yankees to seven hits and allowing only one walk, as the Braves won, 5-0. Posting an ERA of 0.67, Burdette matched the greatest World Series pitching performances by the being the first pitcher since Stan Coveleski in 1920 with three complete-game victories, and the first since Christy Mathewson in 1905 to have two shutouts. As the World Series MVP, Burdette was showered with awards and honors. He gave talks on the lecture circuit, made numerous appearances on television (including "The Steve Allen Show" and Camel cigarette ads), and even cut a novelty record, "Three Strikes and You're Out."

Burdette turned in another great season in 1958 as the Braves repeated as National League champions. At 20-10 he reached the 20-win mark for the first time, and tied with Spahn for the best winning percentage in the National League. His batting even improved significantly, as he finished the season with a .242 batting average and 15 runs batted in. On July 10 against the Los Angeles Dodgers at their temporary home in Memorial Coliseum, Burdette smashed two home runs, one a grand slam off Johnny Podres. This was the second time in two seasons that Burdette had hit two home runs in a game—he had done so against Joe Nuxhall in Cincinnati on August 13, 1957.

Facing the Yankees once again in the World Series, after a Spahn victory in the opener, Burdette cruised to a 13-5 victory in Game Two in which he hit a three-run home run in the first inning. But although Milwaukee jumped to a 3-1 Series lead, Burdette lost Games Five and Seven, giving up a combined 10 earned runs and allowing the Yankees to battle back and win the title.

Vying for their third consecutive pennant in 1959, the Braves relied heavily on their core veterans. Eddie Mathews and Hank Aaron responded with stellar offensive seasons and were among four Braves, along with Burdette and Del Crandall, to finish in the top 12 of the MVP voting that season. Although Burdette had a career-high 21 wins, tying him with Spahn for the league lead, and appeared in both 1959 All-Star Games, he lost 15 games and the heavy workload took its toll as he gave up career highs in home runs (38) and hits allowed (312)—both the highest in the league.

Burdette was a central player in one of the most memorable games in history when he took the mound against Harvey Haddix and the Pirates on May 26, 1959, in Milwaukee. Haddix pitched 12 perfect innings, retiring 36 Braves in order, only to lose in the 13th inning when Joe Adcock drove in Felix Mantilla (who had reached on an error). While not as perfect as Haddix had been, Burdette turned in an excellent performance, giving up 12 hits and no runs. After the game a sympathetic Burdette phoned Haddix to tell him, "You deserved to win, but I scattered all my hits, and you bunched your one." Not sharing Burdette's sense of humor (or at least his timing), the taciturn Haddix hung up on him.

Tied with the Dodgers at the end of the season, the Braves and Dodgers had a best-of-three playoff for the pennant. Down one game after Carl Willey lost the playoff opener, Burdette took a 5-2 lead into the bottom of the ninth inning of Game Two and seemed well on his way to tying the series. However, after giving up three straight singles to Wally Moon, Duke Snider, and Gil Hodges with no outs, Burdette was pulled and could only watch helplessly as the Dodgers drove in all three to send the game to extra innings. In the 12th inning, facing reliever Bob Rush, the Dodgers' Carl Furillo drove in Gil Hodges to end the Braves' season.

After four seasons in which Milwaukee either reached the World Series or came up just short, it was becoming increasingly evident that the Braves dynasty was coming to an end, in large part due to the advancing age of many key players. Burdette performed as consistently as ever, though, going 19-13 with a 3.36 ERA in 275 2/3 innings. On August 18, 1960 facing Philadelphia and former teammate Gene Conley, he pitched a no-hitter, defeating the Phillies, 1-0. Allowing no walks, Burdette faced the minimum 27 batters. The only thing that kept him from a perfect game was hitting the Phillies' Tony Gonzalez with a pitch in the fifth inning. Gonzalez was subsequently erased by a double play.

After dropping to fourth place in 1961 (Burdette was 18-11), the Braves made a concerted effort to bring in younger players in 1962. Birdie Tebbetts, Burdette's former nemesis from Cincinnati, replaced Chuck Dressen as manager late in the 1961 season. Inconsistent all season long in 1962, Burdette was one of the victims of the youth movement, and started only 19 games, about half his usual number. Then his 13 years with the Braves came ended on June 15, 1963, when he was traded to the St. Louis Cardinals for minor-league pitcher Bob Sadowski and utilityman Gene Oliver.

Although Burdette preferred to start, the Cardinals traded for him because they thought he could be used as both a starter and reliever. His first game with the Cardinals, a complete-game victory over the New York Mets on June 18, seemed to suggest a return to form as a front-line starter. Burdette faced his former roommate Spahn when he faced off against the Braves on July 25. Once again going the distance, Burdette won, 3-1. But he struggled most of the season, posted only a 3-8 mark with the Cardinals, and against his wishes, was increasingly relegated to long relief appearances.

Despite again being on a contending team, Burdette was unhappy with his role on the Cardinals and pushed for a trade. He was traded early the next season to the Cubs for pitcher Glen Hobbie, missing out on the Cardinals' 1964 World Series title. Reunited with Bob Buhl, Burdette was again given the chance to start. His struggles continued though and he finished the 1964 season with a 10-9 record and an ERA near 5.00. On May 30, 1965, Burdette was sold to the Phillies. Two starts he made in September represented his continuing struggles and inability to pitch for extended stretches. Against Cincinnati on September 5, he gave up six earned runs in 1 2/3 innings, and in his next start, the Braves scored five earned runs off him in two innings.

Released by the Phillies at the end of the season, Burdette spent his final two seasons in the majors with the California Angels. Adding a knuckleball, Burdette had an excellent season in 1966 when he made 54 appearances out of the bullpen as a key middle reliever. He won his 200th game on July 22 when he entered a game against the Yankees with the score tied 4-4 and the the Angels scored two runs to win, 6-4. But the resurgence was short-lived and Burdette pitched in only 19 games in 1967. His final major-league pitching appearance came on July 16, when he threw a scoreless eighth inning in a loss to the Minnesota Twins. In August the Angels sent him to their Pacific Coast League affiliate in Seattle, his first trip to the minors since 1951. Burdette appeared in 13 games in Seattle before being recalled in September; however, now 40 years old and recognizing that he was not going to be used in any significant capacity, he retired.

After retiring, Burdette took a job scouting pitchers for the Central Scouting System. In 1969 and 1970 he split time between coaching pitchers in the Gulf Coast League and his hometown of Sarasota, where he tried his hand at various businesses, including a gas station and a night club. In 1972 he became the Atlanta Braves pitching coach, and was reunited with longtime teammate Eddie Mathews when Mathews was named manager halfway through the season. Burdette was excited about rejoining the Braves' organization, saying, "They've always been my club. Everything good happened when I was with the Braves. They've been my life."[3] But he left the Braves after the 1973 season, and worked in public relations for a Milwaukee brewery and then in cable television in Florida for 20 years until he retired.

Embracing his connections to the Braves, Burdette was a regular at old-timers games and baseball functions over the years. He appeared on the Baseball Hall of Fame ballot for the first time in 1973, the year that Spahn was elected. Burdette received votes in each of the 15 years he was eligible, peaking in 1984 at 24.1 percent. In 1998 he was inducted to the Florida Sports

Hall of Fame and in 2001 was elected to the Braves Hall of Fame.

Burdette died on February 6, 2007, in Winter Garden, Florida, after battling lung cancer. One of the most fitting tributes came from a longtime teammate, shortstop Johnny Logan, who summed up Burdette's career and personality by remarking, "I don't know if he threw a spitter or not. His ball would really sink. He was a hell of a battler. Whatever Spahnie did, Lew wanted to do better. They had that competition between them. Lew was a big star but he always gave Spahnie the credit."[4]

Sources

Allen, Phil. "Biggest Froggy, Biggest Pond: The Lew Burdette Story." *Baseball Digest,* December 1957: 29-33.

Buege, Bob. *The Milwaukee Braves: A Baseball Eulogy*. Milwaukee: Douglas American Sports Publications, 1988.

Chen, Albert. "The Greatest Game Ever Pitched." *Sports Illustrated,* June 1, 2009: 63-67.

Driver, David. "The Pride of Nitro: Baseball Star Lew Burdette." *Goldenseal*, Fall 1998: 56-62.

Mumau, Thad. *An Indian Summer: The 1957 Milwaukee Braves, Champions of Baseball*. Jefferson, North Carolina: McFarland, 2007.

Schoor, Gene. *Lew Burdette of the Braves*. New York: G.P. Putnam's Sons, 1960.

Sutter, L.M. *Ball, Bat, and Bitumen: A History of Coalfield Baseball in the Appalachian South*. Jefferson, North Carolina: McFarland, 2009.

Vincent, Fay. *We Would Have Played for Nothing: Baseball Stars of the 1950s and 1960s Talk About the Game They Loved*. New York: Simon & Schuster, 2008.

www.baseball-reference.com

Lew Burdette Clipping File at National Baseball Hall of Fame and Museum in Cooperstown, New York.

Notes

1. Phil Allen. "Biggest Froggy, Biggest Pond: The Lew Burdette Story." *Baseball Digest,* Vol. 16, no. 10 (December 1957) : 30.
2. David Driver. "The Pride of Nitro: Baseball Star Lew Burdette." *Goldenseal* (Fall 1998): 59.
3. "Burdette Sees Life on 'Outside.'" Unattributed clipping in Burdette's player file at the National Baseball Hall of Fame.
4. Tom Haudricourt. "Obituary; Lew Burdette 1927-2007; Farewell to a Hero: Crafty Right-Hander Led Braves to to Glory in '57 Series." *Milwaukee Journal-Sentinel* February 7, 2007: C1.

Dick Cole

By Doug Engelman

For young Dickie Cole, growing up in Southern California in the 1930s, dreams of becoming a major leaguer must have seemed as distant as the nearest big-league team, the St. Louis Cardinals, half a country away. Lying on the living-room floor and listening to France Laux doing the Cardinal games on KMOX radio in St. Louis, he could only imagine the sights and sounds of a major-league ballpark. But dreams of a big-league career do come true. Cole's baseball career spanned nearly six decades. After 16 seasons as a player, he remained in the game into the second decade of the 21st century as been a minor-league manager, major-league coach, and a highly respected scout. Cole was valued for his versatility in the field and his studious approach to the game. He played every infield position during his major-league career: 169 games at shortstop, 118 games at second base, 107 games at third base, and two appearances at first base. At 87 years old in 2013, Cole was still active, scouting for the San Francisco Giants organization. It seems dreams do come true!

Richard Roy Cole was born on May 6, 1926, in Long Beach, California, the first of two sons born to Almer and Gertrude (Jones) Cole. His parents were transplants to the Los Angeles area; his father's family migrated from Nebraska and his mother's family from Illinois. They met in California and married in 1924. In the busy and rapidly expanding port city, Almer worked as a salesman and deliveryman for a bread company; Gertrude was a secretary for a fruit-juice company. An athletic youngster, Cole was fixture on the sandlots of Long Beach. In June 1943 he graduated from Woodrow Wilson High School, where he was a standout shortstop, equally adroit with the glove and bat. That August, at only 17, Cole was signed to his first professional contract, by St. Louis Cardinals scout Bob Hughes.[1] On August 25, 1943, he began his professional career playing third base for the Sacramento Solons, the Cardinals' minor-league affiliate in the Pacific Coast League. In his first professional game, according to the account in *The Sporting News*, "Cole singled and scored a run as the Solons bowed to the Padres, 7-4. In the field, he muffed one of three chances, and started a twin-killing."[2] Cole recalled in an interview with the author the frustrating beginning to his professional career, "Our record was 1-14. Nippy Jones (later a major-league first baseman) was on that team, too. He was only 18. I had to hitchhike home from Sacramento, because as a Double-A player, I was broke."[3]

During the offseason, Cole, along with eight other Solon players, was reassigned to the Columbus Redbirds of the Double-A American Association, another Cardinals farm team. Early in the 1944 season he was demoted to the Allentown Cardinals of the Class B Interstate League. At Allentown he batted .281 in 97 games. Like many other ballplayers of that era, Cole found his career interrupted by World War II. In June 1944 he passed an Army physical,[4] and in August he was inducted. (Just before his last game the fans at an Allentown game took up a collection and gave him $138.80.[5]) In 1945, after completing basic training, Cole

Dick Cole (National Baseball Hall of Fame Library, Cooperstown, N.Y.)

was sent to Camp Roberts in Southern California, where he played several games alongside future Hall of Famer Bobby Doerr.

Cole was discharged in 1946, and on June 17, 1946 he rejoined Columbus. Shaking off the rust from two years of military duty, he hit .241 in 37 games with the Red Birds. He began the 1947 season with the Omaha Cardinals of the Class A Western League. Blocked from playing by a logjam in the middle infield, Cole was shipped to the Fresno Cardinals of the Class C California League. There he batted a career-high .386 and led the league in batting.

Considered tall for a middle infielder, the 6-foot-2, 175-pound Cole went to spring training with the Cardinals several times but spent five years shuttling between Columbus, Omaha, and the Rochester Red Wings of the International League. Though he never came close to matching his unexpected hitting success with Fresno (his batting average fluctuated between .236 and .297 between 1948 and 1952), Cole was thought of as a "wizard with the glove."[6] In 1951 he went north with the Cardinals, and made his major-league debut on April 27 when he was inserted as a pinch-runner in the fifth inning, then replaced Marty Marion at shortstop. In the eighth he got his first at-bat, walking and later scoring on Stan Musial's fly ball. He played in 15 games, ten of them as a starter at second base, and batter.194 (7-for-36). On June 15 he was sent to the Pittsburgh Pirates as part of a seven-player trade. (One of the Cardinals traded along with him was Joe Garagiola.) The Pirates optioned Cole to Indianapolis in the American Association, where he batted .297 in 57 games, playing only shortstop. He was recalled by the Pirates in August and started 31 games at second base and eight at shortstop over the last seven weeks of the season, batting .236.

Sent to the Hollywood Stars in 1952, Cole played in 178 games and batted .286 as the Stars won the PCL pennant. With Hollywood Cole encountered manager Fred Haney, who would have a major impact on his playing career. The next season he made the Pirates' roster, and spent the next four years with the club. Cole was a versatile and solid defender, starting at every infield position during his tenure with the Pirates. Primarily a spot starter and defensive replacement, he was a steady but unspectacular infielder for the hapless Pirates, with a .253 batting average.

Cole's finest season as a major leaguer was in 1954. Appearing in 138 games, he had starts at second base, shortstop and third base and batted .270 with 22 doubles, five triples, and one home run. Though fleet of foot, he grounded into 20 double plays, the second-highest total in the National League. Cole's home run, his second and last in the majors, came off the Brooklyn Dodgers' Carl Erskine.

In 1955 Cole lost playing time to Dick Groat who returned to the shortstop position after a stint in the military and to 21-year-old, hard-hitting Gene Freese at third base. Then, in early April 1957, Cole was traded to the Milwaukee Braves even up for utilityman Jim Pendleton, and went from the basement to the penthouse as the Braves won the National League pennant and the World Series over the New York Yankees.

The story of Cole's trade to the Braves shows how closely his fate was tied to manager Fred Haney. In 1952 when Cole was promoted from Hollywood to the Pirates, Haney, his manager with the Stars, also moved up to Pittsburgh, as the manager. By 1957 Haney was managing the Braves, and helped engineer the trade for Cole. Haney had taken a liking to Cole at Hollywood. More than 60 years after their first encounter, Cole was unable to explain why. Perhaps it was his maturity (he was 26 in 1952) or his versatility, he surmised. "I was Fred Haney's little 'Bobo,'" he told sportswriter Jack Heyde. "I guess Fred liked the fact that I worked hard and was a student of the game. Of course, it didn't hurt that I could play all of the infield positions pretty well."[7]

At the end of May Cole was optioned to Triple-A Wichita, then was recalled on June 23. After playing in eight games, primarily as a defensive replacement, he was sent back to Wichita in late July when the Braves called up Bob Hazle. Hazle went on to bat .403 for the Braves in their pennant drive. Cole remained with Wichita, batting .331 in 52 games as Wichita won the American Association pennant. When the Braves expanded their roster in September, they called up infielder Harry Hanebrink and pitchers Phil Paine and

Carl Willey, but Cole never made it back to the big leagues.

In 1958 the 32-year-old Cole hoped for another chance to reach the majors and signed with the unaffiliated Sacramento Solons of the Pacific Coast League. His major-league experience and versatility made him a valuable asset, and he hit .280 for the year. The following year, Cole was reunited with his former Cardinals manager, Marty Marion, who was president of the Houston Buffs of the Texas League. Marion had signed Cole along with several other former big leaguers, eyeing a spot for the Buffs in the planned Continental League. Backed by New York attorney William Shea, the league was conceived as a third major league; Shea's motive was to get another team in New York to replace the departed Dodgers and Giants. Marion and his former big leaguers hoped that this was their opportunity to get back to the majors. After Major League Baseball subsequently announced expansion in 1961 for the American League and 1962 for the National League (including the New York Mets), the Continental League lost its support and folded before it could get started.

After the season in Houston, Cole retired with his wife, Katherine, and their four children, and transitioned into coaching. In 1961 he became part of what some baseball observers consider one of the greatest oddities in major-league managerial history; the Chicago Cubs' "College of Coaches," instituted by Cubs owner Philip K. Wrigley. Cole was one of 11 coaches listed on the roster of the 1961 Cubs. However, he was not one of the principal coach-managers. Along with his rotation as field coach for the big-league club, Cole spent time managing two Cubs farm teams, Wenatchee of the Class B Northwest League and St. Cloud of the Class C Northern League. He was instrumental in the careers of two future stars. "I was sent to work with (future Hall of Famer) Lou Brock on his bunting, and I was the one who moved Kenny Hubbs from shortstop to second base," Cole said. The next year with the Cubs Hubbs was the National League Rookie of the Year." Cole was one of a four-manager rotation along with Rube Walker, Bobby Adams, and Verdie Himsl. He was the only one of the four not to serve a rotation as manager of the Cubs. His stint with the Cubs lasted just one year,[8] and the College of Coaches concept was abandoned after the 1962 season.

In 1962 Cole took the reins of the Auburn Mets of the Class D New York-Pennsylvania League. Still only 36, with a lot of baseball left in him, Cole was one of four designated player-managers in the league that year.[9] However, he had no appearances as a player. That season Cole enjoyed his greatest success as a manager with the New York Mets affiliate. After a third-place finish (62-57) in the regular season, Cole led the team to the league championship and was named Manager of the Year. The following season the league was elevated to Class A status; the club finished in first place, posting a 76-54 record, but lost in the first round of the playoffs. By the late 1960s Cole was back in the Pirates organization; he managed in the Rookie League with the Gulf Coast Pirates in 1970 and tutored Dave Parker in his first year of professional baseball.[10]

Cole began his scouting career with the Pirates. In 1971 he was named scouting supervisor and held that role for the next three seasons. In 1974, after escalating player salaries placed significant financial burdens on major-league organizations, baseball's Central Scouting Bureau, now called the Major League Baseball Scouting Bureau, was founded.[11] Seventeen participating clubs, including the Pirates, contributed some of their best scouts to the combine. Cole was one of the initial 56 scouts who formed the bureau, earning the Scout of the Month designation in December 1976.[12] As of 2013 he resided in Costa Mesa, California, with his second wife, Ada, and continued to work in various scouting capacities with the San Francisco Giants.

As of 2013, Dick Cole had spent all but 17 of his 87 years as a part of professional baseball. In 2008 he was honored by his hometown with induction into the Long Beach Baseball Hall of Fame. He is a member of his high-school athletic hall of fame. In a phone interview with the author, he said, "I dreamed of being a major-league ballplayer, and everything I wanted came true for me." Recalling highlights from his career, Cole said: "Henry Aaron said I was the worst batting practice pitcher he ever faced."

Who wouldn't love to make that claim?

Sources

Telephone interview with Dick Cole conducted by Doug Engelman on February 11, 2013.

Ancestry.com

BaseballAlmanac.com

Baseball-Reference.com

Retrosheet.com

Notes

1 *The Sporting News*, September 2, 1943, 23.
2 *The Sporting News*, August 26, 1943.
3 Telephone interview with Dick Cole on February 11, 2013. All quotations from Cole are from this interview unless otherwise noted.
4 *The Sporting News*, June 29, 1944, 24.
5 *The Sporting News*, August 10, 1944, 22.
6 *The Sporting News*, March 21, 1951, 19.
7 Jack Heyde, *Pop Flies and Line Drives; Visits With Players from Baseball's "Golden Era"* (Victoria, British Columbia: Trafford Publishing, 2004), 75.
8 *The Sporting News*, November 17, 1962, 16.
9 *The Sporting News*, April 4, 1962, 31.
10 *The Sporting News*, August 22, 1970, 44.
11 *The Sporting News*, October 12, 1974, 18.
12 *The Sporting News*, December 4, 1976, 17.

Gene Conley

By John R. Husman

GENE CONLEY EXCELLED at the major-league level of two sports and is the only athlete to own dual-sport championships. Besides pitching for the World Series champion Milwaukee Braves in 1957, he was a member of three NBA championship teams with the Boston Celtics. He was the first player to earn Minor League Player of the Year honors twice and appeared in three major-league All-Star Games. His 15-year career as a professional athlete totaled 23 seasons that included 11 in baseball's major leagues and six in the NBA. At one point he packed 12 major-league seasons into six years with not a day off between those seasons.

The middle of three children of Raymond Leslie "Les" Conley and Eva Beatrice Brewer Conley, Donald Eugene Conley was born on November 10, 1930, in Muskogee, Oklahoma. His heritage includes Irish, German, English, and Cherokee. He was introduced to sports as a boy in Muskogee. He participated in swimming, football, and basketball and was a knothole gang member of the Class D Muskogee Reds.

When Gene was 12 the family moved to Richland, Washington. There at Columbia High School, he earned letters in baseball, basketball, and track. He enjoyed a productive senior year in all three sports. In baseball he lost only one of ten starts (to the eventual state champions) and batted at a nearly .500 clip. In basketball he averaged more than 15 points per game, led the Richland Bombers to their first-ever state tournament berth, and was selected to the all-state team. He was runner-up in the state track meet in the high jump with a leap of 6 feet 3 inches. He has been made a member of the Richland Bomber Hall of Fame.

As an 18-year-old and near his mature height of 6-feet-8, Conley chose Washington State University from the many prominent basketball schools that had offered him scholarships. At WSU he was also afforded an automobile and expenses by a grateful alumnus. Conley captained the freshman basketball team and as a sophomore led the varsity to the Northern Division championship of the Pacific Coast Conference. He was the top scorer for the Cougars, who lost to UCLA for the overall conference championship on a buzzer-beater. Conley represented the Northwest in the 1949 Hearst All-Star (baseball) Game, which pitted all-stars from the greater New York area against the top players from the rest of the country. Gene was named the United States All-Stars captain for the game, played at the Polo Grounds. He was the starting and winning pitcher, besting Frank Torre of the New York team. Conley called the experience of the preliminary games in Seattle, practice in Yankee Stadium, and game itself "as much fun as I ever had in my life." During the spring of 1950, Conley starred for the Washington State baseball team that finished 32-6 and was runner-up for the national championship. He pitched in 16 games, winning five, including two shutouts, saving two more and averaging .417 at the plate. He was inducted into Washington State University's Hall of Fame in 1979.

Gene Conley (National Baseball Hall of Fame Library, Cooperstown, N.Y.)

Conley's pitching attracted scouts from most of the major-league teams. He initially resisted, citing his desire to finish college, but signed with Bill Marshall of the Braves, then in Boston, in October of 1950. He began both his professional sports career and his marriage in the spring of 1951. He married Kathryn Dizney, whom he had met the previous fall.

The Braves assigned Conley to their Class A team at Hartford of the Eastern League for 1951. His debut season was outstanding, with 20 wins, an earned-run average of 2.16, and a strikeout-to-walk ratio well over three to one. He was honored as the league's Most Valuable Player and named Minor League Player of the Year by *The Sporting News*. Conley's success came because of only two pitches, a fastball and a curve, which was his complete repertoire for his entire career.

Basketball re-entered Conley's life late in the 1951 baseball season. Kathryn R. "Katie" Conley told the story in her biography of her husband, *One of a Kind*. She related that during the Hartford club's last trip to Wilkes-Barre, Pennsylvania, Gene was invited to suit up for a scrimmage with the Wilkes-Barre Barons of the American Basketball Association. The Barons' head coach and owner, Eddie White, was impressed and offered him a contract for $5,000. When the Braves learned that Gene was considering playing professional basketball, he was summoned to a meeting with general manager John Quinn. At the meeting, Katie Conley wrote, Gene "had been given a $1,000 check in return for his promise never to play basketball again."[1] Conley honored the deal and labored as an ironworker during the offseason.

Conley's 1951 season earned him a serious look by the Braves, who promoted him to the big-league club as the fourth starter for 1952. His stay was short because of three dismal and winless starts, after which he was assigned to the Braves' top farm club, Milwaukee of the American Association. He did not get his first start there until the season was well into June but still finished with 11 victories for the pennant-winning Brewers. He chipped in with a .338 batting average, aided by a 5-for-5 day against the Indianapolis Indians. Earlier in the 1952 season, on April 26, Conley was the 90th overall pick in the NBA draft, selected by the Boston Celtics. Katie and Gene decided, for financial reasons, that he should try to make the club. He did so and, surprisingly, secured Quinn's permission to play. He played sparingly for Red Auerbach's Celtics, but established that he had the ability to play in the league. The Celtics made the NBA playoffs and were eliminated in the second round. As a consequence, Conley was late in reporting for spring training in 1953.

The year of 1953 was one of promise for Conley as he fully expected to make the big-league baseball club. But he did not. He was again sent to the Braves' top minor club, which had been displaced to Toledo when the Braves moved from Boston to Milwaukee. Conley started fast and kept up the pace until late in the season, when he was sidelined by a troublesome back. He won 23 games before his early exit and was named the American Association's Most Valuable Player. For the second time *The Sporting News* selected him as the Minor League Player of the Year. He was the first player to be so honored more than once. After a week's stay in a Toledo hospital, Conley was fitted with a back brace that he was told to wear for six weeks and then begin a therapy regimen. He immediately discarded the brace and after a couple of weeks his back was feeling fine, enough that he again made the Celtics for the 1953-1954 season. Once again Quinn intervened but this time matched the Celtics' offer of $5,000 to induce Gene not to play basketball. Conley accepted and spent the winter working in Toledo.

En route to Florida for 1954 spring training the Conleys were involved in a serious auto accident. Though their car was demolished, they sustained only minor injuries, and Katie's pregnancy was not compromised. Conley, now well-prepared by his three years and 54-22 record in the minors, made the Braves' Opening Day roster. However, because of the Braves' solid and deep pitching staff, headed by Warren Spahn and Lew Burdette, Gene was not initially placed in manager Charlie Grimm's four-man starting rotation. After he recorded a few solid starts, Grimm revised his plans and went to a five-man rotation. The rookie responded and was selected for the 1954 All-Star Game in Cleveland but was the losing pitcher. By the end of August he had notched 14 wins, but his season was cut short again because of back problems. Conley finished third in an outstanding class for Rookie of the Year honors in 1954. Wally Moon and Ernie Banks finished in the top two spots while Hank Aaron rounded out the group.

As he had the previous summer, Conley recovered quickly from the back ailment with treatment and rest. Once again he tried out for and made the Celtics, but shocked the team by resigning on the eve of the season's opening game. He said he wanted to spend more time with his family and was not sure he would be able to continue as a two-sport athlete. Conley made a difficult decision that he hoped would prolong his baseball career.

Conley went to the Braves' spring training in 1955 without a contract—he was a holdout. Once in camp, he was able to negotiate a $20,000 contract with John Quinn, double his rookie salary. He started the campaign very well and was 8-3 going into a June 15 game against Philadelphia. During that game, according to Kathryn Conley, there was a "horrible sound of something popping or cracking, as he delivered a pitch to Granny Hamner that even our catcher, Del Crandall, heard from his crouched position."[2] This injury to Conley's rotator cuff would plague him for the rest of his career and would have ended it except for regular cortisone injections. He estimated that he had more than 100 injections.

Conley left that game but took his next regular turn five days later and beat the Pirates. He was struck on the injured shoulder by a batted ball in his next start, against Brooklyn, and was forced to leave the game. He missed only a single start before resuming his spot in the rotation, but his pitching arm was still hurting. For the second time in as many years, Conley was selected for the NL All-Star team, but was not slated to pitch as he had only one day's rest. He was forced into action when the NL came back from a 5-0 deficit to send the game into extra innings. Gene was called in to pitch the 12th inning in his home County Stadium and struck out Al Kaline, Mickey Vernon, and Al Rosen in order. Stan Musial slammed a home run leading off the bottom of the 12th to hand the win to the NL and Conley. Gene would not win another game that season. He lost two starts after the All-Star Game and was rested for three weeks before he went on the disabled list for the balance of the season. He was sent to the Mayo Clinic, where he was prescribed exercises, but he self-imposed complete rest.

The shoulder problems were still with Conley at the start of the 1956 season and he was once again on the disabled list. Therapy promoted healing and he returned to the team and won for the first time, in relief, on May 28. Conley was used sparingly by new Braves manager Fred Haney over the remainder of the season. He won only eight times in yet another injury-shortened season as Milwaukee finished in second place, one game behind the Dodgers. The following season, 1957, Gene again alternated between starting and the bullpen, avoided the disabled list for the first time, and won nine games. The Braves continued their fine play and won both the National League pennant and the World Series. Lew Burdette beat the Yankees three times, while Conley had a single lackluster relief appearance, giving up two runs in Game Three.

The pitching career that had been so promising just a few years earlier came unraveled in 1958. Conley's shoulder was still a bother and the Braves' pitching was stronger than ever. Conley, when used, saw mostly relief action and became frustrated, began drinking heavily, and was constantly at odds with manager Haney. He finished the season 0-6 and did not appear in the World Series, again against the Yankees.

After the horrible and disappointing season of 1958, Conley decided to give basketball another try. He called Red Auerbach and was told that Boston did not need him and that Red did not think that he could make the team anyway. Auerbach gave in to Gene's demands for a tryout, but refused to pay the expenses for his trip to Boston. By his sheer determination Conley made the Celtics and signed a contract over the objections of the Braves. On the court he was strong, hustled, could outjump most anyone in the league, and excelled on defense and in rebounding. He would prove that he had staying power as he played three seasons with the Celtics, who were NBA champions all three seasons.

The Celtics' playoff run was cause for Conley not to report to the Braves in the spring of 1959. As a result he was traded to the Philadelphia Phillies on March

31, 1959. The six-player deal was made by the Phillies new general manager, John Quinn, who had just moved over from Milwaukee. The Celtics wrapped up the NBA championship on April 7 and Conley had his second championship ring. He was the first athlete to play on championship teams in two professional sports.

A few days later Conley was in Florida, albeit late, for spring training. It was near the end of April before he made an appearance. He began in relief but was soon moved to the starting rotation and finished with 12 wins for the last-place Phillies. His last win came on August 19, a three-hitter against the Cubs. In the third inning he was hit on the pitching hand while batting against Glen Hobbie. The resulting fracture ended what was Conley's finest season in the making, but not before he completed the game while allowing only a single over the last six innings. He was picked by his former manager, Fred Haney, for the second 1959 All-Star Game in Los Angeles, where he pitched two perfect innings that included strikeouts of Ted Williams and Yogi Berra. He was also named Comeback Player of the Year by the Baseball Writers' Association of America. After the season he signed two contracts, one with the Phillies and another with the Celtics.

The 1960 baseball season was not much different from the previous one, but Conley's wins dropped off to eight. The Phillies offered him $20,000 to forgo basketball the next winter. He made a counter-offer that ended the negotiations and resulted in his being traded to the Boston Red Sox on December 15, 1960. Conley called it the "biggest trade in baseball" because at 6-feet-8-inches he was swapped for Frank Sullivan, who stood 6-feet-6.[3]

Including his previous appearances with the Boston Braves, Conley was about to become the only athlete to appear for three major-league teams in the same city. On April 11, 1961, the Celtics wrapped up another NBA championship, against the St. Louis Hawks at the Boston Garden. Conley was quickly off to Florida for an abbreviated spring training and came back to Boston to start for the Red Sox against the Washington Senators on April 25. Just two weeks removed from the basketball court, he made his first appearance in a Red Sox uniform and pitched eight shutout innings. But after just a few games the pain returned to Conley's pitching shoulder. He kept the recurrence of the rotator cuff injury to himself and continued through the season, pitching just shy of 200 innings and winning 11 games for the sixth-place Red Sox.

Conley had been left unprotected by the Celtics when the NBA held an expansion draft in the spring of 1961. He was selected by the Chicago Packers but did not report, intending to take the winter off. Instead he signed with the Washington/New York Tapers in the fledgling American Basketball League. While with the Tapers, he often accompanied team owner Paul Cohen on sales calls for his Tuck Tape Company. The experience would prove to be valuable when Conley established his own company after his playing days.

The Tapers' season ended in time for Conley to participate in most of spring training with the Red Sox in Arizona. He parlayed a productive spring and a resolve to control his alcohol use into a productive 1962 season. He recorded career highs in wins and innings. The season was not without incident, however, as the shoulder pain returned along with his drinking. After a 13-3 shellacking on July 26 in Yankee Stadium in which he gave up eight runs in two-plus innings, Conley embarked on a venture that has remained signature to him. When the team bus became mired in New York City traffic on the way to the airport, Conley and teammate Pumpsie Green stepped off to find a restroom. This was later dubbed Conley's "intentional walk" by the press.[4] When the players returned, the bus was gone. Left in New York, the pair did some drinking before Green realized he was in trouble and decided to return to the club. Conley continued his binge for a few days and at some point decided to go to Jerusalem. He went so far as to buy a ticket and went to Idlewild Airport (later renamed JFK), but was denied access to the flight because he had no passport. The bizarre incident was well covered by the press and resulted in a substantial fine by the Red Sox, but Conley eventually returned to the good graces of the club.

Before the 1962 baseball season had ended, Conley's NBA rights were traded from Chicago to the New York Knicks. He signed on and played center for what turned out to be the NBA's worst team that year. Two injuries ended his basketball season prematurely, a broken index finger on his pitching hand and a severely sprained ankle.

Because of his early exit from basketball in 1963, Conley was able to participate in an entire spring training. The basketball injuries proved to be a major issue, as was the chronic shoulder injury. He was unable to pitch smoothly and without pain during the exhibition season. He struggled during the early going of the regular season but came back late in the year. He did not know it at the time but when he started and won against the Twins on September 21, 1963, it would be his last major-league appearance.

As was now usual, Conley picked up basketball, again with New York. He was of little use to the Knicks because of injuries and exhaustion. The team was going nowhere and let him leave early to attend spring training. Just after the 1964 baseball season got under way and before he made an appearance, the Red Sox released Conley on April 21. Gabe Paul of the Cleveland Indians signed him the next day for $1 and offered him a trial with the Indians' Burlington (North Carolina) team. Conley pitched in only two games there before becoming convinced that his shoulder would not come around and he could no longer be effective. He retired from baseball.

Gene and Katie made their home in Foxboro, Massachusetts, for 40 years. They established and operated together, for 35 years, the Foxboro Paper Company, which dealt in industrial packaging supplies. Gene had his last drink in 1966. Katie Conley related that a baseball fan told Gene that he was too good to be drinking and that he (the fan) did not like to see him that way. Gene later said, "That was it. I haven't had a drink since." Also in 1966 Conley was asked to try professional basketball again and played and coached in the Eastern League for Hartford and New Haven on weekends for two years.

After his professional sports career, Conley continued to be active with skiing and golf. He never had his rotator cuff repaired. The Conleys were instrumental in gaining pensions for the NBA's pre-1965 players. Conley credited Katie as the catalyst for forming the NBA Old Timers Association, which lobbied their commissioner, David Stern, to provide pensions for players who retired before 1965. Their initiative proved successful in 1988 when the NBA and the Players Association agreed to extend benefits to early players. In 1989 Gene helped Katie through a life-threatening surgery to remove a brain tumor. Together they reared three children who gave them seven grandchildren.

Sources

Conley, Kathryn R., *One of a Kind* (Altamonte, Florida: Advantage Books, 2004).

Crehan, Herbert F., *Red Sox Heroes of Yesteryear* (Cambridge, Massachusetts: Rounder Books, 2005).

Hilton, Michael, "Doubling His Pleasure," *Sports Illustrated*, April 2, 1979.

Paschke, Jim, "Two-Sporters." *Bucks Beat*, April 12, 2002. http://www.nba.com/bucks/news/paschke_020411.html.

Riley, Jim, "Richland's Conley Set Standard Yet Unequalled For 2-Sport Athlete," *Tri-City Herald*, Kennewick, Washington, December 30, 1999.

Greensboro (North Carolina) *Daily News*, August 19, 1949.

Seattle Daily Times, July 26, 1949.

Witter, Greg. "Cougar Baseballers Wake the Echoes of a Legend." Posted at washingtonstate.scout.com/2/867723.html.

apbr.org/pension.html. Congressional Hearings on "Pension Fairness for NBA Pioneers," July 15, 1998.

Husman, John, interviews with Gene Conley by telephone on May 17, 1988; June 4, 2002; January 3, 2010; and February 26, 2013; in Orlando, Florida, on February 14, 2005.

nba.com/bucks/news/paschke_020411.html+Gene+Conley&hl=en.

richlandbombers.1948.tripod.com/Conley/1999-12-30TCHtop100.htm.

baseball-reference.com

basketball-reference.com

nba.com

retrosheet.com

wikipedia.org

Notes

1. Kathryn R. Conley, One of a Kind (Altamonte, Florida: Advantage Books, 2004), 105.
2. One of a Kind, 155.
3. Telephone interview with Gene Conley by author, May 17, 1988.
4. One of a Kind, 321.

Wes Covington

By Andy Sturgill

In the summer of 1952 the Eau Claire (Wisconsin) Bears, the Boston Braves' affiliate in the Class C Northern League, featured two young African-American outfielders who would go on to have long careers in the major leagues. One was Hank Aaron; the other was Wes Covington. Aaron went on to become one of baseball's all-time greats and a member of the Hall of Fame. As a young player, Covington was thought to be in Aaron's class. His skill and potential were so boundless that Aaron, in reference to the Eau Claire team, wrote in his autobiography, "At that point, if people had known that one of our players would someday be the all-time major league home run leader, everybody would have assumed that Covington would be the guy."[1] It was not to be. Covington's injuries and outspokenness combined to keep his potential from ever being fully unlocked. *The Phillies Encyclopedia* put Covington's career succinctly, stating, "Wes Covington lasted 11 years in the major leagues because of a bat that made a lot of noise and in spite of a mouth that did likewise.... (He) specialized in long home runs and long interviews that tended to get people around him a bit testy."[2]

John Wesley Covington was born on March 27, 1932, in Laurinburg, North Carolina, a town 100 miles southeast of Charlotte, near the South Carolina border. He grew up in Laurinburg and was a standout athlete in three sports during his high-school days. Baseball was not one of them, however, as the 6-foot-1, 205-pound Covington excelled in football, basketball, and track. After beginning at Laurinburg High, Covington transferred to Hillside High School in Durham, 100 miles away, primarily because of its athletics program. On the gridiron for Hillside, Wes starred as a running back in the same backfield as future Los Angeles Rams back Tom Wilson, and also excelled as the team's kicker.[3] He was named to the all-state team twice as a fullback, and was clocked at 9.9 seconds in the 100 meters.[4] A "B" student, Covington had offers to play college football at North Carolina State, UCLA, and several small colleges.[5]

In the spring of 1950 Covington gained his first baseball experience on local semipro teams. In 1951, with the North Carolina team in need of an outfielder for the annual North Carolina-South Carolina High School Baseball All-Star Game, Covington was asked to play in the game despite the fact that he had never played high-school baseball. Starting in left field for the North Carolina squad, Covington impressed Boston Braves scout Dewey Griggs enough to be offered a contract. After some convincing, he decided to forgo any possible football future and give professional baseball a try. "You know how it is," he recalled a few years later. "I needed a few dollars, they had a few dollars. Good deal. Besides, my wife, then my sweetheart, asked me to play baseball instead."[6]

The Braves sent Covington to Eau Claire in 1952 for his first taste of professional baseball. There he hit .330 with 24 home runs, including four grand slams. Covington spent the season rooming with Aaron and catcher Julie Bowers at the local YMCA. The trio of young blacks were refused rooms at a hotel in Aberdeen,

Wes Covington (National Baseball Hall of Fame Library, Cooperstown, N.Y.)

South Dakota; and a promotion at an Eau Claire restaurant offering a free steak to any member of the local nine who hit a home run was abruptly canceled when it was learned that Eau Claire's three biggest home run hitters—Aaron, Covington, and Bowers, were black.[7]

During the season Covington was hit in the head by a pitch and spent two weeks in Eau Claire's Luther Hospital. He recounted his experience in Hank Aaron's *I Had A Hammer*:

"I was the first black person who ever went into the hospital there. I felt like a sideshow freak. They assigned different nurses to me every day so they could all get the experience of being in my presence. Actually, I was treated very nicely. The nurses would open my mail and water the flowers for me. All but this one. One nurse, a lady who must've been sixty or seventy years old, had the job of putting water in my pitcher every day. This pitcher was on a tray by the door, and I'd look up and see this arm coming around the door and picking up the pitcher. Then the arm would come around and put the pitcher back. I never saw anything more than the arm. Then one day I was out of bed when she came, and I looked at her. She just froze. I said something, and she just stared at me. She poured the water very nervously, then left. I asked somebody about it later, and they said she had never seen a black person before and didn't know what to expect. Well, one day I was close enough to the door and handed her the pitcher. Then she started to acknowledge me, like bowing her head real fast. Finally, she said something. After that we had a conversation, and by the time I left the hospital, she was sitting at the side of the bed talking to me like an old friend."[8]

In 1953 Covington played in 42 games for Evansville Indiana of the Class B Three-I League before being drafted into the Army. He played for the teams at Fort Knox, Kentucky, and Fort Lee, Virginia, in 1954. With his service commitment completed, Covington was assigned to Jacksonville in the Class A South Atlantic League in 1955. (Hank Aaron had done the same thing in 1953.) Some hailed Covington as "the next Hank Aaron," but he professed to take this hype in stride. "You can't afford to take press clippings seriously," he said. "You have to make the club on the field, not in the newspapers, and you have to do it on your own. I'm not going to try to be another Aaron or another anybody else."[9]

Playing in the Puerto Rican Winter League between the 1955 and 1956 seasons, Covington hit .319 with 12 home runs, led the league in RBIs, and tied Vic Power of the Kansas City Athletics for the lead in hits. Then it was up to the major leagues. Covington made his debut in the Milwaukee Braves' second game of 1956. Pinch-hitting in a tie game against the Chicago Cubs, he singled home Bill Bruton with what proved to be the winning run for the Braves. The next day in St. Louis, Covington was again summoned to pinch-hit. With the Braves trailing by a run and Bruton on second, he homered to put the Braves ahead. After only two games in the major leagues, Covington had twice come up with big hits to help his team win. For the season he hit .283 with two home runs and 16 RBIs. He also began to draw notice for wasting time at the plate, and for his unorthodox batting stance. Regarding his behavior at the plate, *Baseball Digest* opined, "In the time it takes for Covington's ritual of hand dusting, cap adjusting, spike cleaning and deep scowling, the Senate could hold a dozen filibusters."[10] A couple of months later, the magazine described his batting stance as "leaning backward as if in a monsoon, the bat held out straight like a housewife waiting with a mop for hubby to stick his head in the door at 4 a.m."[11]

The next two seasons were banner years for Covington and the Braves. Given a chance to win the everyday left-field job in 1957, he faltered in spring training and found himself back in the minors at Triple-A Wichita when the job was given to veteran Bobby Thomson in May. Covington complained loudly that he got the runaround from the organization when he tried to find out why he was not sticking with the big club. Then in June, when the Braves sought to acquire Red Schoendienst from the New York Giants to play second base, general manager John Quinn almost had to send Covington to the Giants to complete the deal. But Quinn gave up Thomson instead, and with no other options in the organization, the Braves were forced to play Covington every day.

Covington responded by hitting .287 with 21 home runs in 90 games after his return from exile. The Braves went 60-30 in the 90 games on the way to their first pennant since 1948. In the World Series, which the Braves won in seven games over the Yankees, Covington played every inning. He hit only .208 with one RBI, but made two crucial defensive plays though he was not normally known as a stellar fielder (he had more errors than assists during his career and once said; "They don't pay outfielders for what they do with the glove.")[12]

In the second inning of Game Two, with Lew Burdette pitching for the Braves and two men on base, Yankees pitcher Bobby Shantz hit a liner down the left-field line that appeared to be an extra-base hit. But Covington chased the ball down, making a backhand catch on the dead run and saved two runs.[13] He added a go-ahead RBI in the fourth inning as the Braves won the game, 4-2. Covington's catch made him so popular in town that he had to temporarily move out of his house because the phone was ringing off the hook. "I couldn't get any sleep at home," Covington said. "The phone kept ringing. Why, I bet I've got a hundred telegrams so far."[14]

Covington again rescued Burdette from trouble in Game Five when he leaped above the wall in left to steal a home run from Gil McDougald. The Braves won the game, 1-0, and eventually won the Series in seven games.[15]

Covington faced his first major battle with injury in 1958. At the end of an April 8 exhibition game in Austin, Texas during the final week of spring training he suffered a knee injury while sliding into the plate with the winning run and was sidelined until May 2. He appeared in only 90 games during the season, but was productive when he did play, hitting .330 with 24 home runs and 74 RBIs as the Braves won the pennant again. Wes started all seven games of the World Series though this time they lost to the Yankees in seven games.

In 1957 and 1958 Covington finish third on the Braves in home runs and RBIs behind Hank Aaron and Eddie Mathews but he played barely more than half the number of games the two future Hall of Famers played in. In fact, in those two seasons Covington hit a home run every 13.8 at-bats, while Aaron, who won the NL home run crown in 1957, hit one out every 16.4 at-bats.[16]

For Covington, those two seasons were the high-water mark of his major-league career, which had eight more years to go. In 1957 and 1958 he hit more than one-third of his 128 career home runs. In 1959, though he had the most at-bats he of his career, his production declined sharply; his batting average dropped to .279 and his home run total fell to seven, from 24 in 1958. His season ended on August 20 when he tore an ankle ligament. Though manager Charlie Dressen consider him "the key to the Braves pennant hopes,"[17] 1960 was even worse; Covington reported to spring training "grossly out of shape"[18] and still hobbled by the ankle injury. He didn't start a game until May 4, and was benched as an everyday player in July. He struggled his way through a .249 season.

Covington's career continued to slide. He held out before the 1961 season, and some sportswriters questioned whether he had stopped applying himself and was now more interested in tending to the cocktail bar and the rooming houses he had purchased.[19] During his holdout, Covington threatened not to sign "unless certain things were written into (his) contract." Braves general manager John McHale sneered, ".200 hitters don't give ultimatums."[20] Clearly having overestimated his value, Covington ended his holdout on March 8. He started only five games during the first month of the season. The final confirmation of his over-inflating of his value came when he was sold to the Chicago White Sox for the $20,000 waiver price on May 10. Then, after four home runs and 15 RBIs in 22 games for the White Sox, Covington was moved again, this time to the Kansas City Athletics as part of a eight-player deal. Barely three weeks after that, Covington was traded to the Philadelphia Phillies for outfielder Bobby Del Greco, his final stop for the '61 season and his fourth team in less than ten weeks. The Phillies had been the last team in the National League to integrate (employing its first black player, John Kennedy, only as recently as 1957), and Covington was the first African-American to realize a significant role with the team.[21]

Covington found a more permanent home in Philadelphia, and ended up playing more games for them than for any other team. Still, his career with the Phillies was just as volatile as his time with the Braves. He often found himself at odds with manager Gene Mauch. The main source of discord seemed to be Covington's unhappiness with Mauch's platoon system, in which the left-handed hitting Covington rarely played against left-handed pitching. The statistics, however, bear out Mauch's position; Covington hit only .205 against left-handed pitchers from 1962 through 1965. Also, his defense had been made even more suspect by the injuries to his legs, and he was routinely removed in late innings for defensive purposes.

Despite his limitations, Covington was a productive player during his 4 1/2 seasons with the Phillies. He appeared in more than 100 games each of his four full years with the team, the only time during his career when he was healthy enough to do so. His average season was .281 with 14 home runs and 53 RBIs, and in 1963 he hit .303 with 17 home runs and 64 RBIs. Being used in a platoon also gave Covington numerous opportunities to pinch-hit, and he excelled in the role, notching 33 pinch hits as a Phillie. But the defining moment of Covington's stay in Philadelphia was the collapse of 1964.

For the first 5 1/2 months of the 1964 season, everything went the Phillies' way. Sitting atop the National League standings by 6 1/2 games with only 12 left to play, they seemed like a lock to reach their first World Series since 1950. When World Series tickets went on sale, many of the players, with the team in Houston, went shopping with their anticipated bonus money. Covington bought a rifle and brandished it in the clubhouse, saying "This is for the sportswriters."[22] However, as all baseball historians and Philadelphians know, that bonus money never came, as the Phillies went on a ten-game losing streak that turned their huge pennant lead into a second-place tie.

After the stunning end to the 1964 season, Covington spent the offseason pointing the finger for the collapse in every direction except his own, and then showed up for 1965 spring training 15 days late.[23] The *Philadelphia Daily News* wrote, "(Covington) kept hollering and kept popping up. ... Nobody wants to listen to a mean, tough grumbler when that grumbler is hitting .220.

The Phillies lost the pennant, and Covington went around town all winter telling people whose fault it was, and never even mentioned Wes Covington's name."[24] (Covington was being platooned during the disastrous ten-game losing streak and had hit .150 with no home runs, RBIs, or runs scored.)

Covington lasted one more contentious season with the Phillies. At the end of the 1965 season he asked to be released. In early January 1966 he was traded to the Chicago Cubs for Doug Clemens, and Cubs manager Leo Durocher announced his intention to play Covington every day, even against left-handed pitching.[25] Despite Durocher's pronouncements, Covington's Cubs career lasted only nine games before he was released in early May. Shown interest from contenders in both leagues, he signed with the Los Angeles Dodgers, thinking this was his best chance to win. Covington was largely used as a pinch-hitter for the Dodgers, and finally proved to be the veteran leader who was sorely missed during his time in Philadelphia. He was such a vocal supporter from the dugout that at one point Dodgers manager Walter Alston had to explain to an umpire that Covington was only trying to provide his teammates a "loud lift." But his support wasn't just intangible, as he reached base 10 times in 16 pinch-hit appearances during one stretch late in the season.[26] The Dodgers won the pennant but were swept by the Baltimore Orioles in the World Series. Covington made one appearance, striking out as a pinch hitter in Game One. It was his last appearance in the major leagues.

The man who once had said his hobbies were "hitting homers and making money" had handled his money well as a player, and had numerous business operations outside of baseball as he transitioned into post-baseball life. He owned a barbecue restaurant in Philadelphia, held real estate in Pennsylvania, Wisconsin, and Florida, and had a business, Diamond Janitorial Services, that grew into one of Philadelphia's largest janitorial service companies.[27] However, at some point in the late 1970s, tax issues had forced Covington and his wife to Canada.[28] They settled in Edmonton, Alberta, where he operated a sporting-goods store and then spent nearly 20 years working in advertising for the *Edmonton*

Sun.²⁹ Covington also became involved with the Triple-A Edmonton Trappers. In 2003 he returned to Milwaukee for the first time in 40 years at the invitation of the Braves Historical Society, and in 2007 he was one of 14 members of the 1957 champs to gather in Milwaukee to celebrate the 50th anniversary of the Braves' world championship.³⁰ Covington died of cancer on July 4, 2011, in Edmonton.

Sources

Hank Aaron, with Lonnie Wheeler, *I Had a Hammer: The Hank Aaron Story* (New York: HarperCollins, 1991).

Bob Buege, *Milwaukee Braves: A Baseball Eulogy* (Milwaukee: Douglas American Sports Publications, 1988).

Gary Caruso, *The Braves Encyclopedia* (Philadelphia: Temple University Press, 1995).

William Kashatus, *September Swoon* (University Park, Pennsylvania: Pennsylvania Stat University Press, 2005).

Larry Moffi and Jonathan Kronstadt, *Crossing the Line: Black Major Leaguers, 1947-1959*. (Lincoln: Bison Books, University of Nebraska Press, 2006).

Jerry Poling, *A Summer Up North* (Madison: Wisconsin Historical Society Press, 2002).

William Povletich, *Milwaukee Braves: Heroes and Heartbreak* (Madison: Wisconsin Historical Society Press, 2009).

Rich Westcott and Frank Bilovsky, *The Phillies Encyclopedia, 3rd Edition* (Philadelphia: Temple University Press, 2003).

The author also consulted Wes Covington's player file from the National Baseball Hall of Fame and Museum, Baseball-Reference.com, and various issues of *Baseball Digest*, the *Milwaukee Journal*, the *Philadelphia Daily News, Sport, Sports Illustrated,* and *The Sporting News*.

Special thanks to my wife, Carrie, a librarian, for tracking down a seemingly endless list of obscure books I requested as I attempted to learn about Wes Covington's life and career.

Notes

1. Hank Aaron, with Lonnie Wheeler, *I Had a Hammer: The Hank Aaron Story* (New York: HarperCollins, 1991).
2. Rich Westcott and Frank Bilovsky, *The Phillies Encyclopedia, 3rd Edition.*
3. Wes Covington player file, National Baseball Hall of Fame and Museum.
4. Larry Moffi and Jonathan Kronstadt, *Crossing the Line: Black Major Leaguers, 1947-1959.*
5. *Milwaukee Journal,* September 8, 1957.
6. Wes Covington player file.
7. Jerry Poling, *A Summer Up North.*
8. Aaron, op. cit.
9. Moffi and Kronstadt, op. cit.
10. *Baseball Digest,* June 1963.
11. *Baseball Digest,* August 1963.
12. Moffi and Kronstadt, op. cit.
13. Bob Buege, *Milwaukee Braves: A Baseball Eulogy.*
14. Wes Covington player file, National Baseball Hall of Fame and Museum.
15. Moffi and Kronstadt, op. cit.
16. Gary Caruso, *The Braves Encyclopedia.*
17. *The Sporting News,* August 31, 1960.
18. Bob Buege, op. cit.
19. *Milwaukee Journal,* May 12, 1961.
20. *The Sporting News,* February 1, 1961.
21. William Kashatus, *September Swoon.*
22. Ibid.
23. Wes Covington player file.
24. *Philadelphia Daily News,* March 29, 1965.
25. Wes Covington player file.
26. *The Sporting News,* October 1, 1966.
27. *Sports Illustrated,* July 22, 1968.
28. Wes Covington player file.
29. Baseballsavvy.com article accessed at: http://www.baseballsavvy.com/archive/w_wesCovington.html
30. William Povletich, *Milwaukee Braves: Heroes and Heartbreak.*

Del Crandall

By Gregory H. Wolf

Less than four months after his 19th birthday, Del Crandall became the youngest starting catcher in baseball history when he supplanted 32-year-old Bill Salkeld of the Boston Braves in 1949. Returning to the Milwaukee Braves in 1953 after a two-year tour in the military, Crandall was named to eight All-Star teams during the Braves' first ten seasons in Milwaukee (1953-1962) and established his reputation as arguably the best defensive catcher of the era, annually ranking among the league leaders in practically every important defensive statistic. "[Crandall] is like a coach on the field. He can spot a flaw in my motion as soon as it shows up," said teammate Carl Willey.[1] Pittsburgh Pirates general manager Joe L. Brown, quick to point out Crandall's underrated offensive abilities, maintained that "Crandall is the best all-around catcher in the league."[2]

A career in baseball was far from foretold when Delmar Wesley Crandall was born on March 5, 1930, in Ontario, California, the second of three children of Richard and Nancy Crandall. Del and his sisters, Barbara and Betty, grew up with modest means during the Depression in Fullerton, about 25 miles east of Los Angeles in the fertile croplands of Orange County where both of his parents worked in the citrus-packaging industry. In the year-round warm climate, Del was drawn to the local sandlots in Fullerton and began shagging fly balls as a 9-year-old. "I became a catcher," Crandall told the author, "when I was in fifth grade. I was a pudgy little kid and not a very good athlete, but I was enthusiastic. Art Johnson, a coach, came to my elementary school, Maple School. He looked at me with a mask and a catcher's glove and I told him I can catch. That was the first challenge in my young life."[3] Around the same time Del also met Pep Lemon, a former minor-league catcher who ran the local recreation department and managed the semipro Fullerton Merchants. "Everything I learned was from Pep Lemon," he recalled. "He was the most influential man in my baseball career."

A big growth spurt transformed Crandall from a scrawny, 5-foot-tall freshman to a slender, 6-feet-1 high-school senior. Years earlier, Lemon had taken Crandall under his wing and taught him the art of catching and how to throw and release the ball. "At the age of 16, [Pep] let me catch Hal Gregg who was [then] a pitcher for the Brooklyn Dodgers," recalled Crandall of his opportunities to practice with current and former Merchants players and occasionally big leaguers. "That was a boost for my confidence."

A standout catcher at Fullerton High School and in the local American Legion league, Crandall began attracting interest from major-league scouts by the time he was 16 years old. According to Crandall, his father was extremely supportive and invested in his career even though he did not play baseball because of poor eyesight. His father did not want him to sign with the Dodgers, Yankees, or Cardinals because they had

Del Crandall (National Baseball Hall of Fame Library, Cooperstown, N.Y.)

too many prospects in their farm system. Dodgers scout Tom Downey pursued Crandall relentlessly, but Del rejected their $20,000 signing bonus (about 20 times the family's income in 1946) because of the "bonus baby" stipulation requiring him to remain on the big-league roster for two years and lose invaluable minor-league experience. Instead Boston Braves scout Johnny Moore signed Crandall to a two-year contract with the team's Triple-A affiliate, the Milwaukee Brewers, for a $4,000 salary. "That was more money that my parents or I had ever seen," said Crandall.

The still 17-year-old Crandall reported to Austin, Texas, for spring training with the Brewers in 1948, but struggled at the plate and was sent to join the Class C Leavenworth (Kansas) Braves at their camp in Whitesville, North Carolina. A poor hitter in high school, Crandall was batting under .200 when Leavenworth manager Harold "Dutch" Hoffman suggested that he cut down on his swing. "Dutch told me that I have to hit pepper every day, so I did with Joe Nezgoda," Crandall said. "After three or four weeks, I started to hit. I was able to do the same things in a game that I did in pepper." He developed a home-run stroke (his 15 round-trippers were fifth best in the Western Association that year), batted .304, and got an unexpected promotion at the end of the season. "Both catchers with the [Triple-A] Milwaukee Brewers broke their little fingers," said Crandall. "I got called up at the end of the season and then caught all seven games in the American Association playoffs. It was fate and got me exposure."

One of the last players cut during spring training with the Brewers in 1949, Crandall was assigned to the Evansville (Indiana) Braves in the Class B Three-I League, where he fell under the tutelage of manager Bob Coleman, a former big-league catcher who had piloted the parent club a few years earlier. "It was a break to work under him," said Crandall. "He was a defensive-minded coach who encouraged me to throw and pick runners off." Boston manager Billy Southworth and general manager John Quinn personally scouted the young phenom, who batted .351 in 38 games at Evansville. "It was a surprise when told me they were calling me up," Crandall said. "I had just turned 19 years old. [Braves owner] Lou Perini sent a private plane to get me. When I called my parents, I told my mother that I am going to Boston. And she asked 'What for?'"

The reigning National League-champion Braves made room for Crandall by trading backup catcher Phil Masi to the Pittsburgh Pirates. After making his debut as a pinch runner for catcher Bill Salkeld on June 17, Crandall started the next day at Crosley Field in Cincinnati and went hitless in three at-bats. With eight hits in his next 15 at-bats and six runs batted in, Crandall cemented his place as the Braves backstop and started about two-thirds of the games the rest of the season. Named to *The Sporting News*' Rookie All-Star Team, Crandall finished with a .263 batting average and 34 runs batted in (in 228 at-bats) and was runner-up to Brooklyn Dodgers' pitcher Don Newcombe for the Rookie of the Year Award.[4]

With his red hair kept short in the crew-cut style of the era, his fair skin, and his blue eyes, Crandall may have appeared like an all-American boy, but he had a brash, confident personality and was unfazed as a teenager playing in the big leagues. "I was cocky to a degree," he said. He recalled an episode in his rookie year when the Braves flew his parents to Boston to see him play. It was August 27, 1949, and Crandall was the starting catcher after enjoying a three-hit game the previous evening. With one out in the top of the first inning and Johnny Sain pitching to the Reds' Peanuts Lowrey, Crandall took issue with the arbiter just behind him. "Jocko Conlan was the umpire," said the big redhead. "After two pitches right down the center of the plate, I said 'Jocko, I think those two pitches were strikes.' And [Conlan] got furious. He jerked his mask off and came around in front of me. He said, 'No busher is going to come up here and tell me how to umpire.' My response was, 'You can stick that busher up your ass.'"[5] Not surprisingly, that remark earned Crandall his first major-league ejection as a player.

Unlike the short (5-feet-9 or 10) and stocky catchers of the time, Crandall was tall and muscular, weighed about 190 pounds, and blessed with athleticism. Southworth hailed him as the "greatest prospect ever."[6] Ushering in a new style of aggressive play behind the plate, Crandall was known for his bullet arm, catlike, quick movements behind the plate, and his unusual flexibility. However, he drew criticism from some veterans who took offense at how he ran all over the park and threw to all three bases to keep runners on. "When I got to the big leagues, picking off guys was not done that much," said Crandall. "Fielders were just not used to a catcher throwing to pick off a runner. Certainly the manager did not encourage the first or third baseman to cover the bag."

Expecting a breakout season in 1950, Crandall played in only 79 big-league games over the next three years. In his sophomore season, he was sidelined by a broken finger, then returned as a backup after the Braves had acquired the league's best-hitting backstop, Walker Cooper. Crandall's hitting suffered and he finished with a disappointing .220 batting average in 255 at-bats. His career was interrupted for the next two years when he was drafted into the Army during spring training in March 1951. Stationed in Fort Ord, California, Crandall served in the infantry and saw active duty in Japan.

A day before he was inducted into the service, Crandall eloped to Las Vegas with his high-school sweetheart from Fullerton, Frances Sorrells, and got married.[7] They had six children (Del Jr., Ron, Billy, Jeff, Tim, and Nancy) and lived in Fullerton in the offseason, where Del joined his mentor, Pep Lemon, in the park district. In 1959 the Crandalls moved to Brookfield, Wisconsin, just west of Milwaukee.

Rumors about the Braves' future trumped the excitement of Crandall's return to the club's spring training in Bradenton in 1953. "There were so many rumors swirling," he recalled, "and how a move to Milwaukee would also cause scheduling conflicts. No one knew the impact of the move. We didn't know what to expect." Less than a month from Opening Day, National League owners by a unanimous vote allowed owner Lou Perini to move the team to Milwaukee. "We were all surprised by the announcement the Braves were moving," said Crandall. "Teams just didn't move in those days." (It was the first franchise shift in major-league baseball since 1903.)

Crandall returned to a dramatically different team than the one he had left in 1950. Quinn had assembled from the team's farm system a core of youngsters (Billy Bruton, Johnny Logan, and Eddie Mathews, pitchers Lew Burdette and Bob Buhl) for the 1953 season; they were followed by Hank Aaron and pitcher Gene Conley in 1954. Along with the ageless Warren Spahn, these home-grown players created the nucleus for the club's unparalleled success throughout the decade.

Braves manager Charlie "Jolly Cholly" Grimm compared Crandall to his former Cubs teammate, Hall of Fame catcher Gabby Hartnett: "[Crandall] has everything in his favor—perfect poise, sound judgment, and aggressiveness."[8] Known for his patience with youngsters, Grimm gave Crandall time to round into playing shape. He had caught about 40 games each summer for the Fort Ord base team, but suffered from a sore arm during much of spring training.[9] Ready for the traditional Opening Day game in Cincinnati, Crandall caught Max Surkont's three-hitter, stroked a leadoff double and scored in the fifth inning in the club's 2-0 victory. Off to a fast start, Crandall was hitting .301 on June 29 and was named to the first of his eight All-Star teams with the game to be in Cincinnati on July 14. But on July 8 he was nicked on the right hand by a foul tip and missed two weeks. Though he struggled in the second half (.243 batting average), he finished with 15 home runs, 51 runs batted in, and a .272 batting average for the second-place Braves.

The Braves drew 1,826,397 in their first season in Milwaukee, setting set a new National League attendance record that they broke the following year when they became the first NL team to top the 2 million mark. "It was unbelievable to play in Milwaukee," said Crandall. "We drew a lot of fans from Iowa, Minnesota, Wisconsin, and of course Milwaukee. The fans were tremendous." The Braves led the NL in attendance in the first six seasons (1953-1958) in Milwaukee, proving that baseball could thrive in the Upper Midwest; their success paved the way for an unprecedented shift in franchises during the decade. "I do not believe that the Milwaukee Braves experience will ever be duplicated," Crandall said of the city's love for the Braves, especially in the 1950s.

Over the course of the decade, Crandall established a reputation as one of the best defensive catchers of his generation, indeed big-league history. "Pep Lemon had instilled in me the value of defense," Crandall said of his catching philosophy. "I always looked at myself as a defensive catcher first. I think it was the enthusiasm I had playing the game. I didn't get tired and tried to be alert to anything that happened on the field. Hitting did not detract from my catching." In light of various traditional and advanced metrics, Crandall's list of accomplishments is Hall of Fame-worthy. Durable despite broken fingers and annual injuries, Crandall led the NL in games caught five times, in fielding percentage four times, and in putouts three times. Distinguishing himself with his rifle arm, he paced the league in assists six times, in runners caught stealing five times, and in double plays twice.[10] "Good catching demands desire," said Walker Cooper about Crandall's reputation. "That's one reason what Del Crandall is so well regarded by baseball people."[11]

Named team captain as a 24-year-old in 1954, Crandall was a quiet team leader, field general, and capable hitter. Typically batting eighth for most of his career, Crandall annually belted between 15 and 26 home runs, knocked in between 46 and 77 runs, and hit at about a .260 clip between 1953 and 1960. Only Roy Campanella and Yogi Berra exceeded Crandall's offensive output among catchers. As an All-Star in 1954 and 1955, Crandall hit 21 and a career-high 26 home runs respectively (though his batting average dropped to .242 and .236) while the Braves finished in third place and second place to their archrival Dodgers. Crandall's most memorable moment at the plate occurred in 1955 in the first game of a September 11 doubleheader against the Philadelphia Phillies with Herm Wehmeier on the mound. "We had two outs in the ninth inning and the score was 4-1 with the bases loaded," said Crandall. "I fouled off a few pitches and then with a 3-and-2 count I hit a grand slam to win the game." It was one of his four career grand slams and five walk-off home runs.

Crandall became a master at recognizing hitters' weakness and understanding his pitchers' tendencies. His expertise in game-calling played no small role in the success of the Braves in the mid- to late 1950s and for baseball's best righty-lefty duo, Warren Spahn and Lew Burdette. (The third member of the "Big Three," Bob Buhl, preferred Del Rice as his personal catcher.)

"I think he knows more about what I can do in a game situation than I do," Spahn told *The Sporting News*.[12] Asked he handled Spahn and Burdette when they were on the mound, Crandall replied modestly, "Spahn had such great control and was so good—great delivery, deception, and concentration—he'd just hit your glove. He developed a screwball when he couldn't throw as hard anymore." But Crandall was more forthcoming with the fidgety, nervous, and temperamental righty Burdette. "I think I made a contribution with Burdette. I think he relied on me to do things. Sometimes he'd go into his windup before I even gave him a sign. He'd say, 'I knew what you'd call.' We had a close relationship. He trusted me."

The Braves appeared poised in 1956 to take their first pennant since their move to Milwaukee, but got off to a slow start, resulting in Grimm's being fired after 46 games. New manager Fred Haney instituted a more strategic and disciplined approach than the laid-back, players' manager Jolly Cholly. The Braves responded to the manager change, won 11 consecutive games, and enjoyed a 3 1/2-game lead after Labor Day. Despite suffering an injury to his elbow in a collision with the Pirates' Dick Cole on June 19, Crandall seemed to have solved his hitting woes and began September batting .261 and slugging a career-best .481. While the Dodgers won 18 of 28 games in September, the Braves struggled under pressure and won just 14 of 27. Crandall slumped, too, hitting just .157 for the month. In the heat of the pennant race, Haney sent Buhl, Burdette, and Spahn to the mound in 15 of the last 17 games, but lost the pennant by a single game on the season's last weekend. "I view the last weeks of the 1956 season as a sign that we were not ready to win the pennant," Crandall told the author reflectively about the team's collapse. "We had changed managers and Haney had our ballclub doing things that were foreign to us, like Adcock or Mathews bunting. It was a confusing time for us. The veterans in Brooklyn knew how to win."

"I don't have any recollection that we prepared for the 1957 season any differently," Crandall replied when asked how the Braves reacted to their collapse the previous September. However, he noted a change in his skipper. "Haney settled in to manage our ballclub the way it should be. Let the big hitters hit." Lauded by Birdie Tebbetts as "the one man the Braves must have all the way if they hope to win the pennant," the pull-hitting Crandall had been criticized in the offseason for his low batting average (.238) and was the subject of serious trade rumors involving first baseman Frank Thomas of the Pittsburgh Pirates.[13] The "hardest worker in camp," Crandall shortened his powerful swing because of lingering pain from his collision with Cole the previous year and attempted to become more of a spray hitter in 1957.[14] The result was a slight improvement in batting average (.253), but was accompanied by a loss in power as Crandall's slugging percentage dropped 40 points.

A ten-game winning streak from August 4 through 15 catapulted the Braves to the team's first pennant in Milwaukee behind the league's most potent offense (a league-high 199 home runs and 772 runs scored) and arguably its best pitching staff. Crandall said the team's personality reflected their former manager. "The way we played in 1957 goes back to Charlie Grimm and the fact that he let us play. Grimm was not a big one on strategy. Fortunately, we had Mathews, Logan, Adcock, Bruton, and Aaron. We were hard-nosed and that showed up in 1957. We became a ballclub capable of winning the World Series."

According to Crandall, the Braves didn't have a loud, vocal leader; rather, the team came together and each player recognized his role. Nonetheless, opponents acknowledged Crandall as a leader for his inspirational play, knowledge of the game, and manager-like presence on the field. He was undaunted facing the heavily favored New York Yankees in the World Series. "All the players read the papers and knew what was written in New York," he said of the disparaging comments. "We knew we had a good ballclub and had confidence. We weren't intimidated at all."

Notwithstanding his confidence, Crandall recalled how he felt overwhelmed by the historical majesty of baseball's most celebrated park, Yankee Stadium, at the beginning of Game One. "I was intimidated by Yankee Stadium," he said honestly. "I remember warming up Warren Spahn for the first game and my knees were shaking. Spahnie threw a screwball in the dirt and I threw the ball back to second. Then my nervousness was gone." The starter in five of the seven games (Buhl and Rice were batterymates in Games Three and Six), Crandall steadied a nervous Burdette, pitching on two days' rest in the pressure-packed Game Seven. In the eighth inning Crandall connected for a towering home run to left field, giving the Braves a seemingly insurmountable 5-0 lead. "I realized the impact of my home run with bases loaded [with Yankees] in the bottom of the ninth," he said. En route to his third consecutive complete-game victory, Burdette had given up three singles in the inning, but got Moose Skowron to hit a hard two-out grounder to third base. Eddie Mathews backhanded it and stepped on third base to force out Jerry Coleman, giving the Braves an exciting — indeed, unexpected — championship. Crandall noted that the Braves won despite long odds and serious injuries to key players (Bruton, Adock, Buhl). "You talk about destiny, well, you can't rule that out," he said of the magical season.

Hailed as "one of the finest catchers in baseball and a big factor in the brilliant success of the World Champion Braves pitching staff," Crandall, in full catching gear, graced the April 21 cover of *Sports Illustrated* as the 1958 season opened.[15] Abandoning his experimentation with spray hitting, Crandall enjoyed perhaps his best season at the plate, hitting .272 with 18 home runs and 63 runs batted in, while established career highs with 23 doubles, a .457 slugging percentage, and an .805 OPS (slugging percentage plus on-base percentage). Crandall had a discerning eye at the plate and struck out only 477 times in 5,583 career plate appearances. The Braves pulled away from Pittsburgh and San Francisco by going 38-20 in the last two months of the season and cruised to their second consecutive pennant.

In a rematch with the Yankees in the World Series, Crandall started all seven games. His five hits in 14 at-bats helped stake the Braves to a three games to one lead. However, Yankees hurlers limited the Braves to just 20 hits and five runs in the next three games (Crandall went 1-for-11) en route to a come-from-behind World Series championship. "It took a while for us to get over our loss in 1958," said Crandall, admitting that he had fully expected the Braves to win.

"I thought we'd get back and win it in 1959," Crandall told the author. In early June it appeared as though the Braves were well on their way to their third pennant in a row, but they played sub-.500 ball in June, July, and August (42-44) to drop into third place by September. A hallmark of consistency, Crandall caught a career-high 146 games (142 starts), belted 21 home runs, and drove in 72 runs for the high-scoring offense, but the team had one glaring weakness. "I went to Haney because of second base," Crandall said. "Schoendienst was out [with tuberculosis] and we tried [Johnny] O'Brien, [Bobby] Avila, and [Felix] Mantilla. But they were not everyday players and couldn't cover the ground Schoendienst could. I told [Haney] we needed Chuck Cottier. For some reason Haney didn't want to bring him up. We wound up in a tie with the Dodgers, but it should not have been that way." By winning their last two games of the year, the Braves finished the season tied with the Los Angeles Dodgers to force the National League's third best-of-three playoff series. Then the Braves quickly lost two heartbreaking one-run games (the second was a 12-inning affair) and finished in second place. It was the last time they seriously contended for the pennant.

Often overlooked in discussions of the great teams of the 1950s, the Braves had a remarkable four-year run. Twice they lost the pennant during the last games of the season and twice they won in dominating fashion. "We would be looked at as a team a lot differently if we would have been able to pull [four consecutive pennants] off," Crandall said. "We were close. We weren't ready to win in 1956 and did not have the personnel in 1959."

During Crandall's last four years with Milwaukee (1960-1963), the Braves were an aging team in transition. After his final durable season behind the plate (141 games caught) and impressive hitting (a career-high 158 hits, as well as 19 home runs, 77 RBIs, and a .294 average) for the second-place Braves in 1960, Crandall missed almost all of 1961 with a sore arm. In his absence, 20-year-old Joe Torre established himself as the catcher of the future, but Crandall, just 31 years old, thought he had earned the right to come back and compete for the job.

Crandall's relationship with the Braves became strained when general manager John McHale suggested that he play in spring training without a contract because of his arm problems. Crandall was insulted. "I told [McHale], 'You know, I've been a big part of this ballclub for ten years and have represented the Braves on and off the field. I was important to you, and the Braves needed me. I was naïve to think that when I needed the Braves, you'd be there,'" Crandall told the author. "That leaves a sour taste in your mouth." Splitting time with Torre, Crandall rebounded to post a career-high .297 batting average and continued his customary excellent defensive play in 1962. He was named to his final All-Star team and won his fourth Gold Glove Award in five years.

An era came to an end when majority owner Lou Perini sold the Milwaukee Braves to a consortium of six Chicagoans in November 1962. Bobby Bragan, the team's fourth Opening Day manager in five years, installed Torre as the primary catcher; Crandall struggled, batting a career-low .201. "It became increasingly obvious that Bobby Bragan and I did not get along," he said. "We had big disagreements and it led to bad feelings. I told him [Bragan] that I think it time for him to trade me." In the offseason, Crandall was sent to the San Francisco Giants in a seven-player trade that brought outfielder Felipe Alou to the Braves. Crandall wasn't surprised by the trade. "You deal with each year. You take ten years of being important to a ballclub and suddenly in the next year you are not important. That changes your view of the club."

Like many aging veterans, Crandall spent his final years as a baseball nomad, serving as a backup catcher for the Giants (1964), Pittsburgh Pirates (1965), and finally the Cleveland Indians (1966). Serving as Sam McDowell's personal catcher in Cleveland, Crandall was praised for his patience in developing the young fireballer. Indians GM Gabe Paul wanted to sign Crandall to a Triple-A contact in 1967, but, Crandall recalled, "The things that were easiest—the defensive aspects of the game—were now difficult." After 16 years in the big leagues and 1,479 games caught (14th most in history at the time), Crandall announced his retirement. One of the most honored catchers in baseball history, he finished with 179 home runs, 657 runs batted in, a .254 batting average, and a secure reputation as one of the era's best signal-callers.

Crandall embarked on a successful career as manager in 1969. After leading the the Albuquerque Dodgers, a Los Angeles affiliate, to the Texas League championship in 1970, he was one of the most sought-after skippers in baseball.

Hired by the Brewers in 1971 to lead their Triple-A Evansville affiliate, Crandall made it back to the big leagues the following year when he took over the parent club in midseason and guided the Brewers through several lean, talent-poor years (1972-1975). Although the team finished no better than fifth under Crandall, the former backstop was considered an attentive instructor who stressed fundamentally sound baseball. He was largely credited with developing Darrell Porter into a hard-nosed, All-Star catcher in his own mold. Praised for leading essentially an expansion team to respectability by 1974 (76-86 in the tough AL East), Crandall was fired before the last game of the 1975 season amid speculation that Hank Aaron would become the new manager.[16] He finished with a 271-338 record with the Brewers.

Crandall spent the next two years in the Angels organization. He led the Salinas Angels to the league championship in the Class A California League in 1976 and was the first-base coach for the parent club in 1977. The following year Crandall returned to the Dodgers and guided their Albuquerque Dukes affiliate in the Pacific Coast League to four league championships in five years.

In 1983 the Seattle Mariners hired Crandall in midseason to lead a moribund team en route to its third season of over 100 losses during its seventh year as an expansion franchise. The following season he was replaced by former Braves teammate Chuck Cottier prior to Labor Day weekend with the team 17 games under .500. Crandall's résumé also includes work as a color commentator for the Chicago White Sox (1985-1988) and Milwaukee Brewers (1992-1994) Crandall retired from baseball in 1997 after his third minor-league managerial stint in the Dodgers organization. Asked why catchers are successful managers, he said, "Catchers have a better relationship with and exposure to what their manager is thinking. You have a close relationship with the pitching staff and have a chance to manage pitchers better."

As of 2013, Crandall resided with his wife in Brea, California, just a few minutes from Fullerton, where he grew up. Discussing the Braves' victory over the Yankees in 1957, he seemed as excited as he had been more than a half-century earlier. "There is never anything better than winning a World Series," he told the author. Then, in a contemplative moment, he revealed how profoundly his years in Milwaukee had affected him even in retirement. "The things you miss the most are all the friendships you made. You miss all the good times you've had winning baseball. You miss the people and the fans who watched us play. The fans at County Stadium were so enthusiastic."

Sources

Newspapers

Milwaukee Journal.

Milwaukee Sentinel.

The Sporting News.

Websites

Ancestry.com

BaseballLibrary.com

Baseball-Reference.com

Retrosheet.org

SABR.org

Other

Author's interview with Del Crandall on July 30, 2012.

Notes

1. *The Sporting News*, October 1, 1958, 56.
2. *The Sporting News*, December 10, 1958, 19.
3. The author expresses his gratitude to Del Crandall, who was interviewed on July 30, 2012. All quotations from Crandall are from this interview unless otherwise noted.
4. *The Sporting News*, January 16, 1949, 7.
5. The game took place on August 27, 1949.

6   *The Sporting News*, March 8, 1950, 5.

7   Jim Murray, "Murray's Pulling for Pirates," *Milwaukee Sentinel*, September 13, 1965, 12.

8   *The Sporting News*, April 29, 1953, 36.

9   *The Sporting News*, March 11, 1953, 9.

10 Six times Crandall led the league in Total Zone Total Fielding Runs Above Average, an advanced metric that measures the number of runs above or below average the player was worth based on the number of plays made. See Baseball-Reference.com.

11 *The Sporting News*, March 14, 1956, 7.

12 *The Sporting News*, April 6, 1955, 3.

13 *The Sporting News*, January 11, 1956, 11.

14 *The Sporting News*, April 17, 1957, 15.

15 Del Crandall and Len Woodcock, "Del Crandall on the Art of Catching," *Sports Illustrated*, April 21, 1958, sportsillustrated.cnn.com/vault/article/magazine/MAG1002130/index.htm.

16 "Brewers Fire Crandall," (AP), *Meriden* (Connecticut) *Morning Press*, September 29, 1975, 13.

Ray Crone

By Gregory H. Wolf

"Amazing," said Ray Crone when asked by the author to describe fan support in Milwaukee in the 1950s.[1] A tall, lanky right-handed pitching prodigy signed by the Braves in 1949, Crone debuted in 1954 and pitched a ten-inning complete game in his first start in the major leagues. However, after four inconsistent seasons and a 25-20 record with the Braves from 1954 to 1957, Crone was sent to the New York Giants at the trading deadline in 1957 in exchange for Red Schoendienst, thus missing the Braves' historic World Series championship.

On August 7, 1931, Raymond Hayes Crone was born to Gordon and Annie (Gunti) Crone in Memphis, Tennessee. The fifth of six children, Ray was introduced to baseball by his father, who worked for Goodyear and played in a Sunday-morning league for men over 35. In grade school he began to play shortstop and pitch on teams sponsored by the Kiwanis Club and other service organizations. "Halfway through my first year in high school in 1946," Crone said of his high-school freshman team, coached by Hall of Famer Bill Terry, "they promoted me to the varsity team." Over the next three years at Christian Brothers High School and in American Legion ball in the summer, Crone established his reputation as one of the best pitchers Memphis ever produced. Pitching for Lew Chandler, who coached both teams, he led his American Legion team, sponsored by Corbitt Motors, to three consecutive state championships. As a 15-year-old he pitched the title game of the American Legion regional in North Carolina. It ran 18 innings and Crone no-hit the opposition from the sixth through the 16th inning, but lost. "Lew would be put in prison nowadays for abusing kids," Crone joked.

"I never played other positions," said Crone, who threw five no-hitters as a prep phenom. "I pitched and batted ninth." Scouts from the Cardinals, Red Sox, Tigers, and Braves attended his games. "I signed with Bill Maughn of the Boston Braves one day after I graduated high school in 1949, because he was more positive about my career and chances." He was assigned to the Owensboro Oilers in the Class D Kentucky-Illinois-Tennessee (Kitty) League in 1949. Traveling and playing so many games in American Legion baseball prepared him for the physical demands of Organized Baseball and the emotional demands of being away from home for a 17-year-old, he said. "I was calm and remember no anxiety about facing anybody." The youngest player of the team, Crone won nine games, lost three, and posted a 2.93 ERA. He did not attribute his success to any specific coach.[2] "Back then baseball got all the best athletes," Crone said. "There were more than 50 minor leagues. The organization just threw the balls and bats out there and you played. I learned to play by watching semipro games in Memphis."

After Crone's successful seasons with the Evansville Braves in the Class B Illinois-Indiana-Iowa (Three-Eye) League in 1950 and with the Hartford Chiefs in the Class A Eastern League in 1951, where he won 11 and

Ray Crone (National Baseball Hall of Fame Library, Cooperstown, N.Y.)

12 games respectively, the 6-foot-2, 165-pound right-hander was assigned to the Double-A Atlanta Crackers. "In 1952 I went to spring training with Atlanta and Dixie Walker was the manager. We trained in Pensacola, Florida. I made the team and was the opening day pitcher," Crone said. "But I began to lose it. I was just throwing the ball." Having pitched just 19 innings and accumulated a 9.00 ERA, Crone was reassigned to Hartford, where he won 12 games again. Pleased with his development, the Braves signed him to a major-league contract at the conclusion of the season.

In 1953 the 21-year-old Crone was invited to his first spring training with the Braves in Bradenton, Florida. With 45 minor-league wins under his belt, Crone was confident in his abilities. "I thought I threw strikes and had good control when I got to spring training. But from watching guys like Vern Bickford, Warren Spahn, and Lew Burdette, I noticed that certain counts, 3-2 or 2-2, they didn't give in and hit the corners. They threw quality strikes. That made me a better pitcher because I realized what big leaguers did." During the last two weeks of spring training, the Braves, who had just announced their move from Boston to Milwaukee in March, visited their minor-league affiliates. When they arrived in Atlanta, Crone remained there, having been optioned to the Crackers. "I hooked up with Art Fowler and he taught me the slider," Crone said. Despite learning a new pitch, Crone's days in Atlanta were also frustrating. "Gene Mauch was the manager. I was there for about two weeks and he pitched me about four innings in spring training. We were about to start the season and Mauch told me that I am being sent to Jacksonville."

Having trained with major leaguers, Crone was disappointed to be assigned to Class A ball and had serious concerns about his future and even pondered quitting. "The demotion made me upset because I had been in A ball for a couple of years," he said. "You don't have many options to fight the decision. But I was determined and had the only great year I ever had and the slider helped." With a league-high 19 wins to accompany his 2.38 ERA in 253 innings pitched (all career bests), Crone and 19-year-old second baseman Hank Aaron led the Jacksonville Braves to the best regular-season record in the South Atlantic (Sally) League. He won two more games in the playoffs, including a 14-inning complete-game masterpiece over the Savannah Indians, but the Braves lost the league championship.[3]

In preparation for another shot at the big leagues, Crone, along with future Braves teammates Aaron, Bob Buhl, and Felix Mantilla, played for Caguas in the Puerto Rican Winter League in 1954 and led them to the league title. Crone had a 6-1 record in the second half of the season. "At the time I was eager to play anywhere and see the world," Crone said. He credited his success to player-manager Mickey Owen, a former catcher with the Brooklyn Dodgers. "I never pitched to a better catcher than Owen. He really helped me. Not just with words, but with the way he handled me."

After his most successful year pitching, Crone began his second spring training with the Braves in 1954 with more than 60 career wins in Organized Baseball and confidence in his curveball, slider, and control. "I had a changeup," Crone said, "but in those days you didn't throw a changeup much like today." He earned a spot on the team and made his major-league debut in the first game of the year, pitching two-thirds of an inning of scoreless relief against the Cincinnati Reds in a 9-8 loss.

He immediately noticed the difference between the majors and minors. "It made an impression on me in the first game when our manager, Charlie Grimm, got upset because Cincinnati had scored an early run. In the minor leagues, when teams got a run or two, that was no big deal." On May 23 in Chicago Crone notched his first major-league victory by pitching a ten-inning complete game. With two outs in the ninth inning of a scoreless game, Crone lined a single scoring Joe Adcock for his first career RBI; Aaron also scored on a throwing error by right fielder Frank Baumholtz. Up 2-0 with two outs in the bottom of the ninth inning, "Ernie Banks hit one in the seats to tie the game. I threw him a slider, up and away." Crone recalled that it was taken for granted that he would pitch the tenth inning. "No one said anything or asked me how I was doing." After the Braves scored two runs in the extra frame, Crone gave up a two-out single and walk before striking out Gene Baker to earn his first win.

In late July, with only limited relief action after his impressive win, Crone was optioned to the Toledo Sox of the Triple-A American Association, where he won seven of ten decisions and posted a 3.00 ERA. On August 20 against the St. Paul Saints, he pitched a seven-inning no-hitter in the first game of a doubleheader. He was recalled to Milwaukee in mid-September, had three relief appearances, and then ended the season with a start against the Cardinals and pitched nine innings of shutout ball before being replaced by Ernie Johnson. After he finished with a 1-0 record and a 2.02 ERA in 49 innings, Crone's future appeared bright on the third-place Braves, who led the National League in attendance and became the first team in the senior circuit to draw over 2 million fans.

With Warren Spahn, Lew Burdette, Bob Buhl, and Gene Conley, the Braves had one of the strongest pitching rotations in baseball to start spring training in 1955; nonetheless *The Sporting News* reported that Crone had an excellent chance of winning a starting job.[4] No longer bothered by nagging arm injuries, Crone was tabbed as the team's fifth starter. But after giving up three home runs and lasting just 3 1/3 innings in his initial start, he was relegated to the bullpen, where he continued to struggle, and was soon optioned to Toledo again with an unsightly 10.12 ERA in five appearances. At Toledo he pitched spectacularly beginning with a shutout over the Louisville Colonels with Braves owner Louis Perini and general manager John Quinn in attendance. After pitching four consecutive complete-game victories and giving up just 23 hits and three runs (0.75 ERA) during the best stretch of his career, he was recalled to the Braves.[5]

Crone "has excellent stuff" wrote Braves' beat writer Red Thisted during a stretch in which the 23-year-old right-hander gave up just two earned runs in 14 innings in June to earn another shot in the starting rotation.[6] He completed 6 of 13 starts in the second half of the season, including his only career shutout on September 5 when he threw a three-hitter against the Cubs in Chicago. He finished the season with a 10-9 record and 3.46 ERA in 140 1/3 innings for the second-place Braves.

In the 1955 offseason, Ray married Joan Anne Carroll, whom he met while playing in Hartford. Like many of the Braves players, Ray lived in Milwaukee year-round and served as a representative for a local brewery in the offseason.[7]

"Ray has control [and] knows how to pitch," said new Braves pitching coach Charlie Root, who replaced Bucky Harris to start the 1956 season. He predicted that Crone might win 15 games.[8] With a poor spring and an ERA over 5.00, Crone competed for the fourth starting position with Red Murff, a 35-year-old "rookie," who was coming off a 27-win season in the Double-A Texas League. Murff was given the job, but surrendered five runs in five innings in his only start of the season. Due to a quirky schedule and canceled games, Crone made his first start in game six of the season and pitched a complete-game victory over the Cardinals. Manager Charlie Grimm's Big Three, Spahn, Burdette, and Buhl, started the next eight games before Crone got his second start. Not only did he pitch another complete-game victory, he also executed the first successful suicide squeeze bunt for the Braves since they moved to Milwaukee, knocking in Wes Covington, and also scored two runs in his most productive game at the plate.[9]

On May 26 against the Reds in Milwaukee, Crone was involved in one of the strangest and most memorable games of the season. Leading 1-0 through seven innings, he was locked in a pitchers' duel with notoriously wild Johnny Klippstein, who was working on a no-hitter despite issuing seven bases on balls, hitting one batter, and surrendering one run. Reds manager Birdie Tebbetts pinch-hit for Klippstein in the eighth inning, after which Hersh Freeman and Joe Black held the Braves hitless in the eighth and ninth innings, thus completing an unprecedented three-man no-hitter through nine innings. (The MLB Committee on Statistical Accuracy changed the definition of a no-hitter in 1991, thus removing this game from the list of no-hitters.) Crone gave up a two-out game-tying double to Wally Post in the ninth inning and the game finally ended in the 11th inning when Black surrendered a run-scoring single to Frank Torre, giving Crone a complete-game, extra-inning victory.

The 11-inning outing was the longest in Crone's major-league career. "Managers watched pitchers," he said. "When pitchers started to tire, they finished their motion poorly and started throwing high." Three decades before pitch counts dictated how many innings a pitcher could throw, Crone expected to pitch deep into ballgames and confessed that he did not worry about his arm. "The worst thing that happened to pitching was the radar gun," he lamented. "When I pitched no one knew about velocity; they just said, 'He threw hard.' You pitched at your capability. Your arm and your control dictated how you could throw." Never a "hard thrower," Crone relied on his control and threw to all corners of the plate.

After their slow start to the season which resulted in Grimm being replaced by Fred Haney, the Braves were in first place, 2 1/2 games ahead of the Dodgers entering September. Having lost his spot in the starting rotation after a string of several ineffective starts in late July and August and pitching out of the bullpen for the last month of the season, Crone resurrected his season and boasted a 1.69 ERA in 21 1/3 innings over 11 appearances in September; however, the Braves struggled mightily and fell into second place. With the team heading into the final three-game series of the season against the Cardinals and in first place by a half-game, Crone was confident the Braves would win the pennant. "We went into St. Louis with the lead and my roommate Chuck Tanner and I joked that we were going to buy our wives fur coats." The Braves lost two of three while the Dodgers swept the Pirates to win the NL pennant in dramatic fashion.

The stunning loss was traumatic for the Braves and their fans. "One thing I criticize Haney for is he started his Big Three too much at the end of the season," Crone said. Spahn, Burdette, and Buhl started 15 of the team's last 17 games and the final ten. "Burdette and Buhl did not pitch well down the stretch. Haney could have pitched somebody different, but played it safe," Crone opined. Both Buhl and Burdette had their worst months of the season, winning just twice each with 6.39 and 4.46 ERAs respectively. Though he finished with career highs in wins (11) and innings pitched (169 2/3), Crone suggested that Haney lacked confidence in him. Almost immediately after the conclusion of the season, rumors of a trade began to swirl involving Crone and longtime Cardinals second baseman Red Schoendienst, who had been traded to the New York Giants during the 1956 season.[10]

Crone began the 1957 season in the starting rotation and won his first start of the season, surrendering four runs in 7 2/3 innings against the Reds in the third game of the season. But after an ineffective second start, he again lost his spot in the starting rotation. General manager John Quinn continually denied rumors of an imminent trade between the New York Giants and the Braves involving Crone, pitchers Gene Conley, Don McMahon, Juan Pizzaro, or outfielder Wes Covington. After two rough relief outings, Crone found himself lost in the Braves' bullpen. Manager Haney juggled his pitching rotation so that left-hander Warren Spahn did not have to pitch against the Dodgers at Ebbets Field with its short right field and gave Crone a spot start on June 11. Crone took advantage and hurled a complete-game victory that proved to be his last win as a member of the Milwaukee Braves. Four days later he was traded along with Danny O'Connell and Bobby Thomson to the Giants for the 34-year old Schoendienst.

"I was disappointed about the trade," Crone said. "We were in Philadelphia at the time. I remembered seeing something in my hotel mailbox. We were at the trading deadline. O'Connell, Thomson, and I took the train to New York." Crone didn't want to leave the only organization he knew. He lived in Milwaukee year-round with his family, and felt at home in the city. After he was chased in the second inning of his Giants debut in the Polo Grounds on June 16, New York fans voiced their displeasure with the trade. Crone exacted revenge against his former club in his next outing when he relieved Johnny Antonelli and pitched six innings of three-hit shutout ball against Spahn and the Braves to earn his first victory as a Giant. His success was short-lived; he lost his next five decisions as a starter before beating the Phillies in New York on August 9 in the last complete game of his major-league career.

"I didn't respond to the trade well," said Crone of leaving the Braves in their magical championship season. "After the Braves I never felt comfortable." A quiet and mild-mannered person, Ray kept to himself and never sought the bright lights of stardom. After playing with the "down-home" and relaxed Braves, he felt alienated by Giants manager Bill Rigney and his loud and sometimes self-serving personality. "Rigney was a version of Leo Durocher and was not that enamored with me." He finished with a combined record of 7-9 (4-8 with the Giants) and a 4.36 ERA in 163 innings, Crone's season was erratic and unpredictable; nonetheless Giants vice president Chub Feeney expressed his confidence in the 26-year-old, healthy pitcher, saying, "We still think Crone can be a very big winner for us in the future."[11]

Crone played on the last Giants team in New York and on the first in San Francisco. "The fans were excited out there," he remembered. "They had a big banquet and a parade for us." Despite the city's enthusiasm for major-league baseball, Crone thought that the sportswriters and news media were relatively uninformed about the team, other than its star players like Willie Mays and Johnny Antonelli, and consequently may not have been as critical of the team, which had come off a miserable 69-85 season in 1957. Playing in Seals Stadium, so named for the San Francisco Seals of the Pacific Coast League, Crone recalled, "You'd sit in the bullpen and freeze."

Beginning the 1958 season in the bullpen for the Giants, Crone threw four innings of one-run relief on April 24 to earn his first victory of the season and the last in his major-league career. Seeing mainly mop-up duty for the next seven weeks (he appeared in ten consecutive Giants losses), Crone was traded to the Triple-A Toronto Maple Leafs on July 15 for 31-year-old former major leaguer Don Johnson, an inconsistent pitcher with immense potential. Crone languished in Toronto, going winless in two decisions, and never made it back to the major leagues.

Crone admitted that he was affected by the pressure to succeed and pitch consistently well. "In my mind I wasn't doing so well," Crone explained how he thought as a major-league pitcher. "All through my career, I always wanted to do well. When I went to pro ball, I was determined to do well. When I was young, I saw guys who were signed come home with failure and I didn't want to do that. I wanted to make my family proud." Though he never suffered a debilitating injury or a weak or tired arm, after his trade to the Giants Crone never recaptured the fleeting moments of excellence he had with the Braves. He finished his five-year major-league career with 30 wins, an equal number of losses, and a 3.87 ERA in 546 innings.

Despite his poor 1958 season, Crone was determined to make it back to the big leagues and decided to play winter ball with Oriente in the Venezuelan League in 1958-59.[12] He started the 1959 season with Toronto, a franchise owned by Jack Kent Cooke, who specialized in acquiring former major-league players, resurrecting their careers in the International League, and then selling them back to a major-league team. "We opened up in Havana, Cuba," Crone said. "Castro was taking over at the time. There were kids with machine guns near the dugout. The game was held up until Castro arrived." Struggling to regain his form and winless in two decisions, Crone was sold conditionally to the Double-A Birmingham Barons, and began a frustrating odyssey that led him to five teams through 1961. Returned to Toronto after two ineffective starts, he was sold to the Double-A Chickasaws in his home town of Memphis, where he went 6-10 with a respectable 3.19 ERA in 110 innings pitched.

"By 1960 my heart was not in it anymore," Crone said. "I didn't have many options [for a different career] and no college background. I was sold and traded without my control." He felt exploited by teams that viewed him as personal property to be traded or sold for profit without considering how a trade might affect his life, family, and children. Within a span of a year (from late 1959 through the 1960 season), Crone had the unenviable distinction of being the property of, and being sold by, teams in each of the three Triple-A leagues, going from Charleston in the American Association to Portland in the Pacific Coast League, and finally to Dallas-Fort Worth in the American Association. He compiled a 5-12 cumulative record.

Astonished to learn that he was again the property of the Toronto Maple Leafs, Crone reported to their spring training in 1961. Released before the beginning of the season, he signed with the Jacksonville Jets, the expansion Houston Colt .45s' Class A affiliate in the Sally League. Splitting his time as a starter and reliever, Crone won four of nine decisions, but knew it was time to quit. Just 29 years old, he ended his professional baseball career after the 1961 season. In an 11-season minor-league career, he won 90 games and lost 77 with a 3.42 ERA.

Upon retiring, Ray moved permanently to Hartford, Connecticut, where he had been living with his wife and four children in the offseasons since his trade from the Braves. For ten years he was out of baseball, but by 1971 he wanted to become involved again in his lifelong passion. "I didn't feel I could coach," Crone said. "They didn't make much money and I didn't think it was the thing to do with young kids." He began scouting for the Montreal Expos in 1971, moved to the Baltimore Orioles a few years later, and then was named Southwest area scout by Orioles farm director Tom Giordano in 1977. Ray and his family moved to Texas, which he used as a base for his scouting excursions throughout the state and to Louisiana and New Mexico.

At a game in Beaumont game (Texas League) in the 1980s, he noticed a young, hard-throwing pitcher, Kevin Towers, who later became a scout after his playing career ended in 1989. When Towers was named the general manager of the San Diego Padres in 1995, he hired Crone as an area and subsequently local scout, a post he still held in 2012. "I take a lot of pride in being a scout and having been part of this game for so long," said Crone.[13] At the major-league Winter Meetings in 2006, Crone was named the Midwest Scout of the Year. His son, Ray Jr., has served as scout for the Angels, Red Sox, and Tigers.

Involved in baseball for almost his entire life, Crone still resided in Waxahachie, Texas, as of 2013 and scouted Rangers' home games for the Padres. "I went up through the system and paid my dues," Crone said, reflecting on his life in baseball. "I played when baseball was at its height. I look back and know I could have done better. I didn't do that and have to live with it."

Notes

1. The author expresses his sincere gratitude to Ray Crone, who was interviewed on June 19, 2012, for this biography. All quotations from him are from this interview unless otherwise noted.
2. All minor- and major-league statistics have been verified on Baseball-Reference (baseball-reference.com).
3. *The Sporting News*, September 16, 1953, 36.
4. *The Sporting News*, November 3, 1954, 18.
5. *The Sporting News*, June 8, 1955, 40.
6. *The Sporting News*, June 15, 1955, 7.
7. *The Sporting News*, January 4, 1956, 17.
8. *The Sporting News*, February 22, 1956, 10.
9. *The Sporting News*, May 23, 1956, 24.
10. *The Sporting News*, October 24, 1956, 27.
11. *The Sporting News*, September 4, 1957, 16.
12. *The Sporting News*, January 14, 1959, 21.
13. Lyle Spencer, "Crone Named Midwest Scout of the Year." sandiego.padres.mlb.com, December 5, 2006.

John DeMerit

By Steven Schmitt

Before signing a $100,000 bonus contract with the 1957 Milwaukee Braves, John Stephen DeMerit had been a standout athlete since he was a youngster. In the fifth grade he set a record for the 100-yard dash (12.1 seconds) at the Port Relays, an annual event held in his hometown of Port Washington, Wisconsin, 27 miles north of Milwaukee. In high school DeMerit earned 16 letters in four sports—track, football, basketball, and baseball. His father, Sam DeMerit, was the school's athletic director and track coach, a position he held from 1926 to 1962. In football, John played offense and defense and led the team in rushing, passing, placekicking, and punting. In basketball, DeMerit led the Braveland conference in scoring at 24 points per game and set a single-season record for points scored. That spring he pitched and lost, 3-2, in the semifinals of the 1953 state baseball tournament to eventual champion Kaukauna, in Port Washington's first appearance in the tournament.

So how did this versatile but modest athlete get to the major leagues? Born in West Bend, Wisconsin, on January 8, 1936, DeMerit was the youngest of four children, including brothers Samuel Jr. and James and a sister, Nancy. Between high-school years, John played American Legion baseball for the Land O' Lakes team for two summers (and a summer between high school and college), demonstrating for the first time his skills as a five-tool player who could hit for average, hit for power, run, throw, and field. After working out with the transplanted Milwaukee Braves, DeMerit turned down a Class D contract in the Northern League and enrolled at the University of Wisconsin in the fall of 1954 on a basketball scholarship.

"My Dad wanted me to be an engineer," said DeMerit, who soon found that all those mathematical formulas were not for him and switched to physical education and recreation.[1] Playing freshman basketball, DeMerit learned coach Harold E. "Bud" Foster's pattern, set-shot offense that had won an NCAA championship in 1941 and a Big Ten title and NCAA berth in 1947. By this time, DeMerit said, "Every team had scouted us and knew what we were going to do." DeMerit played freshman baseball under coach Gene Calhoun. As a sophomore in 1956, he was on the bubble to make the traveling squad for the spring trip to the Florida State tournament after failing to impress varsity baseball coach Arthur "Dynie" Mansfield in indoor workouts. Mansfield flipped a coin to decide whether DeMerit or another player would make the trip. "That's exactly what happened," DeMerit recalled. "He says, 'Neither one of you guys are good enough to go but I have to take another player.'" DeMerit rode the bench until outfielder Walt Nowicki dusted himself off after sliding into second base, failed to call time, and was tagged out. A disgusted Mansfield, who had virtually zero tolerance for mental errors, turned to his would-be blond bomber and barked, "DeMerit, warm up!" DeMerit led Wisconsin with 14 RBIs on the nine-game journey with five home runs, and finished the season with 12 homers, a school record, and a .349 batting average.

John DeMerit (National Baseball Hall of Fame Library, Cooperstown, N.Y.)

"The ball just hopped off his bat," recalled teammate Wayne "Knobby" Kelliher. "He (also) had an absolute cannon for an arm." Kelliher recalled a 1956 game in which Michigan State shortstop Earl Morrall—who had a 20-year career as an NFL quarterback—tried to score from second on a single to right field. "John threw a one-hop strike to me at home plate," Kelliher, the Badger catcher, remembered. Morrall was still eight feet from the plate when he saw the ball in Kelliher's glove. With his eyes as big as Miami oranges, Morrall was an easy out. "He's thinking, 'Where'd that ball come from?,'" said Kelliher, laughing.[2] Despite DeMerit's "rifle shot" home run and another throw that preserved a tie in the tenth inning, the Badgers lost the second-longest game in Wisconsin history on Morrall's three-run bomb in the top of the 15th inning. Wisconsin finished third in the Big Ten, handing eventual national champion Minnesota its only conference loss, and became the first Wisconsin baseball team to win 20 games.

DeMerit became a "sure-fire prospect" after the team's trip to Arizona in 1957. He slugged three triples against Arizona State in the first of four wins in five games with the Sun Devils. In Wisconsin's only defeat, the Sun Devils intentionally walked DeMerit three times in a row after he belted a two-run homer. Wisconsin's 6-1 record on the road trip (including two wins over the Arizona Wildcats) had scouts buzzing about DeMerit, who batted .553 and drove in 12 runs in ten preseason games.

After the team plane nearly crashed during a severe storm on the way home, the Badgers dropped their first three Big Ten games and finished 3-7.[3] Though DeMerit batted .382 and won his second team MVP award, his home-run production dropped from 12 to 4 and his RBIs from 37 to 17. "The telephone calls, the stands full of scouts—it was just too much for him and the team to handle," said Wisconsin teammate Walter "Bunk" Holt.[4]

Sportswriters correctly predicted that DeMerit would sign a professional contract by season's end. On May 26, 1957, the 21-year-old athlete sat down at a table in the living room of his home and signed a contract with the Milwaukee Braves that included a $100,000 bonus spread over five years. Midwest scout Ed Dancisak, general manager John Quinn, farm director John Mullen, and team president Joe Cairnes were on hand. Dancisak had scouted DeMerit at Port Washington and at the University of Wisconsin. "He's quick with his bat," said Dancisak, "and takes that short stride we like to see in a ballplayer. He knows the strike zone, too."[5]

Dancisak and Quinn believed DeMerit could immediately help the Braves, whose committee of left fielders batted .163 in the first month of play. Milwaukee had failed to acquire sluggers Frank Thomas, Del Ennis, or Lee Walls, had sold Chuck Tanner to the Cubs to make room for bonus player Hawk Taylor, and sent Wes Covington back to Wichita. "Everyone connected with the Braves is more than delighted to have DeMerit with us," said Quinn. "First, because he is an outstanding player; and second, because he is a Wisconsin boy. We would like to develop more home-state boys for the Braves, and are particularly pleased John chose us."[6] Manager Fred Haney said that DeMerit "takes a good cut at the ball. He's a big fellow and I like the way he moves."[7] Wisconsin coach Dynie Mansfield added, "He has good hands and hits for distance to left and center. I think he can definitely step in and help the Braves right now, but the fans shouldn't expect too much until he has a chance to gain confidence and find himself."[8] Twenty-four had scouts watched DeMerit at Northwestern a week earlier. Almost every major-league team sought him but the Braves made the best offer. "I gave my Dad $25,000 to buy a house," said DeMerit, who worked out with the Braves and completed his university exams before playing in his first game on June 18 against the New York Giants at Milwaukee County Stadium.

With some of his Badger teammates watching from the stands, DeMerit debuted as a ninth-inning defensive replacement for left fielder Andy Pafko. Two nights later, pinch-hitting for reliever Dave Jolly, DeMerit singled to center off the glove of Stu Miller, who had given the Braves fits with his Trevor Hoffman-like change-ups. "They fell over on the bench," DeMerit said of the Braves players' reaction to his first plate appearance. "Since I hadn't seen (Miller) before, I probably had an advantage."

As *Milwaukee Journal* sports writer Bob Wolf opined, the Big Ten was not the National League "and the chance that DeMerit will be a star overnight is strictly an outside one."[9] On July 11 center fielder Bill Bruton collided with shortstop Felix Mantilla in the outfield and was lost for the season. Shortly thereafter, the Braves decided to play DeMerit against left-handed pitchers. "He reminds me of Al Kaline," said coach Connie Ryan. "He's loose and takes a good cut at the ball."[10] When Hank Aaron stepped on a drain board chasing a Willie Jones double on July 17 in Philadelphia, DeMerit became the starting center fielder for a week. "DeMerit proved adequate as a center fielder, as was to be expected of a man with his speed and throwing arm," Wolf wrote. "At the plate, though, he showed understandable signs of being unready for major league pitching."[11] For the season, DeMerit collected just five singles in 34 at-bats and fanned eight times. In the World Series against the New York Yankees, DeMerit appeared in the Game Three loss at County Stadium as a pinch-runner for backup catcher Del Rice.

Worst of all, the bonus rule required the Braves to keep DeMerit on the 25-player active roster for two seasons, precluding any minor-league development. "(The contract) was hard to turn down but in retrospect I might have been better off somewhere else," DeMerit said. "You aren't really working your skills. I should have been on my way up through the minors and working toward a major-league career."

With the bonus rule changed in 1958 to prevent teams from "hiding" prospects in the minor leagues, DeMerit played regularly in the Braves system for the next three seasons. In May 1958 he hit four consecutive home runs over two games for the Atlanta Crackers and had a .301 average in mid-June. Because of warts on the fingers of his right hand, DeMerit went on the disabled list. On August 13 he hit his first home run in six weeks and finished the season with a "disappointing" .257 average with 13 home runs and 70 RBIs.[12] In 1959 DeMerit had a 13-game hitting streak in spring training but played most of the season for Class A Jacksonville, batting .251 with 14 home runs and 48 RBIs.[13] Atlanta recalled DeMerit but lost in the Southern Association playoffs. The Braves added DeMerit to their roster in early September after Bruton injured an ankle sliding into second base. DeMerit and Al Spangler shared center field and the Braves tied the Los Angeles Dodgers for the league lead, forcing a best-of-three playoff series. In the Dodgers' second and decisive victory, Spangler batted for DeMerit, who had replaced Pafko in left field.

With one minor-league option left, DeMerit reported early for spring training with the Braves in 1960, with the possibility of platooning with Spangler or Lee Maye at a corner outfield spot for new manager Chuck Dressen. The Braves optioned DeMerit to Louisville, where Ben Geraghty managed the American Association Colonels. "He has all the physical requirements for success," Geraghty said in February. "DeMerit can hit inside pitches all day. On outside pitches, it's a matter of learning the spin on the ball, going after the pitch, and getting his body into the swing. He's strictly an arm-swinger right now."[14]

Because of illness, Geraghty did not finish the season at Louisville. DeMerit did, calling the 1960 season "the most satisfying of my baseball career." The Colonels won the Junior World Series over the International League champion Toronto Maple Leafs, who had won 100 games and took their league title by 17 games. Hitting third in the order as new manager Bill Adair's right fielder, DeMerit batted .268 with 12 home runs and 50 RBIs. His 1957 Milwaukee bonus baby teammate Taylor hit cleanup, batting .270 with 17 home runs and 80 RBIs. Adair (later named American Association Manager of the Year) did little more than make out the lineup card. "No hit-and-runs, no steals, no bunt plays," DeMerit remembered. In the Junior World Series DeMerit homered twice off St. Paul 20-game winner Jim Golden and led the Colonels with a .313 postseason average.

Before the 1961 season began, the Braves traded the popular Bill Bruton to the Detroit Tigers, creating open competition for jobs in left field and center field. DeMerit hit .302 in spring training and beat out Al Spangler for the center-field job. While awaiting delivery of his second daughter, DeMerit started for the Braves in center field on Opening Day, April 11, 1961. The Braves lost to the Cardinals in ten innings, 2-1. Seventeen days later, DeMerit played right field during Warren Spahn's 1-0 no-hitter over San Francisco at frigid County Stadium. "He knew his craft," DeMerit said of Spahn. "He really was a pitcher. He could put the ball where he wanted it. He knew how to set up hitters. The only trouble he had was throwing breaking balls to left-handed hitters. He could get right-handed hitters out with a screwball."

By May 2 DeMerit's average had fallen to .178. The Braves acquired slugger Frank Thomas from the Chicago Cubs to play left field, moved Maye to right and installed Aaron in center. Dressen was willing to give DeMerit a chance to platoon in right field because of his throwing arm. "He hasn't been playing anything like he was in spring training but we've got to give him a chance," the manager said.[15] Instead, DeMerit became a late-inning defensive replacement, pinch-hitter, and pinch-runner, batting .162 with two home runs and five RBIs in 80 at-bats. In June he was on general manager John McHale's alleged "lost worksheet"—a list of players available for immediate trade that a Milwaukee player found in the team's hotel on a road trip.[16]

On October 10, 1961, the New York Mets picked DeMerit in the National League expansion draft. On the Mets, DeMerit joined 1961 teammate Thomas, whom the Braves had traded to the Mets. DeMerit said manager Casey Stengel sometimes dozed off during a game and recalled that the coaches had to translate Stengelese to the players after team meetings. "He shouldn't have been managing," DeMerit said of Stengel. He said the Mets relied on fading veterans to draw fans to the Polo Grounds instead of developing young talent for the future. Thomas hit 34 home runs but ex-Brooklyn Dodgers Gil Hodges, Charlie Neal, and Roger Craig and former batting champion Richie Ashburn were well past their primes. DeMerit reported to camp as one of eight outfielders and did little more than replace Thomas or right fielder Gus Bell in the late innings. Once Stengel had relief pitcher Herb Moford bat for himself in the tenth inning of a tie game on April 17, 1962, with DeMerit available for pinch-hitting.

On May 16, 1962, DeMerit homered and later scored the winning run on ex-Brave Felix Mantilla's 11th-inning single in a 6-5 win over the Cubs at the Polo Grounds. Four days later DeMerit played his final major-league game during a doubleheader against the Braves in Milwaukee. The Mets sold him to Syracuse of the International League and his salary was cut in half, from $10,000 to $5,000. By this time John Quinn was in his third season as general manager of the Philadelphia Phillies. DeMerit recalled a promise from Quinn that he would acquire DeMerit if he was ever released but that never happened. DeMerit got permission to return to Milwaukee to have an injured shoulder treated but he refused to report to Syracuse, opting to retire from the game. The Mets suspended him.[17] Eventually, DeMerit returned to Port Washington, where his promising athletic career had begun.

DeMerit graduated in physical education in recreation with the Class of 1960 at the University of Wisconsin, taking courses in the offseason to complete his degree. With his baseball career over, DeMerit unsuccessfully scoured Madison for jobs in his chosen field—taking summer courses at the university, living in a rented room, and trekking home to "Port" on weekends. When an Equitable Life Assurance agent named Larry McDonald of Sheboygan learned DeMerit was back home, he urged him to become an agent for the company, which happened to be the trustee for the major-league baseball pension fund.

While he enjoyed the work and could have become a district manager, DeMerit found that the feast-or-famine, kitchen-table sales career was not the best fit. In 1967 DeMerit was appointed to the city recreation council. Two years later, the city needed a director of recreation and DeMerit was talked into applying for this job. He got it, and for the next 26 years –from 1969 until his retirement in 1995—DeMerit's department upgraded facilities, supervised a rapidly growing slow-pitch softball program, and staffed local summer playground sites that offered a variety of activities, from tennis to swimming to baseball.

DeMerit said he had no regrets about his career and was grateful for his baseball opportunity and for taking new directions when his major-league career ended. He came back to Port Washington and raised a family of seven children. One of them, Tom DeMerit, was the Los Angeles Dodgers' fourth-round pick in the 1987 amateur draft but never rose above Class A as an outfielder with the Vero Beach Dodgers. DeMerit and his wife, Gladys (Heinen) DeMerit, his high-school sweetheart, were married on February 1, 1958, at St. Mary's

Catholic Church, Port Washington's most visible landmark. As John became famous for his baseball exploits, Gladys accompanied him to Milwaukee, Louisville, and New York and saw a sure-fire prospect take everything in stride and not blow his own horn. "I have never known him to be any other way," she said.[18] That's good enough for John DeMerit and everyone who has known him.

Sources

The Baseball Encyclopedia (New York: Macmillan, 1979).

Louisville Courier-Journal.

The Capital Times (Madison, Wisconsin).

Wisconsin State Journal (Madison, Wisconsin).

Milwaukee Sentinel.

Port Washington (Wisconsin) *Pilot.*

The Sporting News.

Baseball-Almanac.com

Baseball-Reference.com

Retrosheet.com

The BaseballCube.com

University of Wisconsin Athletic Department.

Notes

1. Interviews quoting John De Merit took place by telephone on February 26, 2010, and July 31 and August 2, 2012, and in person at Port Washington, Wisconsin on August 2, 2010.
2. Personal interview. Wayne "Knobby" Kelliher. June 2, 2010, Madison, Wisconsin.
3. Telephone interviews, Bill Rubin, June 11, 2010, and Jim O'Toole, March 10, 2011; personal interview, John Aehl, June 17, 2010.
4. Telephone interview. Walter "Bunk" Holt. Glencoe, Illinois, December 29, 2011.
5. Tony Ingrassia, "Braves Sign UW's DeMerit For Reported $50,000 Bonus," *Milwaukee Sentinel*, May 27, 1957, Part 2, p. 3, 7.
6. "Braves Sign UW's DeMerit."
7. DeMerit Hopes to Help 'in a Pinch,' *Milwaukee Sentinel.* June 3, 1957, Part 2, p. 4.
8. *The Sporting News.* June 5, 1957, 27.
9. *The Sporting News.* June 5, 1957, 10.
10. *The Sporting News.* July 3, 1957, 7.
11. *The Sporting News.* July 31, 1957, 11.
12. *The Sporting News.* November 5, 1958, 13.
13. *The Sporting News.* February 10, 1960, 18.
14. *The Sporting News.* February 17, 1960, 13.
15. *The Sporting News.* May 3, 1961, 8.
16. The Sporting News. June 21, 1961, 15.
17. *The Sporting News.* June 16, 1962, 29.
18. Personal interview with John and Gladys DeMerit. August 2, 2010.

Harry Hanebrink

by Andy Sturgill

A VERSATILE DEFENDER who played as a utilityman in both the infield and outfield, Harry Hanebrink played for the two Milwaukee Braves teams that won the National League pennant in the 1950s, one of which won the World Series. He was also part of a much larger team that captured an even more important victory—the Allied Forces in World War II, during which he served in the US Navy.

Harry Aloysius Hanebrink was born on November 12, 1927, in St. Louis to Harry C. and Christina Hanebrink. He was the Hanebrinks' second child, joining older sister Christine. Their father worked for a newspaper in the St. Louis area.[1]

Harry attended McBride High School, a Catholic school about six miles northwest of downtown St. Louis. (The school closed its doors in 1975.) He joined the Navy on June 21, 1945, shortly after graduating, and served until he was discharged in August of 1946.

Hanebrink signed with the Boston Braves organization and began his professional baseball career with the Eau Claire Bears of the Class C Northern League in 1948. There is some dispute about exactly how Hanebrink came to join the Braves organization; two contemporary accounts offer competing versions. A Braves team publication listed Hanebrink as having signed with scout Bill Maughn, while *The Sporting News* said that Hanebrink signed with the club via Rich Keely, a scout whose brother Bob was a bullpen catcher for the team.[2]

Regardless of the scout who brought Hanebrink into the fold, Hanebrink put up impressive numbers at Eau Claire, leading the team in hits, triples (13), and home runs. His 16 round-trippers tied for the league lead. Hanebrink finished fourth in the league in batting average (.290), trailing among others teammate Chuck Tanner, the only other member of the squad to go on to a major-league career. The left-handed-hitting Hanebrink's power display was an anomaly, likely due in part to the 312-foot right-field fence at Eau Claire's Carson Park. The triple and home-run totals are surprising given Hanebrink's major-league height and weight, which were listed at 6-feet and 165 pounds. After his 16 homers as a 20-year old in 1948, he didn't hit more than eight home runs in a season again until 1956, eight years after his initial outburst.

In 1949 and 1950 Hanebrink put up similar numbers to 1948 as he rose in the minor-league ranks, playing with Evansville of the Class B Three-I League in 1949 and Hartford of the Class A Eastern League in 1950.

In 1951 Hanebrink returned to Hartford and increased his batting average 19 points to .309 (sixth in the league), earning all-star honors. The offensive output was enough to elevate Hanebrink's standing with the Braves, who had always held his fielding prowess in high esteem. Before the 1952 season the Braves initiated

Harry Hanebrink (National Baseball Hall of Fame Library, Cooperstown, N.Y.)

a "Rookie Rocket" tour, in which team executives and media members flew around the country to become familiar with minor-league players the team felt would contribute to the major-league club in the near future. After his strong performance in successive seasons, Hanebrink's St. Louis home made its way onto the list of tour stops.

For 1952 the Braves promoted Hanebrink to the Atlanta Crackers of the Double-A Southern Association. Hanebrink posted a solid season, hitting .291 with six home runs and playing in a team-high 145 games.

Along the way in the minors, Hanebrink made an impression not just because of his play but also because of his unique style at the plate. Of his stance, which he adopted to help him combat overstriding at changeups, he said, "Feet very wide. I don't even take a step, but I come forward with the bat three times then take one fast cut when the pitcher starts to throw. All the fans used to count cadence on every pitch at Hartford, clapping and shouting: 'One, two, three, dip.' I guess it looks funny, but I can hit better that way."[3] His Atlanta teammates nicknamed him "The Stance" because of his unique approach. At one point Hanebrink was in a slump at the plate and Atlanta manager Dixie Walker told him that no one would be able to help him because of his unorthodox style. Hanebrink abandoned the stance for a time but continued to struggle, so he eventually returned to his old reliable way and started hitting again.[4]

After five seasons in the minor leagues, Hanebrink reached the majors in 1953, the Braves' first season in Milwaukee after the franchise moved from Boston, leading baseball's westward migration. He made his big-league debut at Ebbets Field in Brooklyn on May 3, pinch-hitting and grounding out for Braves pitcher Max Surkont in the fifth inning against Brooklyn's Billy Loes. After batting seven times without success (and never more than once in a game), Hanebrink got his first big-league hit on June 6, a two-run pinch-hit home run at Connie Mack Stadium off the Phillies' future Hall of Famer Robin Roberts. Hanebrink did not hit another major-league home run for nearly five years.

Despite spending almost the entire 1953 season with Milwaukee, Hanebrink did not get his first start in the big leagues until August 7, when he played second base and batted eighth in the Braves' 9-2 win over Pittsburgh. That start came the day after he hit a game-winning bases-loaded triple off Russ Meyer of Brooklyn. After the game-winner, Hanebrink started the next 11 games, but after August 16 he started only three more the rest of the season. For his inaugural major-league season Hanebrink hit .238 with one home run and eight RBIs. He appeared in 51 games overall, but came to bat only 87 times, as many of his appearances were as a pinch-hitter or defensive replacement.

After the 1953 season, Hanebrink did not appear in a major-league game again until late 1957. He spent 1954 and 1955 with Toledo, the Braves' Triple-A team in the American Association, and after the franchise was moved to Wichita, he spent all of 1956 and most of 1957 there. During this four-year stretch he hit .272 and saw action primarily at third base, although he played every position except pitcher and catcher for Toledo in 1955. Hanebrink's power jumped substantially at Wichita in 1956 and 1957 (20 and 24 home runs, no doubt due in part to the left-handed hitter taking advantage of another 312-foot right-field fence at Wichita's Lawrence-Dumont Stadium). Hanebrink was called up to the Braves early in September of 1957, going 2-for-7 in six games as the Braves captured the NL pennant by eight games over the Cardinals and then bested the Yankees in seven games in the World Series. As a call-up after the September 1 deadline, Hanebrink did not play in the Series.

Hanebrink spent all of 1958 with the Braves. It was the only one of his 14 professional seasons in which he spent no time in the minor leagues. Not surprisingly, he registered major-league career highs in virtually every counting stat, including games played, at-bats, hits, home runs, RBIs, home runs, walks, total bases, and runs scored. But the numbers are deceptive: Hanebrink struggled at the plate all season, finishing with a batting average of only .188. One highlight for him came on June 15 when his two-run home run in the ninth inning gave the Braves a 4-2 win over the St. Louis Cardinals. With the game taking place in his hometown of St. Louis, it was extra sweet for Harry, whose parents were at the game.

"I've been strangling that bat all season," Hanebrink said of his struggles. "In trying to find a comfortable grip, I've practically squeezed all the sawdust out of it. So when I stepped up to the plate in the ninth I figured I couldn't do any worse and relaxed my grip on the bat. It worked fine, too."[5] But he said he understood that his was a part-time role, and he seemed eager to help the Braves in any way he could. "I can't afford to be choosy," Hanebrink said. "I just want to stay up here and help out wherever I can, whether it's in the outfield or infield."[6] Hanebrink's role developed exactly as he suggested, as his 40 games played in the field saw him in left field 24 times, in right field nine times, and at third base in seven games. That he didn't play more was understandable given that those three positions were manned by sluggers Wes Covington, Hank Aaron, and Eddie Mathews, respectively.

The Braves won the pennant again in 1958, by the same eight games (this time over the Pirates) and again played a seven-game World Series against the Yankees. This time, however, Milwaukee came up on the short end in Game Seven. Hanebrink went 0-2 as a pinch-hitter in Games Three and Five.

Ten days before the start of the 1959 season, Hanebrink was traded to the Philadelphia Phillies with pitcher Gene Conley and infielder Joe Koppe for catcher/first baseman Stan Lopata and infielders Ted Kazanski and Johnny O'Brien. Aside from moving from a team that was within one win of a World Series title to a team that finished in the NL cellar, Hanebrink's role with the Phillies remained similar to what it had been with the Braves. He subbed at second base, third base, and right field, and hit .258 in 97 at-bats. He also spent some time with the Buffalo Bisons, the Phillies Triple-A affiliate.

After 1959 Hanebrink's playing career continued for two more seasons with Buffalo. He played the corner infield spots, and hit only .219 in 310 at-bats in 1960 and '61. After the 1961 season, Hanebrink's 14-year professional baseball career ended.

So who was Harry Hanebrink the player? Modern metrics suggest that he was the prototypical replacement-level player. He played in 177 major-league games in four seasons. He did not have a defined position, but could play second base, third base, and the corner outfield spots. As a fringe major-league player in the 1950s, he almost certainly would have had a longer career had he come along 10 or 15 years later when the major leagues were in the process of expanding from 16 teams (in 1959, Hanebrink's last year in the majors) to 26 teams (1977).

After leaving baseball, Hanebrink returned to his native St. Louis and worked as a real-estate broker with Dolan Realtors for 20 years. In 1992 he began a job as a shuttle bus driver for Quik Park at Lambert-St. Louis International Airport. He remained in this role until his death on September 9, 1996, after a brain aneurysm. He was survived by his wife, Wanda (Powers) Hanebrink; his sister, Christine; two daughters; two sons; and three grandchildren. As a military veteran, Hanebrink was buried at Jefferson Barracks National Cemetery in St. Louis.

Sources

In additions to sources listed below, the author consulted Ancestry.com, the SABR Encyclopedia, and baseball-reference.com.

Notes

1. The 1930 US Census for the St. Louis area appears to conflate two families, the Hanebrinks and the Hanebrands. Using clues derived from other sources, including later hometowns of Harry Hanebrink's sister, Christine, and obituaries for people represented in this census information, I was able to conclude which family was actually Harry Hanebrink's.
2. Steve O'Leary, "Hill Turnover Tips Braves Hand on Deals," *The Sporting News*, October 24, 1951, 18.
3. "Braves Rookie Hanebrink Does Rumba at the Plate," *The Sporting News*, March 12, 1952, 18.
4. Jesse Outlar, "The Stance Goes on Big Bat Spread," *The Sporting News*, May 21, 1952, 29.
5. Red Thisted, "Hanebrink's HR Jars Cards, 4-2," *Milwaukee Sentinel*, June 16, 1958, 5.
6. "Hanebrink's HR."

Bob Hazle

By Nancy Snell Griffith

Until Hugo came along in 1989, Hurricane Hazel (1954) was the strongest storm ever to strike the South Carolina coast. Thus it is fitting that a man from the Palmetto State should be the mighty storm's namesake: right fielder Bob Hazle, who hit the National League with a bang late in the 1957 season. Although that season with the Milwaukee Braves was the highlight of Hazle's very brief major-league career, it is still remembered by sportswriters today. Over a span of 134 at-bats, he hit .403 and helped propel the Braves to the pennant and a World Series victory.

Robert Sidney Hazle was born in Laurens, South Carolina, on December 9, 1930, but grew up in nearby Woodruff. His parents, James Roland (J.R.) Hazle and Ella Belle Bishop Hazle, had six children. In addition to daughters Margaret and Azile, there were four sons: James, Paul, Joseph, and the youngest, Robert. Paul and Joe also signed professional baseball contracts. However, Bob was the only one who made it to the majors; Paul played in the minors from 1944 through 1947 and Joe from 1947 through 1955. Bob starred in four sports at Woodruff High School—football, basketball, and tennis in addition to baseball—and earned 16 letters before he graduated in 1949.

In addition, Bob played ball in the American Legion and in a South Carolina institution, the textile league. He was with teams for Mills Mill in Woodruff—where his father worked—in 1947 and Watts Mill in Laurens in 1946 and 1949. (Catcher Sammy Taylor, three years younger than Hazle, also graduated from Mills Mill to the majors.) Hazle's favorite sport in high school was football, and he had a scholarship offer from the University of Tennessee, but quit after a few days in favor of baseball. He attended Wofford College in Spartanburg, South Carolina, for one semester, but then chose to sign a pro baseball contract instead. To a boy growing up in a poor family, the bonus money of between $6,000 and $8,000 sounded very attractive.

In 1950 Hazle signed with the Cincinnati Reds, who assigned him to their Columbia team in the Sally (South Atlantic) League. The South Carolina state capital was only 80 miles from home. There, manager Gee Walker, the former Detroit Tiger, helped the new pro correct his bad habit of bailing out on pitches. Walker lay on the ground to hold the lefty swinger's foot in place during batting practice, and he then developed a triangular clamp that did the job.[1]

During his initial period in the minors, Hazle played for the Tulsa Oilers (1951, 1953), the Indianapolis Indians (1954), the Nashville Volunteers (1955), and the Wichita Braves (1956). He made the Texas League all-star team in Tulsa in 1951, and the Reds called him up after the major-league All-Star break, but Uncle Sam got to him first, and Hazle spent part of 1951, all of 1952, and the beginning of 1953 in the Army. He was stationed at Fort Jackson, near Columbia, and was able to play a lot of regimental baseball. The Reds called him up for spring training in 1954, but it didn't work out.

Hazle remembered this as the time things began to go a bit sour for him. He wasn't getting much playing time. Even though he had hit around .300 with

Bob Hazle (National Baseball Hall of Fame Library, Cooperstown, N.Y.)

Columbia and Tulsa, he was doing a lot of sitting. And then there was that stint in the military, which came at exactly the wrong time in his career. As he said, "When you get down, especially in the minor leagues, it's hard to get back up."[2] As a minor leaguer, he had a batting average of .287, an on-base percentage of .338 and 249 RBIs—but the 1954 season in Indianapolis was his worst (.224-4-23).

It was while playing winter-league ball in Venezuela in 1954 that Hazle first earned the nickname "Hurricane." (That October the Category 4 Hurricane Hazel had struck the US coast near the border between North and South Carolina.) In 1955, while playing 150 games for the Nashville Volunteers, Hazle batted .314. But while he had never hit for much power before, that year he hit 29 homers and drove in 92 runs. The Reds brought him up to the majors, and he hit a single to center in his first at-bat during his major-league debut on September 8. He played in six games for Cincinnati before the season ended.

Hazle went to spring training with the Reds in the spring of 1956, but just before the season started he and pitcher Corky Valentine were traded to the Milwaukee Braves for first baseman George Crowe. Hazle was never given a reason for the trade, but he recalled, "In those days a ballplayer was like a horse. Open his mouth, look at his teeth, check his legs, and say 'Trade him.'"[3] The Braves immediately sent Hazle down to their Triple-A team in Wichita, where he hit .285 and had 13 homers. Midway through the season, he stepped on something in the outfield and seriously injured his knee. He was forced to hobble through the rest of the season. Hazle almost decided to quit baseball altogether. "I thought I had had it," he said. "I decided that if I didn't make the majors by '57 I would call it quits."[4]

Hazle played at Wichita again in 1957. His manager, Ben Geraghty, showed a lot of confidence in him and refused to send him down to Double-A. His knee began to strengthen, he started playing more regularly, and his batting average soared. Late in July, the Braves brought Hazle up from the minors to replace injured outfielder Bill Bruton. He joined the roster for the 100th game of the season, and shared right-field duties with Andy Pafko. Hazle said he promised himself one thing, "that if I failed, it wasn't going to be for not trying."[5] What followed was a baseball sensation that won the Braves a place in the World Series. Using a bat borrowed from teammate Chuck Tanner, he once again became "Hurricane" Hazle, and this time the nickname stuck. A month later, he was batting .507. An article in the *New York Times* summed it up:

"The Milwaukee Braves' rookie outfielder has stunned the baseball world with his outstanding hitting since he was recalled a month ago from Wichita. He owned a modest .279 batting average at the time. The 26-year-old left-handed hitting South Carolinian has made thirty-four hits in sixty-seven times at bat for an average of .507. … 'It doesn't seem possible that anyone can keep up such a pace,' said Red Schoendienst …'but right now the kid is Stan Musial, Mickey Mantle and Ted Williams all wrapped in one.' … Some say he simply is an overnight sensation. … Others, such as Andy Pafko, the Braves hard-hitting flychaser, say Bob is a natural hitter. 'The kid can really rip the ball,' Pafko said. 'Next to Henry Aaron, he's got the strongest wrists in baseball. And he doesn't swing at too many bad balls, either.'"[6] Hazle's teammate Frank Torre said, "He looked like the best hitter in the world. … He never got fooled." And Eddie Mathews credited him with winning the 1957 pennant for the Braves.[7] Hazle ended the season with a .403 batting average in 41 games. He hit seven home runs and had 27 RBIs. His slugging percentage was .649.

The Braves won the World Series by beating the New York Yankees that year, even though Hazle batted only .154 during the Series. He did, however, have two hits in the seventh game, the first of which sparked a four-run outburst by the Braves. In that game Hazle also tied Mel Ott's record for the most putouts in an inning for a right fielder, three. Even though he had only 134 at-bats for the year, he was fourth in the voting for Rookie of the Year. In an interview done for the 1990 book *When the Cheering Stops*, Hazle remembered his first visit to Yankee Stadium: "I'll never forget coming to Yankee Stadium for the first time. I mean, here I am, a little ol' boy from the little ol' town of Woodruff, South Carolina, and I'm in Yankee Stadium to play in the World Series, the same ballpark where

Babe Ruth played, where DiMaggio played, and all the others. It was simply the ultimate."[8]

There was a bittersweet side to Hazle's wonderful run, though. "The team wanted to give me only a twelve-hundred-dollar raise. Plus I didn't get a bonus I was promised. My World Series share was supposed to take care of that. But I told them I had earned that share and helped the team get there. ...We finally agreed, but maybe that whole thing led to what happened next."[9]

After playing winter ball in the Dominican Republic, Hazle rejoined the Braves for spring training in 1958, but was hit in the head by a pitch from Tom Morgan of the Tigers. Then early in the season he hurt his ankle sliding into second, and was then beaned again by a pitch from Larry Jackson of the Cardinals. He was hospitalized for a week or so, and his equilibrium was thrown off a little. In May of 1958, the Braves sold him to the Detroit Tigers for $50,000. According to the *Chicago Daily Tribune*, "The deal climaxed a disappointing spring for Hazle, who helped propel the Braves to a National League flag last season by hitting .403. His 1958 batting average with the club had shrunk to a mere .179."[10] Jack Tighe, the Tigers' manager, used Hazle to relieve the ailing Al Kaline, and at one point he was hitting .300. But Tighe was fired on June 10, Bill Norman took over, and Hazle was once again riding the bench. He played in 43 games for the Tigers, and had a .241 average in 58 at-bats. His last major-league appearance was with the Tigers on September 28, 1958. Over his major-league career, he played in 110 games and had 261 at-bats and a batting average of .310. He hit nine home runs and batted in 37 runs.

Hazle wasn't called up for the Tigers' spring training in 1959, but was assigned to Charleston in Triple-A. He then played for the Birmingham Barons and the Little Rock Travelers (Double-A) in 1960. Once back in the minors, he said, "My confidence was shot. In the majors, you have it all built up inside you. But when you end up back in the minors there's the small ballparks again with no one coming out. It's very discouraging. And even though I was hitting well, I just didn't feel I would ever get another chance. And as it turned out, I was right."[11]

That winter Little Rock sold Hazle's contract to the Macon Peaches of the Southern Association. Instead, in April 1961, he retired at the age of 30. In a 1987 interview, he told writer David Lamb, "Everything went wrong, and that was the end of it. ... I told the wife it was time to wrap it up."[12] And once he left the game, he "never thought about going back, managing, coaching, or whatever. What's done is done. Besides, the way it ended, I left with kind of a bad taste in my mouth for baseball."[13]

After he returned to South Carolina, Hazle worked first as a salesman for a monument company, and then as a sales representative for Coggins Granite Industries. He and his first wife, Jo Ann, had a son named Robert Jr. (Robbie). Jo Ann died of cancer in 1970, and in 1972 Hazle married his second wife, Pat, who was an accountant. By 1987 the family included four grown children, including two daughters. He ended his career as a salesman for the Ben Arnold Beverage Company, a wholesaler of wine and whiskey. He also worked with an annual charity golf tournament in Ringgold, Georgia, which raised money to benefit the Special Olympics. It was Hazle's job to make sure that former major-league players showed up to play. He had a heart attack in 1981, followed by open-heart surgery. This forced him to slow down his pace a little, and in 1987 his wife, Pat, declared that "The Hurricane, these days ... is really just a gentle breeze."[14]

Bob Hazle died on April 25, 1992, in Columbia, South Carolina, after suffering another heart attack. He was buried in Crescent Hill Memorial Gardens there. This man never bragged about his major league successes. According to his widow, Pat, "That [1957] season was truly a magical whirlwind for him, and he put South Carolina on the map. ... But he would never say he was a hero. He had a true love for baseball."[15] And he was philosophical about his experiences in the sport: "Look at it this way. I'll always have 1957. There was the pennant race and then the World Series. Some players, even great ones, never get there. But I did. And we won it. And we beat the Yankees."[16]

Sources

Baseball-Almanac.com: baseball-almanac.com/players/player.php?p=hazlebo01.

Baseball-Reference.com: baseball-reference.com/players/h/hazle-bo01.shtml.

The Baseball Page: thebaseballpage.com.

Foster, Jim. "Bobby Hazle Glad He Chose Baseball," *Spartanburg (South Carolina) Herald*, August 16, 1957, 14.

"752 Woodruff Fans Send Bob Hazle Good Luck Wire," *Spartanburg (South Carolina) Herald*, October 2, 1957, 1.

"Woodruff Welcomes Home Bob Hazle Today," *Spartanburg (South Carolina) Herald*, October 19, 1957, 8.

Cole, Bob. "Hazle Had Torrid Year for Braves," *The State* (Columbia, South Carolina), April 28, 1992, 1C.

"Hurricane Bob Hazle, Retired Pro Baseball Player, Dies at 61," *Charlotte Observer*, April 27, 1992, 5C.

Paul Hazle obituary, *The State*, July 4, 2009.

Perry, Thomas K., *Textile League Baseball: South Carolina's Mill Teams, 1880-1955* (Jefferson, North Carolina: McFarland and Company, 1993).

McGuire, Mark and Michael Sean Gormley. Moments in the Sun: Baseball's Briefly Famous (Jefferson, North Carolina, McFarland and Company, 1999).

Notes

1. George Stone, *Muscle: A Minor-League Legend* (Haverford, Pennsylvania: Infinity Publishing, 2003), 194.
2. Lee Heiman et al., *When the Cheering Stops* (New York: MacMillan, 1990), 161.
3. Heiman et al., 162.
4. Howard M. Tuckner, "Rookie is Hitting .507," *New York Times*, August 30, 1957, 13.
5. David Lamb, "Hurricane the Hero." *Milwaukee Journal*, September 4, 1987, 3C.
6. Tuckner, "Rookie is Hitting .507."
7. Bob Spear, "1957 a Magical Whirlwind for Hurricane Hazle," *The State* (Columbia, South Carolina), July 26, 2004, C1.
8. Heiman et al., 158.
9. Heiman et al., 166.
10. *Chicago Daily Tribune*, May 25, 1958, A2.
11. Heiman et al., 168.
12. Lamb, "Hurricane the Hero."
13. Spear, "1957 a Magical Whirlwind …"
14. Lamb, "Hurricane the Hero."
15. Spear, "1957 a Magical Whirlwind …"
16. Heiman et al., 170.

Joey Jay

By Joseph Wancho

On Friday, June 13, 1958, the Milwaukee Braves, holding a 1 1/2-game lead atop the National League standings, opened a weekend series in St. Louis. The Braves' starting pitcher was Joey Jay. Connecticut native Jay had not yet succeeded as a major-league pitcher, but he already held two distinctions: He was one of the original "bonus babies"; and he was the first alumnus of the Little League to make the majors. That was back in 1953, and under the bonus rule of the day, Jay had spent most of his time on the Braves' roster, except for one full season, 1956, at Double-A and Triple-A. But in 1958 he was back with the Braves, and on this particular June evening he was making his first start of the season after appearing in four games as a reliever.

In the bottom of the sixth inning, with the Braves holding a tenuous 2-0 lead, the Cardinals' Curt Flood was on second base with two outs. The dangerous Stan Musial stepped up to the plate seeking to tie the game, or at least get the Cardinals on the scoreboard. But Jay got Musial to fly out to right field, ending the inning. The game was then halted because of rain, and eventually the last three innings were rained out, giving Jay his first victory as a starter since his rookie year of 1953.

"I don't remember what the count was," Jay said later of his final pitch to Musial. "But Del Crandall signaled for a changeup. I almost dropped dead. I'd thrown the pitch some in the bullpen, but never in a game, and I would never have dared throw it to a hitter like Musial. But I figured if Del had nerve enough to call for it, I'd better have guts enough to throw it. I read where Stan said I looked pretty good because I could get the change over the plate. I've been doing it ever since."[1] Crandall, Jay's batterymate, said, "You've got to find out fast what a young pitcher's got. After all, he was supposed to be a major-league pitcher. He hadn't been getting anybody out in relief with just his fastball, good as it was."[2] It seemed as though the coming of the bonus baby was at hand for the Braves organization. For Jay, it was the real start of a major-league career that saw him win 20 games twice, albeit with a team other than the Braves.

Joseph Richard Jay was born on August 15, 1935, in Middletown, Connecticut, the only child of Mr. and Mrs. Joseph John Jay. His father had been a semipro baseball player and had a trial with the Boston Braves in 1937. But the need to support his family made the senior Jay give up his dream of playing in the major leagues and return to Middletown, where he worked as a laborer.

Joey was 12 years old when Little League Baseball came on the scene in Middletown. Larger than most boys his age and too old to pitch, Jay played first base. But after "graduating" from Little League he turned to pitching and dominated his opponents from

Joey Jay (National Baseball Hall of Fame Library, Cooperstown, N.Y.)

American Legion ball right through to Woodrow Wilson High School. He pitched three no-hitters while in high school, drawing the attention of a half-dozen big-league teams. Milwaukee scout Jeff Jones got Jay's name on a contract with a bonus offer of $40,000. The 17-year-old Jay, who had just graduated from high school, was going right to the big leagues in Milwaukee.

Although Jay hit the financial jackpot, his growth as a professional pitcher was slowed considerably by the bonus rule imposed by the major leagues in 1953. The various bonus rules were designed to keep teams from spending large sums of money to sign young players. In various forms from 1946 to 1950, it mandated that if a team signed a player for more than $6,000, it could not option him to the minor leagues unless the player cleared waivers. Essentially, the team would be forced to keep the player on its big-league roster. That rule was abolished in 1950, but it resurfaced in 1953 in a slightly different form with the same intent. If a team signed an amateur player to a contract of more than $4,000, it could put him on its big-league roster, where he had to remain for at least two years. If the team started the player in the minor leagues, he was subject to unrestricted draft. This rule was in effect until the 1957 season.

There was plenty of resentment toward rookie Jay in the Braves clubhouse, and the veterans were not afraid to let their disdain show over the next two years. "It was pretty dreadful. I fitted in nowhere," Jay said. "No one was deliberately unkind to me. I was just ignored and felt like the batboy."[3]

But Braves' manager Charlie Grimm did call on Jay to make his first start on September 20, 1953, in Milwaukee. It was only his second appearance of the season, and Jay responded with a 3-0 shutout of Cincinnati in the second game of a doubleheader that was halted after 6 1/2 innings by darkness. He gave up only three hits and struck out four batters. It was the last home game of the season for the Braves, who finished in second place, 13 games behind Brooklyn.

Manager Grimm liked what he was seeing of his prized prospect in spring training the following year. "The kid has looked very good and I am sure he can help us," Grimm said. "When a pitcher shows as much as he has, you have to find a spot for him."[4] But as the team headed north to begin the 1954 campaign, Jay found himself part of the bullpen corps. During the season he appeared in just 15 games, all but one as a reliever. In 18 innings Jay walked 16 batters and struck out 13. He gave up 13 runs for an earned run average of 6.50, to go with a record of 1-0.

After the season, Jay married the former Lois Elizabeth Bruggen on October 19 at St. Sebastian's Catholic Church in Middletown. The couple honeymooned in Puerto Rico, where Jay had signed to play winter ball for Caguas. They also raised five children.

In 1955, with the bonus label now removed, Jay could be sent to the minor leagues to work on his pitching. The Braves had a lot of money invested in the 19-year-old and wanted to exhaust every attempt to get their fair share back on that investment. However, Jay stuck with Milwaukee for the first half of the season. He enjoyed little success, pitching in only 12 games, all out of the bullpen except for one start. He gave up 23 hits and 13 walks in 19 innings. Finally, in early July, the Braves sent Jay to their farm team at Toledo of the Triple-A American Association. He made 11 starts for the Mud Hens and went 3-3, walking 44 batters in 74 innings. Jay could fire the ball, but was having control problems.

The next season, 1956, Jay split his time between Double-A (Atlanta of the Southern Association) and Triple-A (Wichita, American Association). For the first time in his career, he was getting consistent starts and 13 relief appearances. With the Crackers, he was 3-0 with a 2.92 earned-run average, and hurled two shutouts.

Jay pitched a full season for Wichita in 1957, posting a 17-10 record with a 3.31 ERA, despite starting the season 2-6. He struck out 199 batters in 223 innings, and led the league with 18 complete games. In a late-season call-up, he pitched in one game for Milwaukee and was the winning pitcher in the extra-inning contest. He was now 21 years old. What caused the turnaround in his game? After his 2-6 start, he said, "Ben Geraghty (Wichita manager) helped a lot," Jay said. "Besides that I used a slider a lot more and now it's my best pitch.

Bucky Walters taught it to me when he was a Braves coach but I didn't pitch enough then to try it."[5]

Jay was in the majors to stay as the 1958 season rolled around. His confidence was high, as was that of the Braves. Milwaukee had captured the 1957 World Series, besting the New York Yankees in seven games behind Lew Burdette's three victories. The Braves were looking for more of the same with a lineup including Del Crandall, Johnny Logan, Wes Covington, Eddie Mathews, and Hank Aaron. The ageless Warren Spahn, Bob Buhl, and Burdette anchored the pitching staff. It looked as if Jay was falling into an ideal situation for a young player.

Still, Jay didn't get his first start until that mid-June evening in St. Louis. After winning that one, Jay caught fire in July. He started seven games, completed five, and posted a 5-2 record. His ERA was a sparkling 1.39, and he struck out 46 batters in 58 1/3 innings. He was named the NL Player of the Month. Bad luck: On July 29, he pulled a tendon in his right elbow, and had pain up to his shoulder when he threw a curve or changeup. In his next appearance, a start until August 14 against Cincinnati, he was wild, walking eight, but yielded only one hit, and with one inning of relief from Spahn, he defeated the Reds, 3-0. Jay lost his next start, 7-2 to the Los Angeles Dodgers, on the 19th, then didn't pitch again until September 17, in relief of Spahn against the Cardinals, and suffered more bad luck when a hard groundball off the bat of the Cardinals' Irv Noren smashed into Jay's glove hand. He threw Noren out but suffered a hairline fracture to the second knuckle of his ring finger. The Braves won the pennant again, but Jay was a mere spectator in the World Series. The Yankees exacted revenge on Milwaukee, this time winning in seven games. Jay ended the season with a 7-5 record and a 2.14 ERA. He had 74 strikeouts but walked 43 in 96 2/3 innings. Despite the powerful Braves lineup, they could muster only six runs in his five losses. In the games Jay started, his run support was a paltry 2.58 per nine innings.

Braves pitching coach Whitlow Wyatt was pleased with Jay's work. "He's getting it too," said Wyatt. "He uses (the slider) pretty good off his curve now. But he's right—a pitcher has to pitch to improve. For a youngster who hasn't has much of a chance, Joe has been a hard worker."[6]

For all his success in 1958, Jay went in reverse in 1959. He got off to a bad start and was ineffective for the entire season. Veterans Bob Buhl and Bob Rush took up the slack in the rotation, and Joey was demoted to the bullpen. Manager Fred Haney offered another reason why Jay was not having a successful year. "Jay hasn't done a lot of running in the outfield and no pitcher is any stronger than his legs," said Haney. "I don't think he's in shape to pitch—and I don't think he has been all season. Until he shows me that he means business, he's in the bullpen."[7] Jay finished the season at 6-11, with an ERA of 4.09. The Braves tied Los Angeles for first place, but were swept in two games during a best-of-three playoff. Jay pitched 2 1/3 scoreless innings in the second game, a 6-5 loss in 12 innings.

Haney resigned on October 4, saying he wanted to spend more time with his family. He was replaced by Charlie Dressen, who had skippered clubs in Cincinnati, Brooklyn, and Washington. Although Haney may have been harsh at times with Jay, attacking his lazy approach and his unwillingness to get into shape, Dressen chose to start fresh with Joey. He ran Jay in spring training, but encouraged and supported him more than Haney had. Dressen hinted that Jay would become a relief pitcher full time in 1960. Jay made 11 starts during the season, and came out of the bullpen in 21 games. He did not record his first victory until June 20, pitching in relief of Buhl and shutting down the Dodgers over the final 6 2/3 innings of a game the Braves won 4-1. On August 25, he was moved into the rotation and from then until the end of the season, he made seven starts, posting a 5-2 record and a 2.66 ERA in that span. For the year he was 9-8 with an ERA of 3.24.

In the offseason Jay and another young Braves pitcher Juan Pizarro, were traded to Cincinnati for shortstop Roy McMillan. Former Reds manager Birdie Tebbetts had moved to Milwaukee as executive vice president (he eventually stepped in as manager, replacing Dressen) and coveted McMillan, his former Reds shortstop. Jay was unfazed by his move to the Queen City. "I don't think changing clubs will be a handicap," he said. "You change friends and teammates, but you do that when you bounce around in the minors, too. I'll pitch to win no matter what club I'm with. I guess it will be odd the first time or two I face the Braves. But Milwaukee will be the club I'll want to beat most of all."[8]

As it turned out, Jay did not pitch oddly against the Braves at all in 1961. In five starts he was 4-0 with a 2.32 ERA against his former mates. "My years with the Braves are in the past," Joey remarked. "I don't believe in rubbing it in. The Reds are my team now, and I'm happy."[9] And it wasn't just the Braves that Jay got the best of; it was almost every other opponent. Jay pitched his way to a 21-10 record with a 3.53 ERA and a league-leading four shutouts. He struck out 157 batters. His 247 1/3 innings were more than 100 over his previous high, and all 34 of his appearances were starts. Jay had a rocky beginning, losing his first three outings. But he caught fire in May, winning all six starts, and was named the National League Player of the Month. He was selected to the All-Star team, but did not participate in either of the two contests played that season.

Jay's 20th victory was a 1-0, four-hit shutout of the Braves on September 13. He retired Mathews, Aaron, and Joe Adcock in order in the ninth inning. "It's the strongest game I pitched this season," Jay said after the game." I threw everything hard and tried to get it to the spots I wanted."[10] He was the first Reds pitcher to win 20 games since Ewell Blackwell won 22 in 1947. Jay tied his former teammate Spahn in wins and shutouts. He was named the starting pitcher on *The Sporting News* NL All-Star Team. Teammate Jim O'Toole won 19 games and Bob Purkey tallied 16 victories. The strong pitching, combined with the power of the Reds' outfield triumvirate, Frank Robinson, Vada Pinson, and Wally Post, plus the hitting of third baseman Gene Freese, propelled the Reds to the pennant, four games ahead of the Los Angeles Dodgers. Milwaukee finished fourth, 10 games out of first.

"I'm pitching the same way I did when I was with the Braves," he says. "No one taught me any new pitches or anything like that. The difference is that I'm getting a chance to pitch with the Reds. It's hard to work much when you have guys like Spahn, Burdette and Buhl around. Last year I started 11 games and won six of them. This year I started 34 games and won 21. That's the only difference."[11]

The Reds' opponent in the World Series was the New York Yankees. Right fielder Roger Maris had a memorable year as well, his 61 home runs eclipsing Babe Ruth's single-season record by one. Teammate Mickey Mantle hit 54 homers, but his season was cut short by an infected abscess on his right hip.

The Yankees flexed their muscles, winning the Series in five games. Jay won the only game for the Reds, a complete-game 6-2 victory in Game Two at Yankee Stadium. He started the deciding Game Five but was pulled in the first inning with two outs, having given up three runs. The Yankees got two more runs in the inning as they won the game, 13-5, and the Series. Jay had Bobby Richardson picked off first base with two outs, but an error by first baseman Gordy Coleman kept the inning alive for the Yankees. Johnny Blanchard homered, Elston Howard doubled, and the floodgates opened up on Jay and the Reds.

When Jay signed with Milwaukee, he invested some of his bonus money in a poultry farm in Lutz, Florida, about 40 miles from St. Petersburg. Now, with almost a decade in the major leagues, he was preparing for life when his career was over. With a partner, Allen Beard, he formed the J&B Drilling Company in the West Virginia oil country, and the company had some success finding petroleum.

Like most players of his day, when multiyear deals were rare, Jay played on a succession of one-year contracts. Seeking a bigger deal for 1962, he offered to buy out his contract out for a reported $150,000. When owner-general manager Bill DeWitt refused, Jay raised the pot to $200,000. Again DeWitt refused his offer. Eventually Jay signed. "After a while, you just get tired of arguing with them," he said. "Every time you attempt to make a point, they throw a statistic at you."[12]

Jay repeated his 21-victory season in 1962, losing 14 games. He was the first Reds pitcher to have successive 20-win seasons since Bucky Walters in 1939 and '40. Jay set a personal high for innings pitched (273), struck out 155, and posted a 3.76 ERA. He was 3-1 against the Braves in four games, with an incredible 1.35 ERA. In winning his 14th game, against Pittsburgh on July 24, he hurt his pitching shoulder, but received cortisone shots and remained in the rotation. He credited his manager, Fred Hutchinson, for much of his success. "I have to give Hutch a lot of credit," Jay said after defeating the Braves on July 29. "I've gotten a lot of wins this year because he has stuck with me."[13]

But Jay had outings that could annoy a pitcher no end. On August 29 he pitched a career-high 12 2/3 innings but lost to the Dodgers, 2-1, as the Reds left 13 men on base. (He also set a career high in that game with nine walks, none of which figured in the scoring.)

Jay helped himself in two of his victories by hitting his only two major-league home runs. On May 1 he connected for a three-run shot against the New York Mets in an 8-2 win at the Polo Grounds. On May 28 he clouted a two-run homer at Crosley Field against the Houston Colt .45s in a 9-6 win for the Reds.

Bob Purkey won 23 games for the Reds that season, and Jim O'Toole won 16 to go with Jay's 21 victories. But the team finished in third place, 3 1/2 games behind pennant winner San Francisco and 2 1/2 games in back of runner-up Los Angeles. Against the Giants and Dodgers, the Reds were 16-20. Cincinnati was 58-23 at home, but only 40-41 on the road.

Jay touched off a controversy that season over his pitching motion. He was trying out a new way to speed up his delivery, one that San Francisco manager Alvin Dark and Los Angeles skipper Walter Alston claimed was a balk. Dark complained to NL President Warren Giles that Jay pitched "from two different set positions with runners on base."[14] Sometimes he would stand on the rubber, his hands clasped, get the sign from the catcher and pitch. Other times, he went into a quick stretch, came to the set position and pitched. "A guy does something different and right away everyone claims it's illegal," said Reds manager Hutchinson. "What is the difference whether Jay stands on the rubber with his hands clasped or they're hanging at his sides?"[15] Giles allowed Jay's new pitching style, but said it would be subject to review by the league presidents. During the offseason, a rule was enacted prohibiting Jay from using his new method of pitching. In effect, the ruling ended Jay's no-windup delivery, as well as his no-windup move to first base.

Always a slow starter when the season began, Jay in 1963 lost his first six starts before finally winning on May 11 against the Mets. But he could not right the ship, and after dropping a 3-2 decision to St. Louis on August 1, his record stood at 4-15. "It looks as if I'm going to have my third straight 20-game season — 20 losses," he cracked. "I feel bad when I lose because I want to help the club. Personally, though, one more loss now doesn't mean much to me."[16] He finished the season with a 7-18 record and a 4.29 ERA. Although Jay may not have pitched well, his run support was under three runs a game (2.91). He also pitched through a sore right shoulder, and this time a cortisone shot would not do the trick. After August 16 Jay made only one start while pitching six games in relief. Hutchinson may have taken him out of the rotation to keep him from losing 20 games.

Jay's relationship with his manager took a plunge the next season. Joey asked Hutchinson for permission to leave the Reds' 1964 spring training camp in Tampa, Florida, to return home and tend to personal business. Hutchinson denied his request, but Jay left anyway. Hutchinson, backed by Bill DeWitt, said Jay would be penalized financially when he returned to camp. "We can't tolerate any player walking out on us," the manager said. The feud was on and it carried over into the season. Jay wanted out of Cincinnati, and felt that he was on the trading block because of perceived chronic arm trouble. "I wouldn't blame a club for thinking that may be true,"[17] he said.

Jay got little sympathy from *The Sporting News*, which said in an editorial, "A decade ago, Jay received a substantial bonus from the Braves. This club waited patiently for years for a return on the investment, never received it and finally dealt Jay to Cincinnati. There, in 1961 and 1962, Jay developed into an outstanding pitcher. Last year, however, he fell far off the pace of the two preceding years. Despite this, Jay is one of the higher-salaried hurlers in baseball. Jay has little, if any, reason to yelp. Baseball has been more than good to him for over ten years. With good pitching as scarce as it is, all he has to do to stay in the high salary bracket is to correct his attitude and bear down in behalf of the Reds."[18]

For all the off-field fireworks, on the diamond Jay again bounced back. He finished with an 11-11 mark and a 3.39 ERA. In 183 innings he struck out 134 batters and walked only 36. On August 11 he struck out 13, his career high for a game, in a 4-2 victory over Los Angeles. On September 4 he struck out 12 in a 2-0 loss to the Braves. He had some hard luck. On June 30 he fired a two-hitter at Wrigley Field against the Cubs. But Chicago's Larry Jackson was better, giving up only one hit, a single to Pete Rose, in a 1-0 victory over Jay. "What does a guy have to do to win a game?" Hutchinson said in July. "He pitches three complete games, gives up only five runs, and what does he have? Three losses."[19]

Hutchinson became ill and was hospitalized for cancer treatment in late July. Coach Dick Sisler was named interim manager. Sisler, the son of St. Louis Browns great George Sisler, piloted the team to a 32-21 record in the second half of the season. Hutchinson died on November 12 at the age of 45.

On September 13 the Reds were in third place, seven games behind Philadelphia. The Cardinals were also threatening the Phillies' lead. From the 13th to the 27th, the Reds won 13 of 15 games, including nine in a row. Three of those victories were over Philadelphia, and launched the Phillies' ignominious collapse under a ten-game losing streak. On the 27th Jay defeated the New York Mets, 3-1, in the second game of a doubleheader and the Reds moved into first place, one game ahead of the Phillies and a game and a half over St. Louis. But finishing at Crosley Field, the Reds lost four of their last five games and the Cardinals won four of six, winning the pennant by a game.

After Hutchinson's death in November, the Reds removed the "interim" label from Sisler's title. Jay, stricken with the flu, was unable to make his first spring-training start until March 28. But he was ready when the 1965 season began. After a three-inning relief appearance on April 17, Jay made his first start four days later and defeated Chicago, 9-2, at Wrigley Field. He and O'Toole also worked out of the bullpen to bolster the relief corps as Sisler searched for a winning rotation. Jay was sidelined with elbow pain from late June until July 18. He pitched through the discomfort and was 8-2 after a victory on July 23. By September he was pitching out of the bullpen, except for two starts, and did not have much success. After the great start, he produced only one more victory, winding up with a 9-8 record and a 4.22 ERA. The Reds finished fourth in the ten-team NL, eight games behind the pennant-winning Dodgers.

Don Heffner replaced Sisler as the Reds manager in 1966. Jay, who took a pay cut, was sanguine about his future in Cincinnati. "You get 30 and over and you go," he said. "Look at Frank Robinson, he just turned 30 and he left."[20] (Robinson had been traded to Baltimore at the end of the 1965 season.)

As usual, Jay got off to a slow start in 1966. After losing his first two outings, he won his next five. Jay's last start for the Reds came on June 1. He had a no-decision in seven innings against the Pirates, allowing seven hits and striking out four. His record stood at 6 wins and 2 defeats. Two days later, just before the trading deadline, he was traded to the Atlanta Braves for pitcher Hank Fischer. "I was surprised more than anything else," Jay said. "Don Heffner and I were getting along just fine. I don't think he had anything to do with the deal."[21] But Jay failed to win a game with the Braves in eight starts. He was released after the season. He was 30 years old.

Jay signed a minor-league deal with Philadelphia in 1967. When the Phillies ended spring training, Jay stayed behind in Clearwater, Florida, then was assigned to the Tidewater Tides of the Class A Carolina League. After making four starts and going 3-1 there, Jay was released. The Phillies were convinced that the speed he once had was now gone.

In retirement, as he was during his playing career, Jay was an active businessman. J&B Drilling grew to own 75 to 100 oil wells. He also owned or was a part owner of taxicab companies, a fleet of limousines, a carpet-cleaning business and two building maintenance firms. "I started to mingle with all kinds of wheeler-dealers, and before I knew it I owned several oil fields in West Virginia," he said.

Jay, a western Florida resident, adopted a life without baseball. He declined to attend card shows or fantasy camps, and embraced a very low profile contrasted to his former public life. "I don't live in the past, like most ballplayers," he said. "I don't wear my World Series rings, my mother has my scrapbooks, and if someone offered me a baseball job, I'd turn it down in a minute. When I made the break, it was clean and forever. It's infantile to keep thinking about the game. It gets you nowhere. Most ex-ballplayers keep on living in some destructive fantasy world. Not me. I'm happier than ever since I left. And do me a favor. Don't mention where I live."[22]

Sources

The Sporting News.

Baseball Digest.

Sports Illustrated.

National Baseball Hall of Fame Archives.

1930 United States Census.

sabr.org

retrosheet.org

minors.sabrwebs.com/cgi-bin/index.php

cincinnati.reds.mlb.com/index.jsp?c_id=cin

hardballtimes.com

Notes

1. Cleon Walfoort, "The Three Turning Points for Joey Jay," *Baseball Digest*, February 1959.
2. Ibid.
3. Arthur Dailey, "Oversize Little Leaguer," *New York Times*, August 24, 1958.
4. Bob Wolf, "Joey Jay Is Possible Mound Sleeper Among Braves' Mound Hopefuls," *Milwaukee Journal*, March 14, 1954.
5. Bob Wolf, "Poundage No Problem, Says Ponderous Joey Jay," *Milwaukee Journal*, February 25, 1958.
6. Bob Wolf, "Jay," *Milwaukee Journal*, June 19, 1958.
7. Bob Wolf, "Jay Is Demoted to Bullpen Duty by Irate Haney," *Milwaukee Journal*, July 16, 1959.
8. Lou Smith "Presenting Joey Jay," *Cincinnati Inquirer*, February 23, 1961.
9. Earl Lawson, "Hutch Helps Hurler Build Up Confidence," *Cincinnati Post & Times Star*, June 16, 1961.
10. Earl Lawson, "Jay Wins No. 20," *Cincinnati Post & Times Star*, September 14, 1961.
11. Walter Bingham, "Arms and the Men for Cincy," *Sports Illustrated*, October 9, 1961.
12. Earl Lawson, "Joey Jay Trying Out New Pitching Style," Player files, National Baseball Hall of Fame.
13. Earl Lawson, "Shot of Cortisone Kayoes Worries Over Jay's Wing," *The Sporting News*, August 11, 1962.
14. Earl Lawson, "Jay's Speedy New Slab Tempo Triggers Torrent of Squawks," *The Sporting News*, September 29, 1962.
15. Ibid.
16. Earl Lawson, "Jay Can Still Joke, Despite Dismal Year," *The Sporting News,* August 17, 1963.
17. Associated Press, "Jay Goes Home, but Howard Decides to Stay," March 13, 1964. Player files, National Baseball Hall of Fame.
18. Editorial, "Jay Has No Basis for Squawk," editorial, *The Sporting News,* May 30, 1964.
19. Earl Lawson, "Reds Play Riding Hood, Rather Than Wolf in Old Casey's Den," *The Sporting News*, July 25, 1964.
20. Earl Lawson, "Comebacker of '66? Jay Early Choice," *The Sporting News*, April 2, 1966.
21. Furman Bisher, "Memoirs of a Bonus Baby," *Atlanta Journal*, June 22, 1966.
22. Player files, National Baseball Hall of Fame.

Ernie Johnson

By Dana Sprague

A RIGHT-HANDED RELIEF pitcher whose major-league career spanned the entire decade of the 1950s, Ernie Johnson retired with a lifetime record of 40-23 and an ERA of 3.77 in 273 games. "Maybe not the stuff of Cooperstown," remembered Hall of Famer Eddie Mathews, a former teammate, "but damn it, the man could pitch."[1] Johnson's even greater claim to fame, however, was as a television broadcaster for the Atlanta Braves His 52-year association with the Braves was the longest of any person in the organization.

The youngest of three children, Ernest Thorwald Johnson was born in Brattleboro, Vermont, on June 16, 1924. His father, Thorwald, and his mother, Alina "Inkie" Ingeborg, had emigrated from Sweden in the early 1900s. They were lured to Brattleboro by the Estey Organ Company, a world-famous manufacturer of pipe organs. With many Swedes among its 300 employees, Estey was one of the biggest employers in Vermont around the turn of the century, and the neighborhood where Ernie Johnson grew up, close to the Estey factory, was known as Esteyville. Ernie's father worked at Estey for 45 years, and also delivered newspapers on Sundays during the Great Depression.

Johnson recalled that he sometimes went along on those delivery runs "just to be with my father and read the sports page."[2] The children of Esteyville were crazy for sports, and Ernie's first paying job was caddying at the local golf course. "A caddie received 35 cents for nine holes and 60 cents for eighteen," he remembered. He occasionally played a round when he was not caddying, but for the most part his free time was spent in neighborhood games of baseball, football, or basketball, depending on the season. "We played pickup baseball games over on the hospital grounds and neighborhood teams at Oak Grove School," Johnson remembered. "We also played baseball and basketball teams at Austine School for the Deaf. I became friends with several of the deaf students" Growing up in Vermont, Johnson never played Little League baseball; in fact, the Little League field in Brattleboro was not built until 1952, ten years after he made his professional debut.

Ernie's first taste of organized sports came in high school. He always had above-average size and was a good all-around athlete, but most felt that his best sport was basketball. His father installed a hoop outside their house, and Johnson recalled that he and his friends played even in the snow.

Yale University was interested in Ernie as a basketball player. Even after he chose baseball as his profession, Ernie stayed in shape during winters by playing semipro basketball in Vermont and professional basketball in Connecticut.

According to most accounts, Johnson was merely an average baseball player until 1942, his senior year at Brattleboro High School. He actually lost his first game that season, 8-1 to a strong team from Greenfield,

Ernie Johnson (National Baseball Hall of Fame Library, Cooperstown, N.Y.)

Massachusetts, but only one of the runs was earned. Ernie bounced back with a win in his next start, taking a shutout two outs into the ninth inning before yielding a two-run homer.

Johnson's next three games comprise one of the most unusual pitching streaks in the history of high-school baseball in Vermont. On May 8 he pitched a one-hit shutout against Springfield. In his next game, against Bellows Falls on May 13, he pitched another one-hitter, this time taking a no-hitter into the ninth inning before giving up a single. Then on May 20 he took another no-hitter into the ninth inning in a game against Deerfield, Massachusetts. Again his no-hit bid was spoiled, this time by a pair of hits with one out, but he also struck out 20 in what was probably the best game of his high-school career.

For the 1942 season, Johnson pitched all but two of Brattleboro's games, averaging 12 strikeouts, compiling a 6-3 record, a 1.09 earned-run average, and a .409 batting average, and leading the team with 13 RBIs. At the time, though, almost nobody thought he was a potential major leaguer. When asked about it years later, one of Johnson's former teammates replied, "It never entered my mind or any of our other teammates' minds. Baseball players from Brattleboro, Vermont, just don't make it to the major leagues."[3] One man, however, thought differently. Ray Draghetti, Johnson's coach at Brattleboro High School, believed his 6'4", 180-lb. pitcher had the size and talent to make the majors. After graduation, Draghetti took him to Boston for a couple of tryouts, as described in Bob Dubuque's article in the June 19, 1942, edition of the *Brattleboro Reformer*:

"We haven't been asleep, but just careful in not reporting that Ernie Johnson was down in Boston for a few days trying out with the Red Sox. It got pretty well noised around, but we wanted to wait until the kid got home again to find out what the story was.

"Ray Draghetti, who took Ernie to Boston yesterday to work out with the Braves, said the [Red] Sox were interested in the Brattleboro High School star and let him read the fine print on a contract, which he did not sign. The [Red] Sox wanted Ernie to stay home and put on some beef this summer and go south with them on a farm team in the winter. However, it would appear to be a summer wasted here since there is little prospect of semipro ball. That's the story to date."

One week after the tryouts, Casey Stengel's Boston Braves gave Ernie the choice of traveling with the big-league team and throwing batting practice or signing a contract and reporting directly to the minors. He chose the former, and within ten days he was 100 miles from home, pitching batting practice to a team that included future Hall of Famers Paul Waner and Ernie Lombardi. Before his tryout with the Red Sox, Ernie had never been to a major-league game.

After 2 1/2 weeks of traveling with the Braves, Johnson signed a minor-league contract, receiving $125 per month and a signing bonus of $100. The Braves sent him to Hartford of the Class A Eastern League, for whom he made his professional debut on August 9, 1942. Johnson pitched in only eight games that summer, posting a 2-2 record and a 2.84 ERA, but one of them stood out in his memory: "My mom was a homemaker, a great mom. She went to Hartford once to watch me pitch and I gave up a three-run homer. The fans started booing. She turned to some of them and proudly said, 'That's my boy.' They slumped down in their seats quietly."

Before the 1943 season Johnson was drafted into the US Marine Corps. He participated in the Okinawa invasion and was discharged as a staff sergeant in February 1946. His family liked to joke that America was losing the war when he entered the service and had won by the time he was discharged.

Johnson returned to Brattleboro in 1946. That winter, while attending a high-school basketball game, he first noticed Lois Denhard, a cheerleader. They were married a year later. "When we first met, she asked me what I did. I said, 'Play baseball,' and she said, 'No, really, what do you do for a living?' After she saw my first minor-league check, she asked again." The next several years were like a roller-coaster ride for the Johnsons. After only one inning of work with Hartford in 1946, Ernie was demoted to Pawtucket of the Class B New England League. Although he pitched adequately, as attested by his 3.95 ERA, Johnson was 4-7, one of only two losing records in his 14 years as a professional pitcher.

He returned to Hartford and posted winning records in 1947 and 1948, and in 1949 he earned a promotion to the Braves' Triple-A affiliate, the Milwaukee Brewers of the American Association. After only 11 innings, however, the Braves demoted him to Class A Denver. Undaunted, Johnson became one of the best pitchers in the Western League, and his 15-5 record and 2.37 ERA earned him a place on the all-star team.

The Boston Braves invited Johnson to spring training as a nonroster player in 1950. After giving up a home run to Ted Williams in an exhibition game, Johnson remembered manager Billy Southworth saying, "Don't worry, kid, he's hit 'em off better pitchers than you." The resilient Vermonter surprised everyone by breaking camp with the big-league club. For the first time he was earning what he describes as "real money"—$5,000 a year.

Johnson made his major-league debut in Philadelphia on April 28, 1950, becoming the only player from Brattleboro ever to play in the majors. Although he pitched in only 16 games, he managed to hang on with the Braves for most of the season. Johnson was 2-0, but his 6.97 ERA probably accounts for his late-season demotion to Hartford.

The Braves sent Johnson to the minors again in 1951, this time to Milwaukee, but he refused to become discouraged. He went 15-4, led the American Association in ERA (2.62) and winning percentage (.789), and pitched the Brewers to the Governors' Cup and a Junior World Series victory over the Montreal Royals. Including his five postseason victories, Johnson was a 20-game winner in 1951.

Johnson started the 1952 season with Boston, and this time he was in the majors to stay. Bothered by a sore arm, Ernie pitched mostly in relief and went 6-3 for the Braves. He also received ten starting assignments and pitched a shutout in one of them—one of only three complete games he pitched in the major leagues.

For the rest of his career Johnson pitched almost exclusively in relief, which was surprising because as a starter his worst inning was usually the first. Also surprising for a reliever was that his best pitch was his palmball, which was designed to induce groundballs, not strikeouts. "He made my job a lot easier," Eddie Mathews remembered. "His palmball would sink and it kept me busy."

Before the 1953 season, the Braves left Boston, where they were always less popular than the Red Sox, and headed west for Milwaukee, where Johnson had played minor-league ball just two years earlier. It was the first change of cities for a major-league franchise in half a century, and the Braves' success in Milwaukee guaranteed that it would not be the last. From 1953 to 1957, in the major-league city with the smallest population, the Braves averaged 2.1 million in attendance, almost doubling their nearest competitor.

Johnson remembered the euphoria of those early years in Milwaukee: "I've been in baseball for more than three decades, and I've never seen anything remotely close to Milwaukee in the '50s. They were wild, incredible years. Nobody cared in Boston whether we lived or died. Then, in Milwaukee, the town went bananas. We couldn't buy a thing—fans would give us everything free. The players were treated like royalty. Every day was a feast.

"The news of the shift had come in spring training down in Bradenton. When we went north to Milwaukee, they had a huge parade and we went downtown. When we got there, I'll never forget how the people put up a Christmas tree—in April—inside the Schroeder Hotel. They were so beautiful. They said that since we'd missed Christmas with them, they wanted to celebrate it with us now. So there were hundreds of presents under the tree—shaving kits, toiletries, radios, appliances. Just ga-ga from the first day.

"It was like a small town. Some of us lived five minutes from the park. In those first few years we'd go around town, and even when we tried, we couldn't pay for what we bought—the sponsors wouldn't let us." Johnson himself got off to a poor start to the 1953 season—so poor, in fact, that he thought he might be headed back to the minors. But things turned around, and in one stretch of seven days he received credit for three victories. He became a mainstay in the bullpen of a great Milwaukee pitching staff. His 35 relief appearances led the team, and his 2.67 ERA was second on the staff to Warren Spahn's league-leading 2.10.

Johnson followed up that performance in 1954 by posting a 2.81 ERA in 40 games, establishing himself as one of the premier relief pitchers in baseball. Toward the end of that season the citizens of Brattleboro planned a special day in his honor which was recounted in Vic Harrison's article "Toast for a Great Guy" in the *Brattleboro Reformer*.

Though the New York Yankees were the dominant team of the 1950s, the Braves, with future Hall of Famers like Mathews, Spahn, and Henry Aaron, more than held their own. The Braves won the pennant in 1957 and met the New York Yankees in the World Series. Johnson remembered the thrill of pitching in Yankee Stadium: "I remember walking to the mound and all I could think of was, 'Son, you've made it. You've finally made it.' God, I was so happy. I was walking with the ghosts of Ruth and Gehrig—me, just a kid who had lived and died baseball all his life."

The Braves won the 1957 World Series in seven games, and Johnson played a major role. Pitching in Games One, Three, and Six, he gave up only two hits and one run in seven innings, striking out eight and walking one. The only run he gave up was a homer off the foul pole by Hank Bauer that proved to be the winning run in Game Six, but when asked if he thought it was a cheap shot, Johnson replied with characteristic modesty: "There was nothing cheap about that home run. He hit it so hard it may have bent the pole."

After the World Series, Johnson returned to Brattleboro for a welcome-home dinner. He was billed as "Brattleboro's Own World Series Hero," and family, friends, and local dignitaries attended.[4] Among them was Bill Jackowski, a National League umpire from nearby North Walpole, New Hampshire. A story has it that in one game Ernie complained to Bill about his calls on ball and strikes. Jackowski took off his mask and said, "This isn't the West River Valley League in Vermont. Stop complaining and just throw the ball." "That [story] may be true," Johnson said, "but we both had great respect for each other. Billy once told me we were friends off the field, but on the field I don't know you and it was understood that we both had jobs to do."

The 1958 season would be Johnson's last as a player in Milwaukee. Pitching in only 15 games, he once again had a winning record (3-1), but his ERA ballooned to 8.10. Before the season was over, the Braves, who were on their way to another World Series matchup against the Yankees, placed the 34-year-old Johnson on waivers. He remembered it distinctly:

"When the Braves got waivers on me in August, I guess the race was pretty well settled and nobody wanted to pay the $20,000 to claim me along with the salary. Then the Braves were very decent with me and let it be known that I could make my deal or stay with their chain, as I pleased. I know there were stories that I tried to land with the Giants and other National League clubs, but that isn't so. The first man to call me when I was free was [Paul] Richards and I didn't look further."

Richards managed the Baltimore Orioles. Johnson spent his final year in the major leagues with Baltimore in 1959. He pitched respectably, compiling a 4-1 record and a 4.11 ERA, but the Orioles released him after the season. He signed with Cleveland, but arm troubles plagued him in the spring of 1960, and although he appeared on a baseball card that year with Cleveland, he never threw a pitch for the Indians. "They offered to send me to the minors to work things out, but I knew it was time to call it quits."

Johnson returned to Milwaukee and hosted a television show called *Play Ball*, in which he and a guest sat around talking baseball and drinking milk. One of his first guests was Joe Garagiola. When Johnson told the affable catcher that he was nervous appearing on television, Garagiola told him to "just be yourself." It was advice that worked well over the years for Johnson.

For a year Johnson handled the commentary on 20 Braves telecasts and also did some speaking on the banquet circuit, but his main job was selling life insurance for Northwestern Mutual. "I thought I'd be selling insurance the rest of my life," he recalled. But in 1962 the Braves offered him a full-time job in the front office as an administrative assistant to team president John McHale, and Ernie accepted. "Being in the front office had always been my ambition," he said. "From the time I broke into baseball, that was what I wanted to do rather than managing or coaching."

Johnson's job eventually evolved into that of a full-time broadcaster. He moved with the club to Atlanta after the 1965 season and was named Georgia Broadcaster of the Year in 1977, 1983, and 1986. He received three television Emmys. He retired as a full-time announcer at the end of the 1989 season.

Johnson's popularity with Braves fans was never more evident than on September 2, 1989, when the Braves held Ernie Johnson Day. The attendance exceeded 42,000, the largest crowd for a Braves home game that entire season. During the pregame ceremony, Johnson received a television set from his fellow broadcasters, a satellite dish and annual use of a condominium in Florida from TBS, and an automobile from the Braves. He also received proclamations from the Brattleboro selectmen and the governors of Vermont and Georgia. "It was fabulous," Johnson exuded. "… It was the greatest day I have ever had and it is something Lois and the whole family will never forget."[5]

By 2000 Johnson was semiretired, living in Alpharetta, Georgia, and spending lots of time with his wife, three children (daughters Dawn and Chris are teachers, and Ernie Jr., following in his father's footsteps, was a sportscaster for WTBS and on network sports, and seven grandchildren). He still called about 30 games a year on Sports South Network and substituted occasionally on TBS. Over his 32 years in broadcasting, Johnson worked more than 4,100 games, and through it all maintained his grace and gentle humor. For all of the home runs hit by Hank Aaron and knuckleballs thrown by Phil Niekro, nobody spread more goodwill for the Braves than Johnson. "I love baseball," he once said, "and I think it shows."

Johnson was inducted into five Halls of Fame: the Braves Hall of Fame, the Atlanta Sports Hall of Fame, the Georgia Radio Hall of Fame, the Georgia TV Hall of Fame, and the Georgia Sports Hall of Fame.

After an extended battle with congestive heart failure, Johnson died on August 12, 2011, in Cumming, Georgia. While going through the many passages from the online tributes Braves fans had posted about his father, Ernie Jr. read one that buckled his knees. It said, "When you heard Ernie Johnson do a game, it was like summertime would never end."[6]

Sources

A version of this biography originally appeared in *Green Mountain Boys of Summer: Vermonters in the Major Leagues 1882-1993*, edited by Tom Simon (New England Press, 2000).

In researching this article, the author made use of Johnson's file at the National Baseball Hall of Fame Library, the Tom Shea Collection, the archives at the University of Vermont, and several local newspapers.

Notes

1. Atlanta Braves public relations department, no date. Johnson's file at the National Baseball Hall of Fame Library.

2. All quotations, unless otherwise noted, are from the author's interview with Ernie Johnson in 1993.

3. Author's interview with high-school teammate Bob Ratti in 1993.

4. Vic Harrison, *Brattleboro* (Vermont) *Reformer*, no date, no page. Player's file at the National Baseball Hall of Fame Library.

5. Ken Campbell, *Brattleboro* (Vermont) *Reformer*, September 5, 1989, 15.

6. Carroll Rogers, "Ernie Johnson, Jr., emotional, grateful, proud following death of his father," Atlanta Braves with David O'Brien, http://blogs.ajc.com/atlanta-braves-blog/2011/08/13/ernie-johnson-jr-emotional-grateful-proud-following-death-of-his-father.

Dave Jolly

By Chip Greene

Dave Jolly was 28 years old when he made his major-league debut as a member of the Milwaukee Braves. Both he and the team arrived in Milwaukee the same year, 1953. Over the ensuing five seasons the soft-tossing, durable right-handed pitcher became an integral member of the Braves bullpen, throwing 291 innings over that span, winning 16 games and finishing second to Ernie Johnson with 158 relief appearances. By the end of the 1957 season, however, when the Braves won their only World Series for Milwaukee, Jolly's major-league career was over. After bouncing around for a few years in the minor leagues, he settled down in the small town of his birth to raise his family. Almost ten years to the day after his major-league debut, Jolly died, five months shy of his 39th birthday.

David Jolly was born in Stony Point, North Carolina, in the northwestern part of the state, on October 14, 1924, the second of five children of Ralph Jolly, a mill worker, and his wife, Minnie. At Stony Point High School, Jolly excelled at baseball and basketball; he played both sports in the local Tri-County League, too. He graduated from high school in the spring of 1942, and on April 30, 1943, Jolly enlisted in the US Army. Eventually sent overseas, Jolly was assigned to the 54th Field Hospital and saw action in France and Germany. He was discharged in December 1945 and at age 22 returned to the US, unsure of his immediate future.[1]

The origins of Jolly's professional baseball career are unclear. Whether he attended a tryout camp or was scouted around Stony Point is unknown, but in any event, early in 1946 Jolly signed with the St. Louis Browns. The Browns sent him to Mooresville of the Class D North Carolina State League. (Mooresville is 30 miles south of Stony Point.) Joining a pitching staff led by future Hall of Famer Hoyt Wilhelm, Jolly won five games and lost three in 1946, then was 14-7 in 1947 as the Moors captured the league championship. Jolly played first base and the outfield when not pitching, and in the championship season he hit .357 in 155 at-bats, with two home runs. After the season Jolly was drafted by the Cincinnati Reds, based on a recommendation from a scout named Tex Millard. "I was passing through Stony Point one day," Millard said in 1951, when "I saw a sign which said 'baseball today' and decided to take a look. I watched Jolly work and later the Reds signed him."[2]

The next two seasons in the Reds organization were more challenging for Jolly. In 1948 Cincinnati assigned him to the Tulsa Oilers of the Double-A Texas League. He walked an alarming 40 batters in 59 innings, and the Reds sent him to Class A Columbia (Sally League) where the right-hander fared much better, reducing his walks per nine innings to four. In 1949 he returned to Tulsa and spent the entire season there, but again struggled to harness his control, this time walking more than a batter an inning (222 batters in 202 innings). Control problems aside, Jolly was proving to be an innings-eater.

For 1950 the Reds promoted Jolly to Triple-A Syracuse, where he allowed more hits than innings

Dave Jolly (National Baseball Hall of Fame Library, Cooperstown, N.Y.)

pitched (162 in 146 innings) and more walks than strikeouts (76 to 74). Despite Jolly's 5-11 record, Cincinnati invited him to spring training in 1951.

In November 1950 Jolly and Doris Hunter were married; they had met while Jolly was playing with Mooresville. They had two sons, Michael and Craig, and after Jolly's premature death in 1963, mother and sons, as of 2013, continued to reside in Stony Point.

Jolly didn't stick with the Reds in 1951; on April 1 he was optioned once again to Tulsa, where he spent the entire season. The Reds once again recalled Jolly to report the following season, but on October 17 they released him outright to the Oilers. Then a change in organizations propelled him to the major leagues. In January 1952 the Kansas City Blues, the New York Yankees affiliate in the Triple-A American Association, purchased Jolly's contract from Tulsa.

The Blues decided Jolly would be a starter. That role lasted for just two games. As Jolly related a year later, "I got a start and lost that. Then I went on relief and won six."[3] And that was the conversion that sent him to the major leagues. Pitching solely in relief, he finished the season 6-1 with a 3.51 ERA. His 40 appearances were second most on the club. He was now a full-time reliever.

Jolly was particularly effective against the Milwaukee Brewers, who finished in first place, 12 games ahead of the second-place Blues. And after the season the Brewers' parent club, the Boston Braves, took Jolly in the major-league draft. In February 1953 Jolly went to Bradenton, Florida, for spring training with the Boston Braves. By the time spring training ended, he was a reliever for the Milwaukee Braves. He had grown comfortable coming out of the bullpen rather than starting. Indeed, when asked midway through training camp which he'd rather do, he replied, "I like the bullpen. I like to be on relief."[4] The press speculated that Jolly was "likely to be in the … Braves bullpen with Bob Buhl and Larry Jester."[5]

Despite his confidence, there were times during training camp when Jolly worried about making the team. He still had occasional bouts of wildness. During his seven minor-league seasons he'd issued 631 walks, an average of 5.5 per 9 innings, and had never been able to totally conquer his control. Nonetheless, Manager Charlie Grimm showed confidence in him, saying that "Dave showed me he knows how to pitch when he was with Kansas City. There are few relief pitchers with better control when his arm is right."[6] In the end, Jolly made the team.

At 6 feet tall and 160 pounds, Jolly didn't possess overpowering stuff; he had a limited repertoire, and relied on guile rather than speed to keep the batters guessing. Asked during spring training about his approach to working the hitters, he said, "I get them out, I hope, with a slider. I haven't any trick pitch, no knuckler, forkball or fadeaway; just a slider which I try to get over."[7] He kept the slider low and outside and complemented it with a "sneaky" letter-high, inside fastball. Beyond his pitching smarts, Jolly also possessed another attribute that perfectly suited him for the pressures of relief pitching. Jolly was a quiet, reserved man who rarely displayed emotion or got rattled. He carried that calm demeanor to the mound. (Bullpen mate Ernie Johnson dubbed him Gabby, the converse of his nature, and the nickname stuck.) In assessing his rookie reliever that first spring, Grimm described Jolly as "cold as granite … a cold, calculating guy. He looks and acts like a good relief pitcher. He appears to be the type who would enjoy the afternoons in the bullpen, imagining it was Central Park."[8] Jolly told a sportswriter the following season, "I can't afford to get upset when they make an error behind me, or when a dangerous hitter comes to the plate. I just throw the best pitch I have and that's it. If they hit it, they hit it and if they don't, they don't."[9] His was the perfect temperament for pitching the Braves out of trouble.

He got few of those opportunities in his rookie year. The second-place Braves had seven pitchers who totaled over 100 innings each (plus 81 more thrown by Johnson), and there were only so many innings to go around. Moreover, as Jolly said the next season in looking back on 1953, "There were times last year when I had trouble throwing a ball. I got a sore arm early last spring and it stayed with me most of the year."[10] In all, he pitched in only 24 games, working just 38 1/3 innings and losing his only decision.

Things improved noticeably for Jolly in 1954. As the Braves took a step back in the standings, dropping to third place, Jolly enjoyed the finest season of his career. It didn't take him long to stake his claim to the top spot in the bullpen. Jolly earned his first major-league win in his second appearance of the year, on April 23, in St. Louis, coming in to pitch in the bottom of the ninth with the teams tied 4-4. Jolly worked five innings, giving up one run and three hits, and gaining the win when the Braves scored two runs in the top of the 14th. It was the first of several extended outings that year. On June 8, at home against the New York Giants, he threw 7 1/3 innings, allowing five hits and three runs and striking out a career-high nine batters. On July 9 at Cincinnati, he allowed just one hit in 6 2/3 innings. He pitched six innings at Philadelphia on September 13, allowing three hits and two runs, and on the 17th he pitched five innings at St. Louis, giving up no runs and three hits.

Perhaps Jolly's finest outing of the 1954 season took place on July 17, at home against Brooklyn. On that day he made the only start of his major-league career, and pitched ten innings before being lifted for a pinch-hitter in the bottom of the tenth. Jolly allowed just four hits and one run, although he walked six. In the top of the 11th inning, Lew Burdette surrendered the winning run and took the 2-1 loss.

That season Jolly had added another pitch to his arsenal, a knuckleball. He most likely learned it from Hoyt Wilhelm during those first two seasons in Mooresville. Years later Jolly told a reporter, "I had been practicing with a knuckler for about four or five years but I was always afraid to throw it in a game. Finally, I found nerve enough to use it against the Cardinals early in the 1954 season and I was surprised how effectively it worked. I figured if it worked against a gang of hard hitters like the Cardinals, I'd be able to use it against any club. I gained confidence in the pitch and it became my best one."[11]

Indeed, just the thought that he might throw the knuckler made Jolly effective. "Actually, I don't use it much, especially when I'm called on in the middle innings," he said in July 1954. "For one thing, I'd rather have the batters expect it than get it. For another, I never can be sure what my knuckler will do. Sometimes it just hangs out there, waiting to be hit."[12]

It wasn't hit very frequently in 1954. To be sure, Jolly never had another season even close to the one he produced that year. He amassed career highs with 47 appearances, 111 1/3 innings pitched. 10 saves, and a record of 11-6. He had a fine 2.43 ERA. At 29 years old, Jolly was at the top of his game.

Jolly was also handy with a bat in his hands. In 48 at-bats during his five major-league seasons, he had 14 hits, for a .292 batting average. On June 27, 1954, in Philadelphia, Jolly relieved Ernie Johnson in the fifth inning with Milwaukee trailing 3-2. Leading off in the top of the seventh, Jolly hit his only major-league home run, off Curt Simmons, to tie the game, making himself the pitcher of record. In the bottom of the inning the Phillies got a run on a hit by Jolly's mount opponent, Simmons, and Jolly became the losing pitcher.

The remaining three years of Jolly's major-league career were marked by injuries and ineffectiveness; he never again found the form that made him such a stopper in 1954. In 1955, as the Braves again finished in second place, Jolly appeared in 36 games but was hampered throughout the season by an elbow injury that forced him from a game at Cincinnati on May 30. Afterward the right-hander told the press, "It's as if you touched me with a lighted cigarette."[13]

It wasn't the first time he'd suffered through the pain. "I had a similar injury in 1949 with Tulsa," he said, "and was out for a month. It's been bothering me off and on all spring."[14] X-rays revealed a pulled tendon, and Jolly missed much of the 1955 season, finishing with a poor 5.71 ERA and 51 walks in 58 1/3 innings. It was the worst season of his career.

By the spring of 1956 Jolly appeared to be fully recovered. He threw eight hitless innings over his first five regular-season appearances, winning two of the games. Early in the season, however, Fred Haney replaced Grimm as manager and, despite Jolly's return to health, further work became scarce for the 31-year-old. As Haney increasingly called on younger members of the Braves' pitching staff, Jolly appeared in just 29 games, pitching only 45 2/3 innings. He again battled control problems, issuing 35 walks. Returning to Stony Point for the winter, Jolly had reason to be concerned about his future with the team. As it turned out, the 1957 season would be his last in the major leagues.

For Jolly, the Braves' championship 1957 season was largely one of inactivity and speculation about his departure. As June approached and he had yet to pitch in a game, Jolly complained that Haney planned to use him only as a "give-up pitcher in big scoring games." He said, "I don't know why Fred felt that way and I've never asked him for a showdown.... With us, it's mostly hello and goodbye these days. Right now I'm just waiting around to see what he's gonna do. ... You try not to get down in the dumps, but you can't help wondering what's going to happen."[15]

After a quick start out of the gate (9-1 the first two weeks), with the big-three starters, Spahn, Burdette, and Buhl, eating up innings and limiting chances for relievers, the team began to falter in May, at one point losing seven of 12 games and falling two games behind Cincinnati. Looking for more production at the plate, management scoured the league for trade possibilities, and Jolly's name was frequently mentioned as a candidate. It was also reported that the Braves had tried to send Jolly to the minors but apparently couldn't get waivers on him and felt he was worth more than the $10,000 waiver price.[16] It was a frustrating situation for the veteran reliever.

It was not until May 24, at Wrigley Field in Chicago, that Jolly made his first appearance of the season, mopping up in the ninth inning of a 5-1 Milwaukee loss. (Jolly was the last of the Braves' players from the Opening Day roster to get into a game.) So it went for the right-hander in that championship year. He made what turned out to be his last major-league appearance on September 14, 1957, against the Dodgers at County Stadium , By season's end he had pitched just 37 2/3 innings in 23 games. During Milwaukee's World Series victory, Jolly never got into a game. On October 15, five days after the World Series ended, the Braves sold his contract to San Francisco in a straight cash deal (no waivers were involved; the purchase price was unclear).

For the next four years, the right-hander hung on in the minor leagues. At spring training with the Giants in 1958, he developed shoulder tendinitis. Unable to pitch, he was returned to the Milwaukee organization at the end of March, and was sold outright to Wichita of the American Association, for which he made 28 starts and had a 10-11 record. From 1959 through 1961 he also made stops at Houston (11-10 in 1959), Buffalo, Vancouver, Mobile and Portsmouth-Norfolk. He was invited to spring training with the Cubs in 1960, but failed to make the team. After the 1961 season, he retired as a player.

With his baseball career over, the 37-year-old Jolly settled in Stony Point. During the offseasons he had worked in Statesville, North Carolina, for John Boyle and Company, a manufacturer of awnings and industrial fabrics, and now he returned there full time. He also helped coach Statesville's Babe Ruth League All-Stars, which compete for the state championship. He taught the junior boys Sunday school class at his church, for which he'd several years earlier bought an organ with his $8,924.36 slice of the World Series winnings. Jolly became just a regular member of the community.

During this second stint in the minor leagues, Jolly had had several seizures. The first had occurred in 1959 when he was with Houston, in the American Association. Jolly spent several days in the hospital undergoing tests, but nothing conclusive was discovered. Since that time there'd been other periodic episodes as well, diagnosed as small seizures, when he seemed to be staring into space. Doctors sent him to the VA Hospital in Durham for tests, yet none were able to provide an answer. Then one day, during an exam with an ophthalmologist in Stony Point, the doctor found pressure on the optic nerve, and suspected the worst. Soon, Jolly was diagnosed with a brain tumor.

In July 1962 he underwent surgery to remove the tumor, and was listed in critical condition. In October Jolly returned to work, but in December he was again hospitalized at the VA Hospital in Durham. He never went home again. After 149 days in the hospital, with Doris at his bedside, Dave Jolly died on May 27, 1963. He was 38 years old. His sons were ages 10 and 7.

At Jolly's funeral, the Rev. Homer Good, who had been the ballplayer's pastor at Stony Point Baptist Church, summed up Jolly's career. "Dave Jolly was one of America's great athletes," the pastor said. "He played well the game he loved so much. He played well the Game of Life."

Jolly was buried at the Stony Point Cemetery. He was the second of the original Milwaukee Braves to pass away, following fellow pitcher Vern Bickford, who had died of cancer in 1960.

One posthumous remembrance of Jolly can be found near his home town. In the 1970s three ballfields were built about four miles outside of town, between Stony Point and Taylorsville. Ernie Johnson was there for the dedication that day as one of them was named after Stony Point's native son.

Sources

Burlington (North Carolina) *Daily Times News.*

Corsicana (Texas) *Daily Sun.*

Coshocton (Ohio) *Tribune.*

Milwaukee Journal.

Newark (Ohio) *Advocate.*

Rocky Mount (North Carolina) *Evening Telegram.*

Statesville (North Carolina) *Landmark.*

Statesville Daily Record.

Wisconsin Rapids Daily Tribune.

Baseball-Reference.com

Retrosheet.org

My sincerest appreciation to SABR member Bill Mortell for genealogical assistance.

Telephone conversations with Doris Jolly, Dave's widow, on August 2 and 24, 2012.

Dave Jolly player file from National Baseball Hall of Fame, Cooperstown, New York.

Notes

1. Jolly's Army enlistment record indicates that his civil occupation was as a "skilled molder."
2. *Gastonia Gazette,* May 5, 1951.
3. Unidentified article dated March 14, 1953, in Jolly's Hall of Fame file.
4. Ibid.
5. Ibid.
6. Undated and unidentified article in Jolly's Hall of Fame file.
7. Unidentified article dated March 14, 1953, in Jolly's Hall of Fame file.
8. Ibid.
9. *Milwaukee Journal,* July 28, 1954.
10. Undated and unidentified article in Jolly's Hall of Fame file.
11. Jolly's obituary, *New York Times,* June 8, 1963.
12. *Milwaukee Journal,* July 28, 1954.
13. *Wisconsin Rapids Daily Tribune,* May 31, 1955.
14. Ibid.
15. Associated Press via *Janesville Daily Gazette,* May 18, 1957.
16. Ibid.

Nippy Jones

By Dan Fields

THE NUMBERS FOR Nippy Jones in the 1957 World Series don't look like much: three games, three plate appearances, two at-bats, no runs, no hits, one hit-by-pitch. But the "shoe-polish incident" in the tenth inning of Game Four, when Jones was able to confirm that a pitch from Tommy Byrne had struck his foot by showing the plate umpire, Augie Donatelli, a smudge of black shoe polish on the ball, was a turning point in the Series and earned Jones enduring fame among Braves fans. The incident capped a career with many highlights.

Vernal Leroy Jones was born on June 29, 1925, in Los Angeles. His father, Andrew Jones, was a car painter, and his mother, Leona Sims-Jones, worked as a secretary at a manufacturing company. In a 1989 interview the ballplayer explained how he got his nickname: "My father was nicknamed Nip. He liked to take a nip of the bottle now and then. When I'd tag along with him, [people] used to say, 'There goes Nip and Little Nipper.' From then on, Nippy just stuck. With a name like Vernal, I guess you have to have a nickname."[1]

His parents later divorced, and the boy lived most of his early years in the crowded home of his grandparents, George and Dora Sims. According to family lore, young Nippy liked to water the roses. Unfortunately, they were the roses on the carpet of his grandmother's parlor! Jones thought of himself as an only child, because his half-brother (20 years his junior) was born to his father and his wife, Gladys, while Nippy was in the Pacific during World War II. His mother married several times but did not have any more children.

In 1939, while attending Edison Junior High in Los Angeles, Jones met the girl who would become his wife, Nora Frances Graff. However, it wasn't love at first sight: Nora had to fall off her bicycle several times in front of Nippy's house before he really took notice. In a 1997 interview, Nora said of Nippy, "He was a handsome boy and young man. The girls fell all over themselves trying to get his attention. He played all sports—baseball, basketball, and football—and was very popular."[2]

While attending John C. Fremont High School in Los Angeles, Jones, who batted and threw right-handed, played baseball on the school team and also on an American Legion team, Sunrise Post 357. (A fellow infielder with Jones on both teams was Gene Mauch.) In 1942 the Sunrise team won the American Legion World Series in Manchester, New Hampshire, where Jones got to meet Babe Ruth. Scouts at the series were impressed by Jones's play, and after he returned to Los Angeles, he was offered several contracts.

In early 1943, when Jones was still 17 years old, his father signed a contract for him with the St. Louis Cardinals organization. To the dismay of his mother and his girlfriend, Nora, Jones dropped out of high school and traveled north to join the Sacramento Solons (then a Cardinals farm team) of the Pacific Coast League. In the 1943 season he played 129 games at second base, leading the team in doubles (25) and batting average (.304) and tying for most triples (6). Jones

Nippy Jones (National Baseball Hall of Fame Library, Cooperstown, N.Y.)

earned $75 a month and sent most of the money home to his mother.

In September 1943 Jones (now 18 years old) joined the Marines. Cheryl Noss, one of Jones's four daughters, said, "The war in the Pacific was not going well, and Dad decided it was his duty to serve. He was an excellent shot and had a skill for teaching others to shoot. He was promoted to corporal and became a rifle instructor in boot camp at Pendleton. He was in the 38th Replacement Battalion, and they joined the Fifth Marine Division."[3]

Baseball may well have saved Jones's life. According to Noss, "The Fifth Marine Division was getting ready to sail to Iwo Jima when dad and his best friend, Wimpy Quinn, were called back to Pearl Harbor in Hawaii to play baseball for the Admiralty. They boarded a plane for Hawaii ten days before the Fifth Marine Division hit the beach at Iwo Jima. The Fifth Marines suffered 80 percent casualties on the beaches of Iwo Jima. Back home, in Los Angeles, his mother and girlfriend were getting all the horrible news from the Pacific Theater on the casualties that the Fifth Marines were taking on Iwo Jima. His mother kept waiting for the fatal knock on the front door that said her beloved son was a casualty. It was several weeks before my dad was able to contact his mom and let her know he was alive."[4]

Jones spent the rest of his tour at Pearl Harbor playing baseball, football, and basketball on Marine Corps teams for the entertainment of the troops. During that time, he played baseball with or against several major leaguers, including Ted Williams.

In May 1946 Jones, now 20 years old, was discharged from the Marine Corps. On the way home, he called Nora Graff and asked her to meet his ship in San Diego. Between San Diego and Los Angeles, Jones proposed marriage, and the pair wed three days later, on May 29, 1946. Within two weeks Jones made his major-league debut on June 9, replacing Cardinals second baseman Red Schoendienst in the seventh inning of a game against the Philadelphia Phillies. In June, July, and September, Jones played in 16 games with the Cardinals, mostly as a pinch-hitter or pinch-runner. He rapped out four hits in 12 at-bats. He also had one appearance as a pinch-hitter in the 1946 World Series, striking out against Joe Dobson of the Boston Red Sox in Game Five, and won the first of his two World Series rings.

Jones spent the balance of the 1946 season with the Rochester Red Wings, a Cardinals Triple-A team. Playing in 71 games, mostly at third base, Jones batted .344, five points less than the International League batting champion, Jackie Robinson of the Montreal Royals.

In 1947 Jones played in 23 games with the Cardinals during April, May, and September, mostly as a second baseman or pinch-hitter. He had 18 hits in 73 at-bats, for a .247 average. On September 11, Jones hit his first major-league home run, off Ralph Branca of the Brooklyn Dodgers. Jones also hit a double and a single in the game.

With Rochester again in 1947, Jones led the International League in batting average (.337), doubles (36), and triples (12). He hit 10 home runs and drove in 81 runs in 118 games, playing mostly at second base or third.

By 1948 Jones was ready to be an everyday player with the Cardinals, but the lineup was crowded. He was again battling Red Schoendienst for the job at second. "There was no way I was going to beat out Schoendienst," said Jones in a 1991 interview. "So [manager] Eddie Dyer wanted to put me at first base. But they already had Stan Musial and Dick Sisler at first."[5] Just before the season started, Sisler was traded to the Philadelphia Phillies and Musial was moved to the outfield. So Jones became the Cardinals' starting first baseman.

In 1948 Jones played in 132 games and batted .254 with 21 doubles, 9 triples, and 10 home runs. His 81 RBIs, .397 slugging average, and 191 total bases were third highest on the team (behind future Hall of Famers Musial and Enos Slaughter). Jones also grounded into 25 double plays, tied for the most in the major leagues.

On May 23 against the Phillies, Jones had a double, two singles, and two walks (one intentional) and drove in six runs; he had four more three-hit games during the season. On May 31 Jones spoiled a no-hit bid by Ken Raffensberger of the Cincinnati Reds with a single in the eighth inning.

While playing with the Cardinals, Jones became a skilled card player, according to his daughter Cheryl Noss. Card games were a popular pastime on teams' long train trips. Pinochle was the favorite game of manager Eddie Dyer. According to Noss, "Mr. Dyer was a firm believer that if you couldn't strategize and win at pinochle, you had no business being on a baseball diamond. He said pinochle was a thinking man's card game and baseball was a thinking man's ballgame. Needless to say, Dad learned to play pinochle, and all card games, with great skill and cunning!"[6]

Jones also had solid numbers in 1949. Playing in 110 games and often batting fourth between Musial and Slaughter, he batted .300, with 62 RBIs. His .426 slugging average was third highest on the team. On defense, Jones participated in two triple plays. He led NL first basemen with 15 errors. On June 15, 1949, in a game against the Dodgers, Jones had two singles, a double, and a home run and drove in six runs. On August 21 against the Pittsburgh Pirates, he hit three doubles and a single. In the opener of a doubleheader on August 28 against the Boston Braves, Jones hit two home runs and a single, scored three runs, and had three RBIs. In the second game he hit another home run and a single, scored two runs, and had two RBIs. The Cardinals swept the twin bill.

But 1949 was also the year in which Jones suffered a back injury that shortened his career. In a game against the Dodgers, he took a lead off first base. On a pickoff throw he slid feet-first back to the bag as Gil Hodges applied a slap tag. A terrible pain shot through Jones's back, and he was carried off the field on a stretcher. Jones had a herniated disc, which required surgery in the offseason. For a time after the surgery, he was paralyzed from the waist down. In a 1991 interview Jones said, "I was never the same after that. Until the operation, Joe McCarthy [who was scouting for the Yankees] and Eddie Dyer said I was one of the most feared right-handed hitters in the game at the time. After the operation, I could still hit, but not like before. For the rest of my career, baseball people kept asking me about my back. It was a stigma in my career."[7]

Jones played in only 13 games with the Cardinals in 1950, all in July and August. In 1951, he played 80 games with St. Louis between mid-May and early September and batted .263. On May 19 he drove in five runs in a game against the Dodgers. Jones also played in 23 games with Triple-A Rochester.

After the '51 season Jones was taken by the Phillies in the Rule 5 draft. He played in eight games with the Phillies early in the 1952 season, and played in 117 games with the Baltimore Orioles, then a Phillies Triple-A affiliate, and batted just .220. He wondered if his back was so bad that his baseball career was finished.

Jones spent the winter of 1952-1953 playing baseball in Mazatlan, Mexico. He led the league in batting (.386) and hit a game-winning home run that gave Mazatlan the Mexican League pennant. Jones's self-confidence returned.

On February 8, 1953, Jones was sold by the Phillies to the Sacramento Solons of the Pacific Coast League. He was the starting first baseman for the Solons from 1953 through mid-1957, and he wanted to prove that he could make it back to the major leagues. In 1953 Jones led the team in games played (176) and RBIs (102), with a .287 batting average. In 1954 he led the Solons in batting average (.304), hits, doubles, and total bases. In 1955, he led the league in hits (206) and led the last-place Solons in several other batting categories. In 1956 Jones led the Solons in home runs and RBIs.

On June 23, 1957, Milwaukee Braves first baseman Joe Adcock broke his right leg sliding into second base and was expected to be sidelined for six to eight weeks. The Braves needed another first baseman to share time with Frank Torre, and purchased Jones from Sacramento. On July 14 he played in his first major-league game in more than five years. Jones, now 32 years old, played in 30 games with the Braves in 1957 and had 21 hits in 79 at-bats (.266). On July 26, in a game against the New York Giants, he hit a walk-off home run in the 11th inning. On August 24 he hit his last major-league home run, against Johnny Podres of the Dodgers. Jones played his last regular-season game in the majors on September 29.

In the first three games of the 1957 World Series against the New York Yankees, Jones grounded out in two pitch-hitting appearances. But in the bottom of the tenth inning in Game Four, with the Yankees ahead

5-4 and leading the Series two games to one, Jones was sent up to pinch-hit for Warren Spahn against left-hander Tommy Byrne. In a 1991 interview, Jones said, "I knew Byrne when we were both in the Pacific Coast League. I knew he was going to start me out with a bad curve, something low and inside, hoping I'd go after it."[8]

Jones was right. He took the pitch, which skipped past catcher Yogi Berra. Umpire Augie Donatelli called it a ball, but Jones claimed that the pitch had struck his right foot. Charlie Blossfield, a ballboy for the Braves, had let the ball roll to the backstop, and it bounced back toward home plate. Jones scooped up the ball and showed the umpire the black smudge of shoe polish on it. Donatelli reversed his call and awarded Jones first base. Berra and manager Casey Stengel argued the call, to no avail.

Felix Mantilla was sent in to run for Jones, and Bob Grim replaced Byrne. Mantilla advanced to second on a sacrifice bunt by Schoendienst and scored on a double by Johnny Logan. With the game tied, 5-5, Eddie Mathews hit a walk-off two-run home run. The Braves had tied the Series and went on to conquer the Yankees in seven games. The shoe-polish incident was widely regarded as the turning point in the Series. The at-bat was Jones's last in the major leagues.

The Braves sent Jones back to Sacramento after the season. In eight years in the major leagues he had played in 412 regular-season games and batted .267 with 25 home runs.

Jones played two more seasons with Sacramento as the starting first baseman. In 1958 he batted .302 and led the team in most batting categories. In 1959 Jones batted .249. In his final season, 1960, he was the starting first baseman for the PCL's Portland Beavers, batting .249. In 13 years in the minor leagues between 1943 and 1960, Jones batted .292 with 1,678 hits and 119 home runs.

After Jones retired from baseball, he didn't look back. Cheryl Noss said, "My father was a man who prioritized his life. Family always came first, and this is a trait he instilled in his children and grandchildren. My father and mother were only children, raised by divorced and widowed mothers. I believe the strength of my father's love of family allowed him to leave baseball with no regrets. His life wasn't baseball; it was family."[9] She added, "Baseball was a sport he loved, but being away from his family became more difficult as the years passed. He always wanted a large family, and with each subsequent birth of a daughter, it got harder and harder for him to be away from us. He felt he was missing so much."[10]

During offseasons Jones had worked in public relations for Title Insurance and Trust in Sacramento. After retiring from baseball he became the company's head of public relations. "This was his post-baseball dream job," said Noss. "He had a duck/pheasant club and a cabin cruiser on the Sacramento River to entertain clients. He took [real-estate] clients hunting, fishing, golfing, and out to lunches and dinners — all paid for by TI. He brought in a great deal of big business to the title company. He loved the job and the town, and the feeling was mutual."[11]

Jones was well-suited for the position, said Noss: "My dad was easygoing, charismatic, confident, and self-assured in almost all situations. He was soft-spoken and had a relaxed manner. He had the ability to make people want to be around him. He was also humble about his achievements on the playing field. Unless you knew my dad was Nippy Jones, the hometown hero baseball player, you would never find out from him. He was never cocky or arrogant, which was why he had so many friends. Almost all were sportsmen like him who loved hunting, fishing, and the great outdoors."[12]

Jones worked in the title-insurance business for 27 years and retired in 1987 at the age of 62. Then he started the Happy Hooker fishing guide service, on the Upper and Lower Sacramento River. He worked part-time as a fishing guide for the next five years or so. In 1988 Jones appeared at a card show in Milwaukee and autographed the famous baseball that had struck his foot more than 30 years before. Former ballboy Charlie Blossfield, who was given the ball by the umpire, brought the historic ball to the show.

Jones had a major heart attack and emergency open-heart surgery in 1989, but was back on his boat within six months. In 1992 he was diagnosed with colon cancer and underwent surgery and chemotherapy. In 1994 he had a minor stroke. By the time Jones turned 70 in June

1995, said Noss, "We could all tell he was slowing down. His eyes weren't as bright, and he was a little quieter than we had ever seen him. He still loved his fishing and would go out with his son-in-law, grandson, and friends. He would still tell jokes and tell tall tales to his grandson. He had his grandson Chris Jr. believing the water tower on the Sacramento River was stocked with salmon."[13]

Jones was 70 years old when he died of a heart attack while sitting in his favorite chair, on October 3, 1995, less than six months before his and Nora's 50th wedding anniversary. He was buried at Southeast Lawn Memorial Park in Sacramento. Nora died on June 15, 2004, and was buried next to her husband.

Noss recently reread the cards that her mother received after her father died: "Overwhelmingly, the cards said, 'Nippy was a good man.' So simple a statement, yet so complex—just like my dad. Being a "Good Man," to many people, means different things. He was a good son, a good husband, a good father, a good grandfather, a good son-in-law, a good father-in-law, a good friend, a good worker, a good fishing guide, a good sportsman, a good baseball player: a Good Man. I think dad would be more proud of that legacy than any other he could have left."[14]

I thank Cheryl Noss, her sisters Diane Bennett, Debbie Thomas, and Cindi Hayashida, and James Noss (Nippy and Nora's oldest grandchild) for their recollections and for access to newspaper clippings.

Sources

Baseball-Reference.com

Findagrave.com

Retrosheet.org

Jones, Steve, "Ex-Solon 'Nippy' Jones, '57 Series hero, dies at 70," *Sacramento Bee,* October 6, 1995, B1.

Notes

1. Tom Mortenson, "Vernal 'Nippy' Jones: The ballplayer who made shoe polish famous," *Sports Collectors Digest*, March 24, 1989, 146.
2. James Noss, *One of the Boys of Summer: A Biography of V.L. 'Nippy' Jones* (Sacramento: self-published, 1997), 1.
3. E-mail correspondence by the author with Cheryl Noss, January 7, 2013.
4. Ibid.
5. Ben Swesey, " 'Nippy' helped polish off Yankees: Emergency fill-in took one for team in '57 World Series," *Sacramento Bee*, September 22, 1991, D9.
6. E-mail correspondence with Cheryl Noss.
7. Ben Swesey, 1991.
8. Ibid.
9. E-mail correspondence with Cheryl Noss.
10. Ibid.
11. Ibid.
12. Ibid.
13. Ibid.
14. Ibid.

Johnny Logan

By Bob Buege

The first major-league ballplayer to play on championship teams in both the United States and Japan was John Logan, Jr., known to the baseball world as Johnny. For 14 straight years (1948-1961) he was Milwaukee's shortstop, the first five with the American Association Brewers, the last nine with the National League Braves. A four-time All-Star, Johnny helped the Braves win back-to-back pennants in 1957 and 1958 and a World Series in 1957.

John Logan, Jr. was born in Endicott, New York, on March 23, 1926. (All of the standard references say he was born in 1927, but like many actresses and ballplayers, Johnny fibbed to make himself a bit younger.) He was the youngest of three children, who included brother Michael and sister Mary.

Their father, John Logan, Sr., was a native of Russia. "Stalingrad," Johnny says. "He was a guard in the empire."[1] The city would have been called Tsaritsyn back then. Johnny's mother, née Helen Senko, was born in Croatia but also lived in the borderland of Poland. Both parents' families emigrated to America.

"Their families came from Europe and somehow landed in Pennsylvania when they were teenagers," Johnny said. "When they found out that Pennsylvania was kind of depressed, they packed up and went into Endicott, New York, north of the Pennsylvania line. My parents met in Endicott. They started working for the Endicott-Johnson Shoe Company."[2] After marrying and building a small nest egg, John and Helen Logan started their own business.

"They ran a grocery store," Johnny said, "a neighborhood store. When the people didn't have the money, they'd come up to Logan to take the credit. When they had the money, they went to the IGA. But that's where I got to know my neighborhood people. Things were rough then."[3]

The family store did offer one benefit to young Johnny: "I was the most popular kid because every day when I went to school, I had bubblegum. Everybody hung around with me because they always knew I had my dad's free bubblegum. Bubblegum was like a Hershey bar."[4]

As a young boy Logan acquired a nickname by which he would be known as long as he lived in Endicott. "I must have been very active," Johnny said, "and in the Russian language, to settle a young kid, they'd say 'Yah-shoo, yah-shoo. Just be quiet.' The word is a combination of Russian and Croatian. A guy on my street took that and gave me the name Yatcha, or Yatch. The name became very popular in Endicott."[5] To anyone who followed high school athletics in Endicott, in fact, it became a household word.

"My hometown is triple cities — Binghamton, Endicott, and Johnson City. They had a Class A Yankee farm team named the Triple Cities Triplets. When I was 12 I skipped school because the Yankees came in to play the Triplets. I ran nine miles to the ballpark, which was in Johnson City, with no money in my pocket. I go to the entrance of the ballpark and the gate man asks, 'Where is your ticket?' I said, 'You have to pay to watch baseball?' I didn't know it was professional and you've got to pay.

Johnny Logan (National Baseball Hall of Fame Library, Cooperstown, N.Y.)

"I backed away and went down to this green fence. Usually in them days the old ballparks had a green painted fence. There happened to be a knothole in that fence. I looked through that knothole and admired my great ballplayer of the New York Yankees, Joe DiMaggio. He was my big hero."[6]

The date was Friday, May 27, 1938. With the Yanks leading 10-2, the game ended after seven innings because hundreds of kids swarmed onto the field seeking autographs from Lou Gehrig and DiMaggio. Logan said he was not one of them. Asked what he remembered from that game, he said, "Number 5, pinstripes. All I saw was number 5. It was an imagination dream. I didn't see no part of the game. I wasn't interested in no one but Joe DiMaggio."[7]

After the game, Logan recalled, "I had to run nine miles back home to be asked by my mother, 'How was school?' I said, 'Excellent.' Meanwhile I did exactly what I wanted to do, to see my big hero, Number 5 of the New York Yankees. I had the dream of someday playing for my hometown, for the Triplets, to play professional ball. If I could make the Triplets ball team, maybe I could possibly advance to a higher classification."[8]

In an interview 70 years later, Logan still felt a twinge of conscience for not telling his parents the whole truth about that day. "I didn't lie to them, but I didn't tell them. … My parents never knew what sports was. I had a brother that taught me baseball, taught me football, taught me the finer points. I was a batboy for his semipro team. They played every week. Then he played for his factory team, Endicott-Johnson Shoe Company. Anytime they had practice, I was there instead of hitting the books. I was playing with older guys. What happened is, I learned sports is a way of surviving. Back in them days, you could get scholarships."[9]

Not surprisingly, Logan did receive scholarship offers. Dewey Griggs, the baseball scout who ultimately signed Logan for the Boston Braves organization, said, "I knew Johnny was a natural the first time I laid eyes on him. Take a look at his hands. They're big and quick paws, ideal for a shortstop. But then Johnny excelled in any sport. I remember watching him perform at halfback one year during the New York all-state playoffs. That kid was a wonder at football."[10]

As a junior at Union-Endicott High School, Logan became one of the few members of the Orange Tornado, as the school's teams were called back then, to earn major letters in four sports: football, basketball, baseball, and track. Then as a senior, in an undefeated football season shortened to seven games by a polio epidemic, Logan scored 18 touchdowns, three times scoring four in one game, and passed for four others. In their only close game, a 6-0 battle in the mud in the season finale, Johnny scored the only touchdown and protected his team's victory with two pass interceptions.

Logan's gridiron heroics attracted college scholarship offers. "I was pretty good," he said, not boastfully but without false modesty. "I had scholarships (offers) to Syracuse, Colgate, Duke, Notre Dame. We had an assistant coach named Johnny Murphy, from Notre Dame. He was the spark plug of coaching. Ty Cobb (Harold Vernon Cobb) was the head coach, but to learn football, it was Johnny Murphy.

"I think Ty Cobb convinced him that I could be a lot better baseball player than football player because of injuries. (Cobb also coached the baseball team.) I only weighed about 160 pounds then. I'd get crushed by some of them bullies. I never liked football. To me it was an animal game."[11]

Logan summarized his high-school career. "I played basketball, football, baseball, golf, and I ran track. Five-letter man. But you know what I did wrong? I didn't have enough time to look at my schoolwork. After school all I did was go out and play sports with my teammates."[12]

Johnny's main sport, though, was always baseball. "When I was 15 or 16," he said, "every Sunday I'd take a Greyhound bus 40 miles to Homer, New York, to play semipro ball against college boys from Cortland State Teachers College." The manager and GM of Logan's semipro ballclub was Dewey Griggs, who in 1947 would become the New York state and Canada scout of the Boston Braves.

"This is the honest truth," Johnny insisted. "The first workout in Homer, New York—I took a bus ride there—I meet Dewey Griggs. He approached me and said, 'Logan, I've been hearing a lot of things about you, and we're gonna have a workout.' I said, 'Fine.' I went in the dugout—a pretty nice little ballpark there in Homer. I put my little jersey on. I looked in my satchel—two left-footed shoes! So I laced my left foot good, then put my other left shoe on my right foot. He said, 'Logan, you ready to work out?' I said, 'Yep, let's go.'

"He said, 'What position?' I said, 'Shortstop.' So there I am, working out, being a shortstop for about 15 minutes. He hits me groundballs to my left, to my right. About 15 or 20 minutes, and I handled it. Finally we sat in the dugout, and I'm all puffed out, sweating. He said, 'What's with your shoes?' I said, 'What's wrong with them?' He said, 'You've got two left-footed shoes.' The next time I showed up for a ballgame, there was a brand-new pair of shoes sitting there. So that's one way I got a brand-new pair of shoes without no money. By making a mistake."[13]

Logan graduated from Union-Endicott High School in January 1945. His athletic career was put on hold immediately. "I went in the Army right out of high school," he said. "I was drafted. I went to Camp Wheeler, Georgia. I met a great man named Bobby Bragan. He was the manager of the Camp Wheeler baseball team. He's the guy that taught me how to play baseball."[14]

Logan served in the Army in 1945 and 1946, which included duty in Osaka, Japan. After 18 months he was honorably discharged. That made him eligible for benefits under the Servicemen's Readjustment Act of 1944, better known as the G.I. Bill. Like more than two million other former soldiers, Johnny used those benefits to further his education.

"I went to college for a year and a half," he said. "I was a veteran, an Army boy, with no money. I had the privilege of receiving the G.I. Bill of Rights and going to college and getting $75 a month. I went to an extension college in Endicott, an extension of Syracuse University, the one that became Harpur College."[15] What did he major in? "Sports," he answered with a grin.[16]

Logan's excursion into the halls of academe ended in early 1947 when his old friend Griggs, recently hired as a scout by the Boston Braves, signed him to a minor-league contract. The signing of Logan was the first of Griggs's four important contributions to the Milwaukee Braves' 1957 World Series championship team. The others were, in order, Bob Trowbridge, Wes Covington, and Henry Aaron.

Johnny remembered, "I signed my contract for $2,500. In them days it was big money. The first thing I did was I gave my mother $1,500 and I kept a thousand. My family was conservative. They were poor in them days. A thousand dollars was like a million."[17]

The happy young shortstop entered the Braves organization with the Class B Evansville Braves. The Braves told him, "You've got a good manager named Bob Coleman. If he recommends you, someday you'll be in the big leagues." Logan recalled, "Bob Coleman got me 2,500 bucks. He always had a German police dog. That was his buddy. When we went to the ballpark, that dog was always there."[18]

Playing in Bosse Field in Evansville, in the Three-Eye (Illinois, Indiana, Iowa) League, Logan wasted no time in making his mark. He tripled in his first game, smashed an inside-the-park homer in his third game, and quickly earned the *Evansville Courier's* description as "the Braves' super-shortstop."[19] He was chosen to the league's All-Star team and finished the season with a .331 batting average.

Logan's performance in Evansville earned him an invitation to spring training in Bradenton with the Braves in 1948. "I thought I had a good chance of making the Boston Braves," he recalled.[20] To do so, he had to beat out a sensational young shortstop of the 1947 Triple-A Milwaukee Brewers, Alvin Dark.

Johnny remembered, "Seeing Dark and seeing myself, I thought I had a good chance. Unfortunately, Dark was a good hitter. He could hit that ball to right field. I could beat him on defense, but back in the '40s and '50s, everybody was a good defense man."[21] Dark became the Boston shortstop in 1948, earned Rookie of the Year, and helped the Braves win the NL pennant. Logan took over for Dark in Milwaukee, in the American Association, earning $400 a month.

Johnny said, "I was told, 'You're gonna love Milwaukee. It's the capital of beer.' I can remember coming to Milwaukee in 1948, living at the Wisconsin Hotel for five dollars a day. A beer was ten cents a glass. I remember Fazio's, on Jackson Street. The reason why

I got to know Frankie (Fazio) is, after a ballgame, we'd have a big dish of spaghetti, all the Italian bread, butter, and a salad. Frankie would always send us ballplayers a bottle of beer. We ate spaghetti almost every day for a buck and a quarter."[22]

The jump from Class B Evansville to Triple-A Milwaukee was too large for Logan. A month into the season the *Milwaukee Sentinel* bluntly reported, "Johnny is again playing bad ball at short. Logan made only four hits in the last 27 at-bats, and that isn't good enough for this league."[23] He spent some time at Pawtucket (Class B), and at Dallas, Texas, where he enjoyed immediate success. After his third game, the *Dallas Times Herald* wrote, "Johnny Logan, playing short, roamed that side of the infield like a major leaguer."[24]

Logan batted .283 in his five weeks as a Dallas Rebel. "We missed the playoffs by maybe a game or two," he said.[25] In 1949 and 1950 he played every game as the Brewers' shortstop. After a good spring training in 1951, he earned a place in the Opening Day lineup of the Boston Braves. "My first major-league ballgame was against the New York Giants," he remembered, "against Larry Jansen and Bobby Thomson and Don Mueller and Alvin Dark. I recall myself getting 1-for-3 and playing errorless ball. Boy, was I happy!"[26]

Logan's elation was short-lived. Two days later, in the third game of the season, still against the Giants, "I'm in the on-deck circle," he recalled. "I hear from the dugout, 'Hey, Logan, come back to the dugout.' So I was thinking, maybe they're going to tell me what this pitcher's throwing. Billy Southworth, who was the manager then, came over and put his arm around me. He said, 'We're taking you out for a pinch-hitter.' And there I am, waiting for an opportunity. Two on, two out, my third game in the big leagues. I'm very pepped up, and then—I was shocked for being taken out.

"See, Billy Southworth was an experienced manager. He believed in experienced ballplayers. He didn't believe in building up rookies."[27] On May 12 Southworth sent Logan down to Milwaukee. On June 20 Tommy Holmes replaced Southworth as Boston's manager. Two weeks later Logan was recalled by the Braves, but even though he was back in the big leagues, he played in just 51 games during the rest of the season.

At the time Johnny returned to the Braves on the Fourth of July, the *Milwaukee Journal* wrote, "Logan had an amazing fielding record with the Brewers. He had only one error in 57 games this season and handled 264 chances."[28]

Opening Day 1952 found Logan back in Milwaukee playing shortstop for the Brewers. On Memorial Day weekend, Holmes was replaced by Charlie Grimm. "Jolly Cholly's" first managerial move was to send down Buzz Clarkson and call up Logan and insert him in the shortstop position. "Charlie Grimm liked me," Logan explained. "I played for him in the minor leagues in Milwaukee. Charlie Grimm gave me my chance there in Boston."[29]

Logan started the rest of the games that season and rewarded Grimm's confidence in him by batting .283 and leading the NL in fielding for the first of three consecutive seasons. In 1953 Logan and the rest of the Braves made the historic shift to Milwaukee. "I spent five years trying to get out of Milwaukee," Johnny jokingly told a reporter. "I finally get out, so what happens? I'm going back again."[30]

Johnny had a well-earned reputation as a battler, a fighter who never backed down from anyone. Among his fistic rivals during his years as a Brave were Jim Greengrass, Johnny Temple, Hal Jeffcoat, and Don Drysdale. All except Temple were considerably larger than he was. Fortunately for Johnny, he had teammate Eddie Mathews to back him up. "I'd start the fight; Eddie would finish it," Johnny said. "I'm a lover, not a fighter."[31]

After the 1953 season, Logan took a bride. On October 24, in Milwaukee's St. Thomas Aquinas Church, he exchanged vows with Dorothy "Dottie" Ahlmeyer, a beautiful young model from St. Louis. About a month after the wedding, the happy couple's new home was completed in a working-class neighborhood on Milwaukee's south side. The Logans lived together in that house until Dottie died of cancer in 1989.

From 1954 through 1960, Logan anchored the infield for baseball's exciting new franchise, the Milwaukee Braves. He earned All-Star honors four times: 1955, 1957, 1958, and 1959. He helped the Braves win their only World Series in 1957. The Braves had fallen short of the 1956 pennant by one game. On June 15, 1957, however, Johnny acquired a new double-play partner who helped put Milwaukee over the top. "When Red Schoendienst joined our ball team," Johnny recalled, "I went to his locker and hand-shaked him and I said, 'I'm Logan, the shortstop. You're the captain of the infield. You call the steals, who's covering second base. Let me worry about my excellent third baseman, Eddie Mathews.'"[32]

On September 23, 1957, Logan scored the pennant-winning run for the Braves, and in the World Series that followed, featuring Aaron, Mathews, Mantle, and Berra, Logan belted the first home run. In Game Four he set an extra-inning World Series record for shortstops with ten assists. He tied Game Four with a one-out double in the tenth inning before scoring on Mathews' home run in a dramatic Braves' 7-5 win.

Logan and the Braves repeated as NL champs in 1958 but dropped the World Series to the Yankees in seven games. The following year Milwaukee tied the Los Angeles Dodgers for the league crown, necessitating a best-of-three playoff, which the Dodgers won in two straight games. In the deciding game Logan was knocked unconscious at second base by a football-style block thrown by Norm Larker trying to prevent a double play. When Johnny awoke, his first words were, "Did we get the guy at first?"[33] (Yes, they did.)

Because ballplayers in the 1950s did not earn astronomical salaries, most of them, including Logan, needed to find employment during the offseason. Johnny said, "Miller Brewery hired guys to do public relations. They hired Andy Pafko, Billy Bruton, Lew Burdette, clubhouse man Joe Taylor, and some other guys. I went to their employment office. The man there, Bob something, said, 'Fill out an application. We're kind of filled up.' I went over to Blatz and applied for a job over there. Blatz was a great beer back in them days. Meantime, I met the president of Blatz. I told him I was looking for a public-relations job, going out to taverns and going out and making speeches. I told him Miller was close to hiring me but that I wanted to be the only one working for Blatz. I must have convinced him.

"Believe me, I was a shy individual even though I was a good ballplayer. They gave me so many appearances that I got a little more confidence at getting in front of a group of people. I went to these dinners and smokers and banquets and made my little presentation. After five minutes I told them that after my speech I'd start signing autographs, and they all applauded. That's all they wanted was my autograph. But it gave me enough confidence to get in there."[34]

In December 1960 the Braves traded two good young pitchers, Joey Jay and Juan Pizarro, to Cincinnati to obtain Roy McMillan, a classic good-field, light-hitting shortstop. Logan's days in Milwaukee were obviously numbered. On June 15, 1961, he was traded to the Pittsburgh Pirates for outfielder Gino Cimoli. After the 1963 season the Pirates released him.

"After three years with Pittsburgh, I went to Japan in 1964, with the Nankai Hawks. I liked Japan. They were paying me good money. But it was very difficult to communicate. We only had two minor-league ballplayers, Joe Stanka and another kid. I was the only major leaguer. (Stanka had pitched in two games for the White Sox in 1959.) They thought they had a superstar, but unfortunately, at 36 …

"But I enjoyed it. I got to know Japan a little bit — Osaka, Kobe, Tokyo. It was an experience. I took my family there. I have three kids — my Jimmy, the youngest; John (called Danny) is the oldest; and Jeffrey's in the middle. Jimmy happened to be born on March 24, a day after my birthday. I told my wife, 'I want him to be born in America.' Because if you're born overseas you can never become president of the United States. I told my wife, 'When you feel good, you fly over.' Then they flew over about a month later."[35]

The Nankai Hawks won the Japanese equivalent of the World Series on October 10, 1964, seven years to the day after the Milwaukee Braves won their version of the "world championship." Logan's batting average for the year, though, was below .200. Johnny decided to end his baseball career.

"I met Ralph Barnes, the manager of radio station WOKY," Johnny said. "It was the main station in Milwaukee back in them days. I had a sports show, getting interviews from all the big celebrities, like Vince Lombardi and Pat Harder, the referee. He played with the Chicago Cardinals. And I sold advertising to Selig

Ford."[36] In 1973 Logan provided color commentary for Milwaukee Brewers game telecasts. After being appointed to that position, Johnny said, "I'm very, very speechless."[37]

Following his brief broadcasting career, Logan set his course, as the old Johnny Horton song said, north to Alaska. The Trans-Alaska Pipeline, the largest privately funded project in US history, had just been started. Johnny wanted to be part of the project.

"It was frontier terrain," Logan said, "but it's not going to stay frontier terrain. I didn't want somebody telling me how Alaska used to look."[38] On April 27, 1976, he took off to see for himself. He had told his wife he was going, but she didn't believe him. He arrived in Anchorage, age 50, without a job and without experience. After a week of searching, he landed employment.

"I had never done welding," Johnny said with a chuckle. "I was a welder's helper. It was hard work, rough and tough. We lived in barracks in the wilderness. I was with dope addicts, whiskey men, beer drinkers, hard-working men. I never gambled there, never had a drink while I was there. I was like a saint. I'd see these guys in these poker games, a thousand, two thousand dollars. Some guy was gonna work all week for nothing."[39]

Logan earned $11.60 an hour, time and a half after 40 hours. He worked from 6 in the morning until 6 at night, seven days a week. "They furnished your food, and they gave you your lodging," he recalled. "I sent all my money home, my checks. My kid said, 'Mommy, how come he's sending so much money home? What's he doing there?' It was tough work, but I didn't go there for the money. All I did was work, eat, sleep, and write postcards home. For a while I read three-day-old newspapers until I realized, what the hell did I care what was going on?"[40]

In 1978 Logan ran for sheriff of Milwaukee County for the third time. In 1966 he had finished a close second in the Democratic primary in a heavily Democratic county. In 1968 he ran unopposed in the Republican primary, then lost by two to one in the general election. On his third attempt, he reverted to the Democratic Party but was defeated in a landslide by the eight-term incumbent.

Logan maintained his ties to Milwaukee and to the sport he loves. In the early '90s he operated the radar gun at County Stadium. He did scouting for the Milwaukee Brewers.

On August 26, 2005, the Milwaukee Brewers inducted Logan to their Milwaukee Braves Honor Roll in the concourse of Miller Park. On June 6, 2013, he was inducted as the 17th member of the Walk of Fame at Miller Park. In a pregame ceremony before the 1905 induction, Brewers radio announcer Jim Powell highlighted Johnny's baseball and civic achievements. He also described Johnny, with tongue firmly in cheek, as a "superb conversationalist," comparing him favorably to such language stylists as Dizzy Dean and Yogi Berra.[41] Following are just a few oft-quoted Loganisms:

"Rome wasn't born in a day."

"I will perish this trophy forever."

Ordering dessert in a restaurant, Johnny requested pie à la mode, then added, "And put some ice cream on it."

At a banquet, Johnny introduced "one of the all-time greats in baseball, Stan Musial. He's immoral."

When a teammate referred to a mutual acquaintance, Johnny said, "I know the name, but I can't replace the face."[42]

And Milwaukee Braves fans will tell you that nobody will replace Johnny Logan..

Sources

Buege, Bob, "Braves Honor Roll Adds Logan," *The Tepee* newsletter, September 2005.

Chapman, Lou, "John Logan of Braves Weds Model," *Milwaukee Sentinel*, October 25, 1953.

_____, "Johnny Logan Recalls Old Days at County Stadium," *Baseball Digest*, May 2001.

_____, "Logan Returns After Spending 5 Years Trying To Leave Town," *Milwaukee Sentinel*, March 31, 1953.

Jauss, Bill, "Adventure Drew Logan to Alaska Pipeline," *Chicago Tribune*, August 15, 1976.

Thisted, Red, "Brews Bank on Wright," *Milwaukee Sentinel*, May 25, 1948.

Walfoort, Cleon, "We Gave Our Best," *Milwaukee Journal*, September 30, 1959.

"Morning Briefing," *Los Angeles Times*, July 11, 1976.

"Quotebook," *Los Angeles Times*, February 4, 1973.

"Season's No. 1 Crowd Sees John Logan Star," *Evansville Courier*, June 16, 1947.

"Wall Gives Brewers Even Split; Logan Is Recalled by Braves," *Milwaukee Journal*, July 5, 1951.

Binghamton Press & Sun Bulletin, May 1938.

Dallas Daily Times Herald, June 15-August 15, 1948.

Endicott Daily Bulletin, June 1-December 31, 1944.

Evansville Courier, April 1-August 31, 1947.

Milwaukee Journal.

Milwaukee Sentinel.

Baseball-reference.com

In-person interviews with Johnny Logan: December 6, 2005; May 17, 2006; March 23, 2007.

Notes

1. Johnny Logan, in-person interview, March 23, 2007.
2. Johnny Logan, in-person interview, May 17, 2006.
3. Johnny Logan, in-person interview, December 6, 2005.
4. Logan interview, May 17, 2006.
5. Logan interview, May 17, 2006..
6. Logan interview, March 23, 2007.
7. Logan interview, March 23, 2007.
8. Logan interview, March 23, 2007.
9. Logan interview, March 23, 2007.
10. Lou Chapman, "John Logan of Braves Weds Model," *Milwaukee Sentinel*, October 25, 1953.
11. Logan interview, May 17, 2006.
12. Logan interview, December 6, 2005.
13. Logan interview, December 6, 2005.
14. Logan interview, December 6, 2005.
15. Logan interviews, December 6, 2005, and March 23, 2007.
16. Logan interviews, December 6, 2005, and March 23, 2007.
17. Logan interviews, December 6, 2005, and March 23, 2007.
18. Logan interview, May 17, 2006.
19. "Season's No. 1 Crowd Sees John Logan Star," *Evansville Courier*, June 16, 1947.
20. Logan interview, May 17, 2006.
21. Logan interview, May 17, 2006.
22. Logan interview, December 6, 2005.
23. Red Thisted, "Brews Bank on Wright," *Milwaukee Sentinel*, May 25, 1948.
24. *Dallas Daily Times Herald*, June 29, 1948.
25. Logan interview, May 17, 2006.
26. Logan interview, December 6, 2005.
27. Logan interview, December 6, 2005.
28. "Wall Gives Brewers Even Split; Logan Is Recalled by Braves," *Milwaukee Journal*, July 5, 1951.
29. Logan interview, December 6, 2005.
30. Lou Chapman, "Logan Returns After Spending 5 Years Trying To Leave Town," *Milwaukee Sentinel*, March 31, 1953.
31. Lou Chapman, "Johnny Logan Recalls Old Days at County Stadium," *Baseball Digest*, May 2001.
32. Logan interview, December 6, 2005.
33. Cleon Walfoort, "We Gave Our Best," *Milwaukee Journal*, September 30, 1959.
34. Logan interview, May 17, 2006.
35. Logan interview, May 17, 2006.
36. Logan interview, March 23, 2007
37. "Quotebook," *Los Angeles Times*, February 4, 1973.
38. Bill Jauss, "Adventure Drew Logan to Alaska Pipeline," *Chicago Tribune*, August 15, 1976.
39. "Morning Briefing," *Los Angeles Times*, July 11, 1976; Logan interview, May 17, 2006.
40. Bill Jauss, "Adventure Drew Logan."
41. Bob Buege, "Braves Honor Roll Adds Logan," *The Tepee* newsletter, September 2005.
42. Baseball-reference.com

Bobby Malkmus

By Gregory H. Wolf

BOBBY MALKMUS WAS a small, light-hitting, versatile middle infielder who made his major-league debut for the Milwaukee Braves in 1957 during their frantic midseason search for a second baseman. Poor hitting (2-for 22) and the club's acquisition of All-Star Red Schoendienst marked the end of the Malkmus experiment after less than four weeks. Malkmus returned to play in parts of five additional seasons with the Washington Senators and Philadelphia Phillies and established a reputation of having a "big-league glove" at second base, shortstop, and third base.[1]

Robert Edward Malkmus was born on July 4, 1931, in Newark, New Jersey, to Robert and Elizabeth Malkmus. His father was a press setter at a print shop and his mother was a homemaker. In an interview given after his big-league playing days were over, Malkmus said that he started playing baseball because his mother did not allow his two older brothers (Harold and Bill) to play unless they included him. "The competition was good for me," said Malkmus. "[The other] kids didn't like the idea of having a younger kid around, though."[2] Even his older sister, Margaret, was included as the manager one year. Having grown up with modest means during the Depression and war years, Malkmus recalled how special he felt when he had his first uniform: "We didn't have organized leagues. We didn't have uniforms either until one year we scraped up $5 and pitched in to get suits. Man, we thought that was something special, having uniforms."[3]

Malkmus was a standout at basketball and baseball at South Side High School in Newark, but few scouts gave the slightly built (5-feet-9 and about 160 pounds) second baseman a serious look. "After scouts told me I couldn't make it in baseball," recalled Malkmus, "I enrolled in St. Benedict's Prep School [after graduating from South Side in 1949]. I wasn't such a hot student in high school and I was trying to get ready for college."[4] Malkmus continued playing baseball and basketball and caught the attention of Boston Braves scout John "Honey" Russell. "He decided to take a chance and signed me," said Malkmus.[5]

Malkmus's professional career got off to a promising start with the Bluefield (West Virginia) Blue-Grays in the Class D Appalachian League in 1951. Called "Scooter" in one *Sporting News* report, Malkmus played in the All-Star game and was named to the league's All-Rookie team after hitting .273 in 469 at-bats.[6]

Malkmus was drafted into the US Navy and missed the entire 1952 and 1953 seasons. Assigned to the Evansville (Indiana) Braves in the Class B Three-I League in 1954, he excelled as a slick-fielding second baseman who had some pop in his bat. He hit for the cycle on September 4 as Evansville beat the Peoria Chiefs to win the league championship.[7] Finishing the season with a .295 batting average in 522 at-bats, the speedy Malkmus was named to the All-Star team and added to the Milwaukee Braves' 40-man roster at the conclusion of the season.

Malkmus married his high-school sweetheart, Ruth Norma (Bischoff), on September 6, 1952, while he was

Bobby Malkmus (National Baseball Hall of Fame Library, Cooperstown, N.Y.)

still in the Navy. They lived their entire life together in northern New Jersey, where they raised a son and a daughter. A quiet, unassuming person, Malkmus had dark hair, brown eyes, and a dark complexion; however, by the time he debuted in the big leagues, he was almost completely bald.

Each spring from 1955 to 1957 Malkmus reported to Bradenton, Florida, for spring training with the Braves. Second base was seemingly locked up by Danny O'Connell at the time, and utilityman Jack Dittmer was a capable replacement in 1955 and 1956. Nonetheless Malkmus made an impression with his gritty determination and unwavering perseverance. Optioned each year, Malkmus worked his way up the minor-league ladder, going from the Jacksonville Braves of the Class A South Atlantic League (1955) and the Austin Senators of the Double-A Texas League in 1956 to the Wichita Braves of the Triple-A American Association in 1957. Along the way, his batting averaged improved from .243 to .291 making him an even more promising big leaguer.

While *The Sporting News* suggested the Malkmus had a good chance to make the Braves out of camp in 1957,[8] the situation at second base became more complicated with the emergence of Felix Mantilla, an athletic minor-league shortstop, who the Braves thought could be converted to a second baseman.[9] Furthermore, Braves manager Fred Haney acquired light-hitting infielder Dick Cole, one of his trusted players from his days piloting the Pittsburgh Pirates, as O'Connell's primary backup.

Even before the 1957 season began, it was clear that second base was the weak link in an otherwise outstanding Braves infield that had All-Stars at third base (Eddie Mathews) and shortstop (Johnny Logan) and Joe Adcock at first. By late May O'Connell was batting in the .230s and his range at second had worsened considerably. Braves first-base coach Connie Ryan lobbied in favor of promoting Malkmus, whom he had managed in Austin.[10] On May 30 Milwaukee recalled Malkmus to replaced Cole (batting just .125). "[It is a] move of desperation to alleviate a second-base weakness that had grown more acute than ever with the general decline of Danny O'Connell's play," reported *The Sporting News*.[11]

Malkmus's tenure with the Braves was brief—just 13 games and 25 plate appearances before he was reassigned to Wichita on June 23. In the first of six consecutive starts at second base, Malkmus debuted on June 1 by going 0-for-4 as the leadoff hitter in a loss to the St. Louis Cardinals. Hitless in his first 15 at-bats, Malkmus rapped an eighth-inning triple against the New York Giants on June 5 in the Polo Grounds for his first hit, and then scored the game-deciding final run in a 9-8 victory. According to Malkmus, the following game signaled the end of his career with the Braves. "I'm playing second base," he recounted, "and Felix Mantilla is at shortstop. Just as he told me to cover second base if the ball was hit to the mound, it happened, and my mind froze. I just stood there."[12] Malkmus played only three more innings at second base for the Braves. On June 15 the Braves acquired the veteran Red Schoendienst from the Giants in a multiplayer deal that included O'Connell. Reduced to pinch-running and pinch-hitting duties, Malkmus (batting 2-for 22, .091) was reassigned to Wichita and Cole was recalled.

Deeply religious, Malkmus relied on his faith to guide him through setbacks. In fact, his teammates on various minor-league teams and the Braves called him "Preacher," "Rev," and "Deacon" because he was always seen with a Bible and made references to the Bible and religion in the locker room.[13] "When guys found out I was serious," said Malkmus, "they respected me for my beliefs and some even came to me when they had problems and wanted to talk."[14] Throughout his playing career and afterward, Malkmus spoke about faith and sports at churches, youth groups, and YMCA's.

In December 1957 the Washington Senators selected Malkmus in the annual Rule 5 draft. *The Sporting News* noted his "distinguished" minor-league record, but said that "nobody in the Braves organization was overly concerned" with his departure.[15] Senators manager Cookie Lavagetto announced that Malkmus would have first shot at winning the second-base job in 1958.[16] Malkmus started eight of the first ten games of the season but batted just .160 (4-for 25) and lost the job. *The Sporting News* described the team's malaise at second base as a big "disappointment"; the team used five players (Ossie Alvarez, Ken Aspromonte, Malkmus, Herb Plews, and Jerry Snyder) at the position.[17] On the roster the entire season, Malkmus batted .186 (13-for-70).

Malkmus honed his hitting and fielding for Estrellas in the Dominican winter league and arrived at the Senators' spring training in 1959 ready to challenge for the second-base position again. But a weak-hitting spring dropped him to the fourth option behind off-season acquisition and eventual Opening Day starter Reno Bertoia, and backups Aspromonte and Plews. Malkmus was used just six times as a pinch-runner before his contract was sold to the Triple-A Denver Bears (American Association) in early May.

For Malkmus, unable to break through on two teams with major holes at second base, the future appeared bleak. However, he responded in Denver by hitting a career-high .300 and belting 16 home runs. Even more importantly, he had a stroke of luck at the end of the season. Former Braves general manager John Quinn had assumed the same position with the Phillies in 1959. In light of the Phillies' unstable and inexperienced infield, Quinn selected Malkmus in the Rule 5 draft in November 1959.

Malkmus received another break when Gene Mauch was named the Phillies' new skipper two games into the 1960 season. Mauch appreciated Malkmus's versatility and viewed him as an ideal piece in his constant shuffling of players and his strategy of late-inning replacements. Malkmus started games at shortstop (7), second base (17), and third base (8), was a late-inning defensive replacement in all three positions 32 times, and served as a pinch-hitter and pinch-runner. On September 15 at Connie Mack Stadium, Malkmus clubbed his first big-league home run, a grand slam off the San Francisco Giants' Sam Jones to tie the score in the sixth inning of an eventual extra-inning loss. Starting at second base the following evening in Milwaukee, he was involved in a memorable game. With two outs in the ninth inning facing Warren Spahn, Malkmus hit a screeching liner back to the mound. Spahn reached for the ball reflexively, but it ricocheted off his glove, only to be scooped up by shortstop Logan, who threw to Adcock at first to record the final out in Spahn's first career no-hitter. Malkmus finished the season with a .211 batting average (28-for-133) for the last-place Phillies.

Malkmus proved that he had a big-league glove, but he could not overcome his weak hitting to secure a starting position even in an era when infielders were not expected to hit for a high average or for power. The Phillies were an especially weak team in 1961, losing 107 games in the final year before National League expansion, ranking last in runs scored, batting, and earned-run average. Described as a "glove whiz," Malkmus started 55 games at second base, 16 at shortstop, and 10 at third, and served as a defensive replacement on more than 30 other occasions.[18] For the first time in his career, he enjoyed long stretches as a starter when he replaced the injured Tony Taylor at second base in July and September. For the season he hit .231 (79-for-342) and belted seven of his eight career home runs. He exacted a bit of personal revenge against Spahn on August 20, when he hit a two-run homer off the 40-year-old pitcher to account for the Phillies' only runs in a 5-2 loss to the Braves in County Stadium. Malkmus recorded three hits in a game three times and connected for a career-high four safeties, including his last big-league round-tripper, in a 16-inning win over the Pirates on September 23. Despite his utilityman status, Malkmus received one vote for the NL MVP award, the only Phillie to receive any consideration.

Notwithstanding Malkmus's success in 1961, the future of the Phillies' infield rested in the hands of second baseman Taylor and shortstop Ruben Amaro, both just 26 years old, and 27-year-old slugging third baseman Don Demeter. With these middle-infield players healthy in 1962, Malkmus had little opportunity to play. After just five at-bats and one appearance as a defensive replacement through mid-May, Malkmus was optioned to the Triple-A Buffalo Bisons of the International League. He was replaced by 23-year-old shortstop Bobby Wine. Splitting his time among second base, shortstop, and third base, Malkmus hit .278 in 453 at-bats for the Bisons.

A student of the game, Malkmus was groomed by the Phillies to transition into coaching. For the next four years he played for the Phillies' Triple-A affiliates, the Arkansas Travelers (1963-1965) and San Diego Padres (1966), and served as a player-coach under manager Frank Lucchesi in the last three seasons. Still a versatile fielder, Malkmus saw his average fall to .212 in 1965 before he experienced a rejuvenation of sorts in the warm, arid climate of Southern California, where he equaled his career high by batting .300 in 1966, his last full season as a player.

Malkmus finished with a .215 average (123-for-572) in a big-league career spread over six seasons and connected for 1,294 hits, good for a .269 average, in his 12-year minor-league career.

In 1967 Malkmus embarked on a nine-year career as minor-league manager when Philadelphia named him skipper of the Eugene (Oregon) Emeralds of the short-season Class A Northwest League. He guided the team to a second-place finish and was named the league's Manager of the Year.[19] Malkmus led the Spartanburg (South Carolina) Phillies of the Class A Western Carolinas League to the league finals in 1968 before falling to fifth place the following season.

Malkmus was a patient manager who empathized with the young players (most of them right out of high school) who felt pressure trying to fulfill their dreams. "These are young kids and they have a tendency to get down on themselves," he said in an interview in 1971 during the second of two campaigns skippering talent-bare Single-A clubs in the Montreal Expos organization.[20] "Things could always be worse," he often said to his players and then told the story of the 23-game losing streak he experienced as a member of the 1961 Phillies.[21] (The streak ended when the Phillies beat the Braves in Milwaukee, 7-4, and Malkmus went 1-for-3 with a run scored and two runs batted in.)

Malkmus guided four different lower-level teams in the Baltimore Orioles organization to winning records in four consecutive years, including a league championship with the Lewiston (Idaho) Broncs in the Northwest League in 1972. When Hank Peters replaced Frank Cashen as Orioles general manager after the 1975 season, he re-evaluated the club's farm system and let Malkmus go. Malkmus finished with a 508-463 career record as a manager.

In 1980 the Cleveland Indians named Malkmus an area scout responsible for New Jersey, New York, and eastern Pennsylvania. As of 2013, Malkmus still scouted part-time. A baseball lifer, he has been active in various baseball schools, academies, and camps. He served on the board of advisers for the Jack Cust Baseball Academy in Flemington, New Jersey, named after the New Jersey resident and former big leaguer Malkmus scouted. Inducted into the Newark Athletic Hall of Fame in 1995, Malkmus still resided in northern New Jersey as of 2013.

Sources

Newspapers

Chicago Tribune.

Milwaukee Journal.

Milwaukee Sentinel.

The Sporting News.

Websites

Ancestry.com

BaseballLibrary.com

Baseball-Reference.com

Retrosheet.org

SABR.org

Notes

1 *The Sporting News*, August 9, 1961, 20.

2 Tony Petrella, "Bobby Malkmus. The Job: Training Kids to Play Major League Baseball," *Palm Beach Post*, May 30, 1971, E4.

3 Ibid.

4 Ibid.

5 Ibid.

6 *The Sporting News*, July 25, 1951, 31; September 26, 1951, 38.

7 *The Sporting News*, September 15, 1954, 41.

8 *The Sporting News*, October 31, 1956, 6.

9 *The Sporting News*, March 20, 1957, 24.

10 *The Sporting News*, November 6, 1957, 8.

11 *The Sporting News*, June 12, 1957, 11.

12 Petrella.

13 *The Sporting News*, June 19, 1957, 16.

14 Petrella.

15 *The Sporting News*, December 11, 1957, 22.
16 *The Sporting News*, January 1, 1958, 21.
17 *The Sporting News*, April 9, 1958, 16.
18 *The Sporting News*, August 9, 1961, 20.
19 *The Sporting News*, October 7, 1967, 52.
20 Petrella.
21 Petrella.

Felix Mantilla

By Rick Schabowski

VERSATILITY IS THE best word to describe Felix Mantilla's 11-year career, in which he won a world championship with the 1957 Milwaukee Braves, appeared in the All-Star Game, and played every position other than pitcher and catcher.

Felix (Lamela) Mantilla was born on July 29, 1934, in Isabela, a town in the northwest corner of Puerto Rico. His parents were Navidad, of Taino Indian and Spanish descent, and Juan, of African descent. Juan drove a taxi and Felix said that the family "never had much money, but you know, it never seemed to bother us."[1] Felix had two younger sisters, Judith, who graduated from the Interamerican University in San German, Puerto Rico, and Felicita, who became a police officer with the Puerto Rican Police Department.

Puerto Ricans love baseball. There are many different levels of leagues in the country. Mantilla began playing baseball when he was 9 years old, competing in police-sponsored leagues. He was such an excellent third baseman that he was promoted to what Puerto Ricans call Class A ball, playing with older teammates. After a year he was promoted to Arecibo, a city about 45 miles from Isabela to compete in a Class AA league. Later, he became a player on the Puerto Rican National team. Mantilla also played high-school sports, competing in softball, baseball, and track, running in the 100-meter event. One of Mantilla's greatest accomplishments was playing for the Puerto Rican National team that won the Amateur World Series in 1951, defeating Cuba 6-5.

At Caguas in the Puerto Rican league, Mantilla played for manager Luis Olmo, who spent six years in the major leagues with the Brooklyn Dodgers and Boston Braves. Olmo sent Mantilla to the Boston Braves' minor-league camp at Myrtle Beach, South Carolina. "I always wanted to be a big leaguer," Mantilla said. "I guess I looked pretty good at Caguas, so the (team) sent me to the Braves for a trial. They had a kind of working agreement."[2] Braves scout Hugh Wise was so impressed with Mantilla that he offered him a contract. Mantilla remembered signing the final contract and said, "It was for (a bonus of) $400, which seems paltry today, but back then, I can assure you, it was a fortune. Of course I grabbed it and signed." Asked how he spent his bonus, Mantilla said, "Are you kidding? My mother got it."[3]

Before leaving for the camp, Mantilla got a warning from his high-school principal. "The principal knew that I was going to the United States, and he told me, Felix, you might have some problems when you get to the US. You are going to go from San Juan to Miami, then from Miami to Myrtle Beach. Sometimes if you ride a bus, to avoid problems you have to sit in the back."[4] This was all new to Mantilla, since he didn't have to go through this in Puerto Rico, but he was grateful for the advice, and having about ten Puerto Rican players accompany him on the trip made it a little easier.

The Myrtle Beach complex had four baseball diamonds, and in the middle was a tower for the coaches

Felix Mantilla (National Baseball Hall of Fame Library, Cooperstown, N.Y.)

to observe. One day Mantilla was taking batting practice with the Class C Eau Claire team, then "It was the seventh inning of the [Class B] Evansville game, and they needed a third baseman. They sent me over, and I stayed with Evansville. It was a break for me."[5]

Another barrier Mantilla had to overcome was being able to communicate in English. "They wanted me to go for English lessons in Evansville, and I went to school, but they talked too fast," he said. "I picked up my English at the movies, Westerns. There were three or four movie theaters, but there was only one where colored people could sit in the balcony and watch."[6]

At Evansville (Three-I League) Mantilla played for manager Bob Coleman, of whom he said, "He liked me, and I liked the guy. He gave me a chance to play."[7] Mantilla had an impressive 1952 season, playing shortstop and batting .323, and was named the Three-I League's rookie of the year and its All-Star shortstop.

In the offseason, Mantilla played winter ball for Caguas in the Puerto Rican league, where one of his teammates, second baseman Henry Aaron, was moved to the outfield where, Mantilla said, "It seemed he was more at ease than he was at second."[8]

For 1953 Mantilla was promoted to the Jacksonville Braves of the Class A South Atlantic League. He, Aaron, and Horace Garner integrated the team for the first time and helped as it finished in first place. (The Braves lost in the playoff finals.) Mantilla batted .278 and Aaron led the league in batting (.362). "Jacksonville was real bad. I'm talking about 1953, not now," Mantilla said. "They wouldn't boo you because you were playing bad; it was just because you were colored."[9]

Again he spent the offseason playing for Caguas, helping the team capture the Puerto Rican title. For 1954 "They were going to move me to what I think was the Atlanta Crackers at the time, but I wasn't too receptive to that idea, so they moved me to the Triple-A team in Toledo. … It was pretty tough there too, though."[10] Mantilla batted .273 and hit 16 home runs. In a Memorial Day doubleheader sweep at Louisville, he accounted for eight of his team's 12 runs, belting two triples in the opener and a three-run homer in the nightcap. He had a 23-game hitting streak during the season. Still only 20 years old, Mantilla also spent the 1955 season at Toledo, batting .275

At Milwaukee's spring training in Bradenton, Florida, in 1956, Mantilla impressed manager Charlie Grimm, who said he had "one of the best pair of hands I ever saw."[11] For the start of the season he was sent to Sacramento of the Pacific Coast League, but was called up on June 15 to provide backup for shortstop Johnny Logan, who was in a batting slump. He made his major-league debut on June 21 against the Pittsburgh Pirates at Forbes Field, replacing Logan at shortstop. In his first at-bat he popped out to the second baseman. He made his first start on July 1, against the Chicago Cubs in the second game of a doubleheader at Wrigley Field, playing third base and leading off. He went hitless in four at-bats. Mantilla said he was "kind of nervous, but after one inning, I lost my nervousness."[12] He stayed with the Braves the rest of the season, batting .283 in 53 at-bats.

Mantilla earned a spot on the Braves' 1957 roster, impressing manager Haney, who observed that "At third, he's as quick as a cat and has that arm. He can make the pivot on the double play at second."[13] After the newly acquired Red Schoendienst was injured, Mantilla briefly filled in for him.

Mantilla suffered a bruised chest in a collision with outfielder Billy Bruton on July 11 and was sidelined for 18 days. (Bruton was sidelined for the rest of the season.) Mantilla returned to duty on July 29 at County Stadium with a pinch-hit bases-loaded walk that ended a wild extra-inning contest against the New York Giants. The come-from-behind victory kept the Braves in first place by a half-game over St. Louis. In mid-August he filled in at shortstop for Logan, who was recovering from an infected shinbone.

Playing in Milwaukee was an unbelievable experience, Mantilla said. "I remember in spring training, Humberto Robinson said, 'When you get to that city you won't believe it.' I didn't have any idea. I thought maybe it was like Puerto Rico where people got kind of goofy. But when I came here it was a different thing. When I was in the house I could hear at the back door someone was leaving milk. They used to bring a gallon every day for free. There was beer out there. … We used to get Wisco 99 gas and a car from Rank and Son (a Milwaukee car dealer). I had never seen a place like this before. And the fans. If you lost a game they didn't boo you. Coming from a Latin country, when you started losing games you had to watch your back. The park was crowded every day. It was a good feeling every time you went to the ballpark. With the fans behind you, you can't lose."[14]

Mantilla played in four games in the Braves' World Series victory over the Yankees. As a pinch-runner he scored the tying run in Game Four. He replaced second baseman Schoendienst (pulled muscle) in Game Five and started Games Six and Seven at Yankee Stadium. Being on the field for the final out in Game Seven "was the greatest feeling of all time," he said. Mantilla called the World Series victory one of his memorable accomplishments.[15]

Mantilla demonstrated his versatility during the 1958 season, starting 27 games in center field, filling in for the injured left fielder Wes Covington, and also filling in at second base, shortstop and third base. One of his biggest disappointments was the Braves' loss to the Yankees in their World Series rematch, when Milwaukee squandered a three-games-to-one advantage.

At Caguas after the 1958 season, manager Ben Geraghty moved Mantilla from shortstop to second base to help facilitate his probable move to second base to replace tuberculosis-stricken Schoendienst in 1959. As it turned out, Mantilla played 60 games at second, one of six players to fill in for Schoendienst.

In Harvey Haddix's historic pitching feat on May 26, Mantilla became the Braves' first baserunner when he reached first on a throwing error by Pirates third baseman Don Hoak to lead off the 13th inning. Mantilla went to second base on Eddie Mathews' sacrifice and scored the winning run on Joe Adcock's blast. But the season ended on a sour note for the Braces, who were swept by the Los Angeles Dodgers in two games in a best-of-three pennant playoff. Mantilla started Game Two at second base but switched to shortstop after Johnny Logan was injured in the seventh inning. In the 12th inning with two out and Dodgers on first and second, Carl Furillo hit a grounder up the middle. "When the ball came over the pitcher's head," said Mantilla, "I thought I could pick it up and step on the bag. When I got it, I was past the bag and I knew I had to throw to first. I never thought of not throwing to first because I could've gotten him with a good throw. I was off balance when I threw, and that's why it bounced away."[16] Gil Hodges scored on the play, giving the Dodgers the pennant. Braves manager Fred Haney said of Mantilla, "He did the only thing he could, he didn't make a bad play. He was lucky to stop the ball at all."[17]

The 1960 season was another carousel at second base. The Braves were hoping for a return of Schoendienst after his bout with tuberculosis, but the 37-year-old struggled at the plate. Chuck Cottier and Mel Roach also played second base. Mantilla had 148 at-bats with a .257 average and played mainly at second base and shortstop in 63 games.

During the offseason, the Braves changed the makeup of their infield. They acquired Roy McMillan from the Reds to share duties at shortstop with Johnny Logan, and Frank Bolling from the Tigers to play second base. The handwriting was on the wall and Felix knew it, commenting, "They use me in 45 games, and then I see a newspaper got a list of the guys who might go in the draft, Bob Boyd, Al Spangler and me."[18] On October 10, 1961, Mantilla was selected by the brand-new New York Mets in the National League expansion draft.

Given the opportunity to play regularly for the Mets in 1962, Mantilla responded by batting .275 (second highest on the team) in 141 games. The Mets had a horrible season, going 40-120. It was a difficult transition going to a losing team; Mantilla said, "I don't think anyone dreamed the team was going to be that bad. On paper, it didn't look that bad." Casey Stengel, he said, "would bring out the lineup to the umps before the game, then would go back into the dugout and go to sleep. I guess he couldn't bear watching."[19]

After the season Mantilla was traded to the Boston Red Sox for infielder Pumpsie Green, pitcher Tracy Stallard, and shortstop Al Moran. Red Sox manager Johnny Pesky was pleased with the acquisition of Mantilla. "I saw him in 1955 when I was coaching at Denver and he looked like a fine shortstop," Pesky said. "They say he plays a good third and second base. I could use Mantilla in three different positions."[20] Mantilla loved playing in Fenway Park; "it was a great park to see the ball real well. Everything seemed like it was green."[21] While playing for Boston he lived in the nearby Kenmore Hotel.

Mantilla didn't get much playing time during the 1963 season, appearing in just 66 games, but he batted .315. When Ed Bressoud suffered a severe heel sprain and bruise, Mantilla filled in for him, and he began playing second base the last two weeks of the season.

In 1964 he played more often (133 games), filling in at all the outfield positions and at second base, third base, and shortstop. Johnny Pesky had acknowledged before the season, "I should have used Felix Mantilla more (in 1963). He played well in the infield and outfield when I used him. ..."[22]

Mantilla delivered a walkoff two-run, pinch-hit home run in the bottom of the ninth in a 5-4 victory over the Kansas City Athletics on May 23. It was only his second home run of the season. On May 31 he came through again, slugging a pinch-hit double in the ninth inning to beat the Minnesota Twins, 4-3. While replacing an injured Tony Conigliaro in the lineup, Mantilla blasted three homers in two games against the Cleveland Indians on June 27-28. The home run barrage continued and by August 15 Mantilla had 20 home runs.

What caused this sudden power surge? Cleveland manager Birdie Tebbetts, who had also managed Mantilla at Milwaukee, had a theory: "When he went to the Polo Grounds, it became necessary to pull the ball, that he developed a swing that lifted the ball up. It's a swing that's perfect for Fenway and almost every park in our league. He has become probably the most improved man in a career I ever saw."[23]

Mantilla finished the season with 30 home runs in 425 at-bats, an amazing performance considering that he had clubbed only 35 home runs in his previous eight seasons in the majors. He drove in 64 runs, and batted .289. Not bad for a player who saw limited action the first month of the season. Mantilla was honored by the Boston Chapter of the Baseball Writers Association, which gave him the Comeback Player of the Year Award after the season.

Newly appointed Red Sox manager Billy Herman had big plans for Mantilla for the 1965 season, saying he planned to bat him in the fifth spot. "Felix hit 30 homers last year and I want him down where he can drive in the maximum number of runs," Herman said.[24] Mantilla came through with a big season, batting .289, driving in 92 runs, and blasting 18 home runs. He was picked as the American League's starting second baseman for the All-Star Game, his only All-Star Game appearance, and went 0-for-2.

Mantilla spent the offseason working for the Milwaukee police department along with major leaguers Bob Uecker and Don Pavletich in a program instituted by Judge Robert Cannon to help curb juvenile delinquency. Just before the start of the 1966 Mantilla was traded to the Houston Astros for infielder Eddie Kasko. Mantilla had hurt his arm and shoulder during spring training, and he thought the Red Sox decided that this was a good time to move him. He was puzzled that Red Sox told him the trade was for youth but Kasko was two years older.

For the Astros, Mantilla spent most of the first month of the season on the disabled list, then batted .219 with 22 runs batted in in 77 games (151 plate appearances). In the Astros' final game of the season, on October 2 against the Mets at Shea Stadium, Mantilla had a home run, a double, and three runs batted in what turned out to be his last major-league game.

After the 1966 season, Mantilla asked the Astros for his release, which was granted. He considered playing in Japan, but in February 1967 he signed with the Chicago Cubs, who were closer to his home in Milwaukee. While in spring training with the Cubs, Mantilla tore his Achilles tendon during a timing drill. He realized his career was over.

Mantilla played a few games for a team in Sherbrooke, Quebec, but his legs were hurting. The team's manager was fired and Mantilla succeeded him and guided the team to a second-place finish. Mantilla wanted to continue as manager, but the ownership wanted a player-manager, Mantilla returned home to Milwaukee. He worked for the Boys' Club in Milwaukee. A Little League team that competes in the southside of Milwaukee was named after him.

Mantilla has two children from his marriage on September 17, 1953, to Delores Berry, whom he met while playing at Jacksonville. Felix Jr. is a retired attorney and Jose is a retired banker. Mantilla has been married to Kay since 1981, and they reside in the northwest side of Milwaukee. They have five grandchildren. Mantilla said he loves retirement because he can do what he wants to do, when he wants to.[25]

Sources

In-person interviews with Felix Mantilla, November 3 and 8, 1912.

Milwaukee Journal.

Milwaukee Sentinel.

San Francisco Chronicle.

The Sporting News.

Baseball-Reference.com

Retrosheet.org

Baseball Hall of Fame Library: Player file for Felix Mantilla.

Notes

1. Jack Pearson, "The Kid from Puerto Rico decided he liked it here," *50 Plus,* May 2010.
2. Bob Wolf, "Mantilla Now Blocked by Logan at Shortstop but Has Bright Future," *Milwaukee Journal,* April 1, 1956.
3. Pearson, "The Kid."
4. Player interview.
5. Vic Ziegel, "Mantilla Arrives," *Sport,* August 1965.
6. Ziegel, "Mantilla Arrives.".
7. Player interview.
8. Paul Green, "Felix Mantilla," *Sports Collectors Digest,* July 19, 1985.
9. Ziegel, "Mantilla Arrives.".
10. Green, "Felix Mantilla,".
11. Bob Wolf, "Braves' Talent Bin Overflowing With Nifty Kid Infielders," *The Sporting News,* March 21, 1956.
12. Player interview.
13. Cleon Walfoort, "Pennant Rides on 'Felix the Cat,' Now the Club's Only Shortstop," *Milwaukee Journal.* Undated article from the Mantilla file at the Baseball Hall of Fame library.
14. Player interview.
15. Player interview.
16. Player interview.
17. "Crestfallen Mantilla Says He Was Off Balance," *San Francisco Chronicle,* September 30, 1959.
18. Ziegel, "Mantilla Arrives."
19. Pearson, "The Kid.".
20. Hy Hurwitz, "Wanted: Hungry Players, Pesky Tells Hub Hose," *The Sporting News,* February 2, 1963.
21. Player interview.
22. Pesky Will Return in '64; Vows to Correct Mistakes," *The Sporting News,* October 5, 1963.
23. Ziegel, "Mantilla Arrives.".
24. Larry Claflin, "Pleasant Surprise? Watch Morehead, Says Hub's Herman," *The Sporting News,* December 19, 1965.
25. Player interview.

Eddie Mathews

By David Fleitz

EDDIE MATHEWS, THE only man to play for the Braves in Boston, Milwaukee, and Atlanta, burst into stardom in 1953, the team's first season in Milwaukee, when he belted 47 home runs at the age of 21. He hit 370 homers before his 30th birthday, and many believed that if anyone could top Babe Ruth as baseball's all-time home-run king, Mathews was the most likely to do it. Injuries slowed his production as he aged, but when Mathews retired as a player after the 1968 season, he stood in sixth place on baseball's career home-run list with 512 and held the record for games played by a third baseman. Ten years later, he became the second member of the 1957 championship team (after Warren Spahn) to gain election to the Baseball Hall of Fame.

Edwin Lee Mathews, Jr. was born in Texarkana, Texas, on October 13, 1931. His parents moved the family to Santa Barbara, California, four years later. Eddie inherited a passion for baseball from his father, a Western Union telegraph operator and former semipro athlete, though his mother participated as well. "My mother used to pitch to me, and my father would shag balls," he recalled many years later. "If I hit one up the middle close to my mother, I'd have some extra chores to do. My mother was instrumental in making me a pull hitter."[1]

Mathews excelled in football and baseball at Santa Barbara High and received college scholarship offers in football, but his prowess as a third baseman and a left-handed hitter stamped him as one of the most sought-after baseball prospects in the nation. Eddie and his parents weighed offers from several major-league teams during his senior year. The rules then stated that a player could not be signed until he graduated from high school. To be safe, Eddie and Boston Braves scout Johnny Moore waited until midnight on the night of his graduation in June 1949 and signed the contract a few minutes after midnight. Mathews got a $6,000 bonus. Several other teams had offered more money, but Eddie and his father had studied major-league rosters and determined that the Braves, with veteran third baseman Bob Elliott, would likely have an opening at that position a few years down the road.

The Braves sent Mathews to High Point-Thomasville of the North Carolina State League, where he hit .363 and belted 17 homers during the last half of the 1949 campaign. Promoted to Double-A Atlanta in 1950, the 18-year-old Mathews led the Crackers to the pennant with 32 homers, 106 RBIs, and a .272 average. He was considered the best hitting prospect in baseball, and even Hall of Famer Ty Cobb marveled at the youngster's ability. "I've only known three or four perfect swings in my time," said Cobb. "This lad has one of them."[2]

Eddie's career was interrupted by the Korean War, but after a few months in the Navy he received a hardship discharge because of his father's illness and his status as sole support of his family in Santa Barbara. He returned to the Braves organization and played for two teams during 1951, ending the year with the Braves'

Eddie Mathews (National Baseball Hall of Fame Library, Cooperstown, N.Y.)

top farm club, the Milwaukee Brewers. Invited to spring training with the parent team in 1952, Eddie won the third base job, beating out Elliott, just as he and his father had foreseen.

Still only 20 years old, Mathews belted 25 homers as a rookie for the Boston Braves that year. Though he struck out 115 times, batted .242, and drove in only 58 runs, Eddie impressed onlookers with his potential and finished tied for third in the Rookie of the Year balloting. He capped the season on a high note at Ebbets Field in Brooklyn with a three-homer game against the Dodgers on September 27, showing promise for the future. However, his future would not unfold in Boston. After years of declining attendance, the team's owners moved the club to Milwaukee for the 1953 season.

The Milwaukee fans were excited about the arrival of major-league baseball, and in Eddie Mathews they found their first hero. He grew into his own as a hitter in 1953, walloping 47 homers and driving in 135 runs while boosting his average to .302. He continued his hard hitting with 40 homers in 1954 and 41 in 1955, raising expectations that he could someday pass Babe Ruth's career record of 714 round-trippers. On August 16, 1954, the premiere issue of *Sports Illustrated*, with Mathews on the cover, appeared on the nation's newsstands.

Mathews was a hard-working, determined ballplayer who took pride in his fielding as well as his hitting. "Eddie was a below-average fielder when he came up, but he made himself into a good third baseman," longtime teammate Johnny Logan said. "Connie Ryan, one of our coaches, would hit 50 to 100 groundballs to Eddie every day in spring training. He'd knock them down with his chest and pick them up. He broke his nose three times fielding balls."[3] By 1954 Mathews had established himself as a perennial All-Star and the top third baseman in the league, a distinction he held for the next decade.

He was one of the toughest men in the NL and drew almost as much attention for his fighting prowess as for his hitting. In August 1960 Frank Robinson of the Cincinnati Reds slammed into Eddie at third and received several blows to the face from Mathews. "Eddie hit him with three punches that not even Muhammad Ali could have stopped," recalled teammate Warren Spahn years later. "Eddie was a tough competitor and a tough guy. He didn't back down from anybody."[4] A beanball war against the Dodgers in 1957 ended with Eddie pummeling pitcher Don Drysdale, and on August 1, 1954, after Brooklyn pitcher Clem Labine hit Milwaukee's Joe Adcock in the head with a fastball, Mathews nearly came to blows with Jackie Robinson, though no punches were thrown.

"With Eddie, you never worried about anything," said former Braves teammate Lew Burdette. "If somebody charged the mound when you were pitching, you knew he was going to be there. Eddie used to tell me, 'Let the son of a gun charge you and get the hell out of the way.'"[5] Mathews' tenacity, as well as his willingness to protect his teammates at all times, made him one of the most respected players in the NL during the 1950s.

Aside from his fights, however, Eddie rarely showed emotion on the field. "I'm not the type to make a big production out of everything I do," he said. "I think it's a joke when a guy strikes out and throws his bat. If I have to do that to show the fans I'm mad, to heck with it. I shouldn't have to fling bats or kick water coolers. Hustling to me means taking the extra base, beating out the slow roller, breaking up a double play, knocking the ball out of the catcher's glove, backing up throws, and keeping my mind on the game at all times."[6]

The steadily improving Braves finished in third place in 1954 and climbed to second in 1955, largely due to the hitting of another powerful slugger who joined Mathews in the Milwaukee lineup. Hank Aaron, a 20-year-old outfielder from Mobile, Alabama, made his debut with the Braves in 1954 and quickly adapted to major-league pitching. By 1956 Aaron was the NL batting champion and formed a potent left/right hitting combination with Mathews, who hit 37 homers and drove in 95 runs that season. The Braves led the league by 3 1/2 games on Labor Day but faded in the stretch, losing the pennant by one game to Brooklyn.

The Dodgers, with their aging roster, had won their last pennant in Brooklyn, and the Braves were ready to take charge. In 1957 Aaron, the Milwaukee cleanup hitter, announced his arrival as a power threat with 44 home runs, while Mathews, batting in the third spot, chipped in with 32 of his own. Mathews and Aaron were now the best one-two power punch in baseball, and the hard-hitting Milwaukee club, buoyed by the pitching of Spahn, Burdette, and Bob Buhl, won its first pennant, taking the flag by eight games over the second-place St. Louis Cardinals. The Braves entered the World Series as underdogs against the perennial AL champions, the New York Yankees.

All the Braves, except for Aaron, had been hitting poorly during the Series, but the team refused to collapse. The Yankees won two of the first three games and then took a 5-4 lead in the top of the tenth inning of Game Four at Milwaukee. In the bottom of the inning, Braves pinch-hitter Nippy Jones was hit in the foot with a pitch, which he proved to the umpire by showing the black mark made on the ball by the polish on his shoe. Red Schoendienst sacrificed pinch-runner Felix Mantilla to second, and then Logan doubled to score Mantilla and tie the game. This brought Mathews, batting .091 during the Series up until then, to the plate.

First base was open, but the Yankees elected to pitch to Mathews rather than walk him and face Aaron, who was waiting in the on-deck circle. With Milwaukee fans roaring, Mathews belted a Bob Grim pitch over the right-field fence for a game-ending homer and a 7-5 victory. "He didn't get many hits in that Series," recalled Aaron, "but that was the big one. That set up the whole Series for us."[7]

The comeback victory energized the Braves, who won a 1-0 squeaker the next day as Eddie scored the only run of the game. After a 3-2 Yankees win in Game Six tied the Series at three games apiece, Burdette pitched the Braves to the title with a 5-0 shutout in the seventh game. Mathews, who doubled in the first two runs of the contest in the third inning, was the fielding hero as well. The Yankees mounted a threat in the ninth inning, loading the bases with two out, but Mathews backhanded a hard grounder hit by Bill "Moose" Skowron and stepped on third base to end the series. "Without (Mathews) in that Milwaukee lineup," moaned losing manager Casey Stengel, "it would have been a different Series."[8]

The Braves won the pennant again in 1958, but the Yankees enjoyed revenge in the Series. Mathews, who had slumped during the regular season with a .251 average and 31 home runs, managed only four hits and struck out 11 times as the Yankees rebounded from a three-games-to-one deficit and regained the title. Eddie rebounded in 1959 with one of his greatest seasons, leading the league with 46 homers and finishing second in the Most Valuable Player balloting. The Braves finished the campaign in a tie for the league lead with the Los Angeles Dodgers. After his team dropped the first game of a best-of-three playoff, Eddie walloped a solo homer off Drysdale in the second contest, extending the Braves' lead to 4-2 in the fifth inning. However, the Dodgers tied the game in the ninth and won it in the 12th to clinch the pennant.

Mathews and Aaron continued to supply the power for the Braves over the next several seasons, though the team faded from contention after 1959. In 1962 Eddie tore the ligaments in his right shoulder while swinging at a high pitch thrown by Houston's Dick Farrell. He was never as dangerous a hitter after the injury, and his total of 29 homers in 1962 ended a nine-year streak in which he hit 30 or more each season. His first home run of the 1963 season was the 400th of his career, but his output began to diminish because of back and shoulder problems. He rebounded in 1965 with 32 homers and 95 runs batted in for the fifth-place Braves. Home run number 28, smacked on August 20 in Pittsburgh, totaled 773 for the Mathews-Aaron tandem, passing the Babe Ruth-Lou Gehrig mark of 772. Aaron and Mathews combined for 863 home runs between 1954, when Aaron joined the club, and 1966, the team's first season in Atlanta.

Eddie lasted only one season in the Deep South. In November 1966 the Braves obtained Clete Boyer from the Yankees to play third base, then traded the fading Mathews to the Houston Astros a month later. Eddie's career was winding down, though his short tenure with the Astros provided one bright moment. On July 14, 1967, he belted a Juan Marichal pitch into the right-field stands at San Francisco's Candlestick Park to become the seventh member of baseball's 500-homer club. However, Eddie played mostly as a first baseman and occasional pinch-hitter for Houston. He was expendable, and in August, when several AL teams inquired about his availability, the Astros cleared Mathews through waivers. The Detroit Tigers, in need of a third baseman after an injury to Don Wert, acquired Eddie on August 17, 1967, in exchange for a player to be named later. That November, the Tigers sent reliever Fred Gladding to Houston to complete the deal.

Eddie displayed his leadership mettle on his first day as a member of the Tigers when he discovered that not all of his new teammates were content with manager Mayo Smith. When he walked into the Detroit clubhouse for the first time, Mathews spotted a chalkboard on which an anonymous Tigers player had written, "We'll win it despite Mayo." Eddie erased the offending message and gave his teammates a lecture on the importance of supporting their manager. "That little episode made me a friend of the whole team because some idiot had written that down there," recalled Mathews. "Starting from that moment, I was accepted right away."[9]

"You don't appoint guys to be leaders like that," Detroit general manager Jim Campbell said several years later. "They either have it in them to take over, or they don't. And Eddie had it. We knew that when we traded for him. We got him as a player, but we got him to be a leader, too. Even Kaline looked up to him. He took a lot of pressure off Al."[10]

Mathews played third for the Tigers until Wert's return in early September, then shared first base with the slumping Norm Cash for the remainder of the season. He batted .231 in 36 games for Detroit, adding six home runs to raise his career total to 509. On the final weekend of the season, when the Tigers needed to win three out of four from the California Angels at Tiger Stadium to clinch a tie for the AL pennant, Eddie started all four games at first base. He drove in four runs, but the Tigers won only two of the contests and lost the pennant to the Boston Red Sox by one game. In the final game, as Detroit's hopes for victory faded, Eddie nearly tripped over a news photographer while chasing a foul ball. The frustrated Mathews caught the ball and threw it at the unlucky man's feet, earning a chorus of boos from the crowd.

In the spring of 1968, Mayo Smith decided that Eddie's days as a regular third baseman were over. Wert reclaimed the third-base job, while Mathews and Cash competed at first base. Smith even suggested that he might platoon Mathews and Cash, though both were left-handed batters. Cash had struggled against lefties, while Mathews had enjoyed more success against them. Cash, however, established himself as the regular at first with Eddie on the bench. Mathews finally hit his first homer of the 1968 season on May 19 against the Washington Senators. Eight days later Eddie hit the 511th and 512th homers of his career against the Angels, passing Mel Ott for sixth place on the all-time list. The two blows lifted his batting average above the .200 mark for the first time in 1968.

The veteran also gave his team a lift against the Athletics on May 26, after Oakland's Lew Krausse broke Kaline's forearm with a pitch the day before. When Jack Aker hit Detroit's Jim Northrup in the helmet, both benches emptied for what umpire Ed Runge called "the best fight I have ever seen on a baseball field."[11] The charge from the Tigers dugout was led by Mathews, who raced to the mound and clocked Aker in the cheekbone. The skirmish, which raged for more than ten minutes, energized the Tigers, who won 16 of their next 21 games and opened up a 6 1/2-game lead in the pennant race that they maintained to the end of the season.

Unfortunately for Eddie, his back problems flared up again, and in early June the Tigers put him on the disabled list with a ruptured disk. Neither rest nor traction helped ease the pain, and on July 5 doctors at Henry Ford Hospital in Detroit operated to remove the offending disk.

Most observers figured that Eddie's season, and his storied career, were over, but the veteran soon returned to the Tigers and worked hard to get into shape. By early September he was back on the active roster, making a few starts at third and appearing as a pinch-hitter. He lifted his average to .212 by season's end, but the two homers he hit against the Angels in May proved to be his last in the major leagues. Mathews was surprised and pleased that the Tigers decided to put him on the roster for the World Series against the St. Louis

Cardinals, though he had already decided that 1968 would be his last season. His third World Series appearance, coming a decade after his performances in the fall classic for Milwaukee in 1957 and 1958, would mark the end of his playing career.

Mathews played in only two of the seven games against the Cardinals. In Game One he pinch-hit for Don Wert in the eighth inning and struck out against Bob Gibson, who set a Series record by setting 17 Tigers down on strikes in that game. In the fourth game Mayo Smith gave Eddie the starting assignment at third base, with Gibson once again on the mound for St. Louis. Eddie walked once and hit a single, one of only five hits managed by the Tigers in a losing effort. He rode the bench for the rest of the Series as the Tigers won the final three games and claimed their first world title since 1945. Though Eddie modestly described himself as a "cheerleader" for the club—"all I needed was the pompons and the little skirt," he said—he was thrilled to retire as a World Series champion. "We finished on top in Class D in my first year in Organized Baseball, and we finished on top my last year," said Eddie. "What more can a ballplayer ask?"[12] The title eventually made Mathews only the third Hall of Famer, after Joe DiMaggio and Johnny Mize, to retire a World Series winner.

Jim Campbell offered Eddie a job as a scout, but Mathews decided instead to go into business. This effort was a failure; as Eddie later put it, "I didn't like being a salesman. I wasn't a closer. I'd go in and talk baseball for half an hour and walk out without mentioning my product."[13] In 1971 he returned to baseball as a coach with his old team, the Atlanta Braves (which had retired his uniform number 41 in 1969), and in early August 1972 he replaced Luman Harris as manager of the club.

The biggest controversy of Eddie's managerial tenure occurred as his old teammate Hank Aaron, still a fixture in the Atlanta lineup, stood on the verge of breaking Babe Ruth's career mark of 714 home runs. Aaron entered the 1974 season with 713 round-trippers, and hit the record-tying blow on Opening Day in Cincinnati. Eddie then announced that Aaron would sit out the next two games in Cincinnati, the better to break the record at home in Atlanta the following week. Commissioner Bowie Kuhn angrily ordered the Braves to play Aaron against the Reds, threatening to fine or suspend Mathews if Aaron was not in the lineup. After a heated exchange of opinions between Kuhn and Mathews, Aaron sat out the second game of the season, then went hitless in the third and left Cincinnati still tied with Ruth. In the Braves' nationally televised home opener, on April 8, 1974, Aaron hit his 715th homer, breaking the record that many had once expected Mathews to shatter.

The Braves floundered in mid-1974, and in July of that year the Mathews was fired. He spent the next several years coaching and scouting for the Texas Rangers, the Milwaukee Brewers, and the Oakland A's. In 1978 he was elected to the Baseball Hall of Fame in his fifth year of eligibility. Though Eddie had publicly questioned why Ernie Banks, who compiled statistics similar to his, entered the Hall on his first try while he waited five years for induction, he was a happy man at the ceremony in Cooperstown that summer. "I'm just a beat-up old third baseman," Eddie told the crowd. "I'm just a small part of a wonderful game that is a tremendous part of America today."[14]

Eddie's later years were filled with difficulty. Married four times, the hard-drinking Mathews admitted in his 1994 autobiography that his alcohol intake caused him to lose several baseball jobs, including his position as Braves manager. In 1982 he developed a serious case of pneumonia and was hospitalized for months. Fourteen years later, he slipped while boarding a boat, fell into the water and was crushed between the vessel and the pier, smashing his pelvis. The old ballplayer never regained his health after that devastating injury, and on February 18, 2001, he died of pneumonia and respiratory failure at the age of 69.

"I think he was one of the greatest third basemen of all time," Johnny Logan said. "He had one of the sweetest swings I ever saw. There was only one Eddie Mathews."[15]

Sources

Allen, Bob, with Bill Gilbert, *The 500 Home Run Club: Baseball's 16 Greatest Home Run Hitters from Babe Ruth to Mark McGwire* (Champaign, Illinois Sports Publishing, 2000).

Mathews, Eddie, and Bob Buege, *Eddie Mathews and the National Pastime* (Milwaukee: Douglas American Sports Publications, 1994).

Associated Press, February 19, 2001.

Haudricourt, Tom, "Eddie Mathews Overlooked As One of the Game's Greats," *Baseball Digest*, June 2001.

Milwaukee Journal-Sentinel, February 19, 2001.

New York Times, January 20, 1978; August 8, 1978.

The Sporting News, January 15, 1958, 4; August 26, 1978, 12.

The Eddie Mathews page at *www.baseball-almanac.com*

Notes

1. Associated Press, August 8, 1978.
2. *New York Times*, February 19, 2001.
3. Tom Haudricourt, "Eddie Mathews Overlooked As One of the Game's Greats." *Baseball Digest*, June 2001, 74.
4. Haudricourt, 72.
5. "Mathews Remembered," SI.com, February 18, 2001.
6. Bob Allen with Bill Gilbert, *The 500 Home Run Club: Baseball's 16 Greatest Home Run Hitters from Babe Ruth to Mark McGwire* (Champaign, Illinois: Sports Publishing, 2000), 112.
7. *Milwaukee Journal-Sentinel*, February 19, 2001.
8. *The Sporting News*, January 15, 1958, 4.
9. Eddie Mathews and Bob Buege, *Eddie Mathews and the National Pastime* (Milwaukee: Douglas American Sports Publications, 1994), 280.
10. *The Sporting News*, August 26, 1978, 12.
11. Jerry Green, *Year of the Tiger* (New York: Coward McCann, 1969), 58.
12. Mathews, 295.
13. *New York Times*, January 20, 1978.
14. Associated Press, August 8, 1978.
15. Haudricourt, 76.

Don McMahon

By John Vorperian

History has not been kind to Don McMahon. Now largely forgotten, McMahon had a very long —often excellent— career, pitched in the postseason four times, helped win two world championships, and was clearly one of baseball's best relief pitchers in a number of seasons.

Playing in the days before the closer became such a highly prized position, Donald John McMahon worked for seven teams in 18 major-league seasons. Upon his retirement at age 44, only three pitchers (Hoyt Wilhelm, Lindy McDaniel, and Cy Young) had appeared in more games. The two-pitch (fastball and overhand curve), right-handed McMahon pitched in 874 games, racking up 1,310 2/3 innings and 1,003 strikeouts. He notched 153 saves and posted a 90–68 (.570) won-lost record with a career 2.96 earned-run average.

Born on January 4, 1930, in Brooklyn, New York, McMahon grew up there as well. The youngster of Irish American descent went to St. Jerome Elementary School and Brooklyn Prep. In 1948 he graduated from Erasmus Hall High School. McMahon played baseball for the local Flatbush Robins in 1949. He was signed by Boston Braves scout John "Honey" Russell before the 1950 season.

Although mainly a third baseman in high school, McMahon was converted by the Braves into a pitcher. In 1950 at Owensboro (Kentucky) in the Class D Kitty League, the 20-year-old won 20 games, with 143 strikeouts and a 2.72 ERA. He led the league in all three categories. The next year he was sent to Denver in the Class A Western League but appeared in only four games, in relief, before entering the US Army, where he served from May 22, 1951, to May 14, 1953. After completing his service time, McMahon remained in the Braves' organization; the club had relocated to Milwaukee just before the 1953 season.

McMahon was assigned to Evansville (Indiana) in the Class B Three I League and pitched 114 innings in 1953 for a 6-5 won-lost record with 91 strikeouts and a 4.50 ERA. In 1954 he was assigned to the Atlanta Crackers in the Double-A Southern Association, where he improved his game and got his ERA down to 3.56.

On the personal front, 1955 was a big success for McMahon; he married Dolores Darlene Sater on February 5. But it was a dismal baseball year. Now with Toledo of the Triple-A American Association, McMahon finished 2-13 with an ERA that ballooned to 5.01. He returned to Atlanta the following year. McMahon always credited the Atlanta manager, former Brooklyn Dodgers All-Star hurler Whitlow Wyatt, for moving him from the rotation to the bullpen in 1956. It was a switch that proved very successful. That year, McMahon posted a 4-2 mark in 36 innings, struck out 34, and recorded a low 2.00 ERA; he earned a midseason move to Triple-A Wichita in the American Association. He took a while to adapt to the new league, but led off 1957 with a 2.92 ERA in his first 71 innings of relief and got himself a call-up to the big leagues in June. Clyde King also was credited with helping McMahon develop. By this time, McMahon was pitching exclusively in relief.

On June 30, 1957, McMahon made his major-league debut, against the

Don McMahon (National Baseball Hall of Fame Library, Cooperstown, N.Y.)

Pittsburgh Pirates in a doubleheader nightcap before 36,283 in Milwaukee's County Stadium. Called upon to start the ninth inning to replace southpaw Taylor Phillips, he entered the game with the Pirates leading, 4-2. McMahon set down the three batters he faced. In the bottom of the ninth with two outs, the hometown Braves knotted the score on a Felix Mantilla home run with Frank Torre on board. In the Braves' tenth, McMahon popped out to first base in his first major-league at-bat. Taken out in the 12th for a pinch-hitter, McMahon ended his part of the game with four innings pitched, just two hits given up and seven strikeouts. Milwaukee won the match in the 13th by a come-from-behind score of 6-5 when Eddie Mathews hit a two-run home run.

In his first eight appearances, McMahon threw 14 scoreless innings. Milwaukee captured the 1957 National League pennant with a 95-59 record (plus one tie). McMahon ended a great first season with nine saves and a 1.54 ERA. He made three appearances in the 1957 World Series against the Yankees, which the Braves won in seven games. McMahon threw five innings in relief without allowing a run.

After the season McMahon played winter ball for San Juan in Puerto Rico. In December he was traded to Estrellas Orientales in the Dominican League. The idea was to place McMahon with a team that didn't need as much relief help, so he wouldn't get overworked. McMahon pitched very well to open the 1958 season and was named to the 1958 NL All-Star team, but did not appear in the game at Baltimore's Memorial Stadium. He won seven games and lost two, with an ERA of 3.68. It wasn't until June 6 that he gave up his first home run in major-league ball, to Don Zimmer, after 47 appearances without one. McMahon might have become the answer to a trivia question sometime in 1958 at Milwaukee's County Stadium when he was the first pitcher driven from the bullpen to the mound; he arrived in a motor scooter with sidecar. McMahon saved the pennant clincher for Warren Spahn on September 21 in Cincinnati and the Braves repeated as NL champs. McMahon again made three appearances in the World Series but this time Milwaukee fell in seven games to the Yankees.

In 1959 relief specialist McMahon led the NL with 15 saves and in games finished with 49, complementing a 2.57 ERA. He claimed to have counted 132 times he was up and throwing in the bullpen; accurate or not, he was used in 60 games. He helped keep the Braves in the race, but the hitting wasn't sufficient and Milwaukee finished the year tied for the league lead with the Los Angeles Dodgers. The Dodgers took the first two games in the best-of-three playoff to capture the pennant. McMahon got a good pay raise but had a disappointing year in 1960, with a 5.94 ERA and a 3-6 mark. The Braves still contended, finishing second, seven games behind the Pittsburgh Pirates. Bob Wolf wrote in *The Sporting News* that "the Braves' relief pitching was far short of championship caliber. The failure of Don McMahon to regain his form of the last three years was becoming more costly as the season wore on."[1]

Bouncing back from what Wolf called a "season-long slump" in 1961, McMahon brought his ERA back under 3.00 and finished a decent season with a 6-4 mark and a 2.84 ERA. He'd started 1961 very well indeed, but tailed off significantly in August and September, and the team was not convinced that he'd entirely returned to form. The Braves chose not to protect him in the expansion draft as the New York Mets and Houston Colt .45s both joined the NL for 1962. Neither team selected McMahon, and Bob Wolf wrote in February that he "doesn't seem to have the old hop on his fastball, but he does have a good slider and a pretty fair curve."[2]

On May 9, 1962, though, Houston was ready to make a move. Though McMahon had not worked much and not pitched well, the 32-year-old right-hander was purchased by the Colt .45s for a relatively modest $30,000. When the Braves came to Houston in June for the first time, he unleashed a barrage at his former manager Birdie Tebbetts, bitter over the fact that he'd hardly been used by Milwaukee (three innings of work in the first month) and that Tebbetts had told him not to use his fastball except as a waste pitch. On June 7 he blazed several fastballs past Braves batters and got credit for beating his old team. An account in *The Sporting News* June 23 issue mades it clear that there was no love lost between Tebbetts and McMahon. Don later admitted he got a letter from his mother admonishing him. "She told me to quit saying things against Mr. Tebbetts," he reported.[3] He'd also had a flare-up over salary with Braves general manager John McHale, so a change of scenery was probably in order.

McMahon had a gratifying year in 1962. He'd found his fastball again, liked the hot weather, and felt Houston treated its players better (and had a better philosophy of sharing relief work). He appeared in 51 games for Houston and contributed a stellar 1.53 ERA.

In 1963 McMahon put in a full year for Houston, but it wasn't nearly as strong as 1962. His ERA ballooned to 4.05. He did witness teammate Don Nottebart's no-hitter. It was the eighth no-hitter McMahon had seen. McMahon had been the one to recommend signing Nottebart to Houston GM Paul Richards. The day after the 1963 season ended, McMahon was sold to the Cleveland Indians, reuniting him with Tebbetts, now the Tribe's manager. It was Tebbetts who recommended getting McMahon, though it was a cheap enough acquisition at the $20,000 waiver price. The Indians weren't desperate for bullpen help, but Birdie spotted something in Hoot Evers' scouting report on McMahon and thought he saw a bargain.

McMahon lamented leaving Houston, saying that a bad shoulder had hampered him during much of the 1963 season. After the winter off, he established himself as Cleveland's bullpen ace right out of the gate. Coming to a new league gave him a bit of an advantage at first. He still relied mainly on his fastball. "My control isn't so sharp that I can pitch to the inside corner on one guy and the outside on another. All I want to know is whether I should pitch him high or low."[4] By midyear, he had a 1.59 ERA. By year's end, he'd made a career-high 70 appearances in relief, breaking the previous club record of 63 appearances. He was 6-4 with 16 saves. In November he was named Man of the Year for the Indians.

McMahon was a holdout in the spring, and it took a while before Cleveland GM Gabe Paul and his pitcher came to terms—while seated at the February writers' dinner. McMahon contributed a solid and respectable 1965 season (3.28 ERA), though not nearly as spectacular as in 1964. He wasn't being used quite as much in early 1966, throwing 12 1/3 innings in 12 games through the end of May. His ERA was good, though, at 2.92. In early June the Indians traded McMahon and fellow pitcher Lee Stange to the Red Sox for former All-Star relief pitcher Dick Radatz. The Red Sox were on a bit of a swapping spree; the trade was the seventh the team had made since September 1965, as general manager Dick O'Connell moved to remake the team.

Despite Radatz's struggles in 1965 and the early part of 1966, the trade was condemned by many in Boston. Stange was acquired for long relief and spot starts; McMahon was seen as the short-relief specialist—though his first appearance was a four-inning stint on June 4 against the Yankees, and he faced the minimum 12 batters in the seventh through the tenth innings in a game the Red Sox won on a three-run homer by Jim Gosger in the bottom of the 16th. He put out a fire the following night, also against the Yankees. On July 6 he earned wins in both games of a doubleheader at Yankee Stadium and began to win hearts and minds in Boston. The last pitcher to win both ends of a doubleheader from the Bronx Bombers had been Dave Davenport of the St. Louis Browns a half-century earlier, in 1916.

McMahon took over the fireman role, leading the 1966 Boston bullpen with nine saves and a 2.65 ERA. Stange won seven games, but lost nine. Radatz had had his day; he disappointed Cleveland with an 0-3 record and a far higher ERA than either Stange or McMahon. But Boston still wound up just a half-game out of last place. The Boston baseball writers noted McMahon's contribution nonetheless, and voted him the club's most valuable pitcher for 1966.

At the start of 1967, Don, his wife, Darlene, and their six children and two dogs all drove cross-country from his home near Anaheim, California, for Red Sox spring training in Florida. He and John Wyatt were seen as the core of the Boston bullpen. McMahon didn't pitch as well, though, as his ERA was up a run in April and May over his 1966 numbers.

Exactly one year from the day he was acquired by the Red Sox, the team sent him to the Chicago White Sox. It was June 2, 1967, as Red Sox management sought to bolster their infield by trading for veteran utilityman

Jerry Adair. McMahon was not getting a lot of work, having thrown just 17 innings. The White Sox had lost reliever Dennis Higgins, who suffered a detached retina, and were anxious to make a trade, anxious enough to give up a player like Adair. O'Connell found it a very attractive deal, and he pounced on it, throwing in highly touted minor-league pitching prospect Bob Snow (who had gone 20-2 for Class A Winston-Salem the year before).

Boston's 1967 skipper, Dick Williams, told SABR interviewer Jeff Angus that it was "a trade that helped both clubs." He added, "McMahon was disgruntled to leave, but he was just bouncing the ball off the plate with us. When he went over to Chicago, [he] pitched very well for them … [while] Adair played short for us for three weeks when Rico [Petrocelli] was hurt, and contributed."[5] The shift agreed with McMahon; he finished the year with a 1.67 ERA for the White Sox and a 5-0 record, making a key contribution to Chicago's pennant drive that came up three games short. Adair contributed in a number of ways, and a number of writers felt his acquisition was one of the key moves the Red Sox made in their pennant-winning 1967 season.

McMahon didn't last much more than a year in the Windy City. The White Sox really needed another starter, and in a straight-up swap on July 26, 1968, they sent McMahon to the Detroit Tigers for right-hander Dennis Ribant. Chicago was worried about Gary Peters' health and wanted a pitcher with starting capabilities. McMahon again posted a final 1.98 ERA (consistent throughout the year, he was 1.96 for Chicago and 2.02 for Detroit). He'd missed being in the 1967 World Series with the Red Sox, but he found himself with another pennant-winning team as Detroit captured the AL flag in 1968. McMahon collected his second world championship ring as the Tigers beat the St. Louis Cardinals in the fall classic—McMahon himself appearing twice, though briefly and not effectively.

McMahon returned to the NL later the following year, joining his seventh major-league team, when the San Francisco Giants acquired him for a player to be named later (infielder Cesar Gutierrez) on August 8 from the Tigers. Playing with Cooperstown-bound Willie Mays, Juan Marichal, Willie McCovey, and Gaylord Perry must have agreed with McMahon. He was 39 at the time of the transaction, and he still kept getting batters out. He posted a 3.04 ERA for the remainder of 1969 and a 2.96 ERA in 61 appearances in 1970. In 1971 McMahon was still relying on his fastball but admitted he hadn't used his slider for a couple of years. At age 41, McMahon was getting his breaking ball over the plate better than ever, and so featured that more during another season with 61 appearances.

When the Giants re-signed McMahon in 1972, they did so in two capacities. He was to be a pitcher, of course, but he also served as pitching coach, taking over from Larry Jansen. He still got into 44 games, throwing 63 innings and tallying a 3.71 ERA.

Over his first four seasons with San Francisco, McMahon posted an overall 25-15 won-lost record with 30 saves. After the 1972 season, the Giants released him as a player. He continued with his duties as pitching coach. When San Francisco's bullpen began to falter in mid-1973, McMahon was reactivated on June 25. He'd been throwing batting practice all year, so was in excellent shape, and hopped into a game in the eighth inning against Atlanta on July 2. The score was 6-5 Giants, and there was a runner at first and no one out, with Hank Aaron due up. McMahon got Aaron to ground out and closed the game, setting down six straight batters. He notched a 4-0 mark with six saves and an excellent 1.48 ERA. The following year the same situation presented itself. McMahon was the team's pitching coach, returned to the active roster on May 21, and on the following day shut down the Braves in two full innings of work. He threw only 11 2/3 innings, though, appearing in nine games with no decisions and a 3.09 ERA. Six weeks later San Francisco called up Phoenix (Pacific Coast League) farmhand right-hander Ed Halicki and placed McMahon on waivers. Once he cleared waivers, McMahon returned as the pitching coach. His last appearance as a pitcher had been on June 29, 1974, in a home game against the Dodgers. He threw two scoreless innings of relief.

McMahon coached for San Francisco through 1975. In 1976 and 1977 he was a coach with the Minnesota Twins. For a couple of years Don worked in sales for the Rawlings Sporting Goods Company and turned up at Anaheim Stadium in 1979 to present Angels outfielder Rick Miller with a Gold Glove for the 1978 season.

McMahon returned to the major-league ranks to reprise his role as pitching coach with the Giants for three more seasons, 1980-1982. Within a few weeks of his release, he was hired by the Cleveland Indians in the same capacity, 1983-1985. In November 1985 he was hired by the Los Angeles Dodgers to position players from the press box as the team's "eye in the sky."[6] He even worked some in the offseason as a football scout for several years, helping out the Oakland Raiders even while still an active player. He and Raiders owner-coach Al Davis had both attended Erasmus Hall High in Brooklyn.

On July 22, 1987, at Dodger Stadium, while pitching batting practice, the 57-year-old McMahon suffered a heart attack and died a few hours later in a hospital. He had been working for Los Angeles as an instructional coach and scout and threw batting practice almost every Dodgers home game.

The *New York Times* ran a heartfelt appreciation of Don McMahon by Ira Berkow, headlined "He Died With Spikes On."[7] "He had a rubber arm," said longtime friend Frank Torre.[8] The Dodgers wore an armband reading "MAC" in his memory. Survived by his wife and six children, Don McMahon was buried at Good Shepherd Cemetery in Huntington Beach, California, with a baseball in his hand.

Sources

Newspapers

New York Times.

The Sporting News.

Online sources

Ancestry.com

BaseballLibrary.com

Baseball-Reference.com

Retrosheet.com

Books

Looney, Jack, *Now Batting Number....* (New York: Black Dog & Leventhal Publishers. 2006).

Pietrusza, David, Matthew Silverman, and Michael Gershman, eds. *Baseball: The Biographical Encyclopedia* (Kingston, New York: Total Sports/Sports Illustrated. 2000).

Interview

Jeff Angus, Interview with Dick Williams, February 24, 2006.

Notes

1 *The Sporting News*, September 14, 1960, 14.
2 *The Sporting News*, February 28, 1962, 20.
3 *The Sporting News*, June 23, 1962, 19.
4 *The Sporting News*, June 6, 1964, 12
5 Jeff Angus interview with Dick Williams, February 24, 2006.
6 Ira Berkow, "Sports of the Times; He Died with His Spikes On," *New York Times*, August 1, 1987.
7 Berkow.
8 Berkow.

Red Murff

By Michael J. Bielawa

Just before the start of the 1969 World Series, Baltimore Orioles third baseman Brooks Robinson was said to have uttered the rather Grinch-like statement, "We are here to prove there is no Santa Claus."[1] Such unabashed, un-American hubris could only naturally result in a rude October awakening for Baltimore. No presents under the Orange Birds' postseason tree. Just a lump of coal wrapped in pine tar.

Surprisingly, one person who contributed mightily to the Miracle Mets World Series triumph over the Orioles that year was a jolly Texan who never swung a bat or fielded a ball for the New Yorkers: Red Murff. It was this superscout's particular insight and dogged persistence that led to the signing of some of the most beloved players ever to doff a royal blue and orange cap. As a Mets scout, Red was credited with delivering a core of gifted players to the Mets. Jerry Koosman, Ken Boswell, and Jerry Grote all came to New York thanks to Murff's efforts. Red was also credited with discovering a fellow Texan, a lean high-school student the majority of scouts ignored. The only way this pitcher could have got into the Hall of Fame, so they thought, was if he bought a ticket. Murff proved his genius when he signed this fireballer from Alvin, Nolan Ryan.

John Robert "Red" Murff was born in Burlington, Texas, on April 1, 1921, and came to the game late. There was no baseball program at Red's high school in Rosebud, Texas; he only began playing during World War II while a member of an Army Air Corps team. At Maxwell Field, Alabama, Murff hit .466 in 1944 as an outfielder.[2] After the war he played semipro while working as an assistant department manager at Union Carbide and Carbon Corp. in Texas City. He signed on, at the age of 29, with the Baton Rouge Red Sticks of the Class C Evangeline League in 1950 when the club agreed to pay him a higher salary than his day job.[3] Pitching for the Red Sticks, Murff went 17-4, with a respectable 2.96 earned-run average. When he wasn't on the mound, he played the outfield, batting .331 while knocking in 65 runs. He won the league's Rookie of the Year Award. Years later he reflected, "The nicest thing [about the award] was the recognition that helped get me to the big leagues. The award made it known that I was a good player. And I was a rookie nearly 30 years old!"[4]

The following year, at an age when most athletes see their abilities start to decline, Murff decided that he would focus solely on pitching.[5] In the process of amassing 19 wins, he tossed a no-hitter for the Texas City Texans of the Class B Gulf Coast League. He won 23 games for the Tyler East Texans of the Big State League in 1952, and led the Texas League with 17 victories the following year for the Double-A Dallas Eagles (Texas League). Still an Eagle in 1955, he posted a 1.99 ERA, went 27-11, and logged more than 300 innings. *The Sporting News* named him Minor League Player of the Year. His next jump was to the majors, and it was decided in a unique manner. Murff said the Dallas owner, Dick Burnett, and Milwaukee Braves scout Earl Halstead could not finalize a sale price for the pitcher. "Burnett wanted ($100,000) and three players from the Braves 40-man roster. Halstead countered by offering

Red Murff (National Baseball Hall of Fame Library, Cooperstown, N.Y.)

($40,000) and three players. Arguing back and forth for several days, the two decided to sit down and play gin rummy with the winner setting the price for the deal. Eight hours later Halstead emerged victorious, and the Braves paid forty grand and three players to acquire [Murff's] services."[6] Red joined the Milwaukee Braves in 1956, pitched in 14 games (one start) and had a 4.44 ERA. The 35-year-old rookie injured his arm in the third inning of that first start for the Braves, which was his first major-league appearance. Murff, who had also suffered back problems, lamented that there was no real rehabilitation practiced in those days. He never graduated beyond being a bullpen pitcher in Milwaukee. His final game in the major leagues came just 13 months after his debut. He started just twice in 26 games. As a reliever he was retroactively credited with three saves.

Murff remained with the Braves over the 1956 and 1957 seasons, going 2-2 in 1957, but he did not pitch for the Braves after Memorial Day the year they went on to win the World Series. Murff lingered in the minors through 1959, pitching for Triple-A Wichita (11-9 and 11-5 in 1957 and '58) and Louisville (5-5 in 1959). He also hurled in the Puerto Rican League, where he later managed as well.

"Injury only stopped my baseball career as a player," Red philosophically noted. "Baseball was still a part of my life. Baseball was my vocation."[7] In 1960 he became the player-manager of the Jacksonville Braves of the Class A South Atlantic League. Still the ever-competitive Texan, the 39-year-old Murff had a 5-5 record. At Jacksonville he helped a young pitcher named Phil Niekro, who was struggling with his knuckleball. More than 3 1/2 decades later, the 318-game winner said during his 1997 induction speech at the Hall of Fame. "When I played in Jacksonville, Florida, my manager by the name of Red Murff … walked to me and said, 'Son,' he said, 'if you can get that knuckleball over the plate, you can pitch in the big leagues.' And I believed him. I've had a lot of respect for Red and I still do. He's here today and I just want to say thank you for finding someone at that age telling me that I could pitch in the big leagues with that knuckleball."[8]

It was merely Red Murff's first instance of helping a pitcher on the path to Cooperstown.

After scouting for the Houston Colt .45s, Murff joined the expansion team that really needed help. He went to work for the Mets organization in 1963, touring a huge territory that embraced Texas, Louisiana, Oklahoma, and New Mexico. In an attempt to lift the fledgling Mets farm system, Red instituted tryouts for young men enrolled in job-training programs and helped establish winter instructional camps in Mexico. All the while the scout continued to cultivate a keen, almost prescient ability to judge those players being overlooked.

Following up on a lead regarding a lefty hurler at the Army's Fort Bliss in El Paso, Texas, Red was shocked to find a "very fat" Jerry Koosman roaming the outfield.[9] Weight was not the only reason scouts were discouraged about this plump fellow from Minnesota; his lackadaisical approach caused their clipboards to remain blank. Murff persuaded the pitcher to lose weight. He signed Koosman shortly after his military discharge. Murff gave a helping hand to Sam Houston State student Ken Boswell, tutoring the infielder on how to approach the commissioner's office and enter the major-league draft as a special exception. (The Mets took Boswell in the fourth round of the first major-league draft, in 1965.) Jerry Grote, who would become a lifelong friend of Red's, was inked by Murff while he was scouting for the Colt .45s. When Houston lost interest in the catcher, Red's word convinced the Mets brass they should acquire the backstop after the 1965 season.

Nolan Ryan provides a special example of Murff's foresight and determination. Not even his blossoming fastball attracted scouts. The skinny kid's wild delivery did not resemble anything close to big-league potential. It was Murff who stood by the young pitcher, seeing what no one else could. During Ryan's 1999 Hall of Fame induction speech, the man who hurled seven no-hitters praised Murff for making his baseball career possible. "Red is a friend and Red took more of an interest in me at an early age," Ryan said. "He thought when he saw me at 6-foot-2 and 140, he wasn't discouraged by my build and by the way I threw the baseball as many other scouts were. And I appreciate the fact that Red spent so much time with me and worked to help me become a better pitcher."

While Koosman, Ryan, Grote, and Boswell propelled the Miracle Mets into a ticker-tape blizzard in Manhattan, one has to remember that it was Murff who helped bring these gifted players to the team. It is no fairytale for fans and statisticians to look at the contributions of these four members of the 1969 Mets roster and honestly credit Murff with winning 23 regular-season games while collecting 272 strikeouts during that magic season. By bringing Boswell and Grote to the Mets, Murff can also be credited with uncovering 72 RBIs for the club. His postseason numbers for 1969 are even more impressive: the clinching victory in the NLCS, followed by two World Series victories and a save).

By the time the Mets won the Series, Murff was with another club. In September 1968 he had again joined another expansion club that really needed his help, the Montreal Expos. He was named Montreal's Scout of the Year in 1975. Murff also started the baseball program at the University of Mary Hardin-Baylor College, near his home in Belton, Texas, and came up with the innovative method of allowing released professional ballplayers to get an education and still be able to play college ball (games against ex-professionals were deemed exhibitions). The school's baseball ballpark was named Red Murff Field in 1994.

Murff, who was also credited for finding catcher John Bateman (Oklahoma) and pitchers Mike Stanton (Texas) and Norm Charlton (Louisiana), retired from scouting in 1991 after 34 years on the job. He was inducted into the Texas Baseball Hall of Fame in 1989 and the Texas Scouts Association Hall of Fame in 1999. Murff was an uncle to former Yankees and Twins relief pitcher Ron Davis and the great-uncle of Ike Davis, the Mets first baseman). He tried his hand at writing, penning a children's book called *Little Whiskers Fin* after telling his grandson a story. With that under his belt, wrote his own story, *The Scout: Searching for the Best in Baseball* (with Mike Capps).

Murff remained close to the game even in his 80s. After moving to the Tyler, Texas, area in 2003, he took an interest in the University of Texas at Tyler. "Red loved baseball and I loved it as well and we hit it off. …" said the university's former head baseball coach and athletic director, James Vilade. "Early on in our program, Red was the only person who supported our team and our players. He was instrumental with having a scouting day and getting our players ready for professional ball and it really helped them out."[10] Murff was given a Lifetime Achievement Award by the school.

Even when Parkinson's disease, along with heart problems, forced a move into a Tyler nursing home, Murff still talked baseball and went with Vilade to area games on occasion. One of his prize pupils, Nolan Ryan, even paid a visit. Murff died on November 28, 2008, at the age of 87.

Sources

Murff, John "Red" with Mike Capps. *The Scout: Searching for the Best in Baseball*, (Dallas: Word Publishing, 1996).

Cotham, Jeremy, " 'Red' Murff: The Legend of Baseball Legends," *The Patriot Talon* of the University of Texas at Tyler, December 9, 2008.

Daley, Arthur, "The Bubble Bursts," *New York Times*, October 12, 1969.

Wolf, Bob, " 'Won't Muff Big Chance,' Chirps Confident Murff," *The Sporting News*, March 7, 1956.

The Sporting News, 1955-68, 1973.

Niekro, Philip Henry—Baseball Hall of Fame Introduction Speech, August 3, 1997, http://baseballhall.org/node/11259.

Red Murff interviews conducted by Michael J. Bielawa, November 2005.

Red Murff file, National Baseball Hall of Fame, Cooperstown, New York.

Notes

1 Arthur Daley, "The Bubble Bursts," *New York Times*, October 12, 1969.
2 Bob Wolf, " 'Won't Muff Big Chance,' Chirps Confident Murff," *The Sporting News*, March 7, 1956.
3 Wolf, " 'Won't Muff Big Chance'…"
4 Red Murff interview by Michael J. Bielawa November 21, 2005.
5 Wolf, " 'Won't Muff Big Chance,'…"
6 John "Red" Murff with Mike Capps, *The Scout: Searching for the Best in Baseball* (Dallas: Word Publishing, 1996).
7 Red Murff interview conducted by Michael J. Bielawa, November 21, 2005.
8 Philip Henry Niekro—Baseball Hall of Fame Introduction Speech, August 3, 1997. http://baseballhall.org/node/11259
9 Red Murff interview conducted by Michael J. Bielawa, November 30, 2005.
10 Jeremy Cotham, " 'Red' Murff: The Legend of Baseball Legends," *The Patriot Talon* of the University of Texas at Tyler, December 9, 2008.

Danny O'Connell

By Mel Marmer

Instead of being the good-hitting second baseman and field leader that the Milwaukee Braves expected him to be—the player who would make enough of a difference to help lead them to the National League pennant in 1954, Danny O'Connell turned out to be a disappointment, compiling just a .248 batting average in four seasons with the club. The team had dealt six players and $100,000 for him on December 26, 1953, expecting "the brassy, fresh-talking infielder" to hit .300 and become a leader.[1] Instead, O'Connell struggled in three of the four seasons he played for the Braves, hitting .279, .225, .239, and .235 respectively, and showing only occasional glimpses of the .293 hitter and the field leader that he was in his first two big-league seasons with the Pittsburgh Pirates. It was no secret that the Braves coveted All-Star second baseman Red Schoendienst and they made inquiries as to his availability routinely, but couldn't work out a deal for him. In the meantime, everyone hoped O'Connell's hitting stroke would return so a trade would not be necessary. But that didn't happen. O'Connell was benched at times and other players were tried at second base, but O'Connell's play would improve enough that no one dislodged him. Finally, on June 15, 1957, the Braves pulled off the trade that had been rumored for years: O'Connell, outfielder Bobby Thomson, and pitcher Ray Crone were sent to the New York Giants for Schoendienst, who would play a key role in the Milwaukee Braves' winning the pennant and their only world championship that fall.

Regarding the way the situation at the keystone sack played out, Braves pitcher Bob Buhl said, "We had other good second basemen but they couldn't turn a double play or hit .300 like Red."[2] After O'Connell was traded, he continued his struggles at the plate while a member of the Giants in New York and San Francisco. He batted .256 in 1957, .232 in 1958, and just .190 in 34 games in 1959. He was sent down to the Giants' top farm team, Tacoma, in 1960 and began a comeback there at age 31, by hitting .312. O'Connell obtained his release from the Giants and persuaded the expansion Washington Senators to take a chance on him by pointing out that he was a better infielder than almost every draftee available, and his salary was reasonable. He put together two good seasons with the Senators in 1961 and 1962 before retiring as a player. O'Connell "never quite reached the stardom that had been expected of him, but he was a steady and capable player" for ten seasons in the major leagues.[3]

Daniel Francis O'Connell, III, son of Daniel Francis O'Connell, Jr. and the former Myrtle Parliman, was born on January 21, 1929, in Paterson, New Jersey. Five years later brother Robert was born and sister Alice arrived two years after that.

The O'Connells were a working-class Irish family—three generations lived under one roof in a row house on Carlisle Avenue, about a half-hour from New York City.[4]

Danny's father worked as a school janitor and was a semipro pitcher. He took his kids often to see New

Danny O'Connell (National Baseball Hall of Fame Library, Cooperstown, N.Y.)

York Giants' and Brooklyn Dodgers' games. Danny attended St. Bonaventure High School on a basketball scholarship. He was a third baseman on the baseball team and pitched occasionally. His favorite player was Chicago Cubs third baseman Stan Hack. Danny left school before graduation and went to work in a dye plant.

O'Connell began his professional baseball career in the spring of 1946 with the Bloomingdale (New Jersey) Troopers of the Class D North Atlantic League, signed by Brooklyn Dodgers scout Clyde Sukeforth for a $1,500 bonus and a salary of $80 per month. He was 17 years old, a slightly built 5-feet-8-inches tall, and weighed just 140 pounds. He batted .327, with a slugging percentage of .469. In 1947 O'Connell was assigned to the Three Rivers (Quebec) Royals of the Class C Canadian-American League, where he hit .311, and led the team in hits with 151, and in total bases with 195.

In 1948 O'Connell hit .292 for the Greenville (South Carolina) Spinners, of the Class A South Atlantic (Sally) League. The following season he hit .314 with 17 home runs and 102 RBIs for the Triple-A St. Paul Saints of the American Association. In the balloting for the league's most valuable rookie, O'Connell finished second to Milwaukee Brewers second baseman Roy Hartsfield. On October 1, 1949, the Dodgers traded O'Connell to the Pittsburgh Pirates for $50,000 and second baseman Jack Cassini. The outspoken O'Connell commented, "Last year I was playing for (Branch) Rickey, but now I am playing for money."[5]

The once skinny lad filled out to 5-feet-11 and 168 pounds. He played well in spring training in 1950 but was sent to the Triple-A Indianapolis Indians to learn to play shortstop. By July O'Connell was tearing up the American Association, hitting .351 and being named to the all-star team. He got the call to join the parent team on July 11, and made his major-league debut at Forbes Field on July 14, 1950, starting at third base against the New York Giants. O'Connell distinguished himself with an RBI single in his first major-league at-bat, off starter Sheldon Jones, and a single off Sal Maglie in the fourth inning, and scored a run. O'Connell belted his first major-league home run — a ninth-inning solo shot off the Boston Braves' Vern Bickford two days later.

O'Connell was moved to the shortstop position just nine days after his debut when the Pirates purchased veteran third baseman Bob Dillinger from the Philadelphia A's. In 79 games, O'Connell played like a veteran," *The Sporting News* wrote after the season. He batted .292 and "his work in the field was miraculous."[6] He won *The Sporting News*' honors for best rookie third baseman in the majors and showed "exceptional promise during his half-season tenure."[7]

With the Korean War on, O'Connell enlisted in the US Army in February 1951 for two years of active duty. He served in the 3rd Infantry Regiment, primarily a ceremonial unit stationed at Fort Myer, Virginia, next to Arlington National Cemetery. O'Connell played on the regimental baseball team and was a teammate of pitcher Johnny Antonelli of the Braves, catcher Sam Calderone of the Giants, and pitcher Bob Purkey of the Pirates. The Fort Myer nine became the armed forces champion and won the National Baseball Congress Tournament Championship in 1952, sweeping all seven playoff games and defeating Fort Leonard Wood for the title. O'Connell was voted the MVP of the 32 teams in the tournament.[8] The team then traveled to Japan to meet the N.B.C. Japanese champions for the inter-hemispheric nonprofessional championship. The Fort Myer team won the best-of-seven series in five games, and also split a pair of games against two Japanese pro teams.[9]

O'Connell was out of the service and back with the Pirates in 1953. Shortstop Dick Groat was now in the Army, and manager Fred Haney, reflecting on the dearth of infield talent, said he had five capable infielders but that O'Connell was the best he had at each position.[10] Haney decided to employ O'Connell at second base, a new position for him.[11] "I can put him anywhere and he can do better than anybody else," Haney said. "He's our best ballplayer."[12]

Haney picked a special role for O'Connell: "Danny was to all intents the Pirates field captain," Haney's courier who carried messages onto the field and also what Haney called his "stimulator." ... "More than that he is the manager's agitator. He's a holler guy with a loud voice and a needling tongue."[13]

On August 17 at Ebbets Field in Brooklyn, O'Connell singled off Dodgers lefty Johnny Podres, launching a hitting streak that lasted 26 games. The streak ended on September 19 in a game against the New York Giants at the Polo Grounds. For besting a 25-game hitting streak posted by the Pirates' Charlie Grimm in 1923, O'Connell reportedly was given an automobile by his friends from Paterson.

"It was amazing how he handled the bat, because he had no speed at all," teammate Bob Friend said in reflecting on the streak. "He was one of the slower guys on our team. Danny was a guy who knew the strike zone. He couldn't hit for a lot of power, but he could hit to all fields. He was a guy who knew how to play the game."

"He was one of those Punch-and-Judy sort of guys who just put the ball in play," said Nellie King, a Pirates pitcher who faced O'Connell after he was traded to Milwaukee. "He was one of those pesky hitters. ... He would just annoy the heck out of you, like a gnat."[14]

During the streak O'Connell batted .356 (42-for-118). Only five of his hits were for extra bases: one home run, one triple and three doubles. He finished the season with a .294 batting average, 26 doubles and 7 home runs. After that season great things were expected of O'Connell. No one could have anticipated that his first full season in the major leagues would be his best.[15]

Expectations to the contrary, on December 26, 1953, Danny was traded by the Pirates to the Milwaukee Braves for Double-A left-handed pitcher Larry Lasalle, 36-year-old left fielder Sid Gordon, 36-year-old center fielder Sam Jethroe, 20-year-old right-handed pitcher Curt Raydon, 31-year-old right-hander Max Surkont, 26-year-old left-hander Fred Waters, and $100,000.

Coverage of the trade mentioned O'Connell's confidence. "If there is anything that characterizes O'Connell it is confidence. He brims over with it, just as he does with Irish wit and song. He thinks he's good and he has no reluctance to tell anybody what he thinks."[16]

O'Connell's flaws were also examined; one of the most prophetic statements came from Philadelphia Phillies president Bob Carpenter, who said, "There is no assurance that O'Connell can play second base. He's no cat at that spot and if he is shifted to third, there is no proof that Ed Mathews will be a success in the outfield. They are going to have their headaches.[17] Braves pitcher Warren Spahn, welcomed the trade, declaring O'Connell the toughest batter he faced last season and saying he was glad he would not have to pitch to Danny.[18]

Playing in Pittsburgh, there was little pressure to perform for the lowly 1953 Pirates. This wasn't the case in Milwaukee, however, where O'Connell would find that "(e)very game at the County Stadium is a pressure game, every series a World Series."[19]

O'Connell got off to a good start with the Braves in 1954 by reeling off a ten-game hitting streak in which he batted .400 (18-for-45). He was voted Braves player of the week but the distinction it was lost in Milwaukee's mediocre 5-5 start. In early June O'Connell was hitting just .259 and was briefly benched, but he improved and finished the season at .279. The Braves finished in third place with an 89-65 record.

Speaking at a banquet in Waterbury, Connecticut, in January 1955, O'Connell criticized manager Charlie Grimm and his teammates in a way that could have had repercussions. Recalling the beaning of Joe Adcock in August 1954, he said the Braves pitchers needed to stick up for their hitters. And he said the Braves would have won the pennant "if Grimm hadn't been too easy on the players." O'Connell described Grimm as "a nice fellow" and "a great manager to play for."[20] Grimm took the criticism with aplomb, saying that "despite O'Connell, I'll continue to manage the Braves."[21] O'Connell wrote a letter of apology to Grimm.

On January 22, 1955, Danny and Veronica "Vera" Sharkey of Montclair, New Jersey, were married. They would have four children: sons Daniel IV and John, and daughters Maureen and Nancy.

In 1955 spring training O'Connell suffered back spasms warming up before a game. Grimm increased second baseman Jack Dittmer's playing time and Hank Aaron played second base in early June and for 17 days in mid-July. O'Connell's batting average was to .319 on May 20, but drifted down to .225 by season's end. The Braves won 11 of 15 games to move into second place on June 30, never got closer to Brooklyn than ten games behind on August 27, and they finished in second place,

13 1/2 games back. O'Connell's batting average was the lowest among regular players in the major leagues.

O'Connell batted leadoff for most of the 1956 season.[22] In May calcium deposits were found in Red Schoendienst's shoulder, nixing any interest the Braves might have had in him.[23] With the Braves in first place by a game during the first week of June, O'Connell was benched for about a week for lack of hitting. His resurgence was highlighted by a June 13 performance in which he socked three triples off Robin Roberts of the Phillies, lifting his average to .290.[24] In a series against the Pirates in Pittsburgh, June 18-20, O'Connell collected six RBIs, and the Braves, surged back into first place.

O'Donnell batted only .239 for the season, but had a few noteworthy moments. On June 21 he was 3-for-4 with 4 RBIs in the Braves' sixth straight victory. On June 23 O'Connell hit a ninth-inning solo home run off Johnny Antonelli to defeat the Giants, 2-1. On June 24 he hit a a three-run home run off Jim Hearn at the Polo Grounds, a game-winning blooper that just ticked the right field foul pole, 257 feet away. O'Connell helped lead four-game sweeps of Pittsburgh and New York. Meanwhile, manager Charlie Grimm was fired after the Braves fell to 24-22 in July, and was succeeded by Fred Haney.

O'Connell's defense was equally good: "O'Connell turned in his best second-basing of the season in the four-game Cubs series, July 5-8. In one game July 7, he started three double plays," *The Sporting News* wrote.[25] There were still problems. On July 16 he failed to run out a ground ball that appeared to be a routine out. Pirates first baseman Dale Long fumbled the ball and O'Connell would have most likely been safe. O'Connell was fined by manager Haney.[26]

What to do about the second base was becoming a long-running question. After the season Braves beat writer Bob Wolf theorized, "If the Braves can't get the players they want, the most popular way to achieve its purpose would be to shift Mathews to left field and shift O'Connell from second to his natural spot at third base. If they can't get Schoendienst, they could shift (Johnny) Logan to second and have (Felix) Mantilla play shortstop."[27]

The second base situation was finally resolved on June 15, 1957, with the Braves in first place by 1 1/2 games over the Cincinnati Redlegs. O'Connell was traded to the Giants in a deal that brought Red Schoendienst to Milwaukee. O'Connell, outfielder Bobby Thomson, and pitcher Ray Crone went to New York. The trade cost the three traded Braves a share of the team's World Series money.

O'Connell later said that playing for manager Bill Rigney after his trade to the Giants was one of the most frustrating experiences in his career. "I started to lose my confidence. Rigney never used me," he said. "I think the last straw was when we were short of infielders and Rigney played an outfielder, Jackie Brandt, at third over me. My confidence went down to zero."[28] O'Connell played sporadically for the Giants until the team, by then in San Francisco, released him at the end of spring training in 1960.

O'Connell played for the Tacoma Giants of the Pacific Coast League in 1961 and hit .312. After the season he traveled to baseball's winter meetings in search of a job. He signed with the Washington Senators for a $5,000 bonus and salary of about $16,000. He batted .260 in 1961 and .263 in 1962.. He had a career-best .361 on-base percentage in 1961 and led the AL in sacrifice hits with 15, and though he was never a fast runner, pilfered a career-high 15 bases at the age of 32.

Released by the Senators after the 1962 season, O'Connell ended his playing days as a .260 career hitter with 1,049 hits in 1,143 games, 320 RBIs, and 527 runs scored. He was a player-manager for the Senators' York (Pennsylvania) White Roses of the Double-A Eastern League in 1963 before being called up to be a coach with the Senators. In 1964 he was the Senators' third-base coach. After the season he left his coaching job and went to work as a salesman for the Lee Plumbing Supply Company in Denville, New Jersey. He refereed high-school basketball games and was active in his church, St. Thomas the Apostle, in Bloomfield. He was also active in the Catholic Youth Organization in Paterson.

In 1968 O'Connell played in an old timer's game between the Giants and the Dodgers at Candlestick Park that marked the tenth anniversary game of first major-league game played in California. O'Connell victimized Dodgers pitcher Don Drysdale, performing the hidden-ball trick, and doubled off Ed Roebuck to help the Giants to a 2-1 victory in the three-inning contest.[29]

While driving home on the evening of October 2, 1969, the 40-year old O'Connell suffered a coronary occlusion, a blockage of one or more of the arteries in his heart. He lost control of his car in the heavy rain and it skidded into a utility pole near his home. He died from his injuries, leaving behind his wife and four children.

Notes

1 The cash amount of $100,000 is used by Baseball-Reference.com, which the author accessed on June 16, 2013. Other sources, including *The Sporting News*, have given different amounts. Some amounts given are as high as $250,000. The author chose the more conservative amount.

2 Danny Peary, *We Played The Game* (New York: Black Dog and Leventhal, 1998), 353.

3 Obituaries—Danny O'Connell, *The Sporting News*, October 18, 1969, 42.

4 The information about the O'Connell family was obtained from the US Census of 1940, which reported that there were three individuals named Daniel O'Connell living at 136 Carlisle Avenue in Paterson. Daniel Jr. was working as a foreman on road construction. Danny was 11. Grandfather Daniel F. O'Connell, 79 years old in 1940, listed as a saloonkeeper, was born in Norfolk, Connecticut, on January 6, 1864, and died in Paterson on November 6, 1940. Danny's great-grandfather, John O'Connell, was born in Ireland.

5 David Finoli and Bill Ranier, *The Pittsburgh Pirates Encyclopedia* (Champaign, Illinois: Sports Publishing LLC, 2003), 464.

6 *The Sporting News*, October 11, 1950, 11.

7 Bob Broeg, "Strong Rookie All-Stars Show .283 Bat Mark," *The Sporting News*, November 1, 1950, 5.

8 Bob Buege, "Global World Series: 1955-57," *SABR, Baseball Research Journal*, Spring 2012. Accessed online October 1, 2013.

9 *The Sporting News*, March 18, 1953, 31.

10 Milton Gross, "Pirate With a Future." *Sport*, February 1954, 26.

11 *The Sporting News*, March 18, 1953, 10.

12 Gross, 26.

13 Gross, 66.

14 Ray Fittipaldo and Robert Dvorchak, "Obscure Players of Long Ago Atop Streak List." *Pittsburgh Post-Gazette* Sports, May 30, 2003, accessed on August 15, 2013. O'Connell's 26-game hitting streak as of 2014 was still a Pirates record for batters since 1900. It was tied by Kenny Lofton in 2006. The Pirates' all-time consecutive-game hitting record is 27 games, set in 1899 by Jimmy Williams. Also see Pittsburgh Pirates.mlb.com/Pirates history/Individual records, accessed August 31, 2013.

15 Lester J. Biederman, "Streak Reaches 23 Games: O'Connell's Consistent Bat Bright Spot of Dismal Bucs," *Pittsburgh Press*, September 15, 1953.

16 Gross, 26.

17 *The Sporting News*, January 20, 1954, 6.

18 "Spahn Declares O'Connell Toughest Batter To Face," *The Sporting News*, January 27, 1954, 16.

19 Al Hirshberg, "Can Milwaukee Keep It Up?" *Sport*, February 1954, 79.

20 Frank Monardo, "Failure to Return Dusters Costly to Braves—O'Connell," *Waterbury* (Connecticut) *Republican and American*, reprinted in *The Sporting News*, January 17, 1955, 24.

21 *The Sporting News*, February 22, 1955, 27.

22 "Braves' Ifs Vanish—Danny Delivers, Thomson In Stride," *The Sporting News*, May 23, 1956, 11.

23 Joe King, "Schoendienst's Sore Arm Proves Big Pain For Giants," *The Sporting News*, July 4, 1956, 10.

24 Bob Wolf, "Cholly Jolly No Longer—Jaw Sags With Bat Marks in Braves Home Stumble," *The Sporting News,* June 20, 1956, 10.

25 *The Sporting News*, July 18, 1956, 5.

26 Bob Wolf, "Failure to Run Out Grounder Cost Danny One Dollar a Foot," *The Sporting News*, July 25, 1956, 8.

27 "Quinn Denies Deal Pending for Redhead"; Bob Wolf, "Braves Sidewalk Experts Offering Ideas To Fill Holes," *The Sporting News*, November 7, 1956, 17.

28 Obituaries—Danny O'Connell, *The Sporting News*, October 18, 1969, 42.

29 *The Sporting News*, August 4, 1968.

Andy Pafko

By Dale Voiss

HE IS A permanent part of baseball lore. He played for the Chicago Cubs in the 1945 World Series, their last appearance in the fall classic. He stood with his back against the left-field wall as Bobby Thomson's "shot heard 'round the world" flew over his head and into the Polo Grounds grandstand to give the New York Giants a victory over his Brooklyn Dodgers and clinch the 1951 National League pennant. He was the starting right fielder for his home-state Milwaukee Braves in 1953 and 1954. He lost his starting job in 1955 to a young outfielder named Hank Aaron. He played in four World Series for three different teams in his 17-year career. His name is Andy Pafko.

He was born Andrew Pafko on February 25, 1921, in Boyceville, a rural community in northwest Wisconsin between Eau Claire and Minneapolis. His parents were born in Prague (in what became Czechoslovakia), as were the two oldest children. After World War I they moved to the United States and settled in Boyceville. Andy, the third oldest child and first born in America, was raised on a 200-acre dairy farm. The Pafkos later added three sons to the fold, bringing the total to six children.

As a major-league rookie Pafko recalled the days spent milking the 16 cows on the farm. He remembered himself and his brothers trying to find an excuse to go to the pasture and play baseball. Often they wouldn't finish their chores until after dark and wouldn't get to play at all. But he credited milking cows with helping him develop the strong grip that made him a major-league hitter.

Because Boyceville's high school had no baseball team, Pafko's first experience was with the Connersville team of the amateur Dunn County League in 1939. He hit about .500 that summer and this gave him his first inkling that he might have professional potential. In the spring of 1940, now 19 years old, he decided to try out with the Eau Claire entry in the Northern League.

Ivy Griffin, the team's manager, signed him the day he tried out but had to cut him the same day because he realized he had too many players on the roster. Later that season Griffin had an emergency and needed an outfielder, so he drove to the Pafko farm, picked up Andy, and drove him back to Eau Claire for the season's final two weeks. Pafko hit just .209 but his contract was picked up by Madison of the Three-I League that winter. Madison immediately sold his contract to Green Bay of the Wisconsin State League.

Pafko spent the 1941 season playing for the Class D Green Bay Blue Sox. He finished second in the league in hitting with a .349 average. He hit 12 home runs. In November 1941 his contract was purchased by Bill Veeck, then owner of the minor-league Milwaukee Brewers, for $1,000. After reporting to spring training in Ocala, Florida, in 1942 Pafko was assigned to the Macon Peaches of the South Atlantic League, where he hit .300, drove in 85 runs, and led the league in triples with 18.

Summoned twice by his draft board for physicals, Pafko was granted a deferment from military service in World War II because of chronic high blood pressure.

Andy Pafko (National Baseball Hall of Fame Library, Cooperstown, N.Y.)

Pafko was disappointed because he wanted to serve his country. He later said that if he had not been told he would never have known he had high blood pressure, because it did not affect his daily life.

After his season at Macon, Pafko expected to be assigned to Milwaukee in 1943. But over the winter he picked up a Milwaukee paper and read that he had been sold to the Cubs' Los Angeles farm team in in Pacific Coast League. He was deeply disappointed because he wanted his parents to see him play. Pafko was so distraught about having to play so far from home that he considered quitting the game and going back to farming. His older brother John talked him into reporting to the Angels. (Pafko's appearance on the Angels roster meant he had gone from Class D to Double-A in two years.)

At Los Angeles Pafko replaced center fielder Barney Olsen, who had left for the Navy. He opened the season with a two-hit effort against Oakland and never looked back. Angels manager Bill Sweeney adjusted Pakfo's batting stance so he could get out in front of the ball, increasing his power. As a result he led the Pacific Coast League in all three Triple Crown categories for most of the season. In May the Angels moved Pafko to right field, in part due to his strong throwing arm. He was named Southern California's athlete of the month for May by the Helms Athletic Foundation.

Angels president Clarence "Pants" Rowland, a former major-league umpire and manager, was quoted as saying that he would "stake (my) reputation on Pafko," predicting he would become a good big-league hitter eventually. In addition to his ability to hit and hit with power, Pafko was fleet afield. His only weakness was running the bases; he had become gunshy after being picked off second base by the catcher in the season opener. His versatility caused a minor-league manager to give him the nickname Handy Andy.

The PCL's sportswriters voted Pafko the Most Valuable Player after he led the league in batting with a .356 average and runs batted in (118), and hit 18 home runs. The Angels won the league title with a then-record .710 winning percentage, but lost to third-place Seattle in the postseason playoffs.

On September 24, 1943, after the Angels' season was over, Pafko was called up to join the Cubs. He wasted little time in establishing himself as a major-league hitter. He made his major-league debut in front of the smallest crowd in Wrigley Field history; just 314 fans sat through a downpour to watch Pafko go 2-for-3 and drive in four runs in a rain-shortened five-inning victory over Philadelphia. The next day he had three more hits in a victory over the Brooklyn Dodgers. Pafko hit safely in his first nine games and hit .379 with 10 RBIs in 13 games as the season wound down.

Pafko spent the offseason working at a war plant in Los Angeles before reporting to 1944 spring training in French Lick, Indiana, where he won the starting center-field job. In late May St. Louis Cardinals manager Billy Southworth called Pafko the best rookie in the National League. For the fourth-place Cubs, Pafko batted .269 in 128 games with 62 RBIs.

Pafko's open batting stance reminded many of Mel Ott, then still the player-manager of the New York Giants. While Pafko's power was mainly to left field he also had some power to the opposite field. But people seemed most impressed by his ability to make diving catches in the outfield and a cannon arm that netted him 24 assists in 1944.

In 1945 Pafko established himself as a major-league hitter. He batted .298 and drove in 110 runs for the pennant-winning Cubs. His performance was good enough to land him in fourth place in the National League MVP voting. (The award was won by fellow Cub Phil Cavaretta.) Pafko was named to the NL All-Star team, though no game was played because of wartime travel restrictions. He made the All-Star team in four of his next five seasons.

Backed by the bats of Cavaretta and Pafko and the pitching of Hank Wyse (22 victories), the Cubs won the pennant with a 98-56 record, three games better than the second-place Cardinals. Pafko hit just .214 (6-for-28) with two RBIs in the World Series as the Cubs lost in seven games to the Detroit Tigers.

In 1945 Pafko met Chicago native Ellen Kapusta, who had attended a game at Wrigley Field with a mutual friend. She did not seem impressed by Pafko's status as a major leaguer, but that changed when Pafko was able to land her a couple of tickets to the World Series. The two then began a romance that led to marriage on February 1, 1947.

Pafko got off to a slow start in 1946 but picked up the pace in May and was hitting .276 with 21 RBIs on June 1 when he stepped on a ball in pregame practice and suffered an ankle injury that kept him out of action until mid-July. A little more than a month after returning, he was knocked out for the remainder of the season when he fractured his right arm on August 27. He played in just 65 games, hitting .282 and driving in 39 runs as the Cubs fell to third place.

Newly married and with his arm healed, Pafko was raring to go into the 1947 season. He began the season strong, batting .304 through the Cubs' first 32 games. On May 27 Pafko was flown from St. Louis, where the Cubs were playing, to Chicago after developing a kidney infection. He did not return to the lineup until June 18, and wound up batting .302 in 125 games with 13 homers and 66 RBIs. He tied the Cardinals' Whitey Kurowski for the league lead by grounding into 19 double plays.

During the offseason Cubs general manager Jim Gallagher was reported to have rejected two trades involving Pafko, with the Cincinnati Reds and the Dodgers. While they did not trade Andy, the Cubs did make changes for the 1948 season. Among them was moving Pafko from the outfield to third base. He replaced Peanuts Lowrey, who was switched to the outfield and lacked the power that manager Charlie Grimm desired at the hot corner.

On the offensive side, the Cubs did not regret their decision to keep Pafko. He batted .312 with 26 home runs and 101 RBIs, leading the team in all three categories. But Pafko made 29 errors at third base, and seldom played anywhere but the outfield for the rest of his career. The Cubs continued their tumble through the standings, falling from sixth in 1947 to the NL cellar in 1948 with a 64-90 record

On April 30, 1949, Pafko made an embarrassing defensive gaffe at Wrigley Field in front of over 30,000 fans. The Cardinals, losing 3-2, had the tying run on first base with two outs in the ninth inning. Rocky Nelson hit a sinking line drive to center field that Pafko, with a lunge, appeared to have caught for the final out. But umpire Al Barlick ruled no catch. While Pafko argued vehemently that he had caught the ball, the two St. Louis runners scampered around the bases since time had not been called. Pafko finally realized that the ball was still in play and threw home but his throw hit Nelson as he slid safely home with a media-labeled "inside-the-glove" home run. The Cardinals hung on to their 4-3 lead and won the game.

After the Cubs got off to a 19-31 start, Grimm was fired and was replaced by Frankie Frisch. Pafko played third base in 49 games, that season, then returned to the outfield for good. He hit .281 for the season, leading the team with 233 total bases.

In 1950 the Cubs posted a 64-89 record, their fourth straight losing season. But Pafko could hardly be blamed; he hit .304 with a career-high 36 home runs, second in the National League to the Pirates' Ralph Kiner, who had 47. Pafko drew 69 walks to post a career-high .397 on-base percentage. His season was good enough to impress Reds president Giles, who said that if he could choose any player in the NL to help improve his floundering team, he would choose Pafko.

On June 15, 1951, after being the subject of trade rumors practically every season, Pafko was sent to the Brooklyn Dodgers in an four-for-four deal involving some front-line players. He had become an icon in Chicago, and Wrigley Field fans reacted angrily. The Dodgers were playing in Chicago when the trade was made. Pafko changed clubhouses after the first game of a three-game series. It didn't help the mood of the Chicago fans when Pafko hit a solo homer in the seventh inning of a 6-4 Cubs win in his first game in Dodger blue. He hit just .249 for the Dodgers the rest of the season, but contributed 18 home runs and 58 RBIs in 84 games as the Dodgers fought for first place.

Brooklyn had been leading the league by 13 games on August 11, but their crosstown rival, the Giants, rallied to go an amazing 37-7 over the last month and a half to tie the Dodgers. This forced a best-of-three playoff to decide the pennant. After splitting the first two games, the teams met at the Polo Grounds, the Giants' home field. The Dodgers went with 20-game winner Don Newcombe to start the decisive game while the Giants countered with 23-game winner Sal Maglie. The Giants entered the bottom of the ninth down 4-1. After New York scored a run and put runners on second and third with one out, Ralph Branca replaced Newcombe to face Giant third baseman Bobby Thomson. After taking a strike from Branca, Thomson hit a sinking line drive toward Pafko in left field. Pafko went back thinking it might bounce off the wall. Instead the ball cleared the fence for a three-run homer and radio announcer Russ Hodges repeatedly screamed, "The Giants win the pennant!"

In 1952 Pafko roamed the Dodgers outfield with Duke Snider and Carl Furillo. He hit .287 with 19 home runs and 85 RBIs as the Dodgers won their third pennant in six years before losing to the Yankees in the World Series.

In January 1953 the Dodgers traded Pafko to the Braves, who were moving from Boston to Milwaukee and wanted a Wisconsin product on the roster to help draw fans in the early days. Pafko was the starting right fielder in 1953 and 1954, hitting .297 and .286 with home-run power, but in 1955 he lost his starting job to future Hall of Famer Hank Aaron, and was a part-timer for the next five seasons. He did get to play in two more World Series. The Braves beat the Yankees in the 1957 Series but lost to New York in 1958. Pafko started three games in each Series, batting .214 in 1957 and .333 in 1958.

After the two World Series, Pafko played one more season for the Braves before being released as a player in October 1959. He was a coach from 1960 through 1962, and in 1964 he became a minor-league manager in the Braves organization, starting with the Binghamton Triplets of the Class A New York-Pennsylvania League. Among the players on that team was future World Series champion manager Cito Gaston. Pafko, then 43, actually got an at-bat with the Triplets in which he tripled.

In 1965 Pafko managed the West Palm Beach Braves of the Florida State League, and in 1966 and 1967 he led Kinston in the Class A Carolina League. In 1968 Pafko returned for another season to manage at West Palm Beach. He later took a job as a part-time scout with the expansion Montreal Expos. Pafko was a scout for the Atlanta Braves from 1969 to 1973.

After retiring, Pafko and his wife settled in the Chicago area. In 1999 he was named to the Cubs All-Century team. His wife died in 2006. Into his 90s Pafko continued to make occasional trips to Wrigley Field and remained active in the Milwaukee Braves Historical Association, attending the annual meeting each summer in Milwaukee. At the age of 92, he died on October 8, 2013, in a nursing home in Stevensville, Michigan.

Sources

Baseball Digest, September 1954.

The Sporting News, May 5, 1941; November 11, 1941; July 16, 1942; March 4, 1943; July 1, 1943; November 18, 1943.

baseball-reference.com

bleedcubbieblue.com/2007/1/21/6336/1747

discover-net.net/~dchs/history/expafko.html

Phil Paine

By Chip Greene

Tucked in the northwest corner of Rhode Island, just ten miles from both Massachusetts and Connecticut, is the village of Chepachet, where Phillips Steere Paine was born on June 8, 1930. When Paine was a teenager in the 1940s, Chepachet didn't have a high school, so each school day he traveled five miles north to the town of Burrillville to attend Burrillville High School. As of 2013, Paine was the only Burrillville High alumnus to play major-league baseball.

Over parts of six seasons, playing with the Braves both in Boston and Milwaukee, and also with the St. Louis Cardinals, Paine, a tall (6-feet-2), slender (180 pounds) right-handed pitcher, totaled 150 innings in 95 games, all in relief. Between his first game, at the age of 21, and the end of his major-league career at 28, he amassed a sparkling record of 10-1, a .909 winning percentage; served in the Army during the Korean War, and became the first American major leaguer to pitch in the Japanese professional leagues. After his baseball days were over, he settled down with his family to a quiet small-town life in Pennsylvania as the proprietor of a hotel. Much like his baseball career, Paine's life, too, was ended far too soon, but as his family noted at his memorial service, "he accomplished all that he wanted to do." For a young man from a place as tiny as Chepachet, it surely must have been an exhilarating journey; and as his sister Marcia said, "Phil loved every minute of it."

Paine was the only son and the eldest of three children born to Arthur and Celia Paine, and he was named Phillips after Arthur's best friend. (His middle name, Steere, is taken from an old Rhode Island family whose progenitor came to America in the mid-1600s). Arthur Paine had himself been a ballplayer, and from the time her brother was 3 years old, Marcia remembered, "Phil had a glove in his hand." In fact, she said, Phil and his father were often opponents when local teams played each other.[1]

Arthur Paine was also an avid outdoorsman who loved hunting and fishing, and Phil inherited the passion from his father. One of Phil's Burrillville High teammates, George Ducharme, recalled accompanying Phil on several hunting excursions; Ducharme never carried a gun, but he enjoyed walking along as Paine regaled him with stories. So fond was Paine of the outdoors, Ducharme said, that one day during their senior year, Phil skipped baseball practice to go fishing and was summarily benched for one game by his coach.

In addition to his baseball exploits (he played varsity for four years), Paine was a goaltender for three years on the hockey team; during his senior season, the hockey team, in those days a perennial powerhouse in Rhode Island Interscholastic League hockey, was undefeated in league play. On the mound, Paine led the Broncos to four Western Division championships, and as a senior was named to the All-Class-C First Team by the *Providence Journal-Bulletin*. In 2002 Paine was posthumously inducted into the Burrillville High School Athletic Hall of Fame.[2]

In 1948 the Burrillville baseball team won the state high-school championship, as Paine outpitched his more heralded rival, Chet Nichols (whom Paine would later join on the Boston and Milwaukee Braves) in a 3-2 extra-inning victory over Pawtucket East. ("Oh, that Nichols was a hothead," recalled Marcia, who knew Nichols. "He

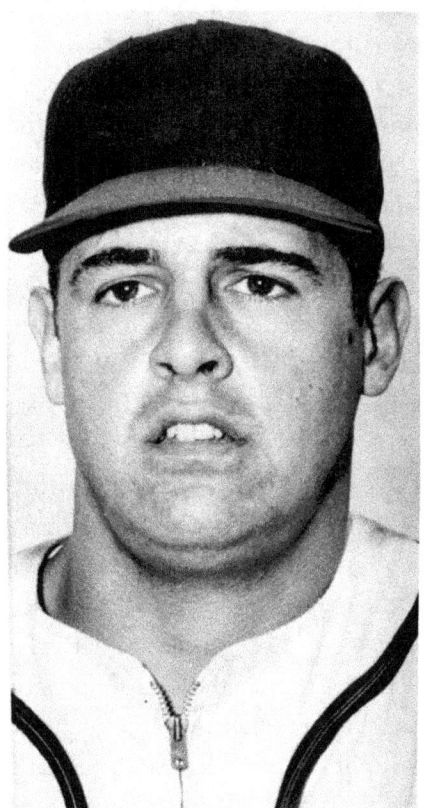

Phil Paine (National Baseball Hall of Fame Library, Cooperstown, N.Y.)

was so mad when Phil beat him.") On that day scouts were out in droves, "mostly to see Nichols," recalled George Ducharme, who played in the game, "but after the game I saw Phil talking to some scouts." Soon thereafter Paine signed a contract with the Philadelphia Phillies, and his professional baseball career began.

Paine joined the Phillies' entry in the Class D Pennsylvania-Ontario-New York League, the Bradford (Pennsylvania) Blue Wings. In 12 games the 18-year-old acquitted himself well. Making eight starts and tossing 97 innings, Paine had a 5-4 record with an impressive 2.41 earned-run average, although, not for the last time, he struggled with his control, finishing with 32 walks (and 35 strikeouts). Despite his low ERA, Paine also proved somewhat inconsistent: While he pitched a 10-0 shutout late in the season to help give Bradford a fourth-place finish in the final standings, he was later shelled in a playoff loss to the Lockport Reds, surrendering eight runs and 15 hits before being pulled in the seventh inning.

Nonetheless, Paine showed much promise, and when the 1949 season opened he had earned a promotion. Beginning the season at Toronto, in the Triple-A International League, the right-hander pitched in two games before settling in for the remainder of the season at Vandergrift (Pennsylvania), the Phillies' team in the Class C Middle Atlantic League. Once again a starter, Paine hurled 202 innings in 35 games and his ERA ballooned to 5.48, as he was again victimized by a lack of control: 136 walks – an average of 6.1 per nine innings.

That was Paine's final season in the Philadelphia organization. After the season he was taken by the Boston Braves in the minor-league draft. (The Braves acted on the advice of their New England scout, Jeff Jones, who in 1948 had signed Chet Nichols.) Within a year and a half the Rhode Island native was pitching in front of Braves fans just 65 miles from his hometown.

Paine arrived in the major leagues via a timely sequence of events. He spent the 1950 season with the Hartford Chiefs, the Braves' team in the Class A Eastern League. Pitching in relief, he appeared in 30 games, posted an 8-3 record with a 3.12 ERA, and, perhaps most importantly, reduced his walks per nine innings to 3.1. It was a solid performance and earned Paine a scheduled promotion to Double-A, where the Braves intended for him to start the 1951 season with the Atlanta Crackers in the Southern Association.

Chance intervened. Before the season Paine learned that he would be inducted into the Army in May. Rather than report to Atlanta, he asked the Braves to return him to Hartford so he would be closer to home until his call-up to the service. Hartford's new manager, Tommy Holmes, was impressed with the tall right-hander. Paine "came to me this spring," the manager recalled that summer, "and told me he felt he could start games as well as pitch in relief. I tried him as a starter and he won four of his first five for me. Showed me he could go the distance, too."

As the weeks passed without a draft notice, Paine remained with Hartford, working both as a starter and in relief. By July 4 he had appeared in 17 games, made seven starts, and pitched 72 innings, amassing a record of 6-6 with a 3.50 ERA. He again suffered bouts of wildness, as his average walks increased to 5 per nine innings. In June, citing ill health, Braves manager Billy Southworth suddenly resigned, and Holmes was named to replace him. On July 4 the Braves called up shortstop Johnny Logan from Milwaukee and Paine from Hartford. After just 96 games in the minor leagues, the 21-year-old from Chepachet was going to the majors.

Paine's addition to the Braves meant there were three Rhode Islanders on the Braves' pitching staff, the first time since the 1800s that three from the state played on the same major-league team. Max Surkont, who had joined the Braves in 1950, had been born in Central Falls, and Nichols, who was in his rookie season, hailed from Pawtucket. Together, the three posted a record that year for Boston of 25-24, very respectable for a team that finished the season with a record of 76-78.

Ten days passed before Paine got into his first game. On July 14, at home against the Cincinnati Reds, he pitched in relief as the Reds shut out Boston, 5-0. Paine, wrote one sportswriter, "made an impressive major league pitching debut for the Braves, striking out four of the six batters who faced him in the last two innings." Nine days later, in a 15-14 Braves win over Pittsburgh, Paine, the third of five Boston pitchers, collected his first victory, allowing three hits in two innings of relief.

By season's end he had logged 35⅓ innings in 21 games, won two without a loss, and posted a 3.06 ERA, though his walks remained problematic (20, or 5.2 per nine innings). That fall Paine was finally inducted into the Army, and it was be two years before he again took the mound for the Braves. When he did, the team no longer called Boston its home.

Paine was sent for basic training to Fort Indiantown Gap, near Harrisburg, Pennsylvania. During off-hours the soldiers often spent time at one of their favorite watering holes, the Warwick Hotel and Restaurant in the nearby town of Hummelstown. There, Paine met Jeannette Orsini, whose father owned the inn, and they began a courtship. After his discharge the two were married, in December 1953. It was a union that lasted 25 years, until Paine's death, and produced three children: sons Dan and Jeff and daughter Sherri, and also eventually four grandchildren. After his marriage, Paine called Hummelstown his home.

With basic training completed, Private First Class Paine was assigned to the 5th Infantry Division and was sent to the US Army Personnel Center at Camp Drake, in Fukuoka, Japan, where he remained throughout 1952 and '53. There he was reunited with George Ducharme, his high-school teammate.

In an interview in 2010 Ducharme told a poignant story: Paine was the star pitcher on the Camp Drake baseball team. When Ducharme arrived, Paine told the Drake coaches about his former teammate's baseball talents and recommended that he be assigned to the team. Subsequently, Ducharme's unit was sent to Korea, where war was still raging, but as a member of the baseball team Ducharme remained behind. All but seven or eight of his unit were eventually killed in the fighting, but, he said, "because Phil Paine got me on the team, I survived and was able to live the life I have led. I'll always be grateful to Paine for that. Without him, I probably would have been killed with the rest of my unit."[3]

Ducharme said that as new soldiers arrived at the camp, Paine would greet them and arrange for their lodging. "It wasn't bad duty," Paine himself later remembered. Most importantly for him, it gave him the chance to keep playing baseball. At some point, Paine signed with the Nishitetsu Lions of the Japanese Pacific Coast League. During his days off from duty the right-hander pitched twice a week for the Lions for $575 per game. In nine games for the Lions, a total of 61 innings pitched, Paine compiled a 4-3 record and a 1.77 ERA. In November 1953 he was discharged from the Army, and he returned to the United States to resume his major-league career.

Paine reported to spring training in Bradenton, Florida, to begin the 1954 season. The year before, the Braves had relocated to Milwaukee. During the 1953 season, Braves pitching coach Bucky Walters, anticipating Paine's return to the mound in '54, had said that "Phil could very well turn out to be a great addition to our staff when he is discharged from the service. He has all the necessary equipment to be a top-notch pitcher." In particular, Walters said, Paine, who threw side-arm, possessed an effective sinker and curve, which made him an ideal candidate for a relief role. His development, it was hoped, would allow Paine to anchor manager Charlie Grimm's overhauled bullpen in 1954. Things didn't quite work out as planned.

Back in major-league harness, Paine simply couldn't find the plate, although perhaps he wasn't given much of a chance to prove himself. Grimm may lacked confidence in Paine, or the right-hander may have had had some undisclosed injury. By mid-July Paine had appeared in only 11 games, and in 14 innings of work he issued 12 walks. On May 22 in Chicago, he was credited with his third career win in an 11-9 Milwaukee victory over the Chicago Cubs (Warren Spahn got a save in relief). But beyond that appearance there were few additional highlights. When the Braves purchased pitcher Dave Koslo from their Toledo farm club on July 19 and assigned Paine to the Triple-A team, it was a clear signal that Paine's future with the Braves was anything but secure.

In the spring of 1955 Paine failed to make the Braves team and was optioned to the Double-A Atlanta Crackers. His stay there was brief. Although he won two games without a loss, his all-too-familiar struggles with control once again predominated, as he walked 19 batters in 23 innings; those walks, along with 20 hits given up, combined to produce a 5.87 earned-run average. After a month in Atlanta (seven relief appearances), Paine was sent to Beaumont, in the Texas League. There, in sweltering summer heat, the Rhode Islander pitched well enough to earn a return to the major leagues.

The Exporters installed Paine as a starter, and the right-hander responded with one of the best stretches of pitching in his career. He once again harnessed his control, and the results were impressive: Paine started 14 games and completed seven, including a two-hit shutout. With a .500 record in 12 decisions for a sub-.500 team, Paine struck out 95 batters in 118 innings; most importantly, he walked just 42. It was the best control he'd exhibited since his first professional season, and the Braves took notice. On July 6, when pitcher Joey Jay was sent to Toledo after the completion of his two-year roster requirement as a bonus player, Paine was recalled to Milwaukee to replace him.

Paine pitched as though this chance would be his last. In one of the best performances of his major-league career, a four-inning stint at Brooklyn on August 2, he allowed just one hit and struck out six to earn his fourth career win. With only one earned run allowed, his ERA was 0.96. He had never pitched better.

After the Brooklyn game Paine told sportswriters, "I came out of the Army overweight. I lost my sinker, one of my best pitches, in the service. Then the trip to Beaumont melted off the extra weight." In the broiling Texas heat, he said, "I lost 17 pounds down there in about five weeks. I lost about 10 pounds a game, even in night games." Now, Paine said, "I can get my curveball over the plate and my sinker is working again."

Although he ended the season with only 25⅓ innings pitched in 15 games, Paine struck out 26 and limited his walks to 14, with a 2.49 ERA. He won two games without a loss, and his career record now stood at 5-0. Despite that performance, in the end it didn't matter; with the exception of two appearances over the next two seasons, 1955 effectively marked the end of Paine's Braves career.

For the next two seasons, Paine toiled almost exclusively in the minors. After making the team in the spring of 1956, he had appeared in just one game when the Braves optioned him to Minneapolis, a New York Giants farm club. (Wichita, the Braves' Triple-A team, wanted Minneapolis first baseman Don Bollweg, so the Braves sent Paine to Minneapolis in exchange.) In 58 games, including five starts, Paine was 8-6 and pitched 116 innings, issuing 4.3 walks per nine innings. On August 29 he was recalled to Milwaukee, to report the following spring, but on October 12, Paine was assigned outright to Wichita.[4] As he returned to Hummelstown in the fall of 1956, the right-hander's immediate future in the major leagues was certainly in doubt.

The following spring provided little reassurance. In 1957, the year Milwaukee won the World Series, Paine failed to make the team in spring training. In April he reported to Wichita – and produced a season that gave Milwaukee one final reason to send him to the mound. In 52 games, all but three in relief, Paine posted a 1.64 ERA in 104 innings pitched, while walking a career-low average of 2.9 batters per nine innings. On September 7 Paine was recalled to Milwaukee, and one week later, at home against Brooklyn, he allowed just one hit in two innings of work (although, perhaps fittingly, he walked three), and held the Dodgers scoreless. It was his final regular-season appearance in a Braves uniform.[5]

Paine attended his last Milwaukee spring training in 1958. By then, in the estimation of manager Fred Haney, the pitcher was one of several who were "on the fringe"; and, exclaimed Haney, "it will be up to them to make [me] keep them around." In the end, Paine wasn't kept.

On April 15, 1958, Milwaukee asked waivers on the right-hander; he was claimed by St. Louis. That season Paine pitched his final 46 major-league games. He got off to a torrid start. On June 24 in Pittsburgh, he won his fourth consecutive game for the Cardinals, lowering his ERA to 0.79 and raising his career record to 9-0. By September, though, Paine had clearly tired and he split two more decisions, finishing the year with a 5-1 record in 73⅓ innings and an ERA of 3.56. It had been a productive performance, but those were Paine's final major-league innings.

After the season Paine joined 19 teammates in an exhibition tour of the Pacific. While he was in Japan Paine was offered another contract by the Nishitetsu Lions, an offer in which, he said upon his return to the

United States, he was "definitely interested." Although Paine ultimately refused the offer, it wasn't the last one he received.

On December 4, 1958, Paine's brief Cardinals career was ended. That day he was part of a deal between the Cardinals and the Los Angeles Dodgers. St. Louis traded outfielder Wally Moon and Paine to the Dodgers for outfielder Gino Cimoli. The Dodgers assigned Paine to Spokane. A few days later Paine agreed to play for the Kintetsu Pearls of Osaka, in Japan's Pacific League in 1959. A month later, however, he announced that he had changed his mind. He needed only 16 days of major-league service to qualify for a pension, so he decided to try to make the Dodgers' team. He notified Kintetsu that he would not join the team after all that season, but that if he failed to stick in the majors he would accept an offer to pitch in Japan in 1960.

In February Paine joined the Dodgers at spring training in Vero Beach, Florida. He told reporters that Kintetsu had offered him "about double my present salary," But that he and his family had decided instead to remain in the United States.

And that ended his deliberations with the Japanese.

Paine failed to make the Dodgers squad in 1959. He spent the entire season in Spokane (5-5, 3.25 ERA). In December Paine was sent to Vancouver, a Baltimore Orioles farm club, and over the next two seasons he appeared in 116 games for the Mounties, all but one in relief. After the 1961 season, Paine retired from baseball at the age of 31.

For the remainder of his life Paine ran the family inn, the Warwick Hotel and Restaurant, in his adopted hometown of Hummelstown. He coached Little League and American Legion baseball. On February 19, 1978, at the age of 47, he died of a brain tumor at the Veterans Hospital in Lebanon, Pennsylvania. He was buried in the Hummelstown Cemetery.

Today, in his hometown of Chepachet, a baseball field is dedicated to the memory of the tall right-hander who made it out of the small town to the major leagues.

Sources

The Era (Bradford, Pennsylvania).

Gazette and Bulletin (Williamsport, Pennsylvania).

Associated Press.

United Press International.

Nashua (New Hampshire) *Telegraph*.

Pacific Stars and Stripes.

Independent (Long Beach, California).

Phil Paine player file, National Baseball Hall of Fame, Cooperstown, New York.

Jeannette Paine, Phil Paine's widow, biographical items.

Marcia Eddy, Phil Paine's sister, telephone interview, March 13, 2010.

George Ducharme, telephone interview, March 6, 2010.

Jeff Farrell, Burrillville High School Hall of Fame Committee, telephone interview, March 9, 2010.

japanesebaseballdaily.com/foreignpitching

retrosheet.org

baseball-reference.com

SABR Baseball Biography Project – Tommy Holmes, www.bioproj.sabr.org-

Notes

1   George Ducharme, a high school teammate of Paine's, said he remembered Arthur Paine, whom he referred to as old "Dan" Paine, as a 45-year-old spitball pitcher in a Sunday league.

2   In his professional career, Ducharme returned to Burrillville High School as assistant principal. During his two-plus decades at the school, it presented the Phil Paine Award to the most promising baseball prospect.

3   Ducharme told me that during Paine's induction into the Burrillville High School Athletic Hall of Fame, he met Paine's widow and family and had the opportunity to share this story with them.

4   There is some discrepancy in the reporting of Paine's return to Wichita. In his Hall of Fame file it is noted among his transactions that Paine was assigned outright on October 12. On October 13, however, the Associated Press reported that "[t]he Wichita Braves announced that Everette Joyner, OF, has been traded to the Milwaukee Braves for three players … Phil Paine (Minneapolis, American Association) and Jack Hannah (Jacksonville, SAL), pitchers, and Tobey Atwell (Miami, IL), catcher." Regardless of the official transaction, as 1956 came to a close, Paine had rejoined Wichita.

5   Although Paine was not on the Braves' World Series roster, he nevertheless supported the team. His sister Marcia lived with Phil and Jeannette in Milwaukee during those days and got to know many of the players. One day, she related, she was watching a documentary about Hank Aaron, and a segment aired from an interview Aaron gave during the 1957 World Series. She was never so surprised as when a player crossed the camera behind Aaron: It was her brother. Marcia laughed with pleasure when she related that story.

Taylor Phillips

By Rick Schabowski

Taylor Phillips had an outstanding career in armed-services baseball, good seasons in the minor leagues, and a six-year major-league career highlighted by being part of the 1957 world champion Milwaukee Braves.

William Taylor Phillips was born on June 18, 1933, in Atlanta, Georgia, to parents Amos and Jewell Phillips. He had a kidney disease as a youngster that prevented him from participating in contact sports, so he began playing baseball. He started pitching when he was young, tossing baseballs to his sister Betty. Phillips' love of the game led him to join the Douglasville, Georgia, town team. (Douglasville, where the family lived, is a suburb of Atlanta.) He recalled, "The boys from Douglasville would choose up sides and play teams from Winston and White City. Back then there were no Little Leagues. We played for fun."[1]

Phillips attended Douglas County High School and earned letters in baseball for three years, graduating in 1950. He attended the University of Georgia on a baseball scholarship for one semester.

Atlanta Crackers scout Skipper Bartlett noticed Phillips while Taylor was pitching for the Marietta (Georgia) Bombers American Legion Junior baseball team during the 1950 State American Legion finals. (Marietta lost to Savannah in the tournament finals.) Phillips was also approached by a New York Yankees scout. The team's manager, Marietta School Superintendent Shuler Antley, who had coached major leaguer Whitlow Wyatt at Cedartown High School, considered Phillips the best pitching prospect he had seen since Wyatt, and thought Phillips had an excellent chance to make the major leagues.

Phillips posted amazing statistics during the Legion season; his record was 23-4, with all four losses decided by one or two runs. In a two-game stretch, he allowed a total of three hits, taking no-hitters into the seventh inning of each contest, while striking out 19 in one of the games. During one stretch, Phillips pitched six games in eight days.

Deciding who to sign with wasn't a difficult decision for Phillips. He said, "The Yankees wanted to sign me, but I wanted to sign with the Crackers (Atlanta of the Southern League). I loved the Crackers because it was my home team."[2] ?? BB Ref says he signed with Milwaukee in 1953

At the age of 17, Phillips began his professional career with the Waycross Bears of the Class D Georgia-Florida League. In 1951 he had a 10-8 record with a 4.25 ERA in 167 innings, walking 162 and striking out 125. His victories included a no-hitter and a one-hitter.

Back in Waycross in 1952, Phillips had a breakout season. He led the league in innings pitched (297), games pitched (46), and wild pitches (23), tied for the lead in strikeouts (265), was second in ERA (1.40), posted a 21-10 record, and was named to the league's All-Star team. On September 4 against Tifton he yielded a lead-off single, then pitched hitless ball the

Taylor Phillips (National Baseball Hall of Fame Library, Cooperstown, N.Y.)

remainder of the game. "I had a super year that year," Phillips commented in a 1990 article in *Sports Collectors Digest*. "There were only two people in baseball, Mike Garcia and Robin Roberts, that pitched more innings than I did in 1952. I played a 140-game schedule in Class D ball, and they played a 154-game schedule in the big leagues. I was proud of that."[3]

The next season Phillips was promoted to the Crackers. "I progressed a little fast and was always the youngest player on each team," Phillips said in the *Sports Collectors Digest* article. "It was a challenge to be playing with my heroes, seeing their names in the paper one year, and playing with them the next. Being put in the same company as those guys was really fantastic for a country boy."[4] One of his biggest thrills took place on July 8, when, as a member of the Southern Association All-Star team, he pitched two innings of shutout baseball to close the game for the All-Stars in their 8-6 victory over Nashville.

Another notable event of the 1953 season was the genesis of his nickname, T-Bone. The Crackers had another Taylor, pitcher Jack Taylor, so to avoid confusion Taylor Phillips was referred to as "T," with the "Bone" being added later.

After the 1953 season Phillips was drafted into the Army. He was stationed at Fort McPherson, near Atlanta. The base team played a 130-game schedule in 1954. Phillips won eight of his first nine decisions and in the first 77 innings he had a 0.81 ERA, striking out 91, giving up 49 hits, and walking 45.

Fort McPherson fielded an impressive 17-man roster for the 1955 season. Eleven of the players had major-league contracts, including pitchers Vinegar Bend Mizell and Billy O'Dell, infielder Frank Bolling and outfielder Norm Siebern. Phillips hurled a no-hitter against Fort Benning (Georgia) and another one against Fort McClellan (Alabama), striking out 21 batters. He finished the season with a 21-0 record, the same as Mizell. At season's end, Phillips's team captured the All-Army World Tournament, held at Fort Belvoir (Virginia).

Discharged from the Army on November 15, 1955, Phillips wasted little time returning to baseball, joining the Caguas-Guayama team managed by Ben Geraghty in the Puerto Rican winter league. Felix Mantilla, Tommy Lasorda, and Wes Covington were also on the Caguas roster. Phillips won outings against National Leaguers Ruben Gomez and Jim Owens. He finished with a 6-3 record as Caguas captured the league title, defeating Santurce, the regular season champ, in six games in the league playoff.

In 1956 Phillips began spring training with Milwaukee in Bradenton, Florida, then was sent to Jacksonville, where the Braves' Wichita and Atlanta farm clubs were training. He began the season with Wichita, where he posted a 2-2 record, including a 1-0 loss in ten innings to Indianapolis on May 28, the winning run scoring on Phillips's own throwing error on an attempted pickoff. Four days later, the Milwaukee Braves, in need of left-handed pitching, help, called him up on the recommendation of Wichita manager George Selkirk. He drove the 600 miles to Milwaukee to begin his major-league career. Meeting Warren Spahn was a big thrill, Phillips said. "He's always been my idol, and it was a great thrill to play with him. He's a great pitcher, and a man to go with it. The first night I was in the majors he came over and patted me on the back, helped me in a lot of things and during the rest of the season he told me what I was doing wrong."[5]

Phillips made his major-league debut on June 8, 1956, in front of 33,360 fans in County Stadium, entering the game against the New York Giants in relief of Ernie Johnson with the bases loaded and two out in the seventh inning. He struck out the first batter he faced, Whitey Lockman. During the 7-2 Braves loss, Phillips pitched 2 1/3 innings, yielding one hit, walking none, and striking out three, including Willie Mays. Giants manager Bill Rigney was impressed, saying, "That kid really showed something. Where did he come from anyway?"[6]

A very excited Phillips went to the clubhouse to shave and shower after the game. "When I came out from shaving, it looked like I had been in a knife fight. I was so scared. I had cut myself in a hundred different places. But the first appearance I had in the major leagues is a thrill a person will never forget."[7]

On July 15 Phillips won his first major-league game in a six-inning relief appearance against the Pittsburgh

Pirates. Relieving Bob Trowbridge, who had been struck on the pitching arm by a line drive, Phillips gave up just three hits (including a home run by Frank Thomas, the first batter he faced) as the Braves won, 4-1. "I wasn't at my best," Phillips said after the game. "My curve wasn't working, I couldn't get it over, so I used the fastball most of the time."[8]

Phillips made his first start on August 9 against the St. Louis Cardinals at County Stadium on August 9, and pitched a three-hitter, winning 4-1 with the Cardinals' only run scoring on an error. He finished the season with a 5-3 record and a 2.26 ERA. He was selected unanimously by Milwaukee sportswriters as the team's Rookie of the Year, and was named to *The Sporting News* 1956 All-Rookie team. "I was real pleased with my rookie year," Phillips said in the *Sports Collectors Digest* interview. "The only thing that bothered me was we didn't win the pennant. We had a lot of chemistry in that team, but the experience wasn't there. We didn't jell like they thought they would, and we lost the pennant by one game. That was a big disappointment."[9]

Phillips played in the Puerto Rican League again after the season. He left the team in early January with a sore arm. Later that month, when he received his Rookie of the Year award, he assured everyone that his pitching arm was OK. "I can't remember I ever had a sore arm. X-Rays showed nothin' wrong with it and the doctor said that I should just rest. That's what I've been doing ever since I got home." [10]

Phillips appeared in 27 games for the Braves in 1957, starting six games and posting a 3-2 record in 73 innings. His 5.55 ERA was largely due to one really bad game. On July 15 Phillips played the role of sacrificial lamb in a game at Brooklyn. Losing 11-4 going into the bottom of the eighth, Braves manager Fred Haney put Phillips into the game and he faced 13 batters, in a nine-run inning, giving up five hits, walking four, hitting a batter, and unleashing a wild pitch as the Dodgers won 20-4. "I wasn't trying to show the kid up," Haney said. "Nobody felt worse about the thing than I did. But I felt I had to leave him in because I've got only nine pitchers and I already used five."[11]

Phillips didn't pitch in the World Series but said, "It was a thrill to just be there and know that you were part of a world championship team."[12]

Phillips didn't have too long to celebrate as a Brave. On December 5 he and catcher Sammy Taylor were traded to the Chicago Cubs for pitchers Bob Rush and Don Kaiser and outfielder Eddie Haas. After the trade he said he looked forward to playing with the Cubs: "Their shortage of left-handed pitching gives me an open shot at a starting job and I think I can make it."[13]

"We're certain Taylor Phillips is going to do the job for us," Cubs manager Bob Scheffing said. "I know he has the stuff. It may take him a while to get into the groove because he only pitched 73 innings last year."[14] Phillips had a rough spring training, but the Cubs needed him to excel as a starter, because Moe Drabowsky was on the disabled list with a serious throat infection.

Phillips picked up his first victory in a Cubs uniform on May 7, defeating the Cincinnati Redlegs in a five-hitter. On the 21st he improved his record to 2-0 with another complete-game five-hitter, against Pittsburgh.

On May 25, before 40,962 at Milwaukee's County Stadium, Phillips started the first game of a doubleheader against his former teammates. He didn't disappoint, giving up just six singles in a 1-0 victory that ran his record to 3-0. After the game he said, "I'll always like to beat this club because I used to play for them, but everybody in the organization treated me fine when I was here. They didn't do me a dirty trick trading me. It was the biggest break of my life. I don't say I'll be a big winner, but at least I'll get the opportunity."[15] Phillips also said he had added another pitch to his repertoire, the knuckleball: "I threw about a dozen knuckleballs against the Braves, and it sure helped me get out of two or three rough spots."[16]

Phillips finished the season with a 7-10 record, appearing in 39 games, starting 27, and posting a 4.76 ERA. "Wrigley Field's not the easiest place in the world to pitch," he commented.[17]

Phillips reported a week early for the 1959 spring training in Mesa, Arizona. He recognized the importance of the coming season, saying, "I figure this is my make-or-break year. Let's face it. I've been up three years now, and I haven't shown anything yet. Oh, I've shown enough to stay on a big-league club, but that doesn't satisfy me."[18] In seven early-season games (two starts) Phillips compiled a 7.56 ERA and posted an 0-2 record. On May 12 he was traded to the Philadelphia Phillies for southpaw Seth Morehead. As he left to join his new team, Phillips said, "I'm just sorry that I couldn't have done better here."[19]

It wasn't much fun playing for the last-place Phillies. In his interview in *Sports Collectors Digest*, Phillips said, "I didn't care for the Phillies at all. That was probably one of the worst teams I've been on. But Philadelphia had one of the best persons I've ever met in my life and that was Robin Roberts. And I was fortunate (that) my roommate was Jim Hegan, a catcher from Cleveland. Some good people, but they were all on the way down."[20] Phillips went 1-4 for the Phillies with a 5.00 ERA. His victory, 3-2 in a rain-shortened six-inning game against Los Angeles on July 19 in Philadelphia, was the only victory of the season by a Phillies southpaw.

Phillips began the 1960 season with Triple-A Buffalo. In midseason he was called up by the Phillies and appeared in ten games, pitching 14 innings and posting an 8.36 ERA. He finished the season back in Buffalo, where he went 6-3 with a 3.65 ERA.

On March 27, 1961, before beginning the season with Buffalo, Phillips married Betty Ferguson of Hiram, Georgia. They had met on a blind date at a square dance three years earlier. The ceremony took place at the Calvary First Baptist Church in Clearwater, Florida.

At Buffalo, Phillips struggled with an 0-1 record and a 7.07 ERA in 14 innings pitched. In early June he was loaned to the Dallas-Fort Worth Rangers, a Triple-A affiliate of the Los Angeles Angels in the American Association. In his first starting assignment, he pitched a three-hit, 3-0 victory over Louisville. He finished the season with an 8-6 record and a 3.46 ERA. After the season Phillips and utilityman Bob Sadowski were traded by Philadelphia to the Chicago White Sox for pitcher Frank Barnes and third baseman Andy Carey. Phillips and Sadowski were assigned to Triple-A Indianapolis. Phillips spent the entire 1962 season with Indianapolis, posting an 8-5 record with a sparkling 2.11 ERA. One of his highlights was a 2-0 two-hitter against Dallas-Fort Worth. The Indians won the American Association title but lost to Louisville in the Junior World Series. Phillips played winter baseball for the Rapinos in Venezuela. (The team was owned by Luis Aparicio.) He had an outstanding season, going 10-4 with a 2.73 ERA and leading the league in strikeouts.

After posting a 4-4 record with a 2.86 ERA for Indianapolis in the first half of the 1963 season, Phillips was called up by the White Sox on July 16. His White Sox debut, on July 23, was anything but auspicious. Entering a tie game in Detroit with two outs, he gave up a grand slam to Norm Cash. He appeared in nine games in all, pitching 14 innings and posting a 10.29 ERA.

After spending the 1963 offseason pitching for Caguas in the Occidental (Venezuela) League, Phillips was again assigned to Indianapolis. He was placed on the disabled list with a muscle tear and pinched nerve in his throwing arm on May 14, 1964. "I didn't get loose and tried to throw hard," Phillips said, "and the first pitch I made was up on the screen. I pulled everything loose in my elbow. It was a whole month before I could throw again."[21]

After coming off the disabled list, Phillips was released. He signed with the Triple-A Atlanta Crackers to finish the season. Phillips was a part of a memorable moment while pitching for Atlanta on September 10, throwing the last pitch at Atlanta's Ponce de Leon Park and retiring Johnny Lewis on a grounder to first. After the game, Phillips took a large chunk of sod from the park, and planted it in his yard, where it remains as green as ever.

Phillips retired after the season. He immediately applied for employment at the post office in Austell, Georgia. He was hired and began his new career the next day, working an overnight shift, which allowed him to take a part-time position as the Atlanta Braves' batting-practice pitcher. "I went out one day, to see some of the guys I knew, and Kenny (Silvestri)?? Who was he? says, 'Do you want to pitch batting practice?' I said sure. 'We'll pay you. When do you want to start? Kenny replied, 'Tomorrow.' So that's how I got hired."[22]

The batting-practice job ended when Phillips had to transfer to another post office and his hours changed.

He stayed involved with baseball, working as a volunteer giving lessons to local players. He estimated that he was helpful in helping around 100 athletes obtain scholarships. One of his more noteworthy pupils was Matt Capps, a pitcher who became a major leaguer in 2005 and was still pitching in 2013. Phillips was also active as a coach in American Legion baseball.

Phillips expressed gratitude to Braves general manager Paul Richards for a roster move he made in the closing weeks of the 1969 season. In 1968 the Braves had activated Satchel Page so he could qualify for a pension, and Richards told Phillips, "If they can do that for one guy, we can do it for you. I had been out of baseball for four or five years, so for the 1969 season, I spent the last three weeks on the active list."[23]

Phillips retired from the Postal Service after 28 years, enabling him to spend time with his children, Debra, Karen, John, Kyle, and an adopted daughter, Beth. Taylor and Betty as of 2013 had nine grandchildren.

Phillips's biggest regret: "I was better than my record showed, was young, single, and I was not as aggressive as I should have been. I took everything for granted."[24] His fondest memory: "The first game I pitched in the big leagues. I pitched a three-hitter against the Cardinals in my first start. I'll never forget that, and how happy I was. I couldn't wait to call home to tell my mother and dad what I had done."[25]

Sources

In addition to a telephone interview with Taylor Phillips on January 25, 2013, the author accessed Phillips's player file from the National Baseball Hall of Fame, and consulted Retrosheet and Baseball-Reference.com. Newspapers consulted include the *Milwaukee Journal*, *Milwaukee Sentinel*, and *The Sporting News*.

Povletich, William, *Milwaukee Braves: Heroes and Heartbreak* (Madison, Wisconsin: Wisconsin Historical Society Press, 2009).

Notes

1. Joe Baggett, "Satisfied: Phillips Reflects Back On His Pro Career," *Neighbor News*, no date, no page (in Phillips's file at the Baseball Hall of Fame).
2. Ibid.
3. Bill Ballew, "Taylor Phillips recalls his days in the majors," *Sports Collectors Digest*, June 15, 1990, 280.
4. Ballew.
5. Al Thomy, "Rookie No Longer, Phillips Aims High in Braves World," *Atlanta Constitution*, February 13, 1957.
6. Bob Wolf, "The Silver Lining: Taylor Phillips, Rookie Lefty Shows Plenty," *Milwaukee Journal*, June 9, 1956, 10.
7. Ballew.
8. Bob Wolf, "Rookie Taylor Phillips Is No Shrinking Violet, Takes Victory Calmly," *Milwaukee Journal*, July 16, 1956, 9.
9. Ballew.
10. *The Sporting News*, February 6, 1957, 6.
11. Bob Wolf, "Braves Still Reeling After Worst Licking," *Milwaukee Journal*, August 16, 1957, 12.
12. Ballew.
13. "Quickly Quoted," *Milwaukee Journal*, December 11, 1957, 21.
14. *The Sporting News*, January 22, 1958, 7.
15. Steve Weller, "New Taylor Phillips is Far Cry from Old; Some Excitement Has Gone Out of Hurling," *Milwaukee Journal*, May 26, 1958, 12.
16. *The Sporting News*, June 6, 1958, 9.
17. Ballew.
18. *The Sporting News*, March 4, 1959, 15.
19. *The Sporting News*, May 20, 1959, 25.
20. Ballew.
21. Ballew.
22. Taylor Phillips, telephone interview with author, January 25, 2013.
23. Phillips telephone interview.
24. Phillips telephone interview.
25. Phillips telephone interview.

Juan Pizarro

By Rory Costello

Juan Pizarro was a talented, durable Puerto Rican pitcher. The lefty pitched in all or part of 18 major-league seasons, starting as a rookie with the 1957 Milwaukee Braves. The Braves rushed him to the big club after one eye-opening season in Class A, yet their very deep pitching staff limited Pizarro's opportunities. He did not come into his own as a big leaguer until 1961, after he was traded to the Chicago White Sox. His best record was 19-9 in 1964—but he never had another season with double-digit wins in the majors. After 1965, Pizarro was primarily a reliever at the top level.

Still, looking at his entire professional career, "Terín" won more than 400 ballgames. His regular-season count is 392: 197 in the US (131 in the majors and 66 in the minors), plus 38 more in Mexico in his late 30s and 157 while playing winter ball in his homeland.[1] Pizarro was one of the most successful pitchers in the history of the Puerto Rican Winter League (PRWL). His career there spanned 22 seasons, from 1955-56 to 1976-77. As of 2012, *El Látigo de Ébano*—The Ebony Whip—ranked second in wins in the league's history. It came as no surprise that when the Puerto Rican Baseball Hall of Fame inducted its first ten members in 1991, Terín Pizarro was one of them.

Pizarro accomplished as much as he did despite his great love of eating, drinking, gambling, and carousing. In a vivid 1982 interview with author Edward Kiersh for the book *Where Have You Gone, Vince Dimaggio?*, he came across as a *boricua* Bo Belinsky. "Yeah, I love to cel-e-brate," he said. "I only remember the parties, the women, the hot times."[2]

Juan Ramón Pizarro Córdova was born in Santurce, Puerto Rico, on February 7, 1937. His father, Zenón Pizarro, was listed in the 1940 census as a construction worker—but Zenón mainly occupied himself as a trainer/gambler in cockfighting (a pastime that remains popular—and legal—in Puerto Rico).[3] Juan's mother, Ramona Córdova, had three daughters before him. They were named Celestina, Ramona, and Alejandrina. In his childhood, he got the nickname that stuck with him for life: Terín. The neighborhood kids likened him to the main character of the comic strip "Terry and the Pirates."[4]

From the age of 13, Pizarro served as a batboy for his hometown team in the PRWL, the Santurce Cangrejeros (Crabbers). Strange to relate, he had not grown up playing baseball. As he explained to Ed Kiersh, though, "I was so busy being bad, I didn't start playing ball until I was fourteen."[5]

It was only after he joined some boys in the neighborhood for a game of *piedritas*—throwing rocks at bottles—that Pizarro found out about his own talent. "I had never done much throwing," he said in May 1956, "even though I had been batboy for Santurce for three years. Some of the boys could throw pretty fast, but I discovered I could throw harder than any of them. And I hit more bottles too." He then began to play amateur league baseball as a high-school junior and proceeded to win 14 games, followed by 19 more as a senior.[6] The team was run by a man named Harry

Juan Pizarro (National Baseball Hall of Fame Library, Cooperstown, N.Y.)

Rexach, a big Santurce fan and friend of the Crabbers' longtime owner, Pedrín Zorrilla.[7]

Pizarro was not big for a pitcher, especially by today's standards. He grew to just 5-feet-11 and weighed only 170 pounds as a young man. Eventually he weighed as much as 190 to 200 — or at least that was the figure in print. "I came to the end of the road a lot quicker because I loved to eat," he freely admitted to Ed Kiersh, patting his stomach and smiling.[8] He had a very live arm, though he did not rely on his fastball alone. His repertoire also included a curveball and — for a time — a screwball, learned from fellow Puerto Rican Rubén Gómez. Mastering his control was a challenge for him in the majors.

Pizarro pitched his first five games as a pro with Santurce in the winter of 1955-56. Pedrín Zorrilla signed him to his first contract. Terín played just 2 1/2 of his 22 winters at home in a non-Crabbers uniform. He was so loyal to winter ball and his team that he turned down an offer for $5,000 from the White Sox not to play following the 1964 season. After the pitcher retired in 1977, the man who then owned the club, Hiram Cuevas, "made sure Pizarro was rewarded with a 20-year coaching contract."[9]

On February 13, 1956, Pizarro signed with Milwaukee. The scout responsible was a fellow Puerto Rican, Luis Olmo. Olmo had finished his big-league career with the Boston Braves in June 1951 and became a full-time scout for them at the end of 1953. Pizarro's first manager in the US, Ben Geraghty, endorsed the young hurler too. Geraghty was also the skipper of another Puerto Rican team, the Caguas Criollos. He said, "When Milwaukee called me up to ask what I thought of Pizarro, I told them he definitely had a major-league arm and could throw harder than anyone in the Milwaukee organization."[10]

According to Pedrín Zorrilla, Santurce received $34,000 from the sale — $2,000 of which went to Terín. His salary for his first year in the US was also to be $2,000 — but that was a raise from the $35 per week that he'd been earning in a San Juan factory.[11] The 19-year-old reported to Jacksonville in the South Atlantic League (Class A). The young man could not speak English then; when Geraghty needed to confer with him on the mound, he needed help from veteran Cuban pitcher Adrián Zabala.

Right from the start, Pizarro was dazzling. In his debut he struck out 14 in six innings before tiring and taking the loss. In his next start, he whiffed 21 in 12 innings.[12] He got 20 Ks against Macon on June 27.[13] For the season, he was 23-6 with a 1.77 ERA. In 274 innings pitched, the Sally League's MVP struck out 318, including at least ten men in 15 of his 31 starts. Pizarro walked 149, which was forgivable in a young flamethrower pitching at that level. That August, Ben Geraghty said, "I'd say there are faster pitchers, even in this league. But his ball really moves. Too many good hitters in this league are swinging and missing. His ball is alive and that is what's going to make him a great big leaguer."[14]

John Quinn, general manager of the big club, "did not rule out the possibility" that Pizarro might get a call-up to Milwaukee.[15] That didn't happen, but another indication of the prospect's promise came from the Sally League's president, Hall of Famer Bill Terry, who raved, "He could be as great as [Warren] Spahn."[16]

During the winter of 1956-57, Pedrín Zorrilla sold the Crabbers. The new owner, Ramón Cuevas, in turn sold the contracts of Pizarro, Roberto Clemente, and second baseman Ronnie Samford to Caguas.[17] Shortly after the deal, Pizarro suffered two broken ribs in an auto accident, and the Braves ordered him to quit for the remainder of the PRWL season.[18] He had shown further promise, however, throwing two shutouts while still with Santurce. The level of competition was generally regarded as just a small step down from the majors.

In January 1957 Milwaukee manager Fred Haney talked about the "southpaw phenom." He said, "The only thing I question is [Pizarro's] bases-on-balls record. Maybe the kid needs another year in the minors to work on his control. Those walks will send a manager to an early grave."[19] During spring training in Florida, Pizarro said of his control, "It's okay." Speaking from the Bradenton rooming house where the Braves of African descent had to reside, the 20-year-old was quite confident. When asked what he had to improve upon to make good in the major leagues, he said simply, "Nothing."[20]

Indeed, Pizarro started the 1957 season with the big club.[21] He did not get a chance in a regular-season game, however, until May 4. At Pittsburgh's Forbes Field, the rookie lost a 1-0 duel to Vernon Law. "Even then it took a couple of 'seeing eye' singles in the seventh inning to beat him."[22] In his next outing, at St. Louis on May 10, the Braves gave Pizarro a big early lead and he went all the way to win, 10-5. Terín helped himself by going 2-for-4 and scoring three runs, including a solo homer off Sam "Toothpick" Jones. He was a respectable batter for a pitcher, hitting .202 lifetime in the majors with eight homers (including three in 1964).

Pizarro was in the starting rotation for six turns from late May through mid-June, but after that, the Braves used him sporadically. They sent him down to Triple-A Wichita "for more experience" on July 3; there he was 4-0 in five starts, though with a fairly high ERA of 4.25. After Pizarro returned in late July, *The Sporting News* wrote, "the young Puerto Rican was counted upon for important assistance as a reliever and spot starter down the stretch."[23]

Yet as it developed, Fred Haney called on him just ten more times with only one start. His most impressive performance came at Cincinnati's Crosley Field on August 31. The Braves gave Lew Burdette a 5-0 lead in the first inning, but Burdette retired just one batter before Haney gave him the hook. Pizarro went the rest of the way for the win, striking out nine and giving up just two runs. He finished his rookie year at 5-6 with a 4.62 ERA in 24 games (10 starts). Control was an issue; he walked 51 men in 99 1/3 innings.

Pizarro got into one game during the 1957 World Series. In Game Three at County Stadium, after the Yankees knocked Bob Buhl out of the box in the first inning, Terín pitched 1 2/3 innings. He gave way to Gene Conley in the third inning after giving up two more runs to New York in the 12-3 loss.

That December Milwaukee beat columnist Bob Wolf wrote, "Juan Pizarro ... was a disappointment, although in his case the problem seemed to be solely one of inexperience. Had he been able to spend the entire campaign at Wichita, pitching every fourth or fifth day instead of rusting away in the Braves' bull pen, he might have been ready for stardom in 1958. But because [Taylor] Phillips failed and nobody else was available to take up the slack, Pizarro had to be kept for all but a month of the season."[24] As Ed Kiersh also noted, though, "Haney ... wondered so much about J.P.'s whereabouts he had to send out groups of players, or even the police, to scour the bars for the missing rookie."[25]

Meanwhile, in the winter of 1957-58, Pizarro's performance with Caguas was simply spectacular. He became the second of four pitchers in PRWL history to win the Triple Crown of pitching.[26] In 19 games, he was 14-5 with a 1.32 ERA. He struck out 183 and allowed just 94 hits in 170 1/3 innings. He broke the league's single-season record with nine shutouts. In addition, on November 21, he broke the league record for strikeouts in a single game — held by Satchel Paige and Bob Turley — with 19 against Ponce.[27] Nine days later he threw a no-hit, no-run game against Mayagüez. He also had a one-hitter and a two-hitter that season. He richly deserved — and won — league MVP honors.

Pizarro had many other excellent seasons at home, and only a few that could be described as so-so or bad. This, however, may have been the best stretch of his entire pro career. It continued in the Caribbean Series. Caguas represented Puerto Rico as PRWL champion, and on February 8, 1958, Pizarro fired 17 strikeouts in an 8-0, two-hit win over Carta Vieja of Panama, shattering the Caribbean Series record.[28] Cuba became tournament champion, though — and a big turning point came two days later, with Pizarro on as a fireman in the ninth inning. The bases were loaded with nobody out, and the tying run would have scored anyway on a long fly to right field, but when an umpire ruled that the ball had been dropped, the irate crowd at San Juan's old Sixto Escobar Stadium started "a small-scale riot." The game was suspended and completed the following night.[29]

Yet despite his brilliance, Pizarro had a disappointing spring camp in 1958.[30] Perhaps he was tired — he'd pitched around 200 innings that winter and had weakened late in another Caribbean Series start. At any rate, there was no room for him on Milwaukee's staff. He went back to Wichita to start the season. Though his record was only 9-10 in 23 games, his ERA was 2.84

and he fanned 158 in 165 innings. The Braves recalled Pizarro in late July, and he responded with three straight complete games, winning two and losing one. Overall with Milwaukee that season, Pizarro was 6-4 with a 2.70 ERA in 16 games (ten starts).

Pizarro's good work in the second half won notice. In early September United Press International wrote, "Juan Pizarro, little more than a spectator in the 1957 World Series, is ready to play a major role for the Milwaukee Braves when they try to make it two in a row over the New York Yankees this year."[31] Again, though, he got to make just one relief appearance in the Series; in Game Five at Yankee Stadium, he was dropped into hot water. New York was ahead 1-0 going into the bottom of the sixth, but Braves starter Lew Burdette weakened, allowing two runs and leaving the bases loaded for Pizarro. By the time the inning was over, the Yankees were up 7-0, and that was where it ended.

Despite some gems, Pizarro never blossomed in Milwaukee. In 1959 he was 6-2, 3.77 in 29 games, interrupted by another stretch at Triple-A in June. During his time at Louisville, he pitched a no-hitter against Charleston at home on June 16. Four days later, this time at Charleston, he was four outs away from back-to-back no-hitters but had to settle for a two-hit shutout.[32]

Before the 1959-60 season in Puerto Rico, Pizarro (plus $10,000) came back to Santurce in return for Julio Navarro and José Pagán.[33] In 1960 he spent the full year with Milwaukee for the first time. The Braves' new manager, Charlie Dressen—who encouraged Pizarro to discard his screwball—compared him to Sandy Koufax (as well as Mike McCormick and Dick Ellsworth).[34] Even so, he was just 6-7, 4.55.

On December 15, 1960, the Braves traded Pizarro and pitcher Joey Jay to the Cincinnati Reds for veteran shortstop Roy McMillan, a top-notch glove man, plus a player to be named later. As part of a three-way deal, Cincinnati moved Pizarro along with pitcher Cal McLish to the Chicago White Sox for third baseman Gene Freese. White Sox president Bill Veeck said, "In the case of Pizarro, who supposedly lacks the drive and aggressiveness to win, if anyone can put a fire under him it is [manager Al] Lopez."[35] This appears to be another example of a stereotype attached to Latino players in those days.

Braves catcher Del Crandall, speaking to author Larry Moffi, gave another indication of why Milwaukee gave up on the talented young Puerto Rican. "With Juan Pizarro, I think in his case his potential was that he could throw the ball at ninety-five miles per hour. Well, that's not necessarily potential, that's somebody with a good fastball. … It was just, throw the ball hard and then turn that little screwball over at times. But I don't think that he was consistent in getting the pitches where he needed to get them in times of trouble."[36]

Looking back, Pizarro's great teammate Henry Aaron wrote, "I've always felt that we would have won some more championships if we had hung onto Pizarro and Jay. We needed young pitchers to take over for Spahn, Burdette, and Buhl, and we never came up with them. … I'm not sure I ever saw a pitcher with more ability than Pizarro had when he came to us out of Puerto Rico at the age of nineteen."[37]

Aaron's book went on to quote another Puerto Rican Brave, Felix Mantilla, who was also of African descent. "I don't think our managers and front office ever understood Pizarro. He was always in shape and ready to pitch, but he was moody. Managers would say things to him about being moody and it would just make him angry." Mantilla then went on to talk at length about the "unwritten rule" in those days against having five black players on the field at the same time, which cost both him and Pizarro playing time.[38] Pizarro himself told Ed Kiersh, "Because I was Latin they thought I was a troublemaker."[39]

Pizarro's breakout year in the majors came at last in 1961—though he did not start or win a game for Chicago until June 10. During that season, he was 14-7 with a 3.05 ERA. His walks were down to 4.1 per 9 innings pitched, and his K/9 ratio was a career-high 8.7, which also led the AL that year. Al Lopez said, "When Pizarro first joined the club in 1961 he was fooling around with a screwball. Here was a young pitcher with control trouble, so I told him to concentrate on finding the plate with his fastball and curve and forget about the screwball. He had enough stuff without it."[40]

"The White Sox didn't give up on me, they didn't punish me, and I pitched my ass off for them," Pizarro told Kiersh.[41] The *bon vivant* backslid in 1962, though—"late-night carousing and skipping practices led to a 12-14 mark, numerous fines, and Lopez's turning gray."[42] Still, he enjoyed another career highlight that winter. Mayagüez, the PRWL champion in 1962-63, signed Terín as a reinforcement for the Inter-American Series. On February 8, 1963, he threw a no-hitter against the Venezuelan champs, Valencia—the only no-no in the history of that tournament.[43]

Pizarro followed with his two best seasons in the majors. He was an American League All-Star in both 1963 (16-8, 2.39) and 1964 (19-9, 2.56). His career-high win total in '64 broke the big-league single-season mark for pitchers born in Puerto Rico.[44] He was also runner-up to teammate Gary Peters among the AL's ERA leaders that year. Despite an anemic offense, the strong pitching of the White Sox led them to challenge the Yankees strongly—they finished just one game back in second place.

Pizarro was able to make only 18 starts for the White Sox in 1965, however; a salary holdout contributed to a sore arm, and he took the mound just seven times through June 23. He didn't get past five innings in any game. Eventually, examination revealed a torn triceps tendon in his pitching shoulder.[45] Pizarro made it back by late July and pitched much better in the season's second half. On August 11—relying heavily on breaking balls[46]—he threw the first of his two one-hitters in the majors, shutting out Washington at Comiskey Park. He wound up at 6-3, 3.43 for the season.

From 1966 onward, Pizarro made just 58 starts in his remaining nine major-league seasons, against 182 relief appearances. He bounced around with six different teams: Pittsburgh, Boston, Cleveland, Oakland, the Chicago Cubs, and Houston. He also returned to the minors for parts of 1970—which included a 9-0 run for the Hawaii Islanders, then a California Angels farm club—1971, and 1973.

The 1971 season with the Cubs had noteworthy performances, though. Chicago called Pizarro up from Triple-A Tacoma in July and used him mainly as a starter (14 times in 16 outings). On August 1 at New York's Shea Stadium, Pizarro went all the way and beat the Mets' ace, Tom Seaver, 3-2. Four days later, he threw his other big-league one-hitter, blanking San Diego at Wrigley Field. On September 17, again at Shea, once more he bested Seaver, who was having his greatest season ever. The score was 1-0—and Juan's solo homer in the eighth inning accounted for the game's only run.

Pizarro didn't do much for the Cubs in 1972. The following year—"admittedly 'fat, lazy, and not giving a s*** at this point'"[47]—he appeared just twice with Chicago before his contract was sold to Houston. After the Astros released Pizarro in April 1974, he went to Mexico, joining the Córdoba Cafeteros. In his first season south of the border, Terín was 13-6 with a brilliant ERA of 1.57, best in the league. He had 15 complete games in his 20 starts, with nine shutouts, including five in a row at one point. Both figures tied Mexican League records. At first it was thought that he had set a new mark with six straight blankings, but the league statistician pointed out that he had given up a run in relief.[48]

As a result of Pizarro's success, the Pirates signed him that August 19. Three days previously, general manager Joe Brown had said, "I might make a move in the next few days that might make you think I'm out of my mind." But Pittsburgh was in third place in the National League East at the time, and it was a low-cost maneuver.[49] Over the next several weeks, Pizarro pitched seven times. Pirates manager Danny Murtaugh made him the starter for the last two of those appearances, and he got his final big-league win on September 26. At Shea Stadium, with a big early lead, he went eight innings, coming out only after the Mets scored two unearned runs in the eighth. Fellow Puerto Rican lefty Ramón Hernández closed out the 11-5 victory. Pizarro also got two hits that day.

Pittsburgh went on to win the NL East in 1974, and Pizarro remained on the postseason roster. His last appearance in the majors came in Game Four of the NLCS on October 9; he got the last two outs as the Dodgers drubbed the Pirates 12-1 to advance to the World Series.

Pizarro was in spring training with the Pirates in 1975 as a nonroster player but did not make the team. Returning to Mexico, he continued to excel for Córdoba in 1975 (14-7, 1.98) and 1976 (11-8, 2.64). He finished his Mexican career with a record of 38-21, 2.04, with 42 complete games and 17 shutouts in his 63 starts.

All along, Pizarro had been playing winter ball at home. He was a member of six PRWL champion teams and appeared in five Caribbean Series tournaments. Caguas won in his Triple Crown year, 1957-58, and added him as a reinforcement for the last edition of the tourney's first phase in 1960. Pizarro won five more PRWL titles with Santurce (1961-62, 1964-65, 1966-67, 1970-71, and 1972-73). The Caribbean Series returned from hiatus in 1970, and Santurce represented Puerto Rico in 1971 and 1973. In between, Pizarro played in the Inter-American Series each year from 1961 through 1964.

Pizarro also reinforced the Bayamón Vaqueros for the 1976 Caribbean Series. He rewarded manager José Pagán's surprise choice by throwing a three-hit shutout against Venezuela on his 39th birthday. "I used my experience in winning that game for Puerto Rico," he said. "It was nice to finish my Caribbean Series career as a winner."[50]

During the winter of 1976-77, Pizarro pitched his last 11 games as a pro for Santurce. His final record in Puerto Rico was 157-110, with a superb 2.51 ERA. Only Rubén Gómez had more wins (174, and he needed 29 seasons to do it). Pizarro pitched 2,403 innings, again second behind Gómez, and allowed just 1,980 hits. He is the PRWL's all-time leader in strikeouts (1,804) and shutouts (46), marks that will almost certainly never be challenged.

In addition to coaching the Crabbers off and on, Pizarro stayed involved with baseball in other ways. As of the early 1980s, he was working for Santurce's Parque Central as an instructor, with the additional goal of keeping kids out of trouble.[51] As late as 1997, he was back in the US, coaching with the Rockford Cubbies of the Midwest League (Class A). The manager was one of his contemporaries in the majors, Rubén Amaro, Sr. "He was very professional for me as well as our young pitchers," said Amaro, "and I know many of those young players were touched by his experience."[52]

In January 2007, Terín told columnist María Judith Caraballo that he was totally retired and enjoying a peaceful life at home in the same section of Santurce, Villa Palmeras, where he grew up. (He mentioned a wife, though not by name, in the Kiersh interview; information on children is also lacking.) After not having been to any ballpark for three years, he was at Game Six of the PRWL finals between the Arecibo Lobos and Gigantes de Carolina. Pizarro told Caraballo stories of his playing days and encouraged young Puerto Rican ballplayers to "work hard, run a lot, and practice enough."[53]

Sources

Internet resources

www.baseball-reference.com

www.retrosheet.org

www.ancestry.com (1940 census records)

www.paperofrecord.com (various small items from *The Sporting News*)

www.checkoutmycards.com (information from Pizarro's baseball cards)

Antero Núñez, José, *Series del Caribe* (Caracas, Venezuela: Impresos Urbina, C.A., 1987).

Crescioni Benítez, José A., *El Béisbol Profesional Boricua* (San Juan, Puerto Rico: Aurora Comunicación Integral, Inc., 1997).

James, Bill, and Rob Neyer, *The Neyer/James Guide to Pitchers* (New York: Simon & Schuster, 2004).

Kiersh, Edward, *Where Have You Gone, Vince DiMaggio?* (New York: Bantam Books, 1983).

Treto Cisneros, Pedro, ed., *Enciclopedia del Béisbol Mexicano* (Mexico City: Revistas Deportivas, S.A. de C.V., 11th edition, 2011).

Van Hyning, Thomas E., *Puerto Rico's Winter League* (Jefferson, North Carolina: McFarland & Company, 1995).

Van Hyning, Thomas E., *The Santurce Crabbers* (Jefferson, North Carolina: McFarland & Company, 1999).

Notes

1. Postseason play—in the minors, Puerto Rico, and international tournaments—got him over 400.
2. Edward Kiersh, *Where Have You Gone, Vince DiMaggio?* (New York: Bantam Books, 1983), 136.
3. Kiersh, *Where Have You Gone, Vince DiMaggio?*, 133.
4. "Puerto Rican Pitcher Gets Sally Loop Praise," United Press International, August 7, 1956.
5. Kiersh, *Where Have You Gone, Vince DiMaggio?*, 132.

6 Joe Livingston, "Ex-Batboy Pizarro Finds Sally Hitters Soft Touch," *The Sporting News*, May 23, 1956, 34.

7 Thomas E. Van Hyning, *The Santurce Crabbers* (Jefferson, North Carolina: McFarland & Company, 1999), 76.

8 Kiersh, *Where Have You Gone, Vince DiMaggio?*, 135.

9 Thomas E. Van Hyning, *Puerto Rico's Winter League* (Jefferson, North Carolina: McFarland & Company, 1995), 100.

10 Joe Livingston, "18-Year-Old Lefty Fans 14 in Six Innings in Sally Debut," *The Sporting News*, April 25, 1958, 32.

11 *The Sporting News*, February 22, 1956, 28; "Puerto Rican Pitcher Gets Sally Loop Praise."

12 Livingston, "Ex-Batboy Pizarro Finds Sally Hitters Soft Touch."

13 "Pizarro Cools Off Slightly in Red Hot Strikeout Pace," *The Sporting News*, July 11, 1956, 41.

14 "Puerto Rican Pitcher Gets Sally Loop Praise."

15 "296 Strikeouts for Pizarro," *The Sporting News*, August 29, 1956, 34.

16 Lou Chapman, "'Pizarro Could Be as Great as Spahn,' Says Bill Terry," *The Sporting News*, October 24, 1956, 8.

17 Van Hyning, *The Santurce Crabbers*, 84.

18 Pito Alvarez de la Vega, "Pizarro, Injured in Auto Crash, Quits Winter Ball," *The Sporting News*, January 9, 1957, 21.

19 Frank Finch, "Pilot Explains His Promise to 'Get Tough,'" *The Sporting News*, January 23, 1957, 4.

20 Bob Wolf, "Phenom Pizarro Sure He'll Make Grad as Brave," *The Sporting News*, March 13, 1957, 17.

21 Bob Wolf," Kid Pizarro Pitches Way Onto Braves' Bulging Staff," *The Sporting News*, April 24, 1957, 9.

22 Bob Wolf, "Braves, Rich in Hill Talent, Put Two More on Display," *The Sporting News*, May 15, 1957, 11.

23 Bob Wolf, "Conley's Comeback Like Oxygen Whiff to Crippled Braves," *The Sporting News*, August 7, 1957, 10.

24 Bob Wolf, "Pitcher-Wealthy Braves Still Seek Bull-Pen Bracer," *The Sporting News*, December 4, 1957, 20.

25 Kiersh, *Where Have You Gone, Vince DiMaggio?*, 133.

26 The others were Sam Jones (1954-55), Wayne Simpson (1969-70), and Edwin Núñez (1981-82).

27 Pat Dobson later broke this record on December 10, 1967, when he struck out 21.

28 Pito Alvarez de la Vega, "Latin Winter Crown Again Won by Cuba," *The Sporting News*, February 19, 1958, 30.

29 "Latin Tempers Explode," "Ump's Ruling Provokes Fan Riot; Series Game Halted," *The Sporting News*, February 19, 1958, 30.

30 Bob Wolf, "Braves Find More Pitching Riches in Depth of Hill Staff," *The Sporting News*, August 6, 1958, 18.

31 "Pizarro Seen Yank-Beater," United Press International, September 5, 1957.

32 "Hit in Eighth Halts Pizarro Bid for Second Gem in Row," *The Sporting News*, July 1, 1959, 27.

33 Van Hyning, *The Santurce Crabbers*, 84.

34 Bob Wolf, "Pizarro Takes Kinks Out of Braves' Staff by Junking Scroogie," *The Sporting News*, June 1, 1960, 15.

35 Edgar Munzel, "Senor to Try Magic on Pizarro, McLish," *The Sporting News*, December 28, 1960, 15.

36 Larry Moffi, *This Side of Cooperstown* (Ames, Iowa: Firehouse Books, 1996), 125.

37 Hank Aaron with Lonnie Wheeler, *I Had a Hammer: The Hank Aaron Story* (New York: Harper Perennial, 2007.)

38 Aaron, *I Had a Hammer*.

39 Kiersh, *Where Have You Gone, Vince DiMaggio?*, 133.

40 Bill Wise, ed., *1965 Official Baseball Almanac* (Greenwich, Connecticut: Fawcett, 1964).

41 Kiersh, *Where Have You Gone, Vince DiMaggio?*, 135.

42 Kiersh, *Where Have You Gone, Vince DiMaggio?*, 132.

43 Van Hyning, *The Santurce Crabbers*, 93.

44 Hiram Bithorn—the first Puerto Rican in the majors—had won 18 for the Chicago Cubs in 1943. Ed Figueroa broke this record in 1978 when he won 20 for the New York Yankees. Javier Vázquez surpassed Pizarro for most career big-league wins by a Puerto Rican native in 2009. Note also that "Nuyorican" John Candelaria won 20 games in 1977 and 177 in his career.

45 Edgar Munzel, "Injury Jinx Hits Sox on Double—Juan and Ward," *The Sporting News*, July 10, 1965, 3.

46 Jerome Holtzman, "Juan Uses His Curve Ball in Twirling a One-Hitter," *The Sporting News*, August 28, 1965, 17.

47 Kiersh, *Where Have You Gone, Vince DiMaggio?*, 135.

48 "Pizarro Streak Ends," *The Sporting News*, August 10, 1974, 42. Gary Ryerson broke the record for total in a season with 10 in 1976. That mark has since been matched twice.

49 Charley Feeney, "Pizarro Back for Another Whirl on Bucco Hill," *The Sporting News*, September 7, 1974, 7, 28.

50 Van Hyning, *The Santurce Crabbers*, 129.

51 Kiersh, *Where Have You Gone, Vince DiMaggio?*, 136.

52 E-mail from Rubén Amaro, Sr. to Rory Costello, December 29, 2012.

53 María Judith Caraballo, "Juan Terin Pizarro La Gloria del Béisbol Puertorriqueño," 1-800-Béisbol website (http://www.1800beisbol.com/baseball/deportes/latinos/juan_terin_pizarro_la_gloria_del_beisbol_puertorriqueno/), unknown date, 2007.

Del Rice

By Norm King

Del Rice was a major-league catcher for 17 years, primarily with the St. Louis Cardinals and Milwaukee Braves. While he was not a good hitter, his longevity was attributable to his excellent defensive skills and his ability to work with pitchers. He also knew how to win as a member of two World Series champions, the 1946 Cardinals and the 1957 Braves.

Long before there was Neon Deion and even when Bo did not know anything, Del Rice was a two-sport star in basketball and baseball. Delbert W. Rice, Jr. was born on October 27, 1922, in Portsmouth, Ohio, the only child of Del Rice, Sr. and Gladys Rice. Del Sr. worked for the city electric company. Del Jr. was an excellent athlete, playing basketball, football, and baseball in high school, but he was destined to be a catcher from his earliest days: "As far back as I can recall, I was always the catcher on the team," Rice once said in an interview. "And I always had a good arm."[1]

That good arm was evident in the neighborhood where Del lived, particularly to one neighbor who happened to be the brother of Branch Rickey, the St. Louis Cardinals' general manager at the time. Frank Rickey was one of the Cardinals' top scouts and he did not have to beat too many bushes to find a tall young catcher with professional potential. Rice was 6-feet-2 and weighed 190 pounds. Rickey signed Rice to a contract in 1941, and the 18-year-old embarked on his baseball career with Williamson (West Virginia) of the Class D Mountain State League.

Rice started off with a bang, well, three bangs, actually, as he went 3-for-4 in his first professional game, including a home run. He also picked a runner off first base. First appearances were indeed deceiving, however, as he went on to hit just .248 in 88 games the rest of the season, with only two more home runs.

Despite the poor hitting stats, the Cardinals were impressed enough to bring Rice back to Williamson for 1942. He caught 121 of the team's 124 games, and the heavy workload seemed to help his hitting as his average improved to .288 with 29 doubles, 3 triples, and 7 home runs. He made the league all-star team.

Rice's knack for being in the right place at the right time continued after his second season. A shortage of players due to World War II (Rice was classified 4-F because of an old injury) caused many teams to suspend their minor-league operations, resulting in Rice's promotion at the tender age of 20 in 1943 from Class D all the way to Double-A with Rochester of the International League. It was clearly too much too soon, as pitchers discovered they could get him out easily with low pitches. A woeful .198 batting average in 66 games was the result, with no home runs, five doubles, three triples, and just 18 runs batted in for the season. On the plus side, he committed only nine errors, after having 20 miscues the year before.

One pitch that did work in Rice's favor was to Mary Alice Ruel (no relation to Muddy) of Portsmouth, whom he married on January 30, 1943.

With the war still raging in 1944, Rice's trials from the previous year bore some fruit that season. In 92

Del Rice (National Baseball Hall of Fame Library, Cooperstown, N.Y.)

games for Rochester, his average climbed to .264, with six homers and a respectable 50 RBIs. He did commit 12 errors, but the increased playing time accounts for the higher total. Overall those numbers were good enough for a one-way ticket to "The Show."

Before the 1945 season started Rice also had good news from the home front, as his son Ronnie was born in March of that year.

Making the 1945 Cardinals was no easy feat. They had won 105 games in 1944 and then defeated the St. Louis Browns in six games in the World Series. Hall of Famer Stan Musial was in the early stages of his career, and the team boasted such solid players as shortstop Marty Marion and third baseman Whitey Kurowski.

The Cardinals' catching situation was a bit unsettled as the 1945 campaign approached. Incumbent Walker Cooper and his brother, pitcher Mort Cooper, threatened to boycott St. Louis's season-opening series against the Chicago Cubs even though they had signed contracts for $12,000.[2] They eventually capitulated, but Walker played only four games before joining the Navy. This gave the starting job to veteran Ken O'Dea, but Cardinals manager Billy Southworth was impressed with rookie backstop Rice. "I know a lot of clubs that would be glad to have Rice for first-string catcher," Southworth said in a May 1945 interview.[3]

The respect was mutual, as Southworth worked closely with Rice to help him overcome his inability to hit the low pitch. "I didn't seem to be able to level off properly on a ball down around my knees," Rice said in a 1945 interview. "But since I've been with the Cardinals, Mr. Southworth, who is a fine batting teacher, has taken me in hand, and I think he has ironed out some of the things I did wrong."[4]

Unbeknownst to Rice, the Cardinals had other irons in the fire between the end of the 1945 season and the start of 1946, which included their intention to trade him to the Dodgers as part of a three-team deal involving Brooklyn, St. Louis, and the Boston Braves. He was supposed to go to the Dodgers and the Cardinals were supposed to receive Mickey Owen, a more experienced catcher, and then send Owen to the Braves in exchange for their primary catcher, Phil Masi. The trade was voided, however, when Owen decided to accept an ill-fated offer to play in the nascent Mexican League.

The trade that did not happen was probably precipitated by the Cardinals selling Walker Cooper to the Giants for $175,000 in January 1946. When Cooper left, he took not only his big bat but a wealth of experience as well. The Cardinals had potential stars in Rice and Joe Garagiola, but they were both inexperienced (Garagiola, in particular was considered a top prospect, even though he was only 20, had only one year of Organized Baseball behind him, and was still in the Army as the season began) and O'Dea was a career backup. "(Manager Eddie) Dyer's chief concern was the catching department, (the) only spot where the Cards aren't at least two deep," wrote W. Vernon Tietjen in *The Sporting News*.[5]

After the 1945 baseball season ended, Rice augmented his income by playing basketball with the Rochester Royals of the old National Basketball League. (The NBL would merge with the Basketball Association of America in 1949 to become the NBA. The Rochester franchise is now the Sacramento Kings.) It was the Royals' first season in the NBL, and they started with a bang. With a roster that included NBA Hall of Famer Red Holzman, NFL Hall of Fame quarterback Otto Graham, and future TV star and baseball player Chuck Connors, the Royals won the league championship in their inaugural season. It was Rice's only year in professional basketball.

The Cardinals started the 1946 season with O'Dea and Rice behind the plate, neither of whom could be considered an everyday catcher. O'Dea had developed back problems, so owner Sam Breadon traded his starting second baseman, Emil Verban, to the Philadelphia Phillies in exchange for journeyman catcher Clyde Kluttz. Garagiola was added to the mix upon his discharge from the Army in May and started his first game on May 26. Although it probably was not the plan, the Cardinals ended up having catcher by committee, with Garagiola behind the plate in 70 games, Kluttz in 49, Rice in 53, and O'Dea in 22.

The catching conundrum did not seem to bother the Cardinals pitchers. They led the league in earned-run average, complete games, and shutouts. As well, all the talent returning from the military helped the Cardinals win the World Series that year in seven games over the Boston Red Sox after winning the major leagues' first-ever best-of-three playoff against the Brooklyn Dodgers in two straight games. Garagiola did the bulk of the catching in the fall classic, while Rice appeared in three games and went 3-for-6 with two runs scored.

The Redbirds were winging it again at the catcher's position in 1947. Kluttz was sold to Pittsburgh, but the Cardinals still retained a trio of catchers with Del Wilber, who had appeared briefly in early 1946, joining Rice and Garagiola on the roster. Although Rice played in more games (97) than either of the others, he was unable to claim the starting job as his own, due partly to a shoulder injury suffered during spring training. He did set a career high for home runs, with 12, but batted only .218 as the Cardinals began three frustrating seasons finishing as the runner-up to the pennant winner.

One season highlight for Rice occurred on August 23 against Philadelphia. In the eighth inning the Phillies had two on, nobody out, and pinch-hitter Charlie Gilbert at the plate. For some reason he tried to bunt with two strikes on him. He made contact, but hit a short foul popup that Rice lunged at and caught with his bare hand. The men on base were running, so Rice gunned the ball to Marty Marion covering second base for the second out; Marion threw it to Musial at first base to complete the triple play. The Cardinals won the game, 5-3.

Rice continued having difficulty claiming the catcher's job for his own as the 1948 season began. "Asked about his catching problems, Dyer said he was quite satisfied with the receiving of Del Wilber, who has been doing the bulk of the Redbirds' mask work this spring," wrote Ray Gillespie in *The Sporting News*. "Eddie indicated, however, that it would be a dogfight for the job, with Del Rice and Joe Garagiola very much in the running in the event the ex-Air Force captain [Wilber] stubs his toe."[6]

It must have been quite a stub, because Wilber ended up catching only 26 games that season. In fact, Rice owned the starting job by early May with his solid defensive work. "He caught a whale of a game as we beat the Cubs 3 to 1, May 3," Dyer said. Del tossed out two base runners and really showed us something when he nailed big Bill Nicholson driving into the plate trying to score."[7]

Besides his stellar defense, Rice was holding on to the job because he was the best from among a sorry group of hitters. By mid-June, Rice was hitting .196, which was Cobbesque compared with Garagiola's .088 and Wilber's .053. These below-average averages prompted the Cardinals to send Garagiola down to their Columbus Triple-A affiliate and bring up 37-year-old Bill Baker, who had not even played in the majors in 1947. Rice still did the lion's share of the catching for the season, appearing in 100 games and hitting a career-low .197 for the year (a mark he equaled in 1955 with the Braves), with only four home runs and 34 RBIs. Of the 100 games he played in, he caught in 99, which under the rules at the time meant that he missed out on qualifying for the league fielding percentage title for his position by one game. He would have won it, too, as he had a league-high .996 fielding percentage, but Masi of the Braves won it with .988.

Rice caught a break during spring training 1949. Unfortunately, the break was in his right thumb, but that did not prevent him from starting on Opening Day in Cincinnati. Garagiola was back up with the big club by then, and Dyer platooned them for the season, with Garagiola playing against right-handers and Rice against southpaws. Rice batted .236 in 92 games and equaled his total for home runs from the previous season with four; but his RBI total dropped to 29.

The catcher's job became Rice's by default early in 1950. Actually, "de" fault was Garagiola's. He began the season as the number one backstop, but on June 1 he separated his shoulder tripping over Jackie Robinson's leg at first base. In 130 games, Rice's average improved to .244 and his production numbers were better as well, with nine homers and 54 RBIs.

Rice's numbers were similar in 1951 (.251, 9 HRs, 47 RBIs), but he made a significant change in his hitting style that improved his confidence going into the 1952 season. He finally heeded the advice of coaches and managers and stopped trying to pull everything to left. His epiphany came in a late-season game against the Giants. "There were runners on first and third, one out, and the count ran to three balls and two strikes," he said. "I made up my mind I was going to right field or else. I guess I fouled off four or five pitches, but finally I shot one to right, for I knew I could do it."[8]

The 1951 season was also significant for Rice because Garagiola, his rival for the catching job, was traded to the Pittsburgh Pirates in June, ensuring that Rice would get most of the work behind the plate.

That is exactly what happened in 1952. Rice played in 147 games that year (in a 154-game schedule), hit double digits in home runs (11) for the second and last time, and set a career high for RBIs with 65. The workload did not affect his defense, either. He made only six errors in 764 chances for a .992 fielding percentage, second in the league to Roy Campanella's .994.

Rice's fine play in 1952 was a prelude to an All-Star season in 1953. His offensive numbers were not as good, but he remained steady defensively, not committing his first error of the season until his 64th game. Campanella won the fan poll for starting catcher in the All-Star Game in Cincinnati that year, but NL manager Charley Dressen chose Del Crandall and Rice, who came in second and third respectively in the balloting, as backups. Rice injured his finger on a foul tip six days before the game, causing him to miss his only chance of making an All-Star appearance.

Injuries and the cumulative effects of a heavy workload took their toll on Rice in 1954. In a June 7 collision at the plate, Campanella, the baserunner, caught Rice in the calf with his spikes, putting him out for a week. Rice's playing time also diminished because his replacement, Bill Sarni, batted .300, hit nine home runs, and had 70 RBIs. As a result, Rice played in only 56 games; his days as a full-time catcher were over.

Not surprisingly, Rice was traded to the Milwaukee Braves on June 3, 1955. His stock had fallen to the point where the Cardinals received Pete Whisenant, who was playing at Triple-A Toledo. With perennial All-Star catcher Crandall on the Braves roster, Rice was clearly going to play a backup role.

Although he was guaranteed diminished playing time in Milwaukee, Rice could get comfort from the fact that he was joining a powerful team that was in the middle of a love affair with the city since moving to Wisconsin from Boston. With a power supply led by Hank Aaron and Eddie Mathews, and with Warren Spahn and Lew Burdette on the mound, the Braves finished second to the Brooklyn Dodgers in 1955 and 1956.

Despite being a backup, Rice certainly contributed to the Braves' 1957 championship. Milwaukee was in the middle of a September swoon, having lost eight games out of 11, caused by, of all things, a hitting slump. Their lead in the NL had dwindled from 8 1/2 to 2 1/2 games, but on September 16 Rice led a 14-hit attack by driving in two runs with a single and home run against the Phillies in a 5-1 win that got the team out of its doldrums. "If Rice didn't get another hit all season, and if his tenure as first-string catcher lasted no more than a game or two, he had done something not even the best hitters on the club could do," wrote Bob Wolf in *The Sporting News*. "He had shown the way out of a batting slump that had threatened to cause the complete collapse of the club."[9]

Rice started that night thanks to pitcher Bob Buhl, for whom Rice was his personal catcher. The pairing worked, as the battery kept going and going until Buhl put together an 18-8 record and led the league with a .720 winning percentage. The World Series was another story, as Buhl had a 0-1 record in two starts with a 10.80 ERA and a total of only 3 1/3 innings pitched. Rice started behind the plate in Games Three and Six and had one hit in seven appearances. The Braves' triumph in seven games over the New York Yankees gave Rice his second World Series ring. The Braves lost a seven-game rematch to the Yankees in 1958, but Rice did not play in that Series.

Rice played for the Braves until he was released after the 1959 season. He signed in October with the Chicago Cubs as a free agent and caught Don Cardwell's no-hitter against the Cardinals on May 15, 1960. He also played for the Cardinals and Orioles that season, and when the American League expanded to ten teams, he became the very first Los Angeles Angel, signing on as a player-coach for the Angels' inaugural season in 1961, Rice's last as a player. On the personal front, Rice also got married for a second time before that season started; his first wife, Mary Alice, had died of leukemia in November 1956. Del married Pat Niebur in February 1961, and the couple had a daughter, Julie Ann, in 1962.

After retiring as a player Rice coached for the Angels and the Cleveland Indians, then began paying his dues as a minor-league manager, starting at San Jose of the Class A California League in 1968. In 1969 he moved up to the El Paso Sun Kings of the Double-A Texas League, where he made a splash right away by being ejected in his first game. Despite that inauspicious start, he managed in El Paso for two years, then took over the Triple-A Salt Lake City Angels (Pacific Coast League) in 1971. Rice skippered this squad to first place in the Southern Division, then defeated Tacoma in the league playoffs, and was named *The Sporting News* Minor League Manager of the Year. For that he was rewarded with the manager's job with the Angels.

Whether it was a reward or a punishment in disguise is an interesting question, because the Angels were a team in turmoil: "There wasn't any fun for the Angels in 1971," wrote Dick Miller in *The Sporting News*. In 1971 Rice's predecessor, Lefty Phillips, wasn't a Captain Bligh, but tensions surrounded the California clubhouse. Tony Conigliaro couldn't bear the stress and quit the game. Alex Johnson was suspended. Chico Ruiz was charged with pulling a gun on a teammate.[10]

It would probably have taken a miracle to turn the 1972 California Angels around quickly, especially when they lost six out of their first eight games. The team ended up with a 75-80 record in a strike-shortened season, and even though the team had a higher winning percentage than the previous season, Rice was given a ticket on the Angels' managerial merry-go-round, becoming the third manager in five years to be fired by the club. He stayed on as a scout, but quit the Angels organization in 1978 when owner Gene Autry asked him to take a $6,000 pay cut.

Rice continued in baseball as a scout with the New York Yankees and San Francisco Giants. He battled cancer for several years and died on January 26, 1983, while waiting to be introduced at a benefit dinner in his honor in Buena Vista, California. He was 60 years old.

Sources

baseball-reference.com/bullpen/Del_Rice

Graham, Frank, Jr., "The Great Mexican War of 1946," *Sports Illustrated*, September 19, 1966.

baseball-reference.com/players/c/coopewa01.shtml

baseball-reference.com/managers/southbi01.shtml

Daly, Jon Daly, biography of Billy Southworth.

baseball-reference.com/bullpen/Joe_Garagiola

baseball-reference.com/players/m/masiph01.shtml

baseball-reference.com/players/o/o'deake01.shtml

paperofrecord.hypernet.ca/paper_view.asp?PaperId=834&RecordId=3&PageId=7749289&iZyNetId={30062EB4-7CFA-4C3D-BD8D-A8950A1AA1E9}&iOrder=2&iOrderDir=0&iCurrentBlock=1

sportsecyclopedia.com/nba/rochester/rochroyals.html

basketball.wikia.com/wiki/National_Basketball_League

baseball-reference.com/minors/league.cgi?code=PCL&class=AAA

Notes

1. Frederick G. Lieb, "Scout Next Door 'Discovered' Del Rice, Card Catching Rookie," *The Sporting News*, July 5, 1945.
2. Frederick G. Lieb, "Coopers, Brother Battery, Call Own Strike, Then Call It Off in Pay Row," *The Sporting News*, April 19, 1945.
3. Frederick G. Lieb, "Cards Start to Hit Fence as Ace Hurlers Hit Stride," *The Sporting News*, May 10, 1945.
4. Ibid.
5. W. Vernon Tietjen, "Cardinals Well-Padded in All Except Pad Corps," *The Sporting News*, April 4, 1946.
6. Ray Gillespie, "Dyer Chuckles Over Redbird Chucking and Nippy's Nifty Work at First Base," *The Sporting News*, April 28, 1948.
7. Ray Gillespie, "Birds, Browns, Show More Power at Gate," *The Sporting News*, May 12, 1948.
8. Bob Broeg, "Younger Redbirds to Get Full Chance to Make Grade—Saigh," *The Sporting News*, November 28, 1951.
9. Bob Wolf, "Buhl-and-Rice Battery Flicks Beacon for Fog-Bound Braves," *The Sporting News*, September 25, 1957.
10. Dick Miller, " 'We'll Have Fun,' Says New Angel Pilot Rice," *The Sporting News*, December 25, 1971.

Mel Roach

By David L. Fleitz

Mel Roach was more a spectator than a player for the 1957 world champion Milwaukee Braves. He played the first part of the season in the minor leagues before the Braves called him up in July. He spent the rest of the campaign as an occasional pinch-hitter and pinch-runner, batting only seven times and stroking only one hit, a single. However, the seldom-used Roach was being groomed for bigger things. With second baseman Red Schoendienst advancing in age, the Braves expected that Roach would step in and claim Schoendienst's spot on the infield in due time. He might have done so, too, had not a debilitating knee injury suffered during the heat of the 1958 pennant race derailed his once-promising career.

Melvin Edward Roach was born in Richmond, Virginia, on January 25, 1933. He was the youngest of five children, all boys, born to Leslie Roach, a Richmond police officer, and his wife, Mable, a housewife. Mel, a right-handed batter and thrower, was a gifted athlete at John Marshall High School in Richmond, starring in football, basketball, and baseball, and serving as captain of all three teams. As a first baseman and cleanup hitter, he led his American Legion team to the national finals in 1950. Graduating from high school in 1951, Mel then attended the University of Virginia in Charlottesville, where he excelled as a quarterback, defensive back, and place-kicker on a football team that amassed a 16-3 record during the 1951 and 1952 seasons. He kicked 37 extra points in 1952, setting a school record at the time. On the Cavaliers basketball team, Roach averaged 10 points per game. Still, his best sport was baseball, and major-league scouts showed interest after Mel, who played mostly at second base in college, led the state in hitting in 1952 and 1953. He had intended to complete his degree in economics and then enter professional baseball, but when a shoulder injury suffered during football season drove him to the sidelines in 1952, Mel decided to listen to major-league offers.

At least ten teams scouted the young Virginia Cavalier intently, with the Milwaukee Braves and the Pittsburgh Pirates expressing the most interest. Reportedly, Pirates scout Rex Bowen called Roach, who stood 6-feet-1 and weighed 190 pounds, the finest prospect he saw at a Forbes Field tryout, but the Pirates had signed too many bonus players to make a serious offer.[1] The Pirates reluctantly passed on the opportunity, and though the Yankees, White Sox, and Indians also courted the young ballplayer, Milwaukee Braves scout Gil English signed Roach to a $40,000 bonus contract in July of 1953.

Because of the "bonus baby" rule in effect at that time, the Braves were required to carry Roach (and a teenage pitcher, Joey Jay, who signed with the club at about the same time) on the major-league roster for two years before allowing him to play in the minors. Roach bided his time on the Milwaukee bench, appearing in five games in 1953 and three in 1954, mostly as a pinch-hitter or pinch-runner. The Braves had agreed to pay the rest of his college expenses, so in 1953 and 1954 he reported to the team in June, after the semester

Mel Roach (National Baseball Hall of Fame Library, Cooperstown, N.Y.)

at the University of Virginia was finished, and left in September to return to campus. As a result, Roach completed his course work in the usual four years, earning his degree in economics in June of 1955. Still, he regretted his lack of playing time. "The big thing was the confidence I got from playing," he said a few years later. "As a bonus player I sat around so much that I got discouraged. I had hopes of making it someday, but I'll have to admit I had serious doubts."[2]

Roach then spent two years in the US Navy. Because he stood a good chance of being drafted into military service, he had decided to enroll in the Naval ROTC (Reserve Officers Training Corps) program while in college, and then go on active duty after graduation to put his military obligation behind him. Gil English, who saw Roach play in a Navy baseball tournament in the fall of 1956, told the Braves that he and Dodgers pitcher Johnny Podres were the two best players in the tourney, calling Roach "an outstanding hitter with fine power."[3] This performance rekindled Milwaukee's interest in Roach, though the youngster's baseball skills had stagnated during his Navy hitch. "Service ball did me no good at all," he told *The Sporting News* in 1958. "It was a good way to stay in shape but the poor competition tended to make a player lazy."[4] Discharged from the Navy in March of 1957, he reported to spring training with the Braves, who sent the 24-year-old infielder to Jacksonville of the South Atlantic League. He batted .311 in 70 games for Class A Jacksonville, then was promoted to Atlanta of the Double-A Southern Association. He batted .293 for Atlanta in 37 games, and despite his lack of power (only six of his 43 hits went for extra bases), the Milwaukee club recalled him in early August. As a returning serviceman, Roach did not count against the 25-man roster limit, so the Braves were able to carry him as an extra player without removing anyone else from the roster.

While the Braves fought for the pennant, Roach spent most of his time on the sidelines, playing mostly in the late innings of blowout wins. Schoendienst, acquired by the Braves in a trade with the New York Giants in June of that year, took control of the second-base job and left little playing time available for the newcomer. As a result, Roach made only four appearances in August and one on September 2 (in a 23-10 win over the Cubs in Chicago). Bothered by arthritis in his throwing arm, he did not take the field again until September 27, when he played a complete game at second base against the Cincinnati Reds and collected his first major-league hit. In all, he batted seven times for the Braves in 1957, reaching base safely once on a single. He watched from the bench as the Braves defeated the New York Yankees in the World Series, and his teammates voted him a one-third share of the World Series money, which came to $2,974.38. "They must have thought I was a nice guy," he recalled many year later.[5]

Roach earned a spot on the team during spring training in 1958 and, though he appeared in only five of Milwaukee's first 24 games, he opened the season on a hot streak. He walloped his first major-league homer, a solo shot off Curt Simmons, in a win over the Phillies on April 19, and belted seven hits in his first 15 times at bat. However, the Braves sent him down to Wichita in early May, leaving many to wonder how a budding star with a .467 batting average could have cleared waivers. Still, Roach did not object. "I've asked the Braves to let me go where I can play every day," he said during spring training. "I don't care where I play. Just let me play."[6] Roach spent a month at Wichita before the club recalled him in June. He pinch-hit and played left field for a few weeks, but in mid-July, when Schoendienst left the lineup with a broken finger, Roach took over the second-base position and began to deliver on his early promise. He kept his average near the .300 mark, showed improvement in his infield play, and performed so well that he retained his hold on the second-base job even when Schoendienst rejoined the team.

On Sunday, August 3, 1958, disaster struck. Roach had played the best baseball of his career in a weekend series against the San Francisco Giants in Milwaukee, belting home runs on Friday and Saturday and going 3-for-4 in the first game of the Sunday doubleheader. He had raised his average to .313 and sparked the league-leading Braves to three wins in a row over the Giants. In Sunday's second game, the thoroughly demoralized Giants fell behind early, and San Francisco shortstop Daryl Spencer, perhaps in an attempt to jolt his teammates to life, took aim at Roach. Spencer, who walked in the top of the fifth inning, advanced to second on a grounder by Valmy Thomas and slid hard into the Milwaukee second baseman. Roach, who took the throw from shortstop Johnny Logan and was airborne when Spencer slammed into him, collapsed in a heap with a severely damaged left knee.

A few weeks before, Braves manager Fred Haney, who selected the reserves for the National League All-Star team that year, bypassed Spencer and chose Milwaukee's Logan instead. Spencer seethed over the slight; indeed, he told an interviewer that he still harbored bitterness over the rejection more than 50 years later.[7] Many observers believed that Spencer's rough play was a form of payback to Haney and the Braves, though Spencer himself never said so publicly. "[Spencer] was definitely out of the baseline, and did a rolling block,"[8] Roach told an interviewer in 2012. The Braves were outraged by Spencer's hard slide, and Milwaukee baserunners made a point of targeting Spencer whenever the opportunity arose during the rest of the game.

Roach was taken to a hospital, where an orthopedic surgeon, Dr. Bruce Brewer, performed a two-hour operation to repair a torn ligament in the player's left knee. Not only was Roach out for the rest of the season, but some feared that his career was over at the age of 25. "It makes me feel plain rotten," he told a reporter after the surgery. "They tell me it could have been much worse, but this is bad enough."[9] He wore a heavy cast on the knee for more than a month, then walked with the aid of crutches and a cane for a few months more. Roach ended the 1958 season with a .309 average in 44 games, and though he could not take part in the World Series that fall against the Yankees, he received a full Series share of $5,896.08.

Recovery was a slow and painful process. As Roach recalled to interviewer Brent P. Kelley in 2006, "I was told by the doctor that I'd never play again, that the knee was in pretty bad shape, so I really had resigned myself that it was over."[10] However, he was determined to rehabilitate the knee, and after sitting out the first part of the 1959 season, he returned to the Braves in June and played in 19 games, though he managed only three singles in 31 at-bats for an .097 average. Still bothered by soreness, he was placed on the disabled list in early August and played no more that season. The Milwaukee club, which lost Schoendienst to a bout of tuberculosis and never found a competent second baseman to replace him, lost the pennant to the Los Angeles Dodgers in two games during a best-of-three playoff.

In 1960 new Braves manager Charlie Dressen used Mel as a utilityman, and Roach, now 27 years old, batted .300 in 48 games. However, he had trouble in the field, probably due to his continuing knee problems, and though he hit well, he could not crack the starting lineup. The Braves finished a distant second to Pittsburgh in the pennant race, and with the second-base situation still unsettled (six different men, including Hank Aaron, saw time at the second sack that season), the club filled the position when it acquired Frank Bolling, a former Gold Glove winner, from Detroit in December of 1960. This move boded ill for Roach's future in Milwaukee.

Roach began the 1961 season in a hitting slump, and on May 3 he suffered an embarrassing lapse in the outfield. Left-hander Warren Spahn had thrown a no-hitter against the Giants five days before, and in Spahn's next start, against the Dodgers, Roach, playing left field, misplayed a third-inning fly ball off the bat of Jim Gilliam that fell for a run-scoring double, the first hit of the game for the Dodgers. Spahn finished the game with a two-hit, 4-1 complete-game victory. The only other hit, which came with two out in the ninth, would not have occurred had Roach caught Gilliam's fly. The miscue cost Spahn the opportunity to match Johnny Vander Meer's feat of throwing two no-hitters in a row, and Roach was despondent. "Don't try to make excuses for me," he said after the game. "It was a fly ball any outfielder should have caught. I just misjudged it."[11] Spahn not only absolved Roach of blame, but was surprised nearly 30 years later when he played a round of golf with Roach and heard his old teammate apologize once again for the long-ago misplay. "Geez, Mel, that was a lifetime ago. Forget it," said the old pitcher.[12]

Roach played only four more games in a Milwaukee uniform, for on May 9, 1961, the Braves traded him to the Chicago Cubs for outfielder Frank Thomas. Roach, who batted only .147 in 1961, played sparingly for the seventh-place Cubs, and at season's end Chicago traded him to the Cleveland Indians for two minor leaguers. Despite his fine spring-training performance, the Cleveland club sent him to the Philadelphia Phillies for pitcher Ken Lehman and outfielder Tony Curry on March 20, 1962.

The Phillies finished the 1962 season in seventh place, ahead of only the Cubs and the expansion Mets and Colt .45s, and the atmosphere around the club did not suit Mel. "We had a pretty sad team [in Philadelphia] — it was a very poor team — and nothing happened there," recalled Roach years later. "… We had Gene Mauch managing, and Gene was more interested in playing golf than managing, in my own opinion, so it was another disaster."[13] Nearing his 30th birthday, Roach began thinking about life after baseball. "My peer group from my graduating class were all getting ahead of me in business and I started thinking in terms of, well, I think I'll get a real job."[14] After the Phillies dropped Mel from their roster and assigned him to the Arkansas Travelers of the Triple-A American Association in October of 1962, the second baseman decided that he had played enough baseball. He retired from the game and entered the banking business.

Mel, who married during the 1962 season, settled in his hometown of Richmond and raised two children with his wife, Marilyn. He eventually became the president of a banking group in Richmond, where he and his wife, both retired, still made their home as of 2013. His only regret, he told Brent P. Kelley in 2006, was the knee injury that shortened his career. "[Daryl Spencer] was a pretty hard-nosed player anyway," he said. "He prided himself on doing it. I saw him many times after that and he never apologized, never said a word about it."[15] An avid golfer, Roach is an active supporter of the Virginia Sports Hall of Fame, into which he was inducted in 1988.

Sources

Kelley, Brent P., *Baseball's Bonus Babies: Conversations with 24 High-Priced Ballplayers Signed from 1953 to 1957* (Jefferson, North Carolina: McFarland and Company, 2006).

Lamb, David, *Stolen Season: A Journey Through America and Baseball's Minor Leagues* (New York: Random House, 1991).

Milwaukee Journal, May 4, 1961.

Rives, Bob, "Daryl Spencer," biography on the SABR BioProject website at sabr.org/bioproj.

The Sporting News, October 31, 1956; December 3, 1958; December 17, 1958.

Telephone interview with Mel Roach, November 18, 2012.

Baseball-reference.com

Notes

1 *The Sporting News*, December 17, 1958, 8.
2 *The Sporting News*, December 3, 1958, 15.
3 *The Sporting News*, October 31, 1956, 6.
4 *The Sporting News*, December 3, 1958, 15.
5 Telephone interview with Mel Roach, November 18, 2012.
6 *The Sporting News*, December 17, 1958, 8.
7 Bob Rives, "Daryl Spencer," biography on the SABR BioProject website at sabr.org/bioproj.
8 Telephone interview with Mel Roach, November 18, 2012.
9 Associated Press, August 5, 1958.
10 Brent P. Kelley, *Baseball's Bonus Babies: Conversations with 24 High-Priced Ballplayers Signed from 1953 to 1957* (Jefferson, North Carolina: McFarland and Company, 2006), 29.
11 *Milwaukee Journal*, May 4, 1961.
12 David Lamb, *Stolen Season: A Journey Through America and Baseball's Minor Leagues* (New York: Random House, 1991), 98.
13 Kelley, 29.
14 Kelley, 29.
15 Kelley, 30.

Carl Sawatski

By Gregory H. Wolf

With his thunderous left-handed home-run stroke, the self-converted catcher Carl "Swish" Sawatski established a reputation as one of the most feared sluggers in Organized Baseball by leading four different leagues in round-trippers in his first five years as a professional (1945 to 1949). Despite his slugging potential, Sawatski bounced around in four different organizations struggling with weight issues before finally earning a permanent spot in the big leagues with the Milwaukee Braves during their magical run to the World Series in 1957. A classic pull hitter, career backup catcher, and effective pinch-hitter, Sawatski retired in 1963 after four productive years with the St. Louis Cardinals.

Carl Ernest Sawatski was born on November 4, 1927, in the small borough of Shickshinny, Pennsylvania, about 130 miles northwest of Philadelphia. Nestled at the mouth of the Shickshinny Creek along the Susquehanna River, Shickshinny is in the heart of coal country in the northern Appalachian Mountains. Carl's parents, Ernest and Stella (nee Gryniewicz), both born in the Keystone State, were the children of Polish-speaking immigrants. Living with modest means in the desperate times of the Depression, Ernest worked on various Works Progress Administration (WPA) projects while Stella found piecework as a seamstress to support their three children, Marcella, Chester, and Carl, born between 1922 and 1927.

Dorothy Sawatski, Carl's widow, told the author in a 2013 interview how Carl grew up with a baseball bat in his hand, hitting everything he could find at home and playing sandlot ball whenever he could. However, hard work and sacrifice defined the period. In an interview near the end of his professional baseball career, Sawatski recounted how he began digging for coal in abandoned local mines as an 11-year-old and carrying it by boat along the Susquehanna River to home.[1] When his parents separated, his mother left the rural confines of Appalachia with her children and moved to Mountain View, New Jersey, in the New York City metropolitan area, where she worked in a factory during World War II. Later his father moved to the vicinity and opened a taxicab business.

A short, stocky youngster, Carl played football and basketball at Pompton Lakes High School, dabbled in boxing at the Diamond Gloves in Paterson, New Jersey, and competed as a third baseman in American Legion baseball in the summer. Known for his towering home-run blasts and his voracious appetite, the left-handed batter attracted the attention of local scouts. "I got a $500 bonus from the Phillies when I signed as a 16-year old [in 1944]," he recalled. "I weighed 188 pounds then. Yes, I was heavy even then."[2]

Finishing high school in 1945, Carl was assigned to the Bradford Blue Wings in the Class D Pennsylvania-Ontario-New York (PONY) League, where he was converted to a right fielder. Notwithstanding his shaky defense, Sawatski tied his manager, Lee Riley, for the league lead with 13 home runs. Promoted to the Schenectady Blue Jays of the Class C Canadian-

Carl Sawatski (National Baseball Hall of Fame Library, Cooperstown, N.Y.)

American League the following season, Sawatski faltered, hitting just .235 with one home run in 136 at-bats, and was released by the club. "I loafed during the winter of 1945-46 and my weight zoomed to 253," he explained."[3] For the rest of Sawatski's baseball career, discussions about his weight were coupled with those about his prodigious power.

No doubt embarrassed by his release, Sawatski caught on with the Bloomingdale Troopers, who played just seven miles from his hometown, for the second half of the 1946 season. His older brother, Chester, was also listed on Bloomingdale's roster that season. Facing less rigorous competition in the inaugural season of the Class D North Atlantic League, he belted seven home runs in 154 at-bats, but he had to reinvent himself if he hoped to continue his career. "I knew I had to do something about my size," he said. "Since I couldn't change my appetite, I changed positions. Due to my build, catching seemed like the best position, so I converted myself."[4] Catching full time in 1947, Sawatski struggled while crouching behind the plate but not while standing at it. Batting .352 for the Troopers, who had a working agreement with the Boston Braves, Sawatski garnered headlines for his hitting. After belting four home runs and knocking in 14 runs in a three-game series against the Kingston Dodgers, the Kingston (New York) Daily Freeman called his performance the "greatest display of batting power in North Atlantic League history."[5] Nicknamed Butch for his stature, Sawatski led the league with 34 home runs and knocked in 138 runs in just 127 games. But the Braves weren't impressed. They sold him to the Chicago Cubs in the offseason.[6]

The Cubs assigned Sawatski to their Class A affiliate in the Western League, the Des Moines Bruins, for the 1948 season. Playing for manager Stan Hack, Sawatski hit home runs in two of his last three at-bats of the season to lead the league with 29 and help the team to a first-place finish. The Cubs rewarded the 20-year-old slugger by calling him up in September. In front of just 1,842 fans at Wrigley Field on September 29, Sawatski made his major-league debut in the fourth inning when he unsuccessfully pinch-hit for pitcher Bob Chipman against the Cincinnati Reds.

Participating in his first major-league spring training in 1949, Sawatski competed with Smoky Burgess for the role of third catcher behind Bob Scheffing and Rube Walker. Limited by a sore arm he developed early in camp, Sawatski was sent to the team's Double-A affiliate in the Southern Association, the Nashville Vols.[7] The "thick torsoed"[8] slugger felt at home at Sulphur Dell with its short right porch which SABR's Warren Corbett has described as "resembl[ing] a ridiculously short par-three hole on a golf course," just 262 feet down the foul line.[9] But the 5-foot-10 Sawatski possessed a power stroke no matter where he played. Opening the season at Joe Engel Stadium in Chattanooga against the Lookouts, Sawatski blasted what some observers thought was the longest home run ever hit and estimated that it traveled 575 feet.[10]

The "huge, powerful catcher" demolished the ball all season, leading the Southern Association with 45 home runs and knocking in 153 runs even though a broken thumb suffered in August forced him to miss three weeks and limited him to 128 games.[11] Sawatski was "a star for the Vols because he prefers catching to dieting," reported a local paper.[12] Nicknamed "Swish" for the sound of his bat launching another home run, Sawatski anticipated a late-season call-up, but the Cubs had obtained former All-Star catcher Mickey Owen in July when he was reinstated after his ban from baseball (for having jumped to the Mexican League in 1945) was overturned.[13] The "most promising" of Cubs prospects and the league's most valuable player led the Vols to the league championship and then put on an unprecedented display of power in the team's Dixie Series championship over the Tulsa Oilers of the Texas League by cranking five home runs in the seven-game series.[14]

Sawatski's improvement as a bona-fide catcher in his first year with the Vols was arguably more important than his slugging accomplishments. In just his third year as a full-time catcher, he played for player-manager Rollie Hemsley, who had a 19-year big-league career as a catcher. According to his widow, Carl credited Hemsley more than any other coach or manager for teaching him the intricacies of being a defensive-minded signal-caller and transforming him into a major-league catcher.

Sawatski made his best catch of the 1949 season when he met local resident Dorothy Lusk at a Vols game against the Travelers in Little Rock, Arkansas. Mrs. Sawatski, a former professional singer, told the author that she did not know much about baseball and was attending one of her first contests when one of her friends introduced her to Carl before the game. Befitting a romantic movie, Dorothy and Carl were married on New Year's Eve. They had two children, John (who was a catcher in the St. Louis Cardinals organization in the early 1970s) and Charles, whom they called Chuck. "I became a big baseball fan," said Mrs. Sawatski. "We rented an apartment or house in every [home] city Carl played in. I never missed a home game, took the kids to the games, and would wait for him with some of the other players' wives after the games. Those were exciting times." In the offseason, the family resided in Little Rock, where Dorothy was an instructor at a local junior college. During his active playing career, Carl held various offseason jobs in his adopted home city, including construction and real estate.

With four minor-league home-run championships in five years, Sawatski had unlimited potential, but *The Sporting News* reported that "the only difficulty seems to be his weight." Cubs scout Pat Monahan, who is given credit for helping the Cubs sign Sawatski in 1948, stunned the baseball world when he announced that the stocky slugger is "the closest in the game to another Babe Ruth."[15] After a productive spring training despite a split finger and pulled back muscle, Sawatski made the team as the third catcher behind Owen and Walker in 1950. But after going 0-for-10 (including his first two major-league starts as a catcher), Sawatski was reassigned to the Vols. "That kid can hit the ball a country mile," said Cubs skipper Frankie Frisch, but the team was upset with his weight and poor fielding.[16] "Frisch was a disciplinarian," said Mrs. Sawatski. "That's what Carl needed at the time. Frisch helped Carl find his way [with the Cubs]. Carl respected Frisch and they had a good relationship." Returning to Nashville, Sawatski publicly declared that he had sworn off drinking beer to lose weight and stated, "I still have confidence I can hit major-league pitching, but I realized that I needed more catching experience."[17] Recalled on August 3, Sawatski went hitless in his first 16 at-bats (extending his major-league hitless streak to 28 at-bats) before he singled off Sal Maglie in the Cubs' 5-4 loss to the New York Giants on August 23. As the Cubs' primary catcher in September, Swish batted .222 (14-for-63) for the month and belted his first big-league home run, a solo shot off the Pirates' Bob Chesnes.

Drafted by the Army in 1951, Sawatski was stationed at Camp Chaffee, near Fort Smith, Arkansas. Without a camp baseball team, Sawatski worked out with the Fort Smith Indians to stay in shape.[18] His two-year tour included active duty in Tokyo, where he provided physical therapy to injured soldiers in Omiya Hospital.

Sawatski returned to the Cubs in time for spring training in 1953, but two years away from baseball had taken their toll. Reporting to camp weighing 240 pounds but winning "his earnest battle against obesity," Sawatski trimmed down to compete for a roster spot.[19] Claiming the spot as third catcher, Sawatski was on the team's active roster the entire season, but spent most of his time in the bullpen warming up pitchers. He made just six starts and batted .220 (13-for-59). Placed on waivers in the offseason, Sawatski was purchased in late November by the Chicago White Sox.

White Sox general manager Paul Richards envisioned Sawatski as an able third catcher, but Swish's two-year stint with the team was filed with frustrations. Sharing backup duties with Matt Batts the entire season, Sawatski batted just .183 (20-for-109); and with just one home run, his nickname faded into distant memory. After honing his defensive skills in the Venezuelan League in the 1954-55 offseason, Sawatski reported to White Sox spring training with a new look. "[I] was sitting in the bullpen, about 420 feet from home plate," he said, "when I covered my left eye and found that couldn't see the pitcher's number."[20] Joining Hank Foiles of the Cleveland Indians as the two most prominent catchers to wear spectacles, Sawatski hoped his corrected vision would help his hitting. It did, but not for the White Sox. The notoriously competitive Richards had tired of Sawatski's weight, hitting, and fielding and optioned him to the Minneapolis Millers, the New

York Giants' affiliate in the Triple-A American Association. Swish the slugger made a comeback. He belted 27 home runs and helped lead the Millers to the American Association title and then hit another three round-trippers to defeat the Rochester Red Wings in the Junior World Series.[21]

Hoping to parlay his success with Minneapolis into another shot at the big leagues, the 28-year-old Sawatski was surprised by his release from the White Sox during spring training and acquisition by Jack Kent Cooke, owner of the Toronto Maple Leafs in the International League. With his reputation of purchasing players and then selling their contract to major-league clubs, Cooke saw a chance to make a few bucks with Sawatski. Despite a broken hand sidelining him for six weeks, Sawatski was the league's best catcher, launching 22 home runs in 332 at-bats, and leading the Maple Leafs to the league playoff finals. On the heels of his record-setting six home runs in 12 playoff games, Sawatski was acquired by the Milwaukee Braves.[22]

With a .187 batting average thus far in his major-league career, Sawatski missed most of spring training with the Braves in 1957 with a broken middle finger on his throwing hand. Nonetheless, manager Fred Haney was impressed with Sawatski's competitive nature and team-oriented attitude, and tabbed him as the team's third catcher behind All-Star Del Crandall and Del Rice, Bob Buhl's personal signal-caller. After an inconsistent first third of the season, the Braves found themselves in second place, tied with the Dodgers, a half-game behind the Cincinnati Reds. Given his first start of the season on June 13 against Brooklyn, Sawatski had one of the best games of his big-league career. Having already smashed two doubles, he got a third hit (in his fourth at-bat), a towering three-run home run to left-center field off reliever Clem Labine to secure the Braves victory and catapult them back into first place. Proving his value to the Braves, Sawatski was unexpectedly productive in the 19 games he started behind the plate, hitting .297 (19-for-73) with five home runs and 13 runs batted in, and finished the season with a .238 average, six home runs and 17 RBIs. After playing in September with a broken right index finger, Sawatski pinch-hit twice in the Braves' exciting World Series victory over the New York Yankees, and struck out both times.

Fresh off a championship and a hefty World Series share worth $8,924.36, Sawatski returned to Little Rock and began officiating football and basketball games.[23] The offseason running and officiating helped Sawatski to overcome his weight issues. Playing between 200 and 215 pounds for the rest of his career, Sawatski impressed teammates with his new stature.

Finding little playing time behind Crandall and Rice and with just ten at-bats by mid-June, Sawatski was traded to the Philadelphia Phillies for catcher Joe Lonnett. Platooning with Stan Lopata, Sawatski was a classic pull hitter and faced primarily right-handed pitchers for the remainder of his career. Against his old teammates on July 4 at County Stadium in Milwaukee, Sawatski had a career-high four hits (in four at-bats) and clouted a solo home run off Gene Conley in a 5-1 victory. Thirteen days later, Swish collected four hits for the second and last time in his career in a loss to the Giants in San Francisco.

With 60 of his 61 games started in 1959 coming against right-handed hurlers, Sawatski developed into a feared hitter, batting .315 against righties (57-for-181), including nine home runs, 43 runs batted in, and a .519 slugging percentage. Facing the Braves on May 25 in Philadelphia, Sawatski launched one of the longest home runs in the history of Connie Mack Stadium; he hit a Buhl fastball over the 60-foot-tall scoreboard in right-center field, 405 feet from home plate. Sawatski pulverized another Buhl fastball two years later while playing for the Cardinals for his only big-league walk-off home run. With the Phillies mired in their second consecutive last-place finish and struggling at the gate, averaging fewer than 11,000 fans per game, Sawatski was unhappy with losing and his paltry salary. "I told [Phillies general manager] John Quinn that if I wasn't traded, I'd hang it up," said Sawatski.[24] Quinn complied with his wish and traded the 32-year-old to the St. Louis Cardinals for pitcher Bill Smith and outfielder Bobby Gene Smith (unrelated despite their identical surnames) on December 4, 1959.

With the short right-field pavilion roof and power alley in Busch Stadium I (formerly known as, and at the time still often referred to as Sportsman's Park), Sawatski landed in the perfect spot. "We got Sawatski for his bat," said Redbirds manager Solly Hemus. "He's not outstanding with his glove."[25] During his four years with the Cardinals, Swish annually put on a Jekyll and Hyde act: He was an unusually productive slugger in St. Louis, where he hit .316 (110-for-348) with 25 home runs and 75 runs batted in.[26] Without the charitable right-field distance on the road, he hit just .193 (64-for-332) with 10 home runs and 41 runs batted in.

Serving as Hal Smith's backup in 1960, Sawatski developed a reputation as a feared pinch-hitter with eight runs batted in on seven hits in just 27 at-bats. The following season he went 11-for-39, including four home runs. *The Sporting News* reported that Sawatski had "great deterrent value. Opposing managers … would have a tired left-handed pitcher in the game rather than bringing in a right-hander who would have to face Sawatski."[27] With his down-to-earth personality, Sawatski had the perfect temperament for a pinch-hitter. "I feel honored when a manager calls on me in tight situations," he said. "I study the pitcher and try to figure out what he's throwing in certain situations. But I do a lot of guessing and regardless of what you hear most hitters do a lot of guessing up there."[28]

After notching career highs in hitting (.299) and slugging (.517) with 10 home runs and 33 runs batted in during the 1961 season, Sawatski hit 13 home runs in just 222 at-bats in 1962 to tie the Cardinals' single-season record for home runs by a catcher (shared by Hal Smith, Walker Cooper, and Eddie Ainsmith). On September 9, 1962, Sawatski tagged Jim Brosnan of the Reds for his only major-league grand slam. The pinch-blast to right field came on an 0-and-2 pitch with two outs in the ninth to lift the Cardinals to a 5-3 win at Crosley Field. With the development of Tim McCarver as a sturdy everyday catcher in 1963, Sawatski saw his playing time diminished and batted just .238 in 105 at-bats.

Sawatski was a player's player and popular clubhouse leader. Known for his jovial disposition, big smile, and thunderous laugh, Swish was called the team's "Judge" who presided over the players' kangaroo court and ruled on petty playing infractions, determining fines when necessary.[29] A joker who enjoyed playing tricks on fellow players, Sawatski was often the target of jokes focusing on the slowest player in baseball. When the 35-year-old Sawatski, in his final season, got the first stolen base in his major-league career, against the Pirates on April 17, 1963, it was called the "most famous theft since the Brinks' robbery."[30] After belting a home run in the second inning off Tom Sturdivant, Sawatski lined a single in the third inning and was given the green light to run. "I guess they figured Sturdivant was going to throw [Julian Javier] another knuckleball with two strikes on the batter," he said, "and Burgess might have trouble handling the ball." Coincidentally, Sawatski repeated the sequence of events later that season against the Phillies when he launched a home run in the seventh inning, then lined a single and stole second base in the eighth inning, just two months before he retired. He was still a threat in St. Louis, where he hit .340 with five home runs and 12 RBIs in 50 at-bats. Swish retired at the conclusion of the season with 58 home runs (all against right-handed pitchers) and 213 runs batted in during his 11-year big-league career and hit another 202 round-trippers in his eight-year minor-league career.

"Carl loved playing for the Cardinals," Mrs. Sawatski said. "He was close friends with Red Schoendienst and Stan Musial and they all retired together after the 1963 season." Musial and Sawatski were both from hard-working Polish families with limited means, and lived in small coal-mining towns in the Pennsylvania Appalachians. "Carl and Stan spent a lot of time together. I think with their background, they understood each other well. Stan's wife, Lillian, was always at the games with us."

Retiring to Little Rock, Arkansas, with his wife and two sons, Sawatski continued to work in construction and real estate. He maintained a close relationship with the Cardinals, appearing regularly at their games, playing in reunion games, and attending special events. In 1966 the Cardinals signed a working agreement with the Texas League's Arkansas Travelers, who played their games in Little Rock, thus providing Sawatski with an opportunity to resume his baseball career. When long-time general manager Ray Winder died in 1967, Travelers team president Max Moses and board member Jack

East, who were instrumental in keeping baseball in the city, offered Sawatski the GM position. "Carl came home one day," Mrs. Sawatski remembered, "and said 'Guess what?' He was excited to get back in baseball. He dedicated his life to the sport."

In 1968 Sawatski was named general manager of the team and just two years later was named *The Sporting News'* Class AA Executive of the Year for his efforts in establishing a model program with strong fan and community support.[31] He was named president of the Texas League before the 1976 season and held the position until his death in 1991. Highly respected for his approach to the game, fairness to teams and players, and understanding of the changing landscape of minor-league baseball, Sawatski received the Warren Giles Award, recognizing outstanding service of a league president, in 1987.[32]

Modest and sometimes shy, Sawatski was a team player who never sought the bright lights of attention or complained about his role on the team. On November 24, 1991, Carl Sawatski, a baseball lifer, died from acute leukemia at the age of 64. He was buried at the Pine Crest Memorial Park in Alexander, Arkansas. In 2005 he was inducted posthumously into the Arkansas Sports Hall of Fame.

Sources

Milwaukee Journal.

Milwaukee Sentinel.

The Sporting News.

Ancestry.com

BaseballLibrary.com

Baseball-Reference.com

Retrosheet.org

SABR.org

Interview with Dorothy Sawatski (Carl Sawatski's wife) on January 6, 2013.

Notes

1. *The Sporting News*, June 23, 1962, 3.
2. Ibid.
3. George Burnham, "Sawatski is at Home in Vols' Dell" Associated Press, *Kingsport News* (Kingsport, Tennessee), July 8, 1949, 9.
4. Ibid.
5. "Bloomingdale Troopers Sweep Three Game Series from Dodgers," *Kingston Daily Freeman*, (Kingston, New York), July 28, 1947, 8.
6. George Burnham, "Sawatski is at Home in Vols' Dell."
7. "Sawatski Has Sore Arm," *Waterloo Daily Courier* (Waterloo, Iowa), March 6, 1948, 43.
8. *The Sporting News*, September 14, 1949, 33.
9. Warren Corbett, "Sulphur Dell (Nashville), *SABR Biography Project*, http://sabr.org/bioproj/park/dac74afo.
10. *The Sporting News*, June 23, 1962, 4.
11. *The Sporting News*, September 21, 1949, 16.
12. George Burnham, "Sawatski is at Home in Vols' Dell."
13. *The Sporting News*, August 24, 1949, 35.
14. *The Sporting News*, November 16, 1949, 6.
15. "Baseball Scout Thinks He Has Successor to Babe Ruth," International News Service, *El Paso Herald* (El Paso, Texas), November 9, 1949, 31.
16. *The Sporting News*, May 10, 1950, 13.
17. *The Sporting News*, June 7, 1950, 33.
18. *The Sporting News*, August 3, 1951, 39.
19. *The Sporting News*, April 1, 1953, 10.
20. *The Sporting News*, June 23, 1962, 4.
21. *The Sporting News*, October 5, 1955, 27.
22. *The Sporting News*, September 26, 1956, 35.
23. *The Sporting News*, October 23, 1957, 9.
24. *The Sporting News*, June 23, 1962, 3.
25. *The Sporting News*, December 16, 1959, 19.
26. *The Sporting News*, December 14, 1963, 19.
27. *The Sporting News*, November 28, 1964, 9.
28. *The Sporting News*, June 23, 1962, 4.
29. Ibid.
30. The Sporting News, April 27, 1963, 32.
31. The Sporting News, December 5, 1970, 35.
32. *The Sporting News*, December 21, 1987, 47.

Red Schoendienst

by Kristen Lokemoen

On October 28, 2011, the St. Louis Cardinals won their 11th World Series championship. Among those celebrating with the team was 88-year-old Red Schoendienst, who had first tasted World Series victory as a young second baseman for the Cardinals in 1946.

Sixty-five years after he savored his first World Series win, Schoendienst was still an integral part of the Cardinals organization. Officially listed as Special Assistant to the General Manager, at heart he was still a coach, donning a uniform for pregame practice at home games, at which he routinely hit fungoes to infielders.

Albert Fred "Red" Schoendienst was born on February 2, 1923, in Germantown, Illinois, a village of about 800 residents 40 miles east of St. Louis. He grew up in a large Catholic family with five brothers and a sister. Three of his brothers would go on to play in the minor leagues.

Schoendienst never saw a major-league game until he played in his first game for the Cardinals in 1945, but the sport was central to his life almost from birth. His father, Joe, had been a catcher in the Clinton County League. By the time his sons were growing up, Joe often came straight from his coal-mining job to umpire a game.

Red's mother, Mary, a homemaker, made baseballs out of sawdust for her sons and their friends. The balls made it through only a few pitches before they disintegrated. The ingenious young players also used items like corncobs, hickory nuts, and rocks as balls and dried pieces of wood to serve as bats.

St. Louis sportswriter Bob Broeg (Baseball Hall of Fame J.G. Taylor Spink Award winner in 1979) compared Schoendienst to Mark Twain's classic character Huckleberry Finn. Never a big fan of school, young Al cared mainly about baseball and fishing—and, in the winter, some hunting. And with all of those brothers and friends, there were always plenty of boys around for a baseball game.

There were two major-league teams in St. Louis while Schoendienst was growing up, and the Germantown boys were split between Browns fans and Cardinals fans. Red favored the Cardinals, but both teams seemed very distant to him. Few games were broadcast on the radio in those days and little was known about their players.

Red preferred playing the game to watching it, anyway. Many of the towns had their own teams in the Clinton County League and the Germantown team's manager, Ed Roach, helped the young player learn baseball fundamentals. Schoendienst said, "He was always telling us how important it was to think when we were on the field, to know where the base runners were and how many outs there were. He always made certain we knew what inning it was and what the score was."

By the age of 16, Schoendienst had had enough of school. He got his Social Security card and joined the

Red Schoendienst (National Baseball Hall of Fame Library, Cooperstown, N.Y.)

Civilian Conservation Corps, one of President Franklin Roosevelt's programs to put the country back to work after the Depression. Schoendienst and two friends were assigned to a camp in nearby Greenville, Illinois, where they made a dollar a day planting trees or working on roads or other projects.

Each camp had its own baseball team. Red and his pal Joe Linneman were only 16 and most of the players were in their early 20s, but Red won the position at shortstop and Joe pitched, winning 17 games and losing only one. Both boys had dreams of playing professional ball, but soon Red's dream would be threatened. He and Joe were building fences one day. Red held the wire tight and Joe hit a staple with his hammer. The staple ricocheted off the post into Red's left eye. He termed it "the most intense pain I've ever felt in my life." His worst fear was losing the eye and not being able to play baseball. He spent five weeks in a St. Louis hospital. The doctors' opinion was that the eye would have to be removed. But Schoendienst found one doctor willing to work with him on exercises to save the eye. His vision gradually improved, but continued to be a problem for him.

When World War II broke out, the CCC was disbanded and some of Schoendienst's brothers went off to fight. Red wanted to play ball as long as he could and took a job at Scott Field (now Scott Air Force Base) in Belleville, Illinois. He heard in 1942 that the Cardinals were holding tryouts and that the prospects could watch a Cardinals game free. That was incentive enough for Red, Joe, and another friend, none of whom had ever seen a major-league game.

The three would-be players hitched a ride into St. Louis. Nearly 400 young men showed up at Sportsman's Park for the tryouts. Red and Joe passed the first round and were asked to come back the next day. Joe spent the night at his aunt's house, but Red, too proud to admit he had nowhere to go, didn't go with him. With a quarter in his pocket, he spent 10 cents on a hot dog at a diner and later, after being driven off a park bench by rain, his last 15 cents for a room in a fleabag hotel—literally. He woke up with bites all over his body.

The Cardinals kept Schoendienst at the camp the rest of that week, but at the end of the week sent him home without offering him a contract. But the Cardinals soon asked him to come back to St. Louis. Their head scout, Joe Mathes, had had to leave town before the camp was finished. When he returned and found Schoendienst unsigned, he rectified that quickly. The Cardinals sent the 19-year-old to their Union City (Tennessee) farm team in the Class D Kitty League. His salary was $75 a month.

Schoendienst gave himself three years to see if he could make a career as a ballplayer. He timed things perfectly, even though he feared that his professional career might end after just one game. He had a good night at the plate, getting four hits. But he made two errors on one key play late in the game. To make things worse, Cardinals general manager Branch Rickey happened to be at the game. Rickey approached his newest hire at his locker and, to Red's relief, consoled him.

"Young man," Rickey said, "this is your first time away from home. You signed your first contract, and you played your first game. That would make anybody nervous. You made a couple of errors tonight. You're a fine ballplayer. But let me tell you something. You're going to make a few more errors before you get out of this game. You look like you could be a pretty good ballplayer. Go out and get them tomorrow."

Schoendienst played just six games for Union City. The Kitty League folded in June, as other minor leagues did in that wartime season. The Cardinals sent Schoendienst and his friend Joe Linneman to another Class D team, Albany, Georgia, of the Georgia-Florida League. Because Schoendienst's injured left eye created problems at the plate against right-handed pitchers, he became a switch-hitter. In the field he made 27 errors in 68 games.

In 1943 the Cardinals moved Schoendienst up to Lynchburg of the Class B Piedmont League. He played mostly at shortstop, but also gained experience at both second base and third base. After just nine games, in which he got 17 hits and batted .472, he was promoted to Rochester, one of the Cardinals' top two farm teams, where the starting shortstop had been hurt.

Playing for manager Pepper Martin, a veteran of the Cardinals' Gas House Gang teams of the 1930s, Schoendienst led the International League in hitting with a .337 average. He was the youngest player to lead the league in hitting since Wee Willie Keeler in 1892 (when it was called the Eastern League).

After playing 25 games at Rochester in 1944, Schoendienst was drafted. After basic training, he was sent to Pine Camp, New York, where he hurt his right shoulder while playing for the camp's baseball team. The recoil from firing weapons aggravated the injury, which would plague Schoendienst throughout his career. Eventually he got a medical discharge because of his eye and shoulder problems. The Cardinals promoted him to the major leagues for 1945, which because so many major leaguers were in the service, was baseball's worst wartime season. But it was the opportunity of a lifetime for Schoendienst. The Cardinals already had an excellent shortstop in Marty Marion. Schoendienst didn't mind, however. He didn't care where they played him, just so they let him play. He started the season in left field, replacing the service-bound Stan Musial, and got his first major-league hit, a triple, on Opening Day. (He also made his first major-league error.) Schoendienst finished his rookie season with a .278 batting average and a league-leading 26 stolen bases.

By the 1946 season the war was over and most of baseball's stars had returned. Musial reclaimed his position in left field. Marty Marion was still at shortstop. Lou Klein had been expected to be the regular second baseman, but he jumped to the Mexican League in May and Schoendienst took over that position. He played in 128 games at second base, and a few games at shortstop and third base. His place on the team was solidified and he had found the position where he would play for the bulk of his career. He batted .281 that season and started at second base for the National League in the All-Star Game. (It was the first of his ten All-Star Game appearances.) The Cardinals defeated the Dodgers in a playoff for the 1946 NL pennant. Schoendienst then played in his first World Series with the Cardinals defeating the Boston Red Sox in seven games.

Schoendienst was now a seasoned major leaguer, a valued part of the Cardinals, and Musial's roommate. They became friends off the field, especially after Schoendienst married Mary O'Reilly, whom he had met on a streetcar while going home after a game in 1945. Wed on September 20, 1947, they had three daughters and a son. The son, Kevin, played two years of minor-league ball.

After their 1946 pennant season, the Cardinals finished second in 1947, 1948, and 1949. Schoendienst settled in at second base, continually improving both defensively and as a hitter. Some tips came from his baseball-savvy wife, Mary, who also was able to negotiate better contracts for him.

The most memorable moment in Schoendienst's ten All-Star Game appearances came in 1950 at Comiskey Park in Chicago. Before the game, he and some other players were kidding around and making predictions on how long a hit they might get. Red pointed to the upper deck in right field and said he was going to hit a ball there. For someone who hit only 84 career home runs, it was a bold statement. But in the top of the 14th inning, Schoendienst came to bat against left-hander Ted Gray. Now that he would bat right-handed, he told his teasing teammates that he'd have to hit the ball into the left-field stands. He did just that—and on the first pitch, providing the winning margin for the National League and laughing all the way around the bases.

Schoendienst reached his peak at the plate in 1953, setting personal highs in batting average (.342), runs (107), home runs (15) and RBIs (79). In early June he was hitting .378, but fell off as the season wore on, and as the season wore on, he battled Brooklyn's Carl Furillo for the batting title. Furillo broke his hand and missed the last three weeks of the season, leaving his average stuck at .344. A mild slump pushed Schoendienst down to .329. He continued to battle and ended the season with a .342 average, knowing that two more hits somewhere during the season would have made the difference.

Those early-'50s Cardinals teams were not particularly good. Manager Eddie Dyer left after 1950 and there were several managers during the period. Changes in managers and players didn't seem to make much difference. In 1953 the team was sold to August A. Busch, Jr., the owner of the Anheuser-Busch Brewery, in a deal that prevented the team from moving to another city. After the 1955 season, Busch hired Frank

Lane, noted for the frequency of his trades, as general manager. Driving to the ballpark on June 14, 1956, Red heard that he had been traded to the New York Giants. It was part of an eight-player deal that brought Alvin Dark to the Cardinals. Mary had been notified at home and said she "just about fell over" from the shock. Musial called losing his friend to another team his "saddest day in baseball." The Schoendienst family had just moved into a new home and had no desire to move from St. Louis. Red went to New York alone. In his first game he hit a pinch-hit home run.

In 1957 the family leased a home in New York so they could be together through the season, but they'd hardly had time to settle in when Schoendienst was traded, again in June, this time to the Milwaukee Braves, for outfielder Bobby Thomson, infielder Danny O'Connell, and pitcher Ray Crone. The Braves were a team loaded with talent—Eddie Mathews, Henry Aaron, Warren Spahn, Lew Burdette, Joe Adcock, Del Crandall, Johnny Logan. When Red donned a Braves uniform, Aaron said, "It made us all feel like Superman. We knew he was going to mean so much to our ballclub that wouldn't show up in the box score. ... (H)e definitely became the leader of that ballclub." Sure enough, the Braves won the pennant, and defeated the Yankees in seven games in the World Series. Schoendienst batted .278 in five games, but had to sit out the last two games with a groin injury. The Braves won the pennant again in 1958, but lost the World Series to the Yankees in seven games.

During that season Schoendienst was concerned about his health. He played in only 106 games and wasn't hitting well or feeling like himself. After the World Series and the birth of his son, Kevin, he went to the doctor. The examination's results showed that Schoendienst had tuberculosis and that he had probably been playing with it for years. Red had noticed that his energy would lag in the second half of the season and that a few days off always helped him. Ahead of him now were months of rest at Mount Saint Rose Sanatorium in St. Louis. He determined to do all he could to get healthy and return to the game. By the end of 1958 he had received more than 10,000 letters and cards, including one from President Dwight Eisenhower, who told him that "anyone with the competitive spirit that you have so often demonstrated can lick this thing."

To speed his recovery, he had surgery to remove part of his lung. The Braves gave him a contract for the 1959 season not knowing whether he would play at all. Schoendienst left the hospital on March 24, 1959, feeling better than he had in years and wondering how much better his career could have been had he been truly healthy throughout it. He didn't return to action until September, when he got a huge ovation from the 18,000 fans at Milwaukee County Stadium when he came out to pinch-hit. Schoendienst had only three at-bats that season, but he was back in the game and that felt good. He was the honorary chairman of the National Tuberculosis Association's Christmas Seal campaign that year.

The Braves' 1960 season started with a new manager. Charlie Dressen had replaced Fred Haney and Schoendienst called Dressen "the only difficult manager I ever played for." Red had worked out all winter with Musial, Ken Boyer, and other players in St. Louis and was in great shape for spring training. But when the season started, Schoendienst found his playing time cut drastically. Never one to question a manager's decision, he reluctantly rode the bench. He played in just 68 games, hitting .257. He knew the Braves were trying to ease him out to make way for someone younger, so it came as no surprise when the team released him at the end of the season. But he still wanted to play. Bing Devine, the Cardinals' general manager, offered Schoendienst a chance to go to spring training in 1961 to try to make the team. Haney, now general manager of the expansion Los Angeles Angels, guaranteed him the Angels' second-base job. But Schoendienst felt that St. Louis was a better place to raise his family. It was home. He also felt confident enough to feel that he'd get a place on the Cardinals.

He did, of course, make the team and more than 50 years later would still be wearing a Cardinals uniform. He knew his role would be as a utility player and he was fine with that. Sitting on the bench allowed him to learn more about what the manager and coaches did. He played in 72 games in 1961 and hit .300.

As the 1962 season came around, Schoendienst signed a contract to coach rather than play. Part of the reason was that each team had to provide players to the expansion New York and Houston franchises. As a coach he was protected from being sent to one of the new teams. He was put on the active roster when the season started.

Schoendienst enjoyed playing out his career with his friend Stan Musial, who was winding down his Hall of Fame career. Both retired as players after the 1963 season. Schoendienst had signed as a coach for 1963 but was reactivated in late June. His last at-bat was on July 7 in San Francisco. He grounded out, just as he had in his first major-league at-bat 18 years earlier.

Schoendienst's first full season of coaching, 1964, was an exciting year in Cardinals history. A June 15 trade with the Cubs brought them Lou Brock, who provided a spark that helped take the Cardinals back to the World Series for the first time since 1946. Their opponent was the Yankees, and the Cardinals beat them in seven games. In a surprise move manager Johnny Keane resigned three days after the Series. He had written his resignation letter before the end of the season, after learning that August Busch wanted to bring in Leo Durocher to manage the Cardinals in 1965.

As it turned out, Durocher didn't get the Cardinals job. Red Schoendienst did. Teams rarely change managers after winning the World Series (although the same thing happened in St. Louis in 2011). Expectations are high after a championship season, making it especially tough on an untested skipper. Some of his veteran players — Ken Boyer, Bill White, Dick Groat, and Curt Simmons — were nearing the end of their careers. The Cardinals finished the 1965 season in seventh place. Still, Gussie Busch believed in Red enough to bring him back for a second season. After a rough start in 1966, St. Louis finished sixth. But they acquired Orlando Cepeda from the Giants and moved into Busch Stadium II during the season.

In 1967 Musial was general manager, Roger Maris was obtained from the Yankees, and Mike Shannon (with Schoendienst's help in spring training) switched from the outfield to third base. The Cardinals won the pennant by 10 1/2 games). The Boston Red Sox were again trying for their first championship since 1918. Again, they were disappointed as the Cardinals won in seven games, led by Gibson, who won three games, and Brock, who hit .414.

The team stayed essentially the same in 1968 and repeated its trip to the World Series, this time playing the Detroit Tigers. The Tigers took the series in seven games, after St. Louis had a three-games-to-one lead.

Schoendienst continued to manage the Cardinals through the first half of the 1970s, but those teams did not enjoy the same success. After a 90-loss, fifth-place finish in 1976, Red was fired. Not knowing any other business, he knew he wanted to stay in baseball, thinking he might even come back to the Cardinals one day. His next job, though, would be in Oakland.

Charlie Finley had just hired Jack McKeon as the Athletics' manager. McKeon hired Schoendienst for his coaching staff. It was Red's first and only foray into the American League. The Athletics were a bad team in 1977, losing 98 games and finishing 38 1/2 games out. McKeon was fired and replaced by Bobby Winkles. Later Winkles was also fired. Schoendienst was offered the job, but had no desire to manage for Finley.

After two years in Oakland, Schoendienst had a chance to go back to the Cardinals in 1979, serving as hitting coach for new manager Ken Boyer, who inherited a team in upheaval. The Cards won 86 games that year, but Gussie Busch wanted more. On June 8, 1980, with the Cardinals in last place, Boyer was fired and Whitey Herzog became the new manager.

Red and Whitey had grown up about 30 minutes apart in southwestern Illinois. They didn't know each other well, but would work together for the next decade. Busch gave Herzog the added role of general manager so that he could obtain the players he wanted to build the kind of team he wanted to manage. Schoendienst stepped in to manage for the last 37 games of the 1980 season so that Herzog could watch the team and scout the Cardinals' minor-league teams for prospects. Red returned to his coaching duties in 1981.

Herzog moved players in and out over the 1981 season and by 1982 had the team he wanted. His teams won National League pennants in 1982, 1985, and 1987. They defeated the Milwaukee Brewers in the 1982

World Series but lost to Kansas City in 1985 and Minnesota in 1987.

Schoendienst was elected to the Baseball Hall of Fame by the Veterans Committee in 1989. In his induction speech he spoke of the day he and his pals had hitchhiked to St. Louis to try out for the Cardinals, commenting, "I never thought that milk truck ride would eventually lead to Cooperstown and baseball's highest honor." He also spoke about his attitude toward playing the game: "I would play any position my manager asked. Whatever it took to win, I was willing to do. All I ever wanted was to be on that lineup card and become a champion."

Another honor came on May 11, 1996, when the Cardinals retired Red's number 2. (Technically it wasn't retired because Schoendienst continued to wear it.)

Mary Schoendienst died on December 11, 1999. She was 76 years old and had loved the game of baseball almost as much as her husband. She was known for reaching out to new players' wives, helping them adjust to life with a major leaguer. Mary sang the National Anthem before many Cardinals games, and she organized the wives' charity group, the St. Louis Baseball Pinch Hitters.

Schoendienst stayed involved with the Cardinals throughout Tony LaRussa's 16-year tenure as manager, there in uniform for most home games. His love of the game never faltered. Nor did the respect and love of fans, players, and managers for him. In his autobiography Schoendienst said, "What makes baseball so great is you can't hold the ball for 24 seconds and take the last shot or run the clock down and kick a field goal. You have to get 27 outs, one way or the other. Time doesn't run out until you get that 27th out. Everything I have in my life I owe to baseball. I've been lucky in so many ways, making a career out of something I loved to do as a kid. It's been a great ride, and I'm not ready to end it yet."

Stan Musial probably summed up his friend best: "A lot of guys had the privilege of playing with or for Red over the years, and I'm proud I was one of them. He is one of the kindest, most decent men I've ever known in my life. Even more important than having been his teammate or roommate, however, is having been his friend for so many years. They don't come any better."

Sources

Bob Broeg. *Memories of a Hall of Fame Sportswriter* (Champaign, Illinois: Sagamore Publishing, 1995).

Jim Hunstein. *1, 2, 6, 9… & Rogers* (St. Louis: Stellar Press, 2004).

Red Schoendienst with Rob Rains. *Red: A Baseball Life* (Champaign, Illinois: Sports Publishing, 1998).

St. Louis Globe-Democrat.

St. Louis Post-Dispatch.

www.baseballhall.org (Hall of Fame).

www.stlouis.cardinals.mlb.com

Ray Shearer

By William H. Johnson

ON THE LAST day of the 1957 season, Sunday, September 29, the Milwaukee Braves entered their final home game against the Cincinnati Redlegs as National League champions after clinching the pennant a week earlier. At the end of six innings the game was a scoreless tie, and when the visiting Redlegs plated three runs in the top of the ninth, overcoming Milwaukee's manufactured runs in the seventh and eighth innings, the Braves could have scarcely been faulted if they'd conceded the contest rather than continue the fight through to the final out.

In the bottom of the ninth, a Joe Adcock single prompted manager Fred Haney to substitute Mel Roach as a pinch-runner, and it became apparent that, even with nothing but pride at stake, the team was simply not going to give up. One out later, an outfielder recently called-up, 28-year-old Ray Shearer, stepped in to pinch-hit for catcher Carl Sawatski, and singled to right field off Cincinnati relief pitcher Bill Kennedy. With two outs, Red Schoendienst singled, scoring Roach and moving Shearer to second. Felix Mantilla then ended the game with a single that pushed Shearer across the plate.

Shearer's hit and subsequent run, decisive acts in an otherwise meaningless game on the final day of a regular season already decided, marked both the apex and the end of his major-league career. The base hit left Shearer with the unusual career batting average of .500, and it afforded him a slice of baseball immortality in a small role with the world champion Braves.

Ray Solomon Shearer, Jr. was born on September 19, 1929, the first child to 19-year-old Ray and 16-year-old Katie (Herman) Shearer, in the borough of Jacobus, Pennsylvania. An outstanding scholastic athlete, the boy excelled at baseball and football at the elite levels in his area, and even spent two seasons with the York City Junior American Legion squads in 1944 and 1945. By the time of his high-school graduation as a multi-sport star, he had enough confidence in his own abilities that he declined a contract offer from the Phillies in order to play football on scholarship at nearby Gettysburg College.[1]

A car trip between Gettysburg and Jacobus is less than 35 miles, yet for a young man experiencing his first separation from home, it seemed much longer. At the time, just after World War II, the level of telecommunications technology meant that while the actual distance was short, a direct phone call home was impossible. In York there were only a few switchboard operators for the entire community, and they were almost exclusively female, so over the span of Ray's college phone calls home he naturally became acquainted with them. Norman Stoner's daughter Joan was one of those operators, and she and Ray got along so well that on September 26, 1952, they were married.[2] The union was both happy and productive. In addition to remaining married for the rest of Ray's life, the couple had four children, daughters Roxanne and Jami and sons Scott and Randy.

Ray Shearer (Photo courtesy of Dave Klug)

After college Shearer finally chose baseball, and signed with the Brooklyn Dodgers as an amateur free agent before the 1950 season. He was dispatched to the lowest level of the organization, the Sheboygan Indians of the Class D Wisconsin State League. There, under the guidance of his manager, former slugger Joe Hauser, Shearer proved the wisdom of the Dodgers' scouting team and showed his slugging potential, by leading the league in hits (160), RBIs (137), and home runs (30), all while batting .317 in 124 games.[3] That squad finished the year in second place, and Shearer was named to the league All-Star team as an outfielder.

He followed that success with a promotion to the Class B Asheville Tourists (Tri-State League), and helped the team to a second-place finish after losing in a four-game sweep) to the Spartanburg Peaches in the 1951 championship series. He was promoted for the 1952 season, this time to Class A and the Pueblo Dodgers, and again in 1953 when he made the jump to the Mobile Bears of the Double-A Southern Association. Although the Bears finished more than 20 games behind the league champion Memphis, the 6-foot, 200-pound Shearer was selected to the league All-Star team in the outfield. He spent the next season, 1954, and much of 1955 with Mobile before earning a seven-game call-up to Triple-A and the Montreal Royals.

Shearer experienced his first setback in 1956 when the Dodgers assigned him to the Fort Worth Cats of the Double-A Texas League after spring training. On June 15 Blackie Sherrod wrote a story on the slugging Cats in *The Sporting News*, noting that Shearer was among the team leaders in homers. Within a few weeks, however, on July 4, the Braves orchestrated a deal with Brooklyn that brought Shearer into the Milwaukee organization in exchange for outfielder Jim Frey. After the trade Shearer remained in the Texas League and simply changed into the uniform of the Austin Senators. A few weeks later, on August 2, he confirmed his value when he hit a three-run homer with two out in the ninth that enabled Austin to defeat Shreveport, 9-7.[4] On August 24 he became the first Austin player that season to homer twice in a single game, and according to *The Sporting News* he continued his slugging heroics throughout the winter with Leones del Escogido, a team that, under manager Red Davis, defeated the Tigres del Licey for the 1956 Dominican Winter League crown.

After eight seasons in the minor leagues, years in which he batted over .300 three times and had shown a power stroke with 26 home runs in 1956 and 29 in 1957 (the latter with Wichita in the Triple-A American Association), the Braves summoned Shearer to the majors as their 1957 pennant run neared conclusion. He made three plate appearances for Milwaukee that September. The first two came in his major-league debut, on September 18, against the New York Giants. He started the game as the left fielder and struck out in his first at-bat against Johnny Antonelli in the bottom of the second inning. He followed that with a walk in the fourth before giving way to pinch-hitter Wes Covington in the fifth inning. His only other appearance, on September 29, yielded his lone major-league hit.

The following spring the Braves returned Ray to Wichita to start the season, but his batting average dipped below .300 and he hit only 18 home runs. At 28 Shearer was already beginning to show the effects of age in the boys' game. In 1959 he was traded to Cincinnati, which assigned him to the Double-A Nashville Volunteers. Shearer batted .320 at Nashville to lead the team that season, and late in the year was sent to help the Triple-A Havana Sugar Kings of the International League. In Game Three of the league championship series against Minneapolis, Shearer "put on a one man show … as Havana beat Minneapolis 3-2 in ten innings and took a 2-1 lead in baseball's Little World Series. The Havana right fielder singled home a run in the eighth to tie the score, 2-2, got off a beautiful throw to third on Stu Lockwood's single in the top of the tenth that put down Minneapolis's Carl Yastrzemski trying to go from first to third, and singled home Tony Gonzalez with the winning run in the last of the 10th with two out."[5]

In 1960 the Reds returned him to Triple-A, again southward to Cuba. With the country in the midst of Fidel Castro's revolution, the US State Department coerced Baseball Commissioner Ford Frick to direct the relocation of the Havana team to New Jersey, and the Sugar Kings became the Jersey City Jerseys during that season. The team's relocation did not help Shearer's bat, as he and the Reds watched his average fall to .261. The aging outfielder split the 1961 season with Triple-A squads in the New York Yankees' and Cleveland Indians' organizations, and in 1962 he split his season at the Class A level with the York White Roses (Eastern League) and the Augusta Yankees (South Atlantic League). Despite hitting .344 in his brief stint with Augusta, time and competition had corralled the slugger. Not only was he battling with himself to try to regain his old hitting stroke, but he was competing with the likes of Tony Oliva and Richie Allen in this league, the new generation of superstar hitters who were ascending their career ladders.

Ray Shearer retired from baseball after the 1962 season, days before his 33rd birthday. He had earned a shot at the big leagues, and boasted a 13-year minor league record of 204 home runs and a .288 batting average in 1,614 games. In his first job out of baseball, he worked for American Machine and Foundry as a maintenance supervisor, a job that allowed him to play for the corporate softball team. Within a few years, using Ray as player and coach, the York AMF softball team was playing so well that it won three consecutive Pennsylvania State Industrial championships, in 1967, 1968, and 1969. After his job at AMF, and now approaching his 40s, Shearer took a job with UPS for a time before settling into a driving position with Preston Trucking.

In the mid-1970s, although only 46 years old and without warning, Shearer suffered a heart attack. He recovered, but at age 51 had a second episode, this one resulting in a consultation with cardiac specialists from Johns Hopkins University. According to Ray's son, Scott, the doctors told the still-young family man that while he might be just over 50 by the calendar, he had the heart muscle of an 81-year-old.[6] On the evening of Friday, February 20, 1982, Ray spent an overdue evening with old friends and acquaintances, sharing memories and—probably—a few laughs. Later that night Ray suffered a final, fatal heart attack. He died the next day in a hospital in York, Pennsylvania, and is buried at the Salem Union Cemetery in Jacobus. Ray Shearer was inducted into the York Area Sports Hall of Fame in Pennsylvania in 1994.

Notes

1. "George Powell and Ray Shearer Jr. Will Be Inducted on Feb. 9; York Area Hall of Fame Grows By Two," *York Daily Record*, January 15, 1994.
2. Emails/telephone conversation with Scott Shearer and family, October 25-26, 2012.
3. Lloyd Johnson and Miles Wolff, eds., *Encyclopedia of Minor League Baseball*, 3rd ed. (Durham, North Carolina: Baseball America, 2007), 446.
4. *The Sporting News*, August 15, 1956.
5. "Shearer Stages Power Display: Havana Wins," *Jefferson City* (Missouri) *Post Tribune*, October 2, 1959.
6. Shearer conversation, October 25, 2012.

Warren Spahn

By Jim Kaplan

THE FIFTH-WINNINGEST PITCHER of all time, Warren Spahn went 363-245 over parts of 21 years from 1942 to 1965. Only by remaining in the game two seasons too long did he fail to finish with an ERA under 3.00 (3.09) and a winning percentage over .600 (.597), and his career totals are all the more impressive considering that he did not record his first big-league victory until he was 25. Spahn should make everyone's list of the ten best pitchers in baseball history, and was the one "sure thing" Braves fans had to cheer for through the team's final five years in Boston — and far beyond.

Named after both President Warren G. Harding and his own father, Warren Edward Spahn was born in Buffalo, New York, on April 23, 1921, the fifth of six children and the first of two sons to Ed and Mabel Spahn. Supporting his family in the city's blue-collar East End, Ed was a $27-a-week wallpaper salesman who did not own a car. His family ate meat maybe once a week, and his children stuffed their shoes with newspapers. A good bowler and semipro baseball player but too small at 5-feet-7 and 130 pounds to dream of a big-league career, Ed sublimated his disappointment by teaching the game to left-handed Warren, the most promising athlete in the family. Ed knew there were only so many positions open for a lefty; so just in case Warren could not hit well enough to play first base (his favorite position), Ed taught him exhaustively how to throw fastballs and curves from a mound he built in the backyard. "You've got to have control," Ed said over and over. "Without control you're nothing!" Warren nodded and kept dreaming of playing first in the big leagues.

"He insisted that I throw with a fluid motion, and the high leg kick was part of the deception to the hitter," Warren told Oklahoma City's *Daily Oklahoman* in 1998. "Hitters said the ball seemed to come out of my uniform."

The secret of Spahn's future injury-free longevity was the foundation laid by his dad. "He taught me how to follow through with my shoulder and body, how to throw without any strain, how to get the most out of my pitch and out of my weight even when I was a skinny kid," Spahn told sportswriter Bob Broeg. "He taught me how to roll a curveball, how to let it go off my fingers at the last moment. He taught me how to pass my knee by my right elbow. I thought it was a lot of drudgery. It was lots more fun just to pick up the ball and throw, but Dad wouldn't let me play catch unless I did it correctly."

Ed and Warren went to Buffalo Bisons minor-league games together, and Warren came to admire Buffalo first baseman Big Bill Kelly, a former major leaguer (Athletics 1920, Phillies 1928) who hit 125 homers for the Bisons from 1922 to 1930 and earlier had played semipro ball with Ed. Warren's father also instructed him to track the motion of Bisons pitcher Charlie "Lefty" Perkins (A's 1930, Dodgers 1934). "Now, if you want to be a pitcher, watch every move Charlie Perkins makes," Ed told his son. "If you want to be a first baseman, watch Bill Kelly."

Warren Spahn (National Baseball Hall of Fame Library, Cooperstown, N.Y.)

Because of his father's connections on the Buffalo club, Warren got to shag balls in practice. When he could not remember names, he called all the players "Kelly," and they in turn called him Kelly Spahn. "After those Bison games my dad gave me the option of an ice-cream cone or a streetcar ride home," Spahn told the *Tulsa Daily World*'s John Ferguson. "Many times we took the ice cream and rehashed the game walking home."

Plainly, Spahn wanted to be another Lou Gehrig. When he was 9, Warren donned a uniform for the Lake City Social Club midgets and played on their team for three years. He graduated to American Legion ball, always a great training ground for future major leaguers. Eventually Warren was playing first base for three local teams six days a week. In a dream sequence on the Lake City Athletic Club team, the 110-pound 13-year-old played with his 37-year-old father and handled Ed's hard throws from third. "You'd think he was going to throw it right through me," Spahn told the *Christian Science Monitor*'s Ed Rumill. "I weighed only about 110 pounds in those days. But he was teaching me to play hard and it did a lot of good."

When Warren arrived at South Park High School, however, he discovered an All-Scholastic player named Bill Benzerman (who later became a professional wrestler) occupying first base; reluctantly, Spahn took up pitching—this time for good. When his coach asked if he had a favorite uniform number, the ever-contrary lefty said 13. "Thirteen, eh? Not the superstitious kind, I see." "Uh-huh," Spahn said. "Thirteen has always been good luck for me."

The youngster led his high school to two city championships, went undefeated his last two seasons, and threw a no-hitter his senior year, but he was spurned by big-league scouts as too skinny. As fate would have it, a disenchanted Red Sox scout named Billy Meyers disagreed with the popular consensus. Meyers did not like the deal the Red Sox were offering one Sebastian Sisti, so he had quit one Boston job and took Sisti with him to the other a few years earlier. (Sibby Sisti would later become a longtime teammate of Spahn's with the Boston and Milwaukee Braves.)

Meyers still worked part time for the Boston Bees (as they were called from 1936 through 1940 before a name change back to Braves) when he was not selling tickets for the New York Central Railroad. Impressed by Spahn's control, he signed the young hurler in 1940 (at Ed's insistence, after he just finished his junior year), for $80 a month. Because his family could not afford expenses, Spahn turned down a partial scholarship from Cornell University and headed straight for the low minors.

Spahn's first pro assignment was the PONY League's Bradford (Pennsylvania) Bees, managed by Jack Onslow. When Spahn asked for number 13, Onslow reportedly replied, "Fella, we don't carry any number thirteens. A guy's liable to run into enough tough luck around here without wearing any number thirteen on his back."

Experimenting with a new delivery for an overhand curve after about one-third of the season, Spahn snapped the pitch too sharply and tore several tendons in his left shoulder. Warren went home with his arm in a sling, and his father went into a depression. Then, after the youngster returned to Pennsylvania two weeks later, he threw his first hard pitch and tumbled off the mound clutching his shoulder. The trainer said he'd need a year off if he was lucky, and Onslow muttered, "You know, maybe I should have given that fellow number 13 after all." Back home, Ed Spahn reacted by going into a deeper depression and was hospitalized. Young Warren spent the remainder of the summer, the fall, and the winter checking baggage at the Buffalo railroad terminal.

With a 5-4 record, 62 strikeouts in 66 innings, and a 2.83 ERA in his brief stay, however, Spahn had showed promise. He recovered by the next season, only to run into more bad luck. In a 1941 appearance at spring training in San Antonio with the Braves, he suffered a broken and permanently disfigured nose courtesy of a teammate's errant throw. He also got some nicknames he did not appreciate: Hooks and the Great Profile. Even his father called him Meatnose.

"When Dad's nose was broken, John Berardino's nose was also broken the same day," Spahn's son, Greg, recalled. "They sent John to a specialist to have it fixed. They called Dad in and told him, 'Warren, we will send you to a specialist to have your nose fixed, but most people that have that done end up with sinus problems and you're not a very good-looking guy.' The ballclub did not want to spend the money on Dad's nose. John Berardino being an actor, that was a different story."

Nonetheless, Braves manager Casey Stengel said, "He's only 20 years old and needs work. But mark my word, if nothing happens to the kid, he can be a great one." Stengel also said, "Some day he's going to be one of the best left-handers in the league."

In the summer of 1941, playing for Evansville (Indiana) in the Three-I League, Spahn led the circuit in wins (19), winning percentage (.760), shutouts (7), and ERA (1.83). With Spahn throwing 42 consecutive scoreless innings and three one-hitters, Evansville won the pennant. Manager Bob Coleman changed Spahn's delivery to put less pressure on his elbow and Warren's roommate, pitcher Willard Donovan, showed him the pickoff move he would eventually perfect.

According to one legend, the old Hall of Fame catcher Ernie Lombardi warmed Spahn up in spring training of 1942. When he threw one of his best fastballs, Lombardi reportedly caught it barehanded, spat tobacco juice on it, and threw it back harder. Turning his back to rub off the juice, Spahn thought, "I'm not sure I belong here."

Even so, Spahn's smooth overhand delivery and flawless follow-though won raves at 1942 spring headquarters in Sanford, Florida, and he made the Boston club. But when he failed to brush back Pee Wee Reese in his second big-league outing as Stengel had ordered, the manager stalked to the mound and growled, "After your shower, pick up your railroad ticket to Hartford." Spahn reported, wowed the Eastern League with a 17-12 record and a 1.96 ERA, and returned to pitch twice more for the seventh-place Braves.

He had no wins over his 15 2/3 abbreviated innings with Boston, but did get credit for an abbreviated complete game on September 26 when Polo Grounds kids who had been admitted for working in a wartime scrap-metal drive swarmed the field in the eighth inning and forced the Giants to forfeit a game in which they were beating him 5-2 (no pitcher gets a win in a forfeit). All of this, Spahn knew, was a prelude to war. He enlisted in the Army in October 1942, and in November Private Spahn was shipped to Camp Gruber, 60 miles southeast of Tulsa, Oklahoma, where he learned to be a combat engineer. It was also where he met his future wife when Buffalo friend Roy Reimann introduced him to LoRene Southard, an oil-company executive secretary with spectacular business acumen who would later help make Spahn rich.

The lefty had a far rougher World War II experience than most big leaguers, who spent the conflict out of harm's way with gloves instead of guns, but before entering the fray he too got to play some ball. Pitching in the summer of 1944 for the Gruber Engineers, with Reimann as his catcher, Spahn won his first 10 games — seven on shutouts — and struck out 186 batters in just 80 innings. The winning streak was snapped when he uncharacteristically committed three throwing errors in a 7-1 loss to the semipro Atlas Electrics of Tulsa at Texas League Park on July 30, 1944. He may have had a lot on his mind, because Spahn was shipped to Europe aboard the line Queen Mary on November 9, 1944. As a staff sergeant in the 276th Engineer Combat Battalion, he arrived in France a few weeks later, and survived for about ten days on peanut-butter sandwiches provided by friendly British soldiers.

Spahn's 9th Armored Division, which preceded much larger groups of Allied troops, was charged with repairing roads and bridges. He fought in the snowy, frozen Battle of the Bulge, getting nicked by bullets in the abdomen and on the back of the head. Crossing France and Belgium, his division arrived at the Rhine River and the Ludendorff railroad bridge at Remagen on March 7, 1945. While retreating, the Nazis had destroyed every intact bridge but the one at Remagen. The demolitions were in place, but for some reason they had never pushed the plunger. The bridge's survival was crucial to the Allies for delivering men, vehicles, and equipment to the German heartland. On March 9 Sergeant Spahn and the 276th were ordered to the bridge to remove the demolitions, repair the bridge, maintain it, and construct a second span for two-way traffic. Working furiously to maintain the girders, Spahn and Co. were bombarded by V-2 rockets while troops, tanks, and trucks crossed above them. A biographer, Al Silverman, later described the scene:

"While the bridge vibrated and twanged like banjo strings, swaying precariously as marching infantrymen tramped across each catwalk, and tanks rumbled across the planked railbed, the units patched holes, bolstered the bridge with heavy supports, repaired damaged flooring and cratered approaches."

Ten days after the first successful crossing, Spahn received an assignment at a meeting over the center of the bridge and walked off to explain to his platoon that they would be taking over the bridge's security at 4 P.M. At 3:56 a platoon member shouted, "Look at the back! The bridge is falling down!" Possibly overloaded, certainly bombarded, the span slipped into the river, leaving 28 soldiers dead, 93 injured, and Sergeant Spahn with shrapnel in his left foot. Having crossed the Rhine, however, the Americans were able to protect a second bridge and other smaller pontoon bridges they built. Surgeons removed Spahn's shrapnel. On June 1, 1945, he was the only ballplayer given a battlefield promotion, from staff sergeant to second lieutenant. In all, he earned a Bronze Star, a Purple Heart, a battlefield promotion, and a Presidential Citation. That made him the most decorated ballplayer in World War II. (Like Spahn, pitcher Hoyt Wilhelm earned a Purple Heart, but Spahn alone received the Bronze Star.)

Aged rapidly by his battle experiences into a partly bald and fully-grown veteran, Spahn also built up stamina, concentration, and discipline during this period. "After what I went through overseas, I never thought of anything I was told to do in baseball as hard work," he insisted. "You get over feeling like that when you spend days on end sleeping in frozen tank tracks in enemy-threatened territory. The Army taught me what's important and what isn't."

Typically, Spahn found humor in the grimmest of situations. Because German spies would wear American uniforms, he said, "Anybody we didn't know, we'd ask, 'Who plays second for the Bums?' If he didn't answer 'Eddie Stanky,' he was dead." Spahn had no use for being labeled a hero. "The guys who died over there were heroes," he told his son, Greg. Nor did Spahn cotton to the view of baseball historians who estimated that he lost 30 or 40 wins to service time. "I matured a lot in those [war] years," he said. "If I had not had that maturity, I wouldn't have pitched until I was 45." (A statement like that says much about character. By contrast, the querulous Bob Feller said that if it weren't for *his* wartime service, "I'd have won more games than Warren Spahn.")

Unaware that the war would end just two months later after the dropping of atomic bombs on Hiroshima and Nagasaki in August 1945, Spahn accepted the battlefield promotion, which forced him to remain in the service until the next May and miss the start of the 1946 baseball season. Instead, he became the hottest pitcher in Germany that spring; working for the 115th Engineers Group, he allowed one run and struck out 73 batters in four games. And when he returned stateside, the Braves immediately promoted him to the majors, on June 10, 1946. "This is the first time in years I've reported to anybody without saluting," he told new Boston manager Billy Southworth.

Spahn appeared in his first postwar game seven days later—Bunker Hill Day in New England—and gave up one run and four hits in four relief innings of a doubleheader opener against the St. Louis Cardinals at Braves Field. "He was all grace," biographer Silverman wrote, "kicking his right leg high in the air, his left elbow passing his right knee, just as his dad had taught him, then uncoiling and the ball snapping to the plate out of flapping sleeves and trousers, the ball streaking in and on the batter almost before he could measure it, blazing in like a freight train coming out of the darkness."

In his fourth start, on July 14, Spahn beat the Pirates, 4-1, and allowed just one runner past second base (Frankie Gustine, who homered). It was his first big-league victory, but Warren was distracted by love. Southworth wanted him to wait until after the season before marrying LoRene Southard—he even offered to be best man and pay for the wedding and honeymoon—but Spahn instead got a day off and married her on August 10.

Chuck Dressen, a Dodgers coach at that time, said Spahn was tipping off his pitches. "We can beat Spahn every time he pitches," Dressen crowed. "We know every pitch he throws." Spahn, who would correct the flaw the following spring with help from pitching coach Johnny Cooney, still went 8-5 with a 2.94 ERA over the second half of the 1946 season. "Pressure? What pressure?" he said. "If I do badly, what's the worst thing that's going to happen? No one is going to shoot at me!"

Because of his military service, balding pate, and relatively advanced age — he won his first game at 25 — Spahn fit in quickly and became an instant elder statesman on the Boston club. "He was born old," a teammate said, and the writers described him as a downright Homeric figure. In a single column, legendary New York sportswriter Red Smith playfully called him "goose-necked, stork-legged," and "a gowky [probably a typo for "gawky"], bat-eared old warrior with the ample nose."

Some pitchers are unapproachable on the days they start. For his part, Spahn played practical jokes. He thought nothing of whacking teammates upside the head, setting their straw hats on fire while they wore them, or leaving mice in their pockets. "When I'm kidding, I'm actually relaxing," he said. "It's my way of coping with pressure."

An act like that can grow old in a hurry if you do not win. But already everyone expected Spahn to be an ace. In a 1946 conversation captured by a Philadelphia sportswriter, Phillies manager Ben Chapman and slugger Del Ennis traded impressions with Giants slugger Johnny Mize:

Chapman: "Spahn has one of the greatest overhand curves I've ever seen."

Ennis: "Never mind the curve. What I have to watch for is the change of pace he throws. I swing at it before it is halfway to the plate."

Mize: "The curve and change of pace are all right, but it's that fastball. It does tricks as it reaches the plate."

Spahn's performance backed up these concerns. In notching a 21-win season that helped the Braves to a third-place finish in 1947, Spahn led the league in ERA (2.33), innings pitched (289 2/3) and shutouts (7) while getting just 11 runs of support in his 10 losses. Most of the 1948 season was a different story; preoccupied by LoRene's pregnancy, the October 1 birth of their only child, Gregory, and an erratic fastball, he was only 15-12, but the 27-year-old Spahn and 30-year-old right-hander Johnny Sain pitched the Braves to a pennant with an incredible stretch run, prompting the "Spahn and Sain and pray for rain" poetry crafted by *Boston Post* sports editor Gerry Hern and repeated around the Hub. The exact words were:

First we'll use Spahn, then we'll use Sain
Then an off day, followed by rain
Back will come Spahn, followed by Sain
And followed, we hope, by two days of rain.

Beginning in a Labor Day doubleheader, Spahn and Sain started 11 of Boston's next 15 games, with Spahn going 4-1 and Sain 5-1. On September 6 Warren threw a 14-inning, 2-1 win over the Dodgers in which he picked Jackie Robinson off first base twice during the extra innings . It was probably the best-pitched game by any Brave all season, and was part of a 14-1 stretch by the club that all but wrapped up the National League flag. Facing Cleveland in the World Series, however, Spahn lost his only start, 4-1 in Game Two. "A few inches the other way and a couple of those hits would have been outs," said Sain, who had beaten Feller 1-0 in the opener. "You gave it a good try." "I pitch to win them all, same as you," Spahn replied.

With the Braves trailing three games to one, Spahn won Game Five with 5 2/3 innings of one-hit, seven-strikeout relief before the largest crowd in World Series history at that time — 86,288 strong in Cleveland's Municipal Stadium. Back in Boston the next day, Southworth asked the weary Spahn if he had anything left, since the manager had to pinch-hit for starter Bill Voiselle in his next at-bat and the Braves were trailing late in Game Six, 3-1 "I'll give it all I've got," Spahn said, but he had trouble warming up. When he relieved in the eighth, the Indians scored an insurance run off him with three straight singles before Spahn stymied the rally with a strikeout followed by a pickoff play during which a Cleveland runner was thrown out at the plate. The Braves' two-run rally in the bottom of the eighth fell just short; Spahn struck out the side in the ninth to give him 12 Ks in his 12 Series innings, but the Braves lost the game, 4-3, and the Series, four games to two.

Members of the Boston Braves Historical Association sometimes speculate: If Spahn had held the Indians scoreless that day and the Braves had won Game Six and, maybe, the Series, would they have left town so soon thereafter? No one knows for sure, but the club certainly did not help matters with an uninspiring title defense. The Braves self-destructed amid dissension, contract disputes, and injury in 1949, finished four games under .500 in fourth place, and began the decline that led to their departure from Boston. Already annoyed by the signing of 18-year-old "bonus baby" pitcher Johnny Antonelli for $50,000 or more in 1948, veteran players balked at Southworth's two-a-day workouts totaling six hours at spring training. Drinking heavily, his nerves in tatters, Southworth had to take a leave of absence two-thirds of the way through the season. Unsatisfied, the players voted him a half-share of their fourth-place Series money. Then, as if things could not get worse, management infuriated players and many fans by trading double-play mainstays Alvin Dark and Eddie Stanky to the New York Giants for four players on December 14, 1949.

But neither these distractions nor even his own salary disputes affected Spahn's concentration: Up to 172 pounds, using his thick wrist and well-developed chest muscles, he went 21-14, 21-17, and 22-14 in 1949-1951, leading the NL in strikeouts all three years and in wins twice. He could go long—he struck out a then-league-record 18 Cubs in during a 15-inning loss on June 14, 1952—and he could talk long. After surrendering a late-May 1951 homer to a rookie named Willie Mays, for instance, he said memorably: "He was something like 0-for-21 [actually 0-for-12] the first time I saw him. His first major-league hit was a home run off me—and I'll never forgive myself. We might have gotten rid of Willie forever if I'd only struck him out."

Spahn was not only a jokester. He notably befriended outfielder Sam Jethroe, the Braves' first black player, and helped start the Jimmy Fund charity in support of the Dana-Farber Cancer Institute. He was also an oracle whose every word on pitching was eagerly awaited. "A pitcher needs two pitches—one they're looking for and one to cross 'em up," Spahn said at one point. On another occasion, he stated, "Hitting is timing. Pitching is upsetting timing." Warren's quotability was a welcome distraction for the 1952 team, which slipped back into the second division when Spahn went 14-19 despite a league-leading 183 strikeouts and a stellar 2.98 ERA (nonsupport again serving as his nemesis). It was his fourth straight strikeout crown.

While negotiating his 1953 contract, Spahn accepted a $25,000 pact but rejected a deal that would have paid him 10 cents for every paid admission over 800,000. That made sense, since the Braves had just drawn a major-league low 281,278 in 1952. Spahn looked for another payday when his business venture opened Warren Spahn's Diner just across Commonwealth Avenue from Braves Field. When the team moved to Milwaukee during spring training, however, Spahn took a double loss: the Braves drew 1,826,397 in their first Midwestern season (which would have meant a $100,000 bonus had he taken the deal), and the restaurant opened without its primary owner.

Financial loss was not the only concern Warren took west. For all his success, his popularity with fans, and the respect of the many teammates and opponents he helped, Spahn was an insecure man who never forgot his youth in Depression-era Buffalo. After ripping cartilage in a knee during 1953 spring training, he didn't tell anyone. "I was one of the senior men on the club, and they'd have let me go in a minute if I went on the disabled list," he told *The Sporting News*'s Dave Kindred. Spahn pitched in pain all year, won the Braves' Milwaukee opener and the All-Star Game in Cincinnati, and led the league in wins (23) and ERA (2.10). Only then did he have offseason surgery.

The Braves finished second, third, and second their first three years in Milwaukee while rebuilding with players like Hank Aaron, Eddie Mathews, Joe Adcock, Del Crandall, Billy Bruton, and Spahn's new running buddy and prankster pal, pitcher Lew Burdette—who, ironically, had been picked up from the Yankees in a trade for the declining Sain. Spahn remained dominant, but with a chance to stay part of the 1956 NL pennant race on the second to last day of the season, after winning 10 of his last 11 games, he lost a 12-inning heartbreaker to the Cardinals when Rip Repulski's double-play ball took a bad hop. He actually cried while leaving the field, and threw his glove at a prying photographer (to whom he later apologized). But the 36-year-old Spahn bounced back in 1957, capturing his only Cy Young Award by going 21-11 with a league-leading 18 complete games and winning six times in 20 pre-stretch-drive days while the Braves took their first pennant in Milwaukee.

Spahn lost the World Series opener to the Yankees, 3-1, but won Game Four, 7-5, in 10 innings. It was perhaps with mixed feelings when he fell sick with the flu that Spahn watched as Burdette took his scheduled start on two days' rest and shut out the Yankees in Game Seven. Although happy to see his buddy win three games and a new car as Series MVP, Warren had no doubt wanted the ball himself.

When both teams repeated as pennant winners the next year, Spahn (22-11 in the regular season) won Game One of the rematch, 4-3, in ten innings, contributing two hits and an RBI himself. Then, locked in a pitcher's zone ("All I can see … is a strike zone waving a bat"), he two-hit the Yankees in Game Four, 3-0, to give Milwaukee a commanding three-games-to-one lead. But called on by manager Fred Haney to pitch on two days' rest, Spahn lost Game Six, 4-3, in ten innings; the Braves might have won the contest (and the Series) in regulation if Bill Bruton had not misplayed a fly ball into a single and third-base coach Billy Herman had not sent 37-year-old Andy Pafko to be tagged out at home on a short fly. Many considered Spahn the outstanding pitcher of the Series, but the Yankees won in seven games.

With extraordinary staying power, the 38-year-old Spahn pitched a league-high 292 innings and went 21-15 for the injury-riddled 1959 Braves, who lost the pennant in two games during a best-of-three playoff with the Los Angeles Dodgers. Then, as the team began slipping, he stayed dominant by throwing his only two no-hitters at the ages of 39 and 40. He fanned 15 Phillies in his first gem, a 4-0 win on September 16, 1960. "All right, just nobody say I've got a no-hitter going," he announced to a shocked Milwaukee bench in violation of the silence code, and he ended with a flourish—deflecting former Brave Bobby Malkmus's line shot to start a spectacular 1-6-3 play for the final out. Seven months later, he faced the minimum 27 batters in a 1-0 no-hit win over the Giants on April 28, 1961, retiring pinch-hitter Matty Alou with a spectacular backhanded flip to squelch a bunt attempt for the second out in the ninth. Spahn allowed two walks in this contest, but double plays wiped out both baserunners, accounting for his 27 men faced.)

This was not his only milestone contest of 1961; Spahn won his 300th game with a 2-1 victory over the Cubs before a crowd of 40,775 on August 11, making him just the 13th pitcher (and the first since Lefty Grove in 1941) to reach the hallowed mark. Even upon getting there, he was far from done; in perhaps the last extraordinary performance of an extraordinary career, the 42-year-old lefty lost a 16-inning duel with the Giants' 25-year-old Juan Marichal, 1-0, thanks to arch-nemesis Willie Mays' homer at 12:31 a.m. on July 3, 1963. Despite this setback, Spahn finished the 1963 season 23-7, led the league with 22 complete games, and even captured several MVP votes.

Explaining his longevity, the usually loquacious Spahn needed just one word: mechanics. "You've got to be a student of pitching," he said. "The way I threw, I never tried to put too much strain on my left arm." Whitlow Wyatt, a Braves pitching coach, said, "He makes my job easier. Every pitch he throws he has an idea behind it."

Spahn's longtime catcher Del Crandall told Spahn's son, Greg, a high-school hitting star who had career-ending surgery in college and later became a successful real-estate executive in Tulsa, that his father showed the batter three things: the sole of his right shoe, the back of his glove, and finally the ball. Spahn leaned forward in an almost courtly bow to the hitters, then rocked back, his right leg raised above his head in what *The Sporting News'* Kindred called a five-minutes-to-six position, followed by an overhand delivery that was as smooth and regular as an oil-field pumping jack back home in Oklahoma, where he now owned a ranch. Since every pitch was thrown with the same motion, the batter had no idea what to expect. "Sometimes the motion deceived me, and I was the catcher," Crandall said.

And there was something else. Because of an old separated shoulder from high-school football, the

6-foot-tall Spahn could not raise his right hand higher than his shoulder. As he moved toward the plate, his glove rose slowly, and then descended quickly through the hitter's line of vision. "People kept telling me that the motion of the glove really bothered hitters," Spahn told Kindred. "So I kept doing it. Whatever bothered hitters, I was for."

This silky-smooth delivery placed a minimum of pressure on Spahn's arm. He also benefited from revolutionary training habits. In his time, pitchers used spring training to get in shape and babied their arms between starts. Spahn headed to camp in tiptop condition, having spent the winters working on his ranch, and threw between starts. Both practices are common today. The same could be said of Spahn's research habits, since he studied hitters' tendencies and rarely gave them the same pitches from one year to the next. He was no slouch at the plate himself; in addition to his 363 victories, he had 363 lifetime hits — including 35 home runs.

As time passed, Spahn adapted. When his fastball began to fade, he learned a screwball, and when that was not enough, he picked up a slider. When his aching knees betrayed him in 1964, he went 6-13 and had to endure manager Bobby Bragan's insinuation that he was hanging on selfishly because of his $80,000 salary. On November 23, 1964, the Mets purchased Spahn from the Braves to be both pitcher and pitching coach. A week later they signed Yankees catching great Yogi Berra. "I don't know whether we'll be the oldest battery in baseball, but I know we'll be the ugliest," Spahn said.

Warren had truly come full circle, as the Mets manager was none other than his first skipper with the Braves back in 1942: Casey Stengel. After finishing sixth or seventh his final five years with Boston, Casey had forged a Hall of Fame career in leading the Yankees to 10 pennants in just 12 seasons. Now he was with a club even more woeful than his Braves; the Mets had lost a record 120 games under Stengel in their maiden 1962 season, and suffered 109 and 111 more setbacks over the next two campaigns.

Although even Spahn could not overcome the hardship of having a club of youngsters and castoffs as his support staff, he was sometimes able to take matters into his own hands. Facing 25-year-old Claude Osteen of the Dodgers early in the 1965 season, for instance, Spahn carried a 3-0 lead into the ninth. After the Dodgers scored two runs and had two runners on base, Stengel, who had admired Spahn with the Braves and saw no reason to change his mind, asked his elderly pitching coach whom he wanted to bring in from the bullpen. Spahn said he wanted to leave the starter in, and then promptly retired the last three batters.

The miracles quickly ran out, though, and Spahn was released and signed by the San Francisco Giants in midseason. He left Gotham with another great quip: "I'm the only guy to play for Casey Stengel before and after he was a genius."

Spahn again faltered, but not before he saw Willie Mays get his 500th homer. "I saw your first, Willie, and now your 500th," he said. Congratulations." Released at season's end with a 7-16 record, Spahn later said, "I didn't retire from baseball. Baseball retired me."

Disappointed or not, Spahn stayed in the game. When he pitched three games for the Mexico City Tigers in 1966 and three games for the Triple-A Tulsa Oilers in 1967, people got the mistaken impression that the 45-year-old was staging a comeback. Actually, he was demonstrating technique to a Mexican team he was coaching, and then trying to improve attendance for an American team he was managing. His Oilers, the top affiliate of the St. Louis Cardinals, won the Pacific Coast League championship in 1968, and Spahn was voted Manager of the Year. Before being fired in August 1971 because he had refused a promotion to be the Cardinals pitching coach the previous year and outstayed his welcome, he racked up 372 wins. He scouted and coached minor-league pitchers for the Cardinals in 1971, then spent two unhappy years as pitching coach for the Cleveland Indians. His spirits lifted when the Hall of Fame called. Only the sixth player elected in his first year of eligibility — his appearances for Mexico City and Tulsa kept his name off the ballot two additional years — Spahn was enshrined in 1973 along with posthumous induction for his son's favorite player, Roberto Clemente.

Spahn instructed the Hiroshima Toyo Carp pitchers in the summers of 1973-1978, then coached minor-league pitchers in the California Angels system for a few years before tiring of travel on "funny little airplanes," as he told writer Rich Westcott, after the 1981 season. Blunt-spoken to the end, he blasted long-haired players and dismissed the idea of a designated hitter, saying, "I think pitchers should be athletes."

On October 16, 1995, Spahn was inducted into the Boston Braves Hall of Fame at the third annual reunion of the Boston Braves Historical Association. In their last day together in Boston, he and Johnny Sain visited what was left of Braves Field and the memories of 1948. Addressing a sizable gathering, Spahn remarked that with that kind of attendance in his day, the Braves might still be playing in Boston.

Thanks to his half-Cherokee wife, LoRene, who got her husband to give up the Buffalo winters and settle in Hartshorne, Oklahoma, Spahn grew rich running a 2,000-acre cattle ranch and leasing some of his land for gas wells. "My mother talked us into buying four beachfront properties in Florida," Greg Spahn said of LoRene, who died in 1978. "They're worth millions now."

In August 2003 the Braves unveiled Shan Gray's nine-foot bronze statue of Spahn kicking high outside Turner Field in Atlanta. Ailing from a litany of mostly age-related difficulties—a broken leg, four broken ribs, a punctured lung, internal bleeding, and fluid buildup in his lungs—Spahn, 82, was wheeled in to see the work. "I took great pride in mooning people," he said. "That's the reason I developed that leg kick."

It was one of the last and best memories of Spahn: kicking and joking. He died on November 24, 2003, and was buried in Elmwood Cemetery back home in Hartshorne. Posthumous honors followed. The city of Buffalo renamed the street to Cazenovia Park, his old high-school field, Warren Spahn Way. Other statues went up at Bricktown Ballpark in Oklahoma City and the Oklahoma Sports Museum in Guthrie. Finally, the Oklahoma Sports Museum established the Warren Spahn Award in 1999 to honor the majors' leading left-handed pitcher.

Should the award have been named for another lefty: a Grove, Koufax, Carlton, or Plank? Not if winning matters most. Spahn's 363 wins are the most of any left-hander, and he was a consistently reliable pitcher, as his ERA's in the regular season (3.09), All-Star Games (3.21), and World Series (3.05) attest. As of 2013 Spahn also held or shared modern major-league records for 20-win seasons (13), most years leading the league in games won (8), career innings by a left-hander (5,246), wins in a season at age 40 (21) and 42 (23), and possibly double plays started by a pitcher (82), which is not an official statistic. His 35 homers are the most by an NL pitcher. Spahn won 75 games after the age of 40, and no matter what his age was, he was great in the clutch. During his career he had a .546 April-July winning percentage, followed by a .676 percentage in August-October—a staggering .130 increase.

In SABR's *Baseball Research Journal* No. 32, Eric Marshall White described Spahn as "the most fantastic finisher of them all." And he did indeed look as if he could go on forever. "I don't think Spahn will ever get into the Hall of Fame," Stan Musial once said. "He'll never stop pitching."

Spahn kept making news in and out of baseball. In 1976 the United States Supreme Court voided a lower court's $10,000 damages award against a man who wrote an unauthorized biography of Spahn. As long as the book contained no reckless disregard for truth and was in the public interest, the judges ruled, the author was within his rights and did not violate a state's right-to-privacy laws. The ruling effectively voided similar suits by Hank Aaron, Don Drysdale, and Eddie Mathews.

Note

This biography originally appeared in the book *Spahn, Sain, and Teddy Ballgame: Boston's (almost) Perfect Baseball Summer of 1948*, edited by Bill Nowlin and published by Rounder Books in 2008.

Sources

Bjarkman, Peter C., *Warren Spahn* (New York: Chelsea House Publications, 1994).

Buege, Bob, *The Milwaukee Braves: A Baseball Eulogy* (Milwaukee: Douglas American Sports Publications, 1988).

Cohen, Richard M., & David F. Neft, *The World Series* (New York: Macmillan, 1986).

Johnson, Richard A., Images of America: Boston Braves (Charleston, South Carolina, Chicago, Portsmouth, New Hampshire, San Francisco: Arcadia Publishing, 2001).

Kaplan, Jim, *The Greatest Game Ever Pitched: Juan Marichal, Warren Spahn and the Pitching Duel of the Century* (Chicago: Triumph Books, 2011).

Kaese, Harold, *The Boston Braves 1871-1953* (Boston: Northeastern University Press, 2004).

Porter, David L., ed., *Biographical Dictionary of American Sports: Baseball* (Westport Connecticut: Greenwood Press, 1987).

Silverman, Al. *Warren Spahn; Immortal Southpaw* (New York: Bartholomew House, Sport Magazine Library No. 9, 1961).

Thorn, John, Pete Palmer, Michael Gershman, and David Pietrusza, eds., *Total Baseball*, fifth edition (New York: Viking/Penguin Books USA, 1997).

Retrosheet.org

Chuck Tanner

By Dan Fields

SOMETIMES NICE GUYS finish first. Chuck Tanner, an eternal optimist who was known as baseball's Mr. Sunshine, managed the Pittsburgh Pirates to a World Series title in 1979. He won more than 1,350 games as a manager of four teams between 1970 and 1988. Tanner also played for eight years in the majors, with the Milwaukee Braves, Chicago Cubs, Cleveland Indians, and Los Angeles Angels. (He spent the first two months of the 1957 season with the Braves before being sent to the Cubs on waivers.) Tanner famously said, "The greatest feeling in the world is to win a major-league game. The second greatest feeling is to lose a major-league game."[1]

Charles William Tanner, Jr. was born in New Castle, Pennsylvania (about 50 miles north of Pittsburgh), on July 4, 1928. Of German-Slovak descent, Tanner was one of three sons of Charles Tanner, Sr., a Pennsylvania Railroad brakeman and conductor, and Anna (Baka) Tanner. He grew up in modest circumstances: "We didn't have electricity until [I was in] tenth grade. No bathroom. We were better off than some because we had a two-holer out back; some people only had one hole. We had a pot-bellied stove, but there were days I'd wake up with snow in my pockets."[2]

As a child Tanner joined a group of older boys in pickup baseball games that would last many hours. He joked that he might have starved if his mother had not shown up every afternoon with peanut-butter sandwiches. His grandfather told him, "You'll be a bum. All you want to do is baseball, baseball, baseball."[3]

Tanner was a ten-letter standout in baseball, basketball, and football while at Shenango High School in New Castle. In June 1946 the Boston Braves signed the 6-foot, 185-pound outfielder, who batted and threw left. In the minors he batted over .300 every year from 1947 through 1954, spending time in Owensboro (Kentucky), Evansville (Indiana), Eau Claire (Wisconsin), Pawtucket (Rhode Island), and Denver. On February 12, 1950, Tanner married Barbara "Babs" Weiss; together, they would have four sons.

In 1954, while playing his fourth year with the Atlanta Crackers in the Double-A Southern Association, Tanner was second in the league in hits (192) and total bases (311). He hit 20 homers and sported a .323 batting average. That year he helped the Crackers win the Southern Association "grand slam": the team won the annual All-Star game, finished first in the regular-season standings, won the league playoffs, and took the Dixie Series over the champions of the Double-A Texas League, the Houston Buffaloes.

In 1955, Tanner's tenth year in professional baseball, he was promoted to the Milwaukee Braves. He made the most of his first appearance: On Opening Day, April 12, he pinch-hit for Warren Spahn in the eighth

Chuck Tanner (National Baseball Hall of Fame Library, Cooperstown, N.Y.)

inning and homered off Gerry Staley on the first major-league pitch he faced to help the Braves defeat the Cincinnati Redlegs, 4-2. Tanner was the seventh player in major-league history to hit a home run on his first pitch and the fifth with a pinch-hit home run in his first at-bat.

In his rookie year, Tanner served as Milwaukee's fourth outfielder. He hit .247, with six home runs and 27 RBIs in 97 games. Tanner was known for his hustle: He would run so hard from left field to the dugout after each inning that he often arrived before the first baseman, Joe Adcock. Tanner saw more limited duty with the Braves in 1956 and 1957, and on June 8, 1957, he was placed on waivers and claimed by the Cubs. In a July 18 game at Forbes Field, both Tanner and Ernie Banks of the Cubs hit inside-the-park home runs, but the Pirates won 6-5. In 95 games with the Cubs that year, Tanner had two four-hit games and six three-hit games. His combined totals for the Braves and Cubs in 1957 were nine home runs and 48 RBIs, with a batting average of .279.

In 1958 with the Cubs, Tanner's 53 pinch-hitting at-bats led the NL. On March 9, 1959, he was traded to the Boston Red Sox for pitcher Bob Smith. Tanner never saw action with Boston and played 152 games that year with a Red Sox Triple-A team, the Minneapolis Millers. On September 9 he was purchased by the Cleveland Indians. Tanner appeared in 14 games with the Indians that month, and he played in 21 games with Cleveland in 1960. Tanner appeared in 70 games during 1961 with the Indians' Triple-A team, the Toronto Maple Leafs, until he was sold in mid-July to the Los Angeles Angels' Triple-A affiliate, the Dallas-Fort Worth Rangers. After he played in 48 games and batted .300 for the Rangers, his contract was purchased by the Angels on September 8.

Tanner played in seven games with the expansion Angels during that team's inaugural season and another seven games in the spring of 1962. He played his final game in the big leagues on May 8, 1962. He spent the rest of the season with Dallas-Fort Worth. During his major-league career, Tanner compiled a .261 batting average, with 21 home runs and 105 RBIs in 396 games. During his 14-season minor-league career, he collected 1,669 hits in 1,454 games.

After the 1962 season Tanner faced a choice. He could play for another year for $18,000, or he could manage a Single-A team in Davenport, Iowa, for $6,000. Tanner made an investment in the future and headed to Iowa. He managed eight years in the Angels' farm system, leading the Quad Cities Angels (1963-1964), El Paso Sun Kings (1965-1966, 1968), Seattle Angels (1967), and Hawaii Islanders (1969-1970). Tanner had a cumulative record of 561-537 (.511), and he won minor-league Manager of the Year honors in 1968 and 1970.

In September 1970 Tanner took over the last-place Chicago White Sox after Don Gutteridge was fired and managed the team for the final 16 games of the season. As the skipper built his players' confidence and got them believing in themselves, the team's fortunes took an upturn. In 1971 the White Sox finished third in the AL West with a record of 79-83, a 23-game improvement over 1970. Tanner moved Wilbur Wood out of the bullpen, and the knuckleball pitcher responded with a breakout year, with 22 wins, an ERA of 1.91, and 210 strikeouts in 42 starts.

In 1972 the White Sox went 87-67 and finished second in their division, and Tanner won the major-league Manager of the Year award from *The Sporting News* and the AL Manager of the Year Award from the Associated Press. Under Tanner's low-key style of handling ballplayers, moody first baseman Dick Allen thrived, leading the league in home runs (37) and RBIs (113) and winning the MVP award. Wood won 24 games and was named the AL Pitcher of the Year by *The Sporting News*. He started 49 games (still tied for second-most starts in a season in AL history) and pitched 376 1/3 innings, the most by an American League hurler since 1912.

In Chicago, Tanner relied heavily on his top pitchers. In 1972, two other White Sox hurlers started at least 40 games, Stan Bahnsen (41) and Tom Bradley (40). In 1973 Wood (48 starts) and Bahnsen (42) again combined for 90 starts; Wood finished with a 24-20 record and again led the majors with 359 1/3 innings pitched. On May 28, 1973, Tanner let Wood complete a game that had been suspended two days earlier against the

Cleveland Indians. He worked five innings, giving up only one unearned run, and picked up the win. Wood then pitched a four-hit shutout in the regularly scheduled game. On July 20, 1973, Tanner started Wood in both games of a doubleheader against the New York Yankees; the pitcher was pinned with both losses.

Under Tanner the White Sox finished in fifth place in 1973, fourth in 1974, and fifth in 1975. After the 1975 season, the team was sold, and new owner Bill Veeck replaced Tanner with Paul Richards. Tanner signed a three-year contract with the Oakland Athletics, and the team was off to the races: In 1976 the A's stole an AL-record 341 bases in 464 attempts. Eight players had at least 20 steals, including pinch-runners Matt Alexander and Larry Lintz, who combined for 51 steals despite only 34 plate appearances. The A's finished second in the AL West with a record of 87 wins and 74 losses.

On November 5, 1976, Tanner was involved in an unusual trade. When Danny Murtaugh, who had managed the Pirates to 1,115 wins and two World Series championships, retired at the end of the season, the team wanted local boy Tanner to replace him. But Tanner was still under contract with the A's, and owner Charlie Finley wanted to be compensated if he was going to release his manager. The Pirates offered either All-Star catcher Manny Sanguillen or $100,000. Finley demanded both, and to Tanner's surprise, the Pirates agreed. It was one of the few times in baseball history that a player was traded for a manager. Tanner was delighted to be returning home: "I can't wait for spring training. This is such a thrill. It's like a dream come true."[4]

With Tanner at the helm, the Pirates won 96 games in 1977 and finished second in the NL East. The team stole 260 bases (the most in a season by the Pirates in 70 years), giving Tanner's teams a total of 601 steals in 1976 and 1977. Dave Parker led the league with a .338 batting average, and 23-year-old John Candelaria sparkled with a major-league-low 2.34 ERA and a 20-5 record.

In 1978 the Pirates were 11 1/2 games behind the Philadelphia Phillies on August 12 after a miserable 4-17 stretch. Ever the optimist, Tanner told his players, "This may not be the end; it may be the beginning."[5]

Over the remainder of the season, the Pirates had a record of 37-12 (.755), including 24 straight wins at home. The Phillies clinched the division on the second-to-last day of the season, and the Pirates finished just 1 1/2 games back with a record of 88-73. It was Tanner's third consecutive second-place finish. Parker was the National League's Most Valuable Player, with a .334 batting average (tops in the majors), 30 home runs, and 117 RBIs. Willie Stargell, who had played in only 63 games the previous year because of a pinched nerve in his left elbow, contributed 28 home runs and 97 RBIs and was named the NL Comeback Player of the Year.

In 1979 Tanner led the Pirates to 98 wins, the most by Pittsburgh since 1908 and good enough to win the National League East by two games over the Montreal Expos. The Pirates adopted the Sister Sledge hit "We Are Family" as its theme song, and their on-field success was a true team effort: No player had as many as 15 wins or 95 RBIs. Tanner was an innovator for using a platoon of relievers, often for an inning each in the same game. Kent Tekulve (94 games), Enrique Romo (84 games), and Grant Jackson (72 games) finished 1-2-3 in games pitched in the NL. The Pirates swept the best-of-five National League Championship Series in three games over the Cincinnati Reds, with Stargell named the series MVP.

In the World Series, Pittsburgh trailed the favored Baltimore Orioles three games to one when Tanner learned that his mother had died. He told his players, "My mother is a great Pirates fan. She knows we're in trouble, so she went upstairs to get some help."[6] The Pirates rallied to win three straight games, including Games Six and Seven on the road. Stargell went 12-for-30, with four doubles and three home runs, and picked up the World Series MVP award. He completed the trifecta by winning the 1979 NL MVP award (along with Keith Hernandez of the St. Louis Cardinals); he was also the third player in eight years to win an MVP award under Tanner. "Having Willie Stargell on your ballclub is like having a diamond ring on your finger," Tanner quipped.[7]

Tanner managed the Pirates for six more years, with winning records in 1980, 1982, and 1983. On May 29, 1983, he became the 35th manager to win 1,000 games in the majors, against 927 losses (.519). Bill Madlock won batting titles in 1981 (.341) and 1983 (.323).

In 1984 the Pirates dropped to sixth place with a 75-87 record, and in 1985, they slid to 57-104. Several players were involved in what became known as the Pittsburgh drug trials of 1985. According to the *Pittsburgh Post-Gazette*: "Seven men—all outside the team—were convicted of selling drugs to baseball players, many of whom testified in exchange for immunity. Mr. Tanner testified he had no more than cursory knowledge of such drug issues, but Dale Berra, a shortstop at the time, contradicted that by testifying that Mr. Tanner warned him to stay away from drug dealers."[8] Tanner was let go by the Pirates and later said, "I would've fired myself."[9] (One bright spot of 1985 was that Tanner's son Bruce pitched ten games for the Chicago White Sox; Tanner's son Mark had pitched in the minor leagues from 1972 through 1975.)

Tanner was hired to manage the Atlanta Braves, who finished last in the NL West in 1986 and fifth in 1987. With a 12-27 record in 1988, Tanner was replaced by Russ Nixon. Tanner had managed a major-league game from September 18, 1970, to May 22, 1988. When he was done, only 18 managers in major-league history had won more games. He finished with a record of 1352-1381 (.495).

But Tanner was not through with baseball. From 1992 to 2002, he served as a special assistant to the general manager of the Milwaukee Brewers. He also scouted for five years for the Cleveland Indians. On July 31, 2004, during the year of the 25th anniversary of the 1979 championship, the baseball field at Shenango High School was dedicated as Chuck Tanner Field. In 2006 Houston Astros manager Phil Garner, an infielder on the 1979 Pirates, honored Tanner by naming him an honorary NL coach in the All-Star Game in Pittsburgh; Tanner also threw out the first pitch. On August 9, 2006, Barbara Tanner, his wife of 56 years, passed away.

In November 2007 the Rotary Club of Pittsburgh presented the first Chuck Tanner Baseball Manager of the Year award to Joe Torre of the Los Angeles Dodgers. Through 2009 the award was given to a major-league manager. In 2010 a second award was presented to the Chuck Tanner Collegiate Baseball Manager of the Year, and the original award was renamed the Chuck Tanner Major League Baseball Manager of the Year award.

In 2008 the Pirates hired Tanner as a senior adviser to the general manager, a job he held until his death on February 11, 2011, in New Castle at the age of 82. He is buried at Castleview Memorial Gardens in New Castle. To honor his passion for teaching baseball, the Pirates created the Chuck Tanner We Are Family Fund, which annually presents an award to the Pirates' minor-league staff person who best exemplifies Tanner's optimism, enthusiasm, work ethic, and leadership. "I've had the greatest life in the world," said Tanner in a 2007 interview. "How many guys can say they won a World Series in their backyard? How can that happen to a kid from Shenango?"[10]

Sources

Baseball-Reference.com

Findagrave.com

Pittsburgh.pirates.mlb.com

Pittsburghrotary.org

Retrosheet.org

Feeney, Charley., "Bucs Give Chuck 1,000th, but It's Not All That Pretty," *Pittsburgh Post-Gazette,* May 30, 1983.

Fenster, Kenneth R., "The 1954 Dixie Series," *The National Pastime,* SABR 40 (2010).

Jaffe, Chris, "10 Things I Didn't Know about Chuck Tanner," Hardball Times (hardballtimes.com), February 14, 2011.

Johns, Walter L., "Tanner—With, Without Shoes," *New Castle* (Pennsylvania) *News,* April 8, 1971.

Liska, Jerry (Associated Press), "Chuck Tanner Cons His White Sox Into Stars," *Tuscaloosa* (Alabama) *News,* August 20, 1972, 3B.

McCollister, John, *Tales from the 1979 Pittsburgh Pirates* (Champaign, Illinois: Sports Publishing L.L.C., 2005).

Porter, David L.,, ed., *Biographical Dictionary of American Sports: Baseball* (volume 3) (Westport, Connecticut: Greenwood Press, 2000).

Spatz, Lyle, ed., *The SABR Baseball List & Record Book* (New York: Scribner, 2007).

Notes

1. *The Sporting News,* July 15, 1985, 18.
2. Sharon Robb, "Tanner 'Positive' Braves Can Climb," *Sun Sentinel* (Fort Lauderdale, Florida), October 31, 1985.

3 David Lamb, *Stolen Season: A Journey Through America and Baseball's Minor Leagues* (New York: Random House, 1991), 201.

4 Craig Brown, "Retracing Chuck Tanner's Path to Pirates," ESPN.com, February 13, 2011.

5 Phil Axelrod, "Never-Say-Die Bucs Created Own Miracle," *Pittsburgh Post-Gazette,* September 7, 1978.

6 Dejan Kovacevic, "Chuck Tanner, Popular Pirates Manager, Dies at 82," *Pittsburgh Post-Gazette,* February 11, 2011.

7 "Pops Go the Pirates," *Time,* October 29, 1979.

8 Dejan Kovacevic, 2011.

9 Ibid.

10 Ron Cook, " 'Fam-a-lee' Blessed With Tanner," *Pittsburgh Post-Gazette,* February 12, 2011.

Hawk Taylor

By Steven Schmitt

In 1972 Metropolis, Illinois, was officially designated as the hometown of Superman, the comic-book character who leaps tall buildings in a single bound. Back in 1957, Robert "Hawk" Taylor was the genuine article when it came to baseball.

Unlike the mild-mannered reporter from the fictitious *Metropolis Daily Planet*, Clark Kent, who left his office, entered a phone booth, and came out as the Man of Steel, Hawk Taylor stepped off the local baseball field and into his high-school graduation gown, then shed the gown and received a "basket of gold," as *Philadelphia Daily News* columnist Sandy Grady put it.[1] At 4:30 a.m. on Saturday, May 30, 1957, just hours after graduating from Metropolis High School, Taylor signed a contract with the Milwaukee Braves for a $6,000 salary and a total bonus of $119,000, at the time the richest-ever deal for a baseball rookie.[2]

Robert Dale Taylor was born on April 3, 1939, in Metropolis, a small town in extreme southern Illinois across the Ohio River from Paducah, Kentucky. He was the oldest of the five children of Vance and Velma Taylor, followed by sisters Sue, Carol, and Jo Ellen, and brother Johnny, who was called Bubber. All male members of the Taylor family had nicknames. Robert got his nickname, Hawk, from a cousin as a child because his favorite movie serial was *Hawk of the Wilderness*. His father, Vance, known as "Flop," was a truck driver with a route from Metropolis to Kankakee, Illinois. An uncle, Benny "Bleek" Taylor, played in 53 major-league games, mainly at first base, for the St. Louis Browns in 1951, the Detroit Tigers in 1952, and the Milwaukee Braves in 1955. Benny also managed at Johnson City, Tennessee, in 1957 for the Philadelphia Phillies' short-season Appalachian League team.

Robert started playing baseball when he was 8 years old in the Khoury League, an age-based organization that started in 1936 in St. Louis and spread rapidly in Missouri and Southern Illinois. By the time he was 12 he was playing on local teams with his uncles. At 13 he was being watched by scouts because of his ability to run, throw, and hit with power. As a senior for the Metropolis High School Trojans, Taylor batted .650 (though he told Jim Enright of the *Chicago American* that he hit over .700 and was intentionally walked at least twice a game) with 10 home runs in a 14-game season. He slugged 21 home runs in his four years on the team, including one that cleared the roof of the local ballpark. He won varsity letters in baseball, football, and basketball, and captured eight medals in two years of track and field competition that included a conference championship in the 100-yard dash. As a junior on the basketball team, Taylor set a single-season scoring mark of 630 points, including 43 points in one game. He had a baseball scholarship offer from the University of Illinois.[3]

Most major-league teams scouted Taylor. The bonus rule in effect at the time required that any player signed for more than $4,000 had to stay on the major-league roster for two calendar years from the signing date. The Milwaukee Braves won the bidding contest for Taylor

Hawk Taylor (National Baseball Hall of Fame Library, Cooperstown, N.Y.)

because they offered more money than the Brooklyn Dodgers. The Dodgers' bid, made over the telephone, was $98,000. "I just about choked," said Taylor, later wondering what kind of career he could have had, especially after Dodger catcher Roy Campanella was paralyzed in a car crash in January 1958 and had to retire.[4] At 1 a.m. on May 30, the Taylors met Braves scout Wid Matthews, a resident of the area and a friend of the family, at the Metropolis Hotel. Matthews topped the Dodgers' bid by $1,000, and added $20,000 for Taylor's father, Vance. "Everything was talked out, and as a result we didn't get out of his room until we signed."[5] The St. Louis Cardinals had made an $80,000 offer but had insisted that Taylor try out at Busch Stadium first.

Taylor's instant riches made him an instant celebrity. The *Metropolis News* carried banner headlines, lengthy articles, and congratulations from well-wishing merchants and organizations, and predicted that there would eventually be such things as an annual Hawk Taylor Day, a Hawk Taylor Street, and Hawk Taylor sodas and gloves. "He's had six marriage proposals and a guy from New York wants to sell him a $125,000 hunting and fishing lodge," the paper wrote. Vance Taylor told the *Milwaukee Journal* that spreading the bonus over five years saved $18,000 in taxes.[6] Sportswriter Bill Harris of the *Paducah Sun Democrat* wrote that local fans would be able to see Hawk in action when the Braves played the Cardinals in night games on July 1 and 2. The community organized bus trips for the games in St. Louis. The Braves and Cardinals were also scheduled for the NBC *Game of the Week* on July 22 and July 29, which would be on local TV. "While watching the Braves on television look for number 19," Harris wrote.[7]

Through it all, Hawk was thrilled but humble. "When you're in baseball, there's only one place to be and that's the majors," he told local writers. Upon his arrival with the Braves on June 4, he acknowledged that he had much to learn and that his money would go into the bank as he earned it. Braves manager Fred Haney had said Hawk would get an opportunity to play when the manager thought he was ready. Taylor believed he could make it and appreciated the help he got from the players and coaches.

As it turned out, Taylor played very little for Milwaukee in its world-championship 1957 season or in several seasons thereafter. On June 9, he made his major-league debut by pinch-running for Frank Torre in the second game of a doubleheader against the Pittsburgh Pirates, and on the 12th he caught the eighth inning against the Dodgers. "We were making up the signals," Braves left-hander Taylor Phillips said. "We didn't have any signals so we just made them up." But the World Series was the ultimate experience of Taylor's half-season of thrills. "Right out of high school, I was rubbing elbows with a team that had four Hall of Famers," he told this writer in an interview at his home in April 2011. "Guys that I had posted on my bedroom wall. It was just a dream come true." And the Series victory? "It was an overwhelming sensation," he reflected. "I thought, 'This is the way it's supposed to be.' I took it for granted that this was big-league life."[8]

Big-league life became minor-league life very quickly. Baseball rescinded the bonus rule retroactively in 1958, and Taylor played most of that season at Cedar Rapids of the Class B Three-I League, batting .297 with 22 home runs and earning a late-season promotion to Class A Jacksonville and then a brief call-up to the Braves during which, on September 27, he got his first major-league hit, a double off Cincinnati's Ted Wieand. In 1959 Taylor played in 99 games for the Atlanta Crackers of the Double-A Southern Association, batting .297 but with just four home runs. In 1960 he had what he called his most satisfying professional season. He played left field and caught for the Junior World Series champion Louisville Colonels. He batted cleanup, hitting 17 home runs with 80 RBIs and a .270 batting average. (His Milwaukee bonus-baby teammate John DeMerit played right field and hit .268 with 12 homers and 50 RBIs.) The Louisville fans voted Hawk the most popular player on the Colonels, who beat the favored Toronto Maple Leafs of the International League in six games.

Ready for another shot at the majors in 1961, Taylor instead was called up to serve in the Army for six months because of the Berlin Crisis, then, after returning and playing in 20 games in 1961, was called up for a second military hitch, and did not return to the Braves until August 11, 1962. On September 15, playing right field in place of Hank Aaron, he ripped five singles, scored a run, and drove in another in a 9-8 win over the Houston Colt .45s. He finished the 1962 season batting .255 in 47 at-bats.

Taylor and Marie Holifield were married in Brookport, Illinois, on October 6, 1962, right after the end of the season. After a honeymoon cruise, Taylor played winter ball in Puerto Rico until just before Christmas.

In 1963 he had his best chance to start for the Braves. He had the left-field job won in spring training, batting .353 in six games ("I was hittin' the dickens out of the ball") when a fluke injury sidelined him for most of the season. Replacing Eddie Mathews at third base in a spring-training game on March 17 against the Minnesota Twins, Taylor got in front of a sharp, top-spinning ground ball hit by the Twins' John Goryl. The ball took a high hop and struck Taylor, breaking his collarbone. Expected to be out four to six weeks, he recovered slowly and had only 29 at-bats during the season, with two hits. After the season the Braves sold Taylor to the Mets, calling their can't-miss prospect "a $119,000 dud."[9]

Taylor saw more action with the cellar-dwelling Mets, playing in the first Opening Day at Shea Stadium, but Casey Stengel's platooning system made him a part-time player. Other than a stretch of eight games as a regular in late June 1964 (4-for-5 on June 20 was his best day as a Met), he spent most of his time on the bench and returned to the minors in 1965 as a catcher for Buffalo of the Triple-A International League. Taylor hit 10 homers with 32 RBIs in 61 games before returning to the Mets for 48 at-bats, four of which produced home runs, and a .152 average in 25 games. Taylor split time with the Jacksonville Suns and the Mets in 1966, hitting a paltry .174 with the big club with three homers and 12 RBIs as an occasional catcher and first baseman. After playing sporadically for the Suns and Mets (catching Tom Seaver on June 18), Taylor was traded to the California Angels. After playing most of the next two seasons in the minors at Syracuse and Seattle, Taylor was selected by the expansion Kansas City Royals in the Rule 5 draft after the 1968 season. In 1969 he had 49 pinch-hitting appearances for the Royals. The leagues had begun experimenting during exhibition games with a designated-hitter rule and Royals manager Joe Gordon said that if the rule had been adopted, Taylor would be the perfect man for the job.

After 46 more pinch-hit at-bats with the Royals in 1970 and a brief return to Louisville (9-for-45 with one homer and seven RBIs) as property of the Boston Red Sox in 1971, Taylor hung up his playing spikes and returned to school. In 1972 he earned two degrees from Murray State University in Murray, Kentucky — a bachelor's in health/physical education with an emphasis on general business, and a master's in health/physical education and recreation. (He had straight A's in his master's program) For three years he taught physical education and coached baseball at Lambuth College in Jackson, Tennessee, then taught and coached at the high-school and junior-college level in Paducah, Kentucky. He worked in the insurance business for a time, and then retired to Murray with no regrets. "I took my retirement seriously," Hawk said, "and when you look out that window there, it's not hard to do."[10]

The last few years of Taylor's life were filled with medical concerns, some of which were dealt with by trips to the Mayo Clinic in Rochester, Minnesota. Taylor improved but needed to take daily rest periods. When the writer visited with him and his wife, Marie, at their home in Murray on April 20, 2011, Hawk was in good spirits and articulate as he recalled memorable moments in his baseball career.

On the 55th anniversary of his major league debut, Hawk Taylor died on June 9, 2012, at Western Baptist Hospital in Paducah, Kentucky, at the age of 73 after battling a series of illnesses that included irregular heartbeat, fibromyalgia, gall-bladder surgery and sleep apnea. He was survived by his wife, Marie Taylor, a pianist and retired professor of music at Murray State University; two sons, Sam and Bruce; and four siblings.

"My hitting and versatility helped my longevity," Taylor said of his professional career, which spanned 15 seasons. "I didn't make the good money." After the bonus year, his highest annual salary in baseball was $25,000. On the game's future, he was optimistic, saying, "Baseball is as healthy as it's ever been. It's done something right."[11]

The same can be said for Robert "Hawk" Taylor. He took advantage of opportunities, responded to adversity, and put his life in perspective. Even with the kryptonite of baseball injuries and a string of illnesses later in life, Hawk may not have been the Man of Steel but he was a super man.

Sources

Besides the sources listed below, information for this biography came from a personal interview with Hawk Taylor on April 20, 2011, material from his scrapbook, and communications from Marie Taylor, Hawk's widow, in 2011 and 2012.

Bradenton (Florida) *Post-Times.*

Louisville Courier-Journal.

Metropolis News.

Milwaukee Journal.

Paducah Sun-Democrat.

Philadelphia Daily News.

Southern Illinoisan, Carbondale, Illinois

The Sporting News.

Obituary, "Mr. Robert Dale 'Hawk' Taylor, age 73, of Murray, Ky.," J.H. Churchill Funeral Home, Murray, Kentucky.

BaseballAlmanac.com

Baseball-Reference.com

Notes

1. Sandy Grady, *Philadelphia Daily News,* June 15, 1957.
2. Taylor interview and *Metropolis News,* June 1, 1957, 1.
3. Taylor and *Metropolis News* clippings from Taylor's scrapbook.
4. Taylor interview.
5. Jim Enright, "Braves' Bonus Kid a Sharp Operator," *Chicago American.* June 5, 1957, 37.
6. "Kankakee '2nd Home' To Dad of $100,000 Bonus Baby," *Milwaukee Journal,* June 26, 1957, 3.
7. Bill Harris, *Paducah Sun Democrat,* June 13, 1957, Sec. 2, p. 1.
8. Taylor interview.
9. *The Sporting News,* December 14, 1963, 18.
10. Taylor interview.
11. Taylor interview.

Bobby Thomson

By Jeff Findley

WHEN NEW YORK Giants announcer Russ Hodges uttered the immortal words "The Giants win the pennant!" the legacy of Bobby Thomson was indelibly etched into baseball history. Despite modest career stats, Thomson's October 3, 1951, home run off Ralph Branca was, in 1999, ranked number one on *The Sporting News*' Greatest Baseball Moments.[1] The "Shot Heard 'Round The World" would forever be the defining moment of his career.

As *New York Daily News* columnist Mike Lupica noted in a 1998 column during Mark McGwire's chase of Babe Ruth's home-run record, "Sometimes you do not need 60 or 61 home runs. Sometimes you just need one, and your life is never the same after that, not for a single day."[2]

"It wasn't just me," Thomson told Lupica. "It was everything. It was New York, it was the Giants versus the Dodgers, it was the way we'd come from so far behind, it was the fact that we came from behind that day in the ninth. It was eight teams instead of all the ones they have now. It was the World Series on the line. You tell me my home run is safe today, and maybe you're right. Sometimes it's like that ball never came down."[3]

In Thomson's own words, "I had a decent major-league career, but if I hadn't been in the right place at the right time in the Polo Grounds, batting against Branca at precisely 3:58 on Wednesday afternoon, October 3, 1951, I would have played my 15 seasons in the major leagues and then vanished from sight and memory, never to be heard from again."[4]

Born Robert Brown Thomson on October 25, 1923, in Glasgow, Scotland, Thomson was the youngest of six children. His father had left Scotland for the United States five days earlier in search of a better life for his family, and in 1926, Robert, his mother, and five siblings landed at Ellis Island in New York Harbor, ultimately settling on Staten Island, part of New York City.[5] Later in life sportswriters often labeled him the Staten Island Scot.

Thomson attended Curtis High School on Staten Island, where he excelled in both soccer and baseball. He drew the attention of the Brooklyn Dodgers, and played for the Dodger Rookies, an amateur team made up of area players the Dodgers wanted to keep an eye on.

Thomson first commanded the Giants' attention in high school as well, playing on an industrial-league team made up of older players. "One night, there was a Giants scout named George Mack at the game. He had come to look at our center fielder, who had been invited to work out for the Giants a few days later at the Polo Grounds," Thomson wrote in *Few and Chosen*. "I had a pretty good game that day, and Mack told our center fielder, "Bring that kid shortstop with you."[6]

Despite the ongoing interest by the Dodgers, Thomson ultimately signed his first contract with the Giants in 1942. "The Giants offered me $100 a month to go to Bristol, Virginia, in a Class D league [Appalachian League]," Thomson said. "The Dodgers said they would give me $125 a month, but I was a Giants fan and I wanted to play for them."[7] Thomson played sparingly at Bristol, and the Giants' front office moved him to Rocky Mount (North Carolina) of the Class D

Bobby Thomson (National Baseball Hall of Fame Library, Cooperstown, N.Y.)

Bi-State League. He played 29 games at third base, hitting .241 with three home runs and 18 RBIs.[8]

Before the 1942 season concluded, Thomson was drafted and entered the US Army Air Corps. Commenting on this chapter of his life, he said, "While I missed out on the chance to improve my skills in the important early years of minor-league baseball, the air force helped me mature. When I got out of the service in 1946, I was invited to spring training in Jacksonville, Florida, with the Giants' Jersey City team of the Triple-A International League. The place was overrun with players who had come out of the service."[9]

Thomson landed in Jersey City, the Giants' top farm team, to start the 1946 season. His first game at Roosevelt Stadium in Jersey City also happened to be Jackie Robinson's first game in Organized Baseball. "As far as what Jackie did in that game, I don't remember," Thomson said. "I just remember he was in all the headlines, and nobody even noticed a scared kid playing center field for the Giants, me."[10] Thomson hit 26 home runs at Jersey City, and joined the Giants late in the season. He played in his first major-league game on September 9 at Shibe Park in Philadelphia, collecting two hits in four at-bats. He hit hit .315 with two home runs in 18 games for the Giants, and was in the major leagues to stay.

Initially slotted into a competition for the job at third base, Thomson began the 1947 season as the regular second baseman but moved to center field after nine games. He fared well as a rookie, batting .283 with 29 home runs, scoring a career-best 105 runs and driving in 85 runs.

Thomson's production fell off in 1948 (.248, 16 HR, 63 RBIs), but he was selected to the NL All-Star team, striking out in a ninth-inning pinch-hitting appearance. The Giants didn't fare much better, finishing in fifth place, 13 1/2 games out of first place. Despite the drop in production, Thomson didn't go unnoticed. The Pittsburgh Pirates, for one, inquired about his services in a potential trade for their own Wally Westlake, but they were unable to offer anything acceptable to the Giants.[11] The Dodgers also showed an interest in Thomson during the winter meetings, but the Giants' price tag of Ralph Branca in return killed the deal.[12]

The Giants didn't fare any better in 1949, but Thomson had what would be considered one of his best seasons, batting .309 with 27 home runs, 109 RBIs, and a .518 slugging percentage. He was a repeat selection as an All-Star, again going hitless in a pinch-hit appearance, but had become a staple in center field for the Giants, playing all of his 156 games at that position. The Giants finished a distant 24 games off the pace. Thomson was still a vital part of their future plans; club officials indicated in the offseason that everyone on the roster was available for trade except Thomson, Whitey Lockman, and pitcher Monte Kennedy.[13] Thomson's defensive skills had matured enough that manager Leo Durocher, commenting on Whitey Lockman, said, "He's the third best outfielder in the league, trailing only Stan Musial and Bobby Thomson."[14]

The Giants went through a major housecleaning before the 1950 season, with a new cast of players built more for speed than power. Thomson led the team with 25 home runs and 85 RBIs, though his batting average fell off to .252. The personnel changes resulted in an improved team that finished third, five games out of first. Thomson hit close to .400 for the final three weeks of the season, a return to form that again earned him mention in trade talks.

Thomson's heroics in 1951 make prior years lose emphasis in establishing his career legacy. The season not only saw a move to third base to make room for rookie Willie Mays (Thomson actually played each outfield position during the season in addition to third base), but the pennant race itself was one of the most exciting in baseball history.

"We got off to a terrible start, and the Dodgers were red hot," Thomson recalled a half-century later. "In July, [Brooklyn manager Charlie] Dressen made his famous remark, 'The Giants is dead,' which really got under our skin. We fell behind 13 games on August 11, but we weren't dead. We began to play better, and the Dodgers slowed down from their torrid first half. By September 14, we had cut their lead to six games, but we only had 12 games left."[15]

The Giants continued to close the gap, and after they beat Boston in their final regular-season game, Brooklyn rallied to beat Philadelphia in 14 innings, setting the stage for a best-of-three-games playoff. Thomson hit his 31st home run in Game One, a 3-1 Giants victory at Ebbets Field. The two-run blast came at the expense of the Dodgers' starter, Ralph Branca. Brooklyn responded with a 10-0 shellacking of the Giants in Game Two, at the Polo Grounds, setting the stage for the deciding game on October 3 at the Polo Grounds.

With Brooklyn leading 1-0, Thomson hit a fly ball in the seventh inning to score Monte Irvin and tie the game, only to see the Dodgers score three runs in the eighth and go up, 4-1. The game entered the bottom of the ninth with Brooklyn's starter, Don Newcombe, still in command. Al Dark and Don Mueller led off with singles, and after Irvin fouled out, Whitey Lockman doubled sharply to left field, scoring Dark and putting runners on second and third with Thomson coming to the plate. "As soon as Whitey hit the ball, I headed for the plate and there's poor Mueller on the ground," Thomson said. "It wasn't until they carried him off the field that I realized he had injured his ankle. The delay kind of broke the tension for a moment. The next thing I remember was Leo Durocher, coming down from the third-base coach's box and putting his arm around my shoulder and saying, 'Bobby, if you ever hit one, hit one now.'"[16] Branca was brought in to relieve Newcombe and get the final two outs.

"Nobody goes up to bat trying to hit a home run in a situation like that," Thomson continued. "If you do, you're almost certain to fail. I was just hoping to make contact."[17]

What happened next remains one of the greatest sporting moments of all time, with Thomson hitting Branca's second pitch into the lower left-field stands, provoking announcer Russ Hodges' unforgettable call and sending the Giants into the World Series against the New York Yankees the next day, a Subway Series they lost in six games.

After the season Thomson's sportswriters' moniker was altered slightly to the Flying Scot from Staten Island. On December 6 he danced a few steps of the highland fling during Bobby Thomson Day, which was celebrated by 1,400 fans in front of the Staten Island Borough Hall.

The dramatic home run linked Thomson and Branca for the remainder of their careers and beyond. The two remained in the New York area for years and developed a friendship, appearing at memorabilia shows and corporate functions. The friendship was tested when the *Wall Street Journal* ran an article in January 2001 headlined "Giants' 1951 Comeback, The Sport's Greatest, Wasn't All It Seemed," that told of an elaborate scheme to steal the signs of the opposition and transmit them to the batter electrically. The article became a book, *The Echoing Green*, published in 2006. For his part, Thomson maintained throughout his life that he didn't receive a stolen sign, telling author Joshua Prager "I was always proud of that swing."[18]

After the pennant winner in 1951, Thomson spent the offseason attending various events, even performing a song with Branca at the annual dinner of the New York baseball writers.[19]

Thomson was an All-Star again in 1952, finally getting a start in the game at third base. He again went hitless, concluding his appearances in All-Star Games without hitting safely in four at-bats. A June 16 game-ending grand slam against Willard Schmidt of the Cardinals spawned memories of the 1951 heroics, and he continued to be productive for the Giants. His 24 home runs again led the the team, but the Giants couldn't recapture the late-season magic of their previous season and finished in second place, 4 1/2 games behind Brooklyn. On December 27 he and Elaine Coley of Plainfield, New Jersey, were married.

By most accounts Thomson was gentle and conservative throughout his career. Author Ray Robinson (*The Home Run Heard 'Round the World*, among others) told of an encounter he had with Thomson at author Dick Schaap's funeral in January 2002. The pair sat together, and after the memorial, Robinson asked Thomson if he had known Dick well. "No, I didn't," Thomson responded. "But he said so many nice things about me, I thought I should come and pay my last respects." Robinson wrote, "It was a typical response for Thomson, who always tried to remain true to his personal ethos: 'If you can bring happiness to somebody, or help somebody, I try to do it.'"[20]

In late 1952 the Braves, soon to move from Boston to Milwaukee, were reported to have an interest in acquiring Thomson, even reportedly offering star pitcher Warren Spahn in a trade.[21] That exchange never came to fruition. With Willie Mays in the Army, Thomson returned to the outfield for the 1953 season and again led the Giants in home runs with 26. The Giants struggled, however, and finished the season in fifth place, 35 games out of first place. With the need for pitching, Thomson's services continued to be a marketable commodity, and on February 1, 1954, the Giants traded Thomson and catcher Sam Calderone to the Milwaukee Braves for pitcher Johnny Antonelli, infielder Billy Klaus, pitcher Don Liddle, catcher Ebba St. Claire, and $50,000. Although the trade was initially a shock, Thomson offered a rational outlook on the change of address. "How do I like it? Why great. What ballplayer wouldn't like being traded to a club that everybody considers a red-hot pennant contender? Naturally, I do feel sorry having to leave New York. However, it's part of baseball to be traded, and this switch I think will do me a lot of good. It was tough keeping up one's spirit with things breaking so badly for the Giants last year."[22]

In their first season in Milwaukee, the 1953 Braves had won 28 more games than in their final season in Boston, and with the addition of Thomson they were considered an instant contender as the 1954 season approached. Optimism was abounding in Milwaukee, and Thomson was slotted to bat cleanup for the first time in his career, a move to protect Eddie Mathews in the lineup. Thomson addressed the opportunity with modesty and appreciation for his new teammate. "I may not get much chance to drive over runs following a guy like Mathews," he said.[23] Thomson didn't get that chance initially. On March 13 he fractured his right ankle sliding into second base in a preseason game against the New York Yankees. The injury hampered Thomson the entire season, and he played in just 43 games, hitting .232 with two home runs.

The injury provided an opportunity for Henry Aaron to join the Braves' starting lineup in his rookie campaign, the second time Thomson had been replaced by a future Hall of Famer (the first was Mays). Suffering from multiple injuries among the ranks, the Braves were left watching at season's end as Thomson's old team, the Giants, won the pennant for the second time in four seasons and carried that momentum to a four-game World Series sweep of the favored Cleveland Indians.

Now 31 years old, Thomson was faced for the first time with the prospect of recovering from a significant injury. With a favorable prognosis by the Braves trainer, Dr. Charles Lacks, manager Charlie Grimm announced early in the winter that Thomson would be his cleanup hitter. Thomson played exclusively in the outfield in 1955, but hit just 12 home runs, and the Braves finished second to the Dodgers. Braves management was disappointed. Trade rumors again mentioned Thomson's name as an expendable, with emerging star Aaron and Bill Bruton considered solid fixtures in the outfield. Once more Thomson endured the offseason, and was still on the Braves roster as the 1956 season opened. His 20 home runs and 74 RBIs, ranked fourth best on a Braves team that now included such sluggers as Aaron, Mathews, and Joe Adcock. Milwaukee finished just one game off the pace to the Dodgers.

Rumors of trades with Thomson's name attached were again prevalent before the 1957 season. Thomson was 33 and considered past his peak by many. The rumors were realized on June 15, when Milwaukee sent Thomson (hitting .236 in 41 games at that point), pitcher Ray Crone, and infielder Danny O'Connell to the Giants for second baseman Red Schoendienst. The move provided minimal benefit to the Giants, as they finished a lowly sixth, 26 games behind the Braves, who won the pennant and went on to win the World Series over the Yankees. For Thomson, it was the second time he was traded from a team that won a World Series the same season.

Traded again at the start of the 1958 season by the Giants (now in San Francisco) to the Chicago Cubs for outfielder/first baseman Bob Speake and cash, Thomson experienced a slight career rebirth, posting respectable numbers of 21 home runs and 82 RBIs to accompany a .283 batting average. He got no closer to a pennant winner, though, as the Cubs were well off the pace, in fifth place.

The story was the same in Chicago in 1959. Although Thomson appeared in 122 games, his career was fading and he was becoming a part-time player, despite contributing a respectable 11 home runs and 52 RBIs. His career and his interest in baseball winding down, Thomson was traded by the Cubs to the Boston Red Sox for pitcher Al Schroll on December 1, 1959. He played just 40 games with the Red Sox in 1960 before being released on July 1. He signed with the Baltimore Orioles and went hitless in three games. His release on July 26, 1960, coincided with his retirement from baseball.

"Times were different then," Thomson said. "I had to work in the offseason, and when I retired, I was married and had a child, and there were no offers for jobs in baseball, as a coach or a scout, so I had to go out and get a job."[24] He worked as a sales executive with the Westvaco paper products Company. "I wanted to get a responsible job, stay home more with my wife and daughter, and live a normal life," Thomson said.[25]

The Thomsons settled in Watchung, New Jersey. They added another daughter and son to their family. Elaine, his wife of over 40 years, died in 1993, and son Bobby Jr. died suddenly the same year, on Father's Day, from a rare virus.

Thomson and Ralph Branca appeared together many times over the years, and their friendship endured all obstacles. "I bleed for Bob about his son," Branca told columnist Dave Anderson in 2001.[26] For his part, Thomson declined to attend the 50th anniversary festivities of the historic home run at a Giants-Dodgers game in San Francisco, mostly in respect for Branca. "They were going to have Ralph and me ride around in a cart," he said. "Ralph doesn't need that."[27]

Thomson finished his career as a three-time All-Star with a batting average of .270 and 264 home runs. He never amassed more than 4.6 percent of the vote in Hall of Fame voting.

Career statistics do not conclusively tell the tale of Bobby Thomson. Remembered throughout his life by one moment in time, in the final analysis, Thomson was a shy and reserved man who consistently tried to fulfill all requests, whether for a story or a simple autograph. "There was no ego in Bobby. He didn't know the word," said Charles "Chick" Harrison, a friend of Thomson's from New Jersey. "He might have been a gem in the baseball world, but he was a gem to everyone who knew him."[28]

"People have asked me if I resent the fact that that 1951 homer is all I'm remembered for," Thomson told *The Scotsman* in 2003. "What I say is, I feel fortunate that I had my one moment in the sun. It's nice to be remembered—and so many people remember where they were when they heard that game on the radio."[29]

Thomson died on August 16, 2010, at his home in Savannah, Georgia. Survived by his daughters Megan and Nancy, he was 86.

Sources

Biegel, Brian, *Miracle Ball* (New York: Crown Publishing, 2009).

Prager, Joshua, *The Echoing Green* (New York: Vintage Books, 2006).

Smith, Ron, *The Sporting News Selects Baseball's 25 Greatest Moments* (Saint Louis: Sporting News Publishing Company, 1999).

Thomson, Bobby with Phil Pepe *Few and Chosen: Defining Giants Greatness Across The Eras* (Chicago: Triumph Books, 2007).

Anderson, Dave, "The Shot Heard 'Round the World: A Fastball, A Swing And Forever." *New York Times*, 2001.

Bathgate, Stuart, "Bobby Thomson: Staten Island Scot brings fame home," *The Scotsman*, 2003.

Biederman, Les, "Meyer Measures Wally for Longer Wallops in Blueprinting Bucco Rise," *The Sporting News*, March 9, 1949.

Burr, Harold C., "Dodgers Seeking First Sacker—Mahatma Admits—But Not Mize," *The Sporting News*, April 13. 1949.

Daniel, Dan, "Thomson, Branca Spark N.Y. Writers' Show," *The Sporting News*, February 13, 1952.

Ellis Nut, Amy, "Baseball legend, ex-N.J. resident Bobby Thomson lived humbled by his 'accidental hero' status," *New Jersey Star-Ledger*, August 18. 2010.

Goldstein, Richard, "Bobby Thomson Dies at 86; Hit Epic Home Run," *New York Times*, August 17, 2010.

Kremenko, Barney, "Lockman, on Tip from Ott, Pegging With More Accuracy," *The Sporting News*, April 15 1950.

Lupica, Mike, "Shot Jolts Bobby Thomson's Memory," *New York Daily News*, September 8, 1998.

Prager, Joshua, "Giants' 1951 Comeback, The Sport's Greatest, Wasn't All It Seemed—Miracle Ended With 'The Shot Heard Round the World'; It Began With a Buzzer—'Papa's' Collapsible Legacy," *Wall Street Journal*, January 31, 2001.

Robinson, Ray, "A Signature Home Run Balanced by Humility," *New York Times*, October 1, 2011.

Smith, Ken, "Only Bobby, Whitey, Monte Left Off Giants' Trade List," *The Sporting News*, October 12, 1949.

Shaikin, Bill, "Bobby Thomson, 1923-2010; his home run was the stuff of legend," *Los Angeles Times*, August 18, 2010.

Thisted, Red, "Bobby the Scot to Get His Fling in Cleanup Spot," *The Sporting News*, March 10, 1954.

Friend, Harold C. "1954 New York Giants Trade Bobby Thomson to Milwaukee Braves for Johnny Antonelli," www.Bleacherreport.com, January 12, 2013.

Baseball-Almanac.com

Baseball-Reference.com

Retrosheet.org

Notes

1. Ron Smith, *The Sporting News Selects Baseball's 25 Greatest Moments* (St. Louis: Sporting News Publishing Company, 1999).
2. Mike Lupica, "Shot Jolts Bobby Thomson's Memory," *New York Daily News*, September 8, 1998.
3. Ibid.
4. Bobby Thomson with Phil Pepe, *Few and Chosen: Defining Giants Greatness Across the Eras* (Chicago: Triumph Books, 2007), X.
5. Bill Shaikin, "Bobby Thomson, 1923-2010; his home run was the stuff of legend," *Los Angeles Times*, August 18, 2010.
6. Bobby Thomson with Phil Pepe, XII.
7. Ibid.
8. "Bobby Thomson, Giant Hero," baseball-almanac.com.
9. Bobby Thomson with Phil Pepe, XIII.
10. Bobby Thompson with Phil Pepe, XIV.
11. Les Biederman, "Meyer Measures Wally for Longer Wallops in Blueprinting Bucco Rise," *The Sporting News*, March 9, 1949, 6.
12. Harold C. Burr, "Dodgers Seeking First Sacker—Mahatma Admits—But Not Mize," *The Sporting News*, April 13 1949, 2.
13. Ken Smith, "Only Bobby, Whitey, Monte Left Off Giants' Trade List," *The Sporting News*, October 12, 1949, 36.
14. Barney Kremenko, "Lockman, on Tip from Ott, Pegging With More Accuracy," *The Sporting News*, April 5, 1950, 15.
15. Bobby Thomson with Phil Pepe, XVI.
16. Bobby Thomson with Phil Pepe, XIX.
17. Ibid.
18. Joshua Prager, "Giants' 1951 Comeback, The Sport's Greatest, Wasn't All It Seemed—Miracle Ended With 'The Shot Heard Round the World'; It Began With a Buzzer—'Papa's' Collapsible Legacy, *Wall Street Journal*, January 31, 2001.
19. Dan Daniel, "Thomson, Branca Spark N.Y. Writers' Show," *The Sporting News*, February 13, 1952, 15.
20. Ray Robinson, "A Signature Home Run Balanced by Humility," *New York Times*, October 1, 2011.
21. Dan Daniel, "Dodgers Offer 4 Players to Reds for Perkowski and Joe Adcock," *The Sporting News*, December 7, 1952.
22. Harold C. Friend, "1954 New York Giants Trade Bobby Thomson to Milwaukee Braves for Johnny Antonelli," *Bleacher Report*, www.bleacherreport.com.
23. Red Thisted, "Bobby the Scot to Get His Fling in Cleanup Spot," *The Sporting News*, 1954, March 10, 1954.
24. Bobby Thomson with Phil Pepe, XXII.
25. Richard Goldstein, "Bobby Thomson Dies at 86; Hit Epic Home Run," *New York Times*, August 17, 2010.
26. Dave Anderson, "The Shot Heard 'Round The World: A Fastball, a Swing And Forever," *New York Times*, October 1, 2001.
27. Ibid.
28. Amy Ellis Nut, "Baseball legend, ex-N.J. resident Bobby Thomson lived humbled by his 'accidental hero' status, *New Jersey Star-Ledger*, August 18, 2010.
29. Stuart Bathgate, "Bobby Thomson: Staten Island Scot brings fame home," *The Scotsman*, December 6, 2003.

Frank Torre

by Norm King

WITH HIS CHARACTER and the way he has given back to the game, Frank Torre is far more than just Joe Torre's big brother.

Frank Torre spent seven seasons in the majors as a first baseman with the Milwaukee Braves and Philadelphia Phillies. He was known more for his defensive prowess at first base than his hitting, leading the National League twice in fielding but hitting only 13 career home runs. During his career he was often platooned with a right-handed hitter or was inserted in the late innings as a defensive replacement.

Torre wasn't your average baseball lifer. True, he remained involved in the game after his on-field career ended, but unlike former players who stayed in the game in a coaching or administrative capacity, Frank got into the business of selling balls and bats to major leaguers and the public alike.

Frank Joseph Torre was born in Brooklyn, New York, on December 30, 1931, the fourth of Joseph and Margaret Torre's five children (brother Joe came 8 1/2 years later). His father was a detective with the New York police department, then became a scout for the Milwaukee Braves from 1955 to 1961 and the Baltimore Orioles from 1962 until he died in 1971. He was physically abusive to their mother and verbally abusive to the children. In the book he wrote with Joe Torre, *The Yankee Years*, Tom Verducci wrote, "He so feared his father that if (Joe) Torre saw his father's car parked outside the house when he came home from school, Torre would just keep on walking."[1]

Joe also told the story about how Frank's courage brought the terror to an end: "One winter, when I was 12, my older brother Frank [then 20] said to my father, 'We want you out of the house. We don't want anything other than the house we live in. We don't want anything from you. Just leave.' And he left."[2]

Despite growing up in a difficult family situation, Frank was an excellent athlete; he was a highly regarded left-handed pitcher at James Madison High School, even though he wanted to play first base. He was so good that he was chosen to pitch in the 1949 Hearst all-star game in New York. The game was founded by *New York Journal-American* sports editor Max Kase in 1945. It pitted players from New York high schools against their peers from across the country and continued until the late 1970s. Pitcher Torre lost the game to future teammate Gene Conley.

Torre finally got his chance as an infielder after he signed with the Boston Braves as a free agent in 1951. The scout who signed him was John "Honey" Russell, for whom scouting was a sideline. Russell was better known as a basketball coach at Seton Hall University in New Jersey, and was also the first coach of the Boston Celtics in the NBA. "I'd like to see him there (first base)," said Russell in a 1954 interview. "His only weak-

Frank Torre (National Baseball Hall of Fame Library, Cooperstown, N.Y.)

ness is that he can't run very fast, but he can do everything else — field, hit and throw."[3]

Russell's assessment that Torre was more effective at first base than on the mound proved correct. "When I reported to Hartford [Class A Eastern League] in 1951, Tommy Holmes, then managing there, gave me my chance to play first base," said Torre. "Later that season, with Denver [Class A Western League], Andy Cohen gave me a chance to pitch in a losing game. The first batter hit a home run almost a mile, but I retired the side and that was the first and only inning I pitched in Organized Ball."[4]

Torre was drafted into the US Army in 1952. He spent 14 months in Korea and was discharged in time for spring training 1954. Before shipping out, he was stationed at Fort Dix, New Jersey, and was the cleanup hitter on the military base's ballclub.

Torre played with Double-A Atlanta (Southern Association) in 1954, and was promoted to Triple-A Toledo (American Association) in 1955 before making it to the big leagues in 1956. While his .327 batting average at Toledo, seven home runs, and 73 RBIs were impressive in themselves, Torre also came to the Braves with a solid reputation as an excellent defensive first baseman. George Selkirk, his manager at Toledo, called him "the greatest fielding first baseman" he had seen in his 29 years in baseball.[5] Torre also had an excellent eye at the plate, having struck out only 53 times in 1,309 minor-league at-bats.[6]

Those numbers and that reputation were essential if Torre was to crack the Milwaukee lineup in 1956. The Braves were an up-and-coming power in the NL, having finished second to the eventual World Series champion Brooklyn Dodgers the previous season. As well, they had an established first baseman in Joe Adcock. Adcock's solid 1956 season, in which he hit 38 home runs and had 103 RBIs, limited Torre's playing time during his rookie year to 159 at-bats with a .258 batting average, no home runs, and only 16 runs batted in. He finished second among the league's first basemen in fielding percentage (.993).

Although Torre's numbers weren't going to win him Rookie of the Year honors, he did have his moments. Adcock's excellent season got off to a poor start, and Torre took over at first base on May 20 after Adcock's batting average dipped to .197. Torre proceeded to hit safely in the first eight games he started. On May 26 he drove in both runs in an 11-inning 2-1 win over Cincinnati, and followed that up the next day with four hits in a 7-2 Braves victory over the Redlegs (the franchise was known as the Redlegs from 1954-1959 because they didn't want their name associated with communism during the McCarthy era). Adcock reasserted his place in the lineup on June 17 when he belted three homers in a doubleheader sweep of the Dodgers. That sweep wasn't enough, however, as the Braves again finished in second place in what turned out to be a last hurrah for the Boys of Summer.

Torre began the 1957 season as a pinch-hitter and late-inning defensive replacement at first base, but that all changed on June 23, when Adcock broke his leg in a collision at second base. While management knew that the team was just as good defensively with Torre at first, he could not produce power numbers as Adcock could. His playing every day also meant that the team's depth took a hit. "Their bench was not overpowering to begin with, and without Torre it became downright weak," wrote Bob Wolf in *The Sporting News*.[7]

The Braves stayed in the race despite Adcock's injury as Torre proved to be more than a capable replacement. In fact, manager Fred Haney didn't rush to reinsert Adcock into the regular lineup when he returned to action on Labor Day. He didn't need to, as Torre's performance on the holiday attested. Frank reached base seven times and tied a modern record for a nine-inning game with six runs scored as the Braves walloped the Cubs 23-10 in the first game of a doubleheader. For the season, Torre batted .272 with five home runs and 40 RBIs. He also had the highest fielding percentage in the NL among first basemen (.996).

That season Milwaukee won the franchise's first pennant since moving to the city from Boston in 1953 by a convincing eight games over the St. Louis Cardinals and defeated the New York Yankees in a World Series that went the distance. The 1957 fall classic is known for Lew Burdette's three victories over the Bronx Bombers, but Torre had a spectacular Series as well, hitting .300 with two home runs (only Hank Aaron, with three, had more, while Adcock didn't have any) and three RBIs, along with a perfect 1.000 fielding percentage. Torre was the only player besides Aaron who both played in all seven games and hit .300 or better. His fourth-inning shot in Game Four was his first home run ever at Milwaukee's County Stadium.

As 1958 spring training got under way, Braves manager Fred Haney was saying that he was going to platoon Torre and Adcock at first base with Torre facing right-handers and Adcock in against lefties. Torre accepted the situation well. "Sure you're sharper if you play all the time, but I've arrived at the point where I'm ready whenever Fred calls on me to play," he said. "It just means I'll have to work harder in practice to stay in shape."[8]

The platoon system worked well early. By mid-May, the two had combined for a .314 batting average, and Adcock had already hit six home runs with 12 RBIs. Torre finally hit his first homer of the season on May 22, his first-ever regular-season home run in front of the hometown fans. Since they were both hitting so well, Haney decided to keep Torre at first and switch Adcock to left field. It had been so long since Adcock had played outfield that he had to borrow the glove he had given his 13-year-old brother-in-law as a present.[9]

Torre ended up having his best offensive season as a major leaguer as Milwaukee repeated as NL champion. He had career highs in games played (138), home runs (six), RBIs (55), and batting average (.309). He also retained his NL fielding percentage title (.994). Then he had a dreadful World Series as the Yankees returned the favor from the previous year and defeated the Braves in seven games. Torre again played every game, but hit only .176 with no homers and only one RBI. He also committed two errors in Game Seven, leading to two Yankee runs.

Adcock began the 1959 season as the regular first baseman until a slow start by the team prompted Haney to return to the platooning system. Each player ended up appearing in 115 games, and while Adcock's numbers remained consistent (.292, 25 home runs, 76 RBIs), Torre's numbers fell off a cliff (.228, one home run, 33 RBIs). He continued his excellent fielding, as he finished second in the league in fielding percentage (.994). As a team, the Braves made a valiant effort to win their third consecutive pennant, but lost a best-of-three playoff to the Los Angeles Dodgers in two straight games.

Frank's 1960 season got off to a poor start when he landed in the hospital briefly with a kidney ailment. It didn't get any better when it became apparent that Adcock had learned to hit the ball the other way. Adcock had an all-star season, batting .298 with 25 home runs and 91 RBIs. Torre, on the other hand, found out that glove was not enough and was optioned along with his .205 batting average to the Triple-A Louisville Colonels of the American Association on June 30. Torre, understandably, was not happy. "I can't afford not to go to Louisville," he said, "but I won't continue playing in the minors after this year. I'd give up the game first."[10]

He stayed with Louisville for most of its season and was a September call-up to Milwaukee but did not appear in a game. All in all, Torre played in only 21 games for the Braves in 1960 and hit .205 with no home runs and five RBIs. He then returned to Louisville to help them win the Junior World Series in six games over the International League's Toronto Maple Leafs. He even contributed a homer in the clincher.

Apparently Torre's threat to quit if he remained in the minors for 1961 proved hollow, as he continued to play in the minor leagues. The Braves assigned him to Louisville in December 1960, but he spent the 1961 season with their other Triple-A affiliate, the Vancouver Mounties. His numbers were respectable: a .307 batting average, 13 home runs (a career best), and 63 RBIs, but he never suited up for Milwaukee again. While he was riding the buses, brother Joe began his major-league career as a catcher with the Braves on May 20. The Philadelphia Phillies purchased Frank's contract on December 2, 1961.

Torre's 1962 season was modest as he again played a backup role behind the Phillies' regular first baseman, Roy Sievers. He was homerless for the third time in his major-league career, although he did hit .310 in 168 at-bats with 20 RBIs. One highlight for Torre was his first game against the Braves, on May 3. He had a double, two singles, and three runs batted in as he led his new team to a 9-8 victory. On that day, Frank played on the same major-league diamond as Joe for the first time, although Joe had to leave the game in the second inning after being hit on the elbow by a pitch.

Frank saw even less playing time in 1963, appearing in only 92 games and batting .250. He hit what turned out to be his last major-league home run on September 28 against Phil Ortega of the Dodgers in a 12-3 Phillies rout of the eventual World Series champions. Torre called it a career for good after his contract was sold to Triple-A Little Rock of the American Association.

After his playing career ended, Frank entered the sporting-goods business. Initially he and Joe operated a sporting-goods store. Frank then joined Adirondack Bats and became manager of the company's professional division. Part of that job consisted of visiting all the major-league spring-training facilities in a trailer that served as a portable bat factory (Yes, the trailer was referred to as a "bat-mobile"[11]) that provided custom-made bats to major leaguers. Inside the trailer were Adirondack craftsmen, as well as a special lathe and other equipment that produced a custom bat in 30 minutes that even included the player's own signature.

Torre later became a vice president at Rawlings Sporting Goods. Both Rawlings and Adirondack were divisions of the same company, A-T-O Incorporated.

The brothers Torre shared the spotlight in October 1996 when Frank underwent heart transplant surgery the night before Joe won his first World Series championship as manager of the New York Yankees. The operation was performed by Dr. Mehmet Oz, who later hosted the *Dr. Oz Show* on TV. That seemed appropriate for the father of five and grandfather of 11, who played with heart and was a wizard with the glove. Torre and Oz celebrated the tenth anniversary of the surgery in 2006.[12]

A new heart gave Torre a chance to continue charitable work and to receive honors for his contributions and achievements. After recovering from the heart transplant, he became active in promoting organ donation and in 1999 received Street and Smith's Mickey Mantle Foundation Courage Award for his efforts in raising awareness about organ donation.

Torre was elected to James Madison High's Wall of Fame in 2002. Other alumni so honored include US Supreme Court Justice Ruth Bader Ginsburg, baseball labor executive Marvin Miller, and Nobel Prize winners Robert Solow (economics) and Stanley Cohen (medicine).

In 2007 Torre needed another organ, this time a kidney; his daughter Elizabeth was the donor.

Living in retirement with his wife, Anne, in Palm Beach Gardens, Florida, he continued his charitable work. He was named to the board of the Baseball Assistance Team, an organization that provides financial assistance to former major- and minor-league players. His son Frank Jr. followed his father into baseball as a high-school coach.[13]

Sources

Greater New York Sandlot Athletic Alliance: http://www.gnysaa.org

James Madison High School Alumni Association: http://www.james-madisonalumni.org

Archives of the New York City's Mayor's Office: http://www.nyc.gov/html/om/html/99a/pr261-99.html

Notes

1. Joe Torre and Tom Verducci, *The Yankee Years* (New York: Doubleday Books, 2009), 13.
2. Safe at Home Foundation website: http://www.joetorre.org/for-youth/stuff-2-know/joe-torres-story/.
3. Dick Young, *The Sporting News*, January 27, 1954.
4. "Sold on Braves by Friendly Scout," *The Sporting News*, January 8, 1958.
5. Bob Wolf, "Rookie Roundup," *The Sporting News*, April 4, 1956.
6. Ibid.
7. Bob Wolf, "Long-Faced Haney Yearns for Long-Ball Replacement," *The Sporting News*, July 3, 1957.
8. "Bunts and Boots," *The Sporting News*, March 26, 1958.
9. "Adcock Returns to Outfield—Idle With Borrowed Glove," *The Sporting News*, July 2, 1958.
10. Bob Wolf, "Torre Accepts Assignment to Minors 'Only for 1960,'" *The Sporting News*, July 13, 1960.
11. Jack Lang, "A Mobile Bat Factory Serves Major Camps," *The Sporting News*, March 21, 1970.
12. Columbia University Medical Centre Department of Surgery website: http://www.columbiasurgery.org/news/2006_hearttx_torre.html.
13. Matt Porter, "With a rich family history in baseball, Frank Torre Jr. rekindles his love for the game," *Palm Beach Post*, February 9, 2011.

Bob Trowbridge

By Nancy Snell Griffith

RIGHT-HANDED PITCHER Bob Trowbridge was one of those players who came into the majors with amazing potential, but, for a variety of reasons, was never able to capitalize on it. After he was signed by the Boston Braves in 1950, he played only one season in the minors before he had to enter the military. While his record at Nellis Air Force Base was amazing, he missed out on three years of big-league competition and skillful coaching. When he finally joined the Braves (by then relocated to Milwaukee) in April 1956, he was part of a high-powered staff that featured Warren Spahn, Lew Burdette, and Bob Buhl, and was used mostly in relief. So although he signed straight out of high school, and appeared in a World Series only seven seasons later, his career was far from outstanding.

Robert "Bob" Trowbridge was born in Hudson, New York, on June 27, 1930. His parents were William (a foreman at a match company, according to the 1940 US Census, most probably Universal Match) and Julia (a machine operator in a sweater mill). He had an older brother, William, 21 at the time of the census and a finisher in a cloth factory.

Trowbridge played high-school baseball, and averaged 15 strikeouts per game.[1] He was soon attracting major-league scouts. Early on, a scout for the New York Giants took him to the Polo Grounds for a tryout. Afterward, the scout tried to persuade him to play Class D baseball, but Bob declined the offer. Trowbridge was also being pursued by scouts from the Brooklyn Dodgers, the Boston Red Sox, and the Cleveland Indians, but it was Dewey Griggs, a veteran scout for the Boston Braves, who eventually signed him as a free agent in 1950.[2]

Trowbridge was assigned to the Eau Claire Bears of the Class C Northern League, where he appeared in 36 games, half of which he started. He compiled a record of 16-8 and a 2.97 earned-run average. He spent the next three years in the military, and pitched for the team at Nellis Air Force Base in Nevbada. There he compiled a three-year record of 60-6 and struck out more than 1,200 batters. Trowbridge refused to kid himself about all those strikeouts, however. In 1955 he told the *Toledo Blade* that "they were mostly against pickups and high school players. … They don't really count."[3]

In 1954, his first year out of the military, Trowbridge did go to spring training with the Braves. Although he "gave Braves' officials quite an eyeful," he did not have a wide enough variety of pitches.[4] He was sent to the minors and pitched in 32 games for the Jacksonville Braves of the Class A South Atlantic League and two games for the Atlanta Crackers of the Double-A Southern Association. Trowbridge struck out 195 batters for Jacksonville[5] and pitched the Braves to the championship in the last game of the season, giving up only five hits and striking out 13.[6] His combined record with the Braves and the Crackers was 18-9, with a 2.90 ERA. In late September, the Braves, who had moved to Milwaukee, got the rights to Trowbridge, Paul Cave, and Bob Giggie, from the Crackers in exchange for catcher Bill Casey.[7]

Bob Trowbridge (National Baseball Hall of Fame Library, Cooperstown, N.Y.)

By January 20, 1955, Trowbridge and Bobby Buhl had signed their contracts.[8] Fans were beginning to learn more about the rookie right-hander. During the offseason he enjoyed bowling, and had an average of around 175. He had cut down on this hobby, however, lest he injure his pitching arm. He was also planning to marry his high-school sweetheart, secretary Frances Leck, in May.[9] Trowbridge was at spring training with the Braves in 1955, and was described as a "rookie fireball pitcher." He had worked on his curve while he was in the minors, and had planned to play winter ball in Puerto Rico, but quickly developed a sore arm and returned home. According to sportswriter Lou Chapman, this sore arm turned out to be a "blessing in disguise," because it limited Trowbridge's ability to throw the fastball and gave him a chance to perfect his curve and learn to pitch a slider from Braves pitching coach Bucky Walters.[10]

Trowbridge spent most of the 1955 season with the Toledo Sox of the Triple-A American Association. On May 27 he pitched a one-hitter, and the *Toledo Blade* called him "one of the Milwaukee Braves' most valuable minor league pitchers," adding, "Bob has one of the fanciest strikeout marks in the minors." Although, as mentioned before, Trowbridge discounted his many strikeouts while he was in the service, the *Blade* declared, "He's chalking up some that do count in his first Triple-A season. He had 10 more last night for a total of 52 in 58 innings. In his last 18 innings he has been hit for only five singles."[11] On July 28 he pitched a two-hitter against Omaha.[12] He pitched 182 innings in 28 starts and one relief appearance for Toledo that year, had a record of 13-8 and an ERA of 3.66, and struck out 135.[13] In late September the Braves sent four players to the minors and called up Trowbridge and Carleton Willey "to bolster their shaken mound staff."[14]

In 1956 Trowbridge was back at spring training once again. According to sportswriter Bob Wolf, he had been transformed from a thrower to a pitcher largely because of the influence of two men and his own determination to be a major-league ball player: "Whitlow Wyatt, who managed Trowbridge briefly at Atlanta two years ago and now is a Philadelphia Philly coach, was one. Charlie Root, coach at Toledo last season and of the Braves now, was the other. 'Wyatt discovered that I wasn't even holding the ball right,' Trowbridge recalled Tuesday. 'When I got that corrected he started teaching me how to throw a slider … didn't use it much until last year at Toledo. Now it's my best clutch pitch, especially against left handers.'" Root "'found that I was standing on the mound wrong,' Trowbridge said. 'He told me to point my right foot straight ahead instead of off to the right. That helped my control a lot.'" Trowbridge felt that he had lost a little speed in order to pick up his new control, but Wolf still felt he was "faster than most of the pitchers around. … If Trowbridge fails to stick this time it probably will be because of the heavy traffic on the Braves' well stocked pitching staff."[15] With a staff that sported Spahn, Burdette, and Buhl, it was an uphill battle for sure.

Trowbridge appeared in his first major-league game on April 22, 1956. He came in during the seventh inning of a losing effort against St. Louis. He gave up a run-scoring single and struck out one in the seventh, held the Cardinals hitless and got one strikeout in the eighth, and then was taken out for a pinch-hitter in the ninth. By mid-May the Braves had optioned him to Wichita subject to a 24-hour recall.[16] He pitched in eight games for Wichita, compiling a record of 3-3. The Braves recalled him in mid-June, but because of their already heavy pitching staff, they switched him from a starter to a long reliever.[17] Although he was hit just below the elbow by a line drive hit by Lee Walls of the Pirates in mid-July, he recovered in time to pitch a one-hit shutout in a 3-0 exhibition victory over the International League all-star team in Toronto a week later.[18]

On August 4 Trowbridge picked up his first major-league win with 4 1/2 innings of relief in Pittsburgh. Four days later he pitched his first complete game, giving up six hits and striking out eight in a 10-1 victory over the Cardinals.[19] He ended the season having appeared in 19 games, only four of which he started. His record was 3-2, he had an ERA of 2.66, and he struck out 40 in 50 2/3 innings.

Trowbridge started the 1957 season with the Braves, but after having pitched only three innings, in mid-May he was once again optioned to Wichita on a 24-hour recall basis.[20] He appeared in three games for Wichita, and had a record of 2-0. By June 1 he was back in Milwaukee. Trowbridge started on June 9 and emerged with a victory in game one of a doubleheader against the Pirates, pitching ten of 11 innings during the contest. According to the United Press, the doubleheader split "proved a couple of things about the Braves' pitching staff: Bob Trowbridge looks like he can hold his own in the majors, but maybe Juan Pizarro is overmatched." (Ironically, Pizarro, who started and lost the second game, eventually ended up with 13 more major-league seasons than Trowbridge.) Trowbridge himself said that his stint in Wichita was "a blessing in disguise.... I got some steady work down there and it helped my control a lot. That was just about what I needed."[21]

Trowbridge seemed to hit his stride during the last month of the season. On September 2, in the second game of a doubleheader against the Chicago Cubs, he pitched a three-hit shutout. In his first major-league shutout, and his first victory since July 29, he struck out nine and did not allow a runner to reach third base.[22] Ten days later, in a victory over the Dodgers, Trowbridge took over from Bob Buhl in the fourth inning and allowed only four hits in the next 5 1/2 innings.[23] On September 17 he pitched a five-hitter against New York; he had allowed only five earned runs during the previous 35 innings he'd pitched.[24] The Braves clinched the NL pennant on September 23. Trowbridge appeared in 32 games (126 innings) during the season, and had 16 starts. His record was 7-5, his ERA was 3.64, and he struck out 75. With a fielding percentage of 1.000, Trowbridge tied ten other National League hurlers for tops in that defensive category.

Trowbridge appeared once during the 1957 World Series, but had a disastrous outing. He entered in the top of the seventh inning of the third game with New York leading 7-3, and gave up two hits (including a home run), three walks, and five earned runs. While the Braves lost that game, they went on to take the series from the Yankees in seven games.

By mid-October Trowbridge, Hank Aaron, and Braves equipment manager Joe Taylor had signed on as sports promotion representatives for a Milwaukee brewery. Trowbridge was slated to travel throughout the country giving talks about baseball.[25] During one of these talks, at the Troy, New York, Kiwanis Club Ladies' Night, Trowbridge, perhaps sensing that his own career was winding down, combined baseball chatter with more serious advice to the parents in attendance. He told them that "young men looking forward to a professional sports career 'should pursue an education first. This sequence,' Mr. Trowbridge said, 'would give the young man an occupational background to fit him for his life after 35, at which time, most sports figures have reached the end of their careers.'"[26]

In 1958 Trowbridge worked mainly out of the bullpen. On July 9 he struck out seven in 4 2/3 innings against the Dodgers. He also gave up five hits, a walk, and three runs, and the Braves lost, 10-3. On August 3 he pitched seven innings of no-hit relief in a 4-3 victory over the San Francisco Giants. With Milwaukee already down 3-0, Trowbridge took over from starter Gene Conley in the third inning with two men on base and no outs. He got Orlando Cepeda to pop out, after which Daryl Spencer hit into a double play. After that, the only two Giant baserunners were on a walk and an error.[27] Trowbridge appeared in 27 games that season, starting four of them. His record was 1-3, his ERA 3.93, and he struck out 31 batters in 55 innings. Milwaukee won the pennant again in 1958, but Trowbridge did not appear during the World Series loss to New York

Trowbridge's career was on the decline. He appeared in 16 games for the Braves in 1959, none of which were starts. His record was 1-0, and his ERA 5.93. He struck out 22 batters in 30 1/3 innings. His last appearance for Milwaukee came on August 18. After the season, on October 12, Milwaukee sold him to the Kansas City Athletics. The Athletics, by all accounts, were happy to have Trowbridge, praising his fastball and curve, and stating that he had never been "given the opportunity to show his stuff with the Braves."[28] He appeared in 22 games for the A's in 1960, only one of which was a start. His record was 1-3, and his ERA 4.61. He had the fewest strikeouts of his professional career, 33 in 68 1/3 innings pitched. He appeared in his final major-league game on July 24, 1960, and was then sent to the Dallas-Fort Worth Rangers of the American Association to make room for Don Larsen.[29] With the Rangers Trowbridge appeared in nine games, compiling a record of 0-5 and an ERA of 4.78. Over the course of his major-league career, he appeared in 116 games, 25 of which were starts. His record was 13-13, and his ERA was 3.95.

Trowbridge spent the 1961 season with the Rochester Red Wings and the Syracuse Chiefs of the International League. In nine games he had neither wins nor losses with an ERA of 4.50. Amazingly, he batted 1.000 that year, albeit in only two trips to the plate. That season proved to be the end of Trowbridge's minor-league career. He appeared in 128 games in the minors, 80 of which he started. He won 52 games and lost 33 and an ERA of 3.29. He returned to Hudson, where he eventually began work at the Hudson Correctional Facility. There he and his wife raised three daughters and a son. When, at the age of 49, he died of a blood clot in his heart on April 3, 1980, he was survived by his children, his wife, Frances, his mother, and his brother William.[30] He is buried in the Cedar Park Cemetery in Hudson. His wife died in 2007. In 2011 Bob Trowbridge was named to the inaugural class at the Capital District Baseball Hall of Fame in Albany.[31]

Sources

Ancestry.com (biographical information, local newspapers)

Baseball-Reference.com (stats, biographical information, minor league information)

Retrosheet.org (Stats, biographical information, information on individual appearances)

Notes

1 Lou Chapman, "Rookie Bob Trowbridge Has Speed to Burn," *Milwaukee Sentinel*, March 23, 1955, 19.

2 Chapman, 19.

3 "Bob (1-Hit) Trowbridge Fans 52 in 58 Innings," *Toledo Blade*, May 29, 1955, 25.

4 Chapman, 19.

5 Jacksonville Joe Reichler, "More Good Pitching Talent on Way to Braves Wigwam," *Waukesha* (Wisconsin) *Daily Freeman*, January 28, 1955, 10.

6 Chapman, 19.

7 "Braves Gain Three Hurlers for Catcher," (United Press) *Oshkosh Daily Northwestern*, September 24, 1954, 15.

8 "Milwaukee Signs Two," (Associated Press) *Bedford* (Pennsylvania) *Gazette*, January 20, 1955.

9 Chapman, 19.

10 Chapman, 19.

11 *Toledo Blade*, "Bob (1-Hit) Trowbridge,"

12 "Regalado Homers in Indians' Win," (Associated Press) *Fergus Falls* (Minnesota) *Daily Journal*, July 29, 1955, 8.

13 "Braves Bank on 4 Rookies," (Associated Press) *Miami* (Florida) *News*, January 18, 1956, 17.

14 "Braves Shift Eight Players," (Associated Press) *Waukesha* (Wisconsin) *Daily Freeman*, September 23, 1955, 10.

15 Bob Wolf, "Bob Trowbridge back at Braves Camp Again and This Time He Has a Good Chance to Stay," *Milwaukee Journal*, February 29, 1956, 26.

16 "Major League Clubs Reduce," (Associated Press) *Frederick* (Maryland) *Post*, May 17, 1956, 9.

17 "Braves Recall Pitcher," *New York Times*, June 18, 1956, 28.

18 "Braves Squelch Listless Pirates," *Sheboygan Press*, July 16, 1956, 20; "Exhibition Results," *Berkshire Eagle* (Pittsfield Massachusetts), July 24, 1956, 5.

19 "Cincy Pulls Within Half Game of Bums," (United Press) *Nevada State Journal* (Reno), August 9, 1956: 10.

20 "Braves Option Pair," (Associated Press) *New York Times*, May 16, 1957, 50.

21 "Trowbridge can Win; Pizarro Overmatched," (United Press) *Wisconsin Rapids Daily Tribune*, June 10, 1957, 6.

22 *Bridgeport* (Connecticut) *Post*, Sept. 3, 1957, 24.

23 "Braves Boost Lead to Five; ChiSox Win," (United Press) *Nevada State Journal (Reno)*, September 13, 1957, 16.

24 "Trowbridge Notches Victories," *Coshocton* (Ohio) *Tribune*, September 18, 1957, 12.

25 "Baseball Was Never Like This," (AP Wirephoto) *Montana Standard* (Butte), October 21, 1957, 7.

26 "Kiwanis Club Observes Ladies Night," *Troy* (New York) *Record*, February 19, 1958, 14.

27 "Braves Sweep Series from Giants…" (Associated Press) *Ironwood* (Michigan) *Daily Globe*, August 4, 1958, 8.

28 "Braves Peddle Bob Trowbridge to Kansas City" (United Press International) *Sheboygan* (Wisconsin) *Press*, October 13, 1959, 24.

29 "Athletics Recall Larsen after 3 Weeks at Dallas," (United Press International) *New York Times*, July 30, 1960, 10.

30 "Bob Trowbridge," *New York Times*, April 5, 1980, 26.

31 Mark McGuire, A Hall Filled With Baseball Talent," *Albany Times Union*, October 30, 2011.

Fred Haney

by Jim Gordon

Fred Girard Haney touched all the bases in a 65-year baseball career that led him from athletic stardom in high school to the general manager's office of the Los Angeles Angels. Along the way, he was a player, coach, scout, World Series-winning manager, broadcaster, and general manager. On the field Fred was a fierce competitor, disputing calls and plays with opponents, umpires, and fans. Off the field he was a devoted family man, with many lifelong friends and a heart for charitable works, particularly those involving youth, veterans, and baseball.

Haney was born on April 25, 1898, in Bernalillo, New Mexico Territory, the fourth and youngest son of William J. and Frances Haney. (Various accounts give his year of birth as 1896, 1897, and 1898, but the latter year is what is on his tombstone.) After the family relocated to Los Angeles, he attended Polytechnic High School, where he was a four-year letterman in three sports. Named twice to the All-California Interscholastic football team, the holder of several swimming titles, a member of the water polo team, and the city's junior handball champion, Haney was one of the first great high-school athletes of Los Angeles.

After spending part of 1919 Portland Buckaroos of the Class B Pacific Coast International League, Haney tried out with the Los Angeles Angels of the Pacific Coast League for the 1919 season and made the team as an infielder. Listed as 5-feet-6 and weighing 170 pounds, he unsurprisingly acquired the nickname Pudge. Despite his weight, he was fast and used his speed to advantage throughout his baseball career.

Haney made the Angels squad again in 1920 as a backup. That June he married his high-school sweetheart and he and Florence began a life and baseball partnership that lasted more than 55 years. Shortly after their wedding, Haney was sent to Omaha of the Class A Western League, where he blossomed. Haney was an aggressive negotiator and for the 1921 season achieved a clause that granted him one-fourth of the purchase price if he was sold to the majors. His play at Omaha attracted the Detroit Tigers, who purchased his contract for $5,000 and four players: Babe Herman, future Hall of Famer Heinie Manush, George Grantham, and Bill Baumgartner. Haney got his $1,250 but when he asked for more because of the players involved, he was asked which quarter of the players he wanted. For years, Haney liked to tell his fellow Angeleno Babe Herman that he owned 25 percent of him, and the Babe usually responded with, "Get out your knife and start cutting."

In 1922 Ty Cobb, beginning his second year of managing the Tigers, developed an affinity for the brash, hustling youngster and gave Haney an opportunity to play a key reserve role. Fred took full advantage of the opportunity, batting a remarkable .352 and playing several positions. He got national attention in midseason in *The Sporting News:* "Manager Ty Cobb has gotten some wonderful work out of recruits on the Detroit Tigers. ... A notable instance is Fred Haney who was called up from Omaha. ... One of the strong points in Haney's favor is that he has the old never-quit spirit highly developed, and that is just what Cobb demands."

Fred Haney (National Baseball Hall of Fame Library, Cooperstown, N.Y.)

Shortly after this article appeared, the fiery rookie got his first suspension and fine.[1] Cobb influenced much of Haney's approach to the game. The two shared a sense of competitiveness, aggressiveness, and desire to win, and remained lifelong friends. Haney stayed with Detroit through the 1925 season. After the season, Haney was traded to the Boston Red Sox for infielder Homer Ezzell and outfielder Tex Vache. The Haneys' only child, Patricia, was born in Michigan during the season.

Haney won the starting third base job for the Red Sox in 1926 but hit only .221 although he did lead the team on stolen bases. In July 1927 he was sold to the Chicago Cubs and subsequently was sold to Indianapolis of the American Association, where he started at third base and hit well.

Haney returned to Indianapolis for the 1928 season and had the best year of his career. He hit well with power and led the league in stolen bases. This was Haney's breakout year as a basestealer, and it would become his hallmark on the field. When the St. Louis Cardinals purchased his contract, he made an unusual demand the negotiations: If he did not make the team, he wanted the right to purchase his release or to be released to a PCL team. By now he had an insurance business with 29 branches in California, and if he was to be in the minors, he wanted to be near his work.

On May 7, 1929, Haney was sold to the Los Angeles Angels of the PCL. He was an immediate sensation, hitting well, stealing bases and energizing the Angels. On September 16 Haney used some of his old football skills by throwing what was termed an illegal block into Hollywood shortstop Dud Lee to break up a double play. The umpire failed to call interference and the Angels rallied for three runs to help their victory. Haney led the league with 56 stolen bases even though he played only two-thirds of the season. The 1930 season was another excellent one for him. Early in the year he had a streak of 36 errorless games at third base. He was the first man to lead the PCL in steals for two consecutive seasons.

Haney's expectation of another banner year in 1931 ended in March when he had surgery to remove and infected kidney. It was thought that he would miss the season, but he was "officially" welcomed back to the team on June 24, when the game was stopped as he came to bat and he was presented a huge basket of flowers by his admirers at Paramount Studios, where he worked as an electrician during the offseason. At the end of August Haney was in the middle of a riot in Seattle after the umpires forfeited a game to the Angels for reasons that are not clear. Police and firemen had to use fire hoses to disperse the crowd of 8,000.

In 1932 Haney was released by the Angels. The next season he signed to play third base for the Hollywood Stars, the Angels' archrivals. Fred played well for the Angels in 1933 and 1934. In June 1934 he severely spiked Angels catcher Walt Goebel; given the bad blood between the teams, the Angels thought it was intentional. In November 1934 he moved to another level in his career when he was hired as player-manager of the Toledo Mud Hens. Haney's fiery nature did not remain in Los Angeles. In June 1935 he protested a doubleheader loss at Columbus after the umpire delayed a game while a telegram was sent to the league president changing the Columbus roster because of an injury. The next day he was still seething and vigorously protested a call. He was ejected and, when he refused to leave the field, was escorted out by the police and suspended. He also made the league all-star team and led the league in stolen bases.

In January 1936 Haney had surgery that ended his everyday playing career but did nothing to stem his fighting spirit. During a game on June 20, he took exception to Louisville manager Burleigh Grimes riding the Toledo pitcher. They came to blows near third base and had to be separated by the police. The 5-foot-10 Grimes made short work of Haney, knocking him down and then trying to carve up his face with his spikes. Haney managed for two more years in Toledo, garnering praise from *The Sporting News* for his fiery leadership that kept the team in the 1937.

Haney's success in Toledo team caught the attention of the lowly St. Louis Browns, who were looking for a new manager who would not command a large salary. Haney took the job, viewing it as an excellent opportunity to deliver a .500 team with improved pitching. It did not happen; the Browns finished last in 1939 and sixth in 1940. After they started the 1941 season poorly, Haney was demoted to manager of Toledo, now a Browns farm team. At the end of the 1942 season, he quit. He blamed the lack of authority to make player deals, but he really wanted to return to Los Angeles, where his daughter, Patricia, was in high school. Haney became the radio playh-by-play announcer for the Angels and the Stars home games. He had kept his Hollywood connections from his days at Paramount and was instrumental in having Bing Crosby wear a St. Louis Browns uniform in the movie *Going My Way*.

Controversy arose late in the 1947 season. Philip K. Wrigley, owner of the Angels, wanted to broadcast road games and sought a broadcaster more partial to the Angels. He also wanted Haney fired from the Stars job, because he feared the new broadcaster would not be able to compete with Haney's style, knowledge, and on-air persona. Haney was defended vigorously through a letter-writing campaign to the Angels. The campaign worked: In 1948 Haney broadcast the Stars' home and away games on KLAC.

On November 4, 1948, the Stars asked Haney to become their manager. He requested a three-year contract with full authority over player deals. Before he took the job he contacted Branch Rickey, then president of the Brooklyn Dodgers, and got a promise that the Dodgers would add Hollywood to their farm system. He was also allowed to continue as program director at KLAC and keep his radio show. Haney's work on the air and his support of youth, charities, public service, and baseball brought him a host of friends and admirers. He ended each broadcast with "This is Fred Haney, rounding third and heading for home." Little did Haney know that in his career, already spanning 30 years, he was only approaching second base.

Haney assessed the Stars as lacking talent, and by the start of 1949 spring training, 16 of the 25 players on the 1948 roster were gone. He warned his players to hustle on every play or be ready to be released. The team was dubbed the Comets, Hurricanes and Shooting Stars because of its running and aggressive play. The Stars won the pennant by 5 1/2 games, and he was named *The Sporting News* Minor League Manager of the Year.

Early in the 1950 season, the Stars dropped a bombshell on the baseball world by appearing on the field in shorts. Haney asserted that the rayon T-shirts and shorts, which resembled track suits and were worn for day games and warm night games, would give his players more speed. The papers called the uniform "scanties," and opposing players teased the Stars mercilessly throughout the season.

Late in 1951 Haney was hospitalized with viral pneumonia. He convalesced in Palm Springs, California. As he recovered, Florence drove him to spring training games and cooked while trying to make sure he got sufficient rest. Haney came back and managed the Stars to the 1952 PCL pennant. After the season Branch Rickey, now with the Pittsburgh Pirates, offered him the job as manager. Haney took the job, saying he did it out of obligation to Rickey for the help he had provided to the Stars. But Haney now had the dubious honor of managing the worst team in baseball. He spent three tough years managing the Pirate "Kiddie Corps." Rickey had signed a large number of players and instructed Haney to play them even if they were not the best, so as to build for the future. The Pirates finished a dismal last each of his three years as manager, and on September 25, 1955, he was fired by Rickey. (Haney's contract would have automatically renewed if he had not been notified by midnight on that day.)

Wanting to remain in the majors, Haney accepted an offer to become a coach for the Milwaukee Braves in 1956. The reaction in Milwaukee was that this was one of the best moves the Braves had made since moving from Boston, that Haney would bring hustle, competitiveness, and baseball strategy. In June, with Milwaukee languishing in fifth place, manager Charlie Grimm was fired and Haney was appointed to replace him. The Braves then went on a tear, winning 11 games in a row, and stayed in contention throughout the season. On September 11, with the Braves one game ahead, Haney was rehired for the 1957 season. The Braves lost the pennant to the Brooklyn Dodgers on the last weekend of the season.

There were reports that some Braves players spent too much time night-clubbing. In his farewell speech to the club after the last game, Haney said, "You had a good time, boys. Have a good time this winter. Because when we meet again next spring, you're going to have the toughest so and so you've ever run into." True to his promise, Haney worked the Braves exceptionally hard during spring training in 1957 and prophetically told the team, "You may hate me in the spring but you'll love me in the fall when you pick up your World Series checks."

When the Braves clinched the pennant, Haney said, "This is the thrill of a lifetime. I knew the boys would come through, and what a great way to do it." In his 40th year in baseball, Haney had made it to the World Series. The Braves and the Yankees fought to the seventh game. For that contest, Haney chose Lew Burdette over Warren Spahn to start. Burdette led the Braves to a 5-0 Series clincher and gave Haney and the Braves the world championship. Haney was now a hero in Milwaukee. He was named National League Manager of the Year by United Press International and was rehired for 1958 with a $40,000 salary, his highest in professional baseball.

Haney led the Braves to another pennant in 1958, but the team lost the World Series in a rematch with the Yankees. In 1959 the Braves and Dodgers tied, and the Dodgers won the pennant by sweeping a two-game playoff. A few days later, during the World Series, Haney resigned as manager of the Braves. In midseason, he had said that this might be his last year. There was speculation over whether he had quit or was pushed out. What is most likely is that he asked Braves owner Lou Perini for more authority and resigned when his request was not granted.

Haney was ready to return home and be with his family. He quickly signed with KCOP-TV in Los Angeles to host *Major League Baseball Presents* on Saturday evenings. Then he landed a three-year contract to televise NBC's *Game of the Week*. A newspaper review of Haney's work said he described the action as though it were radio and had a flair for bringing up colorful anecdotes that added flavor to the telecasts.

When Gene Autry was awarded a Los Angeles American League expansion franchise in December 1960, he quickly hired Haney as the team's general manager. Haney hired Bill Rigney as manager. In the expansion draft, Rigney wanted to select young players for the future but Haney overruled him and the team chose a mix of young players and veterans with reputations to compete with the Dodgers for local attention. Haney also wanted to get power hitters for Wrigley Field in Los Angeles. The Angels drafted 30 players, 28 from the majors and two from the minors. Eight were over 30, 18 were in their 20s, and four were teenagers. The gems were two teenagers, Jim Fregosi and Dean Chance.

Haney's next task was to hire a staff and he brought together a front office including Marvin Milkes, Cedric Tallis, and Roland Hemond. In January Haney and Hemond negotiated a working agreement with their first minor-league club, the Dallas-Fort Worth Rangers of the American Association. Haney organized the refurbishment of Wrigley Field, developed a spring-training facility in Palm Springs and made more than 20 trades to improve the nascent Angels. Although pundits predicted that they would be lucky to win 50 games in their inaugural season, they won 70. This gave the Angels the best record of any of the 14 expansion teams in baseball since 1961. Moreover, Haney's structuring of the team for Wrigley led to a 46-36 home record; the only one of the expansion teams with a winning home record.

For the 1962 season, the Angels moved to the Dodgers' new park in Chavez Ravine, which was pitcher-friendly as opposed to the bandbox Wrigley Field. Haney restructured the team for Chavez Ravine, making multiple trades and bringing up young players. On July 4 the Angels were in first place, but fell to a third-place finish. *The Sporting News* and UPI named Haney Major League Executive of the Year.

Haney continued as general manager of the Angels for six more years, orchestrating the club's move to Anaheim and the development its image in Orange County. After the 1968 season, Gene Autry suggested that it was time for the 70-year-old Haney to retire and offered him a consulting position at the same salary. Haney felt the position had no authority or even formal input but acquiesced out of friendship for Autry.

Haney continued to follow the Angels, attending many games and advising Autry. As his vision began to fail, Florence drove him to the games. On November 9, 1977, Haney suffered a fatal heart attack at his Beverly Hills home. Two years later, in 1979, the Angels won the American League West and entered the playoffs. Gene Autry honored Haney by asking Florence to assist him in throwing out the first ball for Game Three and having her throw out the first ball for Game Four. (The Angels lost the American League Championship Series to the Baltimore Orioles, 3 games to 1.) In 1980 the team established the Fred Haney Memorial Award to recognize the outstanding rookie in spring training.

Florence Haney lived to be nearly 100 before she died in 1998. She and Fred are buried at Holy Cross Cemetery in Culver City, California. Their gravestones represent what was important to them in their lives: "FRED—BELOVED HUSBAND FATHER-GRANDFATHER"; "FLORENCE—BELOVED WIFE MOTHER-GRANDMOTHER." Patricia Haney Franklin, the Haneys' only child, died at the age of 86 in Las Vegas on June 8, 2012.

Sources

Beverage, Richard, *The Hollywood Stars* (Charleston, South Carolina: Arcadia Publishing, 2005).

1999 Anaheim Angels Media Guide.

Ada (Oklahoma) *Evening News*.

Charleston (West Virginia) *Gazette*.

Emporia (Kansas) *Daily Gazette*.

Las Vegas Sun.

Lima (Ohio) *News*.

Massillon (Ohio) *Evening Independent*.

Moberly (Missouri) *Monitor Index and Democrat*.

New York Times.

Oakland Tribune.

The Sporting News.

Waterloo (Iowa) *Daily Courier*.

Bob Keely

By Gregory H. Wolf

A BIG-LEAGUE CAREER is often a product of fate, luck, and timing. Bob Keely would attest to that. In 1944 the St. Louis Cardinals signed the 34-year-old sandlot star as a third-string catcher. Six months later, Keely was a world champion. Keely was originally signed by the Redbirds in 1936, but a knee injury ended his foray into Organized Baseball after two abbreviated summers. Employed by a tiling company, he continued to play in St. Louis area sandlot and semipro leagues until the Cardinals, whose roster had been depleted by World War II, came calling. With only two ninth-inning appearances and just one big-league at-bat in two years with the Cardinals, Keely's major-league playing career was short, but it led to a 50-year career in baseball as a respected bullpen coach for the Boston and Milwaukee Braves from 1946 to 1957, and a long career as a scout.

Robert William Keely was born on August 22, 1909 on the north side of St. Louis to George and Mary Keely. George, a self-employed house painter originally from Michigan, and Mary were wed in 1907. Her parents were German immigrants who had settled in the Mound City in the 1870s. In their first three years of marriage, the Keelys welcomed three boys into the world: Stanley, and then identical twins Robert and Richard. In 1923 their last child, George, was born. In an era when money was tight, Stanley, Bob, and Richard attended school through the eighth grade, before they dropped out to learn trades and support the family. Bob became a plasterer and laid tile, but his passion was baseball, and he played whenever he could. An attempt to go to night school failed because it meant missing too many baseball games. "We were raised in a baseball family," said brother George.[1] Bob began playing in sandlot leagues and made a name for himself as a good-hitting, strong-armed catcher for teams like the Sunrise Packing Company and Damolay in the local municipal leagues, in the early and mid-1930s. "You've got to love baseball — at least I always have. I would have done anything back then to be in baseball. And I'm glad I did. It's been my whole life," Keely once said.[2]

At an age when most men have long since given up on a career in professional baseball, Keely got his chance as a 26-year-old in 1936 when St. Louis Cardinals scout Charley Barrett signed him.[3] Unlike many catchers of the era, Keely was tall and lanky (about 6-feet and 170 pounds); he had quick reflexes, and threw and batted right-handed. The Cardinals assigned him to the Springfield (Missouri) Cardinals in the Western Association, one of their 13 Class C teams among 25 farm clubs.[4] Keely, a backup to future Cardinals All-Star Walker Cooper, did not play and lasted only a few weeks before he was released.[5] He resumed his sandlot career in St. Louis, but was unexpectedly told to report to the Union City (Tennessee) Greyhounds of the Class D Kentucky-Illinois-Tennessee (Kitty) League in 1937.[6] Keely remained with the team until July; it is unclear if he ever played in a game before a hand injury in July shelved him for the remainder of the season.[7]

Bob Keely (National Baseball Hall of Fame Library, Cooperstown, N.Y.)

Keely's minor-league career came to an abrupt close in the offseason. While training at Fairgrounds Park, a municipal park near Sportsman's Park, the Cardinals' home ballpark, Keely's knee locked while he was running downhill. The injury was so severe that the Cardinals' team physician, Dr. Robert Hyland, performed surgery.[8]

After convalescing, Keely continued working as a plasterer and tiler and joined a union, but never gave up on baseball. A bachelor who still lived at home with his parents and three siblings, Keely had the luxury of freedom. In the spring of 1939 he signed with Bob Fischer, who ran the Jennings team in the independent Missouri-Illinois League.[9] (Jennings is a small city in northern St. Louis County near where the Keelys lived.) In subsequent years he played for the Stags of Belleville, Illinois (across the Mississippi River from St. Louis), in the same league, and regularly garnered praise as the league's best catcher who had enough talent for him to play Class B baseball.[10]

World War II had a profound effect on big-league baseball and on Keely. Because of his bad knee, Keely was exempt from military service while hundreds of big-league players were called to serve. Like all teams, the Cardinals suffered a dearth of talent and big-league-ready players.

In a scenario befitting a fairy tale, Cardinals scout Walter Shannon approached Keely after a sandlot game in the spring of 1944 and asked the 34-year-old if he wanted to catch for the Redbirds. The team's third-string catcher from the previous season, 30-year-old Sam Narron, had retired, and the club needed a bullpen catcher. Keely, who was making about $450 per month for a tile company, told his parents about his second chance at professional baseball. "They said they didn't like the idea," remembered Keely, whose salary for the Cardinals in 1944 was $265 per month.[11] "But I loved baseball, and my dad could see that. He said, 'I won't stop you, because I don't want you looking back stating that I kept you from finding out what you could do'."[12]

On the roster for the entire season, Keely was more like a coach than an active player. He threw batting practice, served as bullpen catcher, and most importantly ran the day-to-day operations in the bullpen. Keely was one of the oldest members of the team, but in a time-honored tradition in baseball, he shaved seven years from his age. For the rest of his major-league career, 1916 was given as his birth date in publications and even on his only Topps baseball card (1954). Keely quickly gained manager Billy Southworth's trust. He was charged with warming up relief pitchers but also had the discretion to decide which pitchers were best suited in certain situations and games.

It was a dream come true for Keely to play on the eventual World Series champions. His locker was next to that of another player whose career was revived because of the wartime shortage of players, Pepper Martin, Keely's hero from the 1934 World Series. "We had Walker Cooper and Ken O'Dea, two great ones, so I wasn't going to get much of a chance [to play]," said Keely.[13] On July 25, 1944, Keely made his only appearance of the season under unusual circumstances. With two outs in the ninth inning against the Phillies at Shibe Park in Philadelphia, Cooper went to the mound to confer with his pitcher, Al Jurisich, who was just one strike away from a shutout. Home-plate umpire Jocko Conlan, who had warned Cooper to speed up, ejected him in a 9-0 game, leaving the Cardinals in a predicament. O'Dea was tending to his sick wife at home; Keely was the last and only option. He suited up and caught two pitches—a ball and then a third strike to complete Jurisich's shutout.[14] Keely was on the World Series roster, pitched batting practice, and was one of 21 players to receive a full share of World Series winnings. "[Keely] earned his share," wrote *The Sporting News,* "by catching thousands of deliveries in the Cardinals bullpen and warming up pitchers for that 105-game winner."[15]

In 1945 Keely reported early to the Cardinals' spring training site in Cairo, Illinois, and it appeared as if he would transition into a full-time bullpen coach.[16] In addition to Cooper and O'Dea, the Cardinals had highly touted rookie Del Rice in camp. But when Cooper was called into military service in late April, Keely was added to the active roster.[17] Serving as the bullpen catcher for his second and final season in the big leagues, he played just one inning the entire season, in the next-to-last game of the year, when he replaced

Rice in a game against the Reds in Cincinnati. In the top of the ninth inning he made an out in his only big-league at-bat. He caught the final inning of Glenn Gardner's complete-game, 6-2 victory. The Cardinals finished in second place and released both the 35-year-old Keely and manager Southworth in the offseason.

During their two years together in St. Louis, Southworth and Keely had established mutual trust and respect. When Southworth was named skipper of the Boston Braves for 1946, he invited Keely to spring training in Bradenton, Florida.[18] "Billy Southworth made me feel like one of the greatest guys he ever had work for him," said Keely.[19] When the team broke camp and headed for Boston, Keely was the fourth catcher, behind Phil Masi, Stew Hofferth, and Hugh Poland.[20] Before the season began, he was named bullpen coach, and his playing career was over.

Keely served as a respected bullpen coach for the Braves in Boston and Milwaukee from 1946 until his unexpected retirement in March 1958. Often described as "quiet," "tireless," and "always busy," Keely had a reputation as a patient, astute observer, whose dedication to his pitchers was praised.[21] After winning 20 games in 1946, his first full season, Johnny Sain gave credit to Keely. "There's something that fans and writers didn't realize about me last season. It was the help given me by Bob Keely. Some catchers, in warming up pitchers, look around the stands to see if they can spot some friends. Some like to rib and heckle rival players. But not Keely. The guy really instills confidence into the pitchers."[22]

Keely was especially good at developing young players and was considered "one of the finest characters in baseball."[23] When the Braves signed 18-year-old phenom Johnny Antonelli for a reported $75,000 bonus prior to 1948 season, Keely was part of the club's contract negotiating team. *Life* magazine even reported how Keely, a nondrinker and nonsmoker, was charged with "making Johnny a major-leaguer."[24] They roomed together on the road. Over the course of his coaching career, the soft-spoken, shy Keely, with his gleaming blue eyes, was praised for being a father figure to many of his team's rookies and youngsters.

Opposing managers also recognized Keely's expert handing of the bullpen and pitchers, and twice named him to the NL staff for the All-Star Game. The Braves' Southworth named his trusted coach the batting practice catcher of the 1949 squad,[25] but a bigger honor may have come in 1955 when Leo Durocher, skipper of the New York Giants, named him bullpen catcher for the game in Milwaukee. The recognition was not lost on Lloyd Larson, a sportswriter for the *Milwaukee Sentinel*. "It's a well-deserved award for a swell guy—a hard worker. From opening day of spring training until the season closes, invariably [Keely's] the first man on the field and the last to leave."[26] A player's player, Keely was an ultimate hustler.

In his 12th and final season as a Braves coach, Keely experienced the pinnacle of team success when Milwaukee defeated the New York Yankees in the 1957 World Series. In a startling move just weeks after the season, the Braves fired three of their four coaches (Johnny Riddle, Charlie Root, and Connie Ryan). Asked why he was not included in the axing, Keely responded, "I guess I was too busy minding my own business," a response that pointed to the acrimonious relationship between Ryan and manager Fred Haney and the anger and outrage expressed by Root over his termination.[27] The following spring Keely abruptly resigned. In an open letter to general manager John Quinn, he cited his poor health as the reason for his decision, but also noted, "Money has not been a factor in this matter, nor has anything between me and anyone on the club."[28] The latter remark helped fuel speculation that Keely and Haney no longer saw eye-to-eye.

Keely moved to the Bradenton-Sarasota area in 1960 and became a scout for the St. Louis Cardinals, a job he held until he retired 1978. Keely's twin brother, Richard, was a longtime scout for the Braves. Just as he was during his playing and coaching career, Keely exhibited an unwavering desire and commitment to baseball. "I never tire of baseball," he said of his typical 11-hour days scouting. "I'm the first one [at the park] and if I leave early, it's probably to go see another game at another park. I don't get excited until I see a kid six, eight, or maybe 10 times."[29]

Keely never strayed far from baseball even in retirement. He scouted into his 80s for the Los Angeles Dodgers in the Gulf Coast League and assisted the Pittsburgh Pirates at their spring training site in his home town of Bradenton.[30] "I started my career with a World Series championship team, the 1944 Cardinals, and ended with one, the '57 Braves," Keely said, noting that he had never been on a losing team.[31]

Frail, suffering from the onset of dementia, and living in an assisted-living center the last few years of his life, Bob Keely died at the age of 91 on May 20, 2001, in Sarasota, Florida. Always modest, he often pointed out how lucky and fortunate he was to have the career he enjoyed. "The war gave me a great opportunity," he said, "because I got to work in the big leagues."[32] Upon hearing the news of Keely's passing former Braves pitcher Ernie Johnson remembered Keely as "a hard worker and totally respected by the pitching staff."[33]

Sources

Books

Andrews, Tom, and Rich Wolfe, *For Milwaukee Braves Fans Only* (Covington, Kentucky: Clerisy Press, 2011).

Buege, Bob, *Eddie Mathews and the National Pastime* (Milwaukee: Douglas American Sports Publications, 1994).

Buege, Bob, *The Milwaukee Braves: A Baseball Eulogy* (Milwaukee: Douglas American Sports Publications, 1988).

Caruso, Gary, *The Braves Encyclopedia* (Philadelphia: Temple University Press, 1995).

Klima, John, *Bushville Wins* (New York: St. Martin's Press, 2012).

Mumau, Thad, *An Indian Summer: The 1957 Milwaukee Braves, Champions of Baseball* (Jefferson, North Carolina: McFarland & Co., 2007).

Povletich, William, *Milwaukee Braves: Heroes and Heartbreak* (Madison, Wisconsin: Wisconsin Historical Society, 2009).

Newspapers

Chicago Tribune.

Milwaukee Journal.

Milwaukee Sentinel.

New York Times.

Online Sources

Ancestry.com

Baseball-Almanac.com

BaseballLibrary.com

Baseball-Reference.com

Retrosheet.org

Notes

1. Harold M. Unger, "He had one big league at-bat, but a long career," *Sarasota Herald-Tribune*, May 29, 2001, 1A.
2. Mike Eisenbath, "Playing for love, not for money; In '44 Keely couldn't resist Cards' offer," *St. Louis Post-Dispatch*, August 29, 1994, 5C.
3. Jim Sandoval, "Charley Barrett, The King of Weeds," in Jim Sandoval and Bill Nowlin, eds., *Can He Play? A Look at Baseball Scouts and Their Profession* (Phoenix: Society for American Baseball Research, 2011), 11.
4. "Springfield to Try Sandlot Graduate," *The Sporting News*, April 20, 1936, 2.
5. Eisenbath.
6. Janet Gibson, "Keely was a baseball player, coach, scout," *Sarasota Herald-Tribune*, May 22, 2001, 6B.
7. Eisenbath.
8. Eisenbath.
9. *The Sporting News*, April 20, 1939.
10. "Krepel Names 'Three Eye' League From Illinois-Missouri," *Alton (Illinois) Evening Telegraph*, December 21, 1940, 1.
11. Eisenbath.
12. Ibid.
13. Ibid.
14. Associated Press, "Bob Keely Nearly in Ball Game," *Morning Herald* (Hagerstown, Maryland), September 13, 1945, 10.
15. *The Sporting News*, April 26, 1945, 5.
16. Associated Press, "Flood Waters Keep Cards From Starting Practice," *Morning Herald* (Hagerstown, Maryland), March 20, 1945, 7.
17. Associated Press, "O'Dea Gets Chance with Cooper Gone," *Ottawa (Ontario) Citizen*, April 24, 1945, 14.
18. *The Sporting News*, March 21, 1946, 10.
19. Eisenbath.
20. *The Sporting News*, April 11, 1946, 8.
21. *The Sporting News*, April 11, 1956, 13.
22. *The Sporting News*, February, 19, 1947, 11.
23. *The Sporting News*, July 7, 1948, 6.
24. "Spring Training: The Boston Braves Have a Congenial Camp," *Life*, March 28, 1948, 108.
25. *New York Times*, July 7, 1949, 32.

26 Lloyd Larson, "Durocher Did All Right for Braves in All-Star Selection," *Milwaukee Sentinel*, July 6, 1955, 2.

27 Bob Wolf, "Fred's Coaches Are Angry," *Milwaukee Journal*, November 5, 1957, 18.

28 *The Sporting News*, March 19, 1957, 27.

29 John Brockman, "Baseball Scouts Devoted to Complex Job," *Sarasota Herald-Tribune*, June 6, 1971, 9B.

30 Eisenbath.

31 John Brockman, "Bob Keely Looms Top Cardinal Fan," *Sarasota Herald-Tribune*, October 10, 1964, 14.

32 Eisenbath.

33 Unger.

Johnny Riddle

By Nancy Snell Griffith

Catcher Johnny Riddle had one of the more unusual careers in major-league history. His big-league career spanned 19 years, from his debut with the Chicago White Sox in 1930 until his final game with the Pittsburgh Pirates in 1948. He played for five major-league teams, but he also spent long stretches of time in the minors, the longest from 1931 to 1936. In fact, during the 19 years he appeared in only seven major-league seasons and 98 games. In contrast, in his minor-league career, during which he spent 12 years with the Indianapolis Indians, Riddle appeared in 1552 games. He had earned his nickname, Mutt, by the time he played freshman basketball and football at the University of Georgia, but his son, John, said he didn't use it much in later years.

Riddle made some interesting memories for others. In 1940 he was responsible for what sportswriter Sam Levy called one of the "greatest and oddest double play(s) this veteran reporter has ever seen."[1] Playing for the Kansas City Blues in an all-star game, he tagged out both John Lucadello and Ab Wright at the plate during the same play. He was also one of a brother act in baseball, in fact working a game for the Pirates with his younger brother, pitcher Elmer Riddle. Johnny and Elmer also played together when they were with the Cincinnati Reds, and in the minors with the Indianapolis Indians. During Johnny's last season as a player, in 1948, he was the oldest National League player to appear in a game, and was part of one of the oldest batteries in baseball history when at the age of 42 he caught for Fritz Ostermueller, who was 40. And he was to be a five-time American Association all-star.

John Ludy Riddle, the eldest son of James Ludy Riddle and Susan Rebecca Crosby Riddle, was born on October 3, 1905, in Clinton, South Carolina. The family left Clinton sometime before 1912, and Johnny spent much of his youth in Columbus, Georgia. In 1920 he was living in Columbus with his parents, brothers James, Edward, and Elmer, and sisters Lillian and Frances. The father was working as an overseer in a cotton mill, his son James was a commercial traveler for Moisture Co., and Edward was a timekeeper in a cotton mill. The Riddles were to become quite a baseball family. Besides Elmer and Johnny as major leaguers, Johnny's son John L. Riddle spent several years in the minor leagues, and his nephew, Chase Riddle, managed in the minor leagues, scouted for the St. Louis Cardinals, and later was the longtime baseball coach at Troy University in Alabama.

Johnny attended Riverside Military Academy in Gainesville, Georgia, where he was a star running back on the school's state championship football team, and then spent a year at the University of Georgia. In 1923 he was playing with the Clinton Cavaliers in the South Carolina textile leagues. He played for the Laurens Mill team in 1926 and 1927. In 1927 he moved into Organized Baseball, and played with Sanford in the Class D Florida State League. He spent 1928 first with

Johnny Riddle (National Baseball Hall of Fame Library, Cooperstown, N.Y.)

Quincy, Illinois, of the Three-I League and then with Indianapolis of the American Association. He also played for Indianapolis in 1929. He had fond memories of his early days with Indianapolis: "We used to play twi-night doubleheaders here [Bush Stadium] and go into the stands for a picnic lunch between games," he told a sportswriter. "… And that was nice, because you always got a good meal and made some good friends."[2]

Johnny's father died in 1928, when he was 23 years old, and Johnny helped to support the family and ensure that his younger siblings would be able to stay in school. By 1930 his sister Lillian was also working, having found a job in a candy factory. Johnny spent 1929 with Indianapolis, and in 1930 the Chicago White Sox brought him to spring training. His prospects looked good. In fact, according to a Chicago sportswriter, "(W)ithin a few months [he] will develop into one of the outstanding young catchers of the majors."[3] Riddle made his major-league debut on April 17, 1930, in the Opening Day game against the Cleveland Indians. He played in 25 games with the White Sox that year, the most major-league games he would play in a season. He batted .241 in 58 at-bats. But things didn't pan out as hoped, and Riddle was to spend the next seven years back in Indianapolis. The years were not wasted, however, as it was there that he met his wife, Dorothy Cutshaw, in 1932. They had a whirlwind courtship, meeting on June 18 and marrying on July 30. Despite her father's objections to her marrying a baseball player, their marriage lasted for more than 65 years.

In 1937 the Washington Senators acquired Riddle from Indianapolis in a trade for catcher Shanty Hogan and an unspecified amount of cash. The Senators, however, were not pleased with their acquisition, and protested when an X-ray of Riddle's arm revealed several bone chips and a large growth. After Riddle had played in eight games for the Senators, the trade was voided and the players returned to their teams. Johnny returned to Indianapolis, where he joined brother Elmer on the roster.

On August 30 the Boston Bees acquired Riddle from Indianapolis, and he played with them through most of the 1938 season. He was the Bees' third catcher, but was praised by a local sportswriter as being "a real big leaguer," and "one of those 100 per cent team men."[4] He batted .281 in 19 games with Boston in 1938, and on June 12 he had the best offensive game of his major-league career, going 3-for-4 with a double. On July 4 against the Philadelphia Phillies, he participated in an outstanding force-out at third base, and the *Boston Globe* praised him for his "wonderful faculty of being 'there or thereabouts' on every possible play in his sphere of influence."[5] The next month the Bees included Riddle and several other players in a trade to the New York Yankees for shortstop Eddie Miller.

The Yankees assigned Riddle to the Kansas City Blues, their American Association farm team. He broke his thumb in his first game but managed to catch in 19 games for the Blues that season. He played in 97 games in 1939, and 109 in 1940. In the latter season Riddle batted .280 and had a fielding percentage of .986. In March 1941 his contract was purchased by the Cincinnati Reds. Ernie Lombardi was the Reds' primary catcher, and Riddle played in only ten games. Elmer was a teammate that year; they were to play together with the Reds again in 1944 and 1945.

On November 25, 1941, the Reds named Johnny the playing manager of their Southern Association farm club, the Birmingham Barons. Riddle managed the Barons until August 17, 1944, when the Reds, in the face of wartime player shortages, called him up. He was 38 years old. Although his major-league statistics had been spotty at best, his value to a team was recognized by at least one sportswriter when he was called up: "Riddle was a great minor-league catcher for many years. Swayne Field fans recall his classy work with Indianapolis," a sportswriter wrote of him. "At his best he seemed to be one of those fellows who didn't attract the attention of major-league scouts. He did get a chance or two in the big show, but not until after he had passed his peak. Now, owing to the scarcity of talent, he comes up again, and he may be able to help out, for he knows a lot about baseball."[6]

Riddle played sparingly for the Reds in 1944 and 1945. World War II ended in 1945 and he was released by the Reds on September 11. He returned to Indianapolis, where, now in his 40s, he played in 1946 and 1947. He was one of the most popular players in the Indians' history. In August 1947 the fans showed their appreciation of his long career at a John Riddle Night. He received a $500 check and a Nash Ambassador automobile, and was carried off the field on his teammates' shoulders. He was later named to the All-Indians team by readers of the *Indianapolis News*.

In 19 seasons in the minor leagues, 12 of them in Indianapolis, Riddle appeared as a catcher in 1,296 games, had a fielding percentage of .977, batted .297, and sported a slugging percentage of .390 and an on-base percentage of .302. He batted over .300 during six of those seasons, with his best year coming with Indianapolis in 1930 when his batting average was .359 and his slugging percentage was .486. He even pitched in seven games (11 innings total) at Birmingham in 1944.

In 1948 the Pittsburgh Pirates acquired Riddle to be a player-coach. He served mostly as the bullpen coach until the Pirates activated him when none of the other catchers could handle Kirby Higbe's knuckleball. Riddle caught in ten games, the last one on September 11, and was released after the season, though he continued to coach. In the course of his major-league career, he appeared in 98 games, batted .238, and had a fielding percentage of .983. In four of those years, 1930, 1941, 1945, and 1948, Riddle was error-free defensively. During the 1948 and 1949 seasons, he was again reunited with his brother Elmer on the Pirates' roster.

Johnny was a coach for the Pirates until 1950, and from 1952 through 1955 he was a coach for the Cardinals. Catcher Del Rice, who played under Riddle at St. Louis, called him "one of the smartest and hardest-working coaches in the business," and added, "He's an excellent infield (practice) batter, can pitch and catch batting practice, and is known around the league as a terrific judge of play."[7] In 1953 the Cardinals signed his son, John Louis Riddle, a student at Butler University, to a minor-league contract. John Louis, an outfielder, played in the minor leagues until 1957.

While many players' families remained behind in their hometowns during the baseball season, Dorothy Riddle and her children followed Johnny to many of the places where he played and coached. One of John Louis Riddle's earliest memories was of spending the summer in Boston when his father played for the Bees.

When Johnny managed the Birmingham Barons, the family went to Alabama. During the two years he coached for Pittsburgh, they lived in the Pittsburgh area during the summers, one year in East Liberty and one in Mount Lebanon. And when he went to coach with the Cardinals, the whole family moved to St. Louis for several years.

In 1956 and 1957 Riddle was a coach for the Milwaukee Braves. Riddle often referred to the Braves' World Series victory over the Yankees in 1957 the biggest thrill of his career. After the Braves' World Series triumph, Riddle, third-base coach Connie Ryan, and pitching coach Charlie Root were let go by manager Fred Haney in what Harold Kaese of the *Boston Globe* called "the most surprising shakeup of brass on a championship ballclub since Rogers Hornsby, playing-manager of the St. Louis Cardinals, was traded to the New York Giants after having won everything in 1926."[8] Kaese found Riddle's release particularly mystifying because Riddle had always proved himself to be intensely loyal. In November 1957 Johnny signed as a coach for the Cincinnati Redlegs, replacing Frank McCormick, who was retiring. The following year he coached for the Phillies, his final job in baseball.

In 1958 Riddle went into sales in the beer business in Indianapolis. Around 1961 the family moved to Birmingham, Alabama, where he continued in the beer business for several years. He then went into the retail business in one of the large malls in Birmingham. Eventually the family moved to Connersville, Indiana, where one of their daughters lived. After a few years, they decided they didn't like small-town living, and moved back into Indianapolis.

Johnny Riddle died in Indianapolis on December 15, 1998, at the age of 93. He left behind his wife, Dorothy; children John, Bill, Pat, and Steve Riddle, Linda Weaver, and Barbara Arnold; 19 grandchildren; and 17 great-grandchildren. He is buried in Oaklawn Memorial Gardens in Indianapolis.

Sources

Ancestry.com (1920 and 1930 census records).

Johnny Riddle, Baseball-Reference.com.

"Johnny Riddle," eNotes.com Reference.

"Popular Indianapolis Indians Catcher John L. Riddle…," *Indianapolis Star*, 1998.

"Johnny Riddle," Retrosheet.org.

Biographical and other information provided by Johnny Riddle, his son John L. Riddle, and his nephew, James Riddle.

Notes

1. Sam Levy, "Riddle Unsolved," *Baseball Digest*, April 1951, 82.
2. Kim Rogers, "Baseball Veteran, 90, Remembers the Early Days at Bush Stadium," *Indianapolis Star*, June 30, 1996, B13.
3. Edward Burns, "Bush Sizes Up Sox and Likes Their Looks," *Chicago Daily Tribune*, March 14, 1930, 19.
4. "Southern Pick-Ups," *Christian Science Monitor*, April 6, 1938, 12.
5. "Remarkable Play Is Made by Riddle Forcing Out Klein," *Boston Daily Globe*, July 5, 1938, 6.
6. "Old Johnny Riddle to Catch for the Reds," *Toledo Blade*, August 17, 1944, 20.
7. "Riddle May 'Work' at 3rd," *Milwaukee Sentinel*, June 21, 1956, 10, part 2.
8. Harold Kaese, "Coolness Between Haney and Braves Coaches Apparent in Series," *Boston Daily Globe*, November 5, 1957, 13.

Charlie Root

By Gregory H. Wolf

PERHAPS UNFAIRLY, CHARLIE Root's name and legacy are indelibly intertwined with one of baseball's most enduring and intriguing legends: Babe Ruth's "called shot" in Game Three of the 1932 World Series. Overlooked is Root's reputation as one of the most dependable, durable, and hardest-throwing pitchers of his generation. With the most victories in Chicago Cubs history (201), Root paced the National League with 26 wins in 1927 and helped lead the North Siders to four World Series appearances (1929, 1932, 1935, and 1938) during a ten-season span. After his active playing career, Root was a well respected minor-league manager and major-league pitching coach, most notably for the 1957 champion Milwaukee Braves.

A baseball career was far from foretold when Charles Henry Root was born on St. Patrick's Day, March 17, 1899, the eighth of nine children of Jacob and Mary Root in Middletown, Ohio, situated about halfway between Cincinnati and Dayton. Called the Kaiser for his authoritarian personality and preference for speaking German at home, Jacob worked in the local steel mill, Armco, and envisioned for his four sons a life of hard work in factories.[1] Young Charlie was a class clown in grade school and often found himself in trouble with his teachers. When a teacher reprimanded 13-year-old Charles for his disruptive behavior, "I quit school," he recalled. "And I never spent another day in the classroom."[2] Jacob, who placed little value in formal education and considered athletics folly, accepted his son's decision and demanded that Charlie find a job to help support the financially strapped family. Charlie began "driving a grocery wagon" and then toiled in a box factory, but admitted that he spent more time playing baseball on vacant lots, collecting baseball cards from tobacco packs, and hunting bumblebees. Approaching his 18th birthday, Root took a job at Armco as a patternmaker. Aided by a growth spurt, he pitched and played shortstop for the factory team. Showing promise as a pitcher, Root played semipro ball for the Middletown Eagles, earning $5 a game on Sundays in 1919. When the nearby Hamilton Engine Works offered him $35 per game to pitch for them and a job paying $50 a week, Root jumped at the opportunity, and led manager Carl Link's team to the championship in the Southern Ohio industrial league. Industrial leagues were fertile grounds for professional baseball at the time and were scouted heavily. St. Louis Browns pitcher and scout Carl Weilman, who lived in Hamilton, saw Root pitch several times, including in an exhibition against the Browns, and signed Root to a professional contract.

Almost 22 years old, Root reported to manager Lee Fohl at the Browns' spring-training camp in Bogalusa, Louisiana, in 1921. "A promising youngster" was the report on the tough right-hander, but the Browns, whom some considered to be serious contenders in the American League, had little use for such a green player.[3] Root was optioned to the Terre Haute Tots in the Class B Illinois-Indiana-Iowa (Three-I) League, but his promising maiden season (8-7 with a 3.57 ERA) was

Charlie Root (National Baseball Hall of Fame Library, Cooperstown, N.Y.)

cut short when he broke his leg sliding into third base. Returning to Terre Haute the following season, Root helped lead the Tots to the pennant by winning 16 games, including a no-hitter, and impressed management with his versatility as a starter and reliever.

With a career in the major leagues beckoning, Root joined the Browns at their spring-training facility in San Antonio in 1923 and made the team. Coming off a surprise second-place finish in 1922, the Browns had a veteran staff, led by Urban Shocker, and topped the AL in ERA. Pitching out of the bullpen, Root made his major-league debut on Opening Day, April 18 and retired all three batters he faced in the ninth inning. Throwing almost exclusively fastballs, Root pitched typically in mop-up situations (the Browns lost 23 of the 27 games in which he appeared) and finished with a 0-4 record and 5.70 ERA which earned him a ticket out of the major leagues. "I was glad to go," Root said. "Those fellows just murdered my fast one and they were the best I had in the bag."[4]

In the offseason new Browns manager George Sisler traded Root, utilityman Cedric Durst, pitcher Rasty Wright, and catcher Josh Billings to the Los Angeles Angels in the Pacific Coast League for pitcher George Lyons and catcher Tony Rego in a deal later called Sisler's Folly.[5] Veteran pitcher Doc Crandall took Root under his wing, taught him a hard curveball and helped him develop a changeup. The results were spectacular: Root won 21 games and logged 322 innings. The Chicago Cubs purchased his contract after the season for an estimated $30,000 and two players.[6] After participating in the Cubs' spring training at Catalina Island, Root was optioned back to the Angels for more seasoning. He excelled, winning 25 games, lowering his ERA almost one full run to 2.86, logging 324 innings, and leading the league in strikeouts.

Commencing in manager Joe McCarthy's first year at the helm of the Cubs and marking the advent of 14 consecutive winning seasons for the team (1926-39), including four NL pennants, Root's career has two distinct phases. As the staff workhorse from 1926 to 1933, he averaged 18 wins per season, 40 appearances, (31 starts), and 252 innings pitched; from the age of 35 in 1934 through 1941, Root was an invaluable spot or fourth starter and reliever, averaging 8 wins, 35 appearances (12 starts), and 140 innings per season.

Described as the "pitching find of the season" in 1926, Root (whose first name was spelled both Charley and Charlie in newspaper reports his entire career) began auspiciously, winning his debut by going the distance against the Reds on April 14.[7] Almost immediately, the 27-year-old Root established himself as the staff ace, capable of starting every fourth day and occasionally relieving. More than anything, he earned McCarthy's trust; in turn, McCarthy depended on Root more than any other pitcher in their five years together. Completing 21 of 32 starts (two of them were ten-inning outings) and appearing ten times as a reliever, Root logged 271 1/3 innings and won 18 times; however, had the Cubs provided him even average run support in his losses, he might have won 25, instead of leading the NL with 17 defeats. In 13 of his losses, the Cubs scored two runs or less (a total of 13 runs).

"Cool" and "graceful," Root was one of the great fastball pitches of his era.[8] Though he never led the league in strikeouts, he ranked in the top five for six consecutive seasons (1926-1931) in both strikeouts and strikeouts per nine innings. *The Sporting News* said he had a "mysterious delivery" and could baffle hitters with his overhand, three-quarters, and side-arm delivery depending on the batter or pitch count.[9] With a commanding mound presence, the tobacco-juice spitting Root intimidated batters and freely threw inside, thus earning his nickname Chinski (a ball near the batter's chin). His curveball, a self-described "wrinkle ball" ("It slews a little like the wrinkle in a piece of suit," he said), was known to freeze hitters.[10]

In 1927 Root had one of the best seasons for a pitcher in Cubs history, leading the National League with 26 wins, 309 innings, and 48 games pitched. For the first time since their last pennant, in 1918, the Cubs remained in contention until a September collapse. Hailed as the "best pitcher in the league" and the "sensation of the major leagues," Root won his 22nd game on August 16 by tossing his second consecutive shutout and defeating the Dodgers in Brooklyn, 3-0, giving the Cubs a season-high six-game lead over the Pirates.[11] "Root, once a discarded disappointment, was brought back to life and ambition by McCarthy," lauded the *New York Times*.[12] With six weeks remaining in the season, fans and sportswriters wondered if Root could be the first NL hurler to win 30 since Pete Alexander in 1917. Lacking confidence in his other pitchers and in a tight race, McCarthy pitched Root on short rest and used him in relief between starts. Root won his 24th game on August 27 (after pitching in relief in both games of a doubleheader); overworked, exhausted, and weak (he lost 15 pounds), he won just twice the rest of the season as the Cubs faltered with a 12-17 record in the last month to finish in fourth place.

One constant in Root's rise from semipro ball in Ohio to success with the Cubs was the unwavering support of his wife, Dorothy. Throughout Root's 16 years with the Cubs, she was a permanent fixture at home games at Wrigley Field and often traveled with the team to road games. They were so inseparable that *The Sporting News* labeled them "baseball's ideal family" in a special report about Dorothy.[13] They met in Charlie's hometown, Middletown, eloped to Newport, Kentucky, to marry on May 9, 1918, and had two children, Della and Charley Jr., who were also regulars at the Cubs games.

Largely responsible for keeping the Cubs near the top of the NL in 1927, the 5-foot-10, 190-pound Root reported to camp about 15 pounds overweight in 1928 and battled his waistline all year. After he lost his first three decisions and with an ERA over 5.00, it appeared as though Root was burnt out and suffering the consequences of overwork the previous season. With Pat Malone, Sheriff Blake, Art Nehf, Guy Bush, and Root, McCarthy had five legitimate first-line starters and no longer needed to rely on one pitcher. Root never got untracked and finished with a disappointing 14 wins, a team-high 18 losses, and a 3.57 ERA, and finished only 13 of 30 starts.

Rumors of a trade involving Root for Boston Braves second baseman Rogers Hornsby proved incorrect when the Cubs acquired the cantankerous infielder for five other players and an estimated $120,000 to $200,000, instantly making the Cubs the favorite to win the pennant in 1929.[14] Relying on his fastball and fast curve, Root enjoyed arguably his best season, winning 19 games and leading the league with a .760 winning percentage. Behind Malone, Root, and Bush (who ranked 1, 2, and 4 in the NL in wins), the Cubs demolished competition in July and August, going a combined 44-18, and cruised to the pennant. Consistent the entire season, Root was best when the Cubs needed him, especially in September, when he tossed five consecutive complete games, winning four.

Finishing with 98 wins, their most since 1910, the Cubs faced the juggernaut of the Philadelphia Athletics, winners of 104 games and an 8-1 favorite to win the World Series.[15] Instead of 22-game winner Malone, McCarthy unexpectedly chose 30-year-old Root, noting his "greater experience," to start Game One at home.[16] Unflappable on the mound, Root was temperamentally sound, level-headed, and not easily rattled. In the most effective start of his four World Series with the Cubs, Root surrendered just three hits in seven innings, including a home run by Jimmie Foxx, but was lifted for a pinch-hitter in the seventh inning. His mound opponent, submariner Howard Ehmke, pitched the game of his life, struck out a then-World Series record 13 batters, and won, 3-1. Given the start at Shibe Park in Game Four with Chicago down two games to one, Root cruised into the seventh inning with an 8-0 lead before surrendering a towering home run to Al Simmons. After a single by Foxx, Hack Wilson lost Bing Miller's fly ball in the sun and Root came undone, giving up singles to three of the next four hitters before being replaced by Art Nehf. Owing to another Wilson miscue, Root was charged with six runs in 6 1/3 innings, but not the loss as Philadelphia scored ten runs during the inning in a crushing 10-8 Cubs' loss. The A's closed out the Series two days later with a ninth-inning comeback win.

With great expectations for another pennant, the Cubs got off to a sluggish start in 1930, further enraging team owner Bill Wrigley, who was still smarting from the World Series defeat. Root buttressed the team with nine wins in his first 13 starts, including eight complete games and three shutouts. With their offense firing on all cylinders, the Cubs enjoyed a 5 1/2-game lead over the New York Giants when Root left in the first inning of a defeat to the Pirates on August 27 after surrendering four runs without retiring a batter. Diagnosed with shoulder problems, he was limited to 13 2/3 innings over the remaining five weeks of the season. Chicago lost 13 of its next 19 games to fall out of contention. McCarthy resigned with four games remaining, Wrigley's trust in him irrevocably damaged.

McCarthy's easy-going demeanor was sharply contrasted with new manager Rogers Hornsby's authoritarian and tyrannical rule over players in his year and a half as skipper. Root rebounded in 1931 from a lackluster 1930 season to post 17 wins and led the staff in innings (251), starts (31), complete games (19), and appearances (39, tied with Guy Bush),while lowering his ERA almost one run to 3.48; however, the Cubs were undone by injuries, poor pitching, and age. Alienating players, Wrigley, and general manager William Veeck, the egotistical Hornsby led the team to a disappointing third-place finish.

The mood in the Cubs' clubhouse changed overnight when first baseman Charlie Grimm replaced Hornsby as manager after 99 games in the 1932 season. The tactful and approachable Jolly Cholly let his team play and they responded by winning 26 of 32 games and cruising to the pennant. Root, noticeably relaxed after his relegation to the bullpen for two weeks in July under Hornsby, pitched his best ball of the season after Grimm took over, winning seven of nine decisions in August and September on his way to a 15-10 record. At 33 Root was still a vital member of the staff, which led the NL in ERA and included 22-game winner Lon Warneke and 19-game winner Bush.

With losses in the first two games of the World Series to the overwhelming favorite Yankees in New York, the Cubs returned to Chicago for Game Three. After surrendering a towering three-run blast to Babe Ruth in the first inning and a solo shot to Lou Gehrig in the third, Root entered the fateful fifth inning in a 4-4 game. According to Root, Cubs players had been riding Ruth the entire game. After the first strike Ruth supposedly yelled at him "That's only one strike" and then gestured to him after the second strike.[17] On the next pitch Ruth clouted a shot over the center-field bleachers. Gehrig followed with his second home run and Root was replaced after becoming the first pitcher in World Series history to surrender four home runs in a game. The Bronx Bombers won, 7-5. On the next day, the Yankees completed their resounding sweep of the Cubs.

Neither Root nor Ruth made references to a "called shot" after Game Three and contemporary sportswriters did not mention one either, except for Joe Williams of the *New York Telegram*, whose columns were syndicated nationally. Soon, the story of Ruth's "called shot" spread like wildfire, helped by the sheer stature of the game's greatest player. Eyewitness accounts differ about what actually happened, and an amateur 16mm film of Ruth's at-bat, discovered in the 1970s, has not quelled the enduring controversy. "Ruth most certainly did not call his home run in that game," said Root years later. "I ought to know. I was there."[18] Root claimed that he would never have allowed Ruth to show him up without retaliating: "I'd have put one in his ear and knocked him on his ass."[19] Longtime teammate and friend Grimm added, "Root never squawked as the legend grew that Ruth had called his shot for baseball's most celebrated home run."[20] Never seeking the spotlight, Root, adamantly opposed any dramatizations of the event that exaggerated Ruth's at-bat and refused to cooperate with a Hollywood film of the event.

In 1933, Grimm's first full season as manager, the Cubs plodded along and never challenged for the pennant. The 34-year-old Root pitched solidly, completing 20 of 30 starts, notching 15 wins, and posting a career-low 2.60 ERA. He pitched four extra-inning complete games, including a career-high 13 innings in a 3-2 loss to the Phillies on September 9. The Cubs scored three runs or fewer in all of his ten losses (a total of 15 runs), an oft-repeated refrain for the season.

After a poor spring, Root had an auspicious beginning in 1934 by hurling a complete-game victory on April 21 while hitting a solo home run against rival St. Louis, winning 2-1. A capable hitter with 11 career home runs, Root had a career .180 batting average (196-for-1,086) and 93 RBIs. Failing to get on track after his initial victory, Root, battling his weight, was demoted to the bullpen after a dismal two-inning outing in which he surrendered four runs to the Giants on June 20. Root didn't start another game all season, and finished with a 4-7 record that ushered in suggestions of his demise as a pitcher.

The 1935 season put the suggestions to rest. No longer capable of starting every fourth or fifth day, the 36-year-old Root proved his worth as an effective spot starter, completing six of eight starts while appearing in 16 games as a reliever in the first four months of the season. "I had developed a roll of fat across my shoulders," he said of his problems the season before. "It bothered my delivery."[21] He said that during the offseason he had seriously contemplated quitting the game. But with the endless encouragement of Dorothy, Root began a regimen of rowing and arrived at spring training lighter than in previous seasons, ready to prove he wasn't washed up. His fastball no longer a threat, the 36-year-old Root developed an effective hard knuckleball to go with his breaking balls and transformed himself into a wily, cerebral pitcher whom newspapers called the "grandpappy" of the Cubs staff.[22]

Entering September in the middle of a pennant race, just 1 1/2 games behind St. Louis, the Cubs began an unprecedented run by winning 23 of their last 26 games, including a club-record 21 in a row from September 4 through September 27, on their way to the NL pennant. Joining Warneke, Bill Lee, and Larry French as the primary starters during the September stretch, Root won four consecutive starts, including an 11-inning, complete-game masterpiece over the Phillies on September 5. Root got credit for the Cubs' presence in the pennant race.[23] "[Root] was a big help, not only as a pitcher," recalled first baseman Phil Cavaretta, "but as a coach to our younger pitchers."[24]

Sporting a 15-8 record and a 3.08 ERA in 201 1/3 innings, the sturdily-built Root, whom teammates called Old Bear, started Game Two in the 1935 World Series with a chance to exorcise demons from his performances in 1929 and 1932.[25] Facing the vaunted batting order of the Detroit Tigers boasting four future Hall of Famers (Mickey Cochrane, Charlie Gehringer, Goose Goslin, and Hank Greenberg), Root was lifted after surrendering four runs in the first inning without getting an out. He had one more chance to pitch in the Series (two scoreless innings in relief during Game Four), before the Cubs were defeated in six games.

After an ineffective season as primarily a reliever in 1936 (3-6 with a career-low 73 2/3 innings), Root won 13 games in 1937, prompting *The Sporting News* to report that he "still stands out as the only reliable performer" on a maddening inconsistent staff.[26] When he relieved Roy Parmelee on August 13 and pitched 7 1/3 innings to earn the victory in a 22-6 drubbing of the Reds, the Cubs owned a 6 1/2-game lead over the Giants, but went cold, going 27-24 down the stretch to finish in second place for the second consecutive year.

Used mainly in relief during most of the 1938 season while the Cubs floundered in third or fourth place, Root experienced his final moments of glory in the tension-filled last month of the 1938 season as the Cubs staged a dramatic comeback under the direction of player-manager Gabby Hartnett (who had replaced Grimm in midseason) to win the pennant on the next-to-last day of the season. With the Cubs down by seven games on September 4, Root pitched a complete-game 11-inning 2-1 victory over the Reds at Crosley Field to initiate a 21-5 run the rest of the season. In the best month of his season, Root started five games, relieved in three, won four games, and posted a 2.49 ERA. His last two victories were among the most important of his career: With a scoreless inning of relief against the Pirates on September 28, Root earned a victory when catcher-manager Gabby Hartnett hit his celebrated game-winning "homer in the gloamin'" in the bottom of the ninth to go into first place. Two days later, Root pitched a complete game to defeat the Cardinals 10-3 in Sportsman's Park, securing the pennant for the Cubs. Despite Root's success at the end of the season, Hartnett opted for a three-man rotation of 22-game winner Bill Lee, oft-injured Dizzy Dean, and Clay Bryant for the World Series against the Yankees. The Cubs were swept, and in his only appearance, Root relieved Lee in Game Four and pitched three innings, allowing one run).

On the biggest stage in baseball, Root inexplicably had some of his worst games in his career. In the Cubs' four World Series defeats, Root was winless, lost three, surrendered 26 hits in 22 2/3 innings, and was charged with 18 runs (17 earned) for a 6.75 ERA. Root's woes in the World Series have contributed to his neglected legacy as one of the era's most dependable pitchers.

Never one to make excuses, Root admitted that he never learned to pace himself and had a tendency to overpitch.[27]

Pitching three more seasons and winning an additional 18 games, "Old Mr. Troubleshooter" had the distinction of being the oldest player in 1940 and 1941 and the last player born in the 19th century to play in the major leagues.[28] Released at the end of the 1941 season, the 42-year-old Root finished his career with 201 wins and 160 losses and a 3.59 ERA,. At the end of 2012, Root's 605 appearances as a Cub led the franchise by a wide margin.

A baseball lifer, Root pitched for the Hollywood Stars from 1942 through 1944. In his second season with the club, he was the team's player-manager. In 1945-46 he was the player-manager of the Columbus (Ohio) Red Birds, the Cardinals' affiliate in the American Association. In 1948, at the age of 49, Root pitched his final game in Organized Baseball for the Billings Mustangs in the Class C Pioneer League. He finished with 111 victories in his minor-league career.

Root was the pitching coach of the Cubs for three seasons (1951-53) before former teammate Charlie Grimm hired him in 1956 as a coach for the Milwaukee Braves. Root was known for his "Nine Hill Commandments." With his pitchers he stressed conditioning, ball control, fielding, mastering pitches before experimenting with new ones, running every day, bunting, pacing, developing a changeup, and finally an unteachable quality: "heart."[29] After leading the National League in ERA in 1956, the Braves ranked second in their 1957 championship season. "We all respected Root," eight-time All-Star Del Crandall told the author.[30]

In a surprise move, Root and coaches Johnny Riddle and Connie Ryan were fired within weeks after the Braves won the World Series over the Yankees. "Chances are that no club in major league history went through a shake-up like that after the World Series," reported *The Sporting News*.[31] "Puzzled" by the firing, Root felt insulted by how the Braves, and especially manager Fred Haney, who replaced Grimm in 1956 and wanted his own coaching staff, presented the news to the public. "The club," reported *The Sporting News*, "made it clear that [Root] had been 'replaced' and had not resigned."[32] When Grimm returned as manager of the Cubs in 1960, Root joined him for one final season of coaching before retiring from baseball.

Among the highest-paid players in baseball in the 1930s, Root invested wisely during the Great Depression and lived within his means. After living in Los Angeles during the offseason for many years, he and Dorothy later lived on their 1,000-acre Diamond-R Ranch in Paicines, 120 miles southeast of San Francisco, where Root became a successful cattle rancher and enjoyed hunting and fishing. After an extended illness, Root died on November 5, 1970, at the age of 71 near his home in Hollister, California. He was cremated at Garden of Memories Memorial Park in Salinas, California, and his ashes were scattered.

Sources

Newspapers

Chicago Tribune.

Milwaukee Journal.

Milwaukee Sentinel.

The Sporting News.

Websites

Ancestry.com

BaseballLibrary.com

Baseball-Reference.com

Retrosheet.org

SABR.org

Notes

1. Roger Snell, *Root for the Cubs. Charlie Root and the 1929 Chicago Cubs* (Nicholasville, Kentucky: Wind, 1929), 8.

2. *The Sporting News*, March 2, 1933, 7.

3. "Browns to be in Flag Fight," *New Castle* (Pennsylvania) *News*, March 10, 1921, 20.

4. "Charley Root Has the Makings of a Truly Great Hurler," *Zanesville* (Ohio) *Times Signal*, December 19, 1926, 14.

5. *The Sporting News*, March 7, 1933, 7.

6. "Cubs Pay $50,000 for Charley Root," *Wisconsin State Journal* (Madison), August 10, 1924, 27.

7. *New York Times*, August 2, 1926, 13.

8. "Charley Root Has the Makings of a Truly Great Hurler."

9 *The Sporting News*, June 7, 1926, 1.

10 "Charley Root Has the Makings of a Truly Great Hurler."

11 *New York Times*, March 19, 1928, 27; *Milwaukee Journal*, August 13, 1927, 11.

12 *New York Times*, August 28, 1927, 53.

13 *The Sporting News*, November 9, 1939, 4.

14 Glen Stout, *The Cubs: The Complete Story of Chicago Cubs Baseball* (Boston: Houghton Mifflin Harcourt, 2007), 123.

15 "A's 8-1 Favorite to Win World Series, Associated Press, *Fredericksburg* (Virginia) *Freelance Star,* October 11, 1929, 1.

16 "Root to oppose Grove," Associated Press, *Pittsburgh Press*, October 7, 1929, 20.

17 Peter Golenbock, *Wrigleyville: A Magical History Tour of the Chicago Cubs* (New York: St. Martin's Griffin, 1999), 237.

18 *The Sporting News,* May 12, 1948, 10.

19 Geoffrey C. Ward and Ken Burns, *Baseball: An Illustrated History* (New York: Knopf, 2010), 210.

20 Peter Golenbock, 236.

21 "Charlie Root Tries Again" Associated Press, *Windsor* (Ontario) *Daily Star,* October 7, 1935.

22 "New Yorkers Tumble Far Behind Leaders," *Palm Beach* (Florida) *Post,* September 19, 1935, 6.

23 "Charley Root Main Factor in Chicago's Drive in the National League," *Saskatoon* (Saskatchewan) *Star-Phoenix,* July 23, 1935, 11.

24 Peter Golenbock, 255.

25 Ibid.

26 *The Sporting News*, July 22, 1937, 5.

27 *The Sporting News*, April 4, 1956, 11.

28 *The Sporting News*, March 7, 1940, 1.

29 *The Sporting News*, April 4, 1956, 11.

30 Author's interview with Del Crandall on July 30, 2012.

31 *The Sporting News*, November 6, 1957, 3.

32 *The Sporting News*, November 6, 1957, 3-4.

Connie Ryan

By John McMurray

CONNIE RYAN, a scrappy major-league infielder for a dozen years, had stints with the Braves as a player, coach, and manager in Boston, Milwaukee, and Atlanta, and was Milwaukee's third-base coach in the triumphant 1957 season after managing in the Braves' farm system for the previous two years. He managed the club for five days in June when skipper Fred Haney was ill. In a move that was not unexpected, Ryan and two other coaches, Johnny Riddle and Charlie Root, were fired after the season. (Only coach Bob Keely escaped the noose.) Haney had inherited the coaches when he was hired as the Braves' manager in 1956. During the 1957 season, Ryan and Haney had a relationship that was testy as best, and Ryan occasionally expressed criticisms where they could be heard and relayed back to Haney.[1] According to *The Sporting News*, the two were "scarcely on speaking terms when the campaign ended."[2]

Ryan's seven seasons with the Boston Braves included the pennant-winning year of 1948. That was far from the best season of his career (51 games, .213 batting average), but Ryan was a valuable utility infielder, primarily backing up incumbent Eddie Stanky (and later Stanky's replacement, Sibby Sisti) at second base. Ryan was an intense competitor as well as an occasional sparkplug for the National League pennant-winners, and he could be counted on to play solid defense. Ryan also was not averse to a scuffle now and then.

These qualities stood out to former New York Giants manager Mel Ott, who had scouted Ryan before bringing the young infielder to the major leagues in 1942. "From all the tales that have come on here before Ryan he is a competent and aggressive agent," read one 1942 newspaper account found in his Hall of Fame file. "Ott saw [Ryan] in New Orleans … and admired his fighting spirit as well as his ability. He is a peppery, chip-on-shoulder player like [Dick] Bartell or John McGraw."[3]

Ryan's teammates typically viewed him as pleasant and gentlemanly. Another 1942 account claimed that Connie was "much more articulate than the average rookie getting his first major league chance, and so humble that he ministers to everybody from the bellhops to the bat-boy."[4] Yet Ryan's competitiveness occasionally boiled over. In 1940, while playing second base in the minor leagues for Savannah, he had a scuffle with future teammate Stanky, who was then the second baseman for the opposing Macon team. As Ryan recounted years later, "Every time that I went out to my position, I noticed that my glove was in right field instead of near second base [fielders routinely left their gloves on the field between innings in those days]. I figured somebody was kicking it out there, so I watched—and it turned out to be Stanky kicking it.

"I ran over and took a swing at him, and we got into a little scrape before other players tore us apart. The next thing we knew, we were on the way to the Savannah jail. He was fined $100 and I got off for nothing, for some reason. We got back to the park about a half-hour later and finished the game."[5]

Connie Ryan (National Baseball Hall of Fame Library, Cooperstown, N.Y.)

Occasional bellicosity notwithstanding, Ryan was remembered as "a good team player" and as "an excellent baseball man."[6] Such compliments were traceable to his rookie season of 1942, when an article commented on how Ryan was "an eager and enthusiastic youngster, though a pleasantly restrained and polite one, looking much like [boxing great] Billy Conn and exuding Conn's engaging sureness in himself."[7]

In fact, when he first came to the major leagues that spring with the New York Giants, the 5-foot-11, 175-pound Ryan was reportedly so deferential that he referred to teammates, including Carl Hubbell, as "Mister."[8] At one point, manager Ott took Ryan aside and told him that everyone with the team would prefer that Connie use their respective first names. With that, one newspaper reporter remarked: "Suddenly you remembered who Connie Ryan reminded you of. Another quiet, courteous gentleman from New Orleans, named Mel Ott."[9]

Cornelius Joseph Ryan was born on February 27, 1920, in New Orleans. He was of Irish heritage and had two younger brothers. His father did administrative work for a New Orleans barge line.

Connie's interest in sports was evident from an early age, and the young man played for local American Legion teams in 1935 and 1936. He also saw action on the baseball, football, basketball, and track teams at Jesuit High School in New Orleans. In addition to becoming the first person ever to receive a full baseball scholarship to Louisiana State University, Ryan also played semipro ball in 1938 for Angier, North Carolina, and the next year he was with a developmental team in Colonial Heights, Virginia.

Ryan's love of the game led him to leave LSU over the Christmas break of his sophomore year to play for the Atlanta Crackers in the Class A-1 Southern Association. Ryan reportedly was conflicted between a career in baseball or in the legal profession, but he elected to choose the former. While he was optioned to Savannah of the Class B Sally League during that first season, Ryan was sent back to Atlanta in 1941 after batting .316 in 113 games for Savannah. During the 1941 season with the Crackers, Ryan batted .300 in 151 games with 83 runs batted in and was chosen as Atlanta's Most Valuable Player.

The Giants purchased Ryan's contract from Atlanta on August 7, 1941, and soon began preparing him to be the team's second baseman in place of Burgess Whitehead, who left the team after a subpar 1941 season. According to one 1942 article: "The kid from Atlanta reminds some of Billy Conn, others of Larry Doyle, but despite the ballyhoo, he has managed to remain Cornelius Ryan, Jr., with a great deal of dignity for a 21-year-old. The boy moved stylishly at second base yesterday, but it's no time to put the plug in for him. If he's overly praised now, it might have to be said next week that Ryan doesn't look like Ryan did last week. In brief, he's just a rookie."[10]

In spite of these high expectations, Ryan played in only 11 games in 1942, batting .185 with two RBIs. He also committed an alarming four errors. "The boy is very nervous, all tightened up," said a newspaper account of May 20, 1942. "That is plain, and there is no need to go beyond that into the play by play of the rookie's misadventures. Summing up, Ryan has not hit, has not come through on double plays and has not fielded with assurance."[11]

While noting that Ryan had performed all of these tasks well in the minor leagues, sportswriter Joe King went on to say: "There's a lot of ball-player in him — it will come out again in awhile, but the Giants need it now." The popular perception was that Ryan suffered a nervous breakdown, similar to what Mickey Witek had endured two years prior.[12]

One bright spot in Ryan's abbreviated rookie season was the time he almost turned an unassisted triple play against Pittsburgh. On May 12 at the Polo Grounds, the Pirates' Frank Gustine hit a line drive to Connie in the seventh inning. Rather than touching second base to force Johnny Lanning and then tagging out Pete Coscarart, who were both running on a 3-and-2 pitch, Ryan instead threw to shortstop Billy Jurges, who forced Lanning and tagged Coscarart for the triple play. "Just a few steps," said one report, "and Ryan could have retired the side [himself]."[13]

His part in one of baseball's rarest feats notwithstanding, New York soon optioned Ryan to Jersey City of the International League for more seasoning. And after hitting a disappointing .243 in 112 games there, the highly-touted second baseman never made it back to the Giants. On April 27, 1943, Ryan was traded to the Boston Braves along with catcher Hugh Poland in exchange for catcher (and future Hall of Famer) Ernie Lombardi. There was some controversy surrounding the deal, with rumors that Boston may have received a secret $30,000 as part of the trade, but it was a great move for Ryan, as he was the regular second baseman in 1943 for the sixth-place Braves club managed by Casey Stengel and Bob Coleman (who took over during Stengel's convalescence from a broken leg). In 132 games during his first full major-league season, Ryan batted only .212. He did, however, hit a three-run ninth-inning home run on April 28 to win the game, 3-2, against his former Giants teammates.

Apparently over his nervousness, Ryan dramatically improved his hitting and fielding the next year, and he was chosen for the first and only time to the National League All-Star team. Ryan played all nine innings of the 1944 All-Star Game at second base, got two hits, and had the lone stolen base of the contest during a 7-1 NL victory at Pittsburgh's Forbes Field.

Two weeks later, on July 25, Ryan enlisted in the Navy. At the time, his batting average of .295 was second on the team, he was tied for the NL lead in stolen bases with 13, and his fielding average was on pace to lead the circuit as well. Duty called, however, and so like many ballplayers during World War II, he entered the military while at the top of his game. Ryan played in just 88 games that year, yet he made enough of an impression that he still received votes for Most Valuable Player that October.

Ryan was discharged in January 1946. Returning to the Braves, he stepped right back in as the team's starting second baseman for the 1946 and 1947 seasons. The club was much improved; under new manager Billy Southworth, it rose to fourth place in 1946 and third in 1947. Ryan was a steady contributor on defense and at bat showed surprising offensive production. However, when the team traded for Dodgers second baseman Eddie Stanky shortly before the 1948 season began, Connie became a reserve. Ryan did play briefly in the 1948 World Series, appearing in two games and striking out in his only at-bat.

Connie may be best remembered for an incident that took place on September 29, 1949, at Braves Field, during his last full season with Boston. During a meaningless end-of-season game, as rain fell and the skies darkened at Braves Field, Ryan donned a raincoat while waiting to bat in the on-deck circle. Home-plate umpire George Barr threw him out of the game for his not-so-subtle suggestion that the game be called.

As Ryan later recounted: "They wouldn't listen to us when we hollered at them from the bench that it was raining too hard to play. They wouldn't even take a hint when we built a little fire out of programs and newspapers in front of the dugout. I thought I'd try to convince them some other way, that's all."[14]

Ryan remained with the Braves until May 10, 1950, when he was traded to the Cincinnati Reds for catcher Walker Cooper. Ryan started at second base for the Reds through 1951. The Reds were a sixth-place team, and despite his sharp baseball mind and solid day-to-day contributions—he led the 1951 team with a career-high 16 home runs—Ryan was not in the team's plans as the organization sought to rebuild. On December 10, 1951, Cincinnati traded Connie along with catcher Smoky Burgess and pitcher Howie Fox to the Philadelphia Phillies for catcher Andy Seminick, infielder Eddie Pellagrini, first baseman/outfielder Dick Sisler, and pitcher Niles Jordan. Phillies manager Eddie Sawyer was thrilled to acquire Ryan, saying: "I think Ryan at second with Granny Hamner at short will make a dandy keystone combination."[15]

They did, for a while. Ryan played all 154 games, hit 12 homers in 1952, scored a career-high 81 runs, and he and Hamner turned nearly 100 double plays. A highlight of Ryan's time with Philadelphia was getting six hits in six at-bats during a game at Pittsburgh on April 16, 1953, making him the first Phillies player and just the 31st in major league history to accomplish what at the time was a big-league record. This game was the springboard for another strong year at the plate, as Ryan hit .296 through the first half of the year. But Philadelphia still left Ryan unprotected later that summer, and when released on August 25 he was picked up on waivers by the Chicago White Sox. He played in only 17 games for Chicago (hitting just .222), then was traded back to the Reds with third baseman Rocky Krsnich and pitcher Saul Rogovin for right fielder Willard Marshall on December 10, 1953. Ryan's only appearance in his second stint with Cincinnati, on April 19, 1954, turned out to also be his last game in the big leagues. He finished his 12-year career in the majors with 988 hits in 1,184 games, 56 home runs, 381 RBIs, and a .248 batting average.

Not surprisingly, Ryan's reputation as a tough, heads-up ballplayer helped him to stay in the game. He played the rest of that season for Louisville of the American Association, then in 1955 played for and managed Corpus Christi of the Class B Big State League. After he appeared in 45 games as player-manager of Austin of the Texas League in 1956, Ryan's professional playing days were over, but his managerial career was just beginning. Ryan's other minor-league managerial stints were with Seattle of the Pacific Coast League in 1958, Oklahoma City of the American Association in 1962, and Magic Valley (Idaho) of the Pioneer Rookie League in 1968-1969. Ryan was also an interim manager twice in the major leagues: for 27 games with Atlanta in 1975 and for six games with Texas in 1977. Both times, the full-time position went to others, perhaps because Connie's no-nonsense approach worried management. "I am not concerned with anybody's feelings," he was quoted as saying while Atlanta's interim manager. "I would pinch-hit for my mother to win a ballgame."[16]

After his coaching and scouting days were through, Ryan kept busy in church and civic groups during his retirement. He was a member of the executive board of the Ancient Order of Hibernians, the New Orleans Diamond Club, and the Major League Players Association. According to the *New Orleans Times Picayune*, he was also active in the St. Mary Magdalene and St. Clement of Rome Catholic churches. He was elected to both the New Orleans and the Louisiana Sports Halls of Fame.

Ryan died on January 3, 1996, after a heart attack. He was 75 years old and was survived by his wife, Lorraine Chalona Streckfus Ryan; four children; six grandchildren; and a great-grandchild. He is buried in Metairie Cemetery.

This biography is adapted from one that appeared in the book Spahn, Sain, and Teddy Ballgame: Boston's (almost) Perfect Baseball Summer of 1948, *edited by Bill Nowlin and published by Rounder Books in 2008.*

Sources

Biographical and statistical information from the websites baseball-reference.com, baseball-almanac.com, and baseballlibrary.com, as well as the following clippings from Connie Ryan's player file at the Baseball Hall of Fame, Cooperstown, New York (dates and publications given where known):

Cincinnati Reds biography, 1951.

"Connie Ryan Discharge Today," January 17, 1946.

"Connie Ryan, Veteran of Baseball Battles, Could Rub Some of His Fight on Braves," December 9, 1956.

"Cooper for Connie Ryan," May 19, 1950.

Daley, Arthur, "Triple Play by Ryan and Jurges Marks 7-3 Success for Ott Team," *New York Times*, May 13, 1952.

Daniel, Dan, "Daniel's Dope," April 29, 1943.

"He Reminded You of Someone," Giant Jottings, March 18, 1942.

Kahn, James M., "Ryan Moves Into His First Workout: Connie, Not Yet 22 Years Old, is Ticketed to be Giants' Regular Second Baseman this Year."

King, Joe, "Ryan Touted Early as Rookie of '42: But New Giant Retains His Poise," February 28, 1942.

King, Joe, "Nerves Still Wrecking Ryan's Play: Another Rest May Solve His Problem," May 26, 1942.

King, Joe, "Ryan Relieved of Keystone Job on Giants: Witek Takes Over for Jittery Recruit," March 1942.

King, Joe, "Unassisted Triple Play—Almost: Few Steps Would Have Turned the Trick," May 13, 1942.

King, Joe, "Rookie Ryan Key Player of Giant Infield: Ott Banks on Youth To Fill Keystone Spot," February 24, 1942.

King, Joe, "Nerves Still Wrecking Ryan's Play: Another Rest May Solve His Problem," May 20, 1942.

Lewis, Ted, "Player, coach, scout Ryan dies at age 75," *New Orleans Times Picayune*, January 4, 1996.

Minor league data, apparently from the 1978 Texas Rangers media guide, provided by the Hall of Fame.

Minshew, Wayne, "Trade Winds Send Players Into Motion," September 20, 1975.

Mitchell, Jerry, "Ott Is Sold on Connie Ryan: Rookie Second Baseman's Fielding Impresses," 1942.

"New Orleans Boys Get Break from Mel Ott," February 4, 1942.

Obituary, "Connie Ryan 75," *Sports Collector's Digest*, February 2, 1996.

Obituary, "Infielder 'Connie' Ryan II, N.O. baseball legend, dies," *New Orleans Times Picayune*, January 4, 1996.

"Ott at Last Gets Slugger He Long Has Been Seeking: Mel's Infield Reserve Strength Reduced to Bartell by Trade," April 28, 1943.

"Redleg in a Rhubarb: One of the reasons Connie Ryan has become Cincy's ace second sacker is because he once went to bat in a raincoat when he was with Boston."

Roeder, Bill, "Giants Not Amused by Connie's Con Game," May 7, 1951.

"Ryan of Braves Goes Into Navy," July 25, 1944.

"Ryan Is 31st To Get 6 Hits."

"Ryan First Phil To Get '6 For 6,'" April 17, 1953.

"Sawyer High on Ryan's Hustle," *Boston Daily Record*, March 17, 1952.

Smith, Ken, "Ryan Homer in 9th Shames Giants, 3-2," *New York Daily Mirror*, April 29, 1943.

Tagliabue, Emil, "Ryan's Right Cross Starts Corpus Christi Mass Fight: Park Police Stop Melee Between Teams," August 17, 1955.

United Press, "Braves Sign Connie Ryan To Coach at 3d," October 6, 1956.

"Walker Cooper for Braves' Ryan," May 11, 1950.

Notes

1. *The Sporting News*, November 6, 1957.
2. Ibid.
3. Joe King, "Rookie Ryan Key Player of Giant Infield: Ott Banks on Youth To Fill Keystone Spot," February 24, 1942.
4. Jerry Mitchell, "Ott Is Sold on Connie Ryan: Rookie Second Baseman's Fielding Impresses," 1942.
5. "Connie Ryan, Veteran of Baseball Battles, Could Rub Some of His Fight on Braves," December 9, 1956.
6. Ted Lewis, "Player, coach, scout Ryan dies at age 75." *New Orleans Times Picayune*, January 4, 1996.
7. James M. Kahn, "Ryan Moves Into His First Workout: Connie, Not Yet 22 Years Old, is Ticketed to be Giants' Regular Second Baseman this Year."
8. Joe King, "Nerves Still Wrecking Ryan's Play: Another Rest May Solve His Problem," May 26, 1942.
9. "He Reminded You of Someone," Giant Jottings, March 18, 1942.
10. Joe King, "Ryan Touted Early as Rookie of '42: But New Giant Retains His Poise," February 28, 1942.
11. Joe King, "Nerves Still Wrecking Ryan's Play: Another Rest May Solve His Problem," May 26, 1942.
12. Ibid.
13. Joe King, "Unassisted Triple Play—Almost: Few Steps Would Have Turned the Trick," May 13, 1942.
14. "Redleg in a Rhubarb: One of the reasons Connie Ryan has become Cincy's ace second sacker is because he once went to bat in a raincoat when he was with Boston."
15. "Sawyer High on Ryan's Hustle," *Boston Daily Record*, March 17, 1952.
16. Wayne Minshew, "Trade Winds Send Players Into Motion," September 20, 1975.

John Quinn

By Rory Costello

JOHN J. QUINN spent 47 years working for major-league baseball teams, 28 of those as a general manager. During his tenure as GM of the Boston and Milwaukee Braves (1945-1958), the franchise won three National League pennants and the 1957 World Series. After Quinn went to Philadelphia in 1959, he did another major rebuilding job, though the Phillies never won a pennant on his watch—their collapse in 1964 was his biggest disappointment in baseball.

Quinn was a savvy executive who built his teams the traditional way: by focusing on the farm system and making judicious trades. He also recognized the importance of black and Latino talent. "John was gentlemanly and old school. Always dressed to the nines, he wore a suit and tie with suspenders and a white-starched collar everywhere. And always smelled like 'your father's after-shave.'"[1] On the flip side, Quinn lived up to an Irish stereotype: He liked to drink.[2] He also often knocked heads with players when it came to salary negotiations.

John Jacob Quinn was born on April 1, 1908, in Columbus, Ohio.[3] His father, James Aloysius Robert Quinn (1870-1954), also had a prominent career in baseball at many levels—one may trace much of the son's life history through the father's movements. Bob Quinn, who had been a minor-league catcher and manager in the 1890s, became general manager of the Columbus Senators in 1902 and served in that capacity through 1917. Bob and his wife, Margaret Clark, had four children. John's older brother, Robert, became a Dominican priest, serving as a professor and director of athletics at Providence College. Their two sisters were named Margaret and Mary.[4]

In 1917 Bob Quinn became business manager of the St. Louis Browns. As a result, John went to St. Louis University High School. The family lived around the corner from Sportsman's Park, where John kept busy doing "countless little jobs" and "running errands" for his father. He also got to sit on the bench with the likes of George Sisler and Ken Williams, the stars of the team that nearly won the 1922 American League pennant.[5]

Then in 1923, Quinn *père* led a group of Columbus investors who purchased the Boston Red Sox from Harry Frazee. The family moved east, and John went to Boston College, where he ran track and tried out for the baseball team (coached by Hall of Famer Hugh Duffy) as a "good field, no hit" outfielder.[6] Upon graduating in 1929, Quinn immediately entered a minor position with the Red Sox.[7] In 1963 he remembered working with the groundskeeper and in the ticket office.[8]

After selling the Red Sox to Tom Yawkey in 1933, Bob Quinn served as business manager of the Brooklyn Dodgers during the 1934 and 1935 seasons. He then came back to Boston—but joined the city's other big-league team back then, the Braves, as president and part owner. Upon his father's return to Boston, John Quinn quit the Red Sox and became club secretary for the Braves. He later became farm director.[9] As his father

John Quinn (National Baseball Hall of Fame Library, Cooperstown, N.Y.)

put it wryly in 1945, "He has taken care of what minor-league interests the Braves have had."[10]

In February 1934 John had married Miriam Maloney, from Newton, Massachusetts. They had five children: Joan, Robert, John, Margaret, and Susan.[11] The Quinn family's intimate involvement with baseball came to span four generations. After coming up through the minors as an executive and working as a farm director and scouting director in the majors, the third-generation Bob Quinn was general manager for three big-league clubs from 1988 to 1996. His son, also named Bob, became a major-league executive too. John Jr., or Jack, was a minor-league exec, notably with the Hawaii Islanders, which he owned for several years.[12] In addition, two of John Quinn's daughters were close to baseball. Margaret, better known as Margo, married another longtime farm/scouting director and GM, Roland Hemond. Susan worked for a time in the front office of the California Angels while they were the parent club of the Hawaii Islanders.

In February 1945, at the age of 75, the elder Bob Quinn stepped down as general manager of the Braves, becoming farm director instead. He was named director of the National Baseball Hall of Fame and Museum in July 1948, becoming honorary director in June 1952 following his retirement from the active post. He died in March 1954.[13] John Quinn replaced his father (he had become assistant treasurer when new owners Lou Perini, Joe Maney, and Guido Rugo bought control in January 1944).[14] Praise issued from Ed Rumill, longtime baseball writer for the Boston-based *Christian Science Monitor*: "While the promotion of John Quinn to the general managership of the Boston Braves may have come as a surprise to the fandom section of the Hub, it was accepted as a deserving break for one of the game's most promising young executives by those close to the local baseball situation." The article's subhead read, "Good Background, Hard Worker."[15] Such senior baseball men as Branch Rickey, Larry MacPhail, and George Weiss had all been interested in John in previous years. Previously, when Quinn left the Red Sox, Tom Yawkey had thought so well of the young man that he made a key to Fenway Park his parting gift.[16]

From the moment he took over, Quinn focused on building up the Braves' minor-league chain. He said, "Dad and I have always felt that farms are the only way to develop a winning major-league club. If you have the cash, you can occasionally buy a player who will help you. But most of the time all you can buy is what other clubs don't want. And that type of player won't get you anywhere but down." With an eye toward the end of World War II, he wanted to move fast to secure talent.[17]

Quinn continued to apply this philosophy as he laid the groundwork for success. In early 1947 the Braves added Jack Zeller, the former general manager of the Detroit Tigers, as their chief scout. Zeller said, "I am happy to join such an up-and-coming organization.... the owners of the club have indicated they are going all-out to build a winner and develop a fine farm system." By that point, the Braves either owned or had working agreements with 15 farm clubs. They also had 30 full- or part-time scouts. Zeller added, "I have no intention of reorganizing the scouting staff. It is composed of thoroughly experienced men, who are doing a good job."[18]

Quinn also tended to Boston's Braves Field, which was a modern stadium when former owner Jim Gaffney opened it back in 1915, but had been steadily falling into disrepair. Ahead of the 1948 season, Quinn said, "A conservative estimate of the money spent on Braves Field for improvements and innovations would run to more than a half-million [about $4.8 million in 2012 dollars]. And that doesn't include work we still have in mind and will put into effect as soon as we can."[19]

The Braves then proceeded to win the National League pennant; as of 1963, Quinn called it his biggest single thrill in the game. "You can't beat that first one," he said. He also pointed to his September 1946 trade for heavy-hitting third baseman Bob Elliott as the team's key acquisition.[20] However, he also obtained two other important starters in deals ahead of the 1948 season, left fielder Jeff Heath and second baseman Eddie Stanky. The 1948 Braves were an older team, though; Quinn later noted that their window of success was limited to that year. Boston fell to fourth place in

1949 and stayed there in 1950 and 1951, with sub-.500 records in two of those years.

In September 1951, according to the *Boston Post*, after Ford Frick succeeded Happy Chandler as commissioner of baseball, Quinn was rumored to succeed Frick as National League president.[21] However, the job went instead to Cincinnati general manager and team president Warren Giles.

After a seventh-place finish in 1952, the Braves franchise moved to Milwaukee. The Quinn family didn't find it easy to uproot from Boston, but as John said in 1963, "We went and it turned out great."[22] Meanwhile, he had been turning over the big-league roster, with a continued emphasis on organizational depth. Halfway through the 1953 season, he said, "Harry Jenkins did a fine job rounding up a farm system and in setting up a scouting staff throughout the country which would enable us to match other big league clubs. … Once the scouts have done their job, you must have good minor-league managers."[23]

In summary, he accurately estimated that "the center line of defense and the infield should have 'a reasonable expectancy of eight years.'" Such top players as Eddie Mathews (signed 1949) and Johnny Logan (signed 1947) had sprung from the farm well before the move. A focus on adding talent from the Negro League brought Bill Bruton in 1950 and Hank Aaron in 1952; Quinn rightly regarded landing Hammerin' Hank as his best transaction.[24]

Ironically, Aaron's opening came earlier than the team expected because of a Quinn deal that he acknowledged as a bust: the 1954 trade of pitcher Johnny Antonelli for outfielder Bobby Thomson.[25] A few years later, though, he sent Thomson (plus two other players) back to the Giants and got second baseman Red Schoendienst. "We won twice with him," said Quinn of Schoendienst. "It was no accident."[26]

Even with their foundation of young talent — and the redoubtable Warren Spahn — the Braves could do no better than second place (three times) or third from 1953 through 1956. It took until 1957 before Milwaukee surpassed the Brooklyn Dodgers and New York Giants. The long-term focus proved wise. It's worth examining in further depth how that winning club was constructed:

- Amateur free-agent signings: Spahn (1940), Ernie Johnson (1942), Bob Buhl (1948), Del Crandall (1948), Don McMahon (1950), Bob Trowbridge (1950), Gene Conley (1951), Frank Torre (1951), Wes Covington (1952), Felix Mantilla (1952), Taylor Phillips (1953), and Juan Pizarro (1956).
- Trades: Lew Burdette (1951), Joe Adcock (1953), Andy Pafko (1953), Danny O'Connell (1953), Del Rice (1955), Bob Hazle (1956).

Indeed, after Milwaukee won its first pennant, Quinn said, "You hear a lot about farm systems these days, but I don't think there is another club in the majors that can match us for home-grown players." He credited many of the Braves' scouts by name for their key role, but singled out Johnny Moore, who recommended that the team ask for Lew Burdette while dealing Johnny Sain to the Yankees.[27]

With regard to trades, especially the Schoendienst deal, Quinn said, "My dad often compared baseball to a wagon wheel. It was his theory that if you needed a spoke, it was your job to go and get one. The price, he said, was no object if that was what you needed to keep rolling." He added, "Even with Schoendienst, where would we be without the replacements Fred [Haney] called into action and the tremendous help they furnished? Baseball is still a team game, and nobody ever won without a good team and a lot of luck." It was also interesting to observe that Quinn viewed the clubhouse as outside his domain; he would not visit unless one of the Braves broke an important big-league record or was seriously hurt.[28]

For the most part, the Braves stood pat after winning the World Series. The starting lineup was the same; on the bench, two other farmhands (left fielder Harry Hanebrink and second baseman Mel Roach) earned more action. The main difference between the pennant-winning clubs of 1957 and 1958 was in the pitching staff. Veteran right-hander Bob Rush arrived in a five-player deal in December 1957, and yet more minor-league talent — Carl Willey and Joey Jay — was ready. During the winter meetings, Quinn had sought another lefty, but he couldn't get the man he wanted, Harvey Haddix. He dismissed the idea of dealing Gene Conley for Haddix, saying, "Trading pitcher for pitcher won't work.

It might help our situation by giving us a left-hander, but Cincinnati wouldn't do it because it wouldn't do them any particular good. We would undoubtedly have to throw in somebody else."[29]

On November 17, 1958, Quinn was honored at a testimonial dinner in Milwaukee. Among the baseball dignitaries on hand were the National and American League presidents, Warren Giles and Will Harridge. Some 200 people who sent telegrams, including Richard Nixon, then vice president of the United States but always a keen baseball fan. Charlie Grimm, Haney's predecessor, said, "As long as John is on the job, Milwaukee will never have to worry about a first-division or even a championship club."[30]

Less than two months later, though, Quinn left Milwaukee. On January 13, 1959, he resigned and joined the Phillies on a five-year contract. The Braves in turn recruited John McHale, who had been Detroit's general manager for the previous two seasons. Birdie Tebbetts, executive vice president of the Braves, was an old Tigers teammate of McHale's (though not a close friend). Quinn denied the talk that his departure was related to the appointment of Tebbetts, noting that Phillies owner Bob Carpenter "offered me a proposition I just didn't feel I could turn down."[31] Carpenter said, "I wanted to get the best, and my first choice was John Quinn."[32]

The Phillies needed to get younger and make a break with the past; they were still clinging to several heroes of the 1950 NL pennant winners, the Whiz Kids. Another link to the Whiz Kids, manager Eddie Sawyer, resigned after Opening Day 1960, saying, "I am 49 years old and want to live to be 50." One game later, Quinn installed his choice: Gene Mauch. In 1963 Quinn recalled, "I had placed Gene in his first managerial job at Atlanta [in 1953, a Double-A affiliate of the Braves] and he had great success there."[33]

The hiring of Mauch was rooted in the decision that Quinn came to view as his worst: giving Tommy Holmes the manager's seat in Boston in 1951. "Tommy was our most popular player, and when Billy Southworth quit, I thought promoting Holmes would stimulate interest. But Tommy was lost and it taught me a lesson—unless a man had minor-league managing experience, it was a terrible gamble to turn a major-league club over to him."[34]

As Quinn set about rebuilding, he lured five of the Braves' scouts to Philadelphia.[35] In May 1964 he reiterated his core belief, saying, "When I came here, I said that no major-league club could be successful without a productive farm system. You have to find and raise your own. You can't buy good ballplayers." This, of course, was a decade before the free-agent era dawned. Nonetheless, he continued, "Scouts are the most important people connected with a big-league club."[36]

Yet Quinn also made numerous canny trades. He again credited his father's teaching: "My dad always said never to be afraid to give up three players for one or four for two so long as you got the man you wanted. He was never worried about how much he helped the other team. He was only concerned how much good he did for himself. He wasn't trying to trim anybody."[37]

Still other useful pickups came via the Rule 5 draft. It is also noteworthy that in 1961, Quinn called for Major League Baseball to adopt an amateur draft similar to pro football's. In the past he had paid some big bonuses—Johnny Antonelli's being one example—but he said, "The whole situation has gotten out of hand. ... It's suicide the way it is right now."[38]

The Phillies finished last in 1959, 1960, and 1961, enduring a 23-game losing streak in '61. Things started to look up in 1962; even though the team merely finished in seventh place, the record was above .500 (81-80) for the first time since 1953. The 1963 season was another stride forward, with an 87-75 mark that was good for fourth place. That August Bob Carpenter gave Quinn a vote of confidence, saying that he planned to rehire the GM when his initial five-year contract expired. Carpenter said, "He's built the ballclub and it's starting to arrive. We're getting better and we're going to see this through. We're planning two years from now. If we get first- and third-base help we'll be in good shape."[39]

In October 1963, while attending a luncheon to announce the retirement of farm director Gene Martin, Quinn collapsed. "The condition of the 55-year-old baseball official was so serious for a time that a priest administered last rites as he lay on the floor. ... When Quinn could not be revived he was taken by rescue truck to Jefferson Hospital. There he regained consciousness, sat up and wanted to leave."[40] He made a rapid recovery; "Doctors attributed Quinn's troubles to overwork and tension but found nothing seriously wrong."

A few days after Quinn went into the hospital, he was eager to return to his desk.[41] By November he was back working, but on a limited schedule.[42] Soon he and Mauch were in full swing at the winter meetings. In early 1964 Quinn was also wrangling over salaries. In a way, it was a good problem because younger players were coming into their own. But as Philly beat writer Allen Lewis observed, "Quinn is reluctant to jump youngsters on the way up into the big money after one good year. He feels that it takes at least two good seasons to determine a player's probable future. When they have established themselves, the general manager seems to have little trouble coming to agreement with them."[43]

In later years, though, various players — notably Dick Allen — would say otherwise. As the *Philadelphia Daily News* put it in 1986, the Phillies were "a team he [Quinn] oversaw with great frugality."[44] "I know I'm accused of being too tight," he once said. "But you have to keep in mind it's someone else's money I'm passing out, not my own."[45]

As the Phillies got off to a strong start in 1964 and stayed at the top of the heap, the press had plenty of plaudits for Quinn. That July Jim Foster, sports editor of the *Spartanburg* (South Carolina) *Herald*, called him "a miracle worker," observing, "One of the factors behind his success was disclosed by his visit to the Spartanburg Phillies, the lowest of the Philadelphia farm teams in classification. His presence shows that the big man keeps his eyes focused on the entire operation of the Phillies — even in a year when all goes well. Foster added, "Refusing all credit for himself, Quinn said: 'We have a very good manager in Gene Mauch. He's done wonders with the kids. I'd say it's a case of our young players who we knew had potential coming through for us this year.'"[46]

Yet in June, Allen Lewis issued a Cassandra-like prediction: "Walter Alston may be something of a prophet. When honored by the Philadelphia Sports Writers Association, June 3, at a Baseball Forum luncheon, he told Phillies' officials and fans, 'Enjoy yourselves; things may not always be this easy.'" The Dodgers manager, who had seen his team lose to the Phillies on both previous nights, added, "If I didn't know who was in first place, all I'd have to do would be to look around here ... or see the smiles on the faces of Mauch and John Quinn over there."[47]

Quinn was active when the circumstances dictated in that 1964 season, especially trying to fill the troublesome first-base position when veteran Roy Sievers was no longer producing. Picking up Frank Thomas from the Mets was a great move, and getting Vic Power after Thomas got hurt was the best he could do under the circumstances. The man he really wanted to get from the Angels was Joe Adcock, but Quinn's counterpart in California — none other than Fred Haney — wouldn't make Adcock available.[48]

The Phillies that season seemed ready to capture their first pennant in 14 years, holding a 6 1/2-game lead with 12 to play. However, the team folded, losing ten consecutive games in late September, and lost the pennant to the St. Louis Cardinals by a single game. Then and later, Quinn refused to pin the collapse on Gene Mauch. "We're both responsible," he said. "Mauch gets paid for the managing and I get paid for doing everything else. Don't blame Gene."[49] Needless to say, the disappointment long lingered. In 1972 he told Allen Lewis, "We looked like we had a commanding lead, and that made it all the harder. It looked like the fruit of your efforts and that it would all pay off, and then to lose it like that."[50]

The Phillies remained fairly respectable from 1965 through 1967, winning 85, 87, and 82 games, but finished in the middle of the pack in the National League. During this time, the team acquired veterans (Dick Stuart, Bill White, and Dick Groat, among others) and parted with young talent (Alex Johnson and especially Ferguson Jenkins). Ahead of the 1968 season, the team was described as "in the process of at least a partial rebuilding program."[51] They fell below .500 and to seventh place.

Another notable event for Quinn that year showed his social conscience. Just before Opening Day 1968, Martin Luther King, Jr. was assassinated. All big-league clubs postponed their openers except for the Los Angeles Dodgers, but Quinn said he would rather forfeit the game and pay a fine than take the field. After Dodgers president Walter O'Malley met with NL President Giles and Quinn, the decision became unanimous.[52]

Only the presence of an expansion club, the Montreal Expos, saved the Phillies from finishing last in the NL East in 1969 and 1970. The following year, they dropped to the cellar. Quinn came under pressure for not making trades that winter, but he stuck to his guns. In late January 1972 he remarked, "As I've said right along, I'm not going to make a deal just for the sake of making a deal."[53]

Less than a month later, though, Quinn did make a big move, for a centerpiece of the Phillies' winning teams to come. In his final trade — which some observers rate as his best ever — he acquired future Hall of Fame pitcher Steve Carlton from the St. Louis Cardinals even-up for pitcher Rick Wise.

On June 3, 1972, the Phillies were in fifth place with a 16-27 record, 15 games out of first. Even Steve Carlton, who finished 27-10 that year, had lost five straight starts. Quinn — by then the dean of major-league GMs — was fired. Bob Carpenter declared that he had decided to make a change because of the team's unexpectedly poor showing. He did, however, retain Quinn as a vice president on a consulting basis until the latter became eligible for a pension on his 65th birthday, April 1, 1973.[54] Quinn himself said, "I hope I can remain in baseball because I feel I can still make some fine contributions to this great game."[55]

Indeed, once the consultancy agreement ended, Quinn officially retired from the Phillies organization — and promptly joined the Houston Astros, becoming a special-assignment scout for general manager Spec Richardson.[56] Their friendship went back to the 1950s, when Richardson was business manager for the Jacksonville Braves.

After a long illness, John Quinn died on September 20, 1976, in Stanton, California, at the age of 68. He was survived by Miriam and four of their five children (Joan predeceased him). In his obituary in *The Sporting News*, one Quinn quote ran, "We all make glaring errors and we all make good deals sometimes."[57] Yet he summed up his philosophy even better in May 1964. "You never look back after making a deal. You don't hope the man you give away flops. You simply hope who you get does the job for you."[58]

Sources

baseball-reference.com

retrosheet.org

Notes

1. Steve Bucci and Dave Brown, *Drinking Coffee With a Fork: The Story of Steve Carlton and the '72 Phillies* (Philadelphia: Camino Books, 2011).
2. Quinn's son Bob talked about this and his own drinking in 1992. Paul Daugherty, "The Mighty Quinn," *Cincinnati*, March 1992, 24.
3. "John Quinn Is Now Aiding Astros," Associated Press, April 2, 1973.
4. Loretta J. McLaughlin, "For John Quinns, Almost Everything Comes After Baseball," *Milwaukee Sentinel*, April 6, 1953, Sports-1. Quinn's mother's maiden name came from his brother's obituary: "Rev. Robert G. Quinn; formerly head of P.C. education department, athletics," *Providence Journal*, January 4, 1987, C-10.
5. Barney Kremenko, "He's Putting the Whiz Back in Fizz Kids," *Baseball Digest*, March 1963, 65. Originally published in the *New York Journal-American;* Ed Rumill, "Dad Quinn Coaches Son Into Own Job," *The Sporting News*, February 22, 1945, 7.
6. Rumill, "Dad Quinn."
7. McLaughlin, "For John Quinns."
8. Kremenko, "He's Putting," 64.
9. McLaughlin, "For John Quinns."
10. Rumill, "Dad Quinn."
11. McLaughlin, "For John Quinns."
12. The third-generation Bob Quinn was a minor-league executive with the Braves and Phillies starting in 1959. He was Minor League Executive of the Year for Double-A with the Reading Phillies in 1967. He then became farm director for the Milwaukee Brewers (1971-73) and scouting director for the Cleveland Indians (1973-83). Later, he served as general manager of the New York Yankees (1988-89), Cincinnati Reds (1990-92), and San Francisco Giants (1993-96). His son Bob worked in the Giants front office from 1994 to 2002; he then became a Milwaukee Brewers executive in 2003, where he remained as an executive vice president as of 2013. Jack Quinn was twice Minor League Executive of the Year, in 1962 with the San Jose Bees (lower classifications) and in 1966 with Hawaii (Triple-A). After leaving Hawaii, he was vice president and GM of the Vancouver Canadians, another team in the Pacific Coast League

(1978-83). He then served as GM and later president of the St. Louis Blues franchise in the National Hockey League (1983-86).

13 "Bob Quinn, Former Hall of Fame Director, Dies," *Otsego* (New York) *Farmer*, March 19, 1954, 1.

14 Bill King, "Boston Braves Are Now Home Owned As Joe Maney, Guido Rugo, and Louis Perini, Contractors, Buy Stock Control," Associated Press, January 22, 1944.

15 "Ed Much-Sought-After Young Man," *Christian Science Monitor*, February 15, 1945; Rumill, "John Quinn."

16 Rumill, "John Quinn."

17 Rumill, "Dad Quinn."

18 Howell Stevens, "Jack Zeller Ends 'Retirement' to Become Braves' Chief Scout," *The Sporting News*, February 26, 1947, 16.

19 John Drohan, "Braves' 1915 Park Given $500,000 New Look," *The Sporting News*, January 21, 1948, 2.

20 Kremenko, "He's Putting," 64.

21 "John Quinn Is Mentioned for NL President," *Otsego* (New York) *Farmer*, September 28, 1951, 2.

22 Kremenko, "He's Putting," 66.

23 Joe King, "5-Year Rebuilding Pays Off on Braves," *The Sporting News*, July 1, 1953, 1-2.

24 "John Quinn Dead at 68; Former G.M. of Braves and Phillies."

25 Kremenko, "He's Putting," 66.

26 Kremenko, "He's Putting," 64.

27 James Enright, "Quinn Quiet G.M. of Tepee Tomahawkers," *The Sporting News*, October 2, 1957, 9.

28 Enright, "Quinn Quiet G.M."

29 Bob Wolf, "14 Righthanders—But Braves Still Hungry for Lefty," *The Sporting News*, December 25, 1957, 22.

30 Bob Wolf, "Game's Brass Honor Quinn, 'Great Guy, Real Champion,'" *The Sporting News*, November 26, 1958, 32.

31 "Quinn To Phils, Hamey Back To Yank Office," Associated Press, January 14, 1959.

32 "Big League Executive Switches," United Press International, January 14, 1959.

33 Kremenko, "He's Putting," 63-64.

34 "John Quinn Dead at 68; Former G.M. of Braves and Phillies."

35 Oliver E. Kuechle, "Time Out for Talk," *Milwaukee Journal*, July 11, 1960, Part 2: 9.

36 "Quinn Making Contender Out of Phils," *Pittsburgh Press*, May 17, 1964, Section 2: 4.

37 Kremenko, "He's Putting," 65.

38 "Quinn Urges Majors Adopt Pro Football's Draft Method," *The Sporting News*, June 28, 1961, 11.

39 "John Quinn To Be Rehired, Says Happy Phils' Owner," Associated Press, August 8, 1963.

40 "Phillies Boss Rests After Collapsing," Associated Press, October 11, 1963.

41 "Overwork, Tension Blamed for Collapse of G.M. Quinn," *The Sporting News*, October 26, 1963, 18.

42 Allen Lewis, "Phillie Fodder," *The Sporting News*, November 16, 1963, 20.

43 Allen Lewis, "Phil Salaries Soar; Youngsters in Line for King-Size Hikes," *The Sporting News*, January 25, 1964, 14.

44 "Samuel Strikes Pay Dirt in Settlement," *Philadelphia Daily News*, February 12, 1986.

45 "John Quinn Dead at 68; Former G.M. of Braves and Phillies." *The Sporting News*, October 9, 1976, 53.

46 Jim Foster, "No More Jokes On The Phils," *Spartanburg* (South Carolina) *Herald*, July 16, 1964, 34.

47 Allen Lewis, " 'Live It Up,' Alston Tells Phils; 'You May Run Into Roadblocks,'" *The Sporting News*, June 20, 1964, 6.

48 Allen Lewis, "John Quinn Recalls His Biggest Disappointment in Baseball," *Baseball Digest*, October 1972, 65. Originally published in the *Philadelphia Inquirer*.

49 "John Quinn Dead at 68; Former G.M. of Braves and Phillies."

50 Lewis, "John Quinn Recalls."

51 Ed Rumill, "Phillies: partial rebuilding," *Christian Science Monitor*, March 13, 1968, 7.

52 "Majors' Openers Set Back In Mourning for Dr. King," *The Sporting News*, April 20, 1968, 28.

53 Ralph Bernstein, "John Quinn Prefers To Wait Rather Than Trade, Believing Phillies' Young Men Will Prove To Be Stars In Many Future Years." Associated Press, January 26, 1972.

54 "Phillies' Paul Owens: 'I'd Trade My Mother,'" Associated Press, June 4, 1972.

55 Lewis, "John Quinn Recalls."

56 "John Quinn Is Now Aiding Astros"; "Quinn Now With Astros," *The Sporting News*, April 21, 1973, 36.

57 "John Quinn Dead at 68; Former G.M. of Braves and Phillies."

58 "Quinn Makes Another Winner With Phillies."

County Stadium, Milwaukee, Wisconsin

By Gregg Hoffmann

MILWAUKEE WAS READY for major-league baseball in 1953.

More than 10,000 people turned out for an open house at the ballpark on March 15, three days before the Braves' move to Milwaukee was approved by the National League owners.

Another large crowd turned out on April 6 and braved sleet and cold just to watch an exhibition game against the Boston Red Sox which lasted two innings. When County Stadium opened for the first Milwaukee Braves regular-season game on Tuesday afternoon, April 14, fans lined up hours before the gates opened in order to be among the first to get inside.

Fans that Opening Day started tailgating, a tradition that continues in Milwaukee, while bands played and dignitaries flocked to the new ballpark. A crowd of 34,357 packed the stadium and thousands more listened on radios outside and in homes and pubs around the town. Fans cheered wildly for every hit, every strike, and everything else. It was all new and exciting.

The game lived up to the excitement the day promised, with center fielder Billy Bruton winning the 3-2 contest on a disputed tenth-inning home run that bounced off the glove of a leaping Enos Slaughter, the Cardinals' right fielder.

It had been a long journey to that opener. County officials and others had talked about building a "major league" ballpark in Milwaukee since the 19-teens. Several locations were bandied about over the years, according to Milwaukee County records. Local politicians had differing opinions about where best to situate the stadium. Transportation, parking, and the demolition of existing buildings all factored in, delaying the project by decades.

Officials originally planned to build the stadium for the Milwaukee Brewers of the Triple-A American Association, an affiliate of the Boston Braves. In September 1948, they finally focused on Story Quarry, an abandoned landfill on the west side of the city.

Construction began in October 1950. Officials had to scramble to get materials, in part due to the demands of the Korean War. They were able to convince federal officials that construction had begun before the war rationing was imposed and were thus able to get the necessary steel. Between the material shortage and a required land swap with the adjacent Soldiers Home, the creation of Milwaukee's new ballpark literally required an act of Congress.

The ballpark, whose cost was initially put at $5 million, was the first in the country to be paid for by public funds. The funds came from a combination of city and County of Milwaukee bonds. As for the site, the US Congress in 1949 approved the leasing of 22 acres of federally-owned land for $1 a year and the county bought another 98 acres. A federal agency, the National Production Authority, also had to approve the construction after it had banned any new recreational facilities because of the need for steel and other materials for

County Stadium (National Baseball Hall of Fame Library, Cooperstown, N.Y.)

the Korean War. The stadium project was approved because groundbreaking had taken place a week before the ban was put into effect.

Osborn Engineering was the architect. Hunzinger Construction was the general contractor on the project. The stadium was built primarily for baseball, but was intended to be multipurpose, like Exhibition Stadium in Toronto and Municipal Stadium in Cleveland. (In 1988 home-game scenes for the movie *Major League,* which dealt with the Cleveland Indians, were shot at County Stadium during the summer of 1988, in part because it resembled Municipal Stadium, which was undergoing work at the time.)

The new stadium featured a double-decked grandstand and mezzanine that ran from first base to third base. The lower grandstand extended down the right-field line and to the foul pole. Temporary bleachers occupied the space down the left-field line, as well as several bleacher sections in the outfield. Over the years, a picnic area in left field became a popular feature of the ballpark. So did a grove of fir and spruce trees planted in March 1954, which acquired the name Perini's Woods. Throughout its history, County Stadium was expanded piecemeal, and eventually reached a capacity of 55,000-plus.

It was considered state-of-the-art in its early days and helped to lure the Braves from Boston. The franchise shift also paved the way for other teams, notably the Dodgers and Giants, to join the westward migration.

County Stadium was ready to go by spring 1953, but the Brewers, the Braves' top minor-league team, never played there. Instead, the Boston Braves owners, who had struggled for years at the gate as the second team to the Red Sox, applied for permission to move to Milwaukee.

Lou Perini, principal owner of the Braves, had blocked the St. Louis Browns from moving to Milwaukee earlier. Perini was able to persuade the National League owners to allow his club to move, only three weeks before the season was to start.

With Charlie Grimm, who had piloted the Brewers, as the Braves manager, the club immediately became competitive. Eddie Mathews, Johnny Logan, and others who had come through Milwaukee as minor leaguers, became fan favorites. The 1953 Braves finished 92-62, good for second place, in their first season and set a National League attendance record of 1,826,397.

The Braves continued to contend in their early years in Milwaukee; in fact, they never had a losing season in their 13 years there. Their fewest wins up to the 1957 championship season was 85 in 1955. They finished no worse than third place from 1953 through 1960.

In 1956 the Braves finished only one game behind the Brooklyn Dodgers. They seemed poised to make the move to the top after that season. Fred Haney, a contrast in managing style to the affable Grimm, took over as the skipper in mid-June of 1956 and meant business from the beginning.

The Braves made the move to first in 1957 when they won 95 games. One of the biggest moments in County Stadium history came on September 23, 1957. Henry Aaron, who was the Most Valuable Player that season, homered in the 11th inning off the St. Louis Cardinals' Billy Muffett to give the Braves a 4-2 victory that clinched the pennant. Aaron has often said that that blast against St. Louis was the biggest of his career, even surpassing the homer in Atlanta that broke Babe Ruth's record of 714.

County Stadium was decked out in red, white, and blue for the World Series. One member of the Yankees—reported to be manager Casey Stengel—referred to Milwaukee as "bush," and the fans took that up as their rallying cry, with signs "Bushville Wins" once the Braves won.

The Braves clinched the World Series in New York in Game Seven behind Lew Burdette's third win of the Series. Game Five goes down as one of the great games in the stadium's history. Each team had won two games. Burdette, who had beaten the Yankees 4-2 in Game Two, was opposed by Whitey Ford, who had defeated the Braves 3-1 in Game One. In the sixth inning of a scoreless battle, the Braves broke through with a run. With two out and nobody on base, Mathews bounced a chopper toward second baseman Jerry Coleman. Hustling down the line, Mathews narrowly beat the throw to first. Aaron blooped a single to right-center, sending Mathews to third base. Then Joe Adcock smacked a line-drive single to right that scored

Mathews. The single tally was all Burdette needed. He shut out the Yankees, 1-0, on seven hits.

From 1954 through 1957 the Braves drew more than two million fans each season. On June 12, 1954, journeyman Braves pitcher Jim Wilson fired the first major-league no-hitter in Milwaukee, against the Philadelphia Phillies. The cover of the inaugural issue of *Sports Illustrated*, on August 16, 1954, displayed a photo of Eddie Mathews batting in County Stadium. On July 12, 1955, the stadium hosted its first All-Star Game. More than 45,000 fans saw the National League roar back from a 5-0 deficit to win 6-5 in 12 innings. Attendance peaked at 2,215,404 in 1957 but slipped to 1,971,101 in 1958. In 1959, the year the Braves lost the pennant to the Los Angeles Dodgers in two games during a best-of-three playoff, attendance dropped to 1,749,112.

The subsequent years still had winning seasons and historic events, including two no-hitters by Spahn and one by Burdette, Pittsburgh's Harvey Haddix hurling 12 perfect innings in 1959 only to lose to the Braves in the 13th, San Francisco's Willie Mays hitting four home runs in a game in 1961 and many other thrills. But the magical team that won the championship gradually broke up. The Miracle in Milwaukee had run its course.

From 1960 through 1965, their last season in Milwaukee, the Braves never won fewer than 83 games. Even so, attendance continued to decline, dipping under a million for the first time in 1962. Rumors of the club moving already were circulating.

The 1964 season was marred by rumors about the Braves' status in Milwaukee, and outright feuding began between the ballclub and members of the community. County Board Chairman Eugene Grobschmidt intimated that he thought the Braves weren't making an all-out effort on the field. "I don't think the players or somebody isn't doing something right here," Grobschmidt said with more passion than grammar.[1]

Manager Bobby Bragan, who never caught on with the Milwaukee fans, snapped back at Grobschmidt. Club president John McHale said, "Grobschmidt had better have proof … or be prepared to retract the statement." McHale said the team would even consider a lawsuit.[2]

Congressman Henry Reuss, who represented a Milwaukee district, talked about trying to keep the club in Milwaukee through an antitrust suit against Major League Baseball. Milwaukee County officials indicated a willingness to force the team to stay through the end of 1965 through legal maneuvering.

The final parting of the Braves from Milwaukee was a bitter one. Both sides took legal action and hurled verbal hardballs. Warren Spahn, who was sold to the Mets in November 1964, and Oshkosh native Billy Hoeft, who was released in the spring of 1965, both said the Braves had tried not to win in 1964.[3]

"We should have won the pennant," Hoeft said. "But they didn't want to win."[4] Bragan, a Southerner who supposedly wanted the team below the Mason-Dixon Line, was looked at as the guy who did management's dirty work on the field.

Because of a judge's ruling regarding the County Stadium lease, the Braves had to play the 1965 season in Milwaukee. By July 28 of that season, however, corporation papers were filed for the Milwaukee Brewers Baseball Club, and the search for a new team was on. That served as an admission that the Braves were gone. From 1966 through 1969 Milwaukee was a city in search of a ballclub to call its own.

Perhaps the saddest day in County Stadium's history came when the Braves played their last game there, on September 22, 1965. Mathews recalled his last at-bat. A crowd of 12,577 gave him a standing ovation, and Mathews admitted his eyes teared up. "The fans gave me about a two-minute standing ovation," he recalled. "I was overwhelmed. I tried to bat, but I had to step out of the batter's box three or four times."[5]

Some legal action still took place after the season. Judge Elmer Roller ruled in the spring of 1966 that the Braves and the National League had violated Wisconsin's antitrust laws and must either give Milwaukee a new franchise or return to play in County Stadium. To that verdict, Braves executive William Bartholomay said, "There is as much chance of the Braves playing in Milwaukee this summer as there is the New York Yankees."[6] The Wisconsin Supreme Court overruled Roller.

County Stadium was without baseball. Officials tried to keep some revenue coming in with religious revivals, tractor pulls, wrestling matches, concerts, and other events. The Green Bay Packers, who had played some of their games in the stadium since 1953, continued to play there. But without baseball, the ballpark seemed like a home without a family.

Allan "Bud" Selig, who owned a car-leasing business in Milwaukee, organized a group to get baseball back to Milwaukee and the stadium. They almost bought the Chicago White Sox, who played 20 games at the stadium in 1968 and 1969. But that deal fell through. Selig's group eventually bought the bankrupt Seattle Pilots of the American League, in a move that had almost eerie similarities to the Braves move in 1953, coming only weeks before the opening of the 1970 season.

Milwaukee fans were excited to have baseball back in town, but they warmed up to the Brewers more slowly than they did the Braves; home attendance did not top one million until 1973. The Brewers also struggled on the field in the early years, and even the acquisition of Henry Aaron before the 1975 season didn't move the Brewers out of last place. Aaron hit the final home run (No. 755) of his 23-year career on July 20, 1976, at County Stadium. The Brewers finally built a winning team from the 1978 through the 1982 seasons with Harry Dalton as general manager. In 1982, the World Series returned to County Stadium, and the franchise drew over two million in home attendance in 1983.

The Brewers continued in the stadium for almost two more decades, but by the early 1990s it was clear that the ballpark had become outdated. Selig started talking about the need for a new stadium to keep baseball viable in Milwaukee.

After a contentious political debate about financing, Miller Park was eventually approved. For a couple of seasons, fans could watch the modern facility being built beyond the center-field wall of County Stadium.

The old ballpark had to work overtime after a construction accident killed three workers and delayed the opening of Miller Park for a year. Eventually County Stadium was closed, with its last game on September 28, 2000. Some of the greats who had played there came back for an emotional ceremony to say goodbye to what announcer Bob Uecker called an "old friend." Uecker read a short goodbye for the old park as the lights were turned off, standard by standard. He closed with "So long, old friend, and goodnight everybody."[7]

County Stadium's demolition was completed on February 21, 2001. However, the infield portion of the field was transformed into a youth playing field under the name of Helfaer Park.

Sources

Buege, Bob, *Milwaukee Braves: A Baseball Eulogy* (Milwaukee: Douglas American Sports Publications, 1988).

Gershman, Michael, *Diamonds: The Evolution of the Ballpark* (New York: Mariner Books, 1995).

Hoffmann, Gregg, *Down in the Valley: The History of Milwaukee County Stadium* (Holt, Michigan: Partners Publishers Group, 2000).

Lowry, Philip J., Green *Cathedrals: Ultimate Celebration of All 273 Major League and Negro League Ballparks* (New York: Walker and Company, 2006).

Milwaukee Journal (various issues ranging from 1948 until 2001).

Milwaukee Sentinel (various issues ranging from 1948 to 2001).

Milwaukee County Historical Association documents (1948-53 and 1964-66).

Povletich, William, *Milwaukee Braves: Heroes and Heartbreak* (Madison, Wisconsin: Wisconsin Historical Society Press, 2009).

Wisconsin State Historical Society documents (1948-53).

Interviews (done from 1994 to 1999 for *Down in the Valley*) with baseball commissioner and former Brewers owner Bud Selig, former Milwaukee Mayor Frank Zeidler, former Braves players Eddie Mathews, Henry Aaron, Warren Spahn, Bob Uecker, and Johnny Logan, former Brewers players Robin Yount, and Jim Gantner, and others.

Notes

1. Lou Chapman, "Braves 'Call Off' Suit," *Milwaukee Sentinel*, July 10, 1964, II, 4.
2. Ibid.
3. Milton Gross, "Spahn Wonders What Mets Paid," *Milwaukee Journal*, November 24, 1964, II, 10.
4. Bob Wolf, "'Bragan Tried to Lose'—Hoeft," *Milwaukee Journal*, April 1, 1965, II, 17.
5. Eddie Mathews and Bob Buege, *Eddie Mathews and the National Pastime* (Milwaukee: Douglas American Sports Publications, 1988, 253).
6. Raymond E. McBride, "Braves Say They Won't Return Despite Judge Roller's Decision," *Milwaukee Journal*, April 14, 1966, 1.
7. Crocker Stephenson, "So Long, Old Friend, Crowd Says to Ballpark," *Milwaukee Journal Sentinel*, September 29, 2000, 7A.

Jane Jarvis

By Rory Costello

For generations of fans, the sound of an organ evoked a trip to the ballpark. One of the best-known, best-loved, and simply best baseball organists was Jane Jarvis (1915-2010). Jarvis attracted most attention during her long tenure with the New York Mets (1964 through 1979). However, the one-time child prodigy had a career in jazz both before and after her baseball days. While in New York, she also worked for the Muzak Corp., giving "elevator music" some swing.

It's important to realize, though, that Jarvis came to baseball with the Milwaukee Braves in 1954. She played at County Stadium through 1963 and so provided the soundtrack for both the world champions of 1957 and the National League pennant winners of 1958. Jarvis didn't know anything about the national pastime when she started her job in Milwaukee, but she quickly learned. She became a devoted fan who heightened the crowd's enjoyment with her apt musical selections and flair at the keyboard.

Luella Jane Nossette was born on October 31, 1915, in Vincennes, Indiana. This town is in the southern part of the Hoosier State, and her speech retained the region's drawl.[1] Her first name — which she loathed[2] — came from her mother, a schoolteacher. Jane was the only child of Luella (née Johnson) and her husband Charles Nossette, a lawyer. "I believe I had pre-natal influences," Jarvis said in 1993. "My parents purposefully read poetry and listened to music. As a little bitty thing, I remember my father's reading Shakespeare out loud to me, playing word games and speaking in rhyme."[3]

As one of her obituaries noted, little Jane began picking out melodies on the piano at the age of 4. "A year later her parents, impressed, arranged for her to study classical piano at Vincennes University."[4] Another obit added that the child could play any tune that anyone requested at a department store.[5]

At the age of 5, Jane discovered jazz, courtesy of her uncle's record collection. When she was 11 or 12 (accounts vary), she won a job as house pianist for a radio station in Gary, Indiana. There she accompanied nationally known performers, such as blues/jazz/gospel singer Ethel Waters and singer/comedienne Sophie Tucker.[6] In her teens she also performed in theatricals starring Karl Malden and Red Skelton.[7]

Jane Jarvis with Warren Spahn and Eddie Mathews (Image from **The Hammond Times** (Volume 23, No. 3, 1961), reproduced courtesy of Hammond USA. Enhanced by Seltzer Studio Graphics, Brooklyn, New York (http://seltzerstudio.com/).

Jane's parents were both killed in a road accident—a train collided with their car—when the young girl was 14. It was November 5, 1929, just a week after "Black Tuesday" in the Crash of 1929. Apparently, when Jarvis read about her father's death in the newspaper, it was the first she knew that Charles had Native American heritage.[8]

After the loss of her parents, Jarvis "was basically alone in the world," according to her friend, author Lee Lowenfish (*Branch Rickey: Baseball's Ferocious Gentleman*).[9] "I had lots of relatives," Jane recalled in 2008, "but they were in no position to assist me, and even if they could, they were the wrong kind of people."[10] Her musical studies sustained the teenager. She attended the Chicago Conservatory of Music, the Bush Conservatory (also in Chicago), Loyola University Chicago, and DePauw University in Greenville, Indiana.[11] The depth of her musical knowledge was astounding—she could play 10,000 songs from memory.[12]

In June 1971 Robert Cantwell of *Sports Illustrated* devoted a feature article to Jarvis. He noted, "She always intended to be a concert pianist. As a girl she played with the Indianapolis and Milwaukee symphony orchestras, and she once had a concert tour through several Southern cities. The critics were approving, but they also volunteered kindly advice to the effect that she was too slight and frail to meet the rigorous life demanded of a concert pianist."[13] The blue-eyed brunette was indeed petite—5 feet even. But as New York musician and teacher Ann Ruckert said, "As she played, she somehow became much taller."[14]

Cantwell continued, "Next Jane began playing in Chicago dance bands and at cocktail lounges, but she found this more tiring than the concert stage. 'People drank too much,' she says, 'and talked too much. You heard too much and saw too much and you knew too much and finally you wanted some other kind of life.'"[15]

Jane married Kenneth Jarvis, a chiropractor. They moved to the Milwaukee area in 1946, settling in Oconomowoc, a suburb about 35 miles west. They had two children, Jeanne and Brian. She took a job as staff pianist at radio (and later TV) station WTMJ.[16] She had a show there called *Jivin' With Jarvis*.

In 1960 Robert Cantwell wrote a broader article devoted to "The Music of Baseball." He started by telling how Jarvis came to baseball partway through the 1954 season. "When the Braves moved from Boston to Milwaukee they took with them a fine new Hammond electric organ, which they perched in a makeshift organ loft in the mezzanine box seats behind first base in County Stadium. The organ sounded fine there, but the organist became a fanatical Braves supporter and soon was directing musical Bronx cheers, raspberries, moans, groans, and advice to enemy players and managers. When he began playing 'Three Blind Mice' every time he disagreed with the umpires he had to go."

That organist was an interim performer named Clarence Bosch. The Hammond, which had been in storage, was installed on May 20, 1954, and used for the first time on that date during a charity game between the Braves and the Chicago White Sox. During the 1953 season the Braves used piped-in music under the last year of a contract signed by the minor-league Milwaukee Brewers, for whom County Stadium was built.

As Cantwell recounted, "The task of replacing [Bosch] fell to Joe Cairnes and John Quinn of the Braves' staff, who listened to everybody around Milwaukee and finally selected Jane Jarvis, who—though an accomplished musician—had seen only one baseball game in her life. 'Just don't step on anybody's toes,' said Joe. 'And always remember to play "Take Me Out to the Ball Game" during the seventh-inning stretch,' added John."[17]

"I wasn't a sports fan, and I was uncertain about doing it," Jarvis told the *New York Times* in 1984. "But money overcame my worries."[18] As she told Cantwell in 1971, "They put the fear of God into me—never interfere with the game. Never never never never never never never never never."[19]

A *Milwaukee Journal* feature in June 1957 described some obstacles in the organist's job. For one thing, her cubicle at County Stadium had a very restricted view of the field—a slot that measured one foot by four feet. Jane's son Brian (who also became a musician) saw her quarters when he was a young boy. In 2013, he said with a chuckle, "It was dank in there—like the inside of a battleship! There were all these wires and girders. Today there would be a law against working in a spot like that."[20] Indeed, on cold days Jarvis would play while wearing a heavy coat, gloves, and galoshes.[21]

In addition, Jarvis and Marvin Moran, the Irish tenor who sang the National Anthem, had a very tricky task in coordinating their timing. Moran's microphone near home plate was about 300 feet away from the organ, which was down at the far end of the first-base mezzanine, and so the sound was delayed.[22]

Columnist Donald H. Dooley also wrote at length about what prompted Jane's musical selections. One example was the infamous bench-clearing brawl that broke out in July 1956 after Rubén Gómez of the Giants plunked Braves first baseman Joe Adcock. Jarvis played "The Star-Spangled Banner" in an effort to bring players up short. In 1957 she also showed her sense of humor by breaking into "Where, Oh Where Has My Little Dog Gone?" after a groundskeeper got stuck under the tarp during a rain delay and was crawling around trying to get out. The crowd loved it. [23]

Various players got signature tunes for home runs. Hank Aaron had "Dance With Me, Henry." Eddie Mathews had "California, Here I Come" because he was a native of the Golden State. Johnny Logan had "Oh Johnny, Oh Johnny."[24] When the Braves won, that prompted "Happy Days Are Here Again" or "On, Wisconsin."[25]

In 1960 Robert Cantwell also dwelt on this theme. He noted that the barrage of rainouts at the beginning of the 1956 season in Milwaukee prompted Jarvis to dig deep into the catalog of watery songs. Cantwell also wrote about the campaign Jarvis waged to move the loudspeakers in from a grove of pine trees in center field (because her sound was delayed or lost to wind). But when the speakers were relocated to the stands, the fans in nearby seats suffered, and the speakers went back to the trees.[26]

Jarvis told the *Milwaukee Sentinel* in 1969, "I made up my mind that as long as I was going to be there, I'd really learn the game." She added, "The Braves were a marvelous, precision team, a remarkable assemblage of talent. It was wonderful to watch them." That feature also noted how she developed many lasting friendships with the players and their wives during her years with the Braves. She singled out Henry Aaron—"as exceptionally fine a person in private life as he is an athlete on the field."[27] George Crowe, Bill Bruton, and their wives were also good friends of hers. Eddie Mathews was her favorite player and a lifelong friend.[28]

By means of the dugout phone, Jane also became friends with the likes of Ernie Banks, then the star shortstop (and later first baseman) of the Chicago Cubs. Starting in 1962, she also held lengthy chats with Casey Stengel, manager of the Mets, whom she would come to know even better. She joked that what worried her was, "I think I understood him."[29]

Jarvis was at the keyboard when Warren Spahn won his 300th game in 1961.[30] That year, she also wrote a textbook on the organ.[31]

After the 1963 season, Jarvis moved to New York—"where the center of the music action is," she said.[32] She later called it "the biggest risk I ever took."[33] Previously, she had said, "I moved everything, so that it was impossible to go back."[34] She'd actually tried the Big Apple first as a 17-year-old, but got scared and went home. "No roots, no money," she said in 1984.[35]

Jarvis was divorced by this time; she had previously been married and divorced twice more.[36] The first marriage came when she was a teenager, and ended not long after her first child died at the age of 7; she was married again very briefly to a jazz bassist.[37]

Jarvis worked as a music arranger at a New York TV station until her contract expired. "Out of work, friends of mine from Milwaukee put me in touch with the only person they knew in New York," she said in 1993. "It turned out to be a nun, who knew only one person in the music world, the president of Muzak."[38] Ann Ruckert remembered, "She started as a receptionist and wound up as senior vice president in charge of all production."[39]

By that time, talk was widespread that the Milwaukee franchise would move to Atlanta. John McHale, by then the Braves' general manager and president, apparently wanted to lure Jarvis down from New York. She declined, but McHale gave her a glowing recommendation for the job that had opened up with the Mets, who christened Shea Stadium in 1964.[40]

Meanwhile, the Mets' director of promotion, Tom Meany, had also checked into Jane's background.[41] He had seen her playing while bundled up at County Stadium.

During her first year with the Mets, Jarvis wrote a tune called "Let's Go Mets"; it became a perennial that she played just as the team was ready to take the field. She also stood up to her biggest test of endurance that season. On May 31, 1964, there was a home doubleheader against the San Francisco Giants. She started her workday around noon. The opener took a normal time, just under 2 1/2 hours—but the nightcap went 23 innings, lasting 7 hours and 23 minutes. When the game was over, she played "Gee, How I Hate to Get Up in the Morning."[42]

A little over a month later, the 1964 All-Star Game was held at Shea Stadium. Although Ron Hunt of the Mets went 1-for-3 as the NL's starting second baseman, Robert Lipsyte of the *New York Times* wrote, "The Mets' most significant contribution ... was Jane Jarvis, who was obtained last year (straight cash, no players) from the Milwaukee Braves."[43]

According to Lee Lowenfish, when George Weiss (then the general manager of the Mets) hired Jarvis, he said, "We want to give the fans good music if we can't give them good baseball." Lowenfish also quoted Ralph Kiner, the team's longtime broadcaster: "In those years she was the Mets." Mets broadcaster Gary Cohen added, "She made you feel that anything was possible."[44] Robert Cantwell's 1971 feature talked about the interplay between the crowd and the performers on the field, and Jarvis had the ability to influence the crowd's mood.

In 1969 the Amazin' Mets were no longer downtrodden. As their pennant drive gathered momentum, it was in early September that the *Milwaukee Sentinel* caught up with Jarvis. She said enthusiastically, "I definitely think the Mets will make it next year. ... We might get lucky and win it this year."[45] She was right—she took part in her second World Series championship that October.

Some of the signature tunes that Jarvis bestowed on New York players included "Mr. Wonderful" for Tom Seaver, "When Irish Eyes Are Smiling" for Tug McGraw (who liked to visit Jane at her organ and ask musical questions), and "Felix the Cat" for Félix Millán.

A favorite for audience participation—as it had been in Milwaukee—was "The Mexican Hat Dance." She also slipped in more adventurous jazz offerings, such as Charlie Parker's "Scrapple From the Apple" (for arguments between managers and umpires) and numbers by Miles Davis. Jarvis always insisted that jazz was almost all she played anyway.

After the Mets games, Jane continued to provide musical entertainment at Shea Stadium's Diamond Club. Tommie Agee, another of her favorite players, and his wife enjoyed the scene there, as did Ralph Kiner.

Jarvis was on hand for her fourth pennant in 1973, as the Mets mounted another improbable late surge. She demonstrated her importance to the club in another way during the 1973 National League Championship Series. In Game Three, at Shea, a notorious bench-clearing brawl broke out after hardnosed Cincinnati Reds star Pete Rose took out Mets shortstop Bud Harrelson on a double-play ball. When Rose returned to his position in left field, the fans heaved bottles, cans, and garbage toward him, nearly causing a forfeit. National League President Chub Feeney, in the stands, asked Willie Mays to go out on the field and calm the fans, joined by Mets manager Yogi Berra and team stars Cleon Jones, Tom Seaver, and Rusty Staub. The fans simmered down, with an extra hand from the soothing sounds of Jarvis. At one point, she played excerpts from another of her compositions, "A Prayer for Peace," written during the height of Vietnam War protests.[46]

Perhaps her finest hour, however, came on the night of July 13, 1977, when she kept the fans at Shea calm after a blackout struck New York City in the midst of a heat wave.[47] She was playing in the dark, but her Thomas organ still somehow had power. As the *New York Times* wrote, "In the depths of the blackout Wednesday night at Shea Stadium, the crowd of 22,000 was singing 'White Christmas' along with Jane Jarvis at the organ."[48]

As Jarvis attained greater influence at Muzak Corp., she hired various jazz greats, such as Lionel Hampton, to play on sessions. In fact, said musician Ann Ruckert, "she kept everyone working, recorded the entire catalogs of tunes written by jazz musicians and also helped them set up publishing companies in their own names. We were grateful for the work, and thankful for the business information and help."[49]

However, Jarvis left that firm in 1978. In 1984 she remarked, "I enjoyed producing records for Muzak. But they had a change of policy that didn't fit in with my standards. That was why I left. I thought I'd keep the Mets job for the income, while I started building a career as a jazz pianist. But then I realized that nobody would take me seriously in jazz if I stayed with the Mets. So I left in July 1979. They had no substitute for me, and they never got one. They've been using records ever since."[50]

"I thought I was leaving on my own volition," Jarvis observed in 2008. "It turns out they would have let me go, because there was no organ anymore. The new owners [Doubleday & Co. bought controlling interest in the Mets in January 1980] didn't want it. They made it clear they didn't want the music." She was also saddened that her beloved Thomas organ vanished.[51] Many fans wanted her back—for years at Shea Stadium's annual Banner Day, calls for her return were visible.

According to a 1986 feature about stadium organists, Mets spokesman Dennis D'Agostino said that after Jarvis left, the team's new ownership simply wanted to make a change, and the decision had nothing to do with market research (in contrast to the Seattle Mariners, whose marketing department made a demographic study).[52] In particular, it was new general manager Frank Cashen who brought in programmed music, admitting, "I've never been a disciple of the organ."[53] One may debate whether preference for an organ over canned tunes is generational. Yet even though more than 30 years have passed since Jarvis left the ballpark, fans who heard her play still reminisce fondly.

Meanwhile, as the 1980s progressed, Jarvis was doing nicely as a jazz pianist. She played regularly at a Greenwich Village supper club called Zinno, usually as part of a duo with an old friend, bassist Milt Hinton. In 1985 she also got to play at President Ronald Reagan's second inaugural ball, as part of Lionel Hampton's orchestra. Two years later she played on the silver screen (as "Dance Palace Musician") in Woody Allen's *Radio Days*.

In 1995 a group called the Statesmen of Jazz—featuring musicians past the age of 65—was organized in Florida. Jarvis (who had been living in Cocoa Beach, Florida, since around 1994) became their original pianist. The group traveled around the world. At that time, Jarvis was working on an autobiography.[54] Alas, that work was never finished. However, she released the last two of her five record albums, *Jane Jarvis Jams* (1995) and *Atlantic-Pacific* (2000).

In 2003 Jarvis moved back to New York City. She lived on East 50th Street in Manhattan. In March 2008 a crane collapsed, crushing the building next door. The accident killed seven people, and displaced many others, including the 92-year-old. It was a harrowing experience, but she endured with the help of friends. *New York Times* writer Glenn Collins called her "frail but strong of temperament.... She projected the grandeur of a Gloria Swanson with an impish soupçon of Carol Burnett."[55]

Jarvis was able to return home after a little while. Early in Shea Stadium's last season, journalists Filip Bondy of the *New York Daily News* and Mark Herrmann of *Newsday* reached Jane at her apartment and heard her reminisce about her time with the Mets. As always, she was sunny and optimistic, even though she was very sad that Shea would be gone.

Not long afterward, thanks to Ann Ruckert, Jarvis moved to the Lillian Booth Actors' Home in Englewood, New Jersey, where she spent her final months. She still played her beloved piano—Ruckert said that she and other friends went out to the home for jam sessions.

Jane Jarvis died around 11 A.M. on January 25, 2010.[56] It's noteworthy that the *New York Times* selected Peter Keepnews, a noted writer on the subject of jazz and the son of prominent jazz producer Orrin Keepnews, to write her obituary. However, her passing received notice in the baseball world as well. For example, Lee Lowenfish joined various figures from the jazz scene for a memorial at Manhattan's St. Peter's Church in May 2010 and was one of the speakers.[57] Lowenfish also delivered a talk about Jarvis at the Hofstra University conference in 2012 that celebrated the 50th anniversary of the Mets.

As interesting as this woman was in many ways, her sound is what shapes the popular memory of her. "She had some pretty good jazz chops," said Ron Swoboda of the 1969 Mets, "but she never overplayed the organ. …What made it special was that you knew it was Jane Jarvis playing that music." Howie Rose, who grew up listening to Jarvis before becoming a Mets broadcaster, added, "She had a different lilt to everything she played."[58]

What also came through in that sound was her joy. In 1961 she called her job with the Braves "just a lark."[59] Whenever she was asked how she was doing or what her life had been like, her typical reply was, "Too wonderful for words."

Sources

Thanks to Brian Jarvis, Ann Ruckert, and Lee Lowenfish for their input.

Books

Feather, Leonard, and Ira Gitler, *The Biographical Encyclopedia of Jazz* (New York: Oxford University Press, 2007 edition).

Harvith, John, and Susan Edwards Harvith, *Edison, Musicians, and the Phonograph* (Westport, Connecticut: Greenwood Press, 1987).

Vaché, Warren W., *Jazz Gentry* (Metuchen, New Jersey: Scarecrow Press, 1974).

Internet resources

ancestry.com

fgs-project.com

findagrave.com

allmusic.com

Finding aid, Jane Jarvis papers, Music Division, The New York Public Library for the Performing Arts (nypl.org/ead/137503).

Notes

1 Angela Taylor, "She Spends Her Day Piping In Music, Then Listens to More of Same at Home," *New York Times*, March 12, 1973.

2 Lee Lowenfish, "RIP Jane Jarvis (1915-2010)," Lee Lowenfish blog, February 3, 2010 (http://www.leelowenfish.com/blog.htm?post=663182).

3 Marjorie Kaufman, "She Played the Organ, the Mets Just Played," *New York Times*, January 10, 1993.

4 Peter Keepnews, "Jane Jarvis, Player of Jazz and Mets Music, Dies at 94," *New York Times*, January 30, 2010.

5 Mark Herrrmann, "Mets organist Jane Jarvis remembered as creative soul," *Newsday*, January 30, 2010.

6 John S. Wilson, "Pop/Jazz: From Organ Caterpillar to Jazz Piano Butterfly," *New York Times*, January 20, 1984. Keepnews, "Jane Jarvis, Player of Jazz and Mets Music, Dies at 94."

7 Barbara Laboe, "Stars head to schools," *Moscow-Pullman* (Idaho) *Daily News*, February 20, 1996, 10.

8 Herrrmann, "Mets organist Jane Jarvis remembered as creative soul."

9 Lowenfish, "RIP Jane Jarvis (1915-2010)."

10 Mark Herrrmann, "A good time to cherish Shea's queen of melody," *Newsday*, March 29, 2008.

11 Quite a few stories state that Jarvis went to DePaul University in Chicago. The confusion is understandable, based on both name and location. She is listed in the book *DePauw University People*.

12 Anthony Hiss, "Most Valuable Player," *The New Yorker*, September 28, 1968.

13 Robert Cantwell, "In The Mood—for Baseball," *Sports Illustrated*, June 7, 1971.

14 Ann Ruckert, "Jazz Pianist Jane Jarvis Dies," Annruckert.com, January 26, 2010 (annruckert.com/ann_ruckert/2010/01/jazz-pianist-jane-jarvis-dies.html).

15 Cantwell, "In The Mood—for Baseball."

16 Lee Lowenfish, "Organist Jarvis provided Shea's soundtrack," MLB.com, April 20, 2012 (newyork.mets.mlb.com/news/article.jsp?ymd=20120420&content_id=29206458&vkey=news_nym&c_id=nym). "Jane and the Mets Are in There Pitching," *Milwaukee Sentinel*, September 8, 1969. Cantwell, "In The Mood—for Baseball." Keepnews, "Jane Jarvis, Player of Jazz and Mets Music, Dies at 94."

17 Robert Cantwell, "The Music of Baseball," *Sports Illustrated*, October 3, 1960.

18 Wilson, "Pop/Jazz: From Organ Caterpillar to Jazz Piano Butterfly."

19 Cantwell, "In The Mood—for Baseball."

20 Telephone interview, Rory Costello with Brian Jarvis, August 28, 2013.

21 Cantwell, "In The Mood—for Baseball."

22 Donald H. Dooley, "Musical Double Play Every Day," *Milwaukee Journal*, July 21, 1957, 20.

23 Dooley, "Musical Double Play Every Day."

24 Dooley, "Musical Double Play Every Day."

25 Buck Herzog, "Moon Is Popular Now," *Milwaukee Sentinel*, July 19, 1969. "Jane Jarvis Entertains Braves Fans," *Hammond Times* (magazine of the Hammond organ company), Volume 23, No. 3, 1961, 5.

26 Cantwell, "In The Mood—for Baseball."

27 "Jane and the Mets Are in There Pitching."

28 Hiss, "Most Valuable Player."

29 "Jane and the Mets Are in There Pitching."

30 Lowenfish, "Organist Jarvis provided Shea's soundtrack."

31. Donald H. Dooley, "Milwaukee Studio Notes," *Milwaukee Journal*, December 10, 1961, 25.
32. "Jane and the Mets Are in There Pitching."
33. Erin Walter, "Pianist Took Chances That Happened to Come Her Way," *Lewiston* (Idaho) *Morning Tribune*, February 25, 2000, 2C.
34. "State Performers Do Well in New York," *Milwaukee Journal*, February 12, 1968.
35. Ben Steelman, "Jazz has been love of her life," *Wilmington* (North Carolina) *Morning Star*, November 29, 1984, 1C.
36. Keepnews, "Jane Jarvis, Player of Jazz and Mets Music, Dies at 94."
37. E-mail from Lee Lowenfish to Rory Costello, August 27, 2013.
38. Kaufman, "She Played the Organ, the Mets Just Played."
39. Herrrmann, "Mets organist Jane Jarvis remembered as creative soul."
40. Wilson, "Pop/Jazz: From Organ Caterpillar to Jazz Piano Butterfly."
41. Barney Kremenko, "If Mets Lose, Popular Organist Plays 'Pack Up Your Troubles,'" *The Sporting News*, July 4, 1964.
42. Herzog, "Moon Is Popular Now."
43. Robert Lipsyte, "Mets' Best Off-the-Field Player Knows the Score," *New York Times*, July 8, 1964.
44. Lowenfish, "Organist Jarvis provided Shea's soundtrack."
45. "Jane and the Mets Are in There Pitching."
46. Lowenfish, "Organist Jarvis provided Shea's soundtrack."
47. Filip Bondy, "Jane Jarvis recalls the happy times and tunes at Shea," *New York Daily News*, May 9, 2008. Lowenfish, "Organist Jarvis provided Shea's soundtrack."
48. Paul L. Montgomery, "Night and Day, Mets Are Blacked Out; Mets' Game Blacked Out In Day, Too," *New York Times*, July 15, 1977.
49. Ruckert, "Jazz Pianist Jane Jarvis Dies."
50. Wilson, "Pop/Jazz: From Organ Caterpillar to Jazz Piano Butterfly."
51. Bondy, "Jane Jarvis recalls the happy times and tunes at Shea."
52. Jonathan Karp, "Stadium organists pipe up," *Washington Post*, September 11, 1986.
53. George Vecsey, "The New Sounds of Music at Shea Stadium," *New York Times*, June 30, 1980.
54. Matt Schudel, "Statesmen Show Jazz Never Ages," *Palm Beach Sun-Sentinel*, January 20, 1999.
55. Glenn Collins, "Between Organist and Keyboard, a Crane," *New York Times*, March 22, 2008.
56. Ruckert, "Jazz Pianist Jane Jarvis Dies."
57. Richard Sandomir, "Memorial Tonight for Jarvis, Mets Organist," *New York Times*, May 10, 2010.
58. Herrrmann, "Mets organist Jane Jarvis remembered as creative soul."
59. "Jane Jarvis Entertains Braves Fans."

Headlines and Deadlines: Wordsmiths of the Braves

By Bob Buege

Until the Boston Braves moved to the western shores of Lake Michigan, Milwaukee was strictly minor league. Oh, they had the NBA Hawks, who had transferred to Wisconsin in 1951 as the Tri-Cities Blackhawks (Davenport, Iowa; Rock Island and Moline, Illinois), but the shortened-named Milwaukee Hawks were pathetic. The Hawks never escaped the basement until the franchise moved in 1955 to St. Louis before relocating once again—to Atlanta. And yes, the Green Bay Packers traveled a couple of hours south to play football three times a year and pretended to feel at home, but they were just on loan from a tiny city whose entire population could be seated in New York's Polo Grounds.

Big league meant baseball. Milwaukee had its own interesting ballclub, but they competed in the American Association in a wooden ballpark built in two months in 1888. Then, in March of 1953, the world changed. Overnight, Milwaukee became the center of the baseball universe, home of the handsomest young slugger and the greatest southpaw pitcher and the most gorgeous uniforms on the continent.

Naturally the fans welcomed their new heroes with open arms—and so did the local sports journalists. Milwaukee supported two daily newspapers at the time, the *Sentinel* in the morning and the *Journal* in the afternoon. Both papers fought fiercely for the opportunity to quench the fans' insatiable thirst for information about the glamorous new team performing in County Stadium. Three writers covered the Milwaukee Braves from their arrival in 1953 until their sad departure after the 1965 season.

World Series Button (Courtesy of the Milwaukee Braves Historical Association)

Lou Chapman

By Bob Buege

"Pack a bag." The speaker was Lloyd Larson, sports editor of the *Milwaukee Sentinel*. It was March 18, 1953. Larson was talking to Lou Chapman, one of the members of his staff.

"What for?" came the obvious question.[1]

The answer changed Chapman's life. He was asked to catch a plane for Florida to begin a new beat. The announcement had been made just hours earlier — the National League owners had approved Lou Perini's request to transfer his baseball team, the Boston Braves, to Milwaukee. Chapman would write feature stories and personality sketches of the ballplayers. It was a dream come true.

Nearing age 40, Chapman had been watching the years slip past while he took bowling scores over the phone and tried to manufacture excitement by writing about the least talented team in the National Basketball Association. Catch a flight? Lou would have walked to Florida. Within a day he was sending back a torrent of information from Bradenton about Milwaukee's — about his — new team. For the next 13 years, he never stopped.

Louis Chapman (no middle name) was born in Milwaukee on June 19, 1913. His parents, Dora and Harry Chapman, were Russian Jews who emigrated in 1907 or 1908 from the area around Kiev, now the capital of Ukraine. Harry worked for his father's ice business. In the winter Harry and his brother would drive a truck to Pewaukee Lake, 20 miles west of Milwaukee, cut big chunks of ice out of the lake, and drive them back. They would store the ice and then peddle it during the warm months.

Lou's only sibling was a younger brother named Benward Chapman, who for 35 years was a prominent physician in Milwaukee. Among his better-known patients were the Beatles, Don and Phil Everly, and the perennial host of the Miss America pageant, Bert Parks.

Lou attended Milwaukee's West Division High School. After graduating he enrolled in the Marquette School of Journalism, earning his degree in 1937.

In 1940 Lou met the love of his life, Harriet Grafman, the daughter of Polish immigrants who ran a small grocery store on Milwaukee's north side. "Her eyes were just beautiful," Lou told a reporter. "They were what attracted me to her first."[2] Inspired by her lovely brown eyes, Lou wrote her a poem. She in turn recited poetry to him. They soon began dating in earnest, and the following year they were married.

Harriet was a cultured woman of the arts. During her high-school years she studied piano at the Wisconsin Conservatory of Music. She was an accomplished painter and sculptor. She once helped her son Richard build a model of the Arc de Triomphe out of toothpicks for his school project.[3] She wrote articles for the Milwaukee newspapers. While Lou attended Marquette, Harriet studied at Milwaukee State Teachers' College, graduating in 1934. She became a kindergarten teacher in the public schools and taught until 1965, not including the war years. During World War II she worked in Washington, D.C., in the Office of Strategic Services (OSS), which evolved into the CIA.

Besides her involvement with the fine arts, Harriet also had a baseball connection. Portions of a home movie she made of her husband and his friend Henry Aaron were incorporated into a documentary film, *Hank Aaron: Chasing the Dream*. The movie follows

Lou Chapman (Photo courtesy of Richard Chapman)

Aaron's pursuit of Babe Ruth's career home-run record. It was nominated for an Academy Award in 1996, losing out to a feature about Anne Frank.

Harriet had another connection to "show biz." She and Lou had two sons. Stuart Chapman was a magazine publisher and writer who started a medical publishing firm in New York. His brother, Richard, worked as a screenwriter for both television and Hollywood films. He was the executive producer of the 1980s TV series *Simon and Simon.* He wrote the screenplay for the film *My Fellow Americans,* which starred Jack Lemmon and James Garner. As of 2013 Richard was a senior lecturer in screenwriting at Washington University in St. Louis.

In 1942 Lou received his draft notice. He was initially assigned for basic training at Jefferson Barracks, just south of St. Louis. He was later stationed at Scott Air Force Base, in Illinois. He edited the base newspaper and trained as a radio operator. When World War II ended, Chapman was honorably discharged, having received the rank of sergeant.

Returning to Milwaukee, Chapman worked briefly for the *Milwaukee Journal* and then joined the *Milwaukee Sentinel* in 1948. He labored in obscurity until the Braves arrived, and then suddenly he was a celebrity—well, a minor celebrity. So pervasive was Braves Mania that the team held a series of instructional clinics for women, the theory being that baseball was too sophisticated for their pretty little minds to grasp. Lou was a panelist at each clinic for two seasons.

At the second of the tutorials, on August 11, 1953, an overflow crowd of a thousand women asked questions of a truly impressive panel. Braves players included Eddie Mathews, Warren Spahn, and Joe Adcock. Stan Musial and Enos Slaughter of the St. Louis Cardinals were in town and agreed to sit in. LoRene Spahn, wife of the Braves' star left-hander, served as the panel's token distaff member. Announcer Earl Gillespie and journalists Red Thisted and Chapman rounded out the group.

The ladies had been encouraged to dress in their Sunday finery—hats and all—because the event was being filmed for showing on the NBC *Gillette Cavalcade of Sports.* The women's baseball inquiries ran the gamut from lame to sensible. "Why aren't women allowed to play in Organized Baseball?" one asked. "Why four balls for a walk and only three strikes for a strikeout?" queried another.

The most memorable exchange of the Q&A was handled by Chapman. "What does 'good in the clutch' mean?" was the question.

Without missing a beat, Lou replied, "You must understand first of all that the expression has nothing to do with any activity in the parlor."[4] That was about as bold as television would allow in 1953.

On a rainy Monday evening, May 25, 1953, during a twi-night doubleheader, Chapman was in his customary spot in the press box at County Stadium, witnessing a historic pitching performance. In the nightcap, portly right-hander Max Surkont struck out eight consecutive Cincinnati Reds, the first pitcher to accomplish that feat since 1884. The drama of the moment was heightened by the fact that a 33-minute rain delay separated the seventh and eighth whiffs. After the game, Lou eagerly ran to the clubhouse and interviewed Surkont, who told him straight out that the last strikeout pitch had been a perfect spitball. This win lifted Surkont to 6-0, the first and only time during a nine-year major-league career that he would begin so well.

Chapman revealed to his colleague Red Thisted what Surkont had told him about the spitter. A veteran (and competing) sportswriter overheard the conversation and warned Chapman not to use the information. "It'll damage his career," he cautioned. Chapman was new to covering baseball, and now he faced an ethical dilemma. He pondered it, but not for long. He had a deadline. In the end, he did not use the juicy information. It gnawed at him, though. It was the last time, he said later, that he ever sat on a story.[5] As far as Surkont's baseball career went from that time, he was traded to the Pittsburgh Pirates in December 1953 and pitched for the last time in the major leagues in May 1957.

Generally speaking, Chapman would do nearly anything to get a story. While some writers covered the games from the press box, Lou was a fixture in the locker room or wherever the ballplayers hung out. There was a story, perhaps apocryphal, that he once hid inside a locker during spring training trying to overhear which players would be cut from the roster. Some of the players jokingly referred to Lou as Scoop or Gumby, short for gumshoe, a term for detective. As Lou's son Stuart put it, "My father was the quintessential newspaperman. He relentlessly pursued stories."[6]

Chapman was also fearless. While covering the American League Brewers during the 1970s, he once wrote a story critical of the Kansas City Royals' All-Star third baseman, George Brett. Shortly afterward he encountered Brett in a hotel lobby in Kansas City. As Lou's son Richard described it, "George was waiting for him. He started screaming at my dad, 'I'm going to pinch your (expletive) head off.'"

Lou, who needed thick soles to stand 5 1/2 feet tall, stood his ground. "Go ahead," he yelled back. "I'll show you the biggest lawsuit in Royals history."[7]

Unlike Brett, many of the ballplayers liked Chapman and admired his honesty. On January 25, 1955, Lou wrote in a story that Jackie Robinson criticized Eddie Mathews for being thin-skinned and unable to deal with bench jockeys. "I like to needle him," Robinson said in the article. "He gets hot under the collar. ... Eddie will have to learn how to take it."[8] The remarks stirred some controversy. Soon after that Lou received a letter from Robinson. The note presented Jackie's side of the story but also said he understood why Chapman had written it the way he did. Richard Chapman explained that "Jackie just wanted to make sure their friendship was not at all affected. It was a very complimentary letter that Jackie wrote."[9]

Lou was not stingy with his opinions, though. In 1961 he and *Sentinel* colleague Red Thisted co-authored a three-part series of articles headlined "What's Wrong with the Braves?" The trilogy earned a $500 "Grand Annual" sports writing award as the outstanding sports entry from Hearst newspapers across the country.

And just what was wrong with the Braves? The answer was multilayered: indifferent front office, deadwood on the bench, weak bullpen. Bottom line, though, the finger pointed at manager Charlie Dressen. He had allowed team morale to sink to an all-time low. He was "a petty tyrant, cast in the mold of Captain Queeg of 'Caine Mutiny' ill-fame." He handled the club "as if they belonged in a horse-and-buggy, tough-principled John McGraw era."[10] Chapman and Thisted attributed those opinions to the ballplayers, but they did not use quotes. What's more, the style was pure Chapman. He was dead-on in his thinking, and fans—and ownership—knew it.

Dressen read the articles and got into a shouting match with Chapman in the County Stadium hospitality room, calling him a variety of names, of which "snake" was the mildest.[11]

Lou retaliated in print. For what he claimed was the only time in his career, he let personal enmity color his reporting. He knew Dressen had never attended high school. In a story about Alvin Dark, Lou wrote, "Alvin Dark is a rarity among managers. He has a college degree. Some managers have never gone past the eighth grade."[12] Dressen responded by keeping the reporters out of the clubhouse for 20 minutes after each game. The Braves fired Dressen on September 2, 1961.

Dressen's 20-minute lockout rule, obviously directed at Chapman, was nothing by comparison. Four years later the Braves' front office banned Lou from the locker room altogether. This was during the lame-duck season of 1965. Lou admitted that "I tried to make it as uncomfortable as possible for the carpetbaggers."[13] To do this, every time an opposing player or official came to Milwaukee, Lou would write a story quoting that person being critical of the Braves owners.

On Saturday, June 19, he quoted St. Louis Cardinals reliever Hal Woodeshick as saying, "I feel sorry for the Milwaukee fans, but that's life—everyone's after that almighty dollar." Woodeshick said the Braves would win the pennant if they were playing in Atlanta.[14]

Apparently that was the last straw for the Braves' front office. As Lou wrote, "On Father's Day the Braves disowned me."[15] Assistant general manager Jim Fanning announced, "As of now, the Braves clubhouse is off limits to Lou Chapman."[16] Chapman received the news in a phone call from Bob Wolf of the *Milwaukee Journal*. At the stadium Chapman was physically barred by an attendant, who told him to see Fanning.

"You have had a disquieting effect," Fanning told Lou, "on the players in the clubhouse, the employees in the ticket office, and throughout the stadium. Our people here tingle whenever you come around them."[17] Fanning admitted that none of Lou's articles had been distorted or false. He also told Chapman that he could interview any of the players he wanted to but only in Fanning's executive office, not the clubhouse. Lou named three players plus manager Bobby Bragan. One by one they traipsed into the office to speak with the reporter.

The Milwaukee chapter of the Baseball Writers Association of America immediately filed a letter of protest with the league office and with Commissioner Ford Frick. The indefinite ban was rescinded and ended after one day.

Lou prided himself on being a wordsmith and a voracious reader. He especially admired legendary sportswriter Walter "Red" Smith. Lou's son Richard told of the time after an All-Star Game when his father carried Smith's typewriter across the field for him because Smith was quite elderly. Lou always felt privileged to have done that.[18]

The Braves came and went, but Lou Chapman stayed on the *Sentinel* staff until 1979. He was given a rebirth when the Brewers took over County Stadium in 1970. Nine years later it was time to go.

Lou spent his retirement years in Venice, Florida. He died there on April 30, 2004. His body was returned to Wisconsin for burial in Spring Hill Cemetery, where his grave overlooks Milwaukee's ballpark.

Sources

Chapman, Lou, "Baseball Was My Beat," (three parts), *Milwaukee Sentinel*, November 17, 21, 23, 1979.

Thisted, Red, and Lou Chapman, "What's Wrong with the Braves?" (three parts), *Milwaukee Sentinel*, June 16-18, 1961.

"Chapman, Thisted Win 'Grand' Prize," *Milwaukee Sentinel*, October 13, 1961.

"Harriett G. Chapman," *Wisconsin Jewish Chronicle*, June 29, 2001.

Milwaukee Journal.

Milwaukee Journal Sentinel.

Milwaukee Sentinel.

Retrosheet.org

Chapman, Richard, telephone interview, November 26, 2012.

Notes

1 "Sentinel's Lou Chapman Gives Braves the Color," *Milwaukee Sentinel*, April 11, 1955.

2 Amy Boerema, "Chapman Filled Home with the Arts," *Milwaukee Journal Sentinel*, June 14, 1996.

3 Ibid.

4 Red Thisted, "Clinic for Women Fans Put on TV," *The Sporting News*, August 19, 1953.

5 Lou Chapman, "Grimm Resigned To Soften His Firing," *Milwaukee Sentinel*, November 17, 1979.

6 Richard Chapman, telephone interview, November 26, 2012.

7 Tom Haudricourt, "Sentinel Writer Gave Fans Inside Scoop on Baseball," *Milwaukee Journal Sentinel*, May 3, 2004; Richard Chapman interview.

8 Lou Chapman, "Robinson Flashes Brand New Personality, but Story's Same," *Milwaukee Sentinel*, January 25, 1955.

9 Richard Chapman interview.

10 Red Thisted and Lou Chapman, "Dressen, Players Clash Behind Scenes," *Milwaukee Sentinel*, June 16, 1961.

11 Lou Chapman, "Braves Had Problems Adjusting to Dressen," *Milwaukee Sentinel*, November 23, 1979

12 Ibid.

13 Lou Chapman, "It Was Sportswriter vs. Braves in Battle Over Move," *Milwaukee Sentinel*, November 21, 1979.

14 "Braves Close Clubhouse to Sentinel Writer," *Milwaukee Journal*, June 20, 1965.

15 Lou Chapman, "Our Lou Gets 'Red Carpet' Deal as Braves Lift Ban," *Milwaukee Sentinel*, June 21, 1965.

16 "Braves Close Clubhouse," *Milwaukee Journal*.

17 Lou Chapman, "Our Lou Gets 'Red Carpet' Deal."

18 Richard Chapman interview.

Red Thisted

By Bob Buege

Red Thisted never saw a professional baseball game until he was 20 years old. He made up for lost time, though. Over the course of four decades, he attended every home game played by Milwaukee's ballclub, plus all of the away games when not prevented by wartime travel restrictions. From the start of the 1926 season until the end of the 1965 campaign—a streak of 3,282 games—if professionals were playing baseball in Milwaukee, Red was there. He was not only in attendance but also writing about the game for the *Milwaukee Sentinel*.

Why the late start? When he was a teenager, Red was too busy chasing Mexican bandits and getting shot at by German soldiers.

Red was born on April 8, 1899, in the rural Nebraska village of Lindsay. Red was not his given name, of course. His parents named him Amos, with a middle name of Theodore. The name Amos fit in well with his five siblings: Aaron, Phoebe, Lydia, Moses, and Mary. The Thisted children all bore biblical names because their father, Peter Thisted, was a Lutheran pastor. Both Peter and his wife, Kate, were natives of Denmark. Peter had worked as a coachman, among other menial jobs, while living in Europe. At the urging of a visiting clergyman from California, Peter immigrated to Chicago in 1886 and entered a Lutheran seminary. He became a circuit rider, providing religious services to small Danish congregations scattered around Iowa, Nebraska, Illinois, and Wisconsin. In the Badger state he served three communities: New Lisbon, Camp Douglas, and Big Flats, near the geographic center of the state.

Peter Thisted did not use his actual name. He had been born in the county of Thisted, Denmark, on September 22, 1859, and raised in the town of Lemvig. For whatever reason, when he came to the United States he dropped his last name, Petersen, and adopted his home region as his name. In Chicago he met Katherine Mortensen. They were married there on April 26, 1890. Their first child, Aaron, was born in 1891. Five more children followed, all at two-year intervals. Katherine died in 1907, just 45 years old. Peter remarried in 1912, but on May 19, 1915, he also passed away, in Tomah, Wisconsin.

On March 9, 1916, Mexican revolutionary Pancho Villa, with 40 officers on horseback and an army of a thousand men, carried out a pre-dawn raid on the border town of Columbus, New Mexico. They stole horses and guns and killed 15 Americans. President Woodrow Wilson was furious.

The Commander in Chief ordered General John J. Pershing to lead troops into Mexico and put an end to Villa. The President mobilized the entire Wisconsin National Guard on June 18 at Camp Douglas. Seventeen-year-old Red Thisted lied about his age and joined his older brothers Aaron and Moses and enlisted in Troop "B" of the First Wisconsin Infantry. On July 8 the three Thisteds accepted their first military pay, $22, and boarded a train for Camp Wilson, Texas.

History records that Pershing and two columns of troops crossed the border but failed to apprehend Villa. They did, however, drive him into seclusion. Most of

Red Thisted (Photo courtesy of the Red Thisted family)

the U.S. soldiers never saw action. The greatest danger they faced was surviving a gulf hurricane on August 18 that wrecked three-quarters of the camp. About all they did accomplish was to prepare for active duty as the first American combat troops in Europe.

The First Wisconsin Regiment entrained two days after Christmas and arrived at Fort Sheridan, Illinois, on December 30, 1916. They were not home for long. In late June, as part of the American Expeditionary Forces under General Pershing, the Thisted brothers arrived in France. Before he shipped out for Europe, Red had written a letter home in which he said he "couldn't wait to shoot some Boche,"[1] derogatory slang for Germans. In the bloody battle near Chateau-Thierry during the summer of 1918, Red suffered a serious head wound. Reportedly he would have bled to death, but by a stroke of fortune, his brother Aaron found him and helped get him the necessary medical attention to save his life.

Details of Red's recuperation are not available. What is known, however, is that he returned to the United States on a troop transport vessel in mid-1919. His brothers returned safely as well. Red's ship landed at Boston harbor. In recognition of the soldiers' service to their country, they were invited to Fenway Park as guests of the Red Sox.

"I saw my first professional game at Boston in June, 1919," Red wrote in the *Milwaukee Sentinel* many years later, "on the way back to Milwaukee after the World War I unpleasantness in France."[2] The Red Sox hosted the Washington Senators that afternoon. The names meant nothing to Red at the time, but among the men on the field were the Senators' lanky, hard-throwing right-hander Walter Johnson and the powerfully built Boston left fielder, George Ruth.

"The import of what I saw that day did not reach full significance until many years later," Red confessed.[3] One thing was certain, though. "Professional baseball had made me a convert then and there."[4]

Back in civilian life in Wisconsin, Red enrolled in the Marquette University School of Journalism. Living in Milwaukee allowed Red to attend Brewers baseball games. Right after finishing at Marquette in 1924 he was hired to be part of the sports staff of the *Milwaukee Sentinel*. The baseball beat was filled, of course. Red was assigned to cover golf. His column bore the name "Fore! And After."

Not long after signing on with the *Sentinel*, Red made another long-term commitment. He married Alice Bahr in September 1925. According to their son Joe, Red and Alice were married in one of the newspaper's offices by the religion writer for the paper, who must have been a recognized member of the clergy. Alice was the daughter of a veterinarian in Wausau and a graduate of the state university in Stevens Point. She taught home economics at Waterford High School. Her domestic training undoubtedly came in handy. She and Red raised—correction, Alice raised five children: Dennis, Patricia, George, Joseph, and James. Son Dennis followed his father's example and worked for some years at the *Sentinel*, part-time while he was attending Marquette University, eventually becoming state editor.

Around the time Red got married, the *Sentinel* baseball writer, Bryn Griffiths, filled in for the sports editor a few times. On those days Red rode a streetcar to Athletic Park (he never owned a car or had a driver's license) and wrote the game story about the Brewers. In the process he also received his first baseball bylines, the first of thousands. Beginning the following April the *Sentinel* baseball beat was his permanently.

Red understood the importance of "breaks" and was always thankful that in his first season covering baseball, as he wrote years later, "I got a big one."[5] Beginning in St. Paul on May 26, the Brewers put together a winning streak. As the wins added up, Red's game account became the featured story on the front page of the local section. On June 8 the Brewers extended their victory list to 15 to establish a new American Association record. When the count reached 16, the editors placed the victory number in a rectangular box and displayed it prominently on the page. On page one, above the banner headline, readers were advised to "Turn to Red Thisted's story" for the full game report.[6] This kind of attention given to a writer from the sports department was uncommon, much less one in his first season at his craft. Red was able to ride the wave until June 16. Casey Stengel's Toledo Mud Hens finally defeated the Brewers, ending the streak at 21. Red's story that afternoon began with an allusion to Shakespeare's *Julius Caesar*.[7]

The following year Red's baseball beat put him on the front page. Otto Borchert, the millionaire owner of the Milwaukee Brewers, had been speaking at the annual baseball banquet at the Elks' Club the night before the home opener. In the middle of an anecdote Borchert suffered a cerebral hemorrhage. He had just finished saying "I always made it a point to be loyal to my employers."[8] The words were the last ones he ever spoke. He lurched forward, gasping for breath. After the owner was carried from the podium to an anteroom, the exalted ruler of the Elks' lodge addressed the audience, calling on them to join in singing a verse of "Auld Lang Syne," apparently a significant Elks' ritual. Red was in the audience and was able to provide readers with an eyewitness account of the strange and terrible scene.[9]

Red prided himself on being accurate in his writing. Even the most careful writer can make a mistake, though. In the mid-30's the Brewers had a popular fireplug of an infielder named George Detore. He was a key contributor to the Brewers' 1936 championship. Like a lot of scribes, Red liked to pin colorful nicknames on ballplayers. After Detore had a particularly good day at the plate, Red created an appropriate moniker for him: "The Portuguese Pounder." It may not have rivaled "The Sultan of Swat," but it had a certain ring to it. The only problem was that Detore was a proud Italian.

Besides baseball, Red also wrote about Marquette University football and basketball. On New Year's Day 1937 he traveled to Dallas to cover the inaugural Cotton Bowl game between his alma mater and Texas Christian University. He was disappointed that Slingin' Sammy Baugh had the better of the battle with Marquette's hard-running halfback Ray "Buzz" Buivid, a particular favorite of Red's.

During the last baseball off-season before the United States entered World War II, Red added another dimension to his reporting. Every Monday night at 10:00 he appeared on a radio program called "Hot Stove League." Joining him to chat informally about important topics from the national pastime were fellow journalists Lloyd Larson and Stoney McGlynn and Brewers radio voice Alan Hale. They also featured a weekly guest. Among the visitors were Cleveland third baseman Ken Keltner, Cubs GM Jimmy Gallagher, and Brewers manager "Reindeer Bill" Killefer. The show lasted for only one season, perhaps a victim of the war.

On Red's 54th birthday the Milwaukee Braves arrived by train in their new hometown. After 27 years of covering the Brewers, Red suddenly was in the big leagues, writing game stories about the National League's freshest franchise. He already knew many of the Braves ballplayers. The Brewers had been the Braves' top farm club for six years. Now, though, the likes of Jack Dittmer and Ernie Johnson were playing against Stan Musial and Jackie Robinson. Red covered the Braves for their entire 13-season tenure in Milwaukee.

On August 6, 1955, Sam Levy died of a heart attack. He had been a longtime *Milwaukee Journal* baseball writer as well as the official scorer at County Stadium. Red was called upon to replace him in the scorer's job, which he did until 1962. Following a labor dispute, the *Sentinel* was bought out by their rival publication, the *Journal*. The new owner had an ethics code that precluded Red from being the official scorer lest there be a conflict of interests or a loss of objectivity. Thus ended Red's official scoring career.

While he held the job, however, he became entangled in one of the strangest conclusions a ballgame ever had. On May 26, 1959, Harvey Haddix of the Pittsburgh Pirates pitched 12 perfect innings against the Braves. In the bottom of the 13th, an error, a sacrifice, and an intentional walk put runners on first and second. Joe Adcock blasted a long fly that cleared the center field fence for an apparent home run and a 3-0 Milwaukee victory. Adcock passed Henry Aaron on the base path, though. One runner was ruled out, so the game ended, according to Thisted and the umpires, at 2-0. In an unprecedented decision, league president Warren Giles said the next morning that because of a "secret rule," Aaron was given third base and Adcock second. Adcock's hit over the fence became a double, and the final score (you could look it up) was 1-0.

With the Braves gone to Atlanta in 1966, Red penned a series of articles in the *Sentinel* entitled

"Baseball My Beat: 40 Years with Red." In 14 installments he relived the highlights of his baseball-reporting career. He identified his all-time favorite player—Denny Gearin, a little left-hander that he knew well. He said the toughest competitor he saw was Eddie Mathews, and the finest gentleman was Whitlow Wyatt.[10]

On the night of January 9, 1968, while punching out at the time clock after working late as usual, Red suffered a severe stroke. He was never the same. Six months later he announced his retirement. Red died on June 2, 1977. He was buried near County Stadium in Wood National Cemetery, a graveyard established and reserved for military veterans and their families. His wife Alice rests beside him.

Bud Lea, a colleague at the *Sentinel*, summed up Red's career in eight words: "He had an everlasting love affair with baseball."[11]

Sources

Thisted, Moses N., *With the Wisconsin National Guard on the Mexican Border in 1916-1917*, self-published, 1981.

Chapman, Lou, "Career Comes to End for Thisted," *Milwaukee Sentinel*, July 6, 1968.

Lea, Bud, "Baseball Was Red's Life," *Milwaukee Sentinel*, June 3, 1977.

Thisted, Red, "Baseball My Beat: 40 Years with Red" (series of 14 articles), March 28-April 10, 1966.

_____, "Borchert Tragedy Suspends Opening," *Milwaukee Sentinel*, April 28, 1927.

_____, "Hens Halt Brewer Streak at 21," *Milwaukee Sentinel*, June 17, 1926.

Wells, Robert W., "Wells on Books: When Wisconsin's Troops Protected US Border," *Milwaukee Journal*, February 5, 1981.

"Durable Red's Seen 'Em All Since 1926," *Milwaukee Sentinel*, April 11, 1955.

"Otto Borchert Dies Speaking at Banquet," *Milwaukee Sentinel*, April 28, 1927.

Milwaukee Journal.

Milwaukee Sentinel.

Ancestry.com

Retrosheet.org

Telephone interviews with Bud Lea and Joe Thisted.

Notes

1. Joe Thisted, telephone interview, November 28, 2012.
2. Red Thisted, "Baseball My Beat: 40 Years with Red (2nd of series)," *Milwaukee Sentinel*, March 29, 1966.
3. *Ibid.*
4. *Ibid.*
5. *Ibid.*
6. "Turn to…Red Thisted's Story of the Game" (page one, above banner headline), *Milwaukee Sentinel*, June 16, 1926.
7. Red Thisted, "Hens Halt Brewer Win Streak at 21," *Milwaukee Sentinel*, June 17, 1926.
8. "Otto Borchert Dies Speaking at Banquet," *Milwaukee Sentinel*, April 28, 1927.
9. *Ibid.*
10. Red Thisted, "Baseball My Beat: 40 Years with Red (1st of series)," *Milwaukee Sentinel*, March 28, 1966.
11. Bud Lea, "Baseball Was Red's Life," *Milwaukee Sentinel*, June 3, 1977.

Bob Wolf

By Bob Buege

On the Chicago Cubs' Opening Day in 1930, 7-year-old Bobby Wolf and future President Ronald Reagan had something in common. Neither had ever seen a major-league baseball game. That afternoon young Bobby listened to Pat Flanagan on Chicago radio station WBBM describing the action as the Cubs edged the Cardinals in St. Louis, 9-8. Hack Wilson drove in the first of the 191 runs he would drive in that season. As Wolf later wrote, "After just that one game, I was hooked."[1]

Flanagan was the acknowledged master of radio re-creations of baseball games using a Western Union ticker. A few years later he trained 21-year-old Ronald "Dutch" Reagan in the art. Reagan's baseball broadcasts over Des Moines station WHO eventually led to a screen test with Warner Brothers, a Hollywood career, and the White House. Wolf pursued a career in journalism and became, as one colleague at the *Milwaukee Journal* said, "the star of the sports staff."[2] Such is the transformative power of baseball on the radio.

Robert Argyle Wolf, known professionally as Bob, was born on October 18, 1922, in the posh Chicago suburb of River Forest, Illinois, the fourth of five children. His brother Argyle (it's a family name) was seven years older. He had two older sisters and one younger. Their mother, Pearl, was an Illinois native of English ancestry. Their father, Albert M. Wolf, whose ancestry was German, hailed from Waukesha, Wisconsin, an outer suburb 20 miles west of downtown Milwaukee. Albert attended the University of Wisconsin in Madison, earning a degree in civil engineering in 1909. He followed the Chicago Cubs and Bears, but he remained a Wisconsin Badger sports fan for life.

Bob's father became the president of Wolf, Sexton, Harper, and Trueax, an architectural firm with offices in suburban Chicago. Probably the most remarkable building they designed was the Hotel Baker, a five-story, 55-room structure on Main Street in St. Charles, Illinois. Their client, Col. Edward J. Baker, an heir to part of the Texaco Oil fortune, gave them a huge budget and one simple instruction—create the most wonderful hotel in the Midwest.

Albert Wolf and his associates did as they were told. Built on the bank of the Fox River, the Hotel Baker harnessed the power of the water with its own hydroelectric facility. All materials, from window glass to floor tiles to linens, were of the finest quality. Every room offered a private bath, a luxury in 1928. The Rainbow Room, the hotel's restaurant and ballroom, regularly featured big-name bands fronted by the likes of Louis Armstrong, Tommy Dorsey, and Guy Lombardo. The room's piece de resistance was a dance floor illuminated from beneath by thousands of colored lights, one of only three such surfaces in the United States. More than eight decades later, Albert Wolf's masterpiece still welcomed guests and was designated a historic landmark.

Bob Wolf followed his dad's example and enrolled at the University of Wisconsin in 1941. Small of stature

Bob Wolf (Photo courtesy of the Wolf family.)

but endowed with a zeal for sports, he joined the tennis squad, volunteered as the student manager of the freshman basketball team, and by the end of his third semester started writing sports articles for the student newspaper, the *Daily Cardinal*. His first assignment was to interview the coach of the fencing team.

In the 1940's women did not write sports. When the more senior members of the all-male staff entered the military, Wolf became sports editor from March until the end of the semester. In July 1943, as he later wrote, "I was shouldering a musket for Uncle Sam."[3] His mother would send him sports sections and box scores from back home.

On Easter Sunday (also April Fool's Day) 1945, Wolf was a mortarman with the Army's 96th Infantry Division when it landed on the beach at Okinawa. It was the largest amphibious assault in the Pacific Theater, code-named Operation Iceberg. The plan was for the Allies to use Okinawa as a base for air operations in the impending invasion of the mainland of Japan. The Japanese had prepared their defensive positions, so the fighting that ensued became the bloodiest US battle in the Pacific.

At about 3 A.M. on April 13, Wolf was hit by mortar fire. As he later described it, "One look at my dangling left arm told me my soldiering days were over."[4] His life might have been over if not for the heroic actions of a fellow soldier.

Sgt. Beauford "Snuffy" Anderson, despite bleeding profusely himself from shrapnel wounds, repeatedly picked up mortar shells, smashed them against a rock to arm them, and hurled them at the enemy. He single-handedly killed 25 Japanese soldiers while taking out four mortars and five machine guns. Anderson's bravery earned him the Medal of Honor and enabled Wolf to be evacuated. Wolf's arm was amputated below the elbow the next day.

In autumn 1946 Wolf was back on the Madison campus to finish journalism school. For a semester he again was the sports editor of the *Daily Cardinal*. His regular column appeared under the heading "In the Wolf's Den." During the winter months he again distributed towels and passed out basketballs as student manager of the basketball team, this time coach Bud Foster's varsity. The Badgers won the Big Nine Conference championship, so Bob and the team earned a trip to the NCAA Tournament in Madison Square Garden.

Capturing the conference crown, however, was not as straightforward as usual. The Badgers sat atop the standings when they traveled to the Purdue Fieldhouse in West Lafayette, Indiana, for the next to last game of the season, on February 24, 1947. The score was close through the first 20 minutes. Wisconsin trailed at halftime, 34-33. As the teams trotted off the court, the Purdue students leaped to their feet in a spontaneous moment of joy. Without warning, before most of the players reached their locker rooms, a large section of newly installed wooden bleachers collapsed. Three students were crushed to death and more than 200 were injured; witnesses were surprised the toll wasn't higher. The game was suspended.

It took a week for the league commissioner to decide what to do about the outcome. The conference title was at stake. In the end the game was resumed after the half at a nearby high-school gym with Purdue leading by a point. The Badgers proved worthy of the championship by easily overcoming the Boilermakers, 72-60.

Wolf graduated in June. His timing was perfect. The *Milwaukee Journal* needed a reporter to cover high-school sports. For $40 a week, Bob was their man. He attended four prep football games on a typical weekend, all the while learning the workings of the sports department of a major newspaper. The missing limb proved to be no handicap. Wolf mastered the art of typing with one finger. His customary bow tie was not a clip-on, but the kind that had to be tied, and Wolf managed that with dexterity. Rather than feel sorry for himself, Wolf adapted well to his circumstances.

Wolf's first big assignment at the *Journal* found him covering the National AAU track meet hosted by Marquette University in July 1948. This was a prestigious event, a prelude to the London Olympic Games. Many top-flight athletes competed: football star Ollie Matson, world champion pole vaulter Bob Richards, and the nation's best miler, Gil Dodds, "The Flying Parson." As luck would have it, they were all overshadowed by a 3,000-meter walker who, Wolf wrote, "provided comic relief."⁵ The young man was disqualified for running, not walking, but he refused to leave the track. One of the judges eventually ran him down, tackled him around the neck, and removed him bodily from the premises.

In a 39-year career writing for the *Journal*, Wolf was able to identify his strangest and least enjoyable assignment. It was the Carrera Panamerica, known to gringos as the Pan-American Road Race. In 1950 the Mexican government celebrated the completion of its portion of the Pan-American Highway by sponsoring an open-road auto race. The event quickly earned a reputation as the most dangerous race of any kind in the world. The 1951 race claimed the lives of three drivers. In November 1952 Wolf was sent to report on the third annual competition.

The race ran south to north, starting in the tropical region near the Guatemala border, winding through frightening mountainous terrain that two years previous had been impassable, then traversing stark desert before concluding its five-day chase at Ciudad Juarez, across the Rio Grande from El Paso, Texas. The challenge of following such a trek, nearly 2,000 miles, is obvious. In addition, food and lodging were strictly catch-as-catch-can. Wolf described conditions as squalid, his worst week since Okinawa. To top it off, one of the stories he sent back to the *Journal* arrived in Spanish.⁶

The rules of the race were bizarre. If you stopped to help anyone, you were automatically disqualified. The drivers competed in two-man crews. On the first day a Wisconsin entrant from Fond du Lac fell out of his car on a sharp mountain turn. He survived but was advised to rest for a day before rejoining his partner. Another driver was injured when a low-flying buzzard crashed through the windshield, struck him in the face, and escaped by smashing out the back window. As it turned out, the winner of the stock-car prize was a driver from Milwaukee, who earned $11,628 in his modified Lincoln. It was estimated that between 8 million and 10 million racing aficionados witnessed at least part of the spectacle along the course.

Like all of Milwaukee's sportswriters, Wolf enjoyed a career-changing experience when the Braves became the hometown team in the spring of 1953. He had worked some baseball in 1951 after the *Journal*'s regular man, Sam Levy, suffered a heart attack in June. For the rest of the season Wolf took over the job. The Brewers won the American Association pennant and the Junior World Series. Wolf enjoyed spending five autumn days in Montreal, including two days off because of postponements.

In March 1953 Wolf became the number-two baseball writer. He became numero uno when Levy experienced a fatal heart episode on August 6, 1955. From then on all the excitement of two pennants and two near-pennants was part of Wolf's daily life.

Wolf found true love, or maybe it found him, in a restaurant near Wrigley Field. A young woman named Ruthie Patzke was seated in the dining room with her girlfriend. They had come in with a busload of Braves Boosters from Milwaukee. It was Ruthie's first baseball game. She remembered seeing Bob for the first time. "He was standing in the balcony talking to someone," she said. "He had a blue jacket on. It matched his eyes. Bobby always wore a jacket and tie and shirt." Ruthie told her girlfriend that she wanted to meet that man and would marry him someday.⁷

Long story short, the fire was kindled for Bob and Ruthie that day. He found out where she and her friend would be sitting in the ballpark (upper deck). All through the game she worried that he wouldn't stop to see her, but he did. Bob offered them a ride back to Milwaukee in his car, but this was 1953. That would not have been proper. They rode the bus. He called Ruthie at home, and they started dating.

On September 27, 1954, the day after the National League season ended, Ruthie and Bob were married in a small chapel in a Lutheran church in Milwaukee. (Virjean Lauby and Eddie Mathews were married the same day.) Bob and his bride honeymooned in New York City—for two days. He had to be there to cover the World Series. After Willie Mays made "The Catch" and the Giants took two from the Indians, the Series and the newlyweds shifted to Cleveland. The Indians were awful, and so was the couple's closet-sized hotel room. Wolf got in touch with Braves traveling secretary Duffy Lewis, who saved the day by procuring nicer accommodations for them.

The Braves pulled out of Milwaukee after the 1965 season. Wolf was left without a beat. He received a new one when the National Basketball Association expanded in January 1968 and formed the Milwaukee Bucks. Pretty soon they drafted UCLA's Lew Alcindor, better known later as Kareem Abdul-Jabbar, and the good times were back in Beertown. In April 1970 the one-year-old American League Seattle Pilots became the Milwaukee Brewers and took up residence in County Stadium. Wolf was not tempted, though. Pro basketball offered less travel and a more normal home life. In 1975 he was offered a position as a columnist, and he gladly accepted.

Beginning in 1978, Al McGuire, Marquette's retired basketball coach and later a national TV commentator, hosted a charity event to benefit Children's Hospital. It was a five-mile run through downtown Milwaukee. The fundraiser started small, about 4,000 runners, and grew to be one of the largest in the nation. Twice, in 1982 and again in 1985, Wolf ran alongside McGuire and interviewed him as they jogged. Normally Bob took notes on a stenographer's pad using his own version of shorthand, but for this occasion he made an exception and carried a tape recorder. Ruthie also entered the run. "I always beat him," she said with more than a hint of pride.[8] Wolf continued his running until he was 70.

After 39 years at the *Journal*, Wolf retired in November 1986 so he and Ruthie could live on the beach close to their daughter Debi in California. In retirement he contributed articles and columns to the San Diego edition of the *Los Angeles Times*.

When Wolf turned 80 in 2002, Debi hosted a party for her dad. She knew that his all-time favorite ballplayer was Chicago Cubs slugger Ernie Banks. She arranged for Mr. Cub to call Bob and wish him well on his birthday, which he did.

Wolf suffered a stroke on January 3, 2003. He died at age 81 the day after Thanksgiving of that year in Oceanside, California.

Sources

Wiseman, John B. (ed.), *Joy in Mudville: Essays on Baseball and American Life* (Jefferson, North Carolina: McFarland & Co., Inc., 2010), 89.

D'Amato, Gary, "Wolf Had It Covered," *Milwaukee Journal*, November 30, 2003.

Davis, Richard S., "Bleachers Fall Like Tumbling of Big Wave," *Milwaukee Journal*, February 25, 1947.

Wolf, Bob, "Milwaukee's Chuck Stevenson Wins Mexican Road Race Stock Car Title," *Milwaukee Journal*, November 24, 1952.

_____, "Moments To Remember," *Milwaukee Journal*, November 23, 1986.

_____, "Okinawa: Bloodstain in the Pacific," *Milwaukee Journal*, April 1, 1970.

_____, "State Car Is Third in Mexican Race After Freak Mishap," *Milwaukee Journal*, November 20, 1952.

_____, "39-Year Labor of Love," *Milwaukee Journal*, November 23, 1986.

"Al's Run Rapidly Becomes One of the Biggest in U.S.," *Milwaukee Sentinel*, September 26, 1987.

"Badger Game Disaster! 2 Dead, Over 200 Injured," *Milwaukee Sentinel*, February 25, 1947.

"Beauford T. Anderson, Second Lieut., U.S. Army," arlingtoncemetery.net/btanderson.htm.

"Battle of Okinawa." militaryhistoryonline.com.

"Carrera Panamericana." en.wikipedia.org/wiki/Carrera_Panamericana.

"Haunted Hotels in St. Charles, Illinois/USA Today." traveltips.usatoday.com.

"Hotel Baker." hotelbaker.com.

"Hotel Baker." en.wikipedia.org/wiki/Hotel_Baker.

"Nine Things You Probably Did Not Know About Ronald Reagan's Radio Career," radio.about.com.

"Okinawa: The Last Battle." history.army.mil.

"Soldiers Grove: Beauford T. Anderson," soldiersgrove.com/BT%20Anderson.htm.

Telephone interviews with Debi Wolf and Ruthie Wolf.

Notes

[1] Bob Wolf, "A 39-year labor of love," *Milwaukee Journal*, November 23, 1986.

[2] Gary D'Amato, "Wolf had it covered," *Milwaukee Journal*, November 30, 2003.

[3] Bob Wolf, "Okinawa: Bloodstain in the Pacific," *Milwaukee Journal*, April 1, 1970.

[4] Ibid.

[5] Bob Wolf, "McKenly Sets World Record for 400 Meters in AAU Trials," *Milwaukee Journal*, July 3, 1948.

[6] Bob Wolf, "State Car Is Third in Mexican Race After Freak Mishap," *Milwaukee Journal*, November 20, 1952.

[7] Ruthie Wolf, telephone interview, November 5, 2012.

[8] Ibid.

Voices of the Braves:
Blaine Walsh and Earl Gillespie

By Bob Buege

IN WISCONSIN DURING the mid- and late 1950s, the most recognizable voices in the entire baseball-crazy state belonged to Earl Gillespie and Blaine Walsh, the Milwaukee Braves' tandem of radio broadcasters. In stores, on front porches, in open convertibles at stoplights, their descriptions and accounts of the games was unavoidable. Love-struck residents of the Badger State opened their hearts shamelessly to their new ballclub that arrived from Boston in 1953. Earl and "The Blainer" were the welcome house guests who brought their friends Spahn and Bruton and Mathews into people's homes.

The pairing of Gillespie and Walsh resulted from what Earl called "a shotgun marriage."[1] Gillespie had been broadcasting the games of the American Association Milwaukee Brewers the previous two seasons on radio station WEMP. The Brewers' chief sponsor was Miller High Life, "The Champagne of Bottle Beer." Brewery president Fred Miller, the man behind the scenes who essentially brokered the deal for Lou Perini to move the Braves to Milwaukee, made it known that whichever station received the broadcast rights to the Braves games, he wanted Gillespie to do the play-by-play.

This created a problem. Milwaukee's largest radio and TV stations, WTMJ and WTMJ-TV (owned by the *Milwaukee Journal*), also wanted to carry the Braves. The dilemma was quickly resolved. Both radio stations would carry the identical radio feed, with WTMJ's sports announcer Walsh sharing the microphone with Gillespie. The idea of televising the contests was immediately quashed. For nine seasons Braves owner Perini simply refused to allow any of his team's games to be televised. This was a curious decision since Perini had allowed every home game of his minor-league Brewers to be televised in 1948 and 1949, when hardly anyone even owned a TV.

Actually, Walsh was not Gillespie's original partner in the Braves radio booth. Initially WTMJ assigned Walsh's good friend Bob Kelly. Unfortunately for Kelly, it was expected that announcers would present a telegraphic broadcast of a different game on the Braves' offdays. Kelly had never done one before, and when he messed up one of those re-creations, the station quickly named Walsh to work alongside Gillespie.

Even then the Gillespie and Walsh team was not fully formed. "At first Blaine didn't travel to the games in the East," Gillespie recalled years later, meaning New York and Pennsylvania. "Chris Schenkel was based in New York, and he worked the Eastern games with me."[2] That arrangement was short-lived. The Miller Brewing Company decided "The Blainer" should accompany the Braves on the road.

The chemistry between the two broadcasters was ideal. Gillespie was a high-energy, fast-talking master of the play-by-play. He made even mundane moments

Earl Gillespie (National Baseball Hall of Fame Library, Cooperstown, N.Y.)

sound exciting. Walsh possessed a sonorous baritone voice and an easy, laid-back manner. They shared a sense of humor that often found them laughing uncontrollably on the air. They came across like two good buddies enjoying a ballgame, which they were.

In County Stadium a nylon screen connected the top of the backstop with the bottom of the press box, protecting patrons seated behind home plate from being drilled with a foul ball. Often a foul ball would roll up the screen toward the broadcast booth, and once in a while Gillespie or Walsh would snag one.

On July 28, 1953, the County Stadium crowd included a contingent of 5,000 visitors celebrating Waukesha County Night, honoring the geographic region west of Milwaukee. Waukesha radio station WAUX presented the broadcast team with a large fishnet to help them catch more foul balls. From that night forward the cry of "Blainer, get the net!" became a fixture on Braves broadcasts. The announcers had the horsehide souvenirs autographed by the players and delivered to children in local hospitals. Blaine and Earl quickly became as popular as the Braves on the field.

Commissioner of Baseball Bud Selig, a college student at that time, recalled, "I listened to Earl Gillespie and Blaine Walsh. I lived and died every game. They made a terrific team, as good an announcing team as I've ever heard."[3]

Blaine Luke Walsh was born in Oconto, Wisconsin, on April 17, 1925. His father, Samuel Walsh, was a Republican state legislator at the time. Blaine acquired his rather uncommon first name in honor of Samuel Walsh's political ally John J. Blaine, then Wisconsin's governor. The governor sent the infant a silver ring in appreciation.[4] Later, Governor Blaine successfully ran for the United States Senate, where he authored the bill that repealed Prohibition. Coincidentally, or maybe not, Sam Walsh later became a liquor salesman and ultimately a tavernkeeper in Suamico, a few miles north of Green Bay.

Before opening his first saloon, Samuel Walsh also taught high school for a short time. One of his pupils was Victoria Gierke. After Victoria graduated, they were married. They were both native to the area, he of Irish descent and she Belgian. Their marriage produced three children, Blaine, Richard, and Elizabeth.

At Green Bay West High School, Walsh played two seasons as a guard and center on the varsity football team under coach Faust L. "Frosty" Ferzacca, who later coached Marquette University. After graduating in the spring of 1943, Walsh received his draft notification a few weeks later. His 30 months in the Army included a year and a half assigned to the 248th Combat Engineer Battalion. His main duty was driving trucks as his unit constructed bridges in Germany and France. He was awarded four battle stars and was discharged in January 1946.

Nine days after returning home, Blaine met his future wife, June McClure. Recalling that happy time, June said that her sister Betty was engaged to a man named Jack Olson, who was Blaine's best buddy in Europe. Betty used to send Jack photographs of home while he was in Europe, one of which was a picture of June. When Blaine saw it, he told Jack, "I would like a date with Betty's sister June."[5]

When Blaine returned to Green Bay, June saw him in person for the first time—in church. Jack arranged a blind date, and, according to June, "That was it—love at first sight!"[6] They were married on August 24, 1947, in St. Patrick's Church in Green Bay. In the course of their marriage, June and Blaine raised a family of nine children, six boys and three girls. The large family was perfectly in character. June had grown up in a family of 15 kids.

Home from the war and needing a job, Blaine Walsh tended bar in his father's establishment, the Green Tavern, before finding work in a paper mill. Soon he gave that up and became a dispatcher for the Green Bay Fire Department. Someone from a local radio station heard him and told him, "Blaine, you have a beautiful voice. You ought to come to the station."[7] He did, and WDUZ hired him as a reporter. Later the station gave him the late night news spot. He stayed there for 16 months and then moved to rival station WJPG, newly created by the *Green Bay Press-Gazette*. At WJPG his colleagues included Bob Kelly. It was Kelly who in 1952 told Walsh about a staff opening at WTMJ in Milwaukee. Walsh interviewed and got the job. The day after Christmas 1952 he and June packed up the kids and moved to Wisconsin's biggest media market.

Barely half a year later Walsh was in the limelight of the Milwaukee Braves radio booth at County Stadium alongside his former colleague from WJPG, Earl Gillespie. Together they served as the narrators of the amazing success story of the Milwaukee Braves, partnering for 11 years until Gillespie resigned his position. Blaine continued broadcasting Braves games, on both radio and television, during the club's final two years as a Milwaukee franchise.

Blaine Walsh (Photo courtesy of the Blaine Walsh family)

Broadcasting baseball was not Walsh's sole responsibility for WTMJ. For example, in 1954-55 he dressed up in a space suit and served as the announcer for *Rocky Jones, Space Ranger*. Baseball, though, transcended everything else.

Throughout their years with the Braves, Walsh and Gillespie were like part of the ballclub. They socialized with them and traveled with the players, not seated near the front of the plane with the brass but back among the fun-loving, uninhibited athletes. On Memorial Day 1961, Walsh inadvertently found himself in the midst of one of the more notorious incidents in the brief regime of manager Charlie Dressen.

The Braves had just split a doubleheader with the Phillies in Connie Mack Stadium. On the bus to the airport, en route to Pittsburgh, the players were their customary raucous, high-spirited selves. Walsh was seated on the aisle quietly reading a newspaper. Someone (the usual suspects were Spahn and Burdette) set it on fire — twice. This amused the players no end, but it infuriated Dressen. The little skipper had recently missed five games because of the flu, and he was not in a festive mood. In fact, he had managed that afternoon in street clothes and was still feeling sick. Arriving at the hotel in Pittsburgh, he warned that any player who left the premises that night would face a $500 fine.

Recently acquired Billy Martin piped up from the rear, "Anyone for a $500 sandwich?"[8] Forty-eight hours later Martin was a member of the Minnesota Twins.

Besides doing color and play-by-play of the Braves games, Walsh did an interview show called *Fan in the Stands* starting 25 minutes before each home game. The technology of the 1950s required him to carry a mobile unit the size of a fire extinguisher as he strolled through the lower grandstand area of County Stadium, chatting with early arrivals about where they were from and what they thought of the Braves. They all liked them.

Walsh's duties centered on but were not limited to baseball. He also gave the sports report on the local 6 o'clock news. When a new Sears Roebuck opened at an area shopping center (no malls yet), Blaine was on hand to cut the ribbon. When some civic organization needed a celebrity speaker at their luncheon, the affable Braves broadcaster always drew a good crowd.

Once in a while Walsh could be heard on a national sports hookup. Working with Jack Whitaker, he did the radio broadcast of the National Football League championship game on the day after Christmas 1960, the only important game that Vince Lombardi ever lost. Walsh also teamed with Ernie Harwell on the second 1961 baseball All-Star Game from Fenway Park, the first such contest to end in a tie.

At various times on the state network of WTMJ-620, depending on which station owned the broadcast rights at the time, Walsh also brought listeners the play-by-play of the Green Bay Packers and the Wisconsin football Badgers. In addition, he hosted a ten-minute radio program with coach Johnny Erickson before each home game of the University of Wisconsin basketball team for several years.

After Bobby Bragan became field boss of the Braves in 1963, Walsh served as host-moderator of *The Bobby Bragan Show*, a low-budget production showcasing the winning personality and baseball insights of the former Brooklyn Dodgers catcher and shortstop with the Alabama accent. As it became clear that the Braves were Atlanta-bound, Bragan increasingly became a polarizing figure in the Dairy State, a target of the Milwaukee fans' feelings of betrayal. Nevertheless, June Walsh said she and Blaine found Bragan and his wife to be "a very nice couple."[9] Before Bragan left for Georgia he held a farewell dinner at a Milwaukee hotel. The Walshes were included in a rather exclusive list of invited guests and found the affair and the hosts to be quite charming.

Blaine Walsh also hosted a similar show with the leader of a different Wisconsin sports team. Beginning in 1962, the year in which the Packers won 13 games and lost only one, *The Vince Lombardi Show* took to the air. Lombardi was a living legend in Wisconsin. There is a much-told story, possibly apocryphal, that shortly after moving to Green Bay to coach the Packers, Lombardi, a devout Catholic, was introduced to the archbishop. Lombardi said to His Holiness, "I understand the Green Bay Packers are like a religion around here."

"Oh, no," the archbishop answered, "they're much more important than that."

True or not, Lombardi's TV show quickly became required viewing in Packerland. The show was all business. Walsh would prompt the coach with questions and observations. The gap-toothed Leader of the Pack would show film clips and diagram plays on a chalkboard to explain why the Packers were successful and to prepare the viewing audience for the next Sunday's game.

In order to tape segments with Lombardi, Walsh often had to go to the coach's hotel room. More than once he returned home and told his wife that he had had to wait while the coach finished watching some cartoon on television. Walsh got along well with Coach Lombardi, who once gave him a book that he had inscribed, "To Blaine Walsh, the best interviewer I've ever had."[10]

The Braves' final season in Milwaukee found the fans hostile and few in number. On their final Opening Day in County Stadium, on April 15, 1965, however, a group called Teams, Inc., led by 30-year-old Bud Selig, paid the Braves $35,000 for the team's share of the day's receipts and promoted the game on their own. Their purpose was to pay tribute to the players and to raise money toward bringing in a new ballclub. More than 33,000 attended.

In a pregame ceremony, Walsh stood behind a microphone at home plate, calling off the names of the starting lineup from the 1953 opener. Most of the old-timers were in attendance, and each one ran to his old position as his name was announced. In the background, members of the Eddie Mathews fan club unfurled a huge banner that read, "Atlanta You Can Have the Rest, Leave Us Eddie Mattress Our Hero."[11] Other than the sportswriters, Mathews and Walsh were the only two participants from the '53 season still actively involved with the Braves. One other nostalgic touch was the first-base position. Joe Adcock was in California with the Angels, so pinch-hitting for him was an old Class D first sacker named Earl Gillespie.

In 1966 Blaine Walsh was named Wisconsin Sportscaster of the Year. With County Stadium vacant, he continued his football broadcasting and remained a staff announcer at WTMJ for the next couple of years, but much of his enthusiasm was gone. "He was burned out with WTMJ," wife June said, "He didn't like sitting behind a desk."[12]

For some reason Walsh liked the Atlanta area, so in July of 1969, he and June moved there. Blaine and a couple of partners started a business in the suburb of Dunwoody, a combination service station/car wash with a truck-rental agency included. He also did some free-lance public-relations work. Later he sold the business and took a job with an auto-parts company.

At the start of September 1985, Walsh made plans to fly to Milwaukee. The Pen and Mike Club was honoring his longtime compatriot Earl Gillespie at the Nantucket Shores restaurant. Earl had recently announced that he would be retiring as sports director of WITI-TV6 in December. Walsh wanted to be there. He had not seen Gillespie in six years.

Blaine had not been feeling well recently. While visiting in Florida, June had received a frantic call from their daughter. "Dad had a heart attack!" she exclaimed.[13] Walsh was hospitalized briefly, but the problem did not appear to be serious. Then, on the day when he was supposed to travel to Wisconsin, he felt worse.

"I just can't go," he told June.[14] It pained him to miss his friend's retirement luncheon, but he wasn't up to it. He told June he would call Gillespie the next morning and explain why he had not been there. He knew Earl would understand.

"Be sure to remind me to call him tomorrow," he told June before going to sleep.[15]

At 7:30 the next morning, June said, "I went in the bedroom, and he was gone."[16] He had died in his sleep in the night.

His last words, his last earthly thoughts, had been of his friend Earl Gillespie and the Milwaukee Braves.

Earl Gillespie knew from an early age what he wanted to do with his life. He wanted to be a baseball player.

"I figured if I could make it in the big leagues and earn $9,000 a year, I'd be happy," he recalled many years later.[17]

Of course, every boy in America during the Great Depression had the same dream. Earl's wish, though, came true. He made it in the big leagues, but in a broadcast booth, not on the diamond.

Born in Chicago on July 25, 1922, Earl William Gillespie, Jr. was 7 years old when Wall Street collapsed. Earl and his kid brother, Gordie, knew hard times just like most of the country. They shared a bedroom in the basement of the home of their Grandmother and Grandfather Ross, who had immigrated from Scotland. Their mother, Isabelle Adam Ross Gillespie, was a native of Aberdeen. Grandpa Ross lived near Wrigley Field and worked as a steamfitter. Earl and Gordie's family stayed with them because their mother was in poor health and their father could not find work. He lacked even an elementary-school certificate. Years later he was able to get a job as an accountant.

Gordie and Earl both possessed exceptional athletic ability. Gordie, 3 1/2 years younger, earned all-state honors as a basketball center at Kelvyn Park High School. He achieved his most notable success, however, as a coach in three sports. As head football coach at Joliet Catholic High School, he guided his teams to four consecutive state titles. Among those he coached was the young man who inspired the film *Rudy*. Gordie coached for 59 years. When he finally retired in 2011, his baseball teams had won 1,893 games, almost certainly the highest total of any coach in the nation.

Earl Gillespie saw a clear path to baseball's major leagues, and it ran directly through Chicago's Lane Technical High School. Lane Tech was a massive public high school with a student population of 7,000 boys. The school produced standouts in many sports, and thanks to legendary baseball coach Percy Moore, it produced Phil Cavarretta.

Largely forgotten today, Cavarretta in his day was a sensation in the Windy City. He signed a contract with the Chicago Cubs while still a student. He graduated from Lane Tech in 1934 and within a week was playing ball at Class B Peoria. In his first game as a professional, still only 17 years old, he hit for the cycle. In September he was called up to the big leagues. The following spring, Cavarretta was the Cubs' starting first baseman, and in October he was playing in the World Series.

Earl idolized Cavarretta. Like his hero, Earl was a lefty first baseman. He did not live in Lane Tech's district, but he applied for and received special permission to enroll there. While Charlie Grimm's Cubs were nailing down the pennant, Earl was matriculating at Lane Tech. He had to catch a streetcar very early every morning for the long ride to school, but he was able to play ball for Percy Moore.

Earl missed much of his junior season after he broke his leg while sliding into home plate. As a senior, though, he batted over .500 and led Lane Tech to the city championship game. He slammed a pair of doubles against the left-field wall in Wrigley Field in the title game, but Lane Tech lost to rival Steinmetz High School.

After graduation Earl signed a contract with the Chicago White Sox that, according to brother Gordie, paid Earl $75 a month. The White Sox assigned him to the Jonesboro White Sox in Arkansas, their lowest farm club. Gillespie said that before playing even one game he was sold to the St. Joseph Autos of the Michigan State League. He was beaten out of that job by a 28-year-old veteran. "I was broke," Earl recollected, "and I had to hitchhike home."[18] He worked out with the Madison Blues until he was able to find a place in the Wisconsin State League.

"I stayed at the Cardinal Hotel in Madison," he recalled, "and I did odd jobs. I ran the elevator, dried dishes, and ran the scoreboard in the barroom." He was 17 years old. "I finally caught on with the Green Bay Blue Jays."[19]

In his second year with Green Bay (for that one season they were called the Blue Sox) he was a teammate of Andy Pafko. That was Gillespie's best year at the plate (.283). The Blue Sox finished first in the standings. The postseason tournament fell victim to seven straight days of rain and was canceled.

In 1943 Gillespie's baseball odyssey was interrupted by World War II. He enlisted in the Navy. He passed a test to get into Officer Candidate School in the Marine Air Corps. He received his flight training in Pensacola, Florida. He flew Corsairs off an aircraft carrier. The Corsair was one of the newer fighter planes in the Pacific Theater. Gillespie was sent to Okinawa, but while he was en route, the Enola Gay dropped the atom bomb on Hiroshima and the war quickly ended. Gillespie "reached Okinawa and stayed there doing mop-up stuff for a year or so" before being discharged, his son John said.[20]

In 1942, before entering the military and while playing ball for the Blue Jays, Gillespie had stopped in one night at Oliver's Ice Cream Shop in downtown Green Bay. If this sounds like a Currier and Ives moment, it was. Drawn by the lure of a milkshake or sundae, Earl met a cute young lady named Margery Boland. Earl did not have an automobile; Marge did. They began dating, and on July 22, 1944, they were married in Florida while Earl was on leave before heading to the South Pacific.

In 1946 Gillespie was back playing first base for the Blue Jays for the fourth year. "I think I'm the only guy who played that long in Class D," he often said. "So much for my talent."[21]

During that season Gillespie injured his shoulder. He was called Lippy and Gabby by his teammates because he never stopped talking. While the injury kept him out of the lineup, the team's radio announcer, Al Michaels (no, not *that* Al Michaels), asked him if he wanted to put all that chatter to work by doing a few innings of play-by-play in the radio booth. "That was actually the beginning of my broadcast career," Gillespie often told people.[22]

Gillespie tried selling real estate for his father-in-law's realty firm, but it was not for him. Fortunately for Gillespie, John Walter, the general manager of radio station WJPG, had seen his enthusiasm on the ball field, heard him in the booth with Michaels, and offered him a job. Earl took it.

Earl Gillespie (left), Blaine Walsh (center without cap) and Donald Davidson, Braves traveling secretary (lower right) at County Stadium. (Photo courtesy of Blaine Walsh family.)

Another big break for Gillespie came in 1951. Mickey Heath, radio announcer for the Milwaukee Brewers in the American Association, retired. Red Smith, Gillespie's former manager with the Green Bay Blue Jays, was the Brewers' general manager. He recommended Gillespie, and Earl became the voice of the Brewers. The Brewers proceeded to win the Little World Series under Charlie Grimm in 1951, giving Gillespie even more exposure and adding to his popularity.

Two years later, when Lou Perini moved his Boston Braves franchise to Milwaukee, Gillespie and partner Blaine Walsh were the broadcasters for the most sensational baseball team in America. The Braves set a National League attendance record, and Gillespie and Walsh received much of the credit for helping to create the excitement.

From the very start Gillespie became a trusted member of the Milwaukee ballclub. In spring training he often threw batting practice and worked out with the team. He had a uniform just like the players', with a large number 0 on the back. One time Gillespie was pitching BP when Joe Adcock ripped a vicious line drive that narrowly missed Earl's ear. Batting practice pitchers in those days did not work behind a protective screen as they do today. Manager Charlie Grimm witnessed the near miss and told Gillespie, "That's it. If that ball hits you in the mouth, your career's over."[23] That was Earl's final mound appearance.

Whenever something exceptional occurred on the field, Gillespie could be expected to utter his pet euphemism, "Holy cow!" It was a phrase long associated with St. Louis broadcaster Harry Caray. Earl always denied borrowing it from the Cardinals' announcer. He insisted it just came out naturally. Braves fans loved it. In their home Earl and Marge Gillespie had upward of a hundred knickknacks and statuettes of cows wearing halos, sent by loyal listeners. Gillespie's popularity was further demonstrated by a toy company's creation in 1961 of a statistical card game, the "Earl Gillespie Baseball Game."

Besides Brewers and Braves games, Gillespie also did radio broadcasts of the other major sports teams in Wisconsin: the Milwaukee Hawks of pro basketball, Marquette University basketball and football, the Green Bay Packers, and University of Wisconsin football. In addition, he had numerous national broadcasts and telecasts. He did the play-by-play of the 1954 Detroit Lions vs. College All-Stars contest with Red Grange. He did radio announcing for National Football League championship games in 1953-55, baseball's All-Star Game in 1955 from Milwaukee, the 1957 World Series, and the NFL Playoff Bowl from Miami in 1964.

In 1964 Gillespie took over the telecasts of the Green Bay Packers from Ray Scott. Scott was a legendary minimalist (Starr ... Dowler ... touchdown!) who started doing the Packers' TV games in 1956 when the team was awful and rode the victory train into the Lombardi dynasty. In '64, though, after a dispute with CBS about splitting the game with the other team's announcer, Scott stepped aside and Gillespie moved in, working alongside color man Tony Canadeo. Earl relished the opportunity, but he was also doing Wisconsin Badgers games on Saturdays. His travel schedule became a nightmare. For example, on Saturday, November 14, he worked the Badgers vs. Illinois in Champaign. He left the game during the fourth quarter, caught a plane to Chicago, then caught a different flight to San Francisco to get to Kezar Stadium for the Packers vs. 49ers on Sunday. The next year Scott patched up his differences with the network and returned, so Gillespie's TV career with the Packers expired after one season.

Gillespie's array of broadcasting experiences was impressive, but for Braves fans nothing surpassed his call of the final moments of the 1957 World Series. Here he is in Game Seven, with two out in the bottom of the ninth: "The outfield around to the left. McDougald is on at third, Coleman is at second. Tommy Byrne the baserunner at first. Hank Aaron is pulled around in left center field. A breeze is blowing across from left to right. Burdette's pitch. Swung on, lined, grabbed by Mathews who steps on third—and the World Series is over and the Milwaukee Braves are the new world champions of baseball!"

By far Gillespie's longest-running gig was his 31 years doing radio broadcasts of University of Wisconsin football. In all those hundreds of games, two stood out in his memory. The first was on October 11, 1969, Parents' Day at Camp Randall Stadium. The Badgers had gone

23 straight games without a victory (one tie). Second-year coach John Coatta had yet to find out what winning felt like. Wisconsin was trailing Iowa 10-0 at the half and 17-0 in the third quarter. Somehow the Badgers rallied and won, 23-17, on a fourth-down, 17-yard pass with a minute to go. Sixteen years later Gillespie told Bob Wolf of the *Milwaukee Journal*, "I can see Randy Marks in the end zone after catching the winning touchdown pass. My son John was spotting for me, and he actually cried."[24]

Gillespie's other favorite Badger moment occurred on Homecoming afternoon, November 2, 1985, against Indiana. Once again the Badgers were on a losing streak, this time a modest four games, all of them Big Ten Conference games. This time, however, the thrill was personal for Gillespie. Coach Dave McClain and athletic director Elroy "Crazylegs" Hirsch had arranged for Earl to lead the Badgers as they charged out of the tunnel and onto the field. "You can't imagine how much that meant to me," Gillespie said proudly. "I even talked to the squad in the locker room before the game."[25] To cap the experience, Wisconsin erased a 14-0 deficit and defeated the Hoosiers, 31-20. Gillespie said, "After the Badgers had won, they voted me the game ball."[26]

For 11 years Blaine Walsh and Earl Gillespie brought Wisconsin listeners the excitement, and the disappointments, of the Milwaukee Braves. In 1963, tired of the travel and perhaps foreseeing the sad future of the team, Gillespie resigned to become sports director of WITI TV-6 in Milwaukee. He suddenly had weekends free and a regular schedule. He and a few colleagues presented the news at 6 and 10 P.M. One of those co-workers was a smart-alecky hand puppet of a cat that, at least nominally, forecast the weather. Albert the Alleycat, the creation of puppeteer Jack Du Blon, spoke in a fractured Brooklyn accent, mispronounced words (the humidery is 65 percent) and names (our movie tonight is "The Magnificent Seven" starring Elly Wall-utch), and told outrageous jokes (There's an experiment to cross a turkey and a kangaroo. It would be the first bird you can stuff from the outside). From off-camera came the hearty laugh, à la Ed McMahon, of Earl Gillespie, enjoying himself as always. Said Mary Kay Hayes, Earl's daughter, "Dad loved working with Albert."[27]

Mary Kay also remembered that when her father started working at Channel 6, "They told him the number one sport in Wisconsin is fishing. He took up fishing and fell in love with it."[28] Gillespie developed a whole new audience with his folksy outdoor show *Earl Goes Fishing*. One of his frequent partners in the boat was son John, who followed his dad's footsteps as a TV sports director and then the star of a long-running outdoor adventure program called *Wisconsin's Waters and Woods*.

Earl and Marge had three other children besides Mary Kay and John: Trish, Margie, and Michael. Michael was killed by an automobile when he was just 4. Marge died of cancer in May 1984. In 1985 Earl married Bettye Gilles. She passed away on March 22, 2009.

Gillespie was sometimes criticized for being too close to the athletes, too friendly, to maintain objectivity. He remained unrepentant. "I see nothing wrong with rooting for our guys," he would say.[29]

He told the story of the day the Packers fired Bart Starr as coach. "He walked out of the room, and I followed him into the hallway. There were tears in his eyes, but the first thing he asked me was how my wife was. She had been sick then. Then he asked me if I wanted a one-on-one interview. That's what friendship means."[30]

Earl Gillespie died of respiratory failure on December 12, 2003. He was 81.

Sources

Chapman, Lou, "It Was Sportswriter vs. Braves in Battle Over Move," *Milwaukee Sentinel*, November 21, 1979.

_____, "That's Why the Former Baseball Player Traded His Glove for the 'Mike,'" *Milwaukee Sentinel*, April 15, 1956.

Dobish, Alex, "Blaine Walsh Is a Big Leaguer Now," *Milwaukee Journal*, May 9, 1954.

Drew, Michael H., "Milwaukee Studio Notes," *Milwaukee Journal*, November 22, 1964.

Gonring, Mike, "The Earl of TV Sports," *Milwaukee Journal*, December 14, 1976.

Johnson, Chuck, "New Look, New Voice," *Milwaukee Journal*, September 13, 1964.

Karius, Joe, "State Teams Love of Gillespie's Life," *Milwaukee Sentinel*, July 15, 1985.

Smith, Curt, *The Storytellers,* (New York: Macmillan, 1995).

Silvers, Amy Rabideau, "State Loses Sports Voice of Golden Era," *Milwaukee Journal Sentinel*, December 13, 2003.

Tusa, Rosa, "Earl's Girl—Keeper of the 'Holy Cow!'" *Milwaukee Sentinel*, September 25, 1957.

Vandenberg, Bob, "Living High Life: Milwaukee Was a Magical Place To Be in 1957," *Chicago Tribune*, July 18, 2007.

Wells, Robert W., "Embers of Fans' Old Love for Braves Still Glow," *Milwaukee Journal*, April 16, 1965.

Wolf, Bob, "34-Year Thrill for Gillespie," *Milwaukee Journal*, December 12, 1985.

_____, "Walsh's Voice Lives in Memory," *Milwaukee Journal*, September 12, 1985.

"Blaine Walsh, a Voice of the Braves, Dies," *Milwaukee Journal*, September 5, 1985.

"Gillespie Takes Over for Scott on Packer TV," *Milwaukee Sentinel*, August 5, 1964.

"Scott Replaces Gillespie on Packer TV," *Milwaukee Sentinel*, April 30, 1965.

"Sportscaster Walsh Leaves WTMJ Job," *Milwaukee Journal*, January 8, 1969.

Telephone interviews with Gordie Gillespie, John Gillespie, Mary Kay Hayes, and June Walsh.

Notes

1. Bob Wolf, "34-Year Thrill for Gillespie," *Milwaukee Journal*, December 12, 1985.
2. Bob Wolf, "Walsh's Voice Lives in Memory," *Milwaukee Journal*, September 12, 1985.
3. Bob Vandenberg, "Living High Life: Milwaukee Was a Magical Place To Be in 1957," *Chicago Tribune*, July 18, 2007.
4. June Walsh, telephone interview, November 30, 2012.
5. Ibid.
6. Ibid.
7. Ibid.
8. Lou Chapman, "It Was Sportswriter vs. Braves in Battle Over Move," *Milwaukee Sentinel*, November 21, 1979.
9. June Walsh interview.
10. Ibid.
11. Robert W. Wells, "Embers of Fans' Old Love for Braves Still Glow," *Milwaukee Journal*, April 16, 1965.
12. June Walsh interview.
13. Ibid.
14. Ibid.
15. Ibid.
16. Ibid.
17. Bob Wolf, "34-Year Thrill," *Milwaukee Journal*.
18. Ibid.
19. Ibid.
20. John Gillespie, telephone interview, December 1, 2012.
21. Curt Smith, *The Storytellers* (New York: Macmillan, 1995), quoted in *Milwaukee Journal Sentinel*, December 13, 2003.
22. Earl Gillespie, quoted in *Milwaukee Sentinel* advertisement for WITI TV-6 News, February 16, 1974.
23. Curt Smith, *The Storytellers*, quoted in *Milwaukee Journal Sentinel*.
24. Bob Wolf, "34-Year Thrill," *Milwaukee Journal*.
25. Ibid.
26. Ibid.
27. Mary Kay Hayes, telephone interview, December 1, 2012.
28. Ibid.
29. Amy Rabideau Silvers, "State Loses Sports Voice of Golden Era," *Milwaukee Journal Sentinel*, December 13, 2003.
30. Joe Karius, "State Teams Love of Gillespie's Life," *Milwaukee Sentinel*, July 15, 1985.

1957 Milwaukee Braves Regular Season Summary

Gregory H. Wolf

ALL HEADLINES ARE from the next day's edition of the *Milwaukee Sentinel*, unless otherwise noted.

April 16. BRAVES ON THEIR WAY, 4-1. Spahn's Pitching, Logan's Home Run Highlight Opener. The Braves opened the 1957 season in Chicago on Tuesday afternoon in front of 23,674 spectators in Wrigley Field. Thirty-six-year-old Warren Spahn tossed a complete game, holding the Northsiders to four hits en route to his 204th career victory. The Braves scored all of their runs in the sixth inning, highlighted by Johnny Logan's two-run home run.

The Braves' Opening Day starting lineup was:

Danny O'Connell	2B
Henry Aaron	RF
Eddie Mathews	3B
Joe Adcock	1B
Bobby Thomson	LF
Johnny Logan	SS
Bill Bruton	CF
Del Crandall	C
Warren Spahn	P

April 17. No game scheduled

April 18. NOW IT'S TWO IN A ROW! Burdette Shuts Out Cincy; Aaron Homers. On a sunny afternoon, 41,506 fans turned out for the Braves' home opener. Lew Burdette tossed a six-hit shutout to defeat the Redlegs, 1-0. In the sixth inning Henry Aaron blasted a one-out home run off Hal Jeffcoat into the bullpen in right center field for the game's only run. This contest would be the first of the Braves' four 1-0 complete-game victories thrown by four different pitchers, Burdette, Spahn, Bob Buhl, and Gene Conley, during the season.

April 19. No game scheduled

April 20. O'Connell, Murff Sink Redlegs, 5-4. In the second game of a six-game homestand, Del Crandall went 3-for-4, including a wind-aided second-inning home run, and later scored in the sixth inning on Danny O'Connell double, one of his three hits. Red Murff pitched 1 1/3 innings of scoreless relief to preserve the victory for starter Ray Crone.

April 21. BRAVES ALONE ATOP N.L. Win Fourth in a Row for Spahn's 2nd. The Braves' damage was done by Joe Adcock (three hits and one run batted in) and Del Crandall (two hits and two RBIs) as Warren Spahn scattered nine hits for his second consecutive complete-game victory of the season, 3-1 over the Redlegs.

April 22. BRAVES RIP CUBS FOR FIVE STRAIGHT. Buhl posts Braves 5th win, 9-4; Rush Routed. Behind home runs by Aaron and Adcock, the Braves jumped out to a 9-1 lead after four innings. Bob Buhl held the Cubs to five hits, but walked four in seven innings before yielding to Gene Conley, who pitched the last two innings in a 9-4 victory.

April 23. Neeman's Homer in Tenth Hands Braves First Loss. Cubs rookie catcher Cal Neeman belted his first career home run in the tenth inning off Lew Burdette, who pitched all ten innings but was collared for the hard-luck loss, 3-2. The Braves knocked out starter Elmer Singleton in the fifth inning, but were limited to two hits for the final 5 1/3 innings by journeymen Vito Valentinetti, Dick Littlefield, and Turk Lown.

Eddie Mathews and Del Crandall (National Baseball Hall of Fame Library, Cooperstown, N.Y.)

April 24. BRAVES HOMERS BEAT CARDS. The Braves' three primary home-run threats, Aaron, Adcock, and Mathews, connected off Cardinals starter Herm Wehmeier. Taylor Phillips pitched six innings of relief and earned the victory when Del Crandall launched a dramatic walk-off home run with one out in the ninth inning to defeat the Cardinals, 8-7.

April 25. No game scheduled

April 26. BRAVES FOUR HOME RUNS RIP REDS. The lights at Crosley Field did not bother the Braves as they belted four home runs in their first night game of the season and the first contest of a 16-game road trip. In the second inning Joe Adcock cranked a massive home run to deep right center field, then hit a grand slam in the next inning to record a season-high five runs batted in. Warren Spahn pitched his third consecutive complete game to garner the win, 9-2.

April 27. Burdette Bests Redlegs Again. Lew Burdette matched Warren Spahn with his third consecutive complete game to start the season, holding on for a 5-4 victory over Cincinnati. In the first inning Aaron knocked a pitch from starter Warren Hacker completely over a signboard on top of a factory behind the left-field fence at Crosley Field. Adcock added his fifth home run of the young season, a two-out solo shot, in the fifth inning.

April 28. BRAVES WIN 4TH IN ROW, 3-2. Red Murff relieved Taylor Phillips who issued six walks in 3 2/3 innings (but also secured his first big-league hit in the fourth inning) and held the Redlegs to three hits and one run over 5 1/3 innings to earn his first major-league victory, 3-2, for the three-game sweep of Cincinnati. The two Braves hurlers profited from four double plays; the last twin killing choked off a ninth-inning Redlegs rally. The Braves improved their record to 9-1, their best start since coming to Milwaukee.

April 29. No game scheduled

April 30. HRs by Antonelli and Rhodes Beat Braves. In the first game of a two-game series at the Polo Grounds, the Braves had no answer for former Brave Johnny Antonelli, who limited them to seven singles and struck out nine in a convincing 4-0 win. Dusty Rhodes crushed a pitch from Bob Buhl over the roof in right center field with Red Schoendienst aboard for the first two runs of the game. Antonelli, a capable batter, belted his tenth career home run, a two-run shot off Ray Crone in the seventh inning, to complete the scoring.

NL Standings, after games played on April 30, 1957

Team	Won	Lost	Tie	Pct	GB
Milwaukee Braves	9	2	0	.818	–
Brooklyn Dodgers	8	3	0	.727	1
New York Giants	7	6	0	.538	3
St Louis Cardinals	5	5	0	.500	3.5
Philadelphia Phillies	5	7	0	.417	4.5
Cincinnati Redlegs	5	7	0	.417	4.5
Pittsburgh Pirates	4	8	0	.333	5.5
Chicago Cubs	3	8	0	.273	6

May 1. BRAVES BEAT GIANTS IN 10TH. "My fastball is no longer my ace in the hole," said Spahn. "I came up with my new sinker pitch. Now I am finally a low ball pitcher and it's given me a new lease on life."[1] Going into the top of the tenth tied, 1-1, the Braves scored four runs, including back-to-back home runs by Frank Torre and Bobby Thomson. Spahn pitched a hitless tenth frame to win his fourth consecutive complete game, 5-1 over the Giants at the Polo Grounds in New York.

May 2. BRAVES BEAT PIRATES, 8-5. The Braves scored five unearned runs off reliever Elroy Face, including three in the top of the tenth inning to defeat the Pirates at Forbes Field in Pittsburgh. Hank Aaron rapped a season-high five hits, Danny O'Connell matched his season high with three, and Mathews belted three singles (and knocked in three runs) as part of Milwaukee's 18-hit attack. Red Murff pitched a scoreless tenth frame to preserve Lew Burdette's third victory of the year.

May 3. AARON'S BAT LEAVES BRAGAN SPEECHLESS AFTER BRAVES WIN ONE FROM THE PIRATES, 8-7. (From the *Milwaukee Journal*). The Braves won their third consecutive extra-inning game behind the hot hitting of Hank Aaron (3-for-4 with a double, triple, and home run), while Joe Adcock, Billy Bruton, Del Crandall, and Bobby Thomson had two hits each. Red Murff blew the lead when he surrendered a two-out run-scoring single to Bob Skinner, the first batter he faced in the ninth inning. Thomson singled home Aaron for the go-ahead run in the top of the 11th inning. With men on first and second in the bottom of the 11th, Warren Spahn came on in relief to induce pinch-hitter Danny Kravitz to pop up to center, thus preserving the Braves' exciting win. Pittsburgh used 23 players (including seven pitchers) during this contest.

May 4. BRAVES SHUT OUT, 1-0, BY VERNON LAW. Twenty-year-old rookie Juan Pizarro made his major-league debut against the Pirates, yielding just seven singles and one run. However, Vern Law pitched the first of three career two-hitters (he never threw a no-hitter or a one-hitter) for the shutout. Hank Aaron and Johnny Logan had the only hits for the Braves, who lost for just the third time in 15 games.

May 5. BRAVES BEAT DODGERS, 10-7. Four Aaron Blows Lead 16-Hit Spree. Ernie Johnson, 32, made his first appearance of the year by relieving starter Bob Buhl and Ray Crone, who had been rocked for a combined ten hits and seven runs in the first three innings. Johnson retired the first 16 batters he faced before yielding a bloop single to Gino Cimoli in the ninth. The Braves roared back from a 7-3 deficit with seven unanswered runs, led by Aaron's three-run homer to give Johnson the win, 10-7, at Ebbets Field in Brooklyn.

May 6. BRAVES DROP 14-INNING TILT TO BUMS, 5-4. An "incipient bean-ball battle" began in the first inning when Dodgers starter Don Drysdale knocked down Hank Aaron twice with inside pitches.[2] Lew Burdette retaliated by dusting off Roy Campanella after Carl Furillo's three-run homer was followed by Gil Hodges' deep fly ball to center field. The Braves tied the game on home runs by Mathews, his second of the game, in the sixth, and Joe Adcock in the eighth inning. Given a 4-3 lead in the 12th inning, Burdette surrendered it with two outs in the bottom of the frame. Sandy Koufax pitched a scoreless 14th and earned the win when Gino Cimoli blasted a walk-off shot off loser Red Murff.

May 7. PHILS DEFEAT BRAVES. The Phillies jumped on Warren Spahn for seven hits and five runs in four innings. In the third inning Phillies second baseman Granny Hamner clouted a monster blast into the upper deck in left field of Connie Mack Stadium in Philadelphia. Manager Fred Haney replaced struggling left fielder Bobby Thomson (batting just .156) with little-used Chuck Tanner, who rapped an RBI double in the sixth. Robin Roberts held the Braves to six hits, yielding four runs, for the complete-game victory, 8-4.

May 8. PHILS BEAT BRAVES, 2ND STRAIGHT. Phillies rookie Don Cardwell pitched a complete game seven-hitter, striking out nine, to hand the Braves their third consecutive loss, 2-1. The Braves rallied in the ninth for one run, but Danny O'Connell struck out with two outs and runners on first and third base to end the game.

May 9. No game scheduled.

May 10. PIZARRO, BRAVES WHIP CARDS. Johnny Logan went 4-for-4 with two singles, a double, and a home run to drive in five runs, and Eddie Mathews went 3-for-5 with a double and home run, knocking in three. In his second big-league start, Juan Pizarro hit his first major-league home run (a deep blast into the right-center pavilion seats) and went the distance, overcoming nine hits, four walks, and five runs to earn a 10-5 win over the Cardinals in St. Louis, his first career victory, behind the Braves' 14-hit attack.

May 11. BRAVES LOSE, TIE FOR FIRST. The Braves overcame their third deficit to tie the Cardinals at 7-7 in the eighth inning on Del Crandall's run-scoring single. Reliever Ray Crone extinguished a bases-loaded situation in the eighth, but was the victim of two errors in the tenth. Danny O'Connell bobbled Al Dark's grounder, then Joe Adcock threw Stan Musial's sure double-play grounder into left field. After Crone intentionally walked Jim King, Ken Boyer hit a walk-off single to win the game, 8-7, in the tenth inning.

May 12. BURDETTE, PHILLIPS MUZZLE CARDS IN PAIR, 4-2 and 10-4. In the first game of the Braves' first doubleheader of the season, Lew Burdette tossed a nifty six-hitter and Hank Aaron supplied the fireworks with a two-run homer in the fourth inning. Nursing a two-run lead in the eighth inning, Burdette faced trouble with two on and no outs, but Johnny Logan fielded a grounder to force out Bobby Gene Smith at third. Burdette then induced Al Dark to fly out and Stan Musial to ground out to end the inning.

In the second game the Braves jumped on Herman Wehmeier for two runs in the third inning, when Hank Aaron connected for his ninth home run of the year. In the fourth Danny O'Connell's two-run single knocked Wehmeier out of the game. Eddie Mathews then hit a three-run blast off reliever Willard Schmidt to give the Braves an 8-0 lead. Starter Red Murff surrendered four unanswered runs before reliever Taylor Phillips came on to pitch five scoreless innings of relief and pick up his second win of the year.

The Braves went 10-6 on their first road-trip of the year.

May 13. No game scheduled.

May 14. BRAVES TIP BUMS, TAKE LEAD. In the first game of a seven-game homestand, Joe Adcock belted a triple to score Hank Aaron and scored himself on Chuck Tanner's infield single to give the Braves a two-run lead after one inning. Bob Buhl pitched 6 2/3 innings and matched a career high with nine bases on balls. The Dodgers threatened with two on in the seventh, but Ernie Johnson came on in relief and got Roy Campanella to foul out, ending the rally and saving the 3-2 win for Buhl.

May 15. HOME RUN IN 10TH NIPS BRAVES, 3-2. The Braves reached starter Don Drysdale for only two hits over seven innings, but one of them was Frank Torre's double, scoring Danny O'Connell and Eddie Mathews in the seventh. The Braves' Gene Conley surrendered just three hits over 7 1/3 innings before yielding to Lew Burdette in his first relief appearance of the year. Burdette surrendered a home run to Don Zimmer in the tenth to take the loss.

May 16. BUCS DROP BRAVES TO SECOND PLACE. Bob Friend tossed a seven-hitter. Eddie Mathews' leadoff ninth-inning home-run was his only blemish. Rookie Juan Pizarro had his third consecutive strong outing, yielding only five hits and two runs over eight innings, but was a hard-luck loser, 2-1. The loss dropped the Braves to second place for the first time all season, one game behind the Dodgers.

May 17. Scheduled game with the Pittsburgh Pirates was rained out.

May 18. BRAVES WIN 6-5, HALF GAME OUT (AP, *Racine Journal-Times*). The Braves played their fourth consecutive one-run game and were led by Hank Aaron who enjoyed the first of his two two-home-run games of the season. He went 3-for-4, scored three times, and knocked in four runs. Warren Spahn had his third consecutive poor outing (seven hits and four runs in four innings); however, Burdette tossed one-run ball over five innings to notch his fifth win of the season, 6-5 over the Pirates, to improve the Braves' record to 18-9.

May 19. BRAVES HAND GIANTS VICTORY IN ONE GAME SERIES, 6-3 (*Milwaukee Journal*). In the top of the eighth inning in a 3-3 tie, Danny O'Connell muffed a sure double play with two men on and one out. Reliever Red Murff walked Daryl Spencer, then surrendered a go-ahead two-run single by catcher Ray Katt. Johnny Antonelli pitched three scoreless innings in relief for the Giants to garner the win.

May 20. No game scheduled.

May 21. RAIN ENDS BRAVES, PHILS GAME IN TIE. On a cold, rainy night, the Braves and Phillies played to a 1-1 tie. Starting pitcher Gene Conley singled home Billy Bruton in the bottom of the fifth inning to save the game for the Braves. The Phillies batted in the top half of the sixth, but the game was called after a 31-minute delay in the bottom half of the inning, thus erasing the Phillies' statistics from that half-inning.

May 22. HOMER BEATS PHILS IN 13TH. On a rainy night, Phillies starter Robin Roberts held the Braves batters in check through 12 innings, yielding only three runs, all from Eddie Mathews' game-tying home run in the fifth inning. Leading off the bottom of the 13th, Chuck Tanner hit his first and only career walk-off home run, giving the Braves an exciting 4-3 win. Tough-luck loser Roberts tossed 170 pitches.

May 23. No game scheduled.

May 24. CUBS ROOKIE PACES WIN OVER BRAVES. Warren Spahn was rocked in his fourth consecutive start, yielding six hits and three runs to the Cubs in five innings. Moe Drabowsky tossed a complete-game nine-hitter to earn the win, 5-1, in the first game of a four-game series at Wrigley Field. The Cubs' 26-year-old rookie right fielder Frank Ernaga homered in his first big-league at-bat and tripled in his second at-bat, both off Spahn.

May 25. BRAVES SQUEEZE 7-6 WIN FROM CHICAGO (AP, *Racine Journal-Times*). The Cubs clobbered starter Bob Buhl and reliever Taylor Phillips for seven hits, drew five walks, and scored five runs in 3 1/3 innings before a quartet of relievers (Ray Crone, Dave Jolly, Ernie Johnson, and Warren Spahn) shut them down. Trailing 5-1 after four innings, the Braves roared back with six unanswered runs, led by Johnny Logan and Joe Adcock, who each went 3-for-3. Billy Bruton's run-scoring triple and Hank Aaron's sacrifice fly in the eighth inning proved to be the difference in a 7-6 win.

May 26. BRAVES LOSE PAIR TO CUBS. Twin Loss Drops Club to Third. In the first game of a doubleheader at Wrigley Field, Cubs rookie pitcher Dick Drott set a new club record by striking out 15 batters, including Hank Aaron and Billy Bruton three times each, in a complete-game 7-5 victory. Del Crandall and Chuck Tanner connected for home runs off the 20-year-old right-hander.

Warren Spahn (National Baseball Hall of Fame Library, Cooperstown, N.Y.)

In the second game, Del Rice's first home run of the year, in the sixth inning, and Johnny Logan's run-scoring triple in the eighth gave the Braves a 4-2 cushion. But Juan Pizarro, who had been cruising along, surrendered a home run to Frank Ernaga in the eighth and then came undone in the ninth. After issuing a one-out walk and yielding two singles and the tying run, Pizarro was relieved by Ray Crone with two men on and Ernie Banks at the plate. Banks delivered a walk-off single to win the game. The Braves fell to third place, 2 1/2 games behind the first-place Cincinnati Redlegs. "We've been in a slump the last two weeks," said manager Fred Haney. "I'm not worried about their ability to snap out of it."[3]

May 27. REDS TIP BRAVES IN 'OVERTIME' In the first game of an eight-game homestand, Del Crandall hit a two-run home run in the bottom of the ninth inning to tie the score, 6-6. Reliever Ernie Johnson yielded five runs on four hits in the tenth for the 11-6 loss. Frustration resulted in fisticuffs after a hard slide involving Johnny Logan and Cincinnati's Hal Jeffcoat, who were both ejected. The brief fracas also drew in Eddie Mathews and the Redlegs' 60-year-old third-base coach, Jimmie Dykes. After a seven-game homerless drought, Aaron hit his league-leading 12th home run. Third-place Milwaukee dropped to a season-worst 3 1/2 games out of first place.

May 28. BRAVES' 2 HITS NIP REDLEGS. Don Gross of the Redlegs threw seven hitless innings until Bobby Thomson led off the eighth inning with a triple. Frank Torre's one-out single drove in Thomson for the only run of the game. Spahn bounced back after four ineffective starts to hold Cincinnati to eight hits for his first shutout of the season.

May 29. BUHL'S 4-HITTER HALTS CUBS. Bob Buhl pitched his first complete game of the season and third baseman Felix Mantilla recorded his first three hits of the season to lead the Braves' 12-hit attack. Notoriously poor-hitting Buhl went 2-for-4 with an RBI and scored a run in the 6-2 victory.

May 30. BRAVES, CUBS BREAK EVEN. Home Runs Help Crone Win Opener. In the first game of a doubleheader, Ray Crone pitched an eight-hit complete game (his first of the year) and received help from

Billy Bruton's first home run of the year and catcher Del Rice's second to record the win, 5-2.

Down by two runs in the ninth inning during the second game, the Braves began a two-out rally as Del Crandall and pinch-hitter Chuck Tanner singled, then pinch-hitter Joe Adcock walked. With the bases full, Turk Lown came on in relief and struck out Felix Mantilla to save the win, 4-2, and secure a split in the doubleheader for the Cubs.

May 31. CARDS SHADE BRAVES. Juan Pizarro pitched a complete game, but surrendered 11 hits and lost his third contest in five starts. The Cardinals' Lindy McDaniel went the distance and held the Braves to two earned runs in a 4-3 win. The loss was the Braves' ninth in 20 games decided by one run. Milwaukee finished with a 14-14 record in May, the team's only nonwinning month of the season.

NL Standings, after games played on May 31, 1957

Team	Won	Lost	Tie	Pct	GB
Cincinnati Redlegs	26	14	0	.650	–
Brooklyn Dodgers	23	15	0	.605	2
Milwaukee Braves	23	16	1	.590	2.5
Philadelphia Phillies	23	17	1	.575	3
St Louis Cardinals	19	19	0	.500	6
New York Giants	18	23	0	.439	8.5
Chicago Cubs	12	24	0	.333	12
Pittsburgh Pirates	11	27	0	.289	14

June 1. Cards Drop Braves 7-1 (AP *Racine Journal-Times*). The Braves began the new month with their worst defeat thus far in the season. The Cardinals' Murry Dickson held the Braves to six hits in front of the biggest home crowd since the season's opener, 38,240. Rookie Bobby Malkmus started his first game at second base, the weak spot on the team. Since their 12-2 start, the Braves have played 11-15 ball, and are now just six games above .500. The loss dropped Milwaukee to fourth place, 3 1/2 games out of first and behind Cincinnati, Brooklyn, and Philadelphia.

June 2. BRAVES TOP CARDS, TAKE 3RD. The Braves scored three runs in third inning on RBI singles by Bobby Thomson and Frank Torre. Bob Buhl scattered eight hits and yielded one run in eight innings, but the star of the game was relief pitcher Ernie Johnson. Entering the game in the ninth inning with runners on first base and second base, Johnson got Walker Cooper to hit into a double play and then struck out Don Blasingame to end the game, 3-1.

June 3. No game scheduled.

June 4. GIANTS EDGE BRAVES IN 13TH, 8-7. In New York for the first game of a 14-game road trip, Hank Aaron, Del Crandall, Frank Torre, and Carl Sawatski hit home runs but it was not enough to overcome shaky pitching by starter Ray Crone and relievers Bob Trowbridge and Gene Conley. Dusty Rhodes hit a two-out walk-off single in the 13th inning to drive in Valmy Thomas. Daryl Spencer supplied his own two-out theatrics in the bottom of the ninth inning to tie the game with a single.

June 5. OUTHOMERED 6 TO 3, THE BRAVES TOP GIANTS, 9-8. The two teams combined for nine home runs, one shy of the NL record. In the first inning Joe Adcock hit a line drive that caromed off the 449-foot mark in deep right center field at the Polo Grounds for an inside-the-park home run. Ernie Johnson rescued the Braves again, relieving starter Juan Pizarro in the second inning and pitching 7 1/3 innings for the win. Johnson also hit his only big-league home run, a three-run blast in the third inning. With Giants on first and second in the ninth inning, Taylor Phillips closed out the game by retiring two New York batters.

June 6. GOMEZ SILENCES BRAVES BATS WITH 4-HITTER, 2-0. The Braves endured their third shutout of the season and their fifth loss in seven games. The Giants' Ruben Gomez pitched a quick game (1:55), aided by Red Schoendienst's third-inning home run off loser Bob Buhl.

June 7. SPAHN BLANKS PIRATES FOR 6TH WIN. At Forbes Field, Warren Spahn tossed his second shutout of the season, blanking the Pirates 5-0 on seven singles. Del Crandall knocked in two runs with a single in the second inning. In search of offense, Fred Haney moved Hank Aaron to the cleanup spot for the first time this season.

June 8. Game rained out.

June 9. BRAVES, PIRATES SPLIT. Aaron Gets Homers (AP *Racine Journal-Times*). In the first game of a doubleheader, Bob Trowbridge tossed a career-high ten innings and yielded just one run for the 2-1 win.

Ernie Johnson pitched a hitless 11th inning for the save. Johnny Logan hit the game-winning single in the 11th, knocking in Felix Mantilla. Tough-luck loser Bob Friend went the distance and gave up just five hits. Aaron hit his first home run batting in the cleanup spot.

In the second game Juan Pizarro lost his third consecutive decision. The Braves scored twice in the ninth but came up short, 5-3. Aaron clouted another home run, in the seventh inning.

June 10. BUHL'S PITCHING, MATHEWS' BAT WIN FOR BRAVES, 3-1. Playing in Roosevelt Stadium in Jersey City, New Jersey, against the Brooklyn Dodgers (Brooklyn played seven "home" games at Roosevelt in 1956 and eight in 1957), Bob Buhl tossed a complete-game four-hitter (three of the hits were by Gil Hodges). Eddie Mathews hit his ninth home run of the season, a two-run blast in the fourth to provide Buhl enough runs for his fifth win. The victory moved the Braves back into second place for the first time since May 25.

June 11. BRAVES HOMERS BEAT BUMS. Back in Ebbets Field for the second game of the series, Ray Crone went the distance to pick up his third win of the season. Bobby Thomson smashed a grand slam, Joe Adcock hit his ninth home run, and Billy Bruton went 3-for-5 with two runs scored in a decisive 7-2 victory over Milwaukee's biggest rivals.

June 12. BUMS OUTLAST BRAVES. The Dodgers scored nine unanswered runs, knocking out starter Gene Conley after two-thirds of an inning and reliever Lew Burdette after one inning. The Braves fought back with home runs by Hank Aaron, Frank Torre, and Mathews (his 200th career blast, a new club record breaking Wally Berger's 199 home runs as a Boston Brave/Bee from 1930-1937), but it wasn't enough in an 11-9 loss that left Milwaukee tied with Brooklyn for second place.

June 13. BRAVES REGAIN 1ST PLACE. Starting in place of Del Crandall, who had split his thumb on a foul tip two days earlier, Carl Sawatski had a career day with two doubles and the game-deciding three-run home run in the eighth inning off Brooklyn's Clem Labine. Tempers flared in the second inning after Don Drysdale surrendered a second home run to Bill Bruton, then hit Johnny Logan. After reaching first base and jawing with the intimidating Dodgers pitcher, Logan charged Drysdale and a bench-clearing brawl ensued. The Braves' 8-5 win moved them into first place for the first time since May 15.

June 14. BRAVES ROUT PHILLIES, 10-2. Warren Spahn threw a three-hitter for his seventh victory. The Braves' 2-3-4 hitters (Johnny Logan, Eddie Mathews, and Hank Aaron) went a combined 8-for-15 with seven runs batted in to lead the rout of the Phillies at Connie Mack Stadium.

June 15. BRAVES WIN, BOOST LEAD. GIVE 3 PLAYERS FOR SCHOENDIENST. Bob Buhl pitched his second consecutive four-hitter (he also walked eight) and was supported by the Braves' 16-hit attack to defeat the Phillies, 7-2. However, the biggest news of the day (the trading deadline) was the Braves' acquisition of all-star second baseman Red Schoendienst in exchange for Ray Crone, Danny O'Connell, and Bobby Thomson. "We're giving up plenty, but we feel Red is the key man in our effort to give to the people of Milwaukee and Wisconsin the pennant," said Milwaukee general manager John Quinn.[4]

June 16. BRAVES SPLIT 2 WITH PHILS. Batting in the two hole in his first game with the Braves, Schoendienst went 2-for-5 in the opening game of a Sunday doubleheader as Milwaukee won, 3-2. The game ended when Carl Sawatski gunned down Chico Fernandez on a steal attempt with two outs in the ninth inning. Juan Pizarro tossed a complete-game five-hitter to give the Braves their fourth consecutive win, their longest streak since April 24-28.

In the second game of the doubleheader, Lew Burdette tossed the second of his two career one-hitters, but lost the game, 1-0. The only Philadelphia hit was a leadoff double in the sixth inning by catcher Joe Lonnett, who scored on Richie Ashburn's sacrifice fly. Curt Simmons silenced the Braves bats on six hits. The Braves concluded their road trip with a 9-5 record and a game-and-a-half lead over the second-place Cardinals.

June 17. BUCS BEAT BRAVES IN 9TH. In a makeup game from June 8, the Braves began a 16-game homestand by pounding Pirates' pitchers for 17 hits, but only two for extra bases. Red Schoendienst recorded a season-high four hits. The Pirates erupted for four runs in the top of the ninth off reliever Dave Jolly for the 7-5 victory.

June 18. CRONE, GIANTS BEAT BRAVES. Giants Rout Spahn with 3-Run 6th. The Braves knocked out Giants starter Johnny Antonelli with three runs in the fourth inning, but Ray Crone, who had been traded by Milwaukee three days earlier, silenced his former teammates on three hits over the final six innings to hand the Braves their third consecutive loss, 5-4.

June 19. BRAVES CLIP GIANTS 6-0 (AP *Racine Journal-Times*). Bob Buhl tossed his third consecutive four-hitter and first shutout of the season to defeat the Giants. In his first start of the season, left fielder Wes Covington connected for a three-run home run and Hank Aaron hit a solo shot, his 19th.

June 20. BRAVES LOSE, DROP TO 2ND. The 4-3 defeat to the Giants marked the Braves' 13th loss in 27 one-run games through the first 60 games and their seventh loss in 12 extra-inning contests. In the 12th inning, Taylor Phillips gave up a leadoff triple to Gail Harris, then surrendered a sacrifice fly to relief pitcher Johnny Antonelli, who got credit for his third win of the season against the Braves. After eight consecutive games in first place, the Braves fell to second, but just 2 1/2 games separated the Cardinals, Braves, Redlegs, Dodgers, and the surprising Phillies.

June 21. SIMMONS HANDCUFFS SLUMPING BRAVES, 6-1. In the first game of a five-game series between the two first-division teams, Curt Simmons of the Phillies tossed his second consecutive complete game against the Braves. Burdette was knocked out after five innings having yielding ten hits and five runs.

June 22. PHILS STOP BRAVES 4-2, TAKE OVER SECOND PLACE. (AP *Racine Journal-Times*). The Braves lost their third consecutive game and sixth of their last seven as 28-year-old Phillies rookie Jack Sanford improved his record to 9-1 with a six-hitter (all singles).

June 23. JOE ADCOCK BREAKS LEG. Injury Mars Double Win by Braves. In the first game of a doubleheader, Hank Aaron hit a dramatic two-out ninth-inning walk-off single to left field off starter Robin Roberts, scoring Red Schoendienst from second base to give starter Bob Buhl the victory, 7-6.

In the second inning of the second game, slugging first baseman Joe Adcock broke his right leg and tore ligaments in his knee sliding into second base on Del Crandall's infield hit. Billy Bruton had a double and a triple to go with three runs batted in and Schoendienst had three hits in four at-bats and knocked in two runs to lead the Braves to a seemingly costly 7-3 victory and a sweep of the Sunday twin bill. (Adcock would not return to the starting lineup until nearly mid-September.)

June 24. BRAVES LOSE TO PHILS, DROP TO 3RD. Spahn was rocked for eight hits and six runs in six innings; relievers Dave Jolly and Juan Pizarro yielded four more runs in three innings, as the Braves were defeated, 10-4, and lost the third game of their five-game series with the Phillies. The Braves scorched starter Harvey Haddix for 12 hits in 7 1/3 innings but managed only four runs and left nine runners on base.

June 25. BRAVES LOSE, 2-0, FALL TO 4TH PLACE. In a battle of four-hitters, Dodgers rookie Danny McDevitt tossed his first career shutout. Lew Burdette surrendered a first-inning home run to Duke Snider in his third consecutive tough-luck loss during which the Braves scored one run. The Braves' loss was their eighth in 11 games.

June 26. BRAVES' RALLY BEATS BUMS. In front of 39,233 fans on a Wednesday night, the Braves overcame an early 3-0 deficit behind a home-run barrage started by Carl Sawatski and Eddie Mathews in the third and continued in the fifth inning when Hank Aaron (batting second), Mathews, and Wes Covington hit consecutive home runs off starter Don Newcombe. Trailing by two runs in the eighth, the Braves scored six times on four hits and two Brooklyn errors en route to a 13-9 win.

June 27. BUHL'S FIFTH FOUR-HITTER OF SEASON BEATS DODGERS. (*Milwaukee Journal*). Despite a shaky ninth inning, Bob Buhl continued his wizardry over the Dodgers. After he beat them in eight of nine decisions in 1956, his 2-1 victory over Don Drysdale was his third consecutive complete-game win against Brooklyn during the 1957 campaign. The Braves' two runs came on Hank Aaron's triple in the eighth inning, scoring Buhl and Billy Bruton.

June 28. SPAHN, BRAVES HALT PIRATES, 4-2. Warren Spahn went the distance, yielding just five hits, and hit his 18th career home run (a record for pitchers in the NL). Del Crandall had a season-high three runs batted in. The win put the team back in first place, a half-game ahead of the Cardinals and the Redlegs.

June 29. BRAVES STILL IN FIRST, BEAT PIRATES, 13-6. The offense exploded for 13 runs for the second time in four games. Making his fourth of nine consecutive starts in place of the injured Red Schoendienst, Felix Mantilla hit his first big-league home run. Hank Aaron hit a three-run homer in the sixth and Eddie Mathews followed with a long blast to deep right-center field.

June 30. HOMERS WIN 2 FOR BRAVES. MATHEWS' DRIVE ENDS 2ND IN 13TH. The Braves ended the month by sweeping a Sunday doubleheader from the Pirates to increase their wining streak to six games and end June with a half-game lead over the Redlegs. In the first game, Bob Trowbridge held Pittsburgh to two runs over seven innings and was relieved by Ernie Johnson who got the win (7-4) when the Braves erupted for five runs in the eighth off Pirates starter Vern Law. The damage was done by an unexpected trio of batters: Consecutive singles by Felix Mantilla, Carl Sawatski, and pitcher Johnson accounted for four runs.

In the second game, Hank Aaron had four hits, including a home run, and Felix Mantilla had two singles and a homer, but the hero of the game was Eddie Mathews, whose walk-off two-run blast in the 13th inning off reliever Luis Arroyo gave the Braves a dramatic 6-5 come-from-behind win in front of 36,283 fans. The Braves finished 9-7 on their 16-game homestand.

NL Standings, after games played on June 30, 1957

Team	Won	Lost	Tie	Pct	GB
Milwaukee Braves	42	29	1	.592	–
Cincinnati Redlegs	42	30	0	.583	.5
St Louis Cardinals	38	30	0	.559	2.5
Brooklyn Dodgers	37	32	0	.536	4
Philadelphia Phillies	36	34	2	.514	5.5
New York Giants	36	36	0	.500	6.5
Pittsburgh Pirates	26	46	1	.361	16.5
Chicago Cubs	22	42	2	.344	16.5

July 1. CARDINALS KO BUHL IN THIRD. In St. Louis to play a two-game series against the third-place Redbirds (just 2 1/2 games behind the Braves), Milwaukee got an offnight from Buhl, who surrendered five hits and five runs in 2⅔ innings, and Juan Pizarro, who was tagged for four runs in one inning of relief. But the real culprit in the 9-5 loss was shoddy defense on the left side of the infield as five of those runs were unearned, the product of a season-high four errors. The Braves outhit the Cardinals 11 to 8, but they left ten runners on base.

July 2. BRAVES BEATEN, 4-2, DROP TO 2ND. The Cardinals' 18-year-old rookie Von McDaniel won his fourth consecutive decision to begin his career. Red Schoendienst returned to the lineup (and didn't miss another start all season), allowing Aaron to return to the cleanup spot. The Braves managed just five hits and dropped to second place a half-game behind Cincinnati.

July 3. BRAVES LOSE TO REDS; SLIP TO THIRD. Lew Burdette was knocked out in the sixth inning by first-place Cincinnati and the Redlegs' hitters did not strike out in 35 plate appearances during the game. Aaron, Crandall, and Wes Covington hit homers off starter Hal Jeffcoat, but the Braves lost their third straight, 7-5, to fall to third place behind the Redlegs and Cardinals.

July 4. BRAVES WIN, 10-7; HALF GAME OUT. The two best offenses in the league accounted for 31 hits. Aaron went 3-for-5 with two doubles and his league-leading 26th home run, and Mathews swatted his 17th. With the teams tied 7-7 in the eighth inning, Schoendienst hit a go-ahead single and later scored (along with Bruton) on Redlegs relief pitcher Raul Sanchez's throwing error.

July 5. CUBS BEAT BRAVES, BUHL 7-4. Back in Milwaukee for a three-game series with last-place Chicago, the Braves managed just eight hits in eight innings off rookie Don Elston. Hank Aaron hit a home run for the seventh time in his last eight games. Another Cubs rookie, light-hitting third baseman Jerry Kindall, clubbed his first big-league home run in the second inning to help knock starter Bob Buhl out in the second inning.

July 6. LOWLY CUBS BEAT BRAVES AGAIN, 3-2 (*Milwaukee Journal*). The largest crowd of the year at County Stadium (43,053) saw the Braves lose for the fifth time in their last seven games. Starter Warren Spahn, pitching on three days' rest, surrendered six hits and three runs in seven innings and was tagged for his fourth loss in his last five decisions. Pinch-hitting for Spahn, Andy Pafko hit his first round-tripper of the year.

July 7. BURDETTE BACK ON BEAM, TAMES CUBS, 4-2. BRAVES REGAIN SECOND. Lew Burdette won for the first time since May 18, tossing a six-hitter. Hank Aaron and Wes Covington went a combined 5-for-8 in leading the Braves' nine-hit performance. With the win, the Braves moved to second place (44-34), 2 1/2 games behind the Cardinals, as most players prepared for a three-day respite for the All-Star Game. The Braves and the Pirates would get only a two-day break, in order to play a makeup game in Pittsburgh.

July 8 and 9. No games scheduled.

July 10. BUCS BEAT BRAVES ON AN ERROR. In a makeup game from an early-season rainout, the normally sure-handed first baseman Frank Torre bobbled a hopper by Bob Skinner to load the bases with two outs in the sixth inning and the game tied, 2-2. Then Gene Baker hit a bases-clearing single to hand Bob Buhl his third straight loss, 5-2, in the first contest of a 13-game road trip. The sluggish Braves managed only six hits off starter Bob Purkey, who went the distance.

July 11. BRAVES WIN; 2 GAMES OUT. Bob Trowbridge hurled his first complete game of the year. Johnny Logan hit a two-run home run in the four-run fourth inning. Pittsburgh committed six errors. The Pirates had 12 hits and runners in scoring position in every inning, but managed only two runs as they stranded 11 men on base. The 7-2 Milwaukee win was a costly one, however. Center fielder Bill Bruton and shortstop Felix Mantilla collided violently as they converged on Bill Virdon's short fly ball that went for a double in the first inning. The speedy Bruton was lost for the season with a torn ligament in his right knee. Mantilla suffered a bruised chest and didn't return to the field until August 9.

July 12. BRAVES TIP BUCS; AARON HITS 28TH. After the Braves scored two runs in the ninth — one unearned — they quelled a two-run Pittsburgh rally in the bottom half to win 5-4. Don McMahon relieved Warren Spahn with runners on the corners with one out for the save. Hank Aaron moved to center field to replace the injured Bruton and remained there for the rest of the season.

July 13. 2 HOMERS GIVE BRAVES 4-3 VICTORY. Wes Covington's inside-the-park home run in the second inning and Del Crandall's two-run blast in the seventh highlighted Milwaukee's scoring. Lew Burdette went the distance as the Braves endured another two-run rally by the Pirates in the ninth inning to win by one run.

July 14. HODGES HOMER TIPS BUHL. Bob Buhl tossed a complete game but for the third consecutive game, the opponent mounted a ninth-inning rally.

1957 Milwaukee Braves Yearbook (Courtesy of the Milwaukee Braves Historical Association)

A Gil Hodges walk-off two-run home run in Ebbets Field was the difference in a 3-2 defeat.

July 15. O-W-W-W-W! BUMS, 20!! BRAVES, 4!! The Braves surrendered their most runs since a 24-2 shellacking by the Cubs on July 3, 1945. Reliever Taylor Phillips was clobbered for nine runs on five hits and four walks in the last meaningless frame for the Dodgers. Henry Aaron's 15-game hitting streak ended. Brooklyn's two-game sweep dropped the Braves to third place.

July 16. BRAVES HALT PHILS, 6-2. Warren Spahn tossed a six-hitter and Hank Aaron rebounded to go 3-for-3 with his 29th home run. The Braves' win, coupled with the Dodgers' defeat of the Cardinals, created a three-way tie (Milwaukee, Philadelphia, and St. Louis) for first place with the Dodgers a half-game back.

July 17. BRAVES NEAR LEAD WITH 10-3 WIN OVER PHILLIES. Frank Torre matched his career high with four hits, and Aaron and Schoendienst chipped in with three each to lead a 13-hit attack. Burdette was shaky (eight hits in 5 1/2 innings), but good enough to earn his third straight win with relief help from Don McMahon (3 2/3 scoreless innings). Aaron jammed his left ankle stepping on a drainboard and would be replaced by rookie John DeMerit for the next five games.

July 18. BRAVES BEAT PHILS, LEAD BY ONE. Bob Buhl ended a personal four-game losing streak to give the Braves a three-game sweep of Philadelphia and a one-game lead over St. Louis in the tight NL pennant race. Buhl's personal catcher, Del Rice, hit his fourth home run of the year and knocked in a season-high three runs during the 4-2 Milwaukee win. Don McMahon picked up another save when he struck out Harry Anderson with two runners on and two outs.

July 19. PAFKO'S 2 HOME RUNS HUMBLE GIANTS, 3-1. Batting cleanup in place of the injured Aaron, Andy Pafko accounted for all three Braves runs on two home runs. In his first start since June 12, big Gene Conley tossed his first complete-game win of the year, holding the Giants to seven hits.

July 20. COVINGTON BOMBS GIANTS, 7-5. The Braves blew a five-run lead in the eighth inning but won their fifth consecutive contest in the ninth on Wes Covington's second home run of the game, a two-run blast. Injuries to Milwaukee outfielders continued to mount when right fielder Pafko (who had replaced Aaron after his move to center field) came down with a bad back. He was replaced by Del Crandall, who started his first career game in right field. "We are considering the advisability of bringing up an outfielder from our [Wichita farm team]," said GM Pat Quinn. "Ray Shearer and Bob Hazle have been hitting the ball hard."[5]

July 21. FIELDING LAPSE COSTS BRAVES OPENER AGAINST GIANTS, 5-4. The Braves led 4-3 in the ninth inning of the first game of a doubleheader when Johnny Logan and Wes Convington could not decide who should catch pinch-hitter Ray Jablonski's easy popup for the final out. The ball dropped and the Giants now had runners on second and third. Hank Sauer then lined a pinch-hit two-run single to left to win the game for New York, handing Don McMahon his first big-league loss.

In the nightcap, The Braves scored seven unanswered runs in the last three frames to defeat the Giants 7-4 and maintain their one-game lead over Brooklyn and St. Louis in the pennant race. Johnny Logan matched his career high with five hits; he and Crandall (playing right field) hit home runs and drove in two runs apiece.

The Braves finished the road trip with a 9-4 record.

July 22. No games scheduled

July 23. BUHL BLANKS PHILS ON 2-HITTER. In the first contest of a 16-game homestand, Wes Covington made a diving grab of Solly Hemus's sure double for the first out in the ninth inning to help preserve Bob Buhl's fourth and final career two-hitter. Johnny Logan's two-out RBI triple in the second inning (his seventh consecutive hit) drove in the only run in the game.

July 24. PHILLIES' SANFORD HALTS BRAVES, 3-1. The Braves managed only five hits, including a seventh-inning home run by Wes Covington, off Jack Sanford. Gene Conley was the tough-luck loser, yielding just two runs over eight innings.

July 25. ROBERTS PINS 5-3 LOSS ON BRAVES. After they had led the pennant race for the past seven games, the Braves' loss dropped them into a tie with the Cardinals, with the Dodgers and Redlegs just one game behind and the Phillies three back. The Braves' pitching staff was reduced to eight with Ernie Johnson's sore right elbow. Aaron joined the 30-home-run club for the first of 15 times with a solo shot off Robin Roberts.

July 26. BRAVES WIN ON HOME RUN IN 11TH. After Milwaukee tied the Giants with two runs in the eighth, Nippy Jones' first home run since May 1952 was a dramatic one: a walk-off, three-run blast in the 11th inning to win the game, 6-3, and keep the Braves tied with the Cardinals.

July 27. BRAVES WHIP N.Y. FOR BUHL'S 12TH. The Braves managed only seven hits off two Giants pitchers, but profited from five walks and a wild pitch to win 5-2. Red Schoendienst's hitting streak was snapped at 23 games, but Milwaukee's second consecutive victory over the Giants moved the Braves back into a one-game lead over St. Louis.

July 28. BRAVES BOW TO ANTONELLI, 2-0. In the first game of a Sunday doubleheader in front of 40,503, the Braves had no answer against Johnny Antonelli who limited them to seven hits, including three by first baseman Nippy Jones. Milwaukee was hitless during nine at-bats with runners in scoring position.

Gene Conley tossed a six-hitter and the Braves managed ten singles off four different New York pitchers to win the nightcap, 5-3, to stay tied with the Cardinals for the NL lead.

July 29. BASES LOADED WALK WINS FOR BRAVES. Role players came through in the clutch again. Down 8-4 in the ninth inning, the Braves scored four runs, highlighted by Nippy Jones's two-out RBI single to right field. Andy Pafko scored on the hit, and pinch-runner John DeMerit scored on right fielder Ozzie Virgil's wild throw. Felix Mantilla gave the Braves their fourth win (9-8) against the Giants in the five-game series when he drew a walk with the bases loaded and two outs in the tenth inning.

July 30. BURDETTE BEATS PIRATES, 5-2. The Braves managed nine hits and were aided by two Pirates errors that led to three unearned runs. Lew Burdette pitched an uneventful five-hitter to win his ninth contest and give the Braves a 59-41 record after 100 games.

July 31. BRAGAN ACT STEALS SHOW, BUT THAT'S ALL; BRAVES TIPS BUCS, 4-2. (*Milwaukee Journal*). Bob Buhl tossed his third consecutive complete game and wasn't bothered by Pirates manager Bobby Bragan, who returned to the field in the fifth inning with orange juice for the umpires after he had been ejected. Schoendienst went 3-for-3 with a home run, and Buhl (who hit .082 for the season) notched his second two-hit game of the year. With six wins in their last seven games of the month, the Braves won 18 of 30 in July and remained tied for first with the Cardinals.

NL Standings, after games played on July 31, 1957

Team	Won	Lost	Tie	Pct	GB
St Louis Cardinals	59	40	0	.596	–
Milwaukee Braves	60	41	1	.594	–
Brooklyn Dodgers	57	42	0	.576	2
Cincinnati Redlegs	55	44	0	.556	4
Philadelphia Phillies	56	45	2	.554	4
New York Giants	44	57	0	.436	16
Pittsburgh Pirates	36	66	1	.353	24.5
Chicago Cubs	33	65	2	.337	25.5

August 1. No game scheduled.

August 2. 45,840 SEE CONLEY BLANK BUMS. In front of the largest crowd in any NL game thus far in the season, Gene Conley tossed a four-hitter against Brooklyn to win for the sixth time in 11 decisions, and knocked in the game's only run with a single in the fifth inning that scored Johnny Logan. Despite the win, the Braves remained in second place a half-game behind the Cardinals.

August 3. BUMS' LATE RUSH TIPS BRAVES, 7-1. The Dodgers scored six unanswered runs in the last two innings to hand the Braves their first loss in six games. Milwaukee managed just five hits in six innings off rookie starter Danny McDevitt. Brooklyn reliever Ed Roebuck hurled three hitless frames to earn the victory. Milwaukee fell 1 1/2 games off the pace in the NL pennant race.

August 4. BRAVES TRIM BROOKS, 9-7. Home runs by Hank Aaron, Johnny Logan, Del Rice, and Eddie Mathews gave Bob Buhl a 9-2 lead after six innings before a five-run Dodger rally during the last three innings. With one out and the bases loaded in the ninth inning, Warren Spahn came on in relief and secured the final two outs to record a save and preserve the victory as the Braves took the rubber game of the three-game series in front of 43,109 fans.

August 5. No game scheduled

August 6. BRAVES WIN, 5-4, TAKE LEAD. In front of 41,980 fans on a Tuesday night, Milwaukee managed only five hits off three Redlegs pitchers but scored five runs thanks to two Cincinnati errors. Spahn won his first start since July 16 to move the Braves into a tie for first place.

August 7. BRAVES ROUT REDS, LEAD BY 1 1/2. Gene Conley responded to the birth of his child just hours before the game with his third consecutive complete-game victory. In leading the Braves to a 12-2 win, Wes Covington went 2-for-2 with two round-trippers, four runs scored, and four runs batted in. More than 40,000 fans packed County Stadium for the third consecutive home date to see the Braves win their third game in a row and the eighth in their last nine games.

August 8. BRAVES WIN, 5-3, SWEEP REDS SET. Red Schoendienst hit a two-out, two-run single with the game tied, 3-3, in the eighth inning to give the Braves their 12th win in the 16-game homestand. The three-game sweep of the Redlegs dropped Cincinnati to seven games behind Milwaukee. More importantly, the 5-3 win provided the Braves a 2 1/2-game cushion over the Cardinals and a five-game lead over the Dodgers.

August 9. BRAVES CRUSH CARDS, 13-2. LEAD LEAGUE BY 3 1/2; BUHL WINS 15TH. In the first game of a six-game road trip, right fielder Bob "Hurricane" Hazle went 4-for-5, including his first big-league home run, and Red Schoendienst continued his hot-hitting (4-for-4) to lead an 18-hit attack against the second-place Cardinals. "I'm taking these games one at a time," said manager Haney cautiously. "It's still the old ulcer race, with a five-team scramble down to the wire."[6]

August 10. BRAVES STUN CARDS; LEAD BY 4 1/2. 40TH 'BLANK' FOR SPAHN. Spahn tossed his best game all season, a dominant five-hit shutout to give the Braves breathing room at the top of the NL. "Hurricane" Hazle knocked in three runs; Johnny Logan and Del Crandall drove home two each, and Hank Aaron scored four times to lead the Braves to a 9-0 spanking of the Cardinals.

August 11. BRAVES BEAT CARDINALS FOR 7TH IN A ROW. Gene Conley's fourth consecutive complete game and seventh win in his last eight decisions gave the Braves a resounding sweep of the Cardinals in St. Louis and Milwaukee's season-high seventh straight win. Eddie Mathews' 22nd home run led a modest five-hit attack for a 5-1 win and 5 1/2-game lead in the pennant race. The Braves also displayed their drawing power on the road as the three-game attendance total at Busch Stadium I, with a ballpark capacity of just over 30,000, was almost 81,000 fans

August 12. No game scheduled.

August 13. BURDETTE TURNS INTO A SLUGGER AS BRAVES SHELL REDLEGS, 12-4 (*Milwaukee Journal*). In the first game of a three-game set at Crosley Field, Lew Burdette slugged the first two home runs in his big-league career, drove in four runs, and tossed a complete game to power the surging Braves to their eighth consecutive victory. The Braves opened a 6 1/2-game margin over the Cardinals who continued their "free fall," losing their seventh consecutive contest.

August 14. BRAVES HIKE STREAK TO 9. Leading by two heading into the ninth inning, the Braves erupted for eight runs keyed by Wes Covington's first career grand slam during a 13-3 pounding of Cincinnati. To cap the scoring, rookie reliever Don McMahon also rapped his first big-league hit in the ninth, a double clearing the bases (good for three of his nine runs batted in during an 18-year career). Starter Bob Buhl won his seventh consecutive start, to sport a 16-6 season record.

August 15. WOW — 10 IN A ROW. RIP REDLEGS, 8-1; HANK HITS 2 HRS. Hank Aaron knocked in five runs on two home runs, and Bob Hazle and Eddie Mathews blasted solo shots as the Braves swept the Redlegs in Cincinnati for their season-best tenth consecutive victory and increased their lead to 8 1/2 games. Milwaukee has outscored its opponents 91-27 during the winning streak.

August 16. BRAVES' 'BIG THREE' LEAVES 16 MEN STRANDED AS ST. LOUIS WINS, 6-2 (*Milwaukee Journal*). 45,437 fans packed County Stadium looking for Milwaukee's consecutive win number 11, but the Braves were held to ten singles (four by Red Schoendienst) and were cold in the clutch as their 3-4-5 hitters (Mathews, Aaron, and Crandall) went a combined 1-for-13. On a positive note, Bob Hazle had two more hits (giving him 16 in his last 25 at-bats; for a remarkable .640 batting average covering seven games). For the first time since July 29, a Braves' starter failed to pitch at least seven innings as Gene Conley was knocked out in the second frame.

August 17. AARON'S HIT IN 11TH TRIPS CARDS, 5-4. After the Braves tied the game, 3-3, in the eighth inning on Frank Torre's two-out, run-scoring single, Milwaukee won it in the 11th on Hank Aaron's walk-off, two-run double. Warren Spahn pitched the final 2 2/3 innings in relief to notch his 14th win.

August 18. MORE THAN EIGHT HOURS IS WASTED AS BRAVES DROP PAIR (*Milwaukee Journal*). For just the second time all season, the Braves were swept in a doubleheader. On a rain-soaked day that had two long delays, game one starter Bob Buhl left after facing just two batters in the first inning, complaining of tightness in his right shoulder (he would miss the next three weeks). Behind home runs by Bob Hazle and Eddie Mathews, the Braves jumped out to a 6-1 lead going into the top of the seventh before St. Louis scored five unanswered runs in the final three frames to tie the game and then plated two more runs to win it in the tenth, 8-6.

In the nightcap, Vinegar Bend Mizell blanked the Braves, 6-0, on four hits as the Redbirds clubbed starter Bob Trowbridge for nine hits and five runs before he was replaced in the fifth inning. The Braves lost a series (three games to one) for the first time since they lost two of three to the Phillies on July 23-25, but Milwaukee still maintained a 6 1/2-game lead over St. Louis in the pennant race. The weekend series against the Cardinals attracted more than 130,000 fans to County Stadium.

August 19. No game scheduled.

August 20. BRAVES' LATE RALLY TOPS PIRATES 3-1. In Pittsburgh for just one game to begin a 16-game road trip covering seven cities, the Braves got a seven-hit complete game from Warren Spahn and timely hitting to secure a 3-1 win. With the game tied 1-1 in the top of the ninth, Eddie Mathews belted a one-out triple to score Red Schoendienst and later crossed home on Aaron's single.

August 21. No game scheduled.

August 22. BURDETTE TAMES DODGERS. In his first victory at Ebbets Field in almost two years, Lew Burdette tossed a seven-hitter for his 12th win. Red Schoendienst, Eddie Mathews, and Bob Hazle had three hits each, and Hank Aaron walloped a three-run home run in the first inning to start the Braves toward a 6-1 win. The Braves' consecutive road game winning streak has reached nine.

August 23. BUMS' RALLY IN 9TH TOPS BRAVES, 3-2. Gene Conley held the Dodgers scoreless for eight innings, but Brooklyn rallied for three runs in the bottom of the ninth to win on Gino Cimoli's two-out walk-off single off reliever Don McMahon, who had just made a key throwing error. Starter Sandy Koufax held the Braves to four hits over seven innings, but the win went to Don Drysdale, who pitched a scoreless ninth in relief.

August 24. BRAVES' 21-GUN SALUTE SINKS DODGERS. With the Dodgers' impending move to Los Angeles, the Braves pounded Brooklyn pitchers for 13 hits and 13 runs in their last game at Ebbets Field. Shortstop Felix Mantilla had his best day at the plate with season highs in hits (3), runs scored (3), and runs batted in (4). Mantilla, Hank Aaron, Nippy Jones, and Andy Pafko blasted home runs, while the Dodgers tied a franchise record by using eight pitchers. Lew Burdette pitched the final 2 2/3 innings in relief to notch his second win in three games. The 13-7 win maintained the Braves' 6 1/2-game margin over St. Louis.

August 25. HAZLE'S 2 HOMERS, 6 RBIs WRECK PHILS FOR SPAHN. Bob "Hurricane" Hazle continued his hitting exploits, with three more hits (two home runs and six RBIs) to raise his batting average to a resounding .526. Warren Spahn completed his fifth consecutive start (and hit a solo home run) to win 7-3 and boost the Braves to a 7 1/2-game lead.

August 26. PHILS REBOUND IN 9TH TO TIP BRAVES, 4-3. For the second time in four games, the Braves were victims of a ninth-inning walk-off single. Thirty-seven-year old pinch-hitter Ron Northey (who had not played a complete game in the field since 1950) connected off reliever Ernie Johnson to give the Phillies the win.

August 27. HOME RUNS PLUS M'MAHON WIN FOR BRAVES. Red Schoendienst, Frank Torre, and Eddie Mathews hit home runs to account for all four Braves runs in New York. Reliever Don McMahon stymied the Giants' rally in the eighth inning. With two men on and no outs, he retired six consecutive batters to save the 4-3 win for Lew Burdette. Milwaukee is now 30 games over .500 with a record of 77-47.

August 28. GIANTS BASH ON BRAVES IN 8-RUN 3RD. The Braves got hitting from the top of the order as Schoendienst, Torre, Mathews, and Aaron went a combined 10-for-22 with six runs scored, but the pitching and defense failed. Gene Conley was rocked for eight hits and nine runs (only four earned) in 2 2/3 innings as Bob Hazle's and Felix Mantilla's throwing errors contributed to the Giants' big third inning in a 12-6 loss.

August 29. No game scheduled.

August 30. BRAVES' 4 HOMERS TOP REDS, 9-5. On the strength of home runs by Carl Sawatski, Wes Covington, Frank Torre, and Eddie Mathews, the Braves had a balanced 11-hit attack to give Warren Spahn his 17th win and maintain a seven-game lead over Brooklyn in the pennant race.

August 31. BRAVES BLAST FIVE HOME RUNS BEAT REDS 16TH TIME, 14-4 (*Milwaukee Journal*). The Braves continued to pound home runs during a 15-hit attack at Crosley Field as they improved their season record against the Redlegs to 16-2. Wes Covington, Del Rice, and Eddie Mathews had three runs batted in each to lead an overpowering offense that knocked out Redlegs' starter Joe Nuxhall in the first inning. Cincinnati also chased Braves starter Lew Burdette in the first, but Juan Pizarro pitched 8 2/3 innings of relief and struck out nine to earn the win.

NL Standings, after games played on August 31, 1957

Team	Won	Lost	Tie	Pct	GB
Milwaukee Braves	79	48	1	.622	–
Brooklyn Dodgers	73	56	0	.566	7
St Louis Cardinals	72	56	0	.563	7.5
Philadelphia Phillies	65	63	2	.508	14.5
Cincinnati Redlegs	64	64	0	.500	15.5
New York Giants	62	70	0	.470	19.5
Chicago Cubs	49	76	2	.392	29
Pittsburgh Pirates	48	79	1	.378	31

September 1. BRAVES BLANKED BY REDLEGS, 6-0. Cincinnati's Brooks Lawrence held the Braves to five hits while his counterpart, Gene Conley, was blasted for five hits and four runs before he was replaced with no outs in the fourth inning. Despite the loss, the Braves maintained a 6 1/2-game lead over St. Louis. The 6-0 shutout was certainly not indicative of how the Braves offense lit up the Crosley Field scoreboard during their 11 games in the Queen City this season. Milwaukee hit 29 home runs as the visiting team, slugged .571, and scored 88 runs against the overmatched Redlegs hurlers.

September 2. BRAVES HUMILIATE CUBS, 23-10, 4-0. In Chicago on Labor Day for their last doubleheader of the season, the Braves exploded with ten extra-base hits in the first game for the most runs and most hits (26) since their move to Milwaukee. On the day when first baseman Joe Adcock returned to the team, Frank Torre scored a career-high (and tied a major-league record) six runs; Wes Covington knocked in a career-best six runs, also matched by Hank Aaron; and six Milwaukee batters notched three hits or more. Ernie Johnson relieved starter Lew Burdette and pitched 6 1/3 innings of relief to secure the win.

In the nightcap Bob Trowbridge tossed the best game of his career, a three-hit shutout with nine strikeouts. Covington had three more hits along with two RBIs to total six hits and eight runs driven in for the day. His batting average during the ten at-bats that afternoon went from .280 to .293. The two wins, coupled with double losses by both the Cardinals and Dodgers, gave the Braves an 8 1/2-game lead. "The Braves all but sewed up the league flag," wrote beat reporter Red Thisted.[7]

September 3. SPAHN BLANKS CUBS, 8-0, FOR 41ST SHUTOUT OF CAREER (*Milwaukee Journal*). While Spahn limited the Cubs to six hits to set a modern NL record for the most career shutouts by a left-hander, the top of the order (Schoendienst, Nippy Jones, Mathews, and Aaron) went a combined 8-for-17 with seven runs scored and five driven in. Aaron broke out of his monthlong slump (27-for-110, .245 average but 27 runs batted in during the 28 games) by going 7-for-15 with 10 RBIs in the three-game sweep at Chicago.

September 4. BLASINGAME AND ENNIS RUIN BRAVES' GOOD RELIEF WORK (*Milwaukee Journal*). The Braves were in St. Louis for the last time this season. Juan Pizarro was knocked out in the first inning having surrendered four runs without registering an out. Big Gene Conley came on in relief and pitched nine innings of three-hit ball. Home runs by Del Rice and Eddie Mathews tied the game, 4-4, by the fifth inning, but Milwaukee could not plate another tally during the next six frames. Don McMahon breezed through the tenth and 11th innings before yielding a one-out double to Don Blasingame, who stole third, and then walking two hitters intentionally to load the bases, playing for a double play to end the inning. The plan backfired when Del Ennis hit a fly to right fielder Bob Hazle, who seemed to have an easy catch, but the ball bounced off his shoulder for an error, allowing Blasingame to score the winning run, 5-4.

September 5. MUCH MORE OF THIS COULD BRING TROUBLE. BRAVES LOOK BAD LOSING. In the last game of a 16-game road trip, the Braves looked tired as they managed just four hits off Sam Jones. Slumping Lew Burdette (7 1/3 innings in his last three starts) was knocked out in the fifth inning, and relievers Juan Pizarro (two runs in two innings) and Dave Jolly (five runs in one inning) fared worse in a 10-1 shellacking at Busch Stadium I (still affectionately called Sportsman's Park by many St. Louis fans).

September 6. CUBS HAND BRAVES THIRD LOSS IN A ROW. Returning home to play 18 of their final 21 games and begin a 12-game homestand, the Braves lost their third in a row for the first time since July 1-3. Bob Trowbridge had a four-hit shutout going until the Cubs exploded for five runs in the seventh inning en route to a 5-4 victory.

September 7. SPAHN COOLS CUBS, 7-2, FOR 19TH. Warren Spahn won his ninth consecutive decision by limiting the Cubs to five hits. Every Braves starter managed at least one hit, while Wes Covington and pinch-hitter Andy Pafko belted home runs in a balanced 14-hit attack to help the Braves maintain their 6 1/2-game lead over the Cardinals.

September 8. CUBS BEAT BRAVES; CUT LEAD TO 5 1/2 GAMES. Ernie Johnson gave up a single and four walks in the tenth inning, resulting in two runs and a 5-3 loss. On a positive note, Bob Buhl, in his first appearance in three weeks, pitched three innings of scoreless relief. "We're not feeling any pressure yet," said Spahn after the Braves' fourth loss in five games. "A recession has set in. You've got to expect it after all those runs we've scored and the way we've been winning."[8]

September 9. No game scheduled.

September 10. BRAVES CLIP BUCS, 4-3, TO HOLD 5 1/2-GAME LEAD. Lew Burdette pitched a complete game to pick up his 15th win and scored the decisive run in the seventh inning on Eddie Mathews' single. Hank Aaron launched his 40th home run of the season in the fourth inning and his blast was followed by Mathews' 31st. Shortstop Johnny Logan returned from a shin injury to start for the first time since August 16.

September 11. BUCS CHECK SPAHN'S BID FOR NO. 20, 2-1. In front of just 14,713 fans (the lowest County Stadium turnout since May 29), the Braves lost for the fifth time in their last seven games. In the season's last meeting between the two clubs, the Pirates' Ronnie Kline yielded just six hits (one of them a solo homer by Andy Pafko) while Spahn surrendered just seven hits as the Braves' lead shrank to 4 1/2 games over St. Louis.

September 12. CRANDALL'S HIT TIPS BUMS, 2-1. The Braves got good news as first baseman Joe Adcock started his first game since injuring his leg on June 23 and pitcher Bob Buhl made his first start since August 18. Bob Trowbridge pitched 5 2/3 innings of scoreless relief and pinch-hitter Del Crandall hit a walk-off single to score Johnny Logan with one out in the ninth for the win.

September 13. BRAVES BOW TO BUMS, 5-1; HOLD LEAD AS CARDS LOSE. On Friday the 13th, 40,367 Braves faithful saw their team lose another one. After they managed just four hits the night before, the Braves' hitting woes continued. Don Drysdale overpowered the Braves, limiting them to five hits, and did not allow a baserunner beyond first base after the second inning when Johnny Logan's triple scored Frank Torre for Milwaukee's lone run. Paying his respects to the Braves, Dodgers outfielder Carl Furillo said, "The Braves have got to simply kick each other in the pants and hustle more. It's like the beginning of spring training all over again."[9]

September 14. ERSKINE 4-HITS BRAVES, 7-1; CUTS LEAD TO FOUR. "I have three words for you," said Fred Haney after his team's seventh loss in nine games, "no-hit, no-pitch, no-win."[10] In his only complete game of the year, veteran Carl Erskine continued the Dodgers' mastery of the Braves, who managed just 13 hits in the three-game series. On a positive note, the Braves finished the season with a 12-10 edge over their rivals from Brooklyn; however, their lead over the Cardinals shrank to just four games.

September 15. BRAVES LOSE THIRD STRAIGHT. For the fifth consecutive game, the Braves' anemic offense scored two runs or less, resulting in the team's eighth loss in ten games, 3-2, to the Phillies. Spahn failed in his second attempt to win his 20th game of the season by surrendering the tying run in the ninth. He yielded two singles to start the tenth inning and was charged with the loss when Ted Kazanski greeted reliever Bob Trowbridge with a run-scoring single. The Braves' lead fell to an alarming 2 1/2 games, but things would soon change.

September 16. BUHL HALTS BRAVES' TUMBLE, 5-1. For the first time since September 7, the Braves managed to reach double figures in hits as every starter (except Bob Buhl) had at least one safety. Johnny Logan led the way against the Phillies, going 3-for-4 with two runs scored; the slumping Henry Aaron (2-for-20 in his previous five games) batted fifth and responded by going 2-for-4 and knocking in his first run in six games. Del Rice, Buhl's personal catcher, had a double and home run to help his batterymate win his eighth consecutive decision. The Braves finished the season 12-10 against Philadelphia.

September 17. HOMERS BY ADCOCK, AARON TOP GIANTS. Joe Adcock and Hank Aaron supplied all the power the Braves needed on a cold night in Milwaukee. Each went 3-for-4 and belted home runs; for Adcock it was his first since June 11. But the star of the game was pitcher Bob Trowbridge, a late replacement for Gene Conley. Trowbridge tossed his third complete game of the year (and the final one in his career), limiting the Giants to just five hits in a commanding 3-1 victory. With the victory, the Braves maintained a three-game lead over the Cardinals.

September 18. BRAVES HIKE LEAD TO 4; 2 MILLION YEAR AGAIN. For the fourth consecutive season, more than 2 million fans came out to County Stadium to cheer for their Milwaukee Braves. More importantly on this evening, the Braves beat the Giants, 8-2, for their third straight win and increased their lead over the Cardinals to four games. Lew Burdette pitched a masterful four-hitter, and was aided by the team's biggest offensive outburst since September 3. Del Crandall, 2-for-3 with two runs batted in, led a balanced 11-hit attack against former Braves hurlers Johnny Antonelli and Ray Crone. The Braves finished the season series by taking 13 of 22 against New York.

September 19. No game scheduled.

September 20. BRAVES ROUT CUBS; CARDS EDGE CINCY (AP *Racine Journal-Times*). The Braves traveled 90 miles south for their last road trip of the year, a three-game series at Wrigley Field. In front of just 4,032 fans, all of the Braves' starting position players had at least one hit in a balanced 14-hit attack. Wes Covington belted his 20th home run of the season, a deep shot to left center field off loser Bob Rush. Warren Spahn held the Cubs to three hits and two runs (one earned) in 6 1/3 innings to record his 20th win for the eighth time in the last 11 seasons, as the Braves won, 9-3.

September 21. BRAVES BEAT CUBS, 6-2. Lead by 5. Joe Adcock cranked two long home runs off loser Moe Drabowsky and Hank Aaron continued his hot hitting with two hits (10-for-20 in his last five games) to help Bob Buhl win his ninth consecutive decision and 18th game of the season, a complete-game eight-hitter to give the Braves a five-game lead over the Cardinals with seven games to play.

September 22. HAZLE HOMERS—BRAVES ONE WIN FROM CROWN. The Braves showed their ability to overcome big deficits with the long ball. Down four runs after the first inning, the Braves roared back to tie the game in the fourth behind Hank Aaron's 42nd home run and RBI hits by Bob Hazle and Del Crandall. After the Cubs scored three in the fifth inning, the Braves clawed their way back to tie the game 7-7 in the ninth inning on Eddie Mathews' towering home run to right field. Bob Hazle, who went 4-for-5, led off the tenth inning with his seventh and final home run of the season, and with two outs Mathews singled in an insurance run to complete the Braves' sweep, 9-7, and finish the season series against Chicago with a 13-9 record.

September 23. BRAVES WIN FLAG; IT'S BEDLAM! (*Milwaukee Journal*). The Braves returned to County Stadium for the final six games of the year. The 40,926 faithful fans came out full of hope on a chilly Monday night to watch a pitching duel between crafty veteran Lew Burdette and three Cardinals hurlers for ten innings. Gene Conley tossed a scoreless 11th inning, giving way to the biggest moment thus far in Milwaukee baseball history. With two outs and Johnny Logan on first base, Hank Aaron launched a pennant-clinching walk-off home run for a 4-2 victory.

September 24. BRAVES SPEAR EIGHTH IN A ROW, 6-1. In a routine ballgame, Warren Spahn limited the Cardinals to just five hits en route to his NL-best 21st victory. In his first at-bat since his dramatic blast the night before, Henry Aaron hit his first career grand slam for his major-league leading 44th home run of the season. Spahn and the Braves cruised the final eight innings and let the 30,661 fans in attendance savor Milwaukee's first pennant.

September 25. CARDS SNAP BRAVES' EIGHT GAME WIN STRING, 4-1. In search of his tenth consecutive victory, Bob Buhl pitched 7 1/3 scoreless innings before the Cardinals surprised him with six hits and four runs. The Braves managed just seven hits off Lindy McDaniel and Lloyd Merritt in the loss, and finished the season series with St. Louis tied at 11 games apiece. The big news of the day was the announcement that injured center fielder Billy Bruton, who had not played since his knee injury on July 11, would not be activated for the World Series.

September 26. No game scheduled.

September 27. BURDETTE'S 4-HITTER SILENCES REDS, 2-1. On a chilly night, 23,676 steadfast fans showed up to help the Braves set a new major-league attendance mark (they finished the season with 2,215,404). Redlegs' left-hander Charlie Rabe, in his first big-league start, pitched well, yielding just five hits in seven innings, but two of the hits were solo shots by Del Crandall and Andy Pafko in the fifth inning to account for the Braves' only runs. Lew Burdette was sharp, surrendering just four hits and one run (a homer by Wally Post) in a complete game to win his 17th.

September 28. KLIPPSTEIN TOSSES 1-HITTER AT BRAVES (AP *Big Springs* [Texas] *Daily Herald*). Cincinnati right-hander Johnny Klippstein threw the game of his life, a one-hitter, to defeat Warren Spahn and the Braves, 6-0. With two out in the eighth inning, Bob Hazle lined a single to right field to break up the no-hitter. (Klippstein had pitched seven innings of no-hit ball against the Braves the season before, on May 26, 1956; however, the notoriously wild hurler had walked seven and hit a batter, and was lifted for a pinch-hitter. Relievers Hersh Freeman and Joe Black extended the no-hitter through 9 2/3 innings before the Braves won the game in 11 innings.)

September 29. BRAVES SET 'WIN' RECORD. In the last game of the regular season, Bob Buhl showed his World Series form by pitching five shutout innings in front of 45,000 fans. The Redlegs scored three runs in the top of the ninth to take the lead, 3-2, but in fitting style, the Braves came back. Following singles by Joe Adcock and Ray Shearer, Red Schoendienst singled with two outs to score pinch-runner Mel Roach. Felix Mantilla then belted yet another single to score Shearer and win the game 4-3. The Braves took the season series from Cincinnati, 18 games to 4. Milwaukee finished with 95 wins to break the previous franchise mark of 94 by the 1914 Boston Braves.

Final NL Standings, after games played on September 29, 1957

Team	Won	Lost	Tie	Pct	GB
Milwaukee Braves	95	59	1	.617	–
St Louis Cardinals	87	67	0	.565	8
Brooklyn Dodgers	84	70	0	.545	11
Cincinnati Redlegs	80	74	0	.519	15
Philadelphia Phillies	77	77	2	.500	18
New York Giants	69	85	0	.448	26
Pittsburgh Pirates	62	92	1	.403	33
Chicago Cubs	62	92	1	.403	33

Notes

1. *Milwaukee Sentinel*, May 2, 1957.
2. *Milwaukee Sentinel*, May 7, 1957.
3. *Milwaukee Sentinel*, May 27, 1957.
4. *The Milwaukee Sentinel*, June 16, 1957.
5. *Milwaukee Sentinel*, July 21, 1957.
6. *Milwaukee Sentinel*, August 10, 1957.
7. *Milwaukee Sentinel*, September 3, 1957.
8. *Milwaukee Sentinel*, September 9, 1957.
9. *Milwaukee Sentinel*, September 14, 1957.
10. *Milwaukee Sentinel*, September 14, 1957.

1957 World Series Game-by-Game Summary

By Norm King

Milwaukee Braves

The Braves finished the regular season on a hot streak, winning ten of their last 12 games to capture the NL pennant, thereby erasing the memories of their late-season collapse in 1956. They were the best hitting team in the league, leading in runs scored (772) and home runs (199), and finishing second in batting average. Defensively, the Braves were strong, ranking second in the league in fielding percentage (.981) and double plays (173). That double-play mark would likely have been even better had second baseman Red Schoendienst played a full season with the club. (He joined the team in a trade in mid-June.) The Braves were equally strong on the mound, ranking second in team ERA (3.47) and leading the league with 60 complete games. Above all, the Braves were a resilient club, overcoming injuries to several key players. Both first baseman Joe Adcock and starting pitcher Bob Buhl returned in September from leg and arm injuries. The Braves shuffled their outfield when center fielder Bill Bruton went down on July 11 with a season-ending knee injury. Aaron was inserted into center field and Wichita call-up Bob "Hurricane" Hazle eventually took over in right field. On the eve of the World Series, the Braves team was in good health.

New York Yankees

The methodically brilliant Yankees were at the peak of their dynasty under Casey Stengel in 1957, winning their third of four consecutive pennants under "The Ol' Perfessor." They won the American League flag with a 98-56 record and a comfortable eight-game margin over the second-place Chicago White Sox. No one expected Mickey Mantle to duplicate his numbers from his 1956 Triple Crown season, but his power totals dropped significantly. He batted a career-best .365, but hit only 34 home runs in 1957 after smashing 52 in 1956, and his 94 RBIs in '57 were substantially fewer than his previous total of 130. As a team, the Yankees led the league in numerous offensive categories, including runs scored with 723. The pitching staff's 3.00 ERA was the best in the American League. The team was still fairly young—the average age of the position players was 28.4—and the club was bolstered by Milwaukee-born and -raised 21-year-old Tony Kubek, the AL Rookie of the Year.

Game One—Wednesday, October 2

"Forget That First One! Today'll Be Braves Day. Spahn Bows to Ford in 3-1 Duel."[1]

The actual playing of the 1957 World Series wasn't really necessary because no less a prognosticator than jazz great Lionel Hampton had already predicted a series victory for … the Dodgers?

Hampton was performing at a Milwaukee nightclub a few days before the Series opened, and managed to put his foot through a tom-tom while he was dancing

Managers Casey Stengel and Fred Haney (National Baseball Hall of Fame Library, Cooperstown, N.Y.)

on it. Because such an incident didn't happen very often, he told the audience that, "he knew now that the 'Brooklyn Dodg... er, the Milwaukee Braves, would win the series.'"2

When Schoendienst entered the batter's box in the first inning against the Yankees' left-hander Whitey Ford, it marked the first time the Braves had played in the fall classic since they lost to Cleveland in 1948, when the franchise was located in Boston.

Staff ace Warren Spahn, who led the Braves with 21 wins, lost the battle of southpaws, 3-1, against Ford, who had gone 11-5 during the season for New York. The game was scoreless until the fifth inning, when Yankee second baseman Jerry Coleman scored the Series' first run. The Yankees extended their lead with two more runs in the sixth. The Braves got one back in the seventh when left fielder Wes Covington doubled and came home on a single by Schoendienst.

Game Two—Thursday, October 3

"We Knew We Could Do It! Braves 4, Yankees 2. Covington Hit, Catch, Burdette Pitching Shine"3

The Yankees tossed another southpaw at the Braves in Game Two, 5-foot-6 Bobby Shantz. Lew Burdette countered for the Braves. Any first-game jitters were gone by now as Milwaukee prevailed, 4-2. The Braves broke through first in the second inning when center fielder Henry Aaron tripled and scored on a single by first baseman Joe Adcock. The Yankees tied it in the bottom of the inning and would have added at least two more runs had left fielder Wes Covington not made a leaping, twisting catch of Shantz's two-out line drive. The Braves' Johnny Logan and the Yankees' Hank Bauer traded home runs in the third before Milwaukee scored two more in the fourth when Covington's pop-fly single drove home Adcock and right fielder Andy Pafko also scored when the relay from the outfield got by third baseman Kubek. Burdette went all the way for the victory.

Game Three—Saturday, October 5

"Today We Make History"4

The Soviet Union launched the first Sputnik satellite into space on October 4, 1957, the day before Game Three at Milwaukee's County Stadium. The scientists following Sputnik's flight could be forgiven if they thought the Americans were attacking the satellite because of all the moon shots that flew off the Yankees' bats as the Bronx Bombers lived up to their moniker and trounced the Braves, 12-3. Kubek hit two homers and drove in four runs, while Mantle added a two-run blast for his first (and only) RBIs of the Series. Bob Turley started for the Yankees but was lifted with two outs in the second inning after giving up one run, three hits, and four walks. Don Larsen pitched the remaining 7 1/3 innings for the win.

Loser Bob Buhl led a parade of six Braves pitchers to the mound and was pulled after giving up two hits and a pair of walks for three runs (two earned) in the first inning. In addition to hitting the three home runs, the Yankees received 11 walks in the game.

Fans at County Stadium for the World Series (National Baseball Hall of Fame Library, Cooperstown, N.Y.)

Game Four—Sunday, October 6

"Thar's Joy in Braveland! Mathews' HR Beats NY"5

Game Four had all the elements of a dubious Hollywood script. New York scored in the first inning, but the Braves roared back in the fourth inning with four runs on home runs by Henry Aaron and Frank Torre. The Braves went into the ninth inning with a 4-1 lead and staff ace Spahn on the mound. Spahn blew the lead when he gave up a three-run homer to Elston Howard—with two out, yet—and followed that up by allowing the Yankees to score the go-ahead run by Kubek on a Hank Bauer two-out triple in the top of the tenth inning. Yankee reliever Tommy Byrne hit pinch-hitter Nippy Jones with a pitch leading off the bottom of the tenth, and was replaced on the mound by Bob Grim. Felix Mantilla, running for Jones, was sacrificed to second and scored the tying run on a double to left by Johnny Logan. Eddie Mathews, who had just one hit in the Series up to this point, smacked a 2-2 fastball over the right-field fence to win the thrilling game, 7-5, and send 45,804 Braves fans (along with the hundreds of thousands who swear they were there) home happy.

Game Five—Monday, October 7

"One More Win To Go! Burdette Blanks Yanks, 1-0"[6]

The Braves rode the momentum of their dramatic Game Four win and Burdette's stellar pitching to a 1-0 victory over Whitey Ford in Game Five and a 3-2 Series lead. Left fielder Wes Covington kept the game scoreless in the fourth when he made a spectacular catch over the fence to rob Gil McDougald of a home run. The Braves scored the eventual winning run in the bottom of the sixth. Eddie Mathews got an infield hit, beating out a ground ball to second base that might have been the third out had Yankees second baseman Jerry Coleman played it more aggressively. Mathews went to third on Aaron's bloop single to right-center, and scored on a single by Adcock.

Game Six—Wednesday, October 9

"N.Y. Wins, 3-2, To Tie Series"[7]

The experienced Yankees weren't going to be intimidated by being down three games to two, especially when they were returning back to the House That Ruth Built. Braves starter and losing pitcher Bob Buhl managed to get past the first inning this time, but was gone after 2 2/3, when four hits and four walks had given New York a 2-0 lead. The Braves used the long ball to tie the game up, with solo shots by Frank Torre in the fifth and Henry Aaron in the seventh, but just after the Yankees' fans had finished their seventh-inning stretch, Hank Bauer hit a solo shot high off the screen of the left-field foul pole off reliever Ernie Johnson with one out for the eventual game-winning run in a 3-2 Yankees victory.

Game Seven—Thursday, October 10

"Hail to Our Braves. Best In The World!"[8]

Any tension that might ordinarily accompany a Game Seven disappeared early as the Braves scored four runs in the third inning with hits by Hazle, Mathews, Aaron, and Covington on their way to a 5-0 win and the first championship for the franchise since the Miracle Braves of 1914. Stengel tabbed Don Larsen to start for the Yankees while Braves manager Fred Haney sent Lew Burdette to the mound on two days' rest instead of his ace Warren Spahn (who had the flu). Burdette responded with his second shutout and third complete-game victory of the Series. The Yankees played less like Bronx Bombers and more like Bronx Bumblers as they committed three errors. Braves catcher Del Crandall sealed the deal with a solo home run in the eighth. New York loaded the bases with two outs in the ninth inning but Mathews backhanded a hard shot by Bill "Moose" Skowron and stepped on third base to end the 1957 World Series. Not surprisingly, Burdette was chosen Series MVP.

The Braves Win the World Series! Del Crandall (in catcher's mask), Eddie Mathews, and Lew Burdette hug. Joe Torre (14) and Del Rice join the celebration. (National Baseball Hall of Fame Library, Cooperstown, N.Y.)

Sources

Milwaukee Journal.

Milwaukee Sentinel.

BaseballReference.com

Historicfilms.com

Notes

1. "Forget That First One! Today'll Be Braves Day. Spahn Bows to Ford in 3-1 Duel," *Milwaukee Sentinel*, October 3, 1957.
2. D.H.D., "Hampton's Misplaced Foot Kicks Off Big League Show," *Milwaukee Journal*, October 1, 1957.
3. Red Thisted, "We Knew We Could Do It! Braves 4, Yankees 2. Covington Hit, Catch, Burdette Pitching Shine," *Milwaukee Sentinel*, October 4, 1957.
4. "Today We Make History," *Milwaukee Sentinel*, October 5, 1957.
5. Red Thisted, "Thar's Joy in Braveland! Mathews HR Beats NY," *Milwaukee Sentinel*, October 7, 1957.
6. Red Thisted, "One More Win To Go! Burdette Blanks Yanks, 1-0," *Milwaukee Sentinel*, October 8, 1957.
7. Red Thisted, "N.Y. Wins, 3-2, To Tie Series," *Milwaukee Sentinel*, October 10, 1957.
8. Red Thisted, "Hail to Our Braves. Best In The World!" *Milwaukee Sentinel*, October 11, 1957.

By the Numbers: Milwaukee Braves in 1957

By Dan Fields

1st
And only Most Valuable Player Award won by Hank Aaron, at age 23, and Cy Young Award won by Warren Spahn, at age 36. Red Schoendienst, who came to the Braves in a trade on June 15, finished third in the NL MVP voting, and Spahn was fifth.

1st
Career grand slam by Hank Aaron, off Sam Jones of the St. Louis Cardinals on September 24 (the day after Aaron hit an 11th-inning walk-off home run to clinch the pennant for the Braves). It was his 110th career home run.

2.69
ERA of Warren Spahn, tied for second with Don Drysdale in the National League. Bob Buhl was fourth in the NL with an ERA of 2.74.

3
Doubles each by Frank Torre in a July 14 game and Bob Hazle in the first game of a September 2 doubleheader.

3.47
ERA of the 1957 Braves, second lowest in the NL.

4
Shutouts by Warren Spahn, tied for second most in the NL with Don Drysdale and Don Newcombe.

5
Hits each by Hank Aaron (all singles) in a ten-inning game on May 2 and Johnny Logan (a home run and four singles) in the second game of a July 21 doubleheader.

6
Milwaukee players on the 1957 NL All-Star squad, tied (with the Cincinnati Redlegs) for the most of any NL team. Representing the Braves were Hank Aaron (the starting right fielder), Lew Burdette, Johnny Logan, Eddie Mathews, Red Schoendienst, and Warren Spahn. Burdette gave up no runs in four innings of relief work in the July 9 game, but an error by Schoendienst in the top of the ninth inning led to two unearned runs. The AL won, 6-5.

9
Triples each by Bill Bruton and Eddie Mathews during 1957, tied for third in the majors.

10
Consecutive games won by the 1957 Braves from August 4 through 15.

15
Strikeouts by Milwaukee batters against Dick Drott of the Chicago Cubs, in a 7-5 loss on May 26 (first game of a doubleheader). Hank Aaron and Bill Bruton struck out three times each.

18
Complete games by Warren Spahn, the most in the major leagues. Bob Buhl and Lew Burdette tied for fifth in the NL with 14 complete games.

Hank Aaron (National Baseball Hall of Fame Library, Cooperstown, N.Y.)

21
Wins by Warren Spahn, tops in the majors. Bob Buhl was third in the National League with 18 wins, and Lew Burdette was tied for fourth with 17 wins.

23
Consecutive games in which Red Schoendienst had a base hit, from July 2 through 26. During the streak he had 33 hits in 97 at-bats (.340).

23-10
Score by which the Braves beat the Cubs in the first game of a doubleheader on September 2. Hank Aaron and Wes Covington each had six RBIs, and Frank Torre scored six runs. The Braves won the second game, 4-0.

41
Career shutouts by Warren Spahn on September 3, an NL record for left-handed pitchers. Spahn threw his 63rd and last shutout on May 5, 1964, and as of 2013 still held the league record for career shutouts by a left-hander.

44
Home runs by Hank Aaron, tops in the majors. Eddie Mathews was fifth in the NL with 32 homers.

60
Complete games by Milwaukee pitchers in 1957, the most in the majors.

62
Triples by the 1957 Braves, tops in the major leagues.

77
Extra-base hits by Hank Aaron, the third most in the majors. Eddie Mathews was sixth in the NL with 69.

90
Walks drawn by Eddie Mathews, the third most in the NL.

95
Wins by the 1957 Braves, against 59 losses. The Braves won the pennant by eight games over the St. Louis Cardinals. The last time the franchise had as many wins in a season was in 1899, when the Boston Beaneaters had a record of 95-57. After 1957 the franchise did not reach 95 wins in a season again until 1992, when the Atlanta Braves went 98-64.

118
Runs scored by Hank Aaron, the most in the NL. Eddie Mathews was fourth in the NL with 109 runs.

121
Walks allowed by Bob Buhl, second most in the majors.

124
Home runs allowed by the 1957 Braves, the fewest in the NL.

132
RBIs by Hank Aaron, tops in the majors. Eddie Mathews was seventh in the NL with 94.

199
Home runs by the 1957 Braves, the most in the majors and a franchise record until 1966.

200
Hits by Red Schoendienst (78 with the New York Giants and 122 with the Braves), tops in the majors. Hank Aaron was second in the major leagues with 198 hits.

271
Innings pitched by Warren Spahn, the second most in the majors. Lew Burdette was third in the NL with 256 2/3 innings.

.322
Batting average of Hank Aaron, the fourth highest in the NL.

369
Total bases by Hank Aaron, tops in the majors. Eddie Mathews was fifth in the NL with 309 total bases.

.403
Batting average of Bob Hazle, who played in 41 games from late July through September. In August alone, he had 33 hits (including five home runs) in 67 at-bats (.493), drove in 21 runs, and scored 16 runs.

.442
Slugging average of the 1957 Braves, the highest in the majors.

.600
Slugging average of Hank Aaron, the third highest in the NL. Eddie Mathews was sixth in the NL with a .540 slugging average.

.720
Won-lost percentage of Bob Buhl (18-7), the highest in the NL. Warren Spahn (21-11) was third in the NL at .656, and Lew Burdette (17-9) was tied for fourth at .654.

772
Runs scored by the 1957 Braves, the most in the majors.

.978
On-base percentage plus slugging average of Hank Aaron, the third highest in the NL. Eddie Mathews was sixth in the NL with an OPS of .927.

.981
Fielding percentage of the 1957 Braves, the second highest in the NL.

.996
Fielding percentage as first baseman by Frank Torre, the best in the NL.

2,215,404
Attendance at County Stadium during the 1957 season, the highest of any major-league team. This was a Braves franchise record until 1992.

1957 World Series

0.67
ERA of Series MVP Lew Burdette, who allowed only two runs in 27 innings against the New York Yankees.

2
Shutouts thrown by Lew Burdette, in Game Five and Game Seven. He was the first pitcher to toss two shutouts in one World Series since Christy Mathewson threw three in the 1905 Series.

2
Home runs by rookie Tony Kubek of the Yankees in Game Three; he also hit a single. Kubek scored three runs and drove in four during the game. He was the AL Rookie of the Year in 1957.

3
Complete-game wins by Lew Burdette (including Game Two). The most recent pitcher to accomplish this feat in one World Series had been Stan Coveleski in 1920.

7
RBIs by Hank Aaron, the most by any player in the Series.

9
Years since a team not from New York had won the World Series. After the Cleveland Indians won the Series in 1948, the titles went to the Yankees (1949-1953 and 1956), the Giants (1954), and the Brooklyn Dodgers (1955).

43
Years since the Braves had won the World Series. In 1914 the Boston Braves swept the Philadelphia Athletics.

.209
Batting average of the Braves, the lowest by a World Series winner since the Indians hit .199 in 1948. The Yankees batted .248 in the 1957 Series.

.393
Batting average of Hank Aaron, with 11 hits (including a triple and three home runs) in 28 at-bats.

Around the Majors in 1957

0
Hits allowed by Bob Keegan of the Chicago White Sox in a complete game against the Washington Senators, 6-0, on August 20 (game two of a doubleheader). After this feat, Keegan won only two more games in the majors, finishing in 1958 with a career record of 40-36.

1st
Major-league home run (a grand slam) by Roger Maris of the Indians, on April 18 off Jack Crimian of the Detroit Tigers.

1st
Black player on the Philadelphia Phillies, John Kennedy, when he pinch-ran on April 22 against the Dodgers. It was ten years to the month since Jackie Robinson had debuted with the Dodgers. The Phillies were the last NL team with a black player. (In the AL, the Tigers did not have a black player until 1958, and the Boston Red Sox did not until 1959.)

1st
Career shutout by Don Drysdale of the Dodgers, on June 5 against the Cubs.

1st
Win as Pittsburgh Pirates manager by Danny Murtaugh, on August 6 against the Phillies. His final wins with the Bucs (1,114th and 1,115th) were on October 3, 1976, in a doubleheader sweep of the Cardinals.

1st
Year of the Gold Glove Awards for superior individual fielding. In 1957 one award was given at each position for both major leagues. (Awards for each league began in 1958.) Willie Mays of the Giants won the first of 12 consecutive awards as an outfielder.

2nd
Consecutive year in which Mickey Mantle of the Yankees won the American League MVP Award. He led the majors in runs scored (121), walks (146 in 144 games), and times on base (319) and finished second in the AL in batting average (.365), on-base percentage (.512), slugging average (.665), OPS (1.177), total bases (315), and extra-base hits (68).

2
Home runs hit by pitcher Dixie Howell of the White Sox during 3 2/3 innings of relief work in the second game of a June 16 doubleheader against the Senators.

2.45
ERA of Bobby Shantz of the Yankees, the lowest in the majors. Teammate Tom Sturdivant was second in the major leagues with a 2.54 ERA. Johnny Podres of the Dodgers (2.66) had the lowest ERA in the NL, and teammate Don Drysdale (2.69) was second.

3
Home runs by Ted Williams of the Red Sox in a May 8 game against the White Sox and again in a June 13 game against the Indians. He was the first AL player with two three-homer games in a season.

3
Bases-empty home runs in consecutive at-bats by Ernie Banks of the Cubs, in the second game of a September 14 doubleheader against the Pittsburgh Pirates.

5th
Consecutive season in which Duke Snider of the Dodgers hit 40 or more homers, tying Ralph Kiner's NL record. Snider hit his 39th and 40th home runs on September 22. With 92 RBIs in 1957, he became the first player with 40 home runs and fewer than 100 RBIs in a season.

6
Consecutive games in which Roy Sievers of the Senators hit a home run, from July 28 through August 3.

12
RBIs by Vic Wertz of the Indians during a two-game series against the Red Sox on September 13 (five RBIs, with a three-run homer and two sacrifice flies) and September 14 (seven RBIs, with a grand slam in the first inning and a three-run homer in the second inning).

12
Pinch-hit home runs by the Redlegs, a number not topped by another team in one season until 2001, when the Diamondbacks and Giants each hit 14. Bob Thurman hit four of the 12.

13th
Career grand slam by Gil Hodges of the Dodgers on August 1, an NL record. He hit another grand slam in 1958, and the total of 14 was the NL record until 1974.

13
Stolen bases by the Senators, which remain the fewest by one team in a season (since 1886).

15
Consecutive road wins by the Redlegs, from April 23 through May 27. During the streak, the team had a record of 10-8 at home.

16
Consecutive plate appearances reaching base by Ted Williams, from September 17 to 24. The streak included nine walks (one intentional), four home runs, two singles, and one hit-by-pitch.

19
Saves by Bob Grim of the Yankees, the most in the majors. Clem Labine of the Dodgers led the NL with 17 saves.

20
Triples by Willie Mays, the most in the majors. With 26 doubles and 35 home runs, Mays became the fourth player in major-league history with at least 20 doubles, triples, and home runs each in a season.

20
Wins by Jim Bunning of the Tigers and Billy Pierce of the White Sox, who tied for the most in the AL.

22
Losses by Robin Roberts of the Phillies, the most in the majors; he had ten wins. Chuck Stobbs of the Senators led the AL with 20 losses, against eight wins.

33
Intentional walks drawn by Ted Williams, which is still the AL record for the most in a season.

38
Stolen bases by Willie Mays, the most in the majors. Luis Aparicio of the White Sox led the AL with 28 steals.

42
Home runs (including three extra-inning homers) by Roy Sievers, the most in the AL.

43
Home runs allowed by Pedro Ramos of the Senators, the most in the majors and an AL record until 1986. Robin Roberts allowed 40, the most in the NL.

45 and 74
Years that the Dodgers played at Ebbets Field and in Brooklyn, respectively, before moving to Los Angeles in 1958. In the last game at Ebbets Field, on September 24, 1957, the Dodgers beat the Pirates, 2-0, before a crowd of 6,702.

54.7
Career percentage of runners caught stealing (still a major-league record) by Roy Campanella of the Dodgers, who played his final game on September 29. On January 28, 1958, a car accident in Glen Cove, New York, left the three-time MVP paralyzed from the chest down.

68 and 75
Years that the Giants played at the Polo Grounds and in New York, respectively, before moving to San Francisco in 1958. In the last game at the Polo Grounds, on September 29, 1957, the Giants lost to the Pirates, 9-1, before a crowd of 11,606.

114
RBIs by Roy Sievers, the most in the AL.

188
Strikeouts recorded by NL Rookie of the Year Jack Sanford of the Phillies, the most in the majors. At age 37, Early Wynn of the Indians led the AL with 184 strikeouts.

196
Hits by Nellie Fox of the White Sox, the most in the AL.

331
Total bases by Roy Sievers, the most in the AL.

.388
Batting average of Ted Williams, tops in the majors. At age 39, he was the oldest player to win a batting title, and then he won the 1958 AL title at age 40. Stan

Musial of the Cardinals led the NL in 1957 with a .351 batting average.

.526/.731/1.257

On-base percentage, slugging average, and OPS of Ted Williams, all tops in the majors. Stan Musial led the NL in on-base percentage (.422) and OPS (1.034), and Willie Mays led the league in slugging average (.626).

626

At-bats without a home run by Richie Ashburn of the Phillies

.727

Winning percentage of Dick Donovan of the White Sox and Tom Sturdivant of the Yankees, who tied for the best in the majors. Each had a 16-6 record.

823rd

Consecutive game played by Stan Musial on June 12, an NL record. The streak ended at 895 games on August 23.

1,000

Career RBIs by Gil Hodges on July 19, which happened to be Gil Hodges Day at Ebbets Field.

Sources

Caruso, Gary, *The Braves Encyclopedia* (Philadelphia: Temple University Press, 1995).

Nemec, David, ed., *The Baseball Chronicle: Year-by-Year History of Major League Baseball* (Lincolnwood, Illinois: Publications International, 2003).

Society for American Baseball Research, *The SABR Baseball List and Record Book* (New York: Scribner, 2007).

Solomon, Burt, *The Baseball Timeline* (New York: DK Publishing, 2001).

Sugar, Burt Randolph, ed., *The Baseball Maniac's Almanac,* third edition. (New York: Skyhorse Publishing, 2012).

baseball-almanac.com

baseballlibrary.com/chronology

baseball-reference.com

retrosheet.org

thisgreatgame.com/1957-baseball-history.html

Thirteen Years of Magic

Bob Buege

For Wisconsin's largest city—no, for the state of Wisconsin—the Milwaukee Braves were a dream come true. Beer City had long been a baseball town. Connie Mack had managed the Milwaukee club in the Western League in the 1890's. Baseball's junior circuit, the American League, was born in a Milwaukee hotel room in 1900, with the Milwaukee Brewers a charter member. Almost immediately the Brewers relocated and became the St. Louis Browns. Milwaukee fans quickly turned their attention and loyalty to the city's entry in the American Association. For the next half-century baseball in Milwaukee meant the minor league Brewers in their rickety wooden ballpark, Borchert Field.

On March 18, 1953, the other seven owners of the National League clubs voted unanimously to allow Lou Perini to transfer his Boston Braves to Milwaukee. No franchise had changed cities in 50 years. From the day the team's train pulled into the Chicago and North Western depot at Milwaukee's lakefront, baseball mania reigned in Wisconsin. Some so-called experts questioned whether the rubes in the Dairy State could or would support the Braves. Club officials confidently spoke of drawing a million fans the first year. To say that attendance in County Stadium exceeded expectations would be a gross understatement. Despite frequent rainouts that necessitated doubleheaders, the Braves in just 64 dates counted 1,826,397 and established a new National League attendance record.

The novelty and excitement of being in the major leagues certainly accounted in part for the Braves' success at the turnstiles. So did winning. From the very beginning the Milwaukee Braves were pennant contenders. If not for the existence of the Brooklyn Dodgers, the NL's equivalent of the New York Yankees in the 1950's, Milwaukee would have hoisted a championship flag long before it finally did in 1957.

Most of all, however, Milwaukee fell in love with its new ballplayers. A handful of them were veterans on the downhill side of 30. Southpaw hurler Warren Spahn was a perennial all-star on his way to the Hall of Fame. Backup catcher Walker Cooper was an eight-time all-star. Left fielder Sid Gordon was a two-time all-star with power. Rightfielder "Handy Andy" Pafko was a four-time all-star who grew up milking cows on a farm in northwest Wisconsin. Burly Max Surkont was a Polish-American and a favorite of ethnic Milwaukeeans. He fired a three-hit shutout of the Cincinnati Redlegs in the Braves' first game of 1953. What's more, he won nine of his first ten decisions in that inaugural season.

Overall, though, the new Milwaukee Braves were a team of youngsters. Twenty-one-year-old third baseman Eddie Mathews, the leading home run hitter in baseball, won over the ladies with his matinee-idol good looks. Rookie centerfielder and speedster Billy Bruton was the National League's top base-stealer. Feisty shortstop Johnny Logan led the league's shortstops in fielding percentage. Catcher Del Crandall was a rising star behind the plate. Second baseman Jack Dittmer was a

1957 World Series Program (Courtesy of the Milwaukee Braves Museum)

former Big Ten all-conference football standout who complemented Logan as a double-play partner. Powerful first baseman Joe Adcock, obtained from Cincinnati, hit the longest home runs this side of Mickey Mantle. Freshman hurlers Johnny Antonelli and Bob Buhl won 25 games between them and gave promise of winning many more. The Braves were an exciting team to watch.

The Braves' World Series championship in 1957 provided vindication for their painful collapse the previous year. Fred Haney's club had blown a five-and-a-half game lead in late July but entered the 1956 season's final weekend in St. Louis with a half-game advantage over the Dodgers. The Braves had their "Big Three" starting pitchers—Buhl, Spahn, and Burdette—poised to wrap up Milwaukee's first (of many, it was thought) pennant. The Cardinals sported a losing record that season, but thanks to uncharacteristically heroic efforts from guys like pitcher Herman Wehmeier and center fielder Bobby Del Greco, the Cardinals grabbed the first two games from Milwaukee and dumped the Braves into second place. Wehmeier had lost 20 more games in his career than he had won, but he outdueled Spahn in a 2-1 struggle that lasted 12 innings. Del Greco couldn't hit a lick, but he made two spectacular defensive plays that robbed Milwaukee batters of extra-base hits. Braves fans were devastated.

Nineteen fifty-seven, the Braves' fifth season in Milwaukee, saw the team fulfill its manifest destiny. Thanks to the acquisition of All-Star second baseman Red Schoendienst and the sudden emergence of a force named Bob "Hurricane" Hazle, Haney's troops conquered the National League by eight games. Lew Burdette's deceptive pitches and indomitable spirit carried the club the rest of the way, defeating Casey Stengel's vaunted Bronx Bombers three times as the underdogs from the western shore of Lake Michigan snatched the World Series title that Gotham City thought was its birthright.

Milwaukee fans expected that 1958 would bring more of the same. They were nearly correct. The Braves' offensive production declined a bit, but workhorses Spahn and Burdette won 22 and 20 games, respectively, to lead the club. As in the previous season, the Braves finished first by eight games.

The World Series was another matter. With Spahn winning twice and Burdette once, the Braves took a commanding three-games-to-one lead and seemed invincible. Then, inexplicably, they stopped hitting. New York won three straight, including the final two games in Milwaukee, to lay claim to the title. The Yankees became the first team since the Pittsburgh Pirates in 1925 to come back from a deficit of three games to one and win the Series.

Besides the Braves' post-season stumble, their 1958 chapter produced something even more ominous. Season attendance at County Stadium declined. The total of 1,971,101 was still the best in the National League, better than any other NL team had ever recorded and really just one rainout shy of the magic two million mark. Still, it represented a decrease of 11 percent from the high-water mark of 2,215,404 in 1957. If Braves officials were not concerned, they should have been.

The 1959 season was an enigma. General manager John Quinn, the architect of the Braves' pennants, had quit in January and moved on to Philadelphia. What he left behind, though, looked like a juggernaut. The Braves lineup comprised six starters who had been or would become all-stars, not even counting the Big Three of their mound staff. Baseball's all-time home run tandem, Eddie Mathews and Henry Aaron, had their biggest season with 85 four-baggers. Aaron batted over .400 well into June and led the majors with a .355 average. The major leagues' winningest pair of pitchers of the past 100 years, Spahn and Burdette, were in their prime, each winning 21 games. The supporting cast produced solid performances, the only weakness appearing at second base with Schoendienst out with tuberculosis.

Despite an embarrassment of talent, the Braves struggled to keep pace with the league leaders. Only a strong finish, winning 15 of their last 20 ballgames, allowed them to finish in a dead heat with the Los Angeles Dodgers. Their momentum failed to carry over to the regular season extension, however. The Braves knuckled under in the first two games of the best-of-three playoff. Playing in County Stadium in the opener, Haney's guys appeared listless while receiving no boost from their home surroundings in a 3-2 loss in front of barely 18,000 fans. In their recent heyday, Milwaukee's beloved Tribe would have drawn that many for batting practice. The next afternoon in the Los Angeles Coliseum marked the *coup de grace*. The Braves blew a three-run lead in the ninth and bowed to the Dodgers, 6-5, in 12 innings, snuffing out their quest for a third straight pennant.

Recriminations began at once. Manager Fred Haney naturally bore the brunt of the criticism, which continued for a long time. Many years later, baseball pundit and historian Bill James opined that in 1959 "Fred Haney had the worst season of any major league manager in baseball history."[1]

Those strong words reinforced what some Braves ballplayers said immediately after the season. Shortstop Johnny Logan bluntly stated, "We should have won by ten games without any question."[2]

The feeling was that Haney had relied too heavily on his top two starting pitchers, Spahn and Burdette, to the exclusion of other young but talented hurlers. One of these, former bonus baby Joey Jay, had been relegated to the bullpen in mid-season because Haney thought Jay was lazy and out of condition. Jay did not mince words in assigning blame. "Fred Haney didn't manage the club," he told a reporter. "He sat in one corner of the dugout, gulping down pills and saying to Crandall, 'What should we do, Del?'"[3] Haney tendered his resignation five days after the season ended.

To replace Haney the Braves needed to employ a manager whom the ballplayers would respect and the fans would receive favorably. Instead they hired Charlie Dressen. The fun-loving players bridled at Dressen's egotistical rantings and heavy-handed team management. Baseball historians would tell you Dressen had a brilliant baseball mind. Dressen would have told you that himself. But his personality was a bad fit for the Milwaukee Braves. The fans, meanwhile, found little to warm up to in the five-and-a-half-foot tall master of the pronoun *I*. The result was predictable—the ballclub failed to win the pennant, and attendance declined another quarter-million.

By the 1961 season the Braves were on a steep down slope. To add to the fans' disenchantment, the Milwaukee County Board of Supervisors, who controlled County Stadium, outlawed the longstanding practice of customers bringing in their own beer. In Wisconsin's blue-collar city of breweries, no single action could have done more to keep people away from the ballpark. Three months later the board rescinded the ban, but the damage had been done. Dressen kept his job through most of the campaign, but on September 2, with the Braves seven games out of first, owner Lou Perini fired him. If that was calculated to mollify the fans, it failed miserably. Dressen's successor, Braves executive vice-president Birdie Tebbetts, had always rankled Milwaukee's faithful when he managed the Cincinnati Redlegs. Milwaukee and Cincinnati had numerous bean-ball battles, and Tebbetts repeatedly accused Burdette of throwing spitters. With Tebbetts in charge for the final month the Braves lost more games than they won, and annual attendance fell another 400,000.

Under Tebbetts the 1962 Braves finished fifth in the newly expanded National League and attendance plunged below 800,000. In October Birdie resigned to take the managerial position of the Cleveland Indians. GM John McHale selected yet another skipper who proved unpopular with both the players and the ticket-buying public—Bobby Bragan. The buffoonish Bragan had been fired by the Pittsburgh Pirates after drinking from a carton of orange juice while arguing with the umpires during a game in County Stadium on July 31, 1957. League president Warren Giles fined Bragan and blasted him in a telegram: "Your repeated farcical acts on the field indicate it is not in your nature to take the game on the field seriously."[4] This is the man the Braves hired to manage their club. To Milwaukee fans, Bragan was Dressen with a southern drawl.

On November 16, 1962, the Milwaukee Braves franchise entered its endgame. Lou Perini, apparently weary of the responsibilities of an absentee owner, sold 90 percent of his stock in the Braves to a Chicago syndicate headed by former directors of the Chicago White Sox. Milwaukee civic leaders were at once leery of another out-of-town ownership group. The new owners, however, offered strenuous assurances that they were not seeking to transfer the franchise out of Milwaukee. General manager McHale famously told the community, "The

Braves will be in Milwaukee today, tomorrow, next year, and as long as we are welcome."[5]

The problem of "foreign" ownership, as well as McHale's disingenuous remarks, would have been prevented had it not been for a tragic airplane accident on December 17, 1954. Fred Miller, president of the company that brewed Miller High Life ("The champagne of bottled beer"), died that day when his private plane crashed near Milwaukee's airport. Miller had been an All-American football player at Notre Dame. He was the team's captain at the time of the legendary "Win one for the Gipper" speech. In the early 1950's Miller had been Milwaukee's most civic-minded individual. He led the fundraising for the city's new Arena, for its repertory theater, and for several of its professional sports teams. He was credited with persuading Perini to relocate his Braves in Milwaukee. What's more, it was reported that he had a gentlemen's agreement to purchase the franchise if and when Perini wanted to sell it.

In three years with Bragan as manager, the Braves finished above .500 each season but never climbed higher than fifth place. Beginning about the time of the All-Star break in 1963, rumors surfaced that the Braves were bound for Atlanta. By 1964 there was no doubt. The hot breath of reality told folks in Wisconsin that their baseball team was headed south. The Braves had an ironclad lease on County Stadium for one year longer, however. They tried to buy their way out of the contract, but county officials were in no mood to bargain. As a result, the Braves did something unique in major league history. They played a lame-duck season in 1965.

The Braves still boasted a power-packed lineup. They stayed locked in the pennant race for most of the summer and even captured first place for two days in the latter part of August. Ultimately they collapsed in a heap of pitching dysfunctions, losing six home games in a row to drop out of the race. After that all the action took place in the courtroom of Circuit Judge Elmer Roller. Milwaukee County sued to keep the Braves, claiming a violation of Wisconsin's antitrust law. Judge Roller rendered a verdict in favor of the county in April 1966, but by that time the Braves were already playing in Atlanta. Subsequently the Wisconsin Supreme Court overruled Judge Roller, and that was that.

The legacy of the Milwaukee Braves' 13-year life span probably lies in its pioneer role in baseball's westward migration. Was major league baseball on the West Coast inevitable? Of course. Perhaps the Braves helped speed the process by a few years.

The Milwaukee Braves contributed one other significant thread to the fabric of baseball's rich history. For Opening Day 1965, with County Stadium now acknowledged as the temporary playground of the Atlanta Braves, an organization calling itself Teams, Inc. purchased the right to sell all of the day's tickets. The purpose was twofold: to promote the game as a tribute to the still-beloved ballplayers, and to raise funds to help the group attract a new ballclub to move into County Stadium. The day was a success. The season's largest crowd, 33,874, showed their support, only 483 fewer than the lid-lifter in the happy times of 1953.

The leader of Teams, Inc. was a young automobile salesman named Allan H. (Bud) Selig. From that day forward, Selig was the standard-bearer for Milwaukee big league baseball. He became president and part owner of the Milwaukee Brewers in 1970. Today he stands behind only Judge Kenesaw Mountain Landis as the longest-serving Commissioner of Baseball.

The Milwaukee Braves were unique in American sports history. They never experienced a losing season, yet they existed for only 13 years. Their leaving broke the heart of a city. As the Romans would say, *Venerunt, vicerunt, discesserunt.* They came, they conquered, they departed.

Sources

Bob Buege, *Eddie Mathews and the National Pastime*. Milwaukee: Douglas American Sports Publications, 1994.

Bob Buege, *The Milwaukee Braves: A Baseball Eulogy*. Milwaukee: Douglas American Sports Publications, 1988.

Milwaukee Journal.

Milwaukee Sentinel.

Retrosheet.org

Notes

1. Bill James, *Bill James Guide to Baseball Managers from 1870 to Today*. New York: Scribner, 1997, 202.

2. Milton Gross, "Logan Says He and Most of Braves Have No Regrets Over Fred Haney's Departure," *Milwaukee Journal*, October 22, 1959, 17.

3. Bob Buege, *The Milwaukee Braves: A Baseball Eulogy*. Milwaukee: Douglas American Sports Publications, 1988, 225.

4. Cleon Walfoort, "Bragan Sips Expensive Orange, Offers to Pitch It In Ump's Face," *Milwaukee Journal*, August 1, 1957, 13.

5. Red Thisted, "McHale's Statement Clears Air," *Milwaukee Sentinel*, September 24, 1963, 1.

Contributor Biographies

Michael J. Bielawa has authored histories focusing on New England and Louisiana baseball. His numerous essays have addressed such diverse subjects as baseball symbolism in James Joyce's *Ulysses*, the mysterious disappearance of a Hartford, Connecticut minor-league manager, and New York City baseball curses. Bielawa's work on early Queens, New York baseball and the first All-Star Game (1858) appeared in MLB's *Official 2014 All-Star Game Program*. Mike is also a roving baseball consultant for museums, minor-league clubs, state humanities councils, and libraries.

Bob Buege was born the day after Jess Pike hit his only major-league home run, a three-run blast in the Polo Grounds. A SABR member since 1988, Bob is the author of four books, including *The Milwaukee Braves: A Baseball Eulogy* and *Eddie Mathews and the National Pastime*.

Rory Costello lives in Brooklyn, New York with his wife Noriko and five-year-old son Kai. His Juan Pizarro biography stemmed from a longstanding interest in Latin American ballplayers. His Jane Jarvis biography came from growing up as a Mets fan.

Doug Engelman has enjoyed a lifelong love of the game. As an amateur and semipro player, amateur coach, and fan, he has experienced the heights of joy, and the depths of disappointment (he is a Cub fan) that accompany the passion. As a recent member of SABR, he was truly honored to have the opportunity to participate in this worthy project.

Dan Fields is a manuscript editor at the *New England Journal of Medicine*. He loves baseball trivia, and he regularly attends Boston Red Sox and Pawtucket (Rhode Island) Red Sox games with his teenage son. Dan lives in Framingham, Massachusetts, and can be reached at dfields820@gmail.com.

Jeff Findley is a native of eastern Iowa, where he did the logical thing growing up in the heart of the Cubs/Cardinals rivalry—he embraced the 1969 Orioles and became a lifelong fan. An information security professional for a large insurance company in Illinois, he compiles a daily sports "Pages Past" for his local newspaper.

David Fleitz, a computer systems analyst from Pleasant Ridge, Michigan, has written eight books on baseball history, including biographies of Shoeless Joe Jackson, Louis Sockalexis, and Cap Anson. David's latest work, *Napoleon Lajoie: King of Ballplayers*, was published by McFarland in 2013.

Jim Gordon is a retired aerospace engineer who now spends much of his time attending baseball games and researching Los Angeles-area baseball history. He is co-chairman of the SABR Ballparks Committee and a member of the BioProject Committee and the Games and Simulations Committee as well as managing the Brooklyn/Los Angeles Dodgers in the Great American Fantasy League. He has written biographies of Wrigley Field, Los Angeles and of Fred Haney for the BioProject.

Chip Greene, a SABR member since 2006, is a regular contributor to the BioProject, having written player biographies for books on the 1947 Yankees, 1950s Red Sox, 1970 Orioles, and 1984 Tigers. Additionally, Chip's work has appeared in *Yankees Annual* magazine, and the encyclopedia *American Sports: A History of Icons, Idols, and Ideas*. Chip lives in Waynesboro, Pennsylvania, with his wife, Elaine, and daughters, Anna and Haley.

Gregg Hoffmann has covered baseball in the Midwest for more than 40 years, still writes the Midwest Diamond Report blog and does cover stories for Game Day, the Milwaukee Brewers' program. He is the author of *Down in the Valley: The History of Milwaukee County Stadium* and thousands of articles.

John Richmond Husman has been a SABR member since 1982 and is a former chair of the 19th Century Committee. He is a great grandson of 19th century pitcher J. Lee Richmond and is historian for the Toledo Mud Hens.

William Johnson is a long-time SABR member, currently working for the Iowa Baseball Museum of Norway. He has contributed biographies to several books, including *The Team that Forever Changed Baseball and America: the 1947 Brooklyn Dodgers* among others.

Jim Kaplan is the author of The *Greatest Game Ever Pitched: Juan Marichal, Warren Spahn and the*

Pitching Duel of the Century (Triumph Books, 2011). He covered baseball for *Sports Illustrated* from 1970 to 1986.

Alex Kupfer is originally from Milwaukee, and is currently a doctoral candidate in the Department of Cinema Studies at New York University. His forthcoming dissertation examines the use of nontheatrical motion pictures in higher education, particularly sports films intended for educational or training purposes. This is his second contribution to the SABR BioProject, having written on Dave Campbell for the *Sock It to 'Em Tigers* book on the 1968 Detroit Tigers.

Kristen Lokemoen became a baseball fan as a young girl listening to the Milwaukee Braves games on the radio in her hometown of Merrill, Wisconsin. After a move to Missouri in 1976, Kris became a casual St. Louis Cardinals fan. It was Mark McGwire and the home run race of 1998 that brought her back seriously to the game she loved. Kris became involved in SABR in 2006 as the Bob Broeg St. Louis chapter prepared for the convention in 2007. With a background in group tours, Kris created and escorted the sightseeing tours offered at that convention. Now a chapter board member, Kris is working on a book about baseball, as well as doing other freelance writing.

Norm King is a retired Canadian civil servant who delights in having the time to devote to SABR research. He still misses his beloved Montreal Expos and awaits the day when he will hear an umpire yell "Au jeu" again at the beginning of a ball game.

Russ Lake lives in Champaign, IL, and is a retired college professor emeritus. The 1964 St. Louis Cardinals remain his favorite team, and he was distressed to see Sportsman's Park (aka Busch Stadium I) being demolished not long after he had attended the last game there on May 8, 1966. His wife, Carol, deserves an MVP award for watching all of a 14-inning ballgame in Cincinnati with Russ in 1971—during their honeymoon. In 1994, he was an editor for David Halberstam's baseball book, *October 1964*.

Len Levin, a SABR member since 1977, is a retired newspaper editor and adjunct journalism instructor living in Providence, Rhode Island. Besides editing for SABR publications, he works part-time editing the decisions of the Rhode Island Supreme Court.

Mel Marmer lives in Philadelphia PA and works as a grocer and sign artist for Weavers Way, a local food co-operative. He has been a SABR member for 13 years and enjoys the experience immensely. Mel recently authored and co-edited *The Year of the Blue Snow: The 1964 Philadelphia Phillies* for SABR.

John McMurray is Chair of the Society for American Baseball Research's Deadball Era Committee. He contributed to SABR's 2006 book *Deadball Stars of the American League* and is a past chair of SABR's Ritter Award subcommittee, which annually presents an award to the best book on Deadball Era baseball published during the year prior. He has contributed many interview-based player profiles to *Baseball Digest* in recent years.

Bill Nowlin vaguely remembers when the Braves left Boston, in 1953, but sadly never saw them play when they were one of Boston's teams. Just a very few years later, they won the National League pennant and went on to win the World Series over the New York Yankees, something that made Red Sox fans quite happy. Bill has been VP of SABR since 2004, a noted year in Red Sox history.

Nancy Snell Griffith is the retired Archives and Special Collections Librarian at Presbyterian College in Clinton, South Carolina. She is a lifelong baseball fan, having grown up in Pittsburgh listening to Jim Woods and Bob Prince broadcast the Pirates' games.

Rick Schabowski is a retired machinist from Harley-Davidson and is currently an instructor at Wisconsin Regional Training Partnership in the Manufacturing Program, and is a certified Manufacturing Skills Standards Council instructor. He is President of the Ken Keltner Badger State Chapter of SABR, Treasurer of the Milwaukee Braves Historical Association, and a member of the Hoop Historians.

Steven D. Schmitt has been a SABR member since 2009. At the 40th Convention in 2010, he presented a paper, "Country Hardball", that focused on the Dizzy Dean barnstorming teams of the mid-1930s. He is finishing a history of baseball at the University of Wisconsin, Madison and a biography of former major-league pitcher Ken Johnson for the SABR book on the 1966 Atlanta Braves. Schmitt has a master's degree in journalism and mass communication from the UW—Madison and lives in Madison, Wisconsin.

Former President of North Country Natural, Inc. a natural foods distributorship, **Dana Sprague** may own the largest collection of Ernie Johnson memorabilia that exists. A sixth-generation Vermonter, Dana was born in Brattleboro, Ernie Johnson's hometown, and continues to reside in Brattleboro to this day. He has two grown children, Brandon and Neysa, and has been a SABR member since 1994.

John Henry Stahl is a retired CPA and lives with his wife, Pamela, in suburban Maryland. He's written 19 SABR biographies and recently co-edited a SABR book on the 1964 Cardinals entitled *Drama and Pride in the Gateway City*. He's a longtime fan of the Milwaukee Braves.

A lifelong Philadelphia Phillies fan, **Andy Sturgill** lives in suburban Philadelphia with his wife, Carrie. A college administrator by day, he enjoys reading and visiting ballparks in his free time.

Dale Voiss has a lifelong passion for the game of baseball and its history, and a particular passion for Wisconsin baseball. A member of SABR since 2009, he resides in Madison, Wisconsin.

John Vorperian, a/k/a Johnny V, is host and executive producer, *Beyond the Game*, cablecast in New York (www.wpcommunitymedia.org). The American University alumnus has taught Sport Law & Management topics at Manhattanville College and Concordia College. Aside from a 1994 fantasy camp with Lew Burdette, Mark Lemke, and Ralph Garr, his two fondest Braves moments, were interviewing Milo Hamilton and having a chat with Art Johnson about how to pitch against Stan The Man.

Joseph Wancho is a lifelong Cleveland Indians fan and makes his home in Westlake, Ohio. His has contributed over 50 bios to the SABR BioProject. He edited *Pitching to the Pennant*, a SABR book on the 1954 Indians published in 2014 by University of Nebraska Press.

Saul Wisnia helps keep the legacy of the Braves alive in Boston as senior publications editor for Dana-Farber Cancer Institute/The Jimmy Fund, which the Braves helped start in 1948, and as a founding member of the Boston Braves Historical Association. A longtime SABR-ite, he has written numerous books including *Fenway Park: The Centennial*, *For the Love of the Boston Red Sox*, and *Miracle at Fenway*, and contributed to many others. He lives 5.4 miles from Braves Field and blogs about Boston's "other" baseball team at "Fenway Reflections."

A lifelong Pirates fan, **Gregory H. Wolf** was born in Pittsburgh, but now resides in the Chicagoland area with his wife, Margaret, and daughter, Gabriela. A Professor of German and holder of the Dennis and Jean Bauman endowed chair of the Humanities at North Central College in Naperville, IL, he has published articles on baseball history at *The Hardball Times*, regularly contributes to SABR projects, including the BioProject, and is currently editing a SABR book on the 1929 Chicago Cubs.

SABR BioProject Books

In 2002, the Society for American Baseball Research launched an effort to write and publish biographies of every player, manager, and individual who has made a contribution to baseball. Over the past decade, the BioProject Committee has produced over 2,200 biographical articles. Many have been part of efforts to create theme- or team-oriented books, spearheaded by chapters or other committees of SABR.

THE YEAR OF THE BLUE SNOW:
THE 1964 PHILADELPHIA PHILLIES
Catcher Gus Triandos dubbed the Philadelphia Phillies' 1964 season "the year of the blue snow," a rare thing that happens once in a great while. This book sheds light on lingering questions about the 1964 season—but any book about a team is really about the players. This work offers life stories of all the players and others (managers, coaches, owners, and broadcasters) associated with this star-crossed team, as well as essays of analysis and history.
Edited by Mel Marmer and Bill Nowlin
$19.95 paperback (ISBN 978-1-933599-51-9)
$9.99 ebook (ISBN 978-1-933599-52-6)
8.5"X11", 356 PAGES, over 70 photos

THE MIRACLE BRAVES OF 1914
BOSTON'S ORIGINAL WORST-TO-FIRST CHAMPIONS
Long before the Red Sox "Impossible Dream" season, Boston's now nearly forgotten "other" team, the 1914 Boston Braves, performed a baseball "miracle" that resounds to this very day. The "Miracle Braves" were Boston's first "worst-to-first" winners of the World Series. Refusing to throw in the towel at the midseason mark, George Stallings engineered a remarkable second-half climb in the standings all the way to first place.
Edited by Bill Nowlin
$19.95 paperback (ISBN 978-1-933599-69-4)
$9.99 ebook (ISBN 978-1-933599-70-0)
8.5"X11", 392 PAGES, over 100 photos

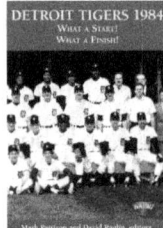

DETROIT TIGERS 1984:
WHAT A START! WHAT A FINISH!
The 1984 Detroit tigers roared out of the gate, winning their first nine games of the season and compiling an eye-popping 35-5 record after the campaign's first 40 games—still the best start ever for any team in major league history. This book brings together biographical profiles of every Tiger from that magical season, plus those of field management, top executives, the broadcasters—even venerable Tiger Stadium and the city itself.
Edited by Mark Pattison and David Raglin
$19.95 paperback (ISBN 978-1-933599-44-1)
$9.99 ebook (ISBN 978-1-933599-45-8)
8.5"x11", 250 pages (Over 230,000 words!)

THAR'S JOY IN BRAVELAND!
THE 1957 MILWAUKEE BRAVES
Few teams in baseball history have captured the hearts of their fans like the Milwaukee Braves of the 1950s. During the Braves' 13-year tenure in Milwaukee (1953-1965), they had a winning record every season, won two consecutive NL pennants (1957 and 1958), lost two more in the final week of the season (1956 and 1959), and set big-league attendance records along the way.
Edited by Gregory H. Wolf
$19.95 paperback (ISBN 978-1-933599-71-7)
$9.99 ebook (ISBN 978-1-933599-72-4)
8.5"x11", 330 pages, over 60 photos

SWEET '60: THE 1960 PITTSBURGH PIRATES
A portrait of the 1960 team which pulled off one of the biggest upsets of the last 60 years. When Bill Mazeroski's home run left the park to win in Game Seven of the World Series, beating the New York Yankees, David had toppled Goliath. It was a blow that awakened a generation, one that millions of people saw on television, one of TV's first iconic World Series moments.
Edited by Clifton Blue Parker and Bill Nowlin
$19.95 paperback (ISBN 978-1-933599-48-9)
$9.99 ebook (ISBN 978-1-933599-49-6)
8.5"X11", 340 pages, 75 photos

NEW CENTURY, NEW TEAM:
THE 1901 BOSTON AMERICANS
The team now known as the Boston Red Sox played its first season in 1901. Boston had a well-established National League team, but the American League went head-to-head with the N.L. in Chicago, Philadelphia, and Boston. Chicago won the American League pennant and Boston finished second, only four games behind.
Edited by Bill Nowlin
$19.95 paperback (ISBN 978-1-933599-58-8)
$9.99 ebook (ISBN 978-1-933599-59-5)
8.5"X11", 268 pages, over 125 photos

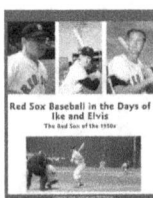

RED SOX BASEBALL IN THE DAYS OF IKE AND ELVIS: *THE RED SOX OF THE 1950S*
Although the Red Sox spent most of the 1950s far out of contention, the team was filled with fascinating players who captured the heart of their fans. In *Red Sox Baseball*, members of SABR present 46 biographies on players such as Ted Williams and Pumpsie Green as well as season-by-season recaps.
Edited by Mark Armour and Bill Nowlin
$19.95 paperback (ISBN 978-1-933599-24-3)
$9.99 ebook (ISBN 978-1-933599-34-2)
8.5"X11", 372 PAGES, over 100 photos

CAN HE PLAY?
A LOOK AT BASEBALL SCOUTS AND THEIR PROFESSION
They dig through tons of coal to find a single diamond. Here in the world of scouts, we meet the "King of Weeds," a Ph.D. we call "Baseball's Renaissance Man," a husband-and-wife team, pioneering Latin scouts, and a Japanese-American interned during World War II who became a successful scout—and many, many more.
Edited by Jim Sandoval and Bill Nowlin
$19.95 paperback (ISBN 978-1-933599-23-6)
$9.99 ebook (ISBN 978-1-933599-25-0)
8.5"X11", 200 PAGES, over 100 photos

SABR Members can purchase each book at a significant discount (often 50% off) and receive the ebook edtions free as a member benefit. Each book is available in a trade paperback edition as well as ebooks suitable for reading on a home computer or Nook, Kindle, or iPad/tablet.
To learn more about becoming a member of SABR, visit the website: sabr.org/join

THE SABR DIGITAL LIBRARY

The Society for American Baseball Research, the top baseball research organization in the world, disseminates some of the best in baseball history, analysis, and biography through our publishing programs. The SABR Digital Library contains a mix of books old and new, and focuses on a tandem program of paperback and ebook publication, making these materials widely available for both on digital devices and as traditional printed books.

CLASSIC REPRINTS

BASE-BALL: HOW TO BECOME A PLAYER
by John Montgomery Ward
John Montgomery Ward (1860-1925) tossed the second perfect game in major league history and later became the game's best shortstop and a great, inventive manager. His classic handbook on baseball skills and strategy was published in 1888. Illustrated with woodcuts, the book is divided into chapters for each position on the field as well as chapters on the origin of the game, theory and strategy, training, base-running, and batting.
$4.99 ebook (ISBN 978-1-933599-47-2)
$9.95 paperback (ISBN 978-0910137539)
156 PAGES, 4.5"X7" replica edition

BATTING by F. C. Lane
First published in 1925, *Batting* collects the wisdom and insights of over 250 hitters and baseball figures. Lane interviewed extensively and compiled tips and advice on everything from batting stances to beanballs. Legendary baseball figures such as Ty Cobb, Casey Stengel, Cy Young, Walter Johnson, Rogers Hornsby, and Babe Ruth reveal the secrets of such integral and interesting parts of the game as how to choose a bat, the ways to beat a slump, and how to outguess the pitcher.
$14.95 paperback (ISBN 978-0-910137-86-7)
$7.99 ebook (ISBN 978-1-933599-46-5)
240 PAGES, 5"X7"

RUN, RABBIT, RUN
by Walter "Rabbit" Maranville
"Rabbit" Maranville was the Joe Garagiola of Grandpa's day, the baseball comedian of the times. In a twenty-four-year career that began in 1912, Rabbit found a lot of funny situations to laugh at, and no wonder: he caused most of them! The book also includes an introduction by the late Harold Seymour and a historical account of Maranville's life and Hall-of-Fame career by Bob Carroll.
$9.95 paperback (ISBN 978-1-933599-26-7)
$5.99 ebook (ISBN 978-1-933599-27-4)
100 PAGES, 5.5"X8.5", 15 rare photos

MEMORIES OF A BALLPLAYER
by Bill Werber and C. Paul Rogers III
Bill Werber's claim to fame is unique: he was the last living person to have a direct connection to the 1927 Yankees, "Murderers' Row," a team hailed by many as the best of all time. Rich in anecdotes and humor, Memories of a Ballplayer is a clear-eyed memoir of the world of big-league baseball in the 1930s.Werber played with or against some of the most productive hitters of all time, including Babe Ruth, Ted Williams, Lou Gehrig, and Joe DiMaggio.
$14.95 paperback (ISNB 978-0-910137-84-3)
$6.99 ebook (ISBN 978-1-933599-47-2)
250 PAGES, 6"X9"

ORIGINAL SABR RESEARCH

INVENTING BASEBALL: THE 100 GREATEST GAMES OF THE NINETEENTH CENTURY
SABR's Nineteenth Century Committee brings to life the greatest games from the game's early years. From the "prisoner of war" game that took place among captive Union soldiers during the Civil War (immortalized in a famous lithograph), to the first intercollegiate game (Amherst versus Williams), to the first professional no-hitter, the games in this volume span 1833–1900 and detail the athletic exploits of such players as Cap Anson, Moses "Fleetwood" Walker, Charlie Comiskey, and Mike "King" Kelly.
Edited by Bill Felber
$19.95 paperback (ISBN 978-1-933599-42-7)
$9.99 ebook (ISBN 978-1-933599-43-4)
302 PAGES, 8"x10", 200 photos

NINETEENTH CENTURY STARS: 2012 EDITION
First published in 1989, *Nineteenth Century Stars* was SABR's initial attempt to capture the stories of baseball players from before 1900. With a collection of 136 fascinating biographies, SABR has re-released *Nineteenth Century Stars* for 2012 with revised statistics and new form. The 2012 version also includes a preface by **John Thorn**.
Edited by Robert L. Tiemann and Mark Rucker
$19.95 paperback (ISBN 978-1-933599-28-1)
$9.99 ebook (ISBN 978-1-933599-29-8)
300 PAGES, 6"X9"

GREAT HITTING PITCHERS
Published in 1979, *Great Hitting Pitchers* was one of SABR's early publications. Edited by SABR founder Bob Davids, the book compiles stories and records about pitchers excelling in the batter's box. Newly updated in 2012 by Mike Cook, *Great Hitting Pitchers* contain tables including data from 1979-2011, corrections to reflect recent records, and a new chapter on recent new members in the club of "great hitting pitchers" like Tom Glavine and Mike Hampton.
Edited by L. Robert Davids
$9.95 paperback (ISBN 978-1-933599-30-4)
$5.99 ebook (ISBN 978-1-933599-31-1)
102 PAGES, 5.5"x8.5"

THE FENWAY PROJECT
Sixty-four SABR members—avid fans, historians, statisticians, and game enthusiasts—recorded their experiences of a single game. Some wrote from inside the Green Monster's manual scoreboard, the Braves clubhouse, or the broadcast booth, while others took in the essence of Fenway from the grandstand or bleachers. The result is a fascinating look at the charms and challenges of Fenway Park, and the allure of being a baseball fan.
Edited by Bill Nowlin and Cecilia Tan
$9.99 ebook (ISBN 978-1-933599-50-2)
175 pages, 100 photos

SABR Members can purchase each book at a significant discount (often 50% off) and receive the ebook edtions free as a member benefit. Each book is available in a trade paperback edition as well as ebooks suitable for reading on a home computer or Nook, Kindle, or iPad/tablet.
To learn more about becoming a member of SABR, visit the website: sabr.org/join

Society for American Baseball Research
4455 E. Camelback Rd., Ste. D-140, Phoenix, AZ 85018
602.343.6455 (phone) • 602.595.5690 (fax)
SABR.org

Become a SABR member today!

If you're interested in baseball — writing about it, reading about it, talking about it — there's a place for you in the Society for American Baseball Research. Our members include everyone from academics to professional sportswriters to amateur historians and statisticians to students and casual fans who enjoy reading about baseball and occasionally gathering with other members to talk baseball. What unites all SABR members is an interest in the game and joy in learning more about it.

SABR membership is open to any baseball fan; we offer 1-year and 3-year memberships. Here's a list of some of the key benefits you'll receive as a SABR member:

- Receive two editions (spring and fall) of the *Baseball Research Journal*, our flagship publication
- Receive expanded e-book edition of *The National Pastime*, our annual convention journal
- 6-8 new e-books published by the SABR Digital Library, all FREE to members
- "This Week in SABR" e-newsletter, sent to members every Friday
- Join dozens of research committees, from Statistical Analysis to Women in Baseball.
- Join one of 60+ regional chapters in the U.S., Canada, Latin America, Japan, England
- Participate in online discussion groups
- Ask and answer baseball research questions on the SABR-L e-mail listserv
- Complete archives of *The Sporting News* from 1886-2003 and other research resources
- Promote your research in "This Week in SABR"
- Diamond Dollars Case Competition
- Yoseloff Scholarships
- SABR research awards

- Discounts on SABR national conferences, including the SABR National Convention, the SABR Analytics Conference, Jerry Malloy Negro League Conference, Frederick Ivor-Campbell 19th Century Conference
- Publish your research in peer-reviewed SABR journals
- Collaborate with SABR researchers and experts
- Contribute to Baseball Biography Project
- List your new book in the SABR Bookshelf
- Lead a SABR research committee or chapter
- Networking opportunities at SABR Analytics Conference
- Meet baseball authors and historians at SABR events and chapter meetings
- 50% discounts on paperback versions of SABR e-books
- 20% discount on MLB.TV subscriptions
- 10% discount on MLB.com Store orders
- Discounts with other partners in the baseball community

We hope you'll join the most passionate international community of baseball fans at SABR! Check us out online at SABR.org/join.

SABR MEMBERSHIP FORM

	Annual	3-year	Senior	3-yr Sr.	Under 30
U.S.:	☐ $65	☐ $175	☐ $45	☐ $129	☐ $45
Canada/Mexico:	☐ $75	☐ $205	☐ $55	☐ $159	☐ $55
Overseas:	☐ $84	☐ $232	☐ $64	☐ $186	☐ $55

Add a Family Member: $15 each family member at same address (list names on back)
Senior: 65 or older before 12/31 of the current year
All dues amounts in U.S. dollars or equivalent

Participate in Our Donor Program!
Support the preservation of baseball research. Designate your gift toward:
☐ General Fund ☐ Endowment Fund ☐ Research Resources ☐ _____
☐ I want to maximize the impact of my gift; do not send any donor premiums
☐ I would like this gift to remain anonymous.

Note: Any donation not designated will be placed in the General Fund.
SABR is a 501 (c) (3) not-for-profit organization & donations are tax-deductible to the extent allowed by law.

Name _____

E-mail* _____

Address _____

City _____ ST_____ ZIP_____

Phone _____ Birthday _____

Dues $_____
Donation $_____
Amount Enclosed $_____

Do you work for a matching grant corporation? Call (602) 343-6455 for details.

If you wish to pay by credit card, please contact the SABR office at (602) 343-6455 or visit the SABR Store online at SABR.org/join. We accept Visa, Mastercard and Discover Card.

* Your e-mail address on file ensures you will receive the most recent SABR news.

Mail to: SABR, 4455 E. Camelback Rd., Ste. D-140, Phoenix, AZ 85018